JOURNAL FOR STAR WISDOM 2013

# JOURNAL FOR STAR WISDOM

## 2013

Edited by Robert Powell

EDITORIAL BOARD

William Bento
Brian Gray
Claudia McLaren Lainson
Lacquanna Paul
Robert Schiappacasse

Lindisfarne Books

LINDISFARNE BOOKS
AN IMPRINT OF STEINERBOOKS/ANTHROPOSOPHIC PRESS, INC.
610 Main Street, Suite 1
Great Barrington, MA, 01230
www.steinerbooks.org

*Journal for Star Wisdom 2013* © 2012 by Robert Powell. All contributions are used by permission of the authors. All rights reserved. No part of this publication may be reproduced, stored in a retrieval system, or transmitted in any form or by any means, electronic, mechanical, photocopying, recording, or otherwise without the prior written permission of the publisher.

With grateful acknowledgment to Peter Treadgold (1943–2005), who wrote the Astrofire program (available from the Sophia Foundation), with which the ephemeris pages in the *Journal for Star Wisdom* are computed each year.

Disclaimer: The views expressed in the articles published in the *Journal for Star Wisdom* are the sole responsibility of the authors of these articles and do not necessarily reflect those of the editorial board of the *Journal for Star Wisdom*.

DESIGN: WILLIAM JENS JENSEN

PRINT: ISBN: 978-1-58420-135-9

EBOOK: ISBN: 978-1-58420-136-6

# CONTENTS

| | |
|---|---|
| *Preface* | 9 |
| The Rose of the World (*Rosa Mira*) <br>    *by Daniel Andreev* | 14 |
| Editorial Foreword <br>    *by Robert Powell* | 18 |
| Working with the *Journal for Star Wisdom* | 21 |
| Earth Chakras <br>    *by Robert Powell and David Bowden* | 22 |
| Finding Jerusalem, Part One <br>    *by David Tresemer* | 34 |
| The Signature of Neptune in World Events <br>    *by David Tresemer* | 38 |
| Finding Ahriman's Influence in the Dark Shadows of Neptune <br>    *by William Bento* | 53 |
| Contemplating America's Camelot at Fifty: The JFK Years and the Christ Rhythm <br>    *by Kevin Dann* | 62 |
| Sophia and the Zodiac <br>    *by Lacquanna Paul* | 68 |
| Discovering the Zodiac in the Raphael Madonna Series Arranged by Rudolf Steiner <br>    *by Brian Gray* | 70 |
| Discussion of Astrological House Systems <br>    *by Robert Powell and Wain Farrants* | 86 |
| Patterns in the Language of the Stars <br>    *by Claudia Mclaren Lainson* | 94 |
| Comet ISON <br>    *by Wain Farrants* | 108 |
| Working with the Star Calender <br>    *by Robert Powell* | 110 |
| Symbols Used in Charts / Time | 112 |
| Commentaries and Ephemerides for January–December 2013 <br>    *by Claudia Mclaren Lainson* <br>    with Monthly Astronomical Sky Watch *by Sally Nurney* | 115 |
| *Glossary* | 232 |
| *References* | 239 |
| *About the Contributors* | 242 |

# ASTROSOPHY

The Sophia Foundation was founded and exists to help usher in the new Age of Sophia and the corresponding Sophianic culture, the Rose of the World, prophesied by Daniel Andreev and other spiritual teachers. Part of the work of the Sophia Foundation is the cultivation of a new star wisdom, *Astro-Sophia* (Astrosophy), now arising in our time in response to the descent of Sophia, who is the bearer of Divine Wisdom, just as Christ (the Logos, or the Lamb) is the bearer of Divine Love. Like the star wisdom of antiquity, Astrosophy is sidereal, which means "of the stars." Astrosophy, inspired by Divine Sophia, descending from stellar heights, directs our consciousness toward the glory and majesty of the starry heavens, to encompass the entire celestial sphere of our cosmos and, beyond this, to the galactic realm—the realm that Daniel Andreev referred to as "the heights of our universe"—from which Sophia is descending on her path of approach into our cosmos. Sophia draws our attention not only to the star mysteries of the heights, but also to the cosmic mysteries connected with Christ's deeds of redemption wrought two thousand years ago. To penetrate these mysteries is the purpose of the yearly *Journal for Star Wisdom*.

U

For information about Astrosophy/Choreocosmos/Cosmic Dance workshops
Contact the Sophia Foundation:
525 Gough St. #103, San Francisco, CA 94102
(415) 522-1150; sophia@sophiafoundation.org;
www.sophiafoundation.org

# PREFACE

## Robert Powell, Ph.D.

This is the fourth edition of the *Journal for Star Wisdom*, which is intended as a help to all people interested in the new star wisdom of astrosophy and in the cosmic dimension of Christianity, which began with the star of the magi. The calendar comprises an ephemeris page for each month of the year computed with the help of Peter Treadgold's Astrofire computer program, and a monthly commentary by Claudia McLaren Lainson (with Sally Nurney). The monthly commentary relates the geocentric and heliocentric planetary movements to events in the life of Jesus Christ.

Jesus Christ united the levels of the earthly personality (geocentric = Earth-centered) and the higher self (heliocentric = Sun-centered) in so far as he was the most highly evolved earthly personality (Jesus) embodying the Higher Self (Christ) of all existence, the Divine "I AM." To see the life of Jesus Christ in relation to the world of stars opens the door to a profound experience of the cosmos, giving rise to a new star wisdom (astrosophy) that is the spiritual science of Cosmic Christianity.

The *Journal for Star Wisdom* is scientific, resting upon a solid mathematical-astronomical foundation and also upon a secure chronology of the life of Jesus Christ, and at the same time it is spiritual, aspiring to the higher dimension of existence that is expressed outwardly in the world of stars. The scientific and the spiritual come together in the sidereal zodiac that originated with the Babylonians and was used by the three magi who beheld the star of Bethlehem and came to pay homage to Jesus a few months after his birth. In continuity of spirit with the origins of Cosmic Christianity with the three magi, the sidereal zodiac is the frame of reference used for the computation of the geocentric and heliocentric planetary movements which are commented upon in the light of the life of Jesus Christ in the *Journal for Star Wisdom*.

Thus, all zodiacal longitudes indicated in the text and presented in the following calendar are in terms of the sidereal zodiac, which has to be distinguished from the tropical zodiac in widespread use in contemporary astrology in the West. The tropical zodiac was introduced into astrology in the middle of the second century AD by the Greek astronomer Claudius Ptolemy. Prior to this the sidereal zodiac was in use. Such was the influence of Ptolemy upon the Western astrological tradition that the tropical zodiac became substituted for the sidereal zodiac used by the Babylonians, Egyptians, and early Greek astrologers. Yet the astrological tradition in India was not influenced by Ptolemy, and so the sidereal zodiac is still used to this day by Hindu astrologers.

The sidereal zodiac originated with the Babylonians in the sixth to fifth centuries BC and was defined by them in relation to certain bright stars. For example, Aldebaran ("the Bull's eye") is located in the middle of the sidereal sign/constellation of the Bull at 15° Taurus, and Antares ("the Scorpion's heart") is in the middle of the sidereal sign/constellation of the Scorpion at 15° Scorpio. The sidereal signs, each 30° long, coincide closely with the twelve astronomical zodiacal constellations of the same name, whereas the signs of the tropical zodiac, since they are defined in relation to the vernal point, now have little or no relationship to the corresponding zodiacal constellations. This is because the vernal point, the zodiacal location of the sun on March 20/21, shifts slowly backward through the sidereal zodiac at a rate of 1° in seventy-two years ("the precession of the equinoxes"). When Ptolemy introduced the tropical zodiac into astrology, there was an almost exact coincidence between the tropical and the sidereal zodiac, as the vernal point, which is defined to be 0° Aries in the tropical zodiac, was at 1° Aries in the sidereal zodiac in the middle of the second century AD. Thus, there was only 1° difference between the two zodiacs. So, it made hardly any difference to Ptolemy or his contemporaries to use the tropical zodiac instead of the sidereal zodiac. But now—the vernal point, on account of precession, having shifted back from 1° Aries to 5° Pisces—there is a 25° difference and so there is virtually no correspondence between the two. Without going into further detail concerning the complex issue of the zodiac, as shown in the *Hermetic Astrology* trilogy, the sidereal zodiac is the zodiac used by the three magi, who were the last representatives of the true star wisdom of antiquity. For this reason the sidereal zodiac is used throughout the *Journal for Star Wisdom*.

Readers interested in exploring the scientific (astronomical and chronological) foundations of Cosmic Christianity are referred to the works listed below under "Literature." The *Chronicle of the Living Christ: Foundations of Cosmic Christianity,* listed on the next page, is an indispensable source of reference (abbreviated *Chron.*) for the *Journal for Star Wisdom,* as, too, are the four Gospels (Matthew = Mt.; Mark = Mk.; Luke = Lk.; John = Jn.). The chronology of the life of Jesus Christ rests upon the description of his daily life by Anne Catherine Emmerich in her four-volume work *The Life of Jesus Christ* (abbreviated *LJC*). Further details concerning the *Journal for Star Wisdom* and how to work with it on a daily basis may be found in the general introduction to the *Christian Star Calendar.* The general introduction explains all the features of the *Journal for Star Wisdom.* The new edition, published 2003, includes sections on the megastars (stars of great luminosity) and on the 36 decans (10° subdivisions of the twelve signs of the zodiac) in relation to their planetary rulers and to the extra-zodiacal constellations, those constellations above or below the circle of the twelve constellations/signs of the zodiac. Further material on the decans, including examples of historical personalities born in the various decans, and also a wealth of other material on the signs of the sidereal zodiac, is to be found in *Cosmic Dances of the Zodiac,* listed below. Also foundational is *History of the Zodiac,* published by Sophia Academic Press, listed below under "Works by Robert Powell."

## LITERATURE

*(See also "References" section)*

*General Introduction to the Christian Star Calendar: A Key to Understanding,* 2nd ed. Palo Alto, CA: Sophia Foundation, 2003.

Bento, William, Robert Schiappacasse, and David Tresemer, *Signs in the Heavens: A Message for our Time.* Boulder: StarHouse, 2000.

Emmerich, Anne Catherine, *Visions of the Life of Jesus Christ* (new edition, with material by Robert Powell). San Rafael, CA: LogoSophia, 2012.

Paul, Lacquanna, and Robert Powell, *Cosmic Dances of the Planets.* San Rafael, CA: Sophia Foundation Press, 2007.

———, *Cosmic Dances of the Zodiac.* San Rafael, CA: Sophia Foundation Press, 2007.

Smith, Edward, *The Burning Bush: An Anthroposophical Commentary on the Bible.* Great Barrington, MA: SteinerBooks, 1997.

Steiner, Rudolf, *Astronomy and Astrology. Finding a Relationship to the Cosmos.* Rudolf Steiner Press: London, 2009.

Sucher, Willi, *Cosmic Christianity and the Changing Countenance of Cosmology.* Great Barrington, MA: SteinerBooks, 1993. *Isis Sophia* and other works by Willi Sucher are available from the Astrosophy Research Center, PO Box 13, Meadow Vista, CA 95722.

Tidball, Charles S., and Robert Powell, *Jesus, Lazarus, and the Messiah: Unveiling Three Christian Mysteries.* Great Barrington, MA: SteinerBooks, 2005. This book offers a penetrating study of the Christ mysteries against the background of *Chronicle of the Living Christ* and contains two chapters by Robert Powell on the Apostle John and John the Evangelist (Lazarus).

Tresemer, David (with Robert Schiappacasse), *Star Wisdom & Rudolf Steiner: A Life Seen Through the Oracle of the Solar Cross*. Great Barrington. MA: SteinerBooks, 2007.

## ASTROSOPHICAL WORKS BY ROBERT POWELL, PH.D.

**Starcrafts (formerly Astro Communication Services, or ACS):**

*History of the Houses* (1997).

*History of the Planets* (1989).

*The Zodiac: A Historical Survey* (1984).

www.acspublications.com

www.astrocom.com

Business Address:

Starcrafts Publishing

334 Calef Hwy.

Epping, NH 03042

Phone: 603-734-4300

Fax: 603-734-4311

Contact maria@starcraftseast.com

**SteinerBooks:**

Orders: (703) 661-1594; www.steinerbooks.org; PO Box 960, Herndon, VA 20172.

*The Astrological Revolution: Unveiling the Science of the Stars as a Science of Reincarnation and Karma,* coauthor Kevin Dann (Great Barrington, MA: SteinerBooks, 2010). After reestablishing the sidereal zodiac as a basis for astrology that penetrates the mystery of the stars' relationship to human destiny, the reader is invited to discover the astrological significance of the totality of the vast sphere of stars surrounding the Earth. This book points to the astrological significance of the entire celestial sphere, including all the stars and constellations beyond the twelve zodiacal signs. This discovery is revealed by the study of megastars, illustrating how they show up in an extraordinary way in Christ's healing miracles by aligning with the Sun at the time of those events. This book offers a spiritual, yet scientific, path toward a new relationship to the stars.

*Christian Hermetic Astrology: The Star of the Magi and the Life of Christ* (Great Barrington, MA: SteinerBooks, 1998). Twenty-five discourses set in the "Temple of the Sun," where Hermes and his pupils gather to meditate on the Birth, the Miracles, and the Passion of Jesus Christ. The discourses offer a series of meditative contemplations on the deeds of Christ in relation to the mysteries of the cosmos. They are an expression of the age-old hermetic mystery wisdom of the ancient Egyptian sage, Hermes Trismegistus. This book offers a meditative approach to the cosmic correspondences between major events in the life of Christ and the heavenly configurations at that time 2,000 years ago.

*Chronicle of the Living Christ: Foundations of Cosmic Christianity* (Great Barrington, MA: SteinerBooks, 1996). An account of the life of Christ, day by day, throughout most of the 3½ years of his ministry, including the horoscopes of conception, birth, and death of Jesus, Mary and John the Baptist, together with a wealth of material relating to a new star wisdom focused on the life of Christ. This work provides the chronological basis for *Christian Hermetic Astrology* and the *Journal for Star Wisdom*.

*Elijah Come Again: A Prophet for our Time: A Scientific Approach to Reincarnation* (Great Barrington, MA: Steiner Books, 2009). By way of horoscope comparisons from conception–birth–death in one incarnation to conception–birth–death in the next, this work establishes scientifically two basic astrosophical research findings. These are: the importance 1) of the sidereal zodiac and 2) of the heliocentric positions of the planets. Also, for the first time, the identity of the "saintly nun" is revealed, of whom Rudolf Steiner spoke in a conversation with Marie von Sivers about tracing Novalis's karmic background. The focus throughout the book is on the Elijah individuality in his various incarnations, and is based solidly on Rudolf Steiner's indications. It also can be read as a karmic biography by anyone who chooses to omit the astrosophical material.

*Journal for Star Wisdom* (Great Barrington, MA: SteinerBooks, annual). Edited by Robert Powell and others in the StarFire research group: A guide to the correspondences of Christ in the stellar and etheric world. Includes articles of interest, a complete sidereal ephemeris and aspectarian, geocentric and heliocentric. Published yearly in November for the coming year. According to Rudolf Steiner, every step taken by Christ during his ministry between the baptism in the Jordan and the resurrection was in harmony with, and an expression of, the cosmos. The journal is concerned with these heavenly correspondences during the life of Christ. It is intended to help provide a foundation for Cosmic Christianity, the cosmic dimension of Christianity. It is this dimension that has been missing from Christianity in its 2,000-year history. A starting point is to contemplate the movements of the Sun, Moon, and planets against the background of the zodiacal constellations (sidereal signs) today in relation to corresponding stellar events during the life of Christ. This opens the possibility of attuning to the life of Christ in the etheric cosmos in a living way.

## Sophia Foundation Press and Sophia Academic Press Publications

PO Box 151011, San Rafael, CA 94915; (707) 789-9062; Email: JamesWetmore@mac.com.
Website: www.logosophia.com

*History of the Zodiac* (San Rafael, CA: Sophia Academic Press, 2007). Book version of Robert Powell's Ph.D. thesis on the *History of the Zodiac*. This penetrating study of the *History of the Zodiac* restores the sidereal zodiac to its rightful place as the original zodiac, tracing it back to fifth-century B.C. Babylonians. Available in paperback and hard cover.

*Hermetic Astrology: Volume 1, Astrology and Reincarnation* (San Rafael, CA: Sophia Foundation Press, 2007). This book seeks to give the ancient science of the stars a scientific basis. This new foundation for astrology based on research into reincarnation and karma (destiny) is the primary focus. It includes numerous reincarnation examples, the study of which reveals the existence of certain astrological "laws" of reincarnation, on the basis of which it is evident that the ancient sidereal zodiac is the authentic astrological zodiac, and that the heliocentric movements of the planets are of great significance. Foundational for the new star wisdom of astrosophy.

*Hermetic Astrology: Volume 2, Astrological Biography* (San Rafael, CA: Sophia Foundation Press, 2007). Concerned with karmic relationships and the unfolding of destiny in seven-year periods through one's life. The seven-year rhythm underlies the human being's astrological biography, which can be studied in relation to the movements of the Sun, Moon, and planets around the sidereal zodiac between conception and birth. The "rule of Hermes" is used to determine the moment of conception.

*Sign of the Son of Man in the Heavens: Sophia and the New Star Wisdom* (San Rafael, CA: Sophia Foundation Press, 2008). Revised and expanded with new material, this edition deals with a new wisdom of stars in the light of Divine Sophia. It is intended as a help in our time, when we are called on to be extremely wakeful during the period leading up to the end of the Mayan calendar in 2012.

*Cosmic Dances of the Zodiac* (San Rafael, CA: Sophia Foundation Press, 2007) coauthor Lacquanna Paul. Study material describing the twelve signs of the zodiac and their forms and gestures in cosmic dance, with diagrams, including a wealth of information on the twelve signs and the 36 decans (the subdivision of the signs into decans, or 10° sectors, corresponding to constellations above and below the zodiac).

*Cosmic Dances of the Planets* (San Rafael, CA: Sophia Foundation Press, 2007), coauthor Lacquanna Paul. Study material describing the seven classical planets and their forms and gestures in cosmic dance, with diagrams, including much information on the planets.

## American Federation of Astrologers (AFA) Publications

PO Box 22040, Tempe, AZ 85285.

*The Sidereal Zodiac*, coauthor Peter Treadgold (Tempe, AZ: AFA, 1985). A *History of the Zodiac* (sidereal, tropical, Hindu, astronomical) and a formal definition of the sidereal zodiac with the star Aldebaran ("the Bull's Eye") at 15° Taurus. This is an abbreviated version of *History of the Zodiac*.

## Rudolf Steiner College Press Publications

9200 Fair Oaks Blvd., Fair Oaks, CA 95628

*The Christ Mystery: Reflections on the Second Coming* (Fair Oaks, CA: Rudolf Steiner College Press, 1999). The fruit of many years of reflecting on the Second Coming and its cosmological aspects. Looks at the approaching trial of humanity and the challenges of living in apocalyptic times, against the background of "great signs in the heavens."

## The Sophia Foundation

525 Gough St. #103, San Francisco, CA 94102; distributes many of the books listed

## Preface

here and other works by Robert Powell.
Tel: (415) 522-1150
sophia@sophiafoundation.org
www.sophiafoundation.org

Computer Program for Charts and Ephemerides, with grateful acknowledgment to Peter Treadgold, who wrote the computer program *Astrofire* (with research module, star catalog of over 4,000 stars, and database of birth and death charts of historical personalities), capable of printing geocentric and heliocentric/hermetic sidereal charts and ephemerides throughout history. The hermetic charts, based on the astronomical system of the Danish astronomer Tycho Brahe, are called "Tychonic" charts in the program. This program can:

- compute birth charts in a large variety of systems (tropical, sidereal, geocentric, heliocentric, hermetic);
- calculate conception charts using the hermetic rule, in turn applying it for correction of the birth time;
- produce charts for the period between conception and birth;
- print out an "astrological biography" for the whole of lifework with the geocentric, heliocentric (and even lemniscatory) planetary system;
- work with the sidereal zodiac according to the definition of your choice (Babylonian sidereal, Indian sidereal, unequal-division astronomical, etc.);
- work with planetary aspects with orbs of your choice.

The program includes eight house systems and a variety of chart formats. The program also includes an ephemeris program with a search facility. The geocentric/heliocentric sidereal ephemeris pages in the yearly *Journal for Star Wisdom* are produced by *Astrofire*. This program runs under Microsoft Windows. Those interested in *Astrofire* may contact:

The Sophia Foundation
525 Gough St. #103, San Francisco, CA 94102
Tel: (415) 522-1150
sophia@sophiafoundation.org
www.sophiafoundation.org

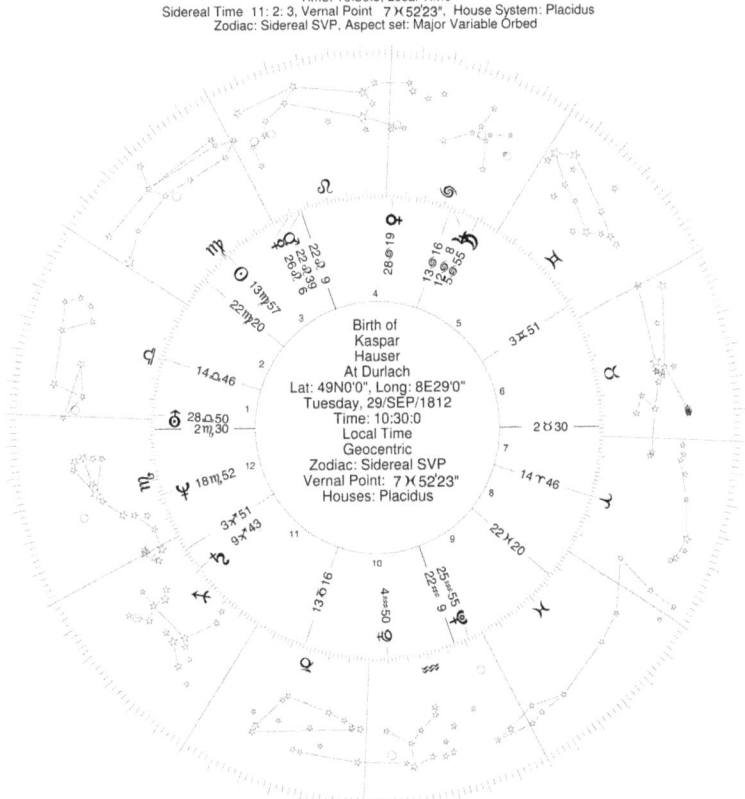

*A horoscope generated by the Astrofire program*

# THE ROSE OF THE WORLD (*ROSA MIRA*)
## *Daniel Andreev*

By warning about the coming Antichrist and pointing him out and unmasking him when he appears, by cultivating unshakable faith within human hearts and a grasp of the meta-historical perspectives and global spiritual prospects within human minds...[we help Sophia bring to birth the new culture of love and wisdom called by Daniel Andreev the "Rose of the World."]...[Sophia's] birth in one of the *zatomis* will be mirrored not only by the Rose of the World; feminine power and its role in contemporary life are increasing everywhere. It is that circumstance, above all, that is giving rise to worldwide peace movements, an abhorrence of bloodshed, disillusion over coercive methods of change, an increase in woman's role in society proper, an ever-growing tenderness and concern for children, and a burning hunger for beauty and love. We are entering an age when the female soul will become ever purer and broader, when an ever-greater number of women will become profound inspirers, sensitive mothers, wise counselors, and far-sighted leaders. It will be an age when the feminine in humanity will manifest with unprecedented strength, striking a perfect balance with masculine impulses. See, you who have eyes.[1]

{These words are those of Daniel Andreev (1906–1959), the great prophet of the coming Age of Sophia and the corresponding Sophianic culture he called the "Rose of the World." In this quote, *zatomis* refers to a heavenly realm within the Earth's etheric aura. Andreev refers to Sophia as *Zventa-Sventana*, "Holiest of the Holy."]

A mysterious event is taking place in the meta-history of contemporary times: new divine-creative energy is emanating into our cosmos. Since ancient times the loftiest hearts and most subtle minds have anticipated this event that is now taking place. The first link in the chain of events—events so important that they can only be compared to the incarnation of the Logos—occurred at the turn of the nineteenth century. This was an emanation of the energy of the Virgin Mother, an emanation that was not amorphous, as it had been before in human history [at Pentecost, when there was an emanation of Sophia into the Virgin Mary], but incomparably intensified by the personal aspect it assumed. A great God-born monad descended from the heights of the universe into our cosmos (ibid., p. 356).

[The words of the great Russian seer, Daniel Andreev, are prophetic. As indicated in *The Most Holy Trinosophia*,[2] he points to the descent of Sophia and the resulting Sophianic world culture, the Rose of the World, in a most inspiring way.]

She is to be born in a body of enlightened ether.... There She is, our hope and joy, Light and Divine Beauty! For Her birth will be mirrored in our history as something that our grandchildren and great-grandchildren will witness: the founding of the Rose of the World, its spread throughout the world, and...the assumption by the Rose of the World of supreme authority over the entire Earth (ibid., p. 357).

[The Sophia Foundation was founded and exists to help usher in the new Age of Sophia and the corresponding Sophianic culture, the Rose of the World, prophesied by Daniel Andreev and other spiritual teachers.

---

1 Daniel Andreev, *The Rose of the World*, p. 358. Words in brackets [ ] here and in the following text are added by Robert Powell.

2 Robert Powell, *The Most Holy Trinosophia: The New Revelation of the Divine Feminine*.

As quoted at the beginning, "warning about the coming Antichrist and pointing him out and unmasking him when he appears" is important. As discussed in the article "In Memory of Willi Sucher" (*Journal for Star Wisdom 2010*).

Humanity's encounter with the Antichrist is part of the initiation trial of humanity as a whole crossing the threshold. The external aspect of this initiation trial is the meeting with the Antichrist as the embodiment of the sum-total of humanity's negative karma, *the double of humankind as a whole*. The inner aspect is the encounter with Christ or the Archangel Michael as the Guardian of the Threshold. The result of successfully passing through this initiation trial is the opening up of conscious awareness of the angelic realm. This is one aspect of the great event at the culmination of the process of humankind as a whole crossing the threshold. Another aspect of this culmination is depicted in the article on World Pentecost.[3]

More than anyone else, Daniel Andreev, as prophet of the coming Sophia culture, the Rose of the World, had a visionary experience of the coming of the Antichrist. His words concerning this are not in the English edition of the *Rose of the World*. Because of the importance of Daniel Andreev's vision of the coming of the Antichrist, his words about this appeared for the first time in English in this journal.

The German translation of Daniel Andreev's book *Rosa Mira: Rose of the World*, in three volumes, comprises a translation of the *whole* original Russian text, whereas the English edition corresponds to volume 1 of the three German volumes.[4]

## The Preparation of Human Beings for the Coming Antilogos

Certainly, humanity has not lacked warnings. Not only the *New Testament* but also the *Qur'an* and even the *Mahabharata* have warned us in the distant past. Have spiritual seers in the East and in the West not proclaimed the Antichrist as an unavoidable evil? All leaders of the Rose of the World will concentrate their forces upon the work of warning about this monster.... This bearer of a dark mission will probably not truly grasp whom he serves and for whom he prepares the way. With all his intellectual genius, his mind will be completely closed to anything of a mystical nature.... He will be greeted enthusiastically: "There he is! The one for whom we have been waiting!" He will show his true force only much later, when the "savior" holds the entire power in his hands....

Is it a matter of a human being? Yes and no. On several occasions [in *Rosa Mira*] I have indicated that this individual was incarnated as a Roman emperor and how, over the centuries and from life to life, he became enveloped in demonic substance. Concerning this monad, whom Gagtungr [Ahriman, or Satan] himself has kidnapped... enough has been said about his previous incarnation [as Stalin] in Russia.... [In that incarnation,] the forces of providence hindered [Satan's attempt] to make of him a dark, universal genius.

[Now, in 1958, he is being prepared] for the successful fulfillment of the historic role of the Antichrist. Stalin's tyrannical genius and his ability to control hypnotically the will of others is well known.... [When he reincarnates as the Antichrist,] he will have at his disposal an enormous capacity for work and a multitude of talents.... He will be uniquely and terribly beautiful. From his facial characteristics, it will be difficult to place him in any particular race or nation. Rather, he will be seen as a representative of the collective of humanity.... [At a certain point in his life, he will undergo a transformation.] His transformation will be noticed by people immediately, yet they will be unable to recognize the meaning or the "how" [of this transformation]. The external appearance of the transformed one will remain virtually unchanged. However, a terrible and frightening energy will proceed from him... Anyone who touches him will receive an electric shock. An invincible hypnotic force [will proceed from him].... The disturbing influence [on spiritually striving human beings] and upon the entire population set in motion by the transformation of the Antilogos will be extraordinary....

---

3  See Robert Powell, *Prophecy-Phenomena-Hope*.
4  The following translation from German into English is by RP.

After a rigged vote, he—the miracle worker—will crown himself.... Humanity will be divided [into those who accept him as world ruler] and those who refuse to acknowledge the usurper.... Of course, force will be used against anyone who refuses to follow the Antichrist. Dark miracles will increasingly occur, shattering the consciousness of people to the very roots of their being. For many, Christ's miracles will pale into insignificance. Crazy enthusiasm will roll in waves across the world.... Eventually, the Antilogos will hold the sole rulership of the planet in his hands. Yet, the true and highest leaders will not subject themselves to this usurper. This will also be the case for millions, perhaps hundreds of millions, of people in every country of the world.

The age of persecution commences. From year to year, they become increasingly extensive, methodical, [and] cruel. Here, the cunning Gagtungr [Ahriman/Satan] even makes use of the heroic protest of the masses. The candidate for the Antichrist who had failed...who had taken his life at the end of World War II,[5] advances now to become the self-appointed leader of the rebels in the struggle against the world ruler.... His thoroughly dark movement will draw the hearts of many into a spiral of raging wickedness and senseless hatred.... Christ's significance will continually be weakened. Then his name will be denied—and finally enveloped in silence....

Shock and terror will take hold of many. Millions of those who had previously distanced themselves from religious matters, who occupied themselves primarily with concerns in their own little world or with artistic pursuits or scientific research, will sense that an irrevocable and very dangerous choice confronts them. In the face of this, even torture and execution pale.... Countless people will turn away from this offspring of hell...from the dark miracles and the charm of the superman, as well as from his immeasurable intelligence and frighteningly cynical wickedness.... The majority of people will fall away from God and allow themselves to be led astray by Gagtungr's protégée....

Stalin wanted not only to be feared; he also wanted to be loved. The Antichrist, however, has need of only one thing: the conviction that everyone [should hold] without exception, [to] believe in his superiority and [to] subject themselves to him without hesitation....

When [during the reign of the Antichrist] the machine civilization begins its total assault on Nature, the entire landscape of the Earth's surface will be transformed into a complete Anti-Nature.... Nature, having become inwardly empty and outwardly crippled, will no longer awaken aesthetic or pantheistic feelings....

Certainly, too, during the complete rule of the tyrant, there will be many whose innermost life will rebel against the senseless existence under the Antichrist. However, psychic control will stifle such thoughts as they arise, and only a few will succeed in acquiring a system of psychic self-defense to protect them from being physically destroyed....

All written or other testimonies that could be dangerous for the Antichrist will be destroyed....

[The suffering of human beings gives nourishment (*gavvach*) to the demons.]...No world wars, revolutions, or repressions, no mass spilling of blood, could have produced *gavvach* in such amounts.... In fact, even humanity in its demonized aspect will not satisfy the Antichrist. He needs humanity as his source of *gavvach*.... [However] even in the most sinful soul, an inextinguishable spark of conscience gleams. However, despair, increasing ignorance, and sheer boredom with life will also take hold of many people, and this will lead to their rejection by the Antichrist. Of what use to him is the intellectual paralysis that sets in after such excesses of despair? Such people are hardly suited to the further development of demonic science and technology or to the conquest of the cosmos or the satanizing of the world....

---

5 Daniel Andreev depicts the two main candidates for the Antichrist in their twentieth-century incarnations: Adolf Hitler and Joseph Stalin. In those incarnations, they competed with each other to become the most evil. In the following incarnation, the most evil one would become the vessel for the incarnation of the Antichrist. According to Daniel Andreev, Joseph Stalin outdid Adolf Hitler to become the chosen one, the prince of darkness.
—R. Powell

[After the Antichrist's death] the world state will rapidly collapse, and only drastic measures will hinder anarchy in various parts of the world.... "And there appears a great sign in heaven: a woman clothed with the Sun" [Revelation 12:1]. Who is the *woman clothed with the Sun*? It is *Sventa-Sventana* [Sophia], embraced by the planetary Logos and chosen to give birth to the Great Spirit of the Second Aeon. The reflection of this event in world history is the Rose of the World, whose utmost striving before, during, and after the time of the Antichrist prepares humanity to become a vessel for the Great Spirit.... An unimaginable jubilation will take hold of this and other worlds as humanity passes through a great, light-filled transformation.

The prince of darkness will terrify human beings.... Christ, however, will take on as many forms as there are conscious beings on Earth to behold him. He will adapt himself to everyone and will converse with all. His forms will simultaneously yield an image in an unimaginable way: *One who appears in heaven surrounded by unspeakable glory*. There will not be a single being on Earth who will not see the Son of God and hear his Word.[6]

[These words by Daniel Andreev are prophetic. They were written shortly before his death in 1959. Now, more than fifty years later, not only is the encounter with the Son of God possible, but also the possibility of hearing his Word. Today, we can experience this meeting with the Son of God in the realm of life forces, also known as the *etheric realm*. This is the most important event that anyone in earthly existence can experience. This spiritual event is the initiatory aspect of human encounters with the Antichrist and the initiation trial for humanity as a whole crossing the threshold.

An example of this spiritual event is related in an account of a young woman of her initiatory experience in meeting Christ as the Greater Guardian of the threshold. She prefers to remain anonymous. This description of her meeting with Christ in the etheric realm—with the etheric Christ, to use Rudolf Steiner's expression—can be a source of inspiration to everyone. She describes how she came to this experience of the etheric Christ through meditating on Christ's experiences during the night prior to the Mystery of Golgotha, the night in the Garden of Gethsemane.]

My focus was again turned to Gethsemane. I entered the light of his deed in the garden and a state of ecstasy—an ineffable, unutterable ecstasy. The light of Christ in Gethsemane enveloped the Earth. Up to that point, I had never merged with such light. My heart soared in ecstasy, lifted into another realm of spirit. I exclaimed, *"This is Life! This is Life eternal, the Life of the world. This is Love! This is eternal Love, which knows no boundaries, for it has penetrated everything in the Earth. It lives within the Earth as an eternal promise of redemption. His love is eternal; His love is free for all who will accept it!"*

Christ then gave me a message for all: *"Love one another and love the Earth. Send your love to your fellow beings and into the Earth that the Earth may be lifted up on wings of peace. There is a body of the Earth, which is a body of love; this is My body that I gave to the Earth. You become one with the body of love by doing works of love, by cultivating feelings of love and by thinking thoughts of love. I invite all to become one with Me in this body of love. I call you home; My arms are around you. Return to love. Remember love. For where love is there am I; and because I desire to have you in My heart, I ask you to love one another, that I may be in you and you in Me. Look for Me to come to you for I am coming and shall gather you to myself and you shall be safely folded in Me because you are precious in My sight; and My sight is ever upon you. Return to Me."*

I then gazed upon him, embracing all of the cosmos. With his arms outstretched across the expanse of Heaven, his voice penetrating the depths of my heart with these words: "I AM eternally here!"

---

6  Daniil Andrejew, *Rosa Mira: Die Weltrose*, vol. 3, pp. 202–226.

# EDITORIAL FOREWORD

## *Robert Powell, Ph.D.*

The *Journal for Star Wisdom* (formerly *Christian Star Calendar*) has appeared every year since 1991. From the beginning the central feature has been the calendar comprising the monthly ephemeris pages together with commentaries drawing attention to the Christ events remembered by the ongoing cosmic events. The significance of following the Christ events in relation to daily astronomical events is an important foundation for the new star wisdom of astrosophy.[1] This new star wisdom is arising in our time in response to the second coming of Christ—known as his return in the etheric realm of life forces—as a path of communing with Christ in his life body (ether body). It should also be mentioned that, with the onset of the second coming of Christ during the course of the twentieth century, Christ is now the Lord of Karma, and this is important to take into consideration in the development of a new relationship of humanity to the stars in our time, particularly with respect to the horoscope as an expression of human karma or destiny.

The events of Christ's life lived two thousand years ago are inscribed into his ether body, and to meditate upon these events at times when they are cosmically remembered is a way of drawing near to Christ. The recently updated version of my article "Subnature and the Second Coming" (in *The Inner Life of the Earth*[2]) outlines the background to contemporary events as a confrontation between good and evil in relation to Christ's descent at this time through the sub-earthly realms and also gives an overview of the various cosmic rhythms unfolding in relation to his second coming, including the thirty-three-and-one-third-year rhythm of his ether body.

The *Journal for Star Wisdom* encourages the reader to engage in the practice of stargazing, which is fundamental to the development of the new star wisdom of astrosophy. One of the foundations of astrosophy lies in the science of astronomy, providing the new star wisdom with a secure scientific foundation, which moreover, can be brought into the realm of experience through the practice of stargazing. In astrosophy there is no longer a separation between astronomy and astrology. For example, when in the *Journal for Star Wisdom* it is indicated that currently Mars in the heavens is at 15° Taurus then, assuming that Mars is visible, the red planet can be seen in conjunction with Aldebaran marking the Bull's eye at the center of the constellation of Taurus, whose longitude, as the central star in this constellation, is 15° Taurus. In astrosophy, the astrological fact of Mars at 15° Taurus is identical with the astronomical reality of Mars' location at the

---

[1] There are many different approaches to astrosophy and not all use the equal-division sidereal zodiac that forms the basis of the approach followed in the *Journal for Star Wisdom*. All references to the zodiac and to planetary positions in the zodiac in the *Journal for Star Wisdom* are in terms of the sidereal zodiac as defined in my book *History of the Zodiac*. Moreover, in astrosophy there are different chronologies of the life of Christ, and the chronology that forms the basis of the approach followed in the *Journal for Star Wisdom* is set forth in my book *Chronicle of the Living Christ*. Thus, all references to planetary positions at the Christ events in the *Journal for Star Wisdom* are in terms of the scientifically established chronology of the life of Christ set forth in my book *Chronicle of the Living Christ*.

[2] O'Leary (ed.), *The Inner Life of the Earth*, pp. 69–141.

center of the constellation of Taurus. Astrosophy thus relates to sense-perceptible reality and to the Divine "background of existence" (the spiritual hierarchies)[3] underlying this reality, whereas astrology is generally practiced in such a way that there is a split between astrology and astronomy (in this example, modern astrology, which uses the tropical zodiac rather than the equal-division sidereal zodiac used in astrosophy, would say that Mars is "in Gemini"). The historical background as to how this separation between astronomy and astrology arose is described in my book *History of the Zodiac*.[4]

The present issue of the *Journal for Star Wisdom* is the twenty-second, but is the fourth published under the new title, as the first eighteen issues were published under the title *Christian Star Calendar*. By way of explanation concerning the new title: this publication is intended as an outreach from the StarFire research group (an astrosophy group) that meets yearly in Boulder, Colorado (sometimes in Fair Oaks, California); see the website www.StarWisdom.org.[5] The *Journal for Star Wisdom* is intended as an organ for the development of the new star wisdom of astrosophy. This was also the purpose of the *Christian Star Calendar*. However, there the focus, at least, initially, was primarily on the calendar—the monthly ephemeris and commentaries. In the course of time, more and more research articles on the new star wisdom of astrosophy came to be published in the *Christian Star Calendar*. A point was reached where it became clear that the publication is more of a journal than a calendar, although the calendar continues to play an important role. It is therefore a natural transition from the *Christian Star Calendar* to the *Journal for Star Wisdom*.

As referred to in my article in this issue of the *Journal for Star Wisdom*, perhaps the greatest prophecy of our time—one that is little known, but which is the reason for the existence of this journal, and is a source of tremendous spiritual light—is Rudolf Steiner's prophecy from the year 1910, just over one hundred years ago. On January 12, 1910, he prophesied that the second coming of Christ would begin in 1933, an event called "Christ's appearance in the etheric realm"—not a return in a physical body but in an etheric (life) body, the realm of life forces. Here with my translation of Marie Steiner's notes from this important, hitherto unpublished lecture:

> 3000 BC: Kali Yuga commenced and lasted until 1899—a time of great transition.
>
> 1933: human beings will appear with clairvoyant faculties, which they will develop naturally. At this time, which we are approaching, the newly beginning clairvoyant faculties have to be satisfied, to experience what they [human beings] should do with them.
>
> I am with you always, even unto the end of the world.
>
> Christ will appear in an etheric form. The physical Christ became the Spirit of the Earth—this was the midpoint, the balance, of Earth evolution.
>
> 5th Letter of the Ap(ocalypse): I will come again; however, take heed that you do not fail to recognize me.
>
> 2,500 years is the time which humanity has to develop again the gifts of clairvoyance. Around 1933 the Gospels must be recognized in their spiritual meaning such that they have worked preparing for Christ. Otherwise untold confusion of the soul will be caused.
>
> Around 1933 there will be some representatives of black magical schools, who will falsely proclaim a physical Christ.

---

3　According to Rudolf Steiner, the constellations are the abode of the first hierarchy, called Seraphim, Cherubim, and Thrones. The movement of the planets takes place against the background of the zodiacal constellations, which—considered as the abode of the first hierarchy—form the Divine "background of existence" in the heavens. "Suppose you wanted to point to some particular [group of] Thrones, Cherubim and Seraphim, one denotes them by a particular constellation. It is like a signpost. In that direction over there are the [group of] Thrones, Cherubim and Seraphim known as the Twins, over there [the group of Thrones, Cherubim and Seraphim known as] the Lion, etc." (Steiner, *The Spiritual Hierarchies*, p. 99; words in brackets added by RP).

4　Robert Powell, *History of the Zodiac*.

5　Other astrosophy websites are www.sophiafoundation.org and www.astrogeographia.org.

Each time that he becomes perceptible, Christ is perceptible for other faculties.[6]

This was Rudolf Steiner's greatest prophecy: the second coming of Christ, which he called the appearance of Christ in the etheric realm, beginning in 1933. It is this event, the presence of the etheric Christ, lasting from 1933 for 2,500 years (until 4433), that is pivotal for the approach to astrosophy (star wisdom) outlined in the *Journal for Star Wisdom*.

[6] Translated from the first page of Marie Steiner's notes, recently published in German for the first time in *Der Europäer,* vol. 14, December/January 2009/2010, p. 3.

In conclusion I would like to express gratitude to our publisher, Gene Gollogly of SteinerBooks, and to the able assistance of Jens Jensen of SteinerBooks, for making this fourth issue of the *Journal for Star Wisdom* available, and to all those who have contributed to make this issue possible, in particular to our authors for presenting their research articles as contributions to the foundations of the new star wisdom of astrosophy, and to all our readers who ultimately are the reason for the existence of the *Journal for Star Wisdom*.

---

"The stars are the expression of love in the cosmic ether...To see a star means to feel a caress that has been prompted by love.... To gaze at the stars is to become aware of the love proceeding from divine spiritual beings.... The stars are signs and tokens of the presence of gods in the universe." (*Karmic Relationships,* vol. 7, June 8, 1924)

"We must see in the shining stars the outer signs of colonies of spirits in the cosmos. Wherever a star is seen in the heavens, there—in that direction—is a colony of spirits." (*Karmic Relationships,* vol. 6, June 1, 1924)

"They looked up above all to what is represented by the zodiac. And they regarded what the human being bears within as the spirit in connection with the constellations, the glory of the fixed stars, the spiritual powers whom they knew to be there in the stars." (*Karmic Relationships,* vol. 4, Sept. 12, 1924)

"All the stars are colonies of spiritual beings in cosmic space, colonies which we can learn to know when, having passed through the gate of death, our own soul lives and moves among these starry colonies...with the beings of the hierarchies.... To understand karma, therefore, we must return once more to a wisdom of the stars. We must discover spiritually the paths of human beings between death and a new birth in connection with the beings of the stars.... There has come forth a certain stream of spiritual life which makes it very difficult to approach with an open mind the science of the stars, and the science of karma.... We can nevertheless go forward with assurance and approach the wisdom of the stars and the real shaping of karma." (*Karmic Relationships,* vol. 4, Sept. 18, 1924)

# WORKING WITH THE JOURNAL FOR STAR WISDOM

The listing of major planetary events each month is intended as a stimulus toward attunement with the Universal Christ, the Logos, whose being encompasses the entire galaxy. The deeds of the historical Christ wrought two thousand years ago are of eternal significance—inscribed into the cosmos—and they resonate with the movements of the heavenly bodies, especially when certain alignments or planetary configurations occur bearing a resemblance with those prevailing at the time of events in the life of Jesus Christ. With the rare astronomical event of the transit of Venus across the face of the Sun that took place June 8, 2004, at exactly the zodiacal degree (23° Taurus), where the Sun stood at Christ's Ascension, a new impulse was given from divine-spiritual realms for the further unfolding of star wisdom, *Astro-Sophia*.

The calendar may be found beginning on page 115. It comprises ephemeris pages for the twelve months of the year with accompanying monthly commentaries on the astronomical events listed on the ephemeris pages. Indications regarding the similarity of contemporary planetary configurations with those at events in the life of Christ are given in the lower part of the monthly commentaries, and the upper part gives a commentary on the notable astronomical occurrences each month. Unless otherwise stated, all astronomical indications regarding visibility mean "visible to the naked eye." See the note concerning time on the page preceding the monthly commentaries.

With this calendar, astronomy and astrology, which were a unity in the ancient star wisdom of the Egyptians and Babylonians, are reunited and provide a foundation for astrosophy, the all-encompassing star wisdom, *Astro-Sophia*, an expression of Sophia and referred to in the Revelation of John as the "Bride of the Lamb."

# EARTH CHAKRAS

## *Robert Powell & David Bowden*

This article is excerpted from chapter 10 of the new book by Robert Powell & David Bowden, *Astrogeographia: Correspondences between the Stars and Earthly Locations—Earth Chakras and the Bible of Astrology* (Great Barrington, MA: SteinerBooks, 2012).

### *The Imprint of the Stars upon the Earth*

We have considered the relationship of the earthly globe to the celestial sphere comprising multitudes of stars, looking at how the stars in the heavens are mirrored on the Earth at various locations, as indicated in Rudolf Steiner's words, *"we can conceive of the active heavenly sphere mirrored in the Earth."*[1] Elsewhere Rudolf Steiner said: *"The continents upon the Earth are held in place from without by the starry constellations. When the constellations change, the continents change, also. On the old maps and atlases these relationships between starry constellations and configurations on the Earth's surface were correctly shown, including also the constellations of the zodiac."*[2]

What we believe to be the correct depiction of the projection of the zodiacal constellations—in particular, of the ecliptic running through the middle of the zodiacal constellations—has been mapped out by David Bowden.[3]

Now there is the question as to whether not only the stars but also the planets might be mirrored upon the Earth? Astrogeographia is concerned primarily with the projection of the stars upon the earthly globe, which is a huge theme. However, the relationship of the planets to the earthly globe is also a vast theme—one which we can only briefly depict here in outline. We ask the reader to bear with us in this sketch, in the understanding that it deserves a much more profound treatment than we are able to give it here.

The relationship of the stars and planets to the Earth are continually changing each hour of the day on account of the Earth's rotation. However, in Astrogeographia we are interested in the *archetypal relationship* of the heavens to the Earth. To express what is meant by "archetypal relationship" an analogy may be drawn with the horoscope at a person's birth.

> If one were to photograph a person's brain at the moment of birth and then photograph also the heavens lying exactly over the person's birthplace, this latter picture would be of exactly the same appearance as that of the human brain. As certain centers were arranged in the latter, so would the stars be in the photograph of the heavens. The human being has within himself a picture of the heavens, and every person has a different one, according to whether he was born in this place or that, and at this or that time. This is one indication that the human being is born from out of the whole cosmos.[4]

The analogy for the Earth to the birth horoscope of an individual is the *thema mundi*, the birth horoscope of the Earth, when at some time

---

1 Steiner, "The Relationship of the Diverse Branches of Natural Science to Astronomy," lect. 10 of CW 323, January 10, 1921, in *Das Verhältnis der verschiedenen naturwissenschatlichen Gebiete zur Astronomie* ["*The Astronomy Course*"], trans. by RP.

2 *Faculty Meetings with Rudolf Steiner*, vol. 2, "Questions and Answers," April 25, 1923. English trans. amended by RP after comparing with the German original.

3 Powell and Bowden, *Astrogeographia*, chap. 8 and appendix 1.

4 Steiner, *The Spiritual Guidance of the Individual and Humanity*, p. 63.

| LOTUS | CHAKRA | PLANET | COLOR |
|---|---|---|---|
| 8-petal | crown | Saturn | violet |
| 2-petal | third eye | Jupiter | blue |
| 16-petal | larynx | Mars | green |
| 12-petal | heart | Sun | yellow |
| 10-petal | solar plexus | Mercury | orange |
| 6-petal | sacral | Venus | red |
| 4-petal | root | Moon | peach-blossom |

in the early history of the Earth an imprint of the starry heavens upon the Earth took place. It is this imprint that is the focus of Astrogeographia. The question now is whether there is also an archetypal relationship of the planets to the Earth? That there is such a relationship is expressly stated by Rudolf Steiner. After saying in relation to the stars, "*We come, then, to a complete mirroring of what is outside in the interior of the Earth,*" he says that the same holds also for the planets:

> Picturing this in regard to each individual planet, we have, say Jupiter, and then a "polar Jupiter" within the Earth. We come to something which works outward from within the Earth in the way that Jupiter works in the Earth's environment. We arrive at a mirroring (in reality it is the opposite way round), but I will now describe it like this: a mirroring of what is outside the Earth into the interior of the Earth.[5]

In addition, another of his indications, which we shall come to below, alludes implicitly to an archetypal relationship of the planets to various continents of the Earth.

### The Seven Planets, the Seven Continents, and the Seven Earth Chakras

There are seven classical planets—Sun (Sunday), Moon (Monday), Mars (Tuesday), Mercury (Wednesday), Jupiter (Thursday), Venus (Friday), Saturn (Saturday)—according to which the seven days of the week are named, and there are seven continents. It is thus worth considering whether there is a correspondence between the seven continents and the seven classical planets. Even though, in the quote from Rudolf Steiner at the start of this article, he indicates that there is a correspondence between the continents and the starry constellations—this being also the core theme of Astrogeographia—the question is whether, over and above this correspondence to the constellations, there is, in addition, also an archetypal relationship between the continents and the seven planets? If there is, we could ask the further question as to whether there is a specific location upon each continent that is the central focus of the in-streaming planetary impulses? Such locations would be special "power points" or "planetary chakras" upon the Earth.

The terminology for describing the chakras in this chapter is tabulated in the table above.[6] This tabulation is based upon indications given by Rudolf Steiner:[7]

In 1967, Robert Coon described in his book *Earth Chakras*[8] the basic principle of one major Earth chakra on each continent, with the exception

---

5 Steiner, "The Relationship of the Diverse Branches of Natural Science to Astronomy," lect. 10, Jan. 10, 1921, *Das Verhältnis der verschiedenen naturwissenschatlichen Gebiete zur Astronomie*.

6 See Paul and Powell, *Cosmic Dances of the Planets*, pp. 179–183.

7 Although Rudolf Steiner indicated not only the approximate locations (larynx, heart, etc.) and the planetary correspondences but also, albeit indirectly (in artistic form), the colors of the lotus flowers in his 1923 sketch "The Human Being in Relation to the Planets," he did not specify either in this sketch or elsewhere the number of petals belonging to the lotus flower located in the region of the crown. See the discussion in the previous reference as to why this lotus flower (crown chakra) is indicated to have eight petals.

8 See Coon, *Earth Chakras*, p. 3.

*Table of Robert Coon's identification of seven Earth chakras on seven continents*\*

| CHAKRA | CONTINENT (COUNTRY) | PLACE |
| --- | --- | --- |
| 7th chakra (crown) | Asia (Tibet, China) | Mount Kailas |
| 6th chakra (third eye) [moving] | Europe (England) | Glastonbury and Shaftesbury |
| 5th chakra (throat) [larynx] | Asia-Africa (Israel/Palestine, Egypt) | Great Pyramid, Mount Sinai, and Mount of Olives |
| 4th chakra (heart) | Europe (England) | Glastonbury and Shaftesbury |
| 3rd chakra (solar plexus) | Australia (Northern Territory) | Uluru and Kata Tjuta |
| 2nd chakra (sexual area) [sacral] | South America (Bolivia-Peru) | Island of the Sun, Lake Titicaca |
| 1st chakra (base of spine) [root] | North America (California) | Mount Shasta |

\* Coon, *Earth Chakras*, pp. 6–16.

of Antarctica. We begin our study of the planetary Earth chakras first by quoting from Robert Coon from the opening chapter to his book *Earth Chakras*:

> Geography teaches us about the continents, oceans, mountains, and rivers of the world. Geology studies stone formations—the skeleton of the Earth. These sciences investigate the more material aspects of the planetary body. The study of Earth chakras is more akin to acupuncture in that we are exploring the more subtle energy structures of the Earth. Earth chakras are like bodily organs that are vital to the health of the world, and to all living beings dependent upon the various environments provided by the world. Each chakra serves a different function, which is twofold:
>
> 1. To maintain the overall global health.
> 2. To transmit and receive energy encoded with information.
>
> There is one great Earth chakra located on each continent.

He gives permanent (fixed) map locations for six of the major chakras and a temporary (moving) location for the Third Eye chakra (see table above), indicating that the current location of this mobile chakra coincides with the place of the heart chakra. He weaves the Earth chakras within a wider context of 156 sacred sites across the planet. This number he derives from fifty-two "inspirational earth chakras,"[9] multiplied by three since each of these fifty-two Earth chakras, he says, "generates a related structural and a related creative gate." He also pointed to a system of spinner wheels and gates for the Earth, that become progressively activated into the future, in nineteen-year cycles. He says that he received his inspiration for the sacred geography of the Earth from the prophet Elijah.

With Robert Coon's basic idea of one chakra on each continent (see table above) as a starting point, we proceed in this article to construct a map of the planetary chakras of the Earth, based on the insights of spiritual science given by Rudolf Steiner—in particular his description of the influences of the planets upon the Earth. In this way we find an assignment of seven planetary chakras to locations on the surface of the Earth—still, however, adhering to the principle of one chakra on each continent, with the exception of Antarctica. We derive our basic insight from Rudolf Steiner's indications given in his lectures *The Mission of Folk Souls*,[10] In the sixth lecture he connects the influence of Mercury with Africa, that of Venus with Southeast Asia, that of Mars with "the broad region of Asia" of the Mongolian peoples

---
9 Ibid., p. 95.
10 Steiner, *The Mission of Folk Souls*, 2005.

(this includes not just Mongolia but also China, Tibet, and other parts of Asia), that of Jupiter with Europe, and that of Saturn with America, whereby it is clear from the context that he means North America. Then in the twelfth lecture of *The Mission of Folk Souls* he is more specific about the key location of a place in Germany as "the point on the continent of Europe from which once the greatest impulses rayed out in all directions." We believe that with these words Rudolf Steiner identified the *Jupiter chakra* of the Earth as the Externsteine. In this lecture it is clear that he meant the Externsteine by his reference to this point lying between "the cities of Detmold and Paderborn," since the ancient site of the Externsteine does in fact lie between Detmold and Paderborn and there is no other noteworthy ancient site between these two cities in Germany. His description of this location as being "the point on the continent of Europe from which once the greatest impulses rayed out in all directions" fits that which can be thought of as the planetary chakra of Europe—the place of in-streaming cosmic forces for the spiritual evolution of Europe.

Having identified, with Rudolf Steiner's help, the Jupiter chakra—i.e., the "third eye" chakra, with the Externsteine on the continent of Europe—the task remains to find the locations of the other planetary chakras on the other continents of the Earth. The seven main continents are: Asia, Africa, North America, South America, Antarctica, Europe, and Oceania, comprising the region of Australia, New Zealand, New Guinea, and neighboring islands (now collectively known as Australasia)—although often simply "Australia" is named as the seventh continent in this list, instead of Oceania.[11]

Leaving Antarctica out of consideration reduces this to six continents. However, Rudolf Steiner considered Southeast Asia separately from the rest of Asia, bringing the number back to seven. Southeast Asia he correlated with Venus, and the rest of Asia—at least, that part of Asia comprising the natural habitat of the "Mongolian peoples"—he brought into connection with Mars. Thus, just as we looked for the Jupiter chakra in Europe, so our search for the Venus chakra is in Southeast Asia, the Mars chakra in Asia, and the Saturn chakra in North America. However, as will be elucidated in our discussion concerning the location of the Sun and Mercury chakras, there is a question—bearing in mind that Africa is correlated with Mercury by Rudolf Steiner—about the position on the globe of the Mercury chakra.

Now let us move forward for a discussion regarding the corresponding resonances of the Sun, Mercury, Venus, and the Moon, with the continents of the Earth. Regarding the Sun chakra: contemplating the Earth as a whole, on numerous occasions Rudolf Steiner referred to the central significance of the location of Golgotha/Jerusalem for the entire Earth. Here Christ's sacrifice took place, which signified on a spiritual level the transition from a descending to an ascending phase of evolution for the Earth and humanity. Astrogeographia connects onto the fundamental significance of Golgotha/Jerusalem and, as discussed in our book—especially in chapter 9—Jerusalem is identified as the location on the Earth's surface that can be regarded as the spiritual center of the Earth, i.e. the heart chakra, corresponding to the Sun.[12] In terms of continents, Jerusalem lies in Asia, but is very close to Africa, and is not far from the southernmost reaches of Europe. However, as discussed in chapter 9 of our book, Golgotha, Mount Sinai, and the Great Pyramid are all spiritually connected with one another, which

---

11  There are widely diverging views as to how the name *Oceania* is defined. Oceania was originally conceived as the lands of the Pacific Ocean, stretching from the Straits of Malacca to the coast of the Americas. It comprised four regions: *Polynesia*, *Micronesia*, *Malaysia* (now called the Malay Archipelago), and *Melanesia* (now called Australasia). Geopolitically Oceania includes Australia and the nations of the Pacific from Papua New Guinea east, but not Indonesian New Guinea or Malaysia. Sometimes Oceania is defined as a continent comprising Australia and nearby islands. This definition is sometimes extended to also include Micronesia, Polynesia, and every island in between, where New Zealand is considered to belong to Polynesia. The widest definition of Oceania includes the entire region between continental Asia and the Americas.

12  Powell and Bowden, *Astrogeographia*.

| Planet | Chakra | Continent | Place/Planetary Chakra |
|--------|--------|-----------|------------------------|
| Saturn | Crown | North America | Mount Shasta |
| Jupiter | Third Eye | Europe | Externsteine |
| Mars | Larynx | Asia | Mount Kailash |
| Sun | Heart | Asia-Africa | Golgotha/Jerusalem |

indicates something of the great outreach of this heart chakra of the Earth.[13]

Taking this into consideration, the Earth's heart chakra is very much linked with the continent of Africa. In fact, Africa looks like a heart! And just as the location of the heart chakra in the human being is not identical to the physical heart, but is nevertheless intimately linked to it, so Golgotha/Jerusalem can be considered as the heart chakra, which is intimately linked to the "physical heart" of the Earth—Africa. As the Sun is the center of our solar system, and as the heart chakra, corresponding to the Sun, is the spiritual center of the human being, so Golgotha/Jerusalem is the spiritual center of the Earth—on account of Christ's sacrifice there, bestowing upon the Earth and humanity the central transforming impulse for the spiritual evolution of the world. And long before the city of Jerusalem existed at this location—in fact, from the time of the *thema mundi*, the birth horoscope of the Earth—on a spiritual level this place was the center of the world, as was recognized later in the Rabbinic tradition: "The innermost sanctuary of the Temple [of Solomon], the Holy of Holies, or *Kodesh Hakodeshim*, where the Ark of the Covenant was placed, *marked the exact center of the world.*"[14]

Apart from identifying Africa's chakra, the heart chakra, with Golgotha (Earth's Sun chakra) and Europe's chakra, the "third eye," with the location of the Externsteine (Earth's Jupiter chakra), we are in agreement with Robert Coon's pinpointing of the locations of four of the other five Earth chakras. However, based on Steiner's research connecting the planets with regions of the Earth, we come to a different correspondence of the chakras to these locations. This is to be expected, because we are looking from a cosmic perspective (*Earth's planetary chakras*), whereas Robert Coon is focused upon *Earth chakras*. We are indebted to Robert Coon for his work in identifying the locations of the Earth chakras, which has served as a starting point for our research. Our work approaches this subject from a cosmic perspective, in order to identify the positions of the planetary chakras upon the Earth. We respect Robert Coon's research and are grateful for his pioneering work in this field, and we believe that in this vast field of inquiry there is room for different perspectives.

Beginning with Robert Coon's identification of Mount Shasta as the Earth chakra on the continent of North America, given the association, according to Steiner, of North America with the planet Saturn, we see Mount Shasta as the Saturn chakra of the Earth, or crown chakra. Proceeding from West to East across the northern hemisphere, North America corresponds to Saturn, Europe to Jupiter, and Asia to Mars. Having identified Mount Shasta as the Earth's Saturn chakra and the Externsteine as the Earth's Jupiter chakra, it is a matter now of finding the Earth chakra on the continent of Asia that corresponds to Mars. According to Robert Coon, the Earth chakra of Asia is Mount Kailash in the Gangdisê Mountains (part of the Transhimalaya) in Tibet—regarded as THE sacred mountain in Buddhism, Hinduism, Jainism, and the Bon religion, a branch of Tibetan Vajrayaha. The Earth's Mars chakra is thus Mount Kailash. Summarizing our findings so far, see the table above.

---

13  For Robert Coon, as indicated in the above table, the great expanse covered by the Great Pyramid, Mount Sinai, and the Mount of Olives comprises the throat (larynx) chakra of the Earth.

14  Lambert Dolphin and Michael Kollen, "On The Location of the First and Second Temples in Jerusalem"; http://www.templemount.org/theories.html.

Whereas these four places belong to the Northern Hemisphere, the other three locations of Earth chakras belong to the Southern Hemisphere. Given that Africa is already accounted for in terms of the Earth's heart chakra at Golgotha being the chakra corresponding to the "heart continent" of Africa, what are the remaining three continents and where are their corresponding chakras? In light of Rudolf Steiner's indication referred to above, it is Mercury that is the planet of Africa in terms of the people indigenous to that continent. Before considering a continent other than Africa in relation to Mercury, let us look further at the question of Africa's relationship to the Sun. As a starting point, it is well-known that Africa is the world's main source of gold, the precious metal corresponding to the Sun. Already from the time of the building of the Great Pyramid, around 2500 BC, during the reign of Pharaoh Khufu (Cheops) of the Fourth Dynasty in Egypt, gold is recorded as having been brought from the "land of Punt"—a trading partner for the ancient Egyptians known for producing and exporting gold. The exact location of Punt remains a mystery. Most researchers now say that Punt was located in the region of the Horn of Africa, where today Northern Somalia, Eritrea, Djibouti, and Sudan (Red Sea coast) are located. In the fifteenth century BC it is recorded that Queen Hatchepsut traded gold from Nubia for myrrh and other goods from the land of Punt. Later, around 1000 BC, agricultural communities south of the Sahara began to resort to gold production for part of the year, and from that time onward transported the gold across the Sahara to trade it for goods. The Phoenecian city-state of Carthage (814–146 BC), located in North Africa on the Gulf of Tunis on the Mediterranean coast, was renowned for its gold, which probably came from the Sub-Saharan region. After the destruction of Carthage, regular trade across the Sahara broke down. Around AD 100 the camel was introduced from Arabia into North Africa by the Romans, making trans-Saharan trade possible again. It is known that from around AD 400 onward camels were regularly transporting gold across the Sahara from West Africa, which for the ensuing eleven hundred years became the world's most important supplier of gold. The Ghana Empire, located in what is now southeastern Mauritania and Western Mali, obtained much of its gold from the Bambuk and Boure goldfields in Sudan. The Ghana Empire was superseded in the thirteenth century by the Islamic Mali Empire, which flourished above all through its gold trade. It contained three immense gold mines within its borders, unlike the Ghana Empire, which was only a transit point for gold. Mali was the source of almost half the world's gold—exported from the goldfields of Bambuk, Boure, and Galam. Then, in 1868 gold was discovered in South Africa—since then the source of nearly forty percent of all gold ever mined, and thought to be still home to an estimated fifty percent of the world's gold reserves. This brief history of Africa's relationship with gold, the metal of the Sun, lends support to the identification of Africa as the Sun (heart) continent on account of its gold reserves—gold being the metal corresponding to the Sun.

On another level, not forgetting that Steiner related the people of Africa to Mercury rather than to the Sun, as the Sun is universal; its influence cannot really be limited to one continent. However, it needs to be borne in mind that Steiner was focusing upon the indigenous people of Africa as the "Mercury race" and not so much upon the continent of Africa as such—and this applies also to the other correspondences between continents and planets referred to in this article. On a physical level, according to the "World Sunshine Map" the continent of Africa receives many more hours of bright sunshine during the year than any other continent of the Earth, and this could also be a reason for considering Africa as the "Sun continent" or the continent where the Sun's influence is greatest.[15] Apart from Africa's relationship to the physical Sun in terms of hours of bright sunshine, and to gold, the metal of the Sun, it is also the natural habitat of the lion; and as Linda Tucker shows convincingly in her book, the lion—especially the white lion—is a symbol both of the Sun

---

15 For the "World Sunshine Map," see http://earth.rice.edu/mtpe/geo/geosphere/hot/energyfuture/Sunlight.html.

and of the spirit of Africa.[16] Moreover, in astrology the heart corresponds to the constellation of Leo, or the Lion, so again we see a correspondence here relating Africa to the heart—and also to the Sun, to which the heart (from another perspective) corresponds.[17]

Relating to the Earth as a living being mirroring in kind the planetary life of our solar system, the lungs are said to correspond to Mercury.[18] If Africa is the heart, where do we find the lungs of the Earth? Everyone knows that trees are the lungs of the Earth and that, in particular, the tropical rainforests are the greatest suppliers of life-giving oxygen on the planet. The Amazon represents over half of the Earth's remaining rainforests and supplies an estimated twenty percent of the planet's oxygen. This is one reason for considering South America, home of the Amazon basin, as the Mercury continent. If Africa is regarded as the Sun (heart) continent, South America can perhaps be identified as the Mercury (lungs) continent. There are various considerations that support this. For example, Mercury is thought of as the planet of movement—Steiner refers to "Mercury's swift-winged movement in our limbs"[19]—and considering the love of movement in South American countries, where an extraordinary number of dance forms have originated, the "Mercurial quality" of South America comes to expression in their penchant for dance.[20] Mercury (lungs) clearly also has to do with breathing, and during breathing the diaphragm contracts and flattens, producing an outward movement of the upper abdominal wall—the epigastric region (solar plexus or "pit of the stomach"), where Steiner locates the Mercury chakra.[21]

There is yet another consideration here, which emerges when we turn our attention to Cuzco, the capital of the Inca civilization and of the whole Tawantinsuyu (Peruvian) empire. According to the Incas the word *Qosqo* (their word for Cuzco) meant "navel of the world." We find here, in this expression, an allusion to a Mercury center. For the navel is related to the solar plexus (Mercury) chakra.[22] Robert Coon identifies Lake Titicaca as the Earth chakra for the continent of South America, and in Inca mythology there is a link between Lake Titicaca and Cuzco. Manco Cápac was said to be the mythological founder of the Inca Dynasty in Peru and the Cuzco Dynasty at Cuzco. He was thought to have arisen from the depths of Lake Titicaca. If Lake Titicaca is the Earth's solar plexus (Mercury) chakra, Cuzco was evidently conceived of as the closely related "navel center of the world" and the Inca connected these two places in the personage

---

16 Tucker, *Mystery of the White Lions*, pp. 253–256.

17 In astrology the Sun is said to be "at home" in Leo. In other words, there is a deep relationship between the Sun and Leo. And just as the heart corresponds to Leo in terms of its physical structure, on a soul/spiritual level it corresponds to the Sun.

18 For the correspondences of the organs with the planets, see Paul and Powell, *Cosmic Dances of the Planets*.

19 Paul and Powell, *Cosmic Dances of the Planets*.

20 The people of Africa, too, have a great love of dance—in line with Steiner's identification of the indigenous African people as the "Mercury race." Further, many people of Black African descent came to Latin America, mainly to Brazil and the Caribbean, but also to Columbia and Venezuela, as part of the Atlantic slave trade.

21 Rudolf Steiner likens the Earth to a human being: "America appears like the breast"; see *Menschheitsentwickelung und Christus-Erkenntnis*, p. 287. It is in keeping with these words of Steiner to relate the lungs to South America. For Steiner's location of the Mercury chakra in the "pit of the stomach" (German: *Magengrube*), or the solar plexus, see *Esoteric Development*, lect. Mar. 16, 1905, p. 110.

22 The close relationship between the navel and the solar plexus (Mercury) chakra is evident in the Hindu tradition, where the location of the 10-petal lotus flower (Sanskrit: *Manipura*) is sometimes identified as the region of the navel and sometimes as the region of the solar plexus. A possible solution to this conundrum comes through Rudolf Steiner's identification—see previous footnote—of the location of the 10-petal lotus flower as the region of the "pit of the stomach," which would seem to indicate the solar plexus (rather than the navel)—that is, the epigastric region rather than the umbilical region. Given that the solar plexus is the location of the Mercury chakra, nonetheless in other traditions—for example, Daoist and Hindu traditions—the navel is of great significance. Thus, according to Ayurvedic medicine, the navel is an important energy center in the human body, with nearly 72,000 subtle nerves (nadis) converging in this area.

of their legendary founder. Thus, Lake Titicaca is identified as the location of the Earth's Mercury chakra, closely linked with Cuzco as the "navel of the world."

In relation to identifying the location of the Earth's Venus chakra, it is helpful if we now turn to an important aspect of Robert Coon's research: that six of the seven Earth chakras all lie along one or the other of two great ley lines of the Earth, which he calls *ley arteries* and names the *Rainbow Serpent* (female) and the *Plumed Serpent* (male). *Ley arteries* is an appropriate expression in terms of their overriding magnitude and significance in comparison with all other ley lines (energy lines) on our planet. Our own research confirms the validity of two principle ley arteries encircling the Earth and that six of the seven planetary chakras of the Earth are indeed located on these arteries—the only one not lying on one of the two lines being the Earth's Sun (heart) chakra at Golgotha/Jerusalem. However, the paths of the two ley arteries that David Bowden has mapped out mathematically differ slightly from the paths of the ley arteries indicated by Robert Coon.

Since Robert Coon in his work does not consider Southeast Asia to be a separate continent from Asia, he does not indicate that one of the seven Earth chakras is located in Southeast Asia. However, in his mapping of the paths of the Rainbow Serpent and the Plumed Serpent around the globe, he identifies two locations where these ley arteries meet and cross one another. One is Lake Titicaca, and the other is the island of Bali. The crossing point on Bali he calls "the World Purification Center," seeing it not as an Earth chakra but as a *sacred gate*—one of the *twelve foundation gates of the world*. He indicates that the sacred sites located on the island of Bali serve in the purification of the Earth's blood. This is exactly the function of the kidneys in the human being, to help in the purification of the blood, removing toxic materials from the body. Just as the heart is the organ corresponding to the Sun, and the lungs are the organ corresponding to Mercury, so the kidneys are the organ corresponding to Venus.[23]

Further research led us to the identification of the highest mountain on Bali, Mount Agung, as the location of the Earth's Venus chakra. The Balinese believe that Mount Agung is a mystical mountain, which they think of as a replica of the mythical Mount Meru, the sacred mountain in Hindu and Buddhist cosmology, considered to be the center of the universe. Moreover, the most important, largest, and holiest Hindu temple on Bali, *Purah Besakih* (the Mother temple of Besakih), is located high on the slopes of Mount Agung. According to our research, it is here on this volcanic mountain that the Earth's Venus chakra is located.

Now, in coming to the task of mapping the flow of the two great ley arteries, we looked for the crossing points of these two circles around the globe connecting the locations of the Earth's planetary chakras. Focusing first upon the crossing point in the Asia/Southeast Asia region against the background of our cosmic perspective (complementary to Robert Coon's Earth-based perspective), the crossing point we found is not on the island of Bali, but interestingly coincides more or less exactly with Mount Kailash, the Earth's Mars (larynx) chakra, which, as described in chapter 9 of our book, lies on the Dubhe meridian—Dubhe being the most luminous of the seven stars comprising the Big Dipper. We found that the other crossing point, located in the Andean highlands in Peru, South America, lies some 854 miles (1,374 kilometers) north-west of Lake Titicaca, the Earth's Mercury (solar plexus) chakra,[24] about 8,900 feet (2,700 meters) above sea level. Like Mount Kailash, it is on the meridian of a very powerful star, since it lies close to the Deneb meridian—Deneb having a luminosity of about 250,000, listed as the thirty-second most luminous star in our galaxy.[25]

---

[23] For the correspondences of the organs with the planets, see Paul and Powell, *Cosmic Dances of the Planets*.

[24] It is also interesting that the Andean crossing point lies some 578½ miles (931 kilometers) north-west of Machu Picchu, the great Inca ceremonial center in the Cuzco region.

[25] See Powell and Dann, *The Astrological Revolution*, chapter 5, concerning the extraordinary significance of the mega star Deneb in the constellation of the Swan.

The Andean crossing point is just 20 miles (32 kilometers) southeast of Kuntur Wasi ("House of the Condor"), the name given to ruins of a religious center with complex architecture and stone sculptures at the headwaters of the Jequetepeque River. Kuntur Wasi is thought to have been constructed around 1000–700 BC and was occupied until around 50 BC. This was the time of the Chavin civilization in Ancient Peru, and lithosculptures found at Kuntur Wasi are similar to the Chavin style. The crossing point of the two great ley arteries is also 19 miles (30½ km.) southwest of Cajamarca, the city that is remembered as the place where the Inca empire came to an end when the Spanish conquistadors captured and murdered the Incan emperor Atahualpa there.

Also very close, just 56½ miles (91 kilometers) southwest of the Andean crossing point, lying on the western outskirts of the Peruvian city of Trujillo on the Pacific coast,[26] is the World Heritage archeological site of Chan Chan, the largest pre-Columbian city in South America—some 500 acres (two square kilometers), with many pre-Columbian palaces. The vast adobe city of Chan Chan on the Pacific coast, which was a triangular city surrounded by walls 50 to 60 feet (15 to 18 meters) high, was built by the Chimú around AD 850 and lasted until its conquest by the Inca Empire in AD 1470. It was the imperial capital of the Chimú until it was conquered by the Incas in the fifteenth century. It is estimated that around 30,000 people lived in the city of Chan Chan, sometimes called the City of the Moon because they worshipped the Moon there. In terms of size and complexity, it has been compared with Teotihuacan in Mexico and with some of the ancient cities of Egypt. Also very interesting is the somewhat older archeological site of the Sun and Moon temples six miles (9½ kilometers) from Chan Chan, on the southeastern outskirts of Trujillo. This complex is dominated by two huge adobe brick buildings: an artificial platform called the Temple of the Moon, and one-quarter of a mile (400 meters) away the Pyramid of the Sun, the largest pre-Columbian structure in Peru. This step pyramid, towering 135 feet (41 meters) above the surroundings, is the tallest adobe structure of the Americas. This major archaeological site was built at the time of the Moche culture (AD 100–800)—perhaps out of a sense of those ancient peoples for this crossing point of two great ley arteries carrying the male solar (Plumed Serpent) and female lunar (Rainbow Serpent) energies.[27]

The balancing of the Sun and Moon energies—manifested by the great Pyramid of the Sun and the Temple of the Moon, near Trujillo, perhaps as an expression of the meeting of the Plumed Serpent and the Rainbow Serpent nearby in the highlands—is an activity of Mercury, the planet closest to the Sun. In the words of Rudolf Steiner:

> *I hold the Sun within me—*
> *As King he leads me into the world;*
> *I hold the Moon within me—*
> *She preserves my form;*
> *I hold Mercury within me—*
> *He holds Sun and Moon together.*[28]

This "holding Sun and Moon together" comes to expression at Lake Titicaca, where there is the Island of the Sun and the Island of the Moon, thus indicating a close resonance between the Earth's Mercury chakra, Lake Titicaca, and the Andean crossing point of the two great ley arteries with the nearby Pyramid of the Sun and the Temple of the Moon on the outskirts of present-day Trujillo.

---

26 Trujillo is the third largest city in Peru and is known as the *Culture Capital of Peru* and the *City of Eternal Spring*. It is an economic hub in Northern Peru—a Mercurial function, recalling that for the Greeks Hermes/Mercury was patron of merchants and commerce.

27 This is an example of what is referred to earlier in this book that often a site connected with a power spot is built not at the actual power spot but, for practical reasons, some distance from the power spot. In this case the practical reasons are obvious: the coastal area is much more hospitable than the Andean highlands. Hence the city of Chan Chan and the nearby ceremonial site with the Pyramid of the Sun and the Temple of the Moon were located on the Pacific coast rather than up in the highlands where the actual crossing point of the two great ley arteries is located.

28 Kirchner-Bockholt, *Rudolf Steiner's Mission and Ita Wegman*, p. 113.

## Earth Chakras

| PLANET | CHAKRA | CONTINENT | PLACE/PLANETARY CHAKRA |
|---|---|---|---|
| Saturn | Crown | North America | Mount Shasta |
| Jupiter | Third Eye | Europe | Externsteine |
| Mars | Larynx | Asia | Mount Kailash |
| Sun | Heart | Asia/Africa | Golgotha/Jerusalem |
| Mercury | Solar Plexus | South America | Lake Titicaca |
| Venus | Sacral | Southeast Asia | Mount Agung |
| Moon | Root | Australia/Oceania | Uluru |

It now remains to determine the location of the Earth's Moon chakra. As mentioned already, leaving Antarctica out of consideration, the remaining continent is Oceania, often simply identified with Australia. According to Robert Coon, the Earth chakra on this continent is Uluru, formerly known to non-Aborigines as Ayers Rock, a large sandstone formation in the center of Australia, which is also a World Heritage site. It is the second largest monolith in the world (after Mount Augustus, also in Australia). Uluru is sacred to the Aborigines and is important in their creation mythology. Archeological research shows that the Uluru area has been inhabited by human beings for at least 10,000 years, and some sources maintain that the Aborigines have been there for at least 20,000 years. Uluru, with its distinctive color, glowing red at dawn and sunset, is one of Australia's most recognizable national landmarks. Our research indicates that Uluru is indeed the location of the Earth's Moon chakra, lying on the great ley artery running through the Externsteine, Mount Kailash, Mount Agung, and Uluru. The other great ley artery runs through Lake Titicaca, Mount Shasta, and Mount Kailash. Golgotha/Jerusalem, as the Earth's Sun (heart) chakra, being of spiritual significance for the whole world, does not lie on either of the two great ley arteries mapped out above.

According to Rudolf Steiner, the region of Oceania was where the Moon was located before it separated out from the Earth.[29] As part of Oceania, Australia comes under the influence of the Moon—also in an evolutionary sense, since the Aborigines, comparing their culture with that of the Lemurians described by Steiner,[30] are evidently descendants from the ancient Lemurians, a culture associated with the lunar influence as an echo of the Ancient Moon stage of evolution. Steiner described Lemuria as a continent very much influenced by the Moon that was located in the region between Australia and Africa, in the general region where now the Indian Ocean is located, which became submerged tens of thousands of years ago.[31] The Aborigines are thought to have inhabited Australia for some 50,000 years—supported by the archeological findings of human remains from Lake Mungo, Australia, dated to about 45,000 years ago—making the Aborigines the oldest continuous population outside of Africa.

The table above offers a summary of our findings identifying the seven planetary chakras of the Earth, where the place of the Christ's resurrection—Golgotha, Jerusalem—is the heart or Sun chakra of the Earth. In Astrogeographia, the latitude of Golgotha corresponds to the alignment of

---

29 See, for example, Steiner, *From Crystals to Crocodiles*.
30 Steiner, *Cosmic Memory*; see chapter on the Lemurian Race.
31 It is conceivable that prior to the destruction of Lemuria there were Lemurians who migrated to regions surrounding the Lemurian continent—to Africa and Australia, for example. In this case, there is a likelihood that Aborigines are descendants of the people who emigrated from Lemuria.

the stars on the Celestial Equator, or 0° declination. The three upper chakras are identified with locations in the northern hemisphere: Mount Shasta, California, with the crown chakra; the Externsteine in Europe with the third eye chakra; and Mount Kailash, Tibet, with the larynx chakra. Conversely, the three lower chakras are identified with locations in the southern hemisphere: Lake Titicaca on the border of Peru and Bolivia with the solar plexus chakra; Mount Agung on the island of Bali with the sacral chakra; and Uluru, Australia, with the root chakra.³²

The Staff of Mercury

Throughout Australia, the Rainbow Serpent is a personification of fertility and rain. In 1926 a British anthropologist Professor Alfred Radcliffe-Brown coined the term "Rainbow Serpent" to describe the recurring myth of a snake of some enormous size living within the deepest waterholes, and described in the Aboriginal stories as descended from the larger being visible as the dark streak in the Milky Way.³³ Robert Coon adopted the term *Rainbow Serpent* to describe the great ley artery that runs through Uluru on its circuit around the globe. For the other ley artery he used the term *Plumed Serpent*, the name of the great deity of various Mesoamerican religions—the Feathered Serpent of the Olmecs, Quetzalcoatl of the Aztecs, and Kukulkan of the Maya.

Bearing in mind the deep truth of the words "as above, so below," relating to the principle of correspondences between the macrocosm ("great world") and the microcosm ("the little world" of the human being), it is interesting, in relation to the idea of two serpents encircling the globe, that Rudolf Steiner draws attention to two "snakes" within the human being:

> There is a symbol that one must enliven within oneself. This is the Staff of Mercury (see Figure 8), the luminous staff with a black snake and a bright luminous shining snake. The snake is a symbol for the astral body. Every night the astral body sheds its skin; it throws off the used-up skin. The black snake is a symbol for this. Overnight it gets a new, shimmering skin, and this newly enlivened, beautiful, shining skin of the astral body is symbolized by the shining snake...this symbol, the Staff of Mercury, who is the "messenger of the gods."³⁴

Applying the principle of correspondences, we believe that Robert Coon's insight into two great ley arteries encircling the Earth is a true one, which is mirrored in the human being in the Staff of Mercury described by Rudolf Steiner, and that this is of significance for the interconnections between the seven planetary chakras located on the seven continents of the Earth.

Readers will have noticed that we do not discuss the well-known power point Glastonbury in England, identified by Robert Coon as both the heart center and the temporary third-eye center of the world. What we found through Astrogeographia is that Glastonbury is indeed highly significant, as it is the location at which the star Botein in Aries, sometimes depicted marking the rear right hoof or flank of the Ram (but "the western one of the three in the tail" according to Ptolemy), is impressed upon the Earth. Botein is the fourth brightest star in Aries. In other words, there are three stars in Aries which are brighter than Botein—these being Hamal ("the star above the head of the Ram"), Sheratan ("the eastern star of the two in the horn"), and Mesartim ("the western star of the two in the horn"). Astrogeographically, Botein is the most important of these four stars, since the projection onto the globe of the other three is in the Northern Atlantic Ocean—that of Hamal is 292½ miles (470½ kilometers) west of Knockfola

---

32 Powell and Bowden, *Astrogeographia*, go into extensive detail concerning the seven chakras of the Earth and give many maps, including the two circles of the two major ley arteries encircling the Earth and intersecting at Mt. Kailash and in the Andes near Trujillo, Peru.

33 See Alfred Radcliffe-Brown, "The Rainbow-Serpent Myth of Australia," *Journal of the Royal Anthropological Institute of Great Britain and Ireland* (vol. 56, 1926), pp. 19-25.

34 Steiner, *Esoteric Lessons 1904–1909*, p. 393.

on the northwest coast of Ireland, Sheratan is 458 miles (737 kilometers) west of Limerick, and Mesartim is 514 miles (827 kilometers) west of Cork. Hence Botein serves astrogeographically as the primary star of Aries in terms of the ordering of stars according to their apparent brightness, being the brightest star of Aries that is projected onto firm land rather than onto the Atlantic Ocean. In addition, since, according to Ptolemy and as confirmed by Astrogeographia, England, as a whole is associated with Aries, Glastonbury assumes special significance for the whole of England and for the entire region falling under the influence of the constellation of the Ram.

Glastonbury, held sacred long before Christianity, was settled already in pre-Christian times by the Celts. According to legend, after Christ's crucifixion Joseph of Arimathea, in whose tomb (the Holy Sepulcher) the body of Christ was laid to rest, went on a mission and came to Glastonbury bearing the cup of the Holy Grail which had been used at the Last Supper and in which some of Christ's blood had been collected as it flowed down from his body on the cross. Legendary accounts relate that through Joseph of Arimathea, there were Celts in the Glastonbury region who converted to Christianity. Under the Celtic monks, a church is said to have been built at Glastonbury, which according to tradition became known as the "Holiest Earth of England," since it was acknowledged as the place where Christianity first came to England. Later, Arthurian legends associated King Arthur with Glastonbury, who supposedly was buried in a grave at the great abbey that grew there from the original church. During the twentieth century a New Age community has grown at Glastonbury, attracting many people with Neopagan beliefs. According to the research of Astrogeographia, Glastonbury is closely aligned with the star Botein, lying exactly on the Botein meridian. Moreover, because of the steady movement northward along this meridian of the projection of Botein, since the beginning of the twentieth century the projection of Botein onto the Earth coincides exactly with Glastonbury, giving grounds to associate the influence of this star with the tremendous growth of interest in Glastonbury as a spiritual center.

We conclude our study of the planetary Earth chakras by quoting from Rudolf Steiner, through whom we came to an understanding of the correspondence between each continent and the seven planets—here contemplating the centrality of Golgotha as the Sun chakra, which, however, is able to be present within the heart of each human being and is thus universal for the whole Earth:

> With the event of Golgotha, when the blood flowed from the wounds of the great Redeemer, when the Cosmic Heart's blood penetrated the Earth and its forces poured down as far as its center, the Earth became illumined from within and light rayed outward into the surroundings.... In the Temple of the human body is the Holy of Holies.... Those who have an inkling of it receive from it the power to purify themselves to such an extent that they can enter into this holiest place. Therein is the Holy Vessel that has been prepared throughout the ages as a container for the blood and life of Christ when the time for it arrives. When one has entered therein, one has found the way to the Holy of Holies in the great Temple of the Earth.... When one discovers oneself within one's innermost sanctuary, one will be allowed to enter in and there discover the Holy Grail... One enters into the Mystery Center of one's own heart and a divine being emerges from this place and unites itself with the God outside, with the Being of Christ.... Because the human being is a twofold being, one is able to pour the Sun forces into the Earth and act as a connecting link between the Sun and the Earth.... It is the mission of every single human being and of the whole of humanity to fill themselves with the Christ Spirit and to recognize themselves as a center living in this Spirit, through which spiritual light, spiritual strength and spiritual warmth can flow into the Earth, thereby redeeming it and raising it aloft into spiritual realms.[35]

---

35 Steiner, *"Freemasonry" and Ritual Work*, pp. 429–430.

# FINDING JERUSALEM, PART ONE

## David Tresemer, Ph.D.

In the tradition of Judaism, Jerusalem was the center and first place of the Earth to congeal. It is where Adam and Eve first stood on land. This accords completely with Rudolf Steiner's comments about Jerusalem as the first place to harden from the plastic and fluid matter during the Lemurian period of history (prior to the Atlantean period). The site of Solomon's Temple is the place Abraham visited, where Solomon built the temple that connected with the holy feminine—the *Shekinah*. Not far from the Temple lies Golgotha, where Christ's blood entered the Earth and revived life for all of earth and humanity. Later, from the site of Solomon's Temple, Muhammad took off to heaven in his magical night journey. Much more could be said of the potent history of this area. I have a very personal connection with the site of the Mystery of Golgotha, finding there the most powerful positivity as well as negativity of any place that I have experienced on this planet, a story for another time.

This brief note asks the question: Is Jerusalem located in a special place on the Earth?

### Golden Proportion

To answer this question, we have to begin with the golden proportion, a number termed *phi* in the nineteenth century, because it was the first letter of the name of the great sculptor Phidias, who used this proportion in his sculptures, as did Leonardo da Vinci much later. Phi has many unique properties, including $1/phi = phi - 1$, and $phi^2 = phi + 1$. $Phi = (\sqrt{5} + 1)/2$, thus relating it to all five-fold geometries, to pentagons and pentagrams. Rudolf Steiner stated that the human etheric (or life or energy) body weaves formative forces through the physical body in pentagonal movements, thus five is connected with the pattern of the life body. Phi is expressed in many kinds of geometries found in nature, including the whorl of pine cones, the spirals in sunflower heads, the pattern of brachiating in all plants, and the relative dimensions of length, width, height of body and extensions of the diverse occupants of ponds and seas.

Phi can be understood as a ratio expressing the principle of growth and productivity. Many proportions in the human body can be found related to phi: the distance of foot to waist compared to the distance from waist to crown of head, the distance from waist to chin compared to the distance from chin to crown of head, the distance from tip of the middle finger to the center of the palm compared to the distance from the center of the palm to the wrist, and many other examples. "The ideal human form is 'built up' according to the golden ratio proportion even down to the greatest detail."[1]

Thus phi is a ratio found in every kind of artistic creation, from architecture to composition in paintings, to design of everyday tools for household use.

Phi is often described with reference to the Fibonacci series, which begins 0, 1, 1, 2, 3, 5...and continues by adding to the last number the number before it. Thus it continues from 5 as follows: 5, (5 + 3 = 8), (8 + 5 = 13), 21, 34, 55, 89, 144, 233, 377, 610.... Take any number divided by

---

[1] Sheen, *Geometry and the Imagination*, p. 110. Many other books have illustrated the varieties of expression of phi, both in physical forms and in the realm of pure mathematics. Note that *phi* summarizes an ideal relation in the examples mentioned. The proportions for measurements of individuals can vary. The averages give the exact ideal proportions, celebrated by artists back even to Egyptian times, as in Schwaller de Lubicz, *The Temple of Man*, wherein the phi proportion is found in many sculptures and paintings of the ancient Egyptians.

its predecessor, such as 89/55, and you have an increasingly accurate estimate of the value of phi: 1.6180339885.

This ratio phi comes alive when thought of as a journey. I wish to find Jerusalem. I start at the zero point. I take one step with my right foot. Then I take one step with my left foot. Good, I've begun. Now I can venture two steps further. Then three steps, then five. Here's what happens along the way: Let's say I've progressed to 144 steps, and I've just completed that, then I take a breather. I reason, "I've just taken 144 steps—I can certainly do that again. And before the 144, I took 89 steps. So certainly I should be able to take 144 + 89 steps more." Thus the journey grows, slowly, by a proportion found to be related to growth patterns in living things. I don't try to double my steps—that was my poor estimate early on, after I had taken only one step in the journey. The sustainable growth pattern means that I do what has already been accomplished. This reliance on what has already occurred in the previous time slot, as well as what occurred in the time slot just before that, lends a great power to one's endurance in the journey. The journey grows in this manner, increasing by 1.618 in each new time slot.

A secret is often overlooked in descriptions of this system: You can get the phi proportion by *choosing any two numbers* at the beginning of the sequence! You follow the rule of building by adding the last two numbers in order to progress, and over time you arrive at the same phi proportion when dividing a number by the previous number.[2] The secret lies not in the initial numbers but in the fact of adding accomplishments in a step-wise fashion to create a foundation for the next step of the journey. Thus the phi proportion summarizes a fundamental principle of natural growth, a process rather than particular numbers.[3]

Architects employed this growth principle in phi proportions between length and width. You may recognize in the 3 x 5 card or the 5 x 8 card the very numbers that we find in the original Fibonacci series. The end facades of the Parthenon in Athens seem to have been designed as height to width in the proportion of 1:phi, as well as many other architectural monuments and designs of household items.

If you place this template in relation to the planet Earth, you can see one side of a rectangle (C – North-pole – J – E) going from the center of the Earth (C in figure 1) up the rotational axis toward the North Pole, and the other side of the rectangle proceeding on the Earth's equator. This creates a rectangle that has a specific angle from the center (angle a in figure 1). That angle is 31.7175°; its complement angle (b) is 58.2825°. The site of the Mystery of Golgotha in Jerusalem lies at the latitude of 31.7786° (from Google Earth), though I have measured it on site with a GPS as being a bit less than that, as 31.74°. This is very close to the angle of a phi-rectangle, which is amazing enough. But why is it not exact? If you consider that the earth is not a perfect sphere, but rather that it is oblate or flattened, you realize that this flattening makes up the difference. The flattening is .00335.[4] This means that an angle of 31.7175° emanating from the Earth's center would indeed find the exact location of the Temple of Solomon and the site of Golgotha in Jerusalem, a fount of spiritual growth for the entire planet continually fed from the creative sources of the Earth itself. The Holy Land and its center in Jerusalem have been famous for many reasons, including its key position on Earth.

---

2  For example, you can pick 4 and 19 as the first two numbers. Their ratio 4.75 is a dismal estimate of phi. However, add the two numbers together, and repeat the process. The eighth term divided by the seventh already gives 1.62, and in successive iterations comes closer and closer to phi.

3  This invites one to find this proportion in steps on a journey, using your physical and etheric (life) bodies as your tool of sensing. Starting in the middle, let's say you've just walked 34 steps. Take a long pause to breathe and take a sip of water. Then walk 34 (you've just done that), short pause, then 21 (the previous number), then a double pause affirming that you've just done 55. Begin again by walking 55, pause, then 34, then a double pause to affirm that you've just completed 89. Begin again by walking 89, pause, then 55, then a double pause to affirm that you've just completed 144. Proceed in this manner, and note your experience.

4  "Flattening" = (horizontal radius – vertical radius)/ horizontal radius. The flattening is about 26 miles in the vertical.

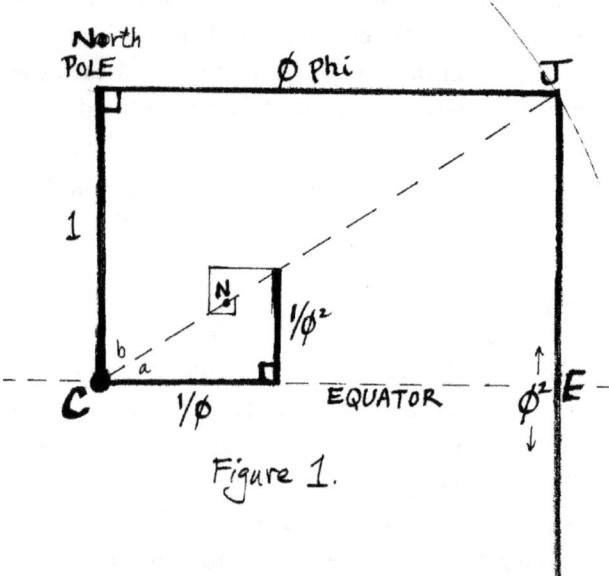

Figure 1.

## Generative Power

The choice of the location of the Temple of Solomon in Jerusalem is often told as a "homely ethical lesson," but relates very strongly to the workings of generative power.

A heavenly voice directed [Solomon] to go to Mount Zion at night, to a field owned by two brothers jointly. One of the brothers was a bachelor and poor, the other was blessed both with wealth and a large family of children. It was harvesting time. Under cover of night, the poor brother kept adding to the other's heap of grain, for, although he was poor, he thought his brother needed more on account of his large family. The rich brother, in the same clandestine way, added to the poor brother's store, thinking that though he had a family to support, the other was without means. This field, Solomon concluded, which had called forth so remarkable a manifestation of brotherly love, was the best site for the Temple, and he bought it.[5]

Not only does this show the generativity of the field, but it shows an interaction with humanity, a going back and forth of gifting. Thus the human beings multiply the generativity of the place by their exchanging. The feature of secrecy in the exchange suggests a connection with hidden forces, which this analysis confirms—forces coming from within the Earth.

## Longitude

Though Jerusalem is placed upon this most growthful of latitudes on the Earth, that would apply to a ring of latitude (31.7°) that runs right round the Earth. Is Jerusalem connected with a particular longitude, in other words, a location determined in the east–west direction? The answer is yes, and requires an introduction.

Three decades ago, Brian Gray, a talented teacher at Rudolf Steiner College in Fair Oaks, California, had the notion that there was once a primal connection between the Earth and the cosmos just as the Earth began to harden and rotate, that is, very long ago. He envisioned that the different continents lay under the supervision of different beings dwelling in the twelve-fold zodiac. He saw this "ur-alignment" in terms of the ecliptic, the plane traversed by Sun and Earth through the twelve realms of the zodiac, which is not presently aligned with the Earth's equator. Ecliptic means the place where eclipses can happen. Thus anything on that plane can come between the Sun and the Earth, as in a lunar eclipse (or the recent Venus eclipse). Since the ecliptic is presently tilted 23.5° off the equator and the Earth's rotational polar axis, the north-pole of the ecliptic when laid upon the Earth is presently on the Arctic Circle (latitude of 66.5°, or 90 minus 23.5). In its present position, the north-pole of the ecliptic acts as a center from which the Earth can be divided into twelve portions each under the tutelage of one of the great living beings of the zodiac. Normally the north-pole of the ecliptic moves around the Arctic Circle, one degree every 72 years, giving us a new astrological age (as in "Age of Aquarius") every 2,160 years.

In Brian Gray's system, the north pole or apex of the primal ecliptic was fixed on the Arctic Circle at the longitude of 143° west.[6] In that

---

5 Ginzberg, *The Legends of the Jews*, p. 154. The evaluation as a "homely ethical lesson" comes from Goldhill, *The Temple of Jerusalem*, p. 36. In 2 Samuel 24:24 (and 1 Chron. 18:25), we find Solomon's father David buying the field, also in relation to issues of generativity, in this case as an antidote to a pestilence (anti-generativity) that had killed seventy thousand people.

6 Brian Gray has different versions that vary between 142 and 143° west, but these variations do not affect the relations to Jerusalem that we are observing here.

system Jerusalem lies at the longitude of 3° to 4° of the Twins (Gemini), opposite to the location of the Galactic Center at 1° to 3° of the Archer (Sagittarius).[7] The Galactic Center has the greatest concentration of suns, the greatest concentration of power, of any location in the heavens. It is truly the origin of the Sun, and therefore our most ancient ancestor. The event of Pentecost took place when the Sun lay at 2° to 3° of the Twins, the event where tongues of fire came into all those most intimately connected with Christ Jesus, staying up through the night, praying in Jerusalem. Thus in this primal location, we can perceive the following alignment for the location of Jerusalem:

GALACTIC CENTER

– 2° to 3° Archer –

– Earth (the line entering in the southern Pacific Ocean) –

– Center of Earth –

– Jerusalem –

– our Sun –

– 2° to 3° Twins –

– Deep Space (away from the galaxy) –

The divine presence of the Galactic Center thus expresses itself on Earth after having passed through the body of the Earth in the place of Jerusalem.[8]

One might wonder about the complement to this location of Jerusalem—that is, a point on the same longitude but 31.7175° to the south of the equator. It lands in the ocean, just off the east coast of South Africa. One might wonder about the direct opposite point through the Earth from Jerusalem, the same latitude in the south and the exact opposite longitude. That point lands in the South Pacific ocean. Perhaps there are tales amongst sailors of crossing those points but I do not know them.[9]

## Implication for the Inside of the Earth

In the accompanying figure, we have relied primarily on the line C – J (for Center – Jerusalem), constructed from the rectangle C – North-pole – J – E, to find our connection with the latitude of Jerusalem at 31.7. However, we can continue the phi-spiral inward, and come to a nodal point N, the beginning of the unfolding phi-spiral. One first observes that the growth spiral ending in Jerusalem does not originate from the center of the Earth. If we take the radius of the Earth as C-J, then that nodal point N lies just over a quarter of the way from the center to the outer surface. One feels that one might reach this causal point by traveling back through the generative spiral, beginning in Jerusalem, from the starting point of the Temple of Solomon of the hill of Golgotha. Is the generative origin point where a portion of the spirits of the dead reside awaiting their release? Is this where Christ visited the prophets during his time in the center of the Earth between crucifixion and resurrection? Is this where the "mothers" mentioned by Goethe at the "center" of the Earth lie? Intuitive inquiry into the nature of that place will reveal its true nature in relation to the events on the surface of our planet. There are several doorways in Jerusalem though I urge caution with some for reasons that I will explain in part 2.

≈

*Part 2 will continue the journey to find Jerusalem*

---

7 Though the center of the Galactic Center can be found at 2°6' of the Archer, the center spans at least a degree in each direction. The place where the celestial equator (the projection of the earth's equator into space) intersects the galactic equator is about 5° of the Archer. See David Tresemer, "Sun, Earth, and the Galactic Center," *Journal for Star Wisdom 2010* (and in revised form for *International Astrologer*). The degrees spanning from 1 to 5 of the Archer are intimately involved with the connection of Earth and Galactic Center.

8 Note that Pentecost occurred at midnight when the Sun lay at 2-3° of the Twins, but Jerusalem was turned away from it – still in this alignment shown here, Jerusalem faced toward the Galactic Center.

9 Though Brian Gray has not yet published his extensive findings, others have taken his basic ideas and created systems of relationship between the heavens and the Earth, though each one with adjustments that put Jerusalem in a different place. These other researchers include Brian Keats, Dennis Klocek, and Robert Powell, whose systems deserve independent study. Thanks to Brian Gray for encouraging me to publish this note on the location of Jerusalem.

# THE SIGNATURE OF NEPTUNE IN WORLD EVENTS

## By David Tresemer, Ph.D.

What is the nature of Neptune? Does it have a discernible signature? Was it aptly named by Le Verrier (the one who calculated its position) as the mythological god of the sea—Neptune? Or does it show signs of the name given first by Galle (the astronomer who first observed it based on Le Verrier's calculations)—Janus, the two-faced god of doorways who looks both forward and back?[1]

We will conclude that Neptune indeed has two faces—mystical, intuitive, revelatory *versus* deceptive, illusory, eroding—and we will show in the following just how far these opposite tendencies reach. As we will see, this goes very deeply into our culture.[2]

In our investigations of the signatures of planets, we have assumed that the planets show more of their true nature when conjunct or opposed to the Sun, as the Sun amplifies the character of the planet to the Earth.[3] In this case, that includes:

Neptune—Sun—Earth (conjunction)
and Neptune—Earth—Sun (opposition)

We extend that phenomenon to a group of favorite stars, which are powerful suns in their own right. Thus the locations that we observe include:

- The Royal Stars of Persia, which are prominent in the fixed signs, Aldebaran at 15° of the Bull, Antares at 15° of the Scorpion, Regulus at 5° of the Lion, and Fomalhaut at 9° of the Waterman.[4]
- Spica, sometimes added to the Royal Stars of Persia and related to the Aldebaran–Antares axis by a close semi-square (45°). As Spica is the exact opposite of the first degree of the Ram (Aries), one might say that Spica is the foundation of the original zodiacal round beginning with 0° of the Ram. I call Spica the Goddess Star, at 29° of the Virgin.
- The greatest concentration of suns in our heavens, the Galactic Center (at 2° Sagittarius).
- The location of the Sun at the Mystery of Golgotha, that series of events that included crucifixion and resurrection of Christ Jesus, and which must be respected as a "mystery" until

---

1   About those who discovered Neptune, and those who nearly discovered it, see David Tresemer, "The Discovery of the Planet Named Neptune," *International Astrologer, The Journal of the International Society for Astrological Research*, Aug. 2012.

2   This study is supplemented by my other research papers on this, "Corporate Personhood" (in preparation) and "Neptune, Christ Jesus, and the Three Johns" (research in progress). The approach to signatures is thoroughly explained in previous articles for the *Journal for Star Wisdom*, on Saturn, Pluto, and Venus, as well as in Tresemer, *The Venus Eclipse of the Sun 2012*. The "we" used in this paper refers to ongoing conversations with William Bento and Robert Schiappacasse about these astrological issues. The comments of Brian Gray and Wain Farrants have also been invaluable for this paper.

3   Richard Tarnas, in *Cosmos and Psyche*, does not emphasize these connections with the Sun, but rather the events occurring close to the discovery of the outer planets (for Neptune, pp. 96–98) and hard aspects (conjunction, opposition, square, with 15° orbs) between the outer planets (for Neptune, especially the interaction with Uranus, pp. 355–451).

4   We use sidereal placements where the fixed stars stay fixed (with "proper motion" that changes their position very slowly over hundreds of years), formally speaking the Babylonian sidereal zodiac. This does not affect the angles of aspects, but does affect the celestial addresses of their locations. The Royal Stars of Persia are described further in Tresemer and Schiappacasse, *Star Wisdom & Rudolf Steiner*, and at www.starwisdom.org. The polarity of Aldebaran and Antares forms the basis for the organization of the zodiac, as we know it (from Powell, *History of the Zodiac*.

deeply contemplated. The Sun was then at 14 to 15° of the Ram (Aries). The position of Neptune at the Mystery of Golgotha was at 3°14' Waterman (Aquarius), thus opposed to Regulus. Anything to do with Regulus in this study can be seen as related also to that position.

- Our own Sun. For the fixed stars and fixed positions, we observe the planet (in this case Neptune) moving and the fixed as stationery. In this case, the Sun moves more swiftly, indeed having each year one conjunction and one opposition with Neptune.

We compare these to events in the world, for which we have collected nearly a thousand events in our dataset. Astrological research is less capable when discussing trends. Though the Black Death is spoken of by historians as an event, it occurred over a span of time, with unknown beginnings and intense middles, then tapering off. However, in this instance we can locate the center (see below). In other cases, as in the Thirty Years War, we can locate the first event—the Battle of White Mountain. In other cases, we can't find dates for cultural trends, such as the rise of the internet. In an early approach to the signature of a planet, we look for clearly defined dates for events.

With other planets, we have looked at historical personages who were born with some of the aspects that we will look at; for want of space, we were not able to go into that for Neptune.

In our studies that span centuries, we normally restrict our observations to very close aspects, 1° of orb in either direction. In our research on the background of the rise of corporate personhood, we began to notice a repeating pattern of a 6° orb. We reasoned that this particular distance had a certain quality important to Neptune. As one friend put it, this is akin to the distance that a bomber must unfurl the electric wire from an explosive charge to the trip-switch. Another way of understanding the importance of this gap in relation to Neptune comes from our understanding of the initiations of Lazarus, where the experience began and ended in a 6° orb (the explanation for which will have to wait until the next issue of this journal).[5] We also reference the teachings of Marc Edmund Jones wherein all the degrees less than ten were understood not as increasing distance but as a quality of relationship. The Babylonian system—that we moderns continue to use for our measurement of time and space—was based on the number 60. Thus 360/60 = 6 was considered a perfect number, with great power.[6] In the study of the discoverers of Neptune, the wider-than-usual 6° orb did not destroy statistical significance. For these reasons we have continued to use it in the case of Neptune.

Thus we consider that an orb of 6° in either direction opens us to the beginning and ending of initiatory sequences in relation to exact conjunctions and oppositions. Nonetheless, we will alert the reader to orbs wider than the more common 4° by putting the Event name in ((doubled parentheses)).

The format is as follows. The event is given in bold. *Celestial* refers first to the location of Neptune, then to the celestial body to which it was aspected, and the kind of aspect and the orb. *Comments* follow. Within each category, the events are given chronologically. Another way of looking at these would be via the quality of the star in action, as well as the quality of the orb. This awaits an expansion of this study. I have added a very few square (90°) connections when they relate to a theme already being developed; even if close, a square also gets parentheses.

## Discoveries and Inventions

In some very important inventions we can see a kind of regime change for culture stemming from technology. Our dataset has many inventions, and the ones connected with Neptune have had widespread impacts on human society.

**Invention by Michael Faraday of the electric motor, December 25, 1821**

*Celestial:* Neptune 10°33' Sagittarius, Sun at 11°17' Sagittarius, conjunction within 1°

*Comment:* What Rudolf Steiner called the "subearthly" forces of electricity (as fallen or degraded light) and magnetism (as fallen sound or tone) were

---

5 In Tresemer "Neptune, Christ Jesus, and the Three Johns."

6 Astrologically, 6° would thus be considered as the sixtieth harmonic.

combined to create the compulsion of movement as rotary motion, which has now powered our entire society. An electrical generator takes powers of nature to produce rotary movement which creates electricity—which then is transmitted down wires to our homes, where we use the electricity to create rotary motion in the dozens of motors in our homes and businesses, thus mimicking nature.

**((Invention by Alexander Graham Bell of the telephone, March 10, 1876))**

*Celestial:* Neptune at 8°14' Ram (Aries), Mystery of Golgotha at 14-15° Ram, conjunction within 6°

*Comment:* An early abstraction of human sensory capacities, which have had positive and negative consequences. We begin here with the extension of sound and speech across distance.

**Invention by Thomas Edison of phonograph, December 6, 1877**

*Celestial:* Neptune at 12°8' Ram (Aries), Mystery of Golgotha at 14-15° Ram, conjunction within 2°

*Comment:* Abstraction from hearing actual instruments and musicians. We can listen to music that occurred in another place and time.

**Invention of electric light by Thomas Edison, October 23, 1879**

*Celestial:* Neptune at 17°54' Ram (Aries), Mystery of Golgotha at 14-15° Ram, conjunction within 3°

*Comment:* Making fallen light (how Steiner understood electricity) into artificial light, which disconnects us from the light of day and permits us to extend our awakeness into the night.

**((Invention of television by John Baird, October 20, 1925))**

*Celestial:* Neptune at 0°15' Lion, Regulus at 5°5' Lion, conjunction within 5°

*Comment:* Abstraction of experience into electron streams hitting a translucent screen. Rudolf Steiner spoke to this invention, even before it occurred: "Many phenomena in the cultural life of today have a destructive effect, especially screen images—which definitely harm the etheric body. Such images also arouse sensuality. True art can bring down into the sense world what comes from higher worlds."[7] For television, we can also see the hope contrasted with the actuality.

**((Invention of long-distance rocket by Robert Goddard, March 16, 1926))**

*Celestial:* Neptune at 28°52' Crab (Cancer), Regulus at 5°5' Lion, conjunction within 7°

*Comment:* Space is collapsed by the ability to send a rocket over distances previously thought too great.

**Invention of the thermonuclear bomb by Edward Teller, November 1, 1952**

*Celestial:* Neptune at 28°0' Virgin (Virgo), conjunct to Spica within 2°

*Comment:* A vast expansion of killing power, marking a regime change. The key to the hydrogen bomb is *fusion* of hydrogen atoms into a helium atom, wherein a portion of the mass is translated (via $E=mc^2$) to energy, as compared to the explosion of neutrons in a regular *fission* atomic-bomb. The atomic bomb is another kind of oxidation reaction, a larger version of TNT. The hydrogen bomb comes from a completely different way of working with matter and energy.

### *The Conundrum*

Right at the very beginning of our researches, the simple and frequent question arises: Is Neptune good or not good? Is it helpful or not helpful? More to the point, would we have been better off without these inventions that have promised a better life but have demonstrably made our lives more fragmented, alienated, and dry? Of course, despite great pressure on the part of astrological clients who seek a quick answer, we cannot be so simple. The conundrum comes in the fact that Neptune functions both ways, simultaneously. The conventional understanding of Neptune includes the notion of creativity, divine inspiration, the ability to generate new images of new possibilities in the world: Neptune generates (or stimulates the generation of) pictures and encourages picture making. It opens human consciousness to new ideologies (which we will soon see in the political realm) and new visions.

---

7  Steiner, *Esoteric Christianity and the Mission of Christian Rosenkreutz* (lect. of 1911), p. 297.

Certainly we can say that many of these inventions are in the realm of pictures, new images as well as the promulgation of images. Telephone, phonograph, television, and electric light: These have all permitted us to ignore the limitations of time (the darkness of night) and distance, and to create more pictures more swiftly about the nature of reality.[8]

The conundrum has two issues working with it. First is the issue of reversal, which we shall tackle more thoroughly in the next section of political and social change. However, we get a taste here. With the inventions of electric light, phonograph, telephone, and television, initially we herald their appearance on the world stage with great happiness, as we predict that they will extend our capacities further. Indeed, this is true—to an extent. We can also observe an ineluctable reversal: The inventions turn in upon themselves and *limit* our capacities as we become enchained to the banality of most telephone conversations (one can include voice messages and texting here), the ubiquity and poor quality of recorded music which lacks the soul of a live performance, the degradation by television images of our ability to see and hear in the real world which has, because of its replacement, become less cared for. One hears of scenes where villagers crowd into a grass hut around a television while their crops fail from want of attention. Instead of new vistas of new visions, television has for the most part delivered us sound bites and advertising jingles. These constitute a reversal of the intended effects of the inventions.

A summary of the effects of the telephone invention comes from Baudrillard's brilliance: "Creating ultra-rapid communication networks immediately means transforming human exchange into a residue."[9] The initial purpose—to ennoble and allow and to open up human communication—becomes subservient to the medium itself, the technology. The invention then becomes not about communication but about swiftness and simulation, the ever-increasing replacement of conversation with mechanism. Conversation—"human exchange"—becomes "residue," a kind of waste that one then tries to minimize. Each of these Neptunian inventions could be seen in this light.

One could say that Neptune's power encourages images of a new world that are cloaked in shining promise, yet deliver over time the opposite. We shall see reversal play out in the political arena with astonishing regularity.

## Conclusions near the beginning

Normally we would save conclusions for the end. However, it would be helpful if you used the conclusions to evaluate the upcoming (and the previous) list of events. Neptune is present in the sky all the time, and frequently in complicated aspects (ranging to semi-sesquadrate and so on) to the Suns that interest us, or in relation to other planets. However, when we limit our view of Neptune to certain aspects (conjunction and opposition) to certain Suns, we can understand its influence when in its full power. We can say that Neptune is related to whole new visions for humankind, to revolutionary new views of reality and possibility, to pictures of the future that are very attractive to many. Adversarial forces—what I have called in *Star Wisdom & Rudolf Steiner* the Illusionist and the Hardener[10]—are independently operating intelligences that can subvert the good that streams from the opportunities of Neptune's alignments with powerful Suns, and turn it into something that increases suffering and misery in the world.

In this view the negativity that shouts out from most (though not all) of the following events does not come from Neptune itself but from the distractions put into place by the clever and destructive adversarial spirits that subvert human progress. One could say that the difficulties are intrinsic to Neptune or that they are swift reactions by adversaries to Neptune's positive possibilities. It makes a difference which way you decide. If you decide

---

8   Having specific dates for these inventions is a privilege. Photography, obviously related to these observations, does not have clear dates when a great breakthrough happened.

9   Baudrillard, *The Illusion of the End*, p. 78.

10   Rudolf Steiner names the Illusionist Lucifer, the "light-bearer," who rebelled against heaven, and the Hardener Ahriman, in the Persian system, the divine adversary of the good.

the former, then you see Neptune as the home of the Hardener and all its minions. If you decide the latter, then you pay attention to Neptune transits of these stars (and of our Sun to Neptune) as positive opportunities. Even though all around you the distractions of tragedy are unfolding, you can then open yourself to the less seen positivity that is available at those times.

The fundamental positivity of Neptune has become my view from research on the events, the inventions that we have already seen as well as the events that we are yet to explore. Neptune holds a great promise for the development of sacred powers of the human being, increased when in conjunction or opposition to the great Suns that we follow. Human beings are not generally ready for these infusions, and unable to grasp them quickly. The retarding forces—Hardener and Illusionist—rush in during the increased flow of positive energy and turn that energy into its opposite, creating destruction where positive change could have existed. I suggest that you meet these events with this in mind. In the case of the inventions above, one doesn't try to "make good" an invention that has gone bad in society, but rather one must travel back to the time of the invention, and pick up the gift that was intended to be positive in its effects. Read on with this dynamic in mind, as it will take an extra twist at the end.

## Regime Change

In our research, I noted an unusual number of events that showed a complete change of political, scientific, and even geological reality, sometimes for a large area, sometimes for the entire world. Arnold Toynbee spoke about this phenomenon in the social/political realm, how people experiencing "spiritual uncertainty" and "moral defeat" seek "a utopian chimera as a substitute for an intolerable present." The people raise cries and sometimes weapons to overcome the vision of the past in order to set up something from the better days of the past (what Toynbee called archaism) or an entirely new age (futurism).

> In both these utopian movements the effort to live in the microcosm instead of the macrocosm is abandoned for the pursuit of an ideal world that would be reached—supposing that this were in fact possible—without any challenge to face an arduous change of spiritual clime.... The vain hope that, if reality is denied with sufficient force, then it will cease to be actual, is also at the root of the futurist form of utopianism.[11]

Liz Greene adds the notion that with Neptune there is a "longing for the lost innocence of the Paradise Garden" in the form of redemption of all past mistakes.[12] We could summarize Toynbee's and Greene's comments astrologically as saying that the struggle to overcome old patterns or old "isms"—capitalism, socialism, communism, religion-ism—and to replace them with new ones shows the influence of Neptune (the ideal world) rather than Saturn ("facing the arduous," "reality"). The restlessness to change the intolerable often brings on a world that is even worse. In relation to the previous section, one could say that the promise or lure of Neptune to advancement is fundamentally correct, but perhaps premature for the present capabilities of human beings and therefore easily subverted.

## Political Regime Change

Whole civilizations have collapsed and been replaced with different forms of organization. New "isms" have taken hold, leaving old ones behind.

**Founding of the Roman Empire by Octavian (Augustus), with constitution and control by the Senate and people of Rome, January 13, 27 BC**

*Celestial:* Neptune at 25°8' Virgo, conjunct Spica at 29°6' Virgo, conjunction within 4° (Neptune applying)

*Comment:* A major development of the political situation in Rome. After this, Octavian changed his name to Augustus ("venerable"), first in the series of emperors to do so. He created what appeared to be a democracy, while retaining great individual power. The appearance of democracy satisfied the demands of the people, though it was subverted by the true plays of power.

---

11 Toynbee, *A Study in History*, p. 245; also Greene, *The Astrological Neptune and the Quest for Redemption*, pp. 289f.

12 Greene, *The Astrological Neptune and the Quest for Redemption*, p. 295.

## Julian the Apostate died on June 26, AD 363

*Celestial:* Neptune at 4°6' Waterman (Aquarius), opposed to Regulus at 5°5' Lion within 1°.

*Comment:* Julian, the last of the Constantines, deposed Christianity as the official religion of Rome, and sought to reinvigorate the Sun mysteries of the pagan religions, while granting religious freedom to everyone. Unlike other emperors, he had studied philosophy, and wrote Neo-Platonist tracts. His death led to great conflicts amongst the religions, a conflict among worldviews for control of the Roman Empire. We see again the conflict of ideological systems.

## Justinian closes the School of Athens in 529

*Celestial:* Neptune around 3° Waterman, opposed to Regulus at 5°5' Lion within 2°, and conjunct Neptune's location at the Mystery of Golgotha

*Comment:* The emperor Justinian has been blamed for closing the School of Athens and the rout of the main school of philosophy of its time. This is contested by several historians, though Rudolf Steiner considers that Justinian closed the School, a major regime change of the intellectual climate of the time, and causing the migration of thinkers to the Arabic courts where they could pursue their studies, to the detriment of humanity because they developed intellectuality too quickly.[13]

## ((Birth of Islam, September 1, 621))

*Celestial:* Neptune at 29°19' Leo, Sun at 5°14' Virgo, conjunction within 6° (Sun separating)

*Comment:* Creation of a new religion, that is, a form to direct human spiritual striving. Though claiming ancestry in Judaism and Christianity, this marked a new era of conflict and wars between the three. The hopefulness of a new message from God quickly turned to violence.

## Crowning of Charlemagne as Holy Roman Emperor, December 25, 800

*Celestial:* Neptune at 2°28' Libra, Spica at 29°6' Virgo; Sun at 0°25' Capricorn, conjunction Neptune and Spica within 4° (Neptune having moved past); Neptune square to Sun within 3°

*Comment:* Conglomeration of many small states into one large empire with a divinely blessed emperor.

---

13 Steiner, *Materialism and the Task of Anthroposophy*, lect. 4.

## ((First Crusade, entry of Jerusalem, July 15, 1099))

*Celestial:* Neptune at 23°23' Cancer, Sun at 15°33' Cancer, conjunction within 8° (Sun applying)

*Comment:* The bloody culmination of the Catholic Church's desire to own and control the property of the events of the Bible. Though a wide orb, it relates to the next regime change.

## Saladin defeats the Crusades at Hattin on July 4, 1187, then takes back Jerusalem

*Celestial:* Neptune at 4°56' Waterman (Aquarius), opposed to Regulus at 5°5' Lion within 1°

*Comment:* The Crusaders had taken Jerusalem violently, enforcing a regime change to all of Christendom in 1099, under another aspect to Neptune. Here is where Saladin took it back. He soon blocked up the Golden Gate so that the Judeo-Christian Messiah could not enter that way, which had been foretold.

## ((Massacre at Beziers, July 22, 1209))

*Celestial:* Neptune at 24°20' Pisces, opposed to Spica at 29°6' Virgin within 5°

*Comment:* Unable to convert the Cathars to Catholicism by persuasion, an army came from northern France led by Simon de Montfort. Their first encounter was at Beziers. The townspeople would not offer up the Cathars, as they were friends and relatives. The southerners expected that nothing would come from this encounter. De Montfort responded by telling his commanders to "kill them all—God will know his own." This massacre of 20,000 people (of whom 200 were Cathars) began the conquest of the south by the north. It also began the Inquisition—the shift from persuasion to thought police and torturers pretending to be Christian. The violence affirmed the Cathars' view that Christianity was satanic, again ideologies that reversed in their effects.

## Execution of the leader of the Templars, Jacques de Molay, March 18, 1314

*Celestial:* Neptune at 13°2' Scorpio, Antares at 15°1' Scorpio, conjunction within 2° (Neptune applying)

*Comment:* Another regime change, showing the end of the Templars, who were the first bankers (noting the connection with banking in the next section).

**Black Death greatest year of death, 75 million dying in Europe, 1351**

*Celestial:* Neptune at 3° Waterman (Aquarius), opposed to Regulus within 2°, and at the exact place of its discovery

*Comment:* The greatest die-off of humanity at any time.

**Martin Luther posts the 95 Theses on the church door, beginning the Protestant Revolution, October 31, 1517**

*Celestial:* Neptune at 3°56' Waterman (Aquarius), opposed to Regulus within 2°

*Comment:* This began a process of change of thinking, and wars to fight about these ways of thinking, that exist to this day. Ideologies and their reversals abound.

**Rapid extinction of the Inca Empire by the Spanish, November 8, 1519**

*Celestial:* Neptune at 8°21' Aquarius, Fomalhaut at 9° 7' Aquarius and Sun at 7°22' Scorpio, conjunction Neptune and Fomalhaut within 1° and square with Sun within 1°

*Comment:* The European (Spanish) thirst for gold created a complete and sudden collapse of an entire civilization, including destruction of all records of that civilization. The thirst for gold and the desire to convert to Christianity led to their opposites. Look at Spain today.

**((Battle of White Mountain, in which the Catholic armies destroyed the kingdom that had supported the free and creative thinkers of the time, November 8, 1620))**

*Celestial:* Neptune at 23°37' Virgo, Spica at 29°6' Virgo, conjunction within 6° (Neptune applying)

*Comment:* Regime change, the alteration of empires and ways of thinking. In this battle, the Catholic armies had come all the way from Spain to crush the Protestant free-thinking culture centered around Prague, wherein the investigations into alchemy, astrology, sacred geometry were being developed, foundational studies upon which we depend for our modern chemistry, psychology, and architecture. From one point of view, a blow against independent thinking. From another point of view, the victory of the forces of the Pope and therefore church-based Christianism. This battle began the Thirty Years War which saw the population of Central Europe reduced by half to two-thirds, a greater catastrophe than the Black Death.

**((Mayflower Compact signed, November 21, 1620))**

*Celestial:* Neptune at 23°37' Virgo, Spica at 29°6' Virgo, conjunction within 6°

*Comment:* The first government of the Europeans arriving to settle the New World.

**Surrender by the British at Yorktown, the last battle of the American Revolutionary War, September 29, 1781**

*Celestial:* Neptune at 13°57' Virgo, Sun at 15° 11' Virgo, conjunction within 2° (Sun separating)

*Comment:* An event that shifted world empires, from Britain to America.

**Philadelphia Convention for American Constitution, September 17, 1787**

*Celestial:* Neptune at 26°1' Virgo, Spica at 29°6' Virgo, conjunction within 4°

*Comment:* Making the vision of a democracy real, in a document that has served as a model for governments around the world ever since. Yet see how this document has been re-interpreted opportunistically (and in reversal) by the Supreme Court, whose task it is to uphold this document.

**Coup d'etat by Napoleon, the "18th Brumaire," November 9, 1799**

*Celestial:* Neptune at 22°56' Libra, Sun at 25°11' Libra, conjunction within 3° (Sun separating)

*Comment:* Regime change wherein Napoleon declared himself First Consul and took over the government. The desire of the people for a single leader was subverted by Napoleon's egocentricity and leading his people to death in futile battles.

**((Battle of Waterloo, June 18, 1815))**

*Celestial:* Neptune at 26°10' Scorpio, Sun at 4°8' Gemini, opposed within 8°

*Comment:* This sealed the downfall of Napoleon. Also the occasion for one of the largest money grabs in history by Nathan Mayer Rothschild, who manipulated knowledge of the outcome of this battle in the bond market.

### First use of "United States of Europe," December 25, 1847

*Celestial:* Neptune at 5°34' Aquarius, Regulus at 5°5' Leo, opposition, exact

*Comment:* The notion of a unified Europe, just as the states of America had united, thus a vision of a regime change.

### ((Fourteenth Amendment, July 9, 1868))

*Celestial:* Neptune at 24°23' Pisces, Sun at 24°46 Gemini, square within 1°. We note squares very rarely here, this one because of the work on corporate personhood (as in next item).

*Comment:* The Fourteenth Amendment to the US Constitution, wherein a "person" is defined in modern terms, recognizing the equality at a soul level of each human being.

### ((Santa Clara Supreme Court case, May 10, 1886, the main event that empowered corporations to be considered as persons))

*Celestial:* Neptune at 1° 54' Taurus, Sun at 26° 41' Aries; Algol at 1° 25' Taurus; Regulus at 5°5' Leo, conjunction of Neptune and Sun within 6° (Sun applying); exact conjunction with Algol; square to Regulus

*Comment:* Algol is the "Eye of Medusa," the most traditionally malefic star in the heavens.[14] From the "Corporate Personhood" research paper, this case marked the key turning point for the award of personhood to corporations.

### Discovery of Pluto by Clyde Tombaugh, February 18, 1930[15]

*Celestial:* Neptune 8°31' Leo, Sun at 6° 7' Aquarius, opposition to Sun within 2°

*Comment:* Pluto and Neptune actually interweave, Pluto being closer to the Earth for twenty-year periods. The revelation of the existence of Pluto, its unveiling, is related to Neptune. One could say that here we have revealed the god of the underworld (Hades) and money (plutocracy). Note that this discovery occurred at the start of a major worldwide economic depression.

### Reichstag Fire, leading to the Fire Decree by the Nazi party, February 27, 1933

*Celestial:* Neptune at 15°1' Leo, Sun at 14° 37' Aquarius, opposition to Sun within 2°; Neptune also square to Aldebaran and Antares

*Comment:* The largest shift of power to the Nazi party, where the communists were blamed for starting the blaze, widely thought to be a set-up by the Nazis. Nonetheless, this justified the seizure of totalitarian powers by the Nazi Party. The people wanted the change, as with Napoleon seeking a single unified leadership in difficult times, causing from this choice a level of suffering even worse than before.[16] Hitler is quoted at the site of the fire as saying, "This is a God-given signal! If this fire, as I believe, turns out to be the handiwork of Communists, then there is nothing that shall stop us now crushing out this murderous pest with an iron fist.... You are witnessing the beginning of a great new epoch in German history. This fire is the beginning."[17] These words are filled with the pictures of the old, the evil, and the new. The "God-given signal" became a radical regime change.

### NATO began, April 4, 1949

*Celestial:* Neptune at 19°45' Virgo, Sun at 20° 34' Pisces, opposed within 1°

---

14 Bento, Schiappacasse, and Tresemer, *Signs in the Heavens*. A great circle with Algol in it meets at a perpendicular to the ecliptic plane at 1°25' Taurus.

15 Of interest for Clyde Tombaugh was the conjunction at his birth of Moon (27°7' Taurus) and Pluto (27°26' Taurus). The discovery occurred when transiting Neptune (8°31' Leo) lay opposite his Birth-Saturn (9°34' Aquarius). Thus personal birth charts interact with historical events, as also shown in the "Discovery of a Planet Named Neptune" article.

16 One might ask about the regime change event of "9/11," the fall of the Twin Towers in New York City on September 11, 2001. Though Neptune seems uninvolved at that point (at 11° 36' Capricorn), Pluto at 17°52' Scorpio lies conjunct Antares (within 3°). There are many events and themes related to Pluto connections, 9/11 showing more the signature of Pluto than of Neptune. We see the discovery of Pluto during a Neptune aspect; however, the discussion of Neptune in relation to Pluto lies beyond the scope of this paper.

17 Recorded by a person on the scene, D. Sefton Delmer, in Carey, *Eyewitness to History*, pp. 507–508.

*Comment:* A cooperation that united many countries in a larger military unit, a picture of cooperation in protection of Western values against the threats of the East.

**((China, Proclamation of beginning of People's Republic, October 1, 1949))**

*Celestial:* Neptune at 20°38' Virgo, Sun at 13°44' Virgo, conjunction within 7° (Sun applying)

*Comment:* An immense empire whose effects are very present today. The view of the human being in a communist state of this size has affected everyone on the earth, as we consume the goods created by those workers whose personhood (see the Fourteenth Amendment and other items related to the definition of "person") was defined in a new "ism"—communism.

**China invades Tibet, October 7, 1950**

*Celestial:* Neptune at 22°54' Virgo, Sun at 19°21' Virgo, conjunction within 4°

*Comment:* This marks the demise of the very complex culture of Tibet, as one ideology overwhelmed another. One wonders why China bothered with the remote area of Tibet, and it comes largely from the compulsion of ideologies to dominate other ideologies, with humans often the pawns in the process.

**Disneyland opens, July 17, 1955**

*Celestial:* Neptune at 1°22' Scales (Libra), conjunct Spica at 29°6' Virgo, within 3°

*Comment:* The largest ever ostensibly non-political picture- and fantasy-creation machine surged into cultural life.[18]

**Brown vs. Board of Education decision by Supreme Court, May 17, 1954, asserting the Fourteenth Amendment in relation to equal schools for all races**

*Celestial:* Neptune at 29°46' Virgo, Spica at 29°6' Virgo, conjunction within 1°

---

18 Disney World in Orlando opened on October 1, 1971, with Neptune at 6°37' Scorpion, with a signature unrelated to a powerful position for Neptune. Likewise, the founding of Pixar on February 3, 1986, has a different signature (Neptune at 10°14' Archer).

*First photo of Earth from space*

*Comment:* This is a major guiding decision that began the entire Civil Rights movement, again grappling with a definition of what it meant to be a person without regard to race.

**((First photo of the Earth from space, the "Blue Marble Photo," on December 7, 1972))**

*Celestial:* Neptune at 11°0' Scorpion, conjunct to Antares at 15°3' Scorpion within 5°

*Comment:* This ability to view the whole earth at one time—a blue ball poised in space—is one of the largest cultural shifts that we have experienced.

**Deepwater explosion and oil spill, April 20, 2010**

*Celestial:* Neptune at 3°23' Waterman (Aquarius), opposed to Regulus at 5°5' Lion within 2°

*Comment:* The largest oil spill, a demonstration of the side effects of an oil-consuming world.

**Adoption of the IPv6 protocol, an expansion of addresses for electronic devices, June 6, 2012**

*Celestial:* Neptune at 8°15' Waterman (Aquarius), conjunct to Fomalhaut at 9°9' Waterman within 1°

*Comment:* This long-awaited Internet Protocol version 6 expanded the list of unique names or identities for electronic devices from about four billion to $2^{128}$, that is, to an identifier with 128 places, each with a "0" or a "1" or "3.4 × $10^{38}$"

(that is 38 zeroes) separate and unique addresses. An "order of magnitude" is the multiplication by ten, and opens an entirely different world (as in the various "Powers of 10" presentations). This expanded the population of potential electronic devices by many orders of magnitude.

⚜

Jesaiah Ben-Aharon argues that all political changes are characterized by one outcome: They all fail.[19] In his view, intrinsic to historical change of this sort is a reversal of one's stated intent. You can look with hindsight at the many regime changes noted in the tables above, and see that this is true. The picture upon one's banner for revolutionary change becomes embarrassing years later, when one realizes that, not only did it not work, it achieved the opposite of what was intended. This is a product of social picture making, that is, a consequence of creating utopian pictures in itself—in other words, a characteristic of Neptune.

### Financial Regime Change

Several events show regime change in the financial sphere.

### Execution of the leader of the Templars, Jacques de Molay, March 18, 1314

*Celestial:* Neptune at 13°2' Scorpio, Antares at 15°1' Scorpio, conjunction within 2° (Neptune applying)

*Comment:* Another regime change, showing the end of the Templars, who were the first bankers—so that the Church and kings could take over these functions. The Templars were known for their honesty and fairness. The Church and kings have not been known for those traits.

### Royal Exchange begun in London, January 23, 1571

*Celestial:* Neptune at 2°14' Twins (Gemini), opposite the Galactic Center within 1°

*Comment:* This marks the beginning of what would later become the London Stock Exchange, by charter from the Queen. See below for other major stock exchanges. What was originally a victory for creating order in buying and selling of shares has turned into its opposite, a method for marginalization and destruction of human exchange.

### Charter of the East India Company on December 31, 1600

*Celestial:* Neptune at 10°47' Lion, opposed to Fomalhaut at 9°7' Waterman within 2°, and conjunct to Regulus at 5°5' Lion within 6°

*Comment:* This company with its own army (similar to Blackwater in Iraq) bullied foreign governments (through severe tactics including bribery, assassination, and even small wars) to grant it exclusive access to trade routes and substances, ranging from spices to sugar to slaves to addictive drugs.

### ((New York Stock Exchange founded, May 17, 1792))

*Celestial:* Neptune at 5°51' Libra, Spica at 29°6' Virgo, conjunction within 7° (Neptune having moved beyond)

*Comment:* The financial sector takes a major step toward control of exchange and trade. Seen positively at its outset, these exchanges have become nexuses of economic dysfunction.

### Tokyo Stock Exchange founded, May 15, 1878

*Celestial:* Neptune at 14°51' Ram (Aries), Mystery of Golgotha at 14-15° Ram, conjunction exact

*Comment:* For a long time, the third largest market in the world. Another nexus for more efficient dysfunction.

### ((Federal Reserve begun, December 23, 1913))

*Celestial:* Neptune at 3°59' Crab, Spica at 29°6' Virgo, square within 5° (Neptune separating)

*Comment:* The Federal Reserve was created and now holds the world's "reserve currency." Though seen originally as a means to make money flows more efficient, this has become (and one could say that this was true from the beginning) a center for the destruction of the currency and its asset base.

---

19 Ben-Aharon, *The Event in Science, History, Philosophy, and Art* (http://virtualbookworm.com).

**New York Stock Market Crash, October 29, 1929**
*Celestial:* Neptune at 9°56' Lion (Leo), conjunct Regulus at 5°5' Lion within 5°, opposed to Fomalhaut at 9°7' Waterman within 1°

*Comment:* The famous beginning of the Great Depression (beginning with America then spreading worldwide), also the temporary end of an era of fiscal and cultural expansion. One could see the manipulations that led to this crash that served the profits of the few.

**((Glass-Steagal Act passed by US Congress, June 16, 1933, limiting powers of banks))**
*Celestial:* Neptune at 13°49' Lion (Leo), opposed to Fomalhaut at 9°7' Waterman within 7°, and square to the main axis of Antares-Aldebaran within 1°

*Comment:* This is the law limiting banks whose repeal has marked, in the mind of many, the dangerous rise of irresponsible power in the banks. Now the banks have created trillions of dollars of derivatives, greater than the combined assets of the earth. The Glass-Steagal act was intended to prevent that sort of wild speculation.

**World Bank founded, December 27, 1945**
*Celestial:* Neptune at 14°35' Virgo, Sun at 11°37' Sagittarius, square to Sun within 3° (Sun applying)

*Comment:* The largest global financial institution, praised for its world-uniting policies, and blamed for destroying many small economies.

**((President Richard Nixon ends the gold standard, creating fiat money as the main currency, August 15, 1971))**
*Celestial:* Neptune at 5°58' Scorpio, Sun at 28°11' Cancer, square within 7° (Sun applying)

*Comment:* This has changed the economies of all nations, steering them away from the discipline of hard assets to paper promises that are now out of control.

**President Nixon opens the gate from the West to China, February 21, 1972**
*Celestial:* Neptune at 10°51' Scorpio, Sun at 7°24' Aquarius, square within 4° (Sun applying)

*Comment:* This meeting began the arrangements for how cheap labor in China would manufacture everything.

*Occupy Wall Street movement*

**((Citizens United Supreme Court case, January 21, 2010, a great advance of empowerment of corporations as "persons"))**
*Celestial:* Neptune at 0° 23' Aquarius, Jupiter 5°55' Aquarius, conjunction Neptune and Jupiter within 6° (Jupiter separating); opposed to Regulus within 5°

*Comment:* The position of Neptune squares the Neptune position of the Santa Clara case, which is its parent. Neptune was quite near the place where it was discovered, which is taken up in the "Neptune, Christ" article. See "Corporate Personhood" article for more references to this event in relation to its predecessors. This decision has unleashed a huge amount of anonymous cash from corporate "persons" to political candidates who therefore no longer serve human beings but rather serve corporate "persons."

**Occupy Wall Street movement, inception September 17, 2011**
*Celestial:* Neptune at 3°57' Aquarius, Regulus at 5°5' Leo, opposition within 2°

*Comment:* A grass-roots uprising hoping for regime change.

### End of the World Prophecies

I have had an interest in the history of prophecies, how few come true, what happens to the believers when they don't, and how to hold prophecy in a helpful manner.[20] Some very major prophecies that

---
20 Prophecy has an important and rightful place in world culture and personal lives. See "Prophecy

attracted the attention of thousands have occurred with strong Neptune placements.

### End of World predicted by Charlie Indian on February 7, 1811

*Celestial:* Neptune at 18°47' Scorpion, conjunct to Antares at 15°1' Scorpion within 4°

*Comment:* Charlie delivered a prophecy to the Cherokee council, including: "The Mother of the Nation has forsaken you because all her bones are being broken through the grinding [of corn and grain by the mills of the white invaders]." He recommended throwing out the technology and getting rid of the white man, as otherwise the earth would come to an end.

### ((End of World predicted by William Miller on March 21, 1844))

*Celestial:* Neptune at 0°3' Aquarius, opposed to Regulus at 5°5' Lion within 6° (and to Neptune's position at the Mystery of Golgotha within 4°)

*Comment:* From a close reading of the Bible, William Miller gave this date for the end of the world, later extended to include two more dates—April 18 and October 22, also opposed to Regulus with the same orb. Many thousands of people prepared for the end of life and the meeting with Jesus Christ. "End of the world" prophecies predict the ultimate regime change.

### ((End of World predicted by Doomsealers on April 14, 1890))

*Celestial:* Neptune at 9°37' Bull (Taurus), conjunct to Aldebaran at 15°3' Bull within 6°

*Comment:* Another large movement readying for the end.

### The date that Jeane Dixon predicted as the birth of the Antichrist, February 5, 1962.

*Celestial:* Neptune at 19°16' Libra, Sun at 21°55' Capricorn, square within 4° (Sun separating); Neptune opposed to Mystery of Golgotha Sun at 15° Aries within 4°

*Comment:* A date much cited by Robert Powell. Whether this prediction about the birth of anti-Christ or Ahriman turns out to be true or not, it

shows a strong relationship to Neptune. Jeane Dixon predicted massive regime change would occur as a result of this human being.

## *Scientific Regime Change: Biology*

Extending the inventions discussed before, we find particularly important discoveries in biology.

### Penicillin discovered by Alexander Fleming on September 3, 1928

*Celestial:* Neptune at 5°37' Lion (Leo), conjunct to Regulus at 5°5' Lion within 1°

*Comment:* Similar to many discoveries, this advance in anti-life (anti-biotics) has saved lives, in this instance many lives, while at the same time weakening the immune systems of human beings. The double nature of many discoveries shows itself quite strongly here.

### James Watson discovers the form of DNA, February 28, 1953

*Celestial:* Neptune at 29°29' Virgo, Spica at 29°6' Virgo, conjunction within 1°

*Comment:* From this eureka-moment (an "aha" realization) came the map of our bodies, which has become another kind of empire and property, patented by corporations.

### Polio vaccine discovered by Jonas Salk on March 27, 1953

*Celestial:* Neptune at 28°52' Virgin (Virgo), conjunct to Spica within 1°

*Comment:* Another lifesaver that has taken lives (the small percent that contract the disease from the vaccination). The double nature of any vaccine is still argued, with one side demonstrating the lives saved, and others demonstrating the weakening of the human immune system.

## *Geological Change*

We have recorded events of many different kinds, including dozens of earthquakes and other disasters. It lifted off the page when we saw that the two most destructive of earthquakes ever, in terms of human life, occurred when there were connections with Neptune, as well as perhaps the most destructive nuclear accident ever to occur, at Fukushima.

---

and Ritual" at www.starwisdom.org (research section).

**Explosion of Mount Vesuvius, August 24, AD 79**

*Celestial:* Neptune at 15°57' Bull (Taurus), conjunct Aldebaran at 15°3' Bull within 1°

*Comment:* Though many more people have died in other natural disasters, this one occurring so close to the capital of the world at that time—Rome—also marked a complete change of thinking about the natural world.

**((Largest earthquake ever, China, January 23, 1556))**

*Celestial:* Neptune at 28°32' Aries, Sun at 23°49' Capricorn, square within 6° (Sun approaching Neptune)

*Comment:* More than 830,000 people perished. Many earthquakes occur. Note that death-by-earthquake means being crushed by something hard, a signature of the Hardener.

**Second largest earthquake, China, July 27, 1976**

*Celestial:* Neptune at 16° 59' Scorpio, Antares at 15° 1', conjunction within 2°

*Comment:* The second largest earthquake killed over 200,000 people by crushing under heavy buildings and collapsing earth.

**Earthquake, tsunami, and destruction of three nuclear power plants at Fukushima, Japan, March 11, 2011**

*Celestial:* Neptune at 4°18' Aquarius, Regulus at 5°5' Leo, opposition within 1°

*Comment:* This event is nowhere near the top of the list in terms of human lives lost; however, the long-term destruction from radioactivity may make it one of the very worst world disasters. It is ongoing, and originated at a connection between Neptune and the King and Queen Star, Regulus, Heart of the Lion.

## *History of Anthroposophy*

Several events in Rudolf Steiner's life can be seen within the context of Neptune. A deeper study comparing the annual conjunctions and oppositions of the Sun with Neptune would reveal more, and awaits further study. However, the point is made that anthroposophy owes something in its origins to connections with Neptune.

**Rudolf Steiner's first lecture on Goethe, November 27, 1891**

*Celestial:* Neptune at 14°30' Bull (Taurus), conjunct to Aldebaran at 15°3' Bull within 1°

*Comment:* Beginning of Steiner's career as a lecturer and public presenter.

**Rudolf Steiner's Festival of Knowledge, wherein he met the being of Christ Jesus, December 2, 1899**

*Celestial:* Neptune at 2°42' Twins (Gemini), opposite the Galactic Center within 1°

*Comment:* This event is given by Steiner as end of the year; the exact date of December 2 was estimated based on other astrological occurrences. Anything in this month would have the same connection with Neptune. An anthroposophist would recognize that here we have an instance where the unusual down-flow of positive energy from Neptune was met—the adversarial forces were set aside and the positive influence was received.

**Rudolf Steiner College founded, September 29, 1976**

*Celestial:* Neptune at 17°47' Scorpion, conjunct to Antares within 3°

*Comment:* Steiner's namesake college chose Michaelmas—September 29—for its founding day, though this also implicated Neptune empowered by the Star of Death and Rebirth (Antares).

## *General Observations about World Events and Neptune*

Each of the foregoing events deserves a complete description of the context of the time, the event itself, the chief actors involved and their birth configurations, the significance of the event for humanity, and a discussion of its implications for our understanding of the qualities emanating from or associated with Neptune. Earthquake-like changes of ideology and empire leave the champions of the new feeling victorious. However, the ones being replaced feel pain, suffering, and crushing loss. From the Spanish conquest of the Incas to the founding of NATO, from Rome to the rise of the Nazis, from the bastions of capitalism in the New York Stock Exchange and the granting of personhood to corporations, we see great shifts of power in the culture. Liz Greene links Neptune to a yearning for redemption, including great political and social changes in service of that restless desire. We can confirm that we have found that pattern displayed here.

Very small orbs are found for two major inventions that have shaped our world, the invention of the electric motor by Faraday and the discovery of the construction of DNA. Both of these have changed the territory of our lives. The new technologies of telephone, phonograph, and television, amongst others, have also changed our lives utterly. Have these marked improvement or its opposite?

We can imagine these phenomena as a swift wiping away of one picture of the world and a replacement by another. Neptune seems to specialize in creating pictures of how-things-are as well as of possibilities for the future. This motivates people to make the changes. No other planetary signature shows so much change. As much as there is destruction, as in the earthquakes and Fukushima, there is perhaps more a rude adjustment of world-views, of ideologies, of what is correct and what incorrect in one's thinking. Such large and sudden changes make life more difficult for everyone. In the terms of Toynbee whom we quoted earlier, this image making, and image destroying yearns for balance from a more Saturnian perspective that reveals reality without veils and that courageously faces the truths before us.

It is tempting to label Neptune as illusion, deception, or materialism, or with names such as Ahriman or Lucifer. Nevertheless, we must avoid this, as making such a process into a noun of any kind actually hides its power. In practical work with clients, one sees that Neptune, by placement in relation to the stars in the heavens or in relation to other planets in one's birthchart, can stimulate imagination in the most compassionate and creative way. But with what guide words or key words can we conclusively label Neptune?

### Enantiodromia

Earlier I voiced the conclusion that Neptune may bring advancement for human beings but that often-adversarial forces get there first, so to speak, and subvert the opportunity into a distracting tragedy. Thus we are hard pressed on whether to award Neptune the list of traits marked A or B:

A: transcendent, spiritual, ideal, symbolic, imaginative, subtle; inspiring of ideals and aspirations, surrender, dissolution of boundaries.

B: bringer of illusion, delusion, deception, self-deception, escapism, intoxication, psychosis, projection.[21]

From the research presented here, I feel that Neptune has to be treated differently. I have concluded from my review of these events that Neptune offers an unusually powerful energy for human development. However, most people are not ready for it. The adversarial forces rush in and turn the positive opportunity into its opposite. Reversal of good intentions into bad effects seems a curse of being human.

This is a characteristic of *enantiodromia*, the turning of a thing into its opposite, noted first by Heraclitus and picked up more recently by Carl Jung, who expressed it as follows: "We can never know what evil may not be necessary in order to produce good by enantiodromia, and what good may very possibly lead to evil."[22] Thus we need not choose between two lists of traits—A vs. B. More importantly, Neptune leads one to a meta-level where both are true at the same time. The *coniunctio oppositorum*—marriage of opposites—that so interested Jung in his study of the alchemists and in his work with depth psychology occurs exactly because a thing is reversed into its opposite.[23] If an integration of the two polarities takes place, that hermaphrodite becomes an entirely new being. Neptune does not offer a list

---

21 These lists from Tarnas *Cosmos and Psyche*, 96. A similar list can be found in Le Grice, *The Archetypal Cosmos*, p. 95.

22 Jung, *The Archetypes and the Collective Unconscious*, par. 397.

23 Heraclitus, fragment 51: "The opposed thing agrees with itself; harmony is the reflexive tension, like the archer's bow and the lyre." Harmony does not come from cessation of activity or calm, but rather from a balance of strongly polarized positions.

of characteristics (such as magnanimity with Jupiter, etc.), but rather a process.

The process of reversal—enantiodromia—is frightening when encountered in Baudrillard's works, because they are couched in the feeling of nihilism that permeates his brilliant commentaries on the modern world. However, the destruction of cultural preconceptions through reversal can be understood in Ben-Aharon's framework as a necessary (and thus ultimately positive) preparation for an infusion of Christ light to all human beings and their cultures.[24]

In the midst of cultural changes—and geological changes as well—that show Neptune's influence, an individual has to become active with each opportunity when Neptune comes into relation to powerful Suns. An individual must seek the intrinsic positivity despite what the newspaper headlines say. One can only persist in paring away the negativity to find the positive pearl at its center. Indeed, Neptune as Janus looks both ways, toward evolution and toward dissolution. When one is able to integrate them, and extend beyond the duality of positive/negative to the process itself, then a new human comes into being.

## APPENDIX: NEPTUNE'S AMPLIFICATION UNTIL 2017

At the beginning of 2013, Neptune lies at 6° of the Waterman (Aquarius), opposite Regulus, the Heart of the Lion, within 1°. It continues into conjunction with Fomalhaut at 9°9' of the Waterman. It reaches the end of the 6° orb from Fomalhaut (at 15°9' Waterman) at the beginning of 2017. (If you include as important Neptune square to the Aldebaran–Antares axis of the heavens at 15° of the Bull and Scorpion, plus an orb of 6°, that takes us to 2019. Neptune next arrives at an opposition to Spica in 2034.) This then is a time when we can attune ourselves to great possibilities streaming from the heavens via Neptune...and we can expect a great number of reversals as the positive opportunities are turned into their opposite.

---

24 Ben-Aharon, *The Event*; Baudrillard, *The Illusion of the End* and *Simulacra and Simulation*.

---

*To starry realms,*
*To the dwelling places of Gods,*
*Turns the Spirit gaze of my soul.*

*From starry realms,*
*From the dwelling places of Gods,*
*Streams Spirit power into my soul.*

*For starry realms,*
*For the dwelling places of Gods,*
*Lives my Spirit heart through my soul.*
—RUDOLF STEINER

*O Spirit of God...*
*Fill the hearts that seek Thee,*
*Seek Thee in deep longing,*
*Deep longing for health*
*For health and strong courage,*
*Strong courage that flows*
    *within our limbs,*
*Flows as a precious divine gift,*
*Divine gift from Thee,*
*O Spirit of God.*
—RUDOLF STEINER

# FINDING AHRIMAN'S INFLUENCE IN THE DARK SHADOWS OF NEPTUNE

## *William Bento, Ph.D.*

When one takes seriously the spiritual scientific research of Rudolf Steiner upon which he made numerous prophetic statements about the times we are living through, there is a justifiable longing to find the phenomenal evidence of such events. With particular regard to the issue of Ahriman's incarnation, there has been a great deal of speculation and posturing going on within anthroposophic circles. Steiner referred to Ahriman, the Persian Prince of Darkness, as the being identified as Satan in the Judaic tradition. Rather than attempting to identify the individual human being who may be bearing Ahriman's incarnation, I find it far more feasible to track the influences of Ahriman throughout the world, and specifically within American society. Many indications for this tracking of Ahriman's influences can be found in Rudolf Steiner's seven lectures in *The Incarnation of Ahriman: The Embodiment of Evil on Earth*.

Rudolf Steiner does not restrict his statements to a single entity known as Ahriman, but also describes a colony of beings he calls the ahrimanic powers. The ahrimanic powers can be regarded as "everything that presses us down upon the Earth, which makes us dull and philistine and leads us to develop materialistic attitudes, penetrating us with a dry intellect" (Steiner, R. 1919). He explains that the ahrimanic beings harbor a firm intention to capture the human kingdom and the entire Earth into their sphere of power. Within this intent is the tactic to create situations that make human beings dependent on ahrimanic beings and their machinations. These ahrimanic beings follow the dictate of the mighty being Ahriman, who has proclaimed to the Heavens that he will control humanity and deprive human beings of any true experience of freedom.

In star-wisdom research I did with David Tresemer and Robert Schiappacasse last year, the theme of Ahriman's activity in the world became focused on a reoccurrence of events that revealed significant aspects to the planet Neptune. The type of phenomena we discovered and explored yielded a disturbing pattern of deception and domination. What we have found in the process of our research was an insidious process of ahrimanic intelligence being incorporated into the very institutions that govern and shape our current world conditions and, in particular, pervade almost every aspect of American culture.

The relation of these historical events to Neptune is not a matter of simple correspondence—that is, Neptune's involvement with these events may or may not indicate a causal relationship between Neptune and Ahriman—but the timing of these events points to the probability that Ahriman chooses to enter human beings while their consciousness is diminished or altered in some way during the times when potent Neptune aspects in the heavens occur. Two questions arise: What role might Neptune play in altering human consciousness—by heightening or diminishing it? And how does Ahriman utilize those periods of time when Neptune heightens or diminishes human consciousness as opportune moments to more effectively attack human beings and harden them?

With regard to the first question, much depends on the planets being aspected and the history or memory of previous events taking place during such aspects. With regard to the second question, only a thorough review of the patterns established over time can lead to credible conclusions, even if those conclusions remain probable and not absolutely definite.

## A Historical Nodal Point of Ahriman's Influence

After the Christmas Foundation Meeting of 1923–1924, Rudolf Steiner's already-prodigious output of esoteric lectures increased dramatically. His sense of the urgency of our time to awaken to the activities of Ahriman was palpable in all lectures given to members and nonmembers of the Anthroposophical Society. However, nowhere is his message to the members about the significant battle between the Archangel Michael and Ahriman given more intimately and more comprehensively than in the lectures published as *Karmic Relationships,* volume 3. These eleven lectures were given in Dornach, Switzerland, from July 1 to August 8, 1924. In the seventh lecture, Steiner addresses the origin and preparation of "The New Age of Michael." Twenty years prior to the end of Kali Yuga (also known as the Dark Age, which began in 3101 BC) and the beginning of the New Age of Light (which began in December AD 1899) the Age of Michael (AD 1879–2233) began. Rudolf Steiner considered that the Michael Age as the time for setting the tone for the future human epochs. He described the Michael Age as a time for two important developments within humanity to take place: the free and personal use of intelligence, and the freedom of the human will.

Despite the spiritual enlightenment that was expected in the Age of Light but did not appear immediately in world events following 1899, the fact remains that, ever since 1900, humanity has been given a golden opportunity to access the illuminating light of a spiritual science. Rudolf Steiner makes it clear that the inertia we experience in this Age of Light results primarily from the old leftover habits of the Age of Darkness. Steiner asserts that the light arising in the twentieth century illuminates the truth. In this light these habits of the age of darkness appear far more evil in form than was possible in the Kali Yuga when they were justified. Two of the tenacious aspects of this inertia are 1) the idea of heredity and 2) the fervor of nationalism. Both aspects stem from an epistemology of materialism, and both aspects deny the concept of the spiritual individuality and the uniting principle of humanity as inclusive and diverse.

In an effort to explicate the context of the origin and preparation of the Michael Age, Rudolf Steiner described the spiritual circumstances of souls connected to Michael from the time of his last reign as the Spirit of the Age from 600 to 246 BC, a time just prior to the Mystery of Golgotha, to the onset of the commencement of the Consciousness Soul Age in AD 1413. In the spiritual world during the fifteenth century, Michael conducted a Supersensible School, wherein his intention to offer cosmic intelligence to human beings on the Earth was revealed. All that once lived as the Michael Mystery knowledge in the Sun Mysteries became alive again in supersensible worlds. As the heavenly teachings of Michael flowed into certain forerunners of the Age of Michael, there were counter-forces at work from the depths of the Earth. Steiner pointed out that the very time when the Intelligence was descending from the cosmos to the Earth, the aspirations of the ahrimanic powers grew ever greater. The Ahrimanic powers strove to wrestle the Cosmic Intelligence from Michael as soon as it became earthly Intelligence. Their intent was to make the intellect dominant on Earth alone, free of Michael. This is the battle between Ahriman and Michael of which we have all participated ever since the fifteenth century. Rudolf Steiner declared that this battle was behind the scenes of the historical events shaping the Age of the Consciousness Soul.

By the time of the beginning of the nineteenth century, Michael gathered those souls dedicated to his service and performed a ritual with mighty imaginations that united the Michaelites through a cultus of courageous souls. This group was predestined to find the Michaelic teachings of the suprasensory school on Earth in the essential ideas and insights of Anthroposophy. At the time of the culmination of the Michaelic Cultus in the spiritual world, and particularly during the 1840s, Ahriman was actively engaged in conducting a subterranean ahrimanic school, wherein the secret laws of the material physical world could be discovered and exploited.

Not only was Ahriman interested in countering Michael's schooling of a cosmic intelligence with remarkable breakthroughs in natural science, but Ahriman was resolved to create an ironclad epistemological basis for materialism—one that would allow a transference of natural scientific principles to shape the emergence of all human and social sciences. Karl Marx and Friedrich Engels offer a striking example of this kind of materialistic thought in their 1848 publication of the *Communist Manifesto*. In this remarkable book the fundamental notion of history was reduced to being the outcome of socio-economic class warfare. Simultaneously, Charles Darwin was writing from his expeditions to South America, the Galapagos Islands, and Australia, contributing to the growing acceptance of the ideas of modern evolutionary synthesis theory (better known as the theory of natural selection), a theory that endorsed a mechanism of power and dominance, wherein the strongest species survive and the weakest degenerate into extinction.

John Stuart Mill published a most defining work in 1846, *Principles of Political Economy*. Although it is unarguably a different approach to social economic issues than what is written in the *Communist Manifesto* of Marx and Engels, Mill's book provides a stimulus for the development of capitalism and the prevailing idea of the "free market." Mill explored the nature of production, beginning with labor and its relationship to nature. He started by stating that the "requisites of production are two: labor, and appropriate natural objects." By "natural objects," he meant the "things" of nature, seeing in nature only "things" to manipulate. Mill emphasized the human connection with the natural world, and how humankind must labor to utilize anything found in the natural world. He used a rich array of imagery, from the sewing of cloth to the turning of wheels and the creation of steam. In Mill's view, humankind had found a way to harness nature. Mill stated that the muscular action needed to harness nature need not be constantly renewed but performed only once and for all. Capitalists could now take full advantage of this great economy of labor. Herein lies the opening in human consciousness to gradually replace the participation of creative human hands in production with machines.

Rudolf Steiner alluded to the fact that since the middle of the nineteenth-century economists have become the new leaders in the world (*Rethinking Economics*, lecture 11). In his lectures in *The Karma of Untruthfulness* (vol. 1) given in Dornach in December 1916, he addressed the unhealthy tendency within modern economics to overwhelm the political and cultural spheres with values that do not apply to social and cultural life. In particular, he cited the emergence of sociology as being infected by the science of statistics, which reduces the human being into a number. In these extraordinary lectures given at the close of World War I, Steiner identified the English and American economists as those who hold the power to dictate world events. This they have indeed done, and continue to do so.

> I have frequently spoken of the significant break that occurred in the spiritual development of the peoples of Europe and America in the middle of the nineteenth century, and especially in the 1840s. I have pointed out that this was the time when the materialistic point of view came to its peak, when a peak was reached in what we may call a way of grasping dead, outer facts with the intellect, refusing to enter into living reality.[1]

The economic decisions in the last century and a half set the stage for the current global market economy. An unholy alliance of mega-corporations and international banking has arisen, and has put the whole world in a terribly precarious situation.

Ahriman's schooling of modern thought was most evident in natural scientific quarters; however, its influence spread into all domains of human life. One of the most exemplary works written during this time, but often overlooked, was Theodor Waitz's book published in 1846, *Foundations of Psychology*. Within this epochal work Waitz criticized Fichte, Shelling and Hegel for intellectualizing the concept of "spirit," which he felt was a mere

---

1 Steiner, *The Fall of the Spirits of Darkness*, p. 136.

fabrication. Waitz proclaimed that psychology was the basis of philosophy. As an anthropologist he perceived the commonalities of various cultures to be the expression of the common psychology of human nature. For him there was no need for an otherworldly explanation of reality. For him aspirations for transcendence had over the course of time turned to the immanence of truth held in the cradle of nature. Waitz's psychology advocated a healthy development of the senses and an objective training of logic. Through these two faculties, he felt all could be known. For Waitz, psychology was the science of sensing life and training logic to interpret it meaningfully. Despite his optimistic humanism, Waitz fell into the trap of advocating a modern form of materialistic thinking.

In 1846 the United States government initiated the Mexican War. This war opened up more land for settlement that could become new states, which raised the debate over Slave State versus Free State in the following Presidential election of 1860. This conflict in the ideology of human rights eventually led to the Civil War in 1861. In these events we can see the ahrimanic influence in turning brother against brother, in inflating the sense of racial inequities, and in clouding the question of the meaning of freedom by displacing it from the cultural sphere into a political issue. The idea of racial heredity and the fervor of nationalism were major factors in what led to the blood bath of the American Civil War.

It should also be noted that in America during the mid-1840s, a widespread interest in spiritualism was taking place. Spiritualism as a pseudo-religion is based on the belief that spirits of the dead residing in the Spirit World have both the ability and the inclination to communicate with the living. Anyone may receive spirit messages, but formal communication sessions (séances) were held by "mediums" that could provide information about the afterlife. This form of mediumism requires a diminishment of consciousness, precisely what Ahriman desires of human beings.

> Now consider this carefully—the powers from the school of Ahriman, which fought a decisive battle in the spiritual world between 1841 and 1879 were cast down into the human realm in 1879. Since then their fortress, their field of activity, is in the thinking, the inner responses, and the will impulses of human beings, and this is specifically the case in the epoch in which we now are.[2]

In this lecture, "The Influence of the Backward Angels," Steiner pointed out how Ernst Haeckel's materialistic monism had been taken up as a basis for an entirely naturalistic religion, that is, nature as the highest ideal based on observable and knowable physical laws. The impact of its popularity resulted in a dismissal of the deeper spiritual realities inherent to esoteric Christianity. The "backward angels," under the influence of Ahriman, aim to enforce a fundamentalist view of Christianity by giving the human being a literal dogma of the Gospels—something Steiner identified as a hollow text when read without spiritual scientific penetration. It is completely within the Ahrimanic strategy to eliminate any understanding of the spiritual evolutionary significance of Christ's deeds upon the Earth.

### The Discovery of Neptune

The date of Neptune's discovery, which was predicted mathematically by Urbain Le Verrier, is September 23, 1846. Such moments as the discovery of a new planet within our solar system cannot be considered a mere accident. I am inclined to state that such a discovery must be given the weight of being a signature of something of great significance within the evolution of humanity on the Earth. As Neptune entered into the consciousness of humanity in 1846, an opportunity was given to deepen our awareness of the accompanying historical phenomena. Reflection on the events mentioned in the above section might imply a connection between the discovery of Neptune and the historical events influenced by the subearthly Ahrimanic school. In the light of Rudolf Steiner's statements, the discovery of Neptune might also be associated with the inspirational and imaginative outpouring of Michaelic intelligence in the supersensible school of Michael during the 1840s.

---

2 Ibid., p. 150.

Neptune's discovery must be considered in the light of both events. The significant distinction in these two cases lies with the consciousness of humanity at the given times of Neptune activity.

It would, therefore, be overly simplistic to claim that the discovery of Neptune is directly related to the Ahrimanic School. Any possible correspondence of Neptune with Ahriman's attack on the human soul needs to be put into a broader esoteric context. In order to do this, further key questions need to be asked: Where did Neptune originate? What is its relationship to humanity? How can we understand the struggles between good and evil as possibly working through the planetary movements in the cosmos?

### Neptune's Origin

Rudolf Steiner presented a cosmogony based on scientific investigation of carefully trained human clairvoyant perceptions. The result of his findings corresponds favorably with the legacy of ancient cosmogonies transmitted from ancient wisdom traditions. Rudolf Steiner asserted that Neptune's origin is found during the period of the Ancient Moon stage of evolution, "when the astral body of the human being was first being bestowed by the Dynamis [Spirits of Movement] to the innocent Sun-like human beings. As the Dynamis began to contract the Ancient Sun sphere (bounded today by Jupiter's orbit) down toward the realm of the Ancient Moon (bounded today by Mars's orbit), Neptune was created outside the boundaries of Saturn and Uranus as a place to house innocent beings who were not yet mature enough to enter into the denser fluid conditions of the Ancient Moon." (Paraphrase of a written communication by Brian Gray) This occurred just before the luciferic rebellion during the Ancient Moon stage, a rebellion that entailed an inflation of egoism into the astral body of humankind.

### Neptune's Relationship to the Human Being

Brian Gray states: "Neptune may be indirectly connected with the pure astral body before the 'War in Heaven' broke out, unsullied by the influences of Lucifer, Ahriman, or the Asuras." In his view, Neptune is purest astrality, purest mirror-like consciousness, undisturbed by outer influences—the pure inner life connected with dreamlike consciousness, reverently beholding the wonders and deeds of spiritual beings. Neptune bestows pure inner picturing, pure dreamlike imaginations, pure longing to retain its inner connection to the lawfulness of spiritual activity surrounding oneself. Yearning to stay connected with the entire soul realm of Sophia; dreamlike atavistic clairvoyance, inner picturing, yearning for reunion with everything that is inwardly mirrored in the pure astral body—that is Neptune's true nature.

However pristine the initial conditions of Neptune were during Ancient Moon, it is hardly possible for me to think that during the unfolding stages of the present Earth evolution that the sphere of Neptune remained immune to the type of ahrimanic rebellion taking place upon the present-day Earth. The ramifications of Ahriman's intentions to divert soul development away from the divine and fix it to mechanistic and materialistic enterprises seem boundless. For Ahriman's plans to succeed fully, he needs not only to contaminate the astral body of humankind—which Rudolf Steiner has identified as the 'battleground' between Michael and Ahriman's influences upon human thinking, feeling and willing—but also to harden the etheric human body. By doing so, he prevents the enlivening of spiritual life within the human being and throughout the social fabric of humanity.

From the perspective of Rudolf Steiner's view of the sevenfold human nature, I understand Neptune to be related to the *budhi*, or life spirit, of the human being. The life spirit is the transmuted life (or etheric) body. This transmutation is the result of the "I" working meditatively into the etheric body to increase the sensitivity to all that surrounds an individual. This sensitivity becomes the seed for compassionate and healing activity. It is derived from the recognition that "I" and the "world" are one. Steiner's description of the sixth region of spirit land in his book *Theosophy* can be related to the planetary sphere of Neptune. He writes, "Everything that human beings do brings about what is best suited to the true and essential nature of the world. Human beings can no longer seek what is to their own advantage, but only what should happen according to the proper progression of the world order."[3] Ahriman's tactic appears to be to reverse this ideal of the Neptune sphere. For example, Ahriman might intend that "everything human beings do brings about what is best suited to the lies of Ahriman about the world. They will seek out only what profits them and what might derail the rightful course of the world order." Such a tactic does not imply that human beings consciously adhere to lies, but that human beings lack the capacity to discern the lie from the truth.

### *Evil within the Planetary Movements*

If we take into consideration the esoteric background of Neptune's existence in our cosmos, then we can realize how critical it is for humanity to undergo a catharsis of the astral body, a purification of soul. What cannot be denied is both Lucifer and Ahriman have had access to the developing astral body of humankind. Both have insinuated their influences into the desire nature of the human being. Pertinent to this article is Ahriman's intention to obstruct any effort at self-transformation. His aim is to convince the human being that he or she is but an intelligent responsive animal that strives to exercise power over the external world...and nothing more. Ahriman is capable of working from any sphere in the cosmos that suits his purposes. In the case of his need to arrest the development of the human capacity to use a higher degree of active spiritual intelligence and to exercise freedom of human will, it appears, through a collection of historical data related to Neptune's planetary position and aspects, that Ahriman has chosen to work in the dark shadows of Neptune's orbital movement around the Sun, in addition to working from the depths of the Earth. Ahriman has cleverly utilized the discovery of Neptune and its planetary movements to cast a spell, a colorless materialistic veil over the soul of the human being. David Tresemer gives numerous examples of this phenomenon by tracking Neptune in important aspects to the Sun and the Royal Stars, citing these positions in relation to historical events that have the characteristics of an Ahrimanic influence in his article, "The Signature of Neptune in World Events."

### *Ahrimanic Deceptions in the Fading US Democracy*

Steiner lectured in Zurich on October 27, 1919, about a specific aspect of Ahriman's deception. His words were filled with a sense of urgency:

> If we inquire: Who stirs up nations against each other? Who raises the questions that are directing humanity today? The answer is the Ahrimanic deception, which plays into human life. And in this area, people very easily let themselves be deceived. They are not willing to descend to the lower strata where reality can be found. You see, Ahriman skillfully prepares his goal beforehand. Ever since the Reformation and the Renaissance, economists have been emerging in modern civilization as the representative governing type. That is a historical fact. If you go back to ancient times—even to those I characterized today as the luciferic—who were the governing types then? Initiates. The Egyptian Pharaohs, the Babylonian rulers, the Asiatic rulers—they were initiates. Then the priest type emerged as rulers, and they were really the rulers right up to the Reformation and the Renaissance. Since then, economists have been in command. Rulers are in fact merely the petty agents and the subordinates of economists. One must not imagine that the rulers of modern times are anything but the subordinates of the economists. Moreover, all that has resulted by way of law and justice—one should study it carefully—is simply a consequence of what economically oriented people have thought. In the nineteenth century, the "economical" person is replaced for the first time by those who think in terms of banking. In the nineteenth century, the organization of finance is created for the first time, swamping every other relationship. We need only to look into these things and follow them up empirically and practically.
>
> All that I stated in the second public lecture here [*The Social Future,* October 25, 1919]

---

3   Steiner, *Theosophy,* p. 146.

is profoundly true. One could wish only that it were followed up in all the details; we could then see how fundamentally true these things are. Nevertheless, just because this rule of the mere "symbol for solid goods" [that is, *money*] has arisen, Ahriman has been given another essential medium for deceiving humankind. If people do not realize that the state of rights and the organism of the spirit must be pitted against the economic order called up through the economists and the banks, then again, through this lack of awareness, Ahriman will find an important instrument for preparing his incarnation. His incarnation is undoubtedly coming, and this lack of insight will enable him to prepare it triumphantly.[4]

These words of Rudolf Steiner were a plea for members of the Anthroposophical Society to take seriously the need to cultivate a free society dedicated to self and social development. Steiner could not have been more prophetic about the power that financial institutions would wield over the generations to come. He actually implied that there must be an awakening and a courageous action on the part of those who had participated in the great suprasensory Michaelic Cultis of the middle of the nineteenth century. For without something of this occurring the world will be at the mercy of the ahrimanic powers. They will work through the global economic market to cause widespread anxiety arising out of illusions of scarcity. With this heightened anxiety, fear easily becomes a pervasive mood of soul. Moreover, in the search to alleviate the fear, the populace is likely to fall into diversions supplied by Ahriman's technological wizardry and be led into the phenomenon so eloquently described by Neil Postman in his book, *Amusing Ourselves to Death.*

One of the more alarming issues occurring in our time is the rapid loss of the sacred singularity of the individual and what once was regarded as the individual's innate right of freedoms. The emergence of the legislated "corporate personhood" in America is a very striking example of this incorporation of ahrimanic intelligence. The body of written rules and privileges awarded to corporations with exclusive profit making motives now have been given more power than anyone imagined. Corporate personhood stands as a phantom being with excessive powers beyond any individual. What transpired 110 years after the Declaration of Independence can be regarded as the antithesis of all that the document stood for as an expression of new forms of liberty, agreement, and fellowship. (See David Tresemer's article, "Corporate Personhood," particularly regarding the Fourteenth Amendment. Now in *The Mountain Astrologer.*)

As I weighed these two bodies of political declaration side by side, an image arose of two mighty archangelic beings. In the Declaration of Independence, I saw clearly the working of the American folk spirit, and in the Supreme Court case ruling of Santa Clara County vs. Southern Pacific Railroad Company of May 10, 1886 (which set the legal precedent of giving corporations rights of an individual), I saw an aspect of the double of the American folk spirit. This imagination is not an entirely new one for me; however, I must mention that these beings can now be seen through the lenses of these two documents. In one, there lives the possibility of the free human being, and in the other lives the human being enslaved and deluded by the forces of the economy, manipulated and controlled by Ahriman.

The innate opportunism of the American folk spirit seems to have been hijacked by the corporate person's power to name, measure, and weigh potential profitability. In this decree we see the abstraction of reducing the individual to a number and measuring and weighing the value of a person with the amount of dollars to be won or lost. The motto *"in God we trust"* has become *"for money we strive."*

Despite all the critical commentary made by champions of the democratic enterprise throughout the first decade of the twenty-first century, the Supreme Court affirmed the notion that a corporation has the same rights as an individual in the Citizens United vs. Federal Election Commission case. On January 21, 2010, the 5-to-4 court decision made it legal for corporate funding of

---

4  Steiner, *The Ahrimanic Desception,* pp. 14–15.

independent political broadcasts in candidate elections to be unlimited and anonymous. This decision expanded the First Amendment rights of free speech of an individual to the corporation. This has led to the formation of the super-PACs that are now buying candidates running for election. We might ask if, unknown to the majority of Americans, this country is now for sale. Granting the right of free speech to corporations may indeed be more of a costly decision than anyone had imagined—with the exception of a smug and cynical Ahriman.

*Neptune in the Water Bearer*

On January 21, 2010, Neptune was moving through the early degrees of the Water Bearer, in the same relative position Neptune was at the time of its discovery on September 23, 1846. One whole orbital cycle of Neptune (163.7 years) had elapsed since its discovery. The many historical events based in materialistic thinking mentioned during the 1840s, during the period when the subearthly Ahrimanic school was fully underway, could be understood as having culminated one Neptune orbit later in this fateful Supreme Court decision reaffirming the concept of "corporate personhood."

Looking further back, we see that Neptune had completed exactly eleven orbits, from its position at 3° in the Water Bearer (Aquarius)—where it stood during the Mystery of Golgotha in AD 33—to the time of its discovery in 1846. Neptune's discovery in 1846 was during the time (1841–1987) that Rudolf Steiner referred to as the height of Ahriman's attack on humanity through materialistic thinking.

Now, in 2010, the twelfth orbit of Neptune since the Mystery of Golgotha has sealed a cycle of twelve (that magic number in celestial realms), during which the spiritual purpose and meaning of the Mystery of Golgotha for human beings on the Earth has been obscured successfully from view. Ahriman's deception has not only been successful in eroding fundamental principles of democracy and replacing them with fear and intense economic strife, but has also thrown a dense veil of materialistic dogma over the esoteric significance of Christ's central deed of overcoming death.

We are left with some serious questions: How long might it be before the one percent of the population with ninety-nine percent of the monetary wealth strips the rights of the individual from participating in any form of democratic activity? How long will it take before the spiritual reality of the resurrection of Christ can be understood as a fact?

Although these political maneuvers are oppressive and call for resistance for the sake of the rights sphere, there are equally more daunting situations to grapple with when we look into the cultural life of America. Materialism, technology, and greed have swept through every cultural institution and forum. The United States of America espouses values that are utopian in nature, yet unobtainable for most and unsustainable as a society. Ahriman's insistence on indoctrinating the human soul with desires for temporal pleasure and self-centered motives can only increase if we remain asleep and unconscious of Ahriman's influences upon our daily lives.

As Neptune now sojourns through the sidereal sign of the Water Bearer, we may lift our thoughts to the initiate who once baptized with water, the archetypal Water Bearer, John the Baptist. His call for *metanoia,* a change of thinking, is as relevant today as it was two millennia ago. John the Baptist was aware of the light shining in the darkness. He saw the One who had come from the Sun to bring a new dispensation of consciousness to humanity. Now it resides in each and every one of us not to succumb to Ahriman's work through the dark shadows of Neptune, but rather to draw from Neptune the soul and spiritual inspiration that empowers us to make all things new.

From the ethereal heights of Neptune stream the true visions of what the human being can become once cleansed in the purest of astral light. It lies within each of us to seek the spiritual insights and purification of soul needed to resist Ahriman's cunning, and in this inner work to find how we may act in accordance with the true being of the world. It is time for all Michaelites to offer their lives selflessly to the service of creating the future world.

As Ahriman's reign falls under its own menacing weight, there needs to be the stalwart company of Michaelites who can cultivate the Sophianic culture of the next age—the Age of Aquarius, the Age of true Spirit Self and goodwill. As Neptune moves through the Water Bearer in 2013, the seeds of the Aquarian Age are being planted in the souls of all who aspire toward the light. May we be prepared to nurture these seeds and see the resurrected "One" who appeared in the garden on April 5, AD 33, in an appearance appropriate for our times and for our current struggles to maintain humanity's sense of dignity.

---

"It became clearer and clearer to me—as the outcome of many years of research—that in our epoch there is really something like a resurrection of the Astrology of the third epoch [the Egyptian–Babylonian period], but permeated now with the Christ Impulse. Today, we must search among the stars in a way different from the old ways. The stellar script must once more become something that speaks to us."
—RUDOLF STEINER (*Christ and the Spiritual World and the Search for the Holy Grail*, p. 106)

---

"In Palestine during the time that Jesus of Nazareth walked on Earth as Jesus Christ—during the three years of his life, from his thirtieth to his thirty-third year—the entire being of the cosmic Christ was acting uninterruptedly upon him, and was working into him. The Christ stood always under the influence of the entire cosmos; he made no step without this working of the cosmic forces into and in him....It was always in accordance with the collective being of the whole universe with whom the Earth is in harmony, that all which Jesus Christ did took place."
—RUDOLF STEINER (*Spiritual Guidance of Man and Humanity*, p. 66)

# CONTEMPLATING AMERICA'S CAMELOT AT FIFTY
## THE JFK YEARS AND THE CHRIST RHYTHM

### Kevin Dann

*"Everything in history rises from the grave in a changed form after thirty-three years."*
—RUDOLF STEINER,
December 23, 1917

Much reflection is invited by the approach (on November 22, 2013) of the fiftieth anniversary of the assassination of President John F. Kennedy, an event that can be seen to have initiated the historical trajectory that culminates in America's Apocalyptic present. As America continues to play a critical role in the fulfillment of the prophecy of Ahriman's incarnation, the presidential office of the United States demands particularly close attention when we consider America's destiny. The coup d'état that occurred in Dallas on November 22, 1963, certainly was an exoteric dynastic crime executed by key members of the military-industrial complex. Was it also an occult crime, whose timing—like so many acts of political assassination carried out by secret, dark brotherhoods—carries the signature of esoteric knowledge of the mysteries of time? No doubt 2013 will bring a cascade of commentary upon both the assassination and legacy of JFK. Is there some perspective that the new star wisdom can lend to this event?

As Robert Powell has perennially pointed out, the "33-year rhythm" is "the 'crown' of astrosophical research."[1] Taken together with Rudolf Steiner's pronouncements in 1917 about the importance of the 33-year rhythm, and given that this year's fiftieth anniversary is halfway to the "fulfillment" rhythm of a full century (3 x 33⅓ years), 2013 seems like an opportune moment to consider the JFK assassination in light of the 33-year historical rhythm. In this essay I will survey the history of the use by anthroposophic authors of Rudolf Steiner's indications about the 33-year rhythm in the human historical process, and reflect upon whether one can detect this rhythm manifesting in relationship to the JFK assassination or events immediately preceding this tragedy.

### 33 YEARS?

Rudolf Steiner first brought this mystery into the open in his "Et Incarnatus Est" lecture in Basel on December 23, 1917. Drawing attention to the phrase from the Latin mass—"*et incarnatus est de spiritu sancto ex virgine Maria*"—he critiqued the modern understanding of the Incarnation by quoting extensively from Ernst Renan's *Life of Jesus* (1863), Heinrich Heine, Edward von Hartmann, and Paul Heyse's *Die Kinder der Welt* (1873). Then, saying that the Magi's conscious action of signaling the Incarnation by "following the star" had also signaled the working of Christ into the historical process, Rudolf Steiner stated the "events happening at approximately the present time (we can only say approximately in such matters) refer back to their historical connections in such a way that we are able to perceive their birthdays or beginnings in the events of thirty-three years ago, and the events of today also provide a birthday or beginning for events that will

---

[1] Quoted from "Robert Powell's Research Confirming the 33⅓-year Rhythm of the Life of Christ," in "By way of a response to Jonathan Hilton's review..." of Powell's article "In Memory of Willi Sucher (1902–1985)," in *Journal for Star Wisdom 2010*. The phrase quoted comes as an addition to a passage excerpted from Robert's "Subnature and the Second Coming" in *Inner life of the Earth*; available online: http://steinerbooks.org/review .html?&id=9780880107136&revid=980.

ripen to fruition in the course of the next thirty-three years."[2]

The sole example given in this lecture of such a relationship between events was of English political interference in Egypt and French attempts to exert colonial power in the early 1880s; without ever saying so directly, Rudolf Steiner implied that these events were connected via the 33-year rhythm to the period 1914 to 1917, and World War I.

When Rudolf Steiner first brought this mystery into the open in 1917, as well as on the three other occasions when he spoke of it, he used the phrase "33 years."[3] The anthroposophical authors who took up this indication of a new Christ-given cosmic Time rhythm employed "33" as an operative principle for their research and writing. In 1937, Walter Johannes Stein examined world political events on either side of the timeline centered on the date of April 8, 1904, the occasion of Great Britain and France signing the "Entente Cordial," and the outbreak of war between Russia and Japan. Stein identified the January 18, 1871, proclamation of the German Empire in the Hall of Mirrors at Versailles as the "Christmas" event leading to the 1904 "Easter." As the "Easter" events 33 years subsequent to this diplomatic deed, Stein pointed to: 1) Japan and Russia's struggle for Manchuria, and Germany's signing of a treaty preparing for an attack on Russian Bolshevism; 2) Germany's withdrawal on January 30, 1937, from the 1919 Treaty of Versailles; 3) the foundation of the Italian "Empire" with the annexation of Abyssinia on June 1, 1936. The intervals between these events vary from 32 years and 11 months to 33 years and 2 months.

In their considerations of the 33-year rhythm, Emil Bock, Willi Sucher, and Ernst Lehrs[4] all passed over the crucial issue of the exact period of time meant by Rudolf Steiner. After pointing out that Rudolf Steiner's 1917 examples were all "negative"—i.e., related to the political turmoil in Europe during the late nineteenth and early twentieth centuries, Lehrs offered as a positive example the event of Rudolf Steiner's founding of Waldorf education in 1919 as the "resurrection" of the period he spent as a tutor in the Specht home in 1886. Lehrs does not specify the months or the particular events chosen as "Christmas" and "Easter." Dr. Steiner's residency in the Specht home actually began in June 1884, and the founding of the first Waldorf school could be considered to range from April 23, 1919, when Emil Molt first asked Rudolf Steiner about the possibility of a school for his employees' children, to August 20, 1919, when Steiner's training of the first teachers began.

In 1955, Guenther Wachsmuth indicated Rudolf Steiner's creation of the *Calendar of the Soul* in 1912 as the "Easter" fulfillment of the 1879 advent of Michael's Archangelic regency. I am unsure of the exact date of the Calendar's genesis, but if one takes October 1879 as the date of the beginning of Michael's reign, the date of publication or conception for the *Calendar of the Soul* would need to be close to October 1912 to qualify this as an example—at least from an exoteric/calendrical standpoint—of the "33-year rhythm."

It is not surprising that Rudolf Steiner's biography became the favorite subject of anthroposophic speculation on the working of the 33-year rhythm. Rudolf Grosse in 1984 connected Rudolf Steiner's deed of the Christmas Conference in 1924 to the "aura" of 1957, seeming once again to employ 33 as the cycle of years. Of course, the Christmas Conference began in the waning days of 1923, suggesting a convenience of arithmetic in the use of 1924 as the initial date.

This sort of imprecise arithmetic occurs frequently in Peter Tradowsky's *Kaspar Hauser: The Struggle for the Spirit*,[5] which examines the

---

2  *Et Incarnatus Est*, p. 15.
3  Lectures in: 1) Basel, December 23, 1917, published as *Et Incarnatus Est: The Time Cycle in Historic Events, op cit*.; 2) Dornach, December 24, 1917 ("A Christmas Lecture," unpublished); 3) Dornach, December 26, 1917, "On the Mysteries of Ancient and Modern Times," lecture 2; 4) Dornach, December 14, 1919, "The Mysteries of Light, of Space, and of the Earth," lecture 3.
4  Bock, *The Three Years*; Sucher, "The 33 Year Rhythm," *Anthroposophical Movement*, 1954;

Lehrs, "The Thirty Three Years Rhythm," *Anthroposophical Quarterly*, 1956.
5  Tradowsky, *Kaspar Hauser*; see also a brief discussion of the 33-year rhythm in his *Christ and Antichrist*, p. 55.

rhythm of 33 years following the birth (in 1812) and death (in 1833) of Kaspar Hauser. Tradowsky's thought-provoking commentary on the political and social events following these two markers fails to go beyond the years—1812 and 1833—to the months and days of Kaspar Hauser's birth and death, and generally employs 99 years, not 100, as his template for the fulfillment after three 33-year rhythms, of the original "Christmas" deeds.

In his book, *Transparent Realities,* Hans Peter von Manen examines the 33-year rhythm in the Anthroposophical Society, from 1956 to 1989, and is the first of the authors considered so far to take up explicitly the question of the exact duration of the rhythm originally indicated by Rudolf Steiner. In a lengthy footnote, von Manen cites a number of German authors[6] who employ a cycle of 32¼ years, as well as two works[7] that take "33" to mean 33⅓. Von Manen also discusses the work of Ormond Edwards, who has argued for both of these cycles.[8]

Readers of the *Journal for Star Wisdom* are most likely aware of Robert Powell's pioneering research regarding the nature and effect of the Christ rhythm in history, but perhaps will find surprising—as I did in preparing this article—the extent to which his findings have not penetrated the anthroposophical community, including those engaged in historical research. Dr. Powell's "'crown' of astrosophical research" remark expresses both its importance as a "first fruit" of his discovery of the exact chronology of Jesus Christ's life, and as a critical underpinning of Powell's research on the metahistorical aspects of Christ's Second Coming. Having first established the "33-year rhythm" as exactly 1½ days short of 33⅓ years,[9] Powell went on to reiterate and extend his statement of this rhythm.[10] Both William Bryant, in *A Journey through Time,* and Kevin Dann have offered evidence from biographical study that affirms the 33⅓—year rhythm.[11]

Few of the authors who have taken up this question have delved into the nature of how this rhythm operates in the historical process. Inspired in part by the writing of Hans Peter von Manen, James Gillen proposed that the rhythm is, like seasonal and diurnal rhythms, a consequence of the activity of the Spirits of Rotation of Time (*Geister der Umlaufzeiten*).[12] This explanation—unlike Robert Powell's, which understands the 33⅓-year rhythm to be strictly a product of Christ's etheric body, merged into the stream of Time—permits more latitude in chronology, akin to the organic and labile rhythms of the natural world. Gillen and von Manen liken the variation in timing of the 33-year rhythm to seasonal rhythms like migration, flowering, etc., which are strictly a product of the interaction of organisms with their local and regional environments, while Rudolf Steiner's use of "approximately" in the *Et Incarnatus Est* lecture refers to the unpredictability of the human social realm.

## CAMELOT'S "CHRISTMAS" EVENTS

*"The 33-year rhythm makes visible the secret activities of the opponents of the spirit. It is capable, if understood correctly, of bringing to light the doings of these practicing occult groups."* —PETER TRADOWSKY[13]

---

6 Bock, *op cit.;* Sucher, *op cit.;* Schulz and Funk, *Zeitgeheimnisse im Christus-leben.*
7 Meyer, *Die Wiedergewinnung des Johannesevangeliums* [Retrieving the Fruits of the Gospel of John]; Ellen Schalk (in *Das Goetheanum,* February 20. 1983).
8 Edwards, *The Time of Christ.*
9 In "The Second Coming," appendix 2 of *Hermetic Astrology Volume I.*
10 In *Hermetic Astrology II,* pp. 335—339; *Chris-*

*tian Hermetic Astrology: Chronicle of the Living Christ,* pp. 415—423; *The Christ Mystery; The Most Holy Trinosophia,* pp. 55—57; p. 125; appendices 3 and 4 in Charles Tidball, *Jesus, Lazarus and the Messiah; The Mystery, Biography, and Destiny of Mary Magdalene,* p. 84; and *Inner life of the Earth* (2008), as well as a number of articles in the journal *Shoreline* in the late 1980s.
11 Bryant, *A Journey Through Time,* pp. 47—54; Kevin Dann, "Henry David Thoreau and the Christ Rhythm," *Journal for Star Wisdom* 2011, pp. 49–53.
12 Personal correspondence with James Gillen, June 8, 9, and 13, 2012.
13 Tradowsky, *Kaspar Hauser: The Struggle for the Spirit.*

There is no ambiguity in the consideration of the JFK assassination as a "Christmas" deed that occurred on a precise date—November 22, 1963. Its first "Easter" anniversary took place on March 22$^{nd}$, 1997. The second cycle will complete on July 22, 2030; the third—and an "octave" in the sense of Rudolf Steiner's 1917 indication that a deed reached its full flowering in the social realm after two rhythms of 33⅓ years—will occur on or about November 22, 2063. Bill Clinton began his second term as President of the United States on January 20, 1997, and was enjoying a period of relative quiescence between the initial allegations of sexual harassment (1991 to 1994) and the House vote to impeach based on these improprieties (1998). The period around March 1997 also saw an easing of international conflicts; Clinton presided over US military operations between 1993 and 1995 in both Somalia and Bosnia, and the Kosovo crisis (1999) and "Operation Desert Fox" against Saddam Hussein (December 1998) had yet to begin. From an exoteric historical perspective, there seems no evidence of an event that might be interpreted as an "Easter" expression of the black deed of the November 22 murder of President John F. Kennedy.

Evil deeds gain power in the social realm when they go unrecognized. Certainly identifying evil was a hallmark of Rudolf Steiner's work, and was likely the primary motivation for his calling attention to the 33⅓—year rhythm in December 1917. The extraordinary efforts by opponents of Kaspar Hauser to continue to suppress the truth about his life and death both immediately after his assassination in 1833 and right up to the present time[14] demonstrate the cascading effect that a lie can have as time progresses, and the obscurantism surrounding the case of Kaspar Hauser should heighten our awareness when we approach the question of the Kennedy assassination (as well as the subsequent murders of Martin Luther King, Jr., Malcolm X, Robert F. Kennedy, and the mass murders committed on September 11, 2001).

A brief survey of past anniversaries of JFK's assassination reveals a sustained and systematic propaganda campaign to reinforce the official government explanation of Lee Harvey Oswald as the "lone gunman" in the public mind, despite massive evidence discrediting it. At the most recent (fortieth) anniversary in 2003, Parkland Hospital (the Dallas hospital where the initial autopsy of JFK was performed), physician Dr. Robert Grossman made the rounds of high-profile radio and television programs, falsely claiming to have been present during the autopsy and that he saw head wounds consistent with the Warren Commission report. These statements institutionalized and reified the falsified autopsy report of still unnamed conspirators operating under government direction at Bethesda Naval Hospital. Curiously, Grossman's falsehood was first introduced in a TV interview on March 22, 1997—one day prior to exactly 33⅓ years after the November 22, 1963 assassination.

Since the publication of James Douglass's *JFK and the Unspeakable*,[15] a growing number of students of the Kennedy assassination take for granted that Kennedy's peacemaking efforts—from his refusal to attack Cuba in the wake of the Bay of Pigs fiasco (April 1961) and the Cuban Missile Crisis (October 1962) to his historic but largely forgotten efforts on behalf of the Nuclear Test Ban Treaty and withdrawal from Vietnam—marked him out for murder by the "deep state." Deep state is Peter Dale Scott's term for the permanent ruling cabal of intelligence agencies and military officials working in collusion with multinational business interests. This cabal is the principle tool of the secret brotherhoods in derailing world destiny. Douglass draws particular attention to JFK's June 10, 1963 American University commencement address, citing early in his book its bold statement eschewing a *Pax Americana*[16] enforced by weapons of war," and including the

---

14 See Terry Boardman, "The Ongoing Struggle for the Truth About the Child of Europe from 1828 to 2004 and Beyond"; at: http://threeman.org/?p=39.

15 Douglass, *JFK and the Unspeakable: Why He Died and Why It Matters*.

16 *Pax Americana* is a term used widely to express the idea of Western hemisphere peace in the twentieth century owing to the political and military power of the US.

entire text of Kennedy's speech as an appendix. In a search for a date for study of the 33⅓-year rhythm in relation to the positive deed of President John F. Kennedy in avoiding catastrophic nuclear war at the height of the Cold War, the June 10th American University address stands out as a good candidate. But a study of Kennedy's public statements in the months leading up to his assassination offers many alternative dates—most notably Kennedy's September 20, 1963, address before the eighteenth General Assembly of the United Nations lauding the Nuclear Test Ban Treaty, in which Kennedy called for "a better weapon than the H-bomb—peaceful cooperation"; and his July 26 radio and television address to the American people on the Nuclear Test Ban Treaty, the day after its signing.

Kennedy's dedication to fostering peaceful cooperation between the US and the Soviet Union was in evidence in almost every speech he gave in 1963, even at relatively inconsequential occasions, like an October 26 appearance to receive an honorary degree at Amherst College, on a day devoted to honoring poet Robert Frost. Kennedy thoughtfully questioned the nature of American ideas and ideals of heroism, pointing to Frost's legacy of increasing not "our self-esteem but our self-comprehension." Acknowledging the contribution of powerful men to America's greatness, Kennedy lauded as even more indispensable those who question power. This commitment to peace tragically continued right up to the day of his assassination, when he had ventured right into the heart of the Gunslinger Nation, and a city and state notorious for its pugnacious, often violent, vigilante frontier ethic—a place where his pacific political views were hardly welcome. In remarks prepared for delivery to the Texas State Democratic Committee in Austin, JFK predictably stressed growth and prosperity, but began by reminding his audience that he was "determined this land we love shall lead all mankind into new frontiers of peace and abundance."

## SMALL GESTURES, LARGE WAVES

Secrecy can ensure victory for evil for a time, and thus must be overcome by those who labor for disclosure of the truth about historic events. Secrecy can also be a tool for truth, justice, and peace. James Douglass places great emphasis upon the secret negotiations conducted between Kennedy and Nikita Khrushchev in the months leading up to the signing of the test ban treaty, and he draws particular attention to a passage in a twenty-seven-page letter from Khrushchev, in which he proposes Noah's Ark to JFK as a symbol of the world situation: "We're all on the Ark in the nuclear age; let's not argue over who's clean and unclean." Calling the Kennedy–Khrushchev alliance a "miracle," Douglass's language comes close to suggesting the cooperation of the spiritual world in some of these deeds. He also approaches an understanding of Kennedy's assassination as a deed of sacrifice; in a number of intimate vignettes, Douglass demonstrates how keenly aware Kennedy was of his own mortality.

Peter Tradowsky has beautifully brought into focus Rudolf Steiner's indications that Kaspar Hauser performed a deed of sacrifice of world historic magnitude, and—given the precarious balance of the nuclear-armed superpowers in the 1960s and the psychopathic attitude of people like "Dr. Strangelove" (General Curtis LeMay)—one can easily entertain the thought that JFK, too, chose a sacrificial path when he "turned" (Douglass's term) from Cold Warrior to peace promoter.

James Douglass's sensitivity to the emotional power of small gestures allows him to approach JFK's essential humanity in a beautiful, revealing way. He stresses how deeply affected JFK was by the death of his infant son Patrick; receiving the news while he was meeting with Norman Cousins and other allies in his efforts to eliminate the nuclear threat, Kennedy had already been haunted by the prospect of the deadly effects of radioactive fallout upon innocent children. The loss of his son in utero seemed to intensify this horror for the President. Perhaps Patrick, too, performed a sacrifice that helped intensify his father's peacemaking resolve.

Both Rudolf Steiner and Robert Powell have given us the bright promise that the Christ rhythm has been working more effectively since the advent of the New Age of the etheric Christ in 1899. In so many of the reports of encounters with the etheric Christ, we know that Christ comes as intimate, compassionate friend. In our efforts to discern the activity of the Christ rhythm in history, we would do well to turn our attention from the heavily documented and discussed deeds of powerful men and women, from the treaties signed or battles fought, to the spontaneous gestures of friends and allies of humble rank. On the morning of October 5, 1963, while President Kennedy was meeting in the Rose Garden with his National Security Council (some of whom were undoubtedly privy to the conspiracy to take his life), his 6-year-old daughter Caroline approached him, wanting his attention. JFK shooed her away, but she persisted, and he then let her speak. Caroline began to recite her father's favorite poem, "Rendezvous": "I have a rendezvous with death." While the President and the NSC members watched and listened Caroline spoke the entire poem.

Might it be that the 33⅓-year rhythm for which we should search in relation to the tragedy of the Kennedy assassination is actually the one that ripples out silently from the morning of October 5, 1963, when a young daughter of a President facing the "unspeakable" evil of his own Cabinet and the CIA feels the call to speak a poem, whose meaning she herself cannot understand? Might there be in the days leading up to and falling away from February 5, 1997, some echo of Caroline's small deed? And might we, as we look forward another 33⅓ years to February of 2030, begin to imagine how this sublime rhythm of time may burst forth and blossom as the Christ-imbued timing of new initiatives for peace and justice?

In light of the current apocalyptic unfolding of events expressing both imperial excess abroad[17] and tightening state control over civil liberties at home[18] one would hope that the coming year would see American citizens reflecting upon the contemporary state of America's mission in the world. The commentaries in this volume offer scores of opportunities—based on planetary rhythms against the zodiac—to bring to mind both founding "Christmas" impulses toward the Good, and adversarial efforts to thwart the Good. At this critical time, when the etheric Christ calls to us to cultivate the Good as earnestly as we seek to recognize evil, may we also take great solace and strength from the knowledge that this Christ-given rhythm of Resurrection pulses eternally through Time.

---

17 Military adventurism in the Middle East and North Africa; persistent State Department belligerence toward Iran, China, and Russia; the CIA drone program of "targeted killings," now conducted under a new Orwellian definition of militants as "all military age males in a strike zone."

18 Widespread police brutality against citizens participating in the "Occupy" movement; the frightening provisions (such as indefinite detention) of the National Defense Authorization Act [NDAA].

# SOPHIA AND THE ZODIAC

## *Lacquanna Paul*

Following a conversation with a friend in which she described an encounter with Sophia and her holy awe in beholding "Sophia's head in the middle of the zodiac, her robes, covered with stars, hung down to the Earth," I sat down to ponder this grace-filled encounter. First I emptied myself and became inwardly silent, and then the following impression began to flow into my consciousness. Sophia was teaching me—gently—allowing each image to unfold into the next. The teaching came through a kind of inner resonance that utilized my own heart and thinking process. The words recorded here cannot possibly hold the fullness of the resonance she imparted to me, and afterward I felt eternally grateful, nourished, and held.

The zodiacal constellations could be thought of Sophia's crown—the inner workings of her consciousness—and could be likened to the human crown chakra. In contemplating this, it was as though I was lifted inwardly into cosmic space, there to experience Sophia as sound and blazing light. Sophia is like a womb, with ever-unfolding forms flowing from within a radiant mandorla of light, one form inside another, forever giving birth.

The way creation works is that it has to be fructified by God's substance, which is Christ (Sophia is the Bride). This Life substance flows continually, as sparks of fire, from the Galactic Center, the Heart of God and is "ejected" into her body. What we experience of Sophia in cosmic space as sound is created through this ejecting movement inside her body.

To work with the constellations at this time in history is of particular significance. It is attuning to a matrix (perfect pattern) that has a deep and profound resonance in the human being. Now in our time this resonance is being enlivened through her presence and is thus particularly potent as a way of aligning us with the zodiac. Each zodiacal sign offers a key to tomes of wisdom. The zodiac can be thought of as her necklace, with our Sun as the heart. The Sun is like a crystal, able to receive from the necklace of the zodiac and then stream out qualities of informing light. In the same way, the human heart is capable of receiving the sounds of the constellations and reflecting their nature. Most important, here, is the listening of the heart, which is capable of perceiving the sounds and qualities of the constellations.

The eye receives; it is normally an organ of reception. However, when it becomes active, aligned with the heart's radiance, beholding spiritually through the fire of love, it also radiates. Yet imagine that there are blind spots in our vision; so it is when the heart is not picking up all twelve streams. We need the streaming from all twelve constellations to be able to manifest the full radiance of the heart, to become fully human. Sophia helps us to hold the twelve in consciousness, and they then open up as "halls of wisdom." They are as keys connected to the whole of creation—a looking glass. Everything is in her. She holds all potential, which unfolds in time.

Sophia is coming now to set things right, to right our course. With her approach, we are more and more magnetized to our original matrix of order in time. As she approaches, she is also enfolding us, taking us up. She is a being of intense and unimaginable love; this is the key to her wisdom. When a human being receives her, there is a feeling of being nourished, sustained, and protected. To hear her name is something of significance, because the name itself calls her forth. By calling her forth, She calls forth a memory in the human being—a memory that serves to awaken untapped reservoirs in the soul.

To sound her name into the Earth's atmosphere is important. "Hallowed be thy name"—carry her name in your heart and awareness and one will experience her presence everywhere. "May the holiness of thy name shine anew in our remembering."

How is Sophia working in our world situation today? In every situation? Sophia is the ever-renewing Isis, who calls us to live in a continual process of unveiling her creation. Isis unveiled! To experience the unveiling of Isis is to come to know that she is a fecund goddess and always to remember her fecundity. Life is a fertile field, upon which we are to learn to plant seeds and to work with her fertility.

If Christ is the One whose seed she bears—"Not I, but Christ in me"—planting seeds would be to do deeds that are Christ inspired. We live in her body and she is fertile. We need to be careful what we plant. We need to take care daily to "weed the garden" and tend it. We are "swimming" in her ocean of fertility.

Like the Magician in the first chapter of the book *Meditations on the Tarot*, we can attune to Divine Love, and with this intention she can guide our actions. "Hallowed be thy name"; in her hallowed halls all things are timeless, eternal. What are Sophia's hallowed halls? By way of contrast, think of genetic engineering. Genetically modified creations will ultimately die, for they cannot sustain themselves. They cannot remain, because in God's creation they are not real. In God's creation only what is born of Divine Love is real. Only what is REAL exists eternally. Disease and famine happen, but cannot extinguish her fertility, because she is forever creating—she IS creation!

---

*"If you lift your arm and point upward, you have up there the realm of particular Thrones, Cherubim, and Seraphim. If you move and again point upward, you would find other Thrones, Cherubim, and Seraphim above you.... Suppose you wanted to point to some particular Thrones, Cherubim, and Seraphim. They are by no means identical, like a group of twelve similar soldiers, for instance. They differ considerably from one another. Each bears its individual stamp, so that as one looks upward from various points, one sees quite separate beings. In order to locate particular Thrones, Cherubim, and Seraphim, one denotes them by a particular constellation. It is like a signpost. In that direction over there are the Thrones, Cherubim, and Seraphim known as the Twins, over there, the Lion, and so on. The constellations of the zodiac are more than mere signposts.... It is important to realize that, when we refer to the zodiac, we are speaking of spiritual beings."*

(The Spiritual Hierarchies and the Physical World: Zodiac, Planets & Cosmos, April 17, 1909)

# DISCOVERING THE ZODIAC IN THE RAPHAEL MADONNA SERIES ARRANGED BY RUDOLF STEINER

## Brian Gray

*"In the different arts...we are presented with different languages that give expression to certain truths living in the human soul. They are often the most secret truths, the most secret knowledge, which cannot readily be reduced to rigid concepts nor clothed in abstract formula, but seek artistic expression."*[1]

Rudolf Steiner praised Raphael's portrayals of the divine human form. "Raphael is valued so highly because, to a greater degree than any other painter, he was able to clothe the spiritual in sense-perceptible representation."[2] Raphael's paintings of the Madonna express secret truths. Rudolf Steiner described the healing effects of Raphael's Madonnas in August 1908, and between 1908 and 1911 he directed Dr. Felix Peipers to arrange fifteen images—thirteen images from nine of Raphael's paintings, plus a Donatello relief and a Michelangelo sculpture—as a therapeutic meditation for patients suffering from emotional disturbances. Sometimes called the Raphael Madonna Series, these fifteen pictures invite our active contemplation.[3] Those who employ them in curative education and at Camphill Villages know their therapeutic value, particularly when the pictures are viewed just before going to sleep (see figure 1 and figure 2).

Contemplating these fifteen images has a remarkable effect upon the human soul. Each image can awaken inner pictures that lift us into communion with realms beyond the physical world, stirring our feelings of wonder and reverence and opening our souls to divine mysteries. These images were chosen and arranged by Rudolf Steiner for certain reasons. They stimulate and ennoble our inner perceptions—that is, these pictures can help us refine and purify our *astral body*. But these pictures also directly engage and quicken movements of the human *etheric body*—our mobile body of formative life-forces—in ways that bring healing forces to our *physical body*.

### TEMPLE SLEEP, HOLY ISIS AND THE MADONNA PICTURES

In ancient Egypt (2907–747 BC), a patient suffering illness would be put into the condition of "temple sleep" by priest-initiates. In 1908, Rudolf Steiner described the experience of "temple sleep":

> During this sleep the patient perceived etheric forms in the spiritual world, and the wise priests understood the art of influencing these etheric pictures which passed before the sleeper; they could control and guide them.... Powerful forces were liberated during the etheric visions, and these restored to order and harmony the forces of the body which had fallen into disorder and discord.[4]

Holy Isis, the ancient spiritual companion of humanity, appeared to the patient during the temple sleep and brought etheric forces to heal the patient's soul and body. This pure maternal being is present in the spiritual world. Holy Isis virginally formed human beings in earliest stages of Earth evolution, prior to the Fall in mid-Lemurian times,

---

1 Steiner, "Isis and Madonna." April 29, 1909.
2 Steiner, *True and False Paths in Spiritual Investigation,* lect. 11, August 22, 1924.
3 At http://www.wynstonespress.com/Website/pages/Prints/Madonna1-15_prints.html. The set of Madonna Series post cards is also available from Rudolf Steiner College Bookstore, Fair Oaks, CA.

4 Steiner, *Universe, Earth, and Man,* lect. 2, August 5, 1908.

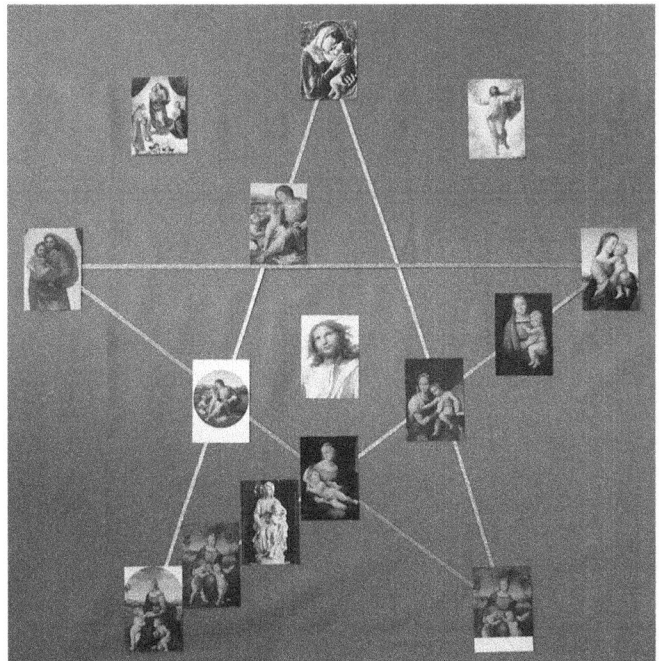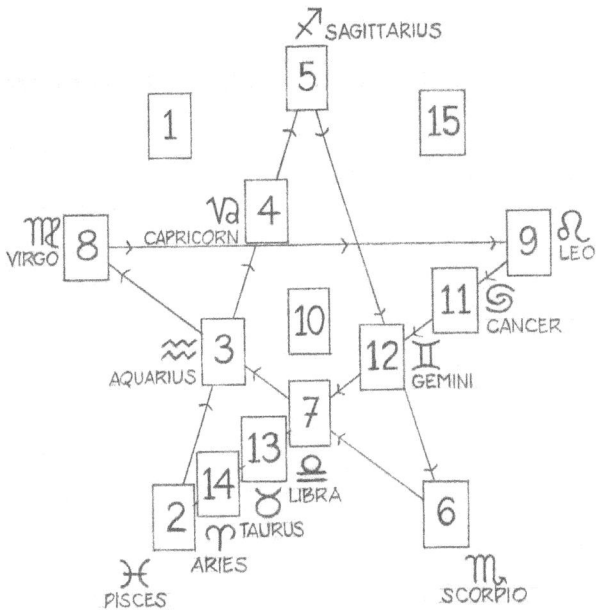

*Figures 1 and 2*

when the human "I" began to incarnate into physical bodies and sexual reproduction began. In the earliest primeval times, when Holy Isis had been active, "there were no unhealthy forces; disease did not exist; there was no death such as we know it. It was only when, with sexual reproduction, the human being was endowed with the "I," that sickness and death entered."[5]

As Adam and Eve incarnated, their previously whole male/female etheric bodies were divided into female or male counterparts. With sexual reproduction and the beginning of ego-involvement with Earth evolution, human beings gradually lost sight of Holy Isis, the virginal mother of humanity. Nevertheless, she remains connected to humanity and continues to be actively involved with our healing. Temple priests brought the human soul into direct communion with Holy Isis:

> The invalid who lay in the temple sleep beheld the form of her who was the mother of her kind without having received fertilization from her kind. Before the invalid stood the generating woman, the woman with child, yet who is virgin; the Goddess who in the Lemurian epoch was the companion of the human being, and who has since disappeared from human sight. In ancient Egypt she was called Holy Isis.[6]

Rudolf Steiner described the creative activity of Holy Isis as bearing "the great healing principle to which humanity will again attain when it steeps itself anew in Spiritual Wisdom. We see what has remained of this in the wonderful symbol of the Virgin Mother with the child.... We see it in many pictures of the Madonna. *We assert these pictures have a curative effect;... a picture of the Madonna is a means of healing.* When it is viewed and studied in such a way that it has an after-effect upon the human soul, when this human soul can dream during sleep about the Madonna picture, it then possesses a healing power even today."[7]

In ancient times temple priests conjured healing visions in the souls of patients, who received them passively. But in the Age of the Consciousness Soul (from AD 1414 to 3574), we must take initiative to contemplate the artistic pictures of the Madonna Series with our full attention if we hope to awaken comparable healing visions, which can arise like dream images in sleep as after-effects of our meditation.

---

5  Ibid.

6  Ibid.

7  Ibid.

## Movements of the Etheric Body

Why did Rudolf Steiner select these pictures of the Madonna and arrange them in this sequence? Observing how artistically he designed the Raphael Madonna Series, we realize that Rudolf Steiner was himself an artistic genius[8] with therapeutic insights. He perceived that certain currents of our mobile, flowing etheric body weave through our physical body in the pattern of a five-pointed star. While we rhythmically contemplate the fifteen images of the Raphael Madonna Series, these currents of our etheric body can weave through the physical body in a healing manner. These pictures help prepare us to commune with Holy Isis and to receive her curative effects.

In 1907, Rudolf Steiner drew a diagram (see figure 3) and explained how certain currents of our etheric body move as a five-pointed star—a pentagram—through the physical body:

> The human being possesses this physical body in common with the whole of the mineral kingdom surrounding us; the forces at work in our physical body are the same as those operating in the whole of so-called inanimate nature.
>
> This physical body is, however, permeated by still higher forces...only under the influence of the etheric body can they be held together in this form.... The physical materials have the constant tendency to group themselves according to their own nature; this signifies the destruction of the living body and the etheric body fights continually against this destruction.... The etheric body continually combats the destruction of the physical body....
>
> The clairvoyant sees in the etheric body of the human being certain currents that are exceedingly important. Thus, for example, there is a stream which rises from the left foot to the forehead (see figure 3), to a point which lies between the eyes, about half an inch down within the brain; it then returns to the other foot; from there it passes to the hand on the opposite side; from thence through the heart into the other hand, and from there back to its starting-point. In this way *it forms a pentagram* 

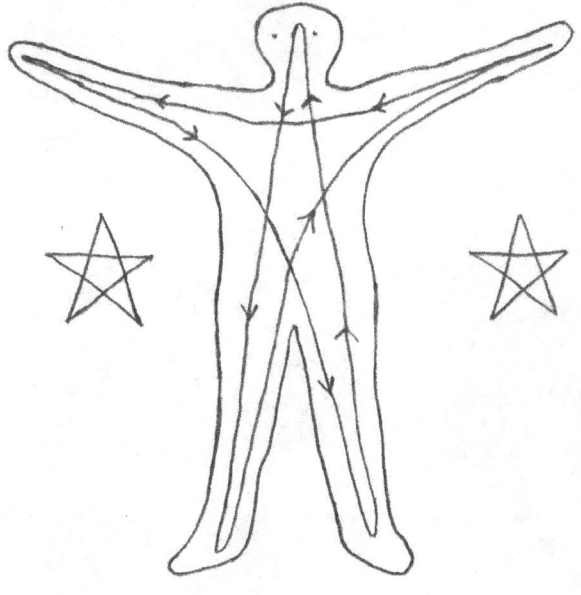

*Figure 3*

> *of currents of force....* This current is not the only one in the etheric body, there are very many of them. *It is to this stream of force that the human being specially owes her or his upright position.*"[9]

Notice in figure 3 how this stream of etheric currents flows from our left foot to our forehead, from our forehead to our right foot, from our right foot to our left hand, from our left hand to our right hand, and from our right hand to our left foot. As we observe the arrangement and sequence of pictures in the Raphael Madonna Series as shown in figure 1, our gaze and the movements of our etheric body follow the same directional flow. In the images we find "mirror-reflections" of this directional movement, as we are facing the pentagram of pictures as though looking into a mirror. With our attentive gaze moving from image to image, healing etheric currents can move more harmoniously through our physical body in the directions of this pentagram.

---

8 See Brian Gray, "Rudolf Steiner: The Artist." *Journal for Star Wisdom 2011*, pp. 54–60.

9 Steiner, *The Gospel of St. John*, lect. 2, November 17, 1907.

*Discovering the Zodiac in the Raphael Madonna Series Arranged by Rudolf Steiner*

## ETHERIC CURRENTS, PHYSICAL BODY, AND ZODIAC

How do the pictures in the Raphael Madonna Series depict the healing currents of the etheric body moving through the twelve forms of the physical body? After contemplating these images and their gestures for many years, one day I realized that the twelve pictures that lie along the pentagram depict the twelve parts of the physical body creatively formed from the zodiac. According to Rudolf Steiner, "the physical body is the echo of the zodiac."[10] Spiritual beings dwelling in the zodiac form the twelve parts of our physical body. How does each picture in the Madonna Series correspond to one of the twelve signs of the zodiac? As there are fifteen pictures in the series, what do the "extra three" images contribute to our experience?

As shown in figure 1, twelve pictures lie on the pentagram, while three key adjoining pictures—one at the upper left, one at the heart of the pentagram, and one at the upper right—are particularly helpful to us in purifying our *astral body*. These profound pictures prepare our souls to receive deep truths of mystery wisdom; they "set the stage" for the other twelve. Just to be clear, please note that all pictures within the Madonna Series images help purify our astral body. The twelve pictures that lie along the pentagram emphasize the forms and gestures of the *physical body* as it is shaped from the twelve realms of the zodiac. The child's movements up, down, and across the body of the Madonna from one picture to the next reveal how the healing *etheric currents* flowing through the physical body along the pentagram shown in figure 3 can be strengthened. Moreover, all fifteen images work to purify our astral body.

---

10 Steiner, "The Alphabet." December 18, 1921; see also Brian Gray, "Anthroposophic Foundations for a Renewal of Astrology." *Journal for Star Wisdom 2012*, pp. 98–130.

## ZODIACAL CORRESPONDENCES IN THE FIFTEEN IMAGES OF THE RAPHAEL MADONNA SERIES

The following are the fifteen images of the Raphael Madonna Series and their zodiacal correspondence:

1. Sistine Madonna (complete image)
2. Beautiful Gardener (*La belle jardinière*)—Pisces, the Fishes ♓
3. Alba Madonna (*Madonna Della casa d'Alba*)—Aquarius, the Water Bearer ♒
4. Detail of Alba Madonna (*Madonna Della casa d'Alba*)—Capricorn, the Goat-Fish ♑
5. Pazzi Madonna (*Madonna di casa Pazzi*)—Sagittarius, the Archer ♐
6. (Veiled) Madonna of the Goldfinch (*Madonna del Cardellino*)—Scorpio, the Scorpion ♏
7. Bridgewater Madonna—Libra, the Scales ♎
8. Sistine Madonna (Detail)—Virgo, the Virgin ♍
9. Tempi Madonna—Leo, the Lion ♌
10. Head of the Transfigured Christ—Heart of the Pentagram
11. Granduca Madonna—Cancer, the Crab ♋
12. Madonna of the Fish—Gemini, the Twins ♊
13. Bruges Madonna—Taurus, the Bull ♉
14. Madonna of the Goldfinch (*Madonna del Cardellino*)—Aries, The Lamb of God ♈
15. The Transfigured Christ—Our Highest Human Ideal

### Image 1: Sistine Madonna—
### *Spirit Cosmos birthing Human Soul birthing Creative Spirit*

The opening image into the Raphael Madonna Series is the *Sistine Madonna* painting in its entirety (next page). Rudolf Steiner placed three "setting images" by Raphael "outside" the pentagram of twelve pictures: 1) the *Sistine Madonna*, 10) the head of Christ from *The Transfiguration on Mount Tabor*, and 15) the transfigured body of Christ from the painting of *The Transfiguration*. As stated, these three images effectively help us purify our astral body and attune our soul to the

*Image 1:* Sistine Madonna

mystery of the virginal woman giving birth to the higher human being. This higher human being is our true human spirit, who survives death by communing with the being who bestows eternal life. These three pictures reveal the mystery of the virginal human soul—which, when purified through catharsis, becomes the pure "Virgin Sophia"—giving birth to the child of the eternal human spirit.

Image 1: *Sistine Madonna* embodies a pentagram in the positioning of the upper figures and two cherubic angels forming the feet of the pentagram at the bottom of the painting. Rudolf Steiner described the *Sistine Madonna* with these words in 1908 and 1909:

> The artist has surrounded the Madonna with clouds out of which develop a great number of similar little children, a crowd of angelic forms.... Do not these cloud angels surrounding the Madonna say something to us? Yes...something whispers in our soul, "Here before us is a miracle in the best sense of the word." We do not think that this child whom the Madonna bears in her arms is born in the ordinary way from the woman. No! These wonderfully delicate angel forms we see in the clouds seem to be in process of development, and the child in the Madonna's arms seems to be only a more condensed manifestation of them, like something that had crystallized somewhat more than these fleeting angelic forms, which seems as if brought down from the clouds and held fast in her arms. It is thus this child appears to us, and not as if born from the woman. We are directed to a mysterious connection between the child and the virgin mother."[11]

> If we try to make a picture of the soul that gives birth to the higher human being out of itself, out of the spiritual universe, we need only call to mind the picture of the *Sistine Madonna*.... in the *Sistine Madonna* we have a picture of the human soul born of the spiritual universe, and springing from this soul the highest that a human being can bring forth—the human being's own spiritual birth, what within the human being is a new begetting of cosmic creative activity."[12]

In figure 1, the *Sistine Madonna* is placed above and to the left of the pentagram, like an overture. As the opening image, the *Sistine Madonna* establishes a "spiritual mood" for the entire sequence of pictures. We will continue by considering each Image's position along the pentagram of healing etheric currents and its relationship to the formative forces streaming from the zodiac.

### Image 2: Beautiful Gardener (La belle jardinière)—Pisces, the Fishes

Following the *Sistine Madonna*, the first image on the pentagram, *Beautiful Gardener* (*La belle jardinière*) anchors the left foot of figure 1. It is first of the four pictures ascending from the left "foot" toward the "head" of the pentagram. An unclothed child comfortably and joyfully stands with both of his feet resting upon the Madonna's foot, one leg slightly bent. Our attention moves from the feet anchoring the left corner through the line of the child's gaze up to the head of the

---

11 Steiner, *Universe, Earth, and Man*, lect. 1, August 4, 1908.
12 Steiner, "Isis and Madonna." April 29, 1909.

*Image 2*: Beautiful Gardener—*Pisces, the Fishes*

*Image 3*: Alba Madonna—*Aquarius, the Water Bearer*

Madonna. A second child, partially clothed, anchors the right foot of the picture, holding a cross that parallels the left side of the pentagram. A book rests on the Madonna's forearm, and the unclothed child reaches across her lap to touch her book with his left hand. The Madonna cradles the child's forearm in her left hand, while her right hand caresses his back.

This picture emphasizes gesturing hands and feet of three figures—six feet and six hands in a variety of poses, all twelve extremities touching, embracing, holding, supporting, and caressing the physical body. This image reflects creative forces streaming from the Fishes, Pisces, the twelfth sign of the zodiac, which form our hands and feet. Rudolf Steiner identified Pisces as our "home" constellation, and stated that our hands and feet most fully express our humanity. The gesture of Pisces is "the event becomes destiny." In future stages, human beings will become Spirits of Freedom and Love. Raphael's *Beautiful Gardener* echoes our primeval experiences in the Garden of Paradise, communing with Holy Isis before the Fall. Holy Isis is preparing the human child to become the vessel of the "I AM." Jupiter is the "ruling planet" of Pisces.

### *Image 3:* Alba Madonna (Madonna Della casa d'Alba)—*Aquarius, the Water Bearer*

In this circular painting by Raphael, the younger child ascends up the left side of the pentagram behind the lower leg of the Madonna, which appears prominently in the foreground of the painting. Forearms and lower legs of the two central figures are emphasized, while hands and feet are less prominent than in image 2). Both children hold the cross, with the older child gazing up in wonder at the Madonna and young child. The Madonna holds a folded book in her left hand, a finger marking her place, while she and the child serenely and majestically gaze out toward our left horizon, as if contemplating distant mysteries of the future.

The circular *Alba Madonna* painting is cosmic, atmospheric, expansive, and filled with vitality. It expresses the formative forces from the Water Bearer, Aquarius, that form our forearms and lower legs. Aquarius is connected to the human

*Image 4:* Alba Madonna *(detail)—*
*Capricorn, the Goat-Fish*

*Image 5:* Pazzi Madonna—*Sagittarius, the Archer*

etheric body and the realm of the angels, who provide the life-activity in our thinking. The gesture for Aquarius is "the human being in balance." Are the Madonna and child envisioning the future Age of Aquarius, when human beings will begin to work out of our true, higher selves? Saturn is the ruling planet of both Aquarius and Capricorn.

### *Image 4:* Alba Madonna *(detail)* (Madonna Della casa d'Alba)—*Capricorn, the Goat-Fish*

A close-up detail of the *Alba Madonna* painting serves as the third picture along the left side of the pentagram. Rudolf Steiner brings our attention here to the knees of both Madonna and child, which are placed prominently, near the center of the image. This closer view stimulates our appreciation for the noble inner lives expressed in the gestures of these three rosy-cheeked figures, and awakens our feeling for their vitality and intimate affinity with each other.

This detail of the *Alba Madonna* expresses the creative forces of the Goat-Fish, Capricorn, the realm of the archangels and of the human astral body. The archangels interweave among angels and between human beings, creating the basis for our feeling relationships with one another. From Capricorn streams the formative forces that shape our elbows, knees, and all our joints—allowing flexible interrelationships between the otherwise rigid bones of our body. As Aquarius and Capricorn are both "ruled" by Saturn, it seems appropriate for Rudolf Steiner to repeat the *Alba Madonna* image for both; the two views convey different impressions. Capricorn's task is to "bring thoughts to the world." Our astral body bears our thinking, feeling, and willing activity.

### *Image 5:* Pazzi Madonna (Madonna di casa Pazzi)—*Sagittarius, the Archer*

The *Pazzi Madonna,* a relief by Donatello, is placed at the apex of the five-pointed star. Madonna and child are focused in deep communion, their foreheads touching at the bridge of their noses. It as if the two-petaled lotus flower (the brow chakra, or third eye) of each is gazing into the infinitely rich spiritual visions of the other.

Could a more fitting image for the "head" of the pentagram be found than this remarkable relief? The movement from left foot up to the head of the pentagram is arrested, turned, and focused downward toward the right side of the pentagram by the gesture of this image. The Madonna bows her head down toward our right, as if anticipating the child's sharp descent to the bottom right foot of the pentagram that will follow.

The overall gesture of this picture—focusing our attention upon the brow chakra, which is ruled by Jupiter—expresses forces streaming from the Archer, Sagittarius, that form the large bones and muscles of our upper arms and thighs. Jupiter is the ruling planet of Sagittarius. The intensity of concentration, strength, and focus of this image is that of resolve—the key gesture for Sagittarius. One can feel the Madonna's upper-arm strength holding the child's body in position, so that their foreheads may touch. One hand holds the child's upper arm, while her other hand supports his weight. The Archai, Spirits of Time dwelling in Sagittarius, provide human beings with our attentive will power. In the Archer we also find the exact center of our Milky Way galaxy—a realm that Robert Powell and others consider to be a central dwelling place for the Father in the heavens. Are we witnessing the Madonna and child communing with the will of the Father, kindling the "I AM" and resolving to perform sacrificial deeds of will, in this striking image?

## Image 6: (Veiled) Madonna of the Goldfinch (Madonna del Cardellino)— *Scorpio, the Scorpion*

With this fifth image, our gaze plunges from the apex of the pentagram all the way down to its right foot. The seated Madonna holds an open book in her left hand; the unclothed child nestles between her open legs. The line between the Madonna's head and the tilt of the child's body terminates the descending line of the pentagram. Positioned between her legs, the unclothed child leans back to gaze above the brow of the second child while lifting his arm to stroke the head of the goldfinch held by the second child. The unclothed child's gaze and uplifted arm redirects our attention to

*Image 6:* (Veiled) Madonna of the Goldfinch— *Scorpio, the Scorpion*

the line of the pentagram ascending from right foot toward left hand. A rhythmic spacing appears between the two heads of the children and the open book.

Puzzlingly, Rudolf Steiner veiled the lower portion of this painting so that the genitals of the unclothed child are hidden from view. Why did he chastely veil this picture, while others in this series show the innocent nakedness of the child? The veiling expresses secret mysteries of the Scorpion (Scorpio), the constellation of the zodiac from which the Exusiai (Spirits of Form) shape the human form, reproduce it, and prepare it to receive the "I AM" during Earth evolution. From Scorpio, our organs of sexual reproduction were formed at the time of the Fall. But the Madonna Series pictures portray conditions prior to the Fall, before sexual reproduction began, when Holy Isis still virginally formed human beings. This part of the zodiac was originally the eagle, the majestic bird flying closest to the Sun and whose feathers bear the Sun's thoughts. In an innocent gesture of sacrifice, the eagle here descends into the form of the goldfinch, the bird that feeds among the thorn bushes from which the Crown of Thorns will be fashioned. The eagle and the scorpion both express "conception"—conception of thoughts and children. The gesture of Scorpio is "intelligent, clear thought." John the Evangelist is associated with the eagle. Life is bestowed through the eagle, but when life must be withdrawn from the body, the scorpion's sting brings death. This child will incarnate, unite with the being who is the source of life, go through the sting of death, and overcome it, like the dove. Mars is the ruling planet of Scorpio.

## Image 7: Bridgewater Madonna— Libra, the Scales

In one of Raphael's most dynamic and beautiful compositions, the child actively stretches across the Madonna's lap, his body twisting and turning with great mobility. The child turns his head up toward the Madonna's face, and her body twists to one side. These two figures accentuate the directional line ascending from right foot toward the left hand of the pentagram, the child moving toward the Madonna's right side. This image is rightfully placed at the fulcrum point in the lower notch of the pentagram. Despite the child so actively twisting on her lap, the serene Madonna remains composed and inwardly balanced, her hands gracefully held paralleling the child's body.

This dynamic picture expresses the creative forces streaming from the Scales (balance), Libra, that form our pelvic structure, providing uprightness and balanced movement to the human body. The Dynamis (Spirits of Motion), who dwell in Libra, bestowed the astral body upon the human being during the ancient Moon stage. From the Dynamis, human beings receive the capacity to form inner pictures, feelings, thoughts, and impulses of will within the astral body, as well as to move gracefully through the etheric and physical body. The gesture of Libra is "weighing the thought." Venus is the "ruling planet" of Libra, and Venus's movements around the Sun create a beautiful five-pointed star over eight years. We are led to ask: Are the healing etheric currents stimulated by the Madonna Series connected with the movements of the Venus pentagram?

*Image 7:* Bridgewater Madonna—*Libra, the Scales*

## Image 8: Sistine Madonna *(detail)*— Virgo, the Virgin

This close-up view of the Madonna holding the child at her right side is among Raphael's most sublime works of art. The Madonna and child gaze out of the picture directly into the soul of the viewer, as if petitioning us to awaken. Their loving gaze is filled with wakeful expectation, wisdom-filled understanding, tender compassion, and conscience. What are they asking of us? In the Madonna Series, this picture forms the left hand of the pentagram, the child held above the liver side of the Madonna. Remarks already made about the *Sistine Madonna* (image 1) apply here, as well.

From its placement on the pentagram, Rudolf Steiner presents the *Sistine Madonna* to us as the purest portrayal of the Virgin, Virgo. This cosmic feminine being, known as Holy Isis–Sophia–Mary, births the body, soul, and spirit of the human being. The Kyriotetes, the Spirits of Wisdom who serve Sophia and child, dwell in Virgo. Virgo sends

*Image 8:* Sistine Madonna *(Detail)—Virgo, the Virgin*

*Image 9:* Tempi Madonna—*Leo, the Lion*

forth the formative forces that shape our digestive and metabolic system, the female womb, and they also activate our seven life processes. The Kyriotetes first bestowed the etheric body to humanity during the ancient Sun stage of creation. Mercury, the planet of healing, is Virgo's "ruling planet." The gesture of Virgo is "soberness, inward turn." The Madonna and child might say to us: "Human Being, know thyself."

## *Image 9:* Tempi Madonna—*Leo, the Lion*

The child has moved across from the left hand to the right hand of the pentagram. The Madonna joyfully hugs the child to her left side, their hearts jubilantly touching one another as if beating in unison. The child is embraced upon her bosom, their rosy cheeks united tenderly in affection and love. The change in mood from the sober inwardness of the *Sistine Madonna* to the joy-filled embracing of the *Tempi Madonna* is remarkable.

The *Tempi Madonna* expresses the creative forces streaming from the Lion, Leo, that form our heart and lungs—our rhythmic system of breathing and blood circulation. From the lion the Thrones, Spirits of Will, initiated the forming of the human physical body during ancient Saturn. Even today, the Thrones enthusiastically offer themselves with devotion and self-sacrifice. The Thrones pour forth love, courage, good will, perseverance, and warmth through the lion. They generously allow their pure spiritual being to be condensed into the denser substances of spiritual light, inner warmth, fire, air, water, and earth needed to clothe human bodies and the kingdoms of nature in matter. The Sun is the "ruling planet" of Leo. From the *Tempi Madonna* we feel the Sun streaming from the hearts of the Madonna and child in the gesture of Leo: "flaming enthusiasm."

We can picture Christ resting in the bosom of the Father, radiating as the heart of the Father, performing the will of the Father. We can also picture Christ dwelling within the bosom of the Mother, radiating the Mother's life, healing, individuality, relationship, compassion, forgiveness, creativity, freedom, and love. In this way, the head of the Christ can awaken our highest human ideal within our hearts—the Universal Human toward whom we strive. But why portray the head of the transfigured Christ? What happened during the Transfiguration, and how is it related to our soul birthing the human spirit and the healing currents of the etheric body?

Christ's incarnation into the body of Jesus was accomplished in definite stages. Jesus was carefully prepared as the Grail vessel who could receive and assist the Christ's incarnating into humanity and the Earth. At the Baptism in the Jordan, the Cosmic Christ became the "*I AM*" of Jesus. Then, by facing and overcoming three Temptations after forty days of fasting, Christ penetrated and purified the *astral body* of Jesus. The third stage of Christ's incarnation required purification of the *etheric body* of Jesus, which was achieved at the Transfiguration event. According to Matthew 17:1–2, Christ ascended a high mountain with three disciples, "and was transfigured before them: and his face did shine as the Sun, and his raiment was white as the light."

As Christ purified the etheric body of Jesus at the Transfiguration, that etheric body began to radiate pure light like the Sun. During the ancient Sun, the etheric body was first bestowed upon humanity by the Kyriotetes, who serve Christ and Sophia from the realm of Virgo. The Madonna serves as the mediator and maternal source of the life spirit of Christ, which she transforms into the healing currents of our etheric body. During Earth evolution, our waking "I" lives primarily in the sensory world, experiencing it through our physical body. In the future times, evolving human beings will ascend into higher selfhood and begin to work more directly through the etheric body, learning to employ the healing etheric currents moving along the pentagram. Here we begin to

*Image 10: Head of* The Transfigured Christ

### Image 10: The Transfigured Christ *(detail)*— Heart of the Pentagram

At the heart of the pentagram Rudolf Steiner placed the head of Christ from Raphael's painting of the Transfiguration. Contemplating this picture and its placement, we recall Rudolf Steiner's words: "In the *Sistine Madonna* we have a picture of the human soul born of the spiritual universe, and springing from this soul *the highest that a human being can bring forth—the human being's own spiritual birth.*"[13]

Christ is the forerunner, benefactor, and teacher of our spiritual birth; his transfigured head appears at the heart of the pentagram. We know Christ as the Lamb of God, the Logos, the bestower of the I AM, the substance and meaning of existence, the source of divine love, compassion, and forgiveness—the being and source of divine life. Christ serves as the head of the spiritual hierarchies in service to the will of the Father.

13 Steiner, "Isis and Madonna," April 29, 1909.

*Image 11:* Granduca Madonna—*Cancer, the Crab*

*Image 12:* Madonna of the Fish—*Gemini, the Twins*

trace only one thread of the many relationships between Christ's purifying the etheric body at the Transfiguration and positioning of the head of the Transfigured Christ at the heart of the pentagram. There are many more levels of this sublime mystery to contemplate.

### Image 11: Granduca Madonna— Cancer, the Crab

The serene Madonna holds the child on her left side, supporting him with her left hand held near her waist. The Madonna's right hand touches his chest, while the child's left hand reaches up to rest upon her breastplate. Both figures are looking down with an inward gesture. With their heads tilted slightly to one side, we might imagine both of them listening to a beautifully played symphony. In the pentagram sequence, the child begins descending down the body of the Madonna. The movement we perceive is from the right arm down toward the left leg of the pentagram

The gestures of the Madonna and child—each gently touching the ribs of the other—express the forces streaming from Cancer, the Crab, that form our rib cage. Our twelve pairs of ribs serve as a musical instrument tuned to the twelve tones of the scale. The Cherubim, the Spirits of the Harmonies, dwell in Cancer. Our breathing and heartbeat rhythmically play the inner musical tones within our rib cage. The Madonna and Child both sound forth this cosmic music and listen to the harmony of the spheres. Cancer's gesture is "initiative," and the Moon is its "ruling planet."

### Image 12: Madonna of the Fish— Gemini, the Twins

The Madonna sits demurely on a throne, her eyes gazing down to our left. Her face reveals wakeful interest and perhaps a bit of concern. Her right shoulder slightly forward, the Madonna raises her right arm and places her hand on the child's torso as if to steady or restrain him. The child sits on the arm of the throne with one foot on her lap, his other foot placed against the side of the chair arm, as if poised to propel his body forward. His left hand holds open a book while he leans forward, reaching his right hand down toward our left. The parallel arms of Madonna and child resemble the Roman numeral II. The counterpoise is striking. The child appears to be intent to descend to our left, while the Madonna seems equally intent upon holding him back. Their gestures emphasize the descending line from the right hand of the pentagram toward the left foot.

The parallel arms and counterpoised gestures characterize the formative forces streaming from the Twins, Gemini, that create the symmetry of the human body. The forces from Gemini establish polarities and weave interrelationships between them, forming opportunities for dynamic interchanges between what appear to be opposite extremes. The Seraphim, the Spirits of Love who dwell in Gemini, are the hierarchy closest to the Trinity. They mediate between the Godhead and the rest of the spiritual hierarchies, all of whom the Seraphim lovingly serve like brethren. As it is placed along the pentagram of the Madonna Series, this picture sets up tensions—between incarnating or holding back in the spiritual world, between mortality and immortality. We feel the child's intention to enter incarnation, as well as the Madonna's concern for the child's well-being. The gesture of Gemini is "capacity for action." Mercury is the "ruling planet" of Gemini.

## *Image 13:* Bruges Madonna— *Taurus, the Bull*

Michelangelo's sculpture, the *Bruges Madonna*, portrays a large-headed child, willfully descending toward incarnation. The child holds the Madonna's hands and supports himself by wrapping an arm around her thigh as he steps down toward Earth. Though he is still partially enveloped in her protective garments, the Madonna seems resigned to accept the child's willful determination to touch down and fulfill his intention. That time has not yet fully come—the child's feet

*Image 13:* Bruges Madonna—*Taurus, the Bull*

rest on a step, hovering just above the Earth until the proper moment arises.

The willful child in the *Bruges Madonna* conveys to us the gesture of Taurus: "limb system, will, deed." Taurus, the bull, streams formative forces that shape our neck, throat, mouth, and ears. The Holy Spirit, the spirit of communion, understanding, and right speaking, works through Taurus, inspiring our ability to listen and to speak, to commune with one another. Venus, the "ruling planet" of Taurus, bears the capacity for loving sacrifice. We approach the final stages of the child's incarnation; the Word is about to become flesh.

## *Image 14:* Madonna of the Goldfinch (Madonna del Cardellino)— *Aries, The Lamb of God*

As our gaze descends toward the left foot of the pentagram, we arrive at the "final" image of the twelve zodiacal pictures and the incarnation of the Lamb of God. Remarkably, at the left foot of

*Image 14:* Madonna of the Goldfinch—
*Aries, the Lamb of God*

the pentagram we find the unveiled picture of the Madonna of the Goldfinch—the same image that Rudolf Steiner veiled at the right foot of the pentagram! (There are wonderful mysteries here to explore more fully.) Now that this complete picture is unveiled for us, previously hidden details emerge. We see the unclothed child is standing with his right foot upon the Madonna's right foot, similar in some ways to the gesture depicted in the *Beautiful Gardener* (image 2). In fact, many similarities can be found when comparing the *Beautiful Gardener* with the *Madonna of the Goldfinch*. Both Images share the terminal position near the left foot of the pentagram. Since the healing etheric currents flowing along the pentagram don't stop abruptly at the left foot but rather turn and continue to ascend toward the head of the pentagram, we might imagine that the *Madonna of the Goldfinch* gestures could gradually metamorphose into the *Beautiful Gardener*. The biggest differences between the two pictures are the reversal in the positioning of the two children, and the shift in the Madonna's gaze upon the two children.

Profound mystery wisdom lies hidden in the relationship between the two children and the Madonna that would lead us too far afield to articulate in this brief article. The unveiled Madonna of the Goldfinch picture manifests the formative forces streaming from the Ram, Aries, that form our head and nerve-sensory system. The Christ penetrates and works through all twelve constellations of the zodiac, but St. John's designation "Lamb of God" signifies a particularly strong connection between Christ and realm of Aries. How does the Madonna of the Goldfinch manifest the formative forces streaming from Aries? The key gesture for Aries is "the event." The Madonna and the two children, each and together, play essential roles in preparing humanity and the Earth for the incarnation of Christ. Perhaps the words of Christ from Matthew 18:20 apply here: "For where two or three are gathered in my name, there am I in the midst of them." Certainly, the Madonna and the two children are gathered to serve in the name of Christ. The Lamb of God expressed infinite love and gratitude to all humanity for allowing him to incarnate and serve our evolution. One might imagine the glyph of Aries as hidden within the arrangement of the three figures in the Madonna of the Goldfinch.

## *Image 15:* The Transfigured Christ—
## Our Highest Human Ideal

Rudolf Steiner placed the picture of the transfigured Christ as the "closing image" of the Raphael Madonna Series. The body of the transfigured Christ appears to float above the dense gravity of the sense world. He streams forth life into the etheric world of levity, his head, arms, and legs outstretched into a pentagram. Christ's gesture in Raphael's painting is similar to Rudolf Steiner's sketch in figure 3, depicting the flow of healing etheric currents from left foot to head to right foot to left hand to right hand to left foot. Raphael here artistically portrays our own potential future stages of human development. In future times, human beings will actively work from the level of Spirit Self through our etheric bodies. The solid

*Image 15:* The Transfigured Christ

material Earth must be spiritualized by human creative activity and human love, and human beings must learn to become creative within the etheric world. Christ now dwells in the etheric world, as our highest human ideal. Remarks made about image 10 apply here, as well.

## Closing Considerations

We have just begun to draw back the veil of profound mysteries and deep spiritual truths hidden within the artistry of the Raphael Madonna Series. We don't know whether or not Raphael intended to paint pictures that could be used as the basis for what Rudolf Steiner selected and assembled so beautifully here. Rudolf Steiner held Raphael in highest esteem as a fellow Sun initiate in service to human evolution through Sophia and the Christ, and it is wonderful to contemplate how one initiate creatively works with and builds upon the contributions of the other. This remarkable artistic work is "apocalyptic" in the true sense of that word. The Raphael Madonna Series invites us "to draw back the veil."

We discover through this article that a zodiacal structure forming the *physical body* underlies this sequence of pictures arranged by Rudolf Steiner. We can follow the healing currents of the *etheric body* moving through the human form along the pattern of a five-pointed star. We can experience that the Madonna images help us purify our *astral body*, and that they reveal the mysteries of the birth of our true human selfhood—the *I AM* and the possibility of achieving the stage of *spirit self* in future stages. We pose the possibility that the pentagram of healing etheric currents depicted in the Madonna Series might well be related to the Venus pentagram. Rudolf Steiner remarked that other patterns of etheric currents also flow through our physical body, and that our etheric body is "the echo of the moving planets."[14] Infinitely more riddles and truths await further exploration and discovery. Some brief considerations are offered here.

One might ask: Why does the zodiac appear to move "backward" along the pentagram sequence? Why does the series start with Pisces and end with Aries? Over astronomical ages of time, the vernal Sun appears to "fall back" along the zodiac by one degree in 72 years, or by 30° in 2,160 years. Hence, long cosmic cycles of evolution follow the "backward" movement through the zodiac—from Pisces to Aquarius to Capricorn—that we discover in the Raphael Madonna Series. This movement is connected with the "precession of the equinoxes."

From another perspective, one stream of child development follows this same "reverse" sequence through the zodiac. The very young child's spirit lives primarily in the limbs in the first seven years; when the child's spirit ascends into the rhythmic system, the child goes to grade school; finally, the spirit of the teenager ascends into the head and gradually awakens to adult intelligence. The limbs can be correlated to the constellations Pisces, Aquarius, Capricorn, and Sagittarius. The metabolic and rhythmic system can be correlated with

---

14 Steiner, *Universe, Earth, and Man*, lect. 1, August 4, 1908.

Scorpio, Libra, Virgo, and Leo. And the upper human being can be correlated with Cancer, Gemini, Taurus and Aries. In 1923, the first three panels of Rudolf Steiner's "Foundation Stone Verse" unfold through a similar "reverse" sequence: the human soul lives in the limbs, in the beat of heart and lung, and in the resting head. Thus we see the "backward" sequence through the zodiac suggested here is not unique.

We have not specifically identified the two children who appear in certain pictures. Nor have we considered Rudolf Steiner's deep spiritual relationship to Raphael and their roles as Sun Initiates serving Sophia, Michael, and the Christ. May this brief article serve to stimulate the reader's further research into the profound mysteries of the Raphael Madonna Series.

NOTE: Post cards of the Raphael Madonna Series can be ordered online through Wynstones Press, or phone orders can be placed through Rudolf Steiner College Bookstore at 916-961-8729.

---

*"He said there was something called the Grail, whose name—how it is known—he had read clearly in the stars.*

*"A [heavenly] host left it upon the Earth, and then flew up above the stars on high."*

—WOLFRAM VON ESCHENBACH, *Parzival*, 454,21–25

The Russian poet and mystic Daniel Andreev also had a vision of the Holy Grail in the starry heavens and revealed its name:

*"I remember seeing a glowing mist of stunning majesty, as though the creative heart of our universe had revealed itself to me in visible form for the first time. It was Astrofire, the great center of our galaxy."*

—DANIEL ANDREEV, *The Rose of the World*, p. 198

# DISCUSSION OF ASTROLOGICAL HOUSE SYSTEMS

## *Robert Powell & Wain Farrants*

Robert: Regarding the houses in astrology, in last year's issue of this journal Brian Gray offered a very thoughtful appraisal, which should be read by everyone interested in the question of the astrological houses.[1] Also, my booklet on the houses is relevant, as it offers an overview of the history of the houses.[2] Astrologer Marina E. Partridge in her discussion of the houses[3] refers to my booklet *History of the Houses*, but misses the point that at the end of the booklet I refer to Rudolf Steiner's statement about the clockwise eurythmy zodiac being the zodiac during the cycle of the day. It is this statement, taken together with the research of Michel Gauquelin (discussed at length by Marina) and with early historical evidence from Egypt and elsewhere (referred to in my booklet), which subsequently led me to conclude that the clockwise house system is appropriate in relation to the birth of the soul into the earthly reality of the clockwise daily movement of the Sun, the Moon, the planets, and the stars.

Jacques Dorsan's book on the clockwise house system is essential reading for the clockwise house system in the birth horoscope, and his book gives many examples of applying the clockwise system.[4] As was anticipated, the publication of this book has started a discussion among astrologers regarding the clockwise house system. First, here is a review by astrologer Helen Stokes. This review was published in the March/April 2012 issue of the (British) *Astrological Journal*:

> Astrologers in the West have traditionally interpreted the houses as though they rotate in the same anticlockwise direction as the signs of the zodiac. In 1984, Jacques Dorsan published the first edition of this book [*The Clockwise House System*] after his extensive practice of astrology had convinced him that the houses actually move in the opposite direction to the zodiac signs. This book [*The Clockwise House System*] represents a new English translation of Dorsan's original work, edited and supplemented by Wain Farrants and Robert Powell.
>
> Dorsan described himself as a siderealist; he considered planets and houses according to the natural zodiac, structured on the fixed stars. Therefore it made sense to him to consider the houses from a clockwise direction. Helpfully, for those of us who are more accustomed to viewing houses from the opposite direction, he explains in the preface that his theories should also be of interest to those using the tropical zodiac, and I did indeed find this to be the case.
>
> Dorsan's text considers the quadrants, the planets in the houses, the meanings of the twelve houses, the angles, which house to assign to the father and which to the mother, and the techniques behind his philosophies. The book also includes more than 80 charts used to illustrate the author's hypotheses. These are taken from the original 1984 French work, with edits and additions carried out by the editor of this edition.
>
> *The Clockwise House System* is a fascinating read, helped immensely by the plethora of carefully chosen and introduced examples.

---

1 Gray, "Anthroposophic Foundations for a Renewal of Astrology," *Journal for Star Wisdom 2012*, see especially part 2: "A Fresh Look at the Astrological Houses," pp. 116–130.

2 Powell, *History of the Houses*; http://www.astrocom.com/astrology/booklets/history-of-the-houses.

3 See http://darkstarastrology.com/house-system-astrology/.

4 Dorsan, *The Clockwise House System*.

Many astrology books suffer from a lack of examples or throw too many in without adequate explanation, but here the balance is very good. It is easy to follow the author's train of thought, and interesting to consider a different take on the houses. Many useful and interesting ideas can also be taken away. This is a well-edited, accessible book and worth a read for any astrologer open to a different way of looking at the birth chart.

In the US, a reviewer (H.S.) from Pensacola, Florida, posted the following review of Jacques Dorsan's book on the Amazon.com website:

I don't know what made me decide to buy this book; the concept itself seems to defy "logic"—at least from the traditional view of astrology. Clockwise houses? Hmmm. I am glad I did, however. This is a fascinating read, one that will make you think. I highly recommend it to any student of astrology who is struggling with the (apparent) inconsistencies and contradictions that traditional (tropical) astrology seems to be replete with. If you already accept the sidereal zodiac as being closer to reality in terms of planet/sign descriptions, this is just another small step in realigning your thinking. The author is a siderealist.

No doubt traditional astrologers will have a problem with the ideas in this book (especially adherents of the tropical zodiac—for siderealists, this may just be a short leap), regarding it as an amusing deviation at best, and a professional threat at worst. I myself am not a practicing astrologer; I have no reputation or body of work to defend in embracing something as radical as the concept this book presents. I am, however, a serious student of astrology and like to think for myself. So I have no problem with investigating alternate rationales, testing them and coming to my own conclusions. If you are of a similar mind-set, you will find this a very interesting and stimulating read.

Mr Dorsan was a dedicated and serious astrologer. He didn't wake up one day and decide the houses should be viewed in reverse. He worked with this concept for years, testing and applying it, and cites numerous examples of how much more effective this approach was with helping his clients. Included are lots of charts of famous personalities, with short bios and descriptions illustrating the efficacy of his approach. There is also a complete description of the houses based on his system, along with brief descriptions of the planets in the 'new' houses.

The concept is simple enough: why should the 1st house be the house 'below' the horizon, and the 12th house 'above' the horizon in the full light of day? Would it not make more sense to reverse that? This house system agrees more closely with the sectors identified by Gauquelin in his research. Another interesting point is the confusion about the 11th house often being considered a 'money' house. With clockwise houses, the 11th house becomes the 2nd house of money and the old 2nd house becomes the 11th.

From the author: "Just to give one single example, the transits that the slow planets make in the radical chart (that of birth); let us suppose that a slow Jupiter-Saturn sextile comes about in your second house (gains) and in the fourth house (profession); it is quite simple and rapid to conclude that your professional income will progress for the months during which this sextile is maintained. Previously, you would not have arrived at a prediction as exact as this since the significations attributed to each of these two above houses, were falsified. This examination alone, repeated in several horoscopes, will convince you of the rectitude of my method."

I plan to further explore this concept with my own charts. In my humble opinion, if you are serious about getting results with your astrology, and not adverse to exploring new concepts, this is a rewarding must-read.

***Addendum to my above review (19 May 2012): As a further refinement, I have been using the Equal House method to demarcate the house cusps and am finding it to be more reliable in terms of results. Previous to that, I had been using Whole Signs. The ascendant degree seems to be a better house divisor and demarcator, especially in terms of transit and progression timing...I have stopped using the MC/IC (an abstractly calculated axis which breaks down at the north/south poles anyway);

I'm getting better results from the ascendant-based method. House rulership based on traditional methods has always been "iffy" to me, and with this clockwise house system there are, in effect, 'two' house rulers. However, by relying more on the ruler of the equal house degree as the 'true' house ruler, I am getting better results there as well with the clockwise house system.

All in all, I am convinced that this house system is valid. If for no other reason than that it works. And works well. As an aside, I know of only one other astrologer who uses the clockwise house system, Robert Powell. If anyone is curious, you might want to read his book: *The Astrological Revolution*. You may not agree with his beliefs on reincarnation, karma, etc., or his use of Placidus house cusps (an error in my judgment), but his book will definitely stimulate your brain cells and get you thinking.[5]

Wain: I am open to the use of Equal Houses, commencing at the Ascendant, but not centered on the Ascendant. I have a horoscope in my database of a woman with Jupiter in the third equal house but the fourth Placidus house, who fits Dorsan's delineation of Jupiter in the Third House perfectly, "As though by miracle, one could escape unharmed from a car, train or airplane accident." In her case it was a car, which drove over the edge of a cliff.

Robert: Also on the Amazon.com website a second review of Dorsan's book was posted by Joseph Arechiga from North Hollywood, California:

Excellent book —

I've wanted to use houses for years. I really have. But I never get consistent results — But with clockwise houses — not only are results consistent — But I think I'm finally getting stable enough results to do so. Excellent book —

If you've never wondered who came up with the counter clockwise standard Western houses and why — this book explains it. Why would you trust a system who's origins are totally unknown to most. Can't recommend this book enough. You won't even need to memorize the meanings of houses anymore as with the clockwise system the meanings are obvious. Gazillions of sample charts about half the book (and it's a really big book). Half the book is history and theory. If you seek consistent results with houses you need to read this book.[6]

Returning to Brian Gray's article on the astrological houses, Brian indicates:

It is important to note that the houses in the original house system were *numbered counterclockwise*, corresponding to the movements of the planets through the signs of the zodiac. The clockwise diurnal rotation of the heavens is accounted for by the role of the *horoscope* (Ascendant), which views each succeeding degree of the zodiac as it rises after birth. Since the *horoscope was the key reference point for the original birth charts*, as the day progresses and the heavens turn clockwise, the *horoscope* continues to view the zodiac as each later degree of the ecliptic rises along the eastern horizon. Thus the houses are always numbered in counterclockwise sequence from the viewpoint of the *horoscope*. Gauquelin's and Dorsan's idea that house systems should be numbered clockwise arises from ignoring the significance of the *horoscope as the key viewpoint for the entire birth chart*. We find even deeper reasons for the original house system being numbered counterclockwise from Robert Powell's research.

Robert Powell calls the whole-sign houses—the oldest known horoscopes with 12 houses—the *ancient hermetic system* of houses. He beautifully explains the origin of the houses in relation to *the horoscope of conception*, as expressed by the ancient rule of Hermes:

Robert: One of the earliest references to the houses is that found on four demotic horoscopes, drawn up on four ostraca from Medinet Habu in Egypt. The horoscopes are dated AD 13, 17, 18 and 35. These horoscopes reveal an early definition of the houses, as originated in Egypt in the hermetic astrology of antiquity. In this early definition each house is simply equated with a sign of the sidereal zodiac: the first house with the rising sign, the second house with the next sign, and so on. The houses in this original definition were therefore each 30° long, identical

---

5 See http://www.amazon.com/gp/pdp/profile/A7X2G1GDGSKJG/ref=cm_aya_bb_pdp.

6 See http://www.amazon.com/clockwise-house-system-foundation-astrology/product-reviews/1584200952/ref=sr_1_1_cm_cr_acr_txt?ie=UTF8&showViewpoints=1.

with the zodiacal signs. The first house in this early definition of the houses was the house containing the Ascendant, i.e. the zodiacal sign rising on the eastern horizon at the moment of birth.[7]

Before considering the meanings traditionally associated with the twelve houses, it is important to grasp the origin of the houses.... The origin of the house system, in fact, can only be understood against the background of *the horoscope of conception*, as determined by the rule of Hermes. The hermetic rule specifies that the Moon at the moment of conception indicates the place of the Ascendant – or its opposite, the Descendant – at birth.... during the Moon's orbits of the zodiac between conception and birth the entire course of destiny for the spiral of life is elaborated, whereby each lunar orbit of the sidereal zodiac corresponds to seven years of life.[8]

The goal of the incarnating human being is the birth configuration, whereby the moment of conception is an important point of transition....at the moment of conception, as determined by the hermetic rule, the imprint of the image begins to work into the building up of the physical body (embryo), and at the same time the etheric body begins to be formed through the orbits of the Moon around the sidereal zodiac. Simultaneously...the karma for the coming life on Earth is woven into the etheric body reflecting the planetary movements taking place during the embryonic period. Thus the planetary movements between conception and birth indicate the weaving of destiny into the etheric body, and the formation of the etheric body itself—concurrent with the Moon's orbits of the zodiac—occurs in such a way that *one lunar orbit of the sidereal zodiac corresponds to seven years of life*.[9]

Brian: Here we find the deeper spiritual reasons why the world's oldest house system numbered the houses *counterclockwise* from the Ascendant (*horoscope*). The Moon's position at conception becomes the Ascendant/Descendant horizon at birth, and the counterclockwise motion of the Moon, Sun and planets through the signs of the zodiac between conception and birth patterns the interweaving of individual destiny for the coming life. The motion through the signs of the zodiac is *counterclockwise*, agreeing with the sequence of how the signs of the zodiac rise at the Ascendant (*horoscope*) following the moment of birth. The deeper wisdom at work in the original house system has been lost in recent times.[10]

Robert: Brian quotes here from my research into the hermetic house system in *Hermetic Astrology*, volume 2, originally published in 1989 (republished in 2006). There, as indicated in the above quote, I point to the appropriateness of the counterclockwise house system at conception and during the embryonic period, as applied in astrological biography. However, as mentioned at the start of this article, it was when I subsequently came across Rudolf Steiner's statement about the clockwise eurythmy zodiac being the zodiac during the cycle of the day, together with other research findings—primarily the findings of Michel and Françoise Gauquelin and Jacques Dorsan—that in the course of time, and in light of much research, I came to the conclusion that the clockwise house system is appropriate at the birth of the soul into the earthly reality of the clockwise daily movement not only of the Sun, but also of the Moon, the planets, and the stars, which is why in my later books I employ the clockwise house system.[11]

From the perspective of the soul's descent from the Moon sphere (counterclockwise perspective) to the Earth sphere (clockwise perspective), this explains why *both* the clockwise and the counterclockwise house systems are true, in which case there are four levels to consider—see, for example, my description in the article "Horoscopes Old and New"[12]:

---

7 Powell, *History of the Houses*, p. 3.
8 Powell, *Hermetic Astrology*, vol. 2, p. 248.
9 Ibid., pp. 253–254.

10 Gray, "Anthroposophic Foundations for a Renewal of Astrology," *Journal for Star Wisdom 2012*, see especially part 2: "A Fresh Look at the Astrological Houses," pp. 116–130.

11 See, for example, Powell, *Elijah Come Again* and *The Astrological Revolution* (coauthored with Kevin Dann).

12 See http://www.astrogeographia.org/features/horoscopes_old_new/.

Wain: My big question is whether or not houses are relevant in the conception chart, and if so what house system to use? Transits appear to work in conception charts. Transits to birth and epoch chart houses will naturally work for equal houses because it will simply be the same as a semi-sextile, sextile, square, trine or quincunx to the Ascendant.

Robert: Clearly, further research needs to be done into the validity of clockwise and counterclockwise house systems. At present, we stand at the beginning of coming to clarity regarding this theme, and we can be grateful to researchers such as Brian Gray, Michel Gauquelin, and Jacques Dorsan for publishing their ideas and research into such fundamental aspects of the science of the stars.

Wain: I have made a small start to this. I am studying the birth and epoch charts of athletes,

| Level of the "I" | Hermetic (Tychonic) birth chart | clockwise houses |
| --- | --- | --- |
| Level of the soul (astral body) | Geocentric birth chart | clockwise houses |
| Level of the life body (etheric body) | Geocentric conception chart | counterclockwise |
| Level of the physical body | Hermetic conception chart | counterclockwise |

## MARTINA NAVRATILOVA

| Epoch Hermetic Physical Body | Epoch Geocentric Etheric Body | Birth Geocentric Astral Body | Birth Hermetic "I" |
| --- | --- | --- | --- |
| Uranus 6 Cancer 18 | Uranus 5 Cancer 41 | | |
| | Mercury 6 Capricorn 54 | | |
| Earth 17 Cancer 21 | Sun 17 Capricorn 21 | | |
| Venus 18 Aries 6 | | | Mercury 18 Cancer 56 |
| | | Venus 20 Leo 17 | Jupiter 21 Leo 19 |

## JACK NIKLAUS

| Epoch Hermetic Physical Body | Epoch Geocentric Etheric Body | Birth Geocentric Astral Body | Birth Hermetic "I" |
| --- | --- | --- | --- |
| Uranus 6 Cancer 18 | Saturn 29 Pices 57 | Moon node 0 Libra 21 | Venus 27 Pisces 38 |
| | Mercury 6 Capricorn 54 | | Mercury 14 Sagitarius 31 |
| Chiron 16 Gemini 24 | Chiron 12 Gemini 20 | | |
| | Mars 28 Sagittarius 29 | Mercury 29 Sagittarius 24 | |
| | Mercury 22 Pisces 44 | Chiron 22 Gemini 15<br>Mars 17 Pisces 54 | Jupiter 20 Pisces 27 |

## MAURICE (ROCKET) RICHARD

| Epoch Hermetic Physical Body | Epoch Geocentric Etheric Body | Birth Geocentric Astral Body | Birth Hermetic "I" |
| --- | --- | --- | --- |
| | Sun 3 Gemini 22 | | Mercury 2 Sagittarius 5 |
| Jupiter 0 Leo 16 | Ascendant 3 Leo 20 | Moon 3 Aquarius 21 | |
| | Saturn 12 Leo 49 | | |
| | Uranus 12 Aquarius 1 | | Uranus 12 Aquarius 24 |
| Saturn 18 Leo 33 | | Jupiter 16 Leo 48<br>Uranus 14 Aquarius 6 | |
| | | Mercury 23 Aquarius 6 | Jupiter 22 Leo 39 |

## PELÉ

| Epoch Hermetic Physical Body | Epoch Geocentric Etheric Body | Birth Geocentric Astral Body | Birth Hermetic "I" |
|---|---|---|---|
| | Mars 1 Aries 28 | | |
| | Saturn 2 Aries 15 | | Chiron 1 Cancer 43 |
| | | Jupiter 18 Aries 9 | |
| | | Saturn 18 Aries 19 | |
| Venus 29 Aries 32 | | Mercury 29 Libra 55 | Uranus 29 Aries 36 |
| Chiron 24 Gemini 4 | Ascendant 23 Sag 32 | Moon 23 Gemini 32 | |
| Mercury 23 Aquarius 26 | | Venus 24 Leo 54 | |
| | Neptune 1 Virgo 2 | | |
| | Venus 3 Pisces 43 | Neptune 2 Virgo 24 | Neptune 1 Virgo 22 |
| | Midheaven 16 Virgo 26 | Moon Node 16 Virgo 57 | |
| | Jupiter 13 Pisces | Mars 17 Virgo 30 | |

## BABE RUTH

| Epoch Hermetic Physical Body | Epoch Geocentric Etheric Body | Birth Geocentric Astral Body | Birth Hermetic "I" |
|---|---|---|---|
| Venus 25 Aries 33 | | Mars 24 Aries 7 | Mercury 25 Aries 17 |
| | | | Uranus 23 Libra 31 |
| | Jupiter 2 Gemini 53 | Jupiter 3 Gemini 17 | Mars 3 Gemini 10 |
| | Ascendant 12 Sag 53 | Moon 12 Gemini 53 | Jupiter 11 Gemini 51 |
| Mars 12 Aquarius 53 | | Mercury 12 Aquarius 12 | |
| | | Venus 10 Aquarius 44 | |

because one source of their skill must be a coordination among their physical, etheric, astral bodies, and the "I." Here are some examples:

Martina Navratilova, tennis player, birth and epoch in Prague, Czech Republic. Birth October 18, 1956, at 16:39:43 CET. Epoch February 1, 1956, at 8:41:59 GMT.

Her physical and etheric bodies are connected by Uranus opposition Mercury. Her astral body and "I" are connected by Venus in conjunction with Jupiter in Leo in the seventh clockwise house, and Moon conjunction Mars in Pisces rising in the first clockwise house. Her physical body and "I" are connected by Venus in Aries square Mercury in Cancer.

Jack Niklaus, golfer. birth and epoch in Columbus, Ohio. Birth January 21, 1940, 3:06:10 EST. Epoch May 4, 1939, 12:07:36 GMT.

Jack Niklaus has connections between his four "bodies," showing that his "I" could work into his astral, etheric and physical bodies.

Maurice (Rocket) Richard, hockey player for the Montreal Canadiens, birth and epoch in Montreal, Quebec. Birth on April 4, 1921, at 2:30:00 EST. Epoch June 18, 1920, at 14:12:39 GMT.

Richard's physical body is totally under the control of his emotions and life body, whereas his etheric body has connections to both his astral body and "I."

"Pelé" Edson Arantes do Nascimento, birth and epoch in Coracoes, Brazil. Birth October 23, 1940, at 2:58:42 BZT. Epoch February 10, 1940, at 6:22:17 GMT.

Pelé was one of the greatest and most well-known soccer players.

Pelé had connections between all of his bodies.

## Muhammed Ali

| Epoch Hermetic Physical Body | Epoch Geocentric Etheric Body | Birth Geocentric Astral Body | Birth Hermetic "I" |
|---|---|---|---|
| Saturn 22 Aries 26 | Jupiter 21 Aries 37 | | |
| Jupiter 29 Aries 24 | Uranus 29 Aries 43 | Saturn 27 Aries 44 | |
| | | Uranus 2 Taurus 36 | Saturn 3 Taurus 22 |
| Mars 20 Scorpio 31 | | Jupiter 18 Taurus 2 | Mars 18 Taurus 54 |
| | Chiron 1 Cancer 21 | Sun 3 Capricorn 21 | |

## O. J. Simpson

| Epoch Hermetic Physical Body | Epoch Geocentric Etheric Body | Birth Geocentric Astral Body | Birth Hermetic "I" |
|---|---|---|---|
| | Jupiter 8 Libra 25 | Chiron 8 Libra 21 | |
| | Mars 14 Libra 25 | | Mars 14 Aries 54<br>Chiron 14 Libra 44 |
| | Chiron 1 Libra 7 | Mercury 0 Cancer 39 | |
| Saturn 17 Cancer 27<br>Pluto 18 Cancer 52 | Saturn 15 Cancer 0<br>Pluto 18 Cancer 10 | | |
| Mars 0 Scorpio 31 | Venus 1 Scorpio 6 | | Jupiter 3 Scorpio 3 |
| Mercury 10 Scorpio 2 | | Mars 12 Taurus 1 | Venus 15 Taurus 36 |

Babe Ruth, birth and epoch, Baltimore, Maryland. Born February 6, 1895, at 13:36:45 EST. Epoch July 29, 1894, at 22:25:37 GMT.

Babe Ruth was a well-known American baseball player.

Babe Ruth had connections between all aspects of the fourfold human being.

Muhammed Ali, birth and epoch in Louisville, Kentucky. Born on January 17, 1942, at 18:25:31 CST. Epoch on March 23, 1941, at 19:42:26 GMT.

Muhammed Ali, world champion boxer and outspoken Muslim, in particular about America's involvement in Vietnam.

Like Pelé, Muhammed Ali has the royal conjunction of Jupiter and Saturn, but in his epoch chart. Pluto and Chiron are rising in the first clockwise house in both the epoch and birth charts, hermetic and geocentric. Geocentric Mars in the birth chart is high in the clockwise fourth house.

O. J. Simpson, birth and epoch in San Francisco. Birth July 9, 1947, at 8:08:00 PST. Epoch October 7, 1946, at 0:58:34 GMT.

O. J. Simpson, American football star, later accused of murder. He is now in prison (though for other offences).

The Saturn–Pluto conjunction (not a surprise that it appears in both the geocentric and hermetic charts of the epoch, as they move so slowly) rises in the first clockwise house and makes a T-square with the opposition of Mars in the epoch geocentric chart (etheric body) and Mars-Chiron in the hermetic birth chart ("I"). His fourfold being is also connected by four planets in Scorpio and Taurus, connected to one another by conjunction and opposition.

These are just a few examples. This requires further research, looking at more horoscopes. For example, it would be interesting to look at the horoscopes of those who are not so skilled with their bodies, to investigate whether they have connections between the epoch and birth, geocentric and hermetic charts.

Robert: It is clear that further research is needed, in order to come to clarity regarding the houses. Again, as suggested at the start of this article, Brian Gray's article published in last year's issue of this journal offers a good starting point regarding the question of the astrological houses (see reference 1), and also my booklet *History of the Houses* offers helpful indications, including (1) an outline of Michel Gauquelin's epoch-making research verifying the validity of the astrological houses, and (2) Rudolf Steiner's statement about the clockwise eurythmy zodiac (see reference 2). I use the expression "epoch-making" because the research of Michel Gauquelin, in collaboration with his first wife Françoise Schneider-Gauquelin, scientifically established the authenticity of the astrological houses.[13] This offers encouragement to all researchers in this field to investigate further what the truth underlying the astrological houses really is. Apart from the fundamental question as to whether the houses are to be counted in a clockwise or counterclockwise direction, the various methods of house division (Whole Sign, Equal House, Placidus, Topocentric, etc.) need to be investigated in terms of their validity, as well as the question as to whether the first house begins with the Ascendant or whether the Ascendant is regarded as delineating the middle of the first house.

This article is intended as a stimulus to encourage further research into the fundamental astrological reality of the houses, comprising the relationships of the Sun, Moon, and planets to the Earth, just as the other fundamental astrological reality is that of the positions of the Sun, Moon, and planets against the background of the zodiacal constellations (sidereal signs), comprising their relationships to the starry heavens. The third fundamental astrological reality is that of the relationships of the Sun, Moon, and planets to one another—known as the *astrological aspects*. Brian Gray's excellent article in the *Journal for Star Wisdom* 2012 goes into each of these three levels: zodiacal constellation/signs—planetary aspects—houses.

---

13 See http://en.wikipedia.org/wiki/Michel_Gauquelin, which offers an overview of the life and research of Michel Gauquelin, including a bibliography of his many books summarizing his research findings.

---

"The mission to which his birth called him [the birth of the Old Testament patriarch Jacob] was revealed to him through the realm of the angels...conscious perception of the angels came to him....The first stage...is attained when one enters conscious interaction with the beings of the angelic hierarchy.... [This] does not involve knowledge of universal laws, but entering conscious interaction with the beings who know the mysteries of birth. The true horoscope will not be reached by a path of calculation but through a path of interaction with suprasensory beings. What angels have imparted to humankind, that is the 'horoscope' in the true sense."
—Valentin Tomberg, *Christ and Sophia*, p. 47

# PATTERNS IN THE LANGUAGE OF THE STARS
## THE 2013 JUPITER-PLUTO OPPOSITION
## AND THE JUPITER RETURN OF 9/11

### *Claudia Mclaren Lainson*

The stars are the dwelling places for beings of the first hierarchy—Thrones, Cherubim and Seraphim. These are great and lofty beings who spiritually direct the course of evolution from their hallowed thrones on high. The planets carry their god-born messages in order to guide humanity and human affairs upon the Earth. Stars and planets live and teach in patterns that span decades, centuries, and even millennia. To follow these patterns through time helps us understand the spiritual guidance that is leading us along the path of love and wisdom reflecting the Hermetic axiom: As above, so also below.

An aspect is a particular angular relationship between two planets, or between a planet and a star. Over time, the various aspects create patterns of influence that affect our history. Through events in history, it can be revealed whether humanity has followed the divine influences issuing from the stellar patterns—or whether, instead, adversarial forces were allowed, through the passivity of human beings, to invert and corrupt these divine prophecies that serve to guide us along the arduous path of evolutionary progress.

An important aspect in 2013 is the opposition between Jupiter and Pluto on August 7, which will occur within 3° of the opposition that took place between these two planets at the Mystery of Golgotha. This opposition is coincident with the Jupiter return of the 9/11 event. Jupiter in her twelve-year orbit around the Sun will this year return to its location of September 11, 2001. These two stellar events contribute to a larger macrocosmic story that has been developing over the past thirteen years. To understand the potency of this year's events, it is helpful to place them into a greater context wherein we observe a whole series of planetary patterns that began in the year 2000.

To follow the movements of the stars and planets in this way since the beginning of the twenty-first century helps us understand the broad strokes of history. Each stellar event is like one piece in a multifaceted jigsaw puzzle. Imaginatively we can place these various pieces together to see what patterns are emerging that serve to sculpt the history of our time. This takes concentration and presence of mind, yet it is just these attributes that are now diminishing. For in our modern techno-culture we tend to fracture even meaningful events into mere twitters and bytes, which are limited to relentlessly serving our ephemeral awareness of news flashes—to the detriment of depth and interconnectivity. Patterns cannot be discerned in this manner.

The stars work through spatial relationships. Imagine space as an ocean of forces at rest. As the various angles and patterns, created by planetary aspects, cause movement within this ocean, forces are released into time. These forces are meant to become active within human beings on Earth. We can imagine that if these forces cannot be grasped by awakened human beings, they are then being spilled. We are the vessels through which these spiritual forces are to resound. Spilled forces can be seized by adversarial powers, whereby they are then used for agendas that work as caricatures of the beautiful intentions of creation. These stellar angles and patterns, ever newly being born into time, are holy messages from the star beings. Since the time of ancient Egypt we have been gradually forgetting the language the stars once spoke to us. Now, we live in a time when we must learn how to speak to the stars. Left to the spiritually bankrupt machinations of sciences that are ignorant of spirit, infrared forces are able to create what is indecent in the eyes of God, yet parade as wisdom in the eyes of human beings who have forgotten that there ever was a language in the stars. This leaves history vulnerable to subversive agendas. For there are black occult brotherhoods who do remember the ocean of forces at rest and the powers released when cosmic events activate these forces from their rest. The success of these brotherhoods is the result of diminished consciousness in human beings whose endless tracking of the pieces results in missing that which is perceivable in the cosmic patterns.

The adversaries who spawn subversive agendas are mighty fallen spirits. They know well the art of inversion. They work through human pawns infected with greed and raw ambition. With humanity thus increasingly distracted and disinterested, historical events can become "authored" by these fallen spirits—who do track the larger story, and are able to fashion history through their misuse of stellar forces. When cosmic forces fall into the hands of those who are pupils in the school of Ahriman, they are misused through inversions. Through inversion pain takes the place of pleasure, hatred takes the place of love, egoistic power takes the place of "Not my will, but thy will be done," and evil takes the place of good. Tutelage by Ahriman teaches the way of using the activity released by the ocean of forces at rest through insidious methodologies that work against divine creation.

Thus there is an entire spectrum of possibilities in every star message, from the highest to the lowest. The mid-point between the two is what we might call "ordinary reality"—the narrow region of visible light, above which is the ultraviolet and below which the infrared. Beneath the midpoint (the realm of visible light) the inversion occurs—in a way similar to how divine love becomes divine wrath, whereby the lofty star stories are grasped by forces that stand in direct opposition to the holy beings of the higher hierarchies who serve the source of all star wisdom—the Central Sun in the heart of the Milky Way. We collectively decide, as a society and through either activity or apathy, what will be done with the possibilities the stars proclaim in their constant communion with the Earth.

The apparent duality of ultraviolet and infrared, which assumes every frequency in between, is in reality one continuum upon which the same force can manifest in various ways. Therefore this is an imagination for full spectrum possibilities within one continuum. Here Newton's third law of motion applies (every action has an equal and opposite reaction), as does Einstein's theory of parallel universes.[1] For the purpose of this article, the spectral terms used here refer to heaven-born ultraviolet, and ahrimanically inverted infrared. In the space between is the world in which human beings stand as the connecting link between the heights and the depths. It is in this middle realm that Christ is working, and just as he was in constant union with the stars at his first coming, so is he now in constant communion with the stars at this time of his second coming. His presence can help us reawaken to the wisdom streaming from the starry worlds. In this in-between place where humanity lives, good simply *is!* The battle between evils rage around us, but, in the last analysis, all we are asked to do is to take up the good; for if the good is taken up, evil has no place in the world. The battle for the human soul is apparent. We are encouraged to live into, and embody our wholeness, through uniting with the in-streaming revelation born from the ultraviolet spheres of the great star beings. To ignore this taking up of divine light would result in entire cultures falling prey to the dark beings and their brilliant agendas of deception. Understanding the patterned language of the stars, however, alerts humanity to the nature of forces that are being released from the ocean of forces at rest in the ultraviolet realms. This awareness provides spiritual guidance.

Since the beginning of the twenty-first century some of the major aspects between the planets have been the Jupiter-Saturn conjunction and oppositions, the Saturn-Uranus opposition, and the Jupiter-Uranus conjunction. Also of note was

---

1 Einstein helped discover the Einstein-Rosen Bridge, the area at the singularity of a rotating black hole, where one can cross into a parallel universe.

the crossing of Pluto three times, in 2010, over its exact location at the third temptation of Christ in the wilderness.[1]

### *Pluto over the Third Temptation*

During this period of transits that echoed the third temptation (from January 2010 through mid-November 2010), there were the Pakistan floods and the eruption of Eyjafjallajökull, as well as three significant earthquakes—in Haiti, in Chile, and in the Yushu region of China. Directly following the last Pluto transit over this degree, the Arab Spring began in December of 2010. As the third temptation was the temptation to turn stones into bread, we may imagine the earthquakes, volcanoes, and floods as offering a picture of how the Earth and her elemental beings respond when human beings invert the star stories. In lectures on the manifestation of karma, Rudolf Steiner remarked on the connection between human beings' immorality and the Earth's natural disasters. This link is not one of a punitive God, but one wherein the Earth must release the toxicity of aberrant human astral forces. These messages of the starry heavens can be viewed as the Earth's sacraments. Christ's answer to the third temptation was: Man does not live by bread alone, but by every word that issues from the mouth of God. The rampant disharmony that is wreaking havoc on the Earth is evidence that those dictating the course of human affairs, whether it be through politics, economics, or cultural indoctrination, are not serving as connecting links between Heaven and Earth, but are instead passively allowing, or even actively pursuing, agendas that are representative of the insatiable hunger of the serpent who endlessly toils to cause the human body and soul to become mechanized. This is the ahrimanic threat. This is a picture of turning what is living into that which is dead; and turning what is dead into what is living. Ahriman speaks to Christ during the last temptation:

> Look at the dead earthly phenomena, the stones; they can come to life as bread if you only command them to do so. They will become as bread because, from the Earth's interior, I can supply a lifelike force to all dead matter. You must simply will what is dead to live.

Here it is clear that Ahriman uses the will of human beings as he once sought to use the will of Christ. His use of our will forces allows him to create in our world. Ahriman is causing that which is dead to appear living (virtual realities and beyond), and he is causing that which is living (our etheric bodies and our seeds) to become dead. Three times this temptation was magnified in 2010 as Pluto transited this place where it was during the third temptation. We can see these aspects as the calling card of ahrimanic powers. For the memory of this temptation was inscribed into the zodiac at this degree, and it is this memory that is activated as Pluto, in particular, returns again to this place in the heavens. We are to keep in mind that when historic memories are activated by planetary movements, they call into action what is there being remembered. The success of the third temptation will continue to grow to the extent we allow this to happen. For the more we engage in altering nature's archetypes (as done in GMOs or weather modification), or through excessive exposure (especially in childhood) to the virtual worlds, the more we accommodate Ahriman's creation of an alternate world to the world of divine creation.

Pluto's transit over this degree of the third temptation in the wilderness was, and continues to be, a clarion call for all humanity. What so long ago was the temptation of Christ alone has now become the continuation of the temptation to turn stones into bread for all of humanity. This temptation has everything to do with money and the exploitation of the natural world. Another example of Ahriman's success in achieving his third temptation is the Gulf oil spill that began with the explosion of the British Petroleum offshore oil-drilling rig Deepwater Horizon on April 20, 2010, causing an extraordinary amount of damage to the environment. Here oil was extracted from the depths of the ocean under exceedingly difficult and dangerous circumstances. GMOs and dangerous drilling practices are examples of insatiable hunger for power, profit, and control of resources.

---

1 See Powell and Dann, *Christ and the Maya Calendar,* chap. 2, "The Apocalypse Code."

Beginning in 2008, and overlapping in 2010 with this Pluto transit over the third temptation, were the oppositions of Saturn–Uranus.

## Saturn–Uranus

Saturn-Uranus oppositions happen approximately every forty-four years. In the twentieth century these two planets came into opposition between 1917 and 1920, and later between 1964 and 1967. WWI and the Bolshevik Revolution dominated the first period of opposition. The second period was dominated by the US Civil Rights movement (led by Dr. Martin Luther King), the Vietnam War protests, and—shortly past the opposition—the Six-Day War between Israel and Arab nations. These events testify to the upheavals and transformations possible during this particular aspect. The last periods of conjunctions between the two planets occurred in 1942 and again in 1988. The year 1942 was dominated by the events of World War II, and 1988 saw technology preparing for the World Wide Web that would transform cultures. In this same year, Congress funded the Human Genome Project, a massive effort to map and sequence the human genetic code as well as the genomes of other species.

An entire spectrum of possibilities open with each and every stellar pattern. To read the gesture developing in history, one is urged to notice what general proclivity is manifesting against the background of historic memories. This informs us as to the nature of the spectrum (ultraviolet or infrared) being played out globally; and it reveals whether we are in communion with divine spiritual beings or, inversely, dark adversarial beings. Individuals are to perceive their own truths. The danger comes when it seems no one notices anything.

In the twenty-first century, between November 2008 and July 2010, there were five oppositions of Saturn and Uranus. An example of the ultraviolet spectrum of this aspect is Padre Pio receiving the five wounds of the stigmata on September 20, 1918. In their oppositions these planets tend to manifest by calling forth new, radically unconventional and higher intelligence (Uranus) that inherently wants to break free from the conformity of the past—in opposition to the long-established, conventional, and stoic (Saturn) patterns of rule. Padre Pio's experience of opening to a new light, and the forming of the organ of the will (stigmata) that could receive the light, gestures this aspect's grace. In a similar fashion we can imagine the release of illumination helping human beings of good will to conscientiously open to the light of new imaginations, and then forming this light into deeds of spirit-willed action. Inversely, old paradigms may push through, exerting the will-to-power. Just prior to the first opposition came the banking crash of September 2008, followed by the exact opposition on November 4, 2008—which was the Election Day for the US President Barack Obama. Also in this aspect, the young soldier Adolf Hitler was poisoned by mustard gas on the battlefields of World War I (October 15, 1918) and then slipped into a coma. When he recovered, his friends observed that he was another person, with enhanced power and diminished morality. These events give further evidence of the influences particular to this aspect. These two planets remained in close opposition through the inauguration of the US President in 2009.

The next exact opposition was on February 5, 2009. This date was marked by the inception of the Tea Party Movement. One year later, Sarah Palin would deliver the keynote address at the first Tea Party Convention in Nashville, where some 600 people were in attendance. In her speech she claimed: "America is ready for another revolution." It is sometimes the case that apparently rival streams are used in the pretense of fighting against each other. This may on the surface appear real, even to those fighting. It can also be true that such conflicts are used by those with dark agendas in order to achieve their predetermined goals. That is, extremist points of view can serve to turn conflicting people unwittingly into the arms of the one who has all along been the intended favorite. Revolution is certainly an attribute of Uranus; and the Tea Party was, and is, a party of revolution, utilizing the American iconic event of throwing British tea into the Boston Harbor as a prelude to the American Revolution. By the time of the final opposition between Saturn and Uranus, on July

26, 2010, the new American President (Obama) was settling into the White House while mounting opposition to him from the Tea Party continued to gain influence. The banking debacle—called by some a great and ominous coup—had changed the world of finance. Causing great harm to millions of people throughout the world, it threw many nations into economic downturns that continue to undermine the very existence of a middle class, as well as threaten the viability of the European Union and the euro community in particular.

As Pluto transited the third temptation, and Saturn-Uranus remembered various dramatic events in recent history (the Bolshevik Revolution, the Civil Rights movement, Vietnam War protests, Israeli Arab conflicts, world wars, explosions in technology, Padre Pio, Hitler, and Obama's election) the great conjunction between Jupiter and Saturn arched high above in its twenty-year cycle, outpacing these shorter cycles as it stretched its long arm of influence toward 2020.

### Jupiter–Saturn

Conjunctions between Jupiter and Saturn, which take place every twenty years, are called great conjunctions. The Jupiter-Saturn cycle is the longest cycle that doesn't involve any of the outermost planets (Uranus, Neptune, or Pluto[2]). These conjunctions set the tone for widespread social change, generational themes, cultural conditions and social interaction. As the last great conjunction—on May 28, 2000—happened in Aries (the first of the zodiacal signs, which actively forms the human head), it proclaimed innovation and new leadership born of high ideals. It asked for cooperation between peoples in respect for differences that would otherwise tend to provoke them against each other. It called for the light of wisdom to shine into communities; for communities to form around new ideals; for the awakening to moral laws that would be protective of the Earth and her elemental beings; and for obedience toward the way of peace in all kingdoms of the Earth. It was the onset of a new millennium and a time for new beginnings.[3]

These twenty-year great conjunctions of Jupiter and Saturn have periods of waxing and waning. For ten years, the efforts toward attaining the "stellar possibility" of the conjunction expand, giving loft to new wings of hope, leading up to the period of the opposition between them. Then, for another ten years, the outcomes of how humankind has used the broad spectrum of stellar possibilities contracts into form. The ideal is that progressive change will have truly occurred through the activity of those who are in alignment with the divine will of the stars and the preciousness of the Earth's intended destiny. Ultimately, the collective/cultural use of the stars' energy patterns, inscribed in planetary cycles, creates the world in which we dwell. Whether we create peace and harmony depends on whether humanity has used the higher spectrums of stellar possibilities. Alternatively, tyrants (negative Jupiter) and oppressors (negative Saturn) invert the star energies, laming the wings of hope and instead creating havoc in the kingdoms of nature and in human affairs on Earth. During the first ten years, Jupiter reigns over Saturn—it has a "leading" role. After this, Saturn forces tend to dominate. Jupiter is expansive; Saturn contractive. Then, after this twenty-year period of waxing and waning has elapsed, a new great conjunction occurs. The next great conjunction between Jupiter and Saturn will take place in 2020, in the constellation of Capricorn.

From 2000 through 2011, Jupiter called for several things: expansion from constrictions, optimism toward new paradigms, the struggle for human freedom, and new opportunities in community. From 2012 to 2020, Saturn influences will dominate. Kronos (Saturn), the father of Zeus (Jupiter), is known to have swallowed his offspring as they were born. Will there be more restrictions on liberty? Will there be far-greater economic trials, fear, a turning against civilians by

---

2 Even though Pluto has been declassified and assigned a "dwarf planet" status, there is evidence of Pluto's continued planetary-like influence as exemplified in the life of Christ, and through the work of various researchers. For these reasons the author recognizes Pluto as a planetary influence.

3 See Powell, "The Cosmic Beginning of the New Millennium," *Christian Star Calendar 2000* (now at sophiafoundation.org).

the governments appointed to protect them? Will authorities and subjugates, oppressors and rebels continue to clash? Will the strong arm of oppression squeeze the life out of Jupiter's optimism?

Are we to become like Zeus and use thunderbolts and lightning in our striving toward the achievement of wisdom? We have seen much of the expansion through 2011. Now we stand as historical witnesses to the dominating Saturn forces of the waning years. Was the hope offered in the last several years real? Or was it all a clever guise leading freedom into the jealous mouth of Kronos, who indeed will swallow his children whole? Alternatively, Saturn can be thought of as a portal to the realm of our Heavenly Father. This is a portal we are to open, for it creates a flow of inspiration guiding us to apply the proper measure of restraint that apportions judiciousness to expansion—thus taming what can become inflated. In the upcoming Pluto opposition to Jupiter, which can be read in the light of the influence of this twenty-year Jupiter–Saturn cycle, we will be asked: Have we opened the higher portal to the Father, thus becoming vessels for the divine principles of spiritual guidance (ultraviolet Pluto), or have we instead ignored the wonder-filled possibilities and unleashed destructive forces by opening the gates of Hell (infrared Pluto)? This is a tricky slope. We are living in extreme times and the middle way is no longer what it once appeared to be. Choices are being called for. Not a yes, no, or maybe, but a bold statement that is punctuated with "I will" do this or that. Humanity is in the process of achieving its fullness as the tenth hierarchy—the hierarchy of freedom. We are free to accept or reject the guidance from spiritual worlds. Not to choose opens the possibility that we are silently chosen, through passivity, or disinterest.

Less than one month before this first Jupiter-Saturn opposition, the 2010 Gulf Oil Spill occurred. (This was also 6 days before the fourth Saturn–Uranus opposition.) Shortly before the last opposition, there occurred the Christchurch earthquake (February 2011) as well as the Japanese earthquake and tsunami (March 2011). The seriousness of the nuclear disaster in Japan has (to date) been underreported and continues to threaten the Earth and her inhabitants. Rudolf Steiner refers to the sixth sub-earthly sphere as a layer containing unharnessed passions, a layer that reacts strongly to excesses of human will. It can push through into physical forces such as earthquakes, tsunamis, and volcanic eruptions. Ahriman predominates in this sixth sphere, which is also known as the Fire Earth. An imbalance between human and divine will agitates this sub-earthly region. Then, shortly after this last opposition between Jupiter and Saturn, was the severe tornado outbreak (considered to be the deadliest on record) in the southern US in 2011. According to data from the Storm Prediction Center, the number of preliminary tornado reports during March of 2012 was over 270 percent of the average monthly count. Extreme fires, heat, floods, and droughts continued through the summer of 2012.

Taking the start of the current millennium as a beginning point, the great conjunction of 2000 between Jupiter and Saturn in Aries was quite significant in that it proclaimed a keynote for the following twenty years, which are now more than halfway past. This great conjunction heralded a new Christ-like leadership and asked us to found communities that are devoted to the Earth, communities replete with a wisdom-filled response to the tragedies occurring within nature. We have seen a rise in teachings of peace and equality, along with the cultivation of radically new ideas and the fostering of ideals of collaboration and togetherness. On other fronts, however, we have seen the opposite: oppressive tyrants, reckless greed, losses of civil liberties, detainment without representation, decisions that support corporations as beings, and weather anomalies that define the utter chaos we are all seeing in nature. Where will we be led as the contracting forces of Saturn become more dominant? Will the motives rising from the infrared spectrums, as inversions to divine inspirations, take precedent over the ultraviolet spectrums of truth?

Saturn is the keeper of cosmic memory. We are wise to serve the memory of our divine origins. We are spiritual beings striving to realize the magnificence of being truly human. This necessitates that we find the will to confront evil. Christ overcame death; we are to overcome evil through the power invested in us through his sacrifice. It will be through Christ that we achieve our rightful rank of becoming the tenth hierarchy. Morality is key.

Human morality is a state of being wherein the individual is in alignment with the divine powers of love and peace. This is alignment with the upper ultraviolet spectrums of possibility. From this active mode of participation, we can become co-creators in the spiritually directed evolution of the Earth. To lose this moral high ground could cause us to fall into the increasingly prevalent worlds that are being created as an alternative reality to evolution as it is divinely ordained. All planetary aspects can manifest goodness, and each aspect also has its inverted equivalent. Infinite possibilities can be chosen. The spiritual beings guiding our evolution send initiates into time in order that new capacities can be developed. High initiates are the Great Teachers who achieve capacities during their lives on Earth that are thereafter to be modeled by us, so as to become our individual capacities. We are all seeking initiation into the secrets of evolution. We stand in the middle with Christ. What will we do?

The stellar conjunction between Jupiter and Saturn in 2000 occurred exactly where Venus was at the death of Novalis—a poet whose heart was attuned to Sophia. This points to a resonance with this conjunction, between the love of Sophia and her Mother in the depths of the Earth; and it is John who is the guardian of the Sophia mysteries. In his Last Address, Rudolf Steiner promised that the John being would be with us at the end of the twentieth century to help us through the great challenge we would then be facing.[4] The John being is John the Baptist (who was the reincarnation of the prophet Elijah, who later reincarnated as Raphael and later still as Novalis); he is a guide for all communities striving to accomplish what this conjunction has proclaimed. Just as John was the one who recognized Christ at his first coming, so, too, will communities working with him be those that recognize Christ in his Second Coming in the Earth's etheric realm.

Who are the teachers summoned by this great conjunction? They are Christ, as the Lamb of God sounding forth from Aries; Sophia, as the Bride of the Lamb resurrecting from the poetry of Novalis; and John, who is one of our most powerful leaders in this time of dire trial. John the Baptist was beheaded by one of the dark masters of illusionary deception, and we are cautioned to keep our heads and hold fast to our crowns—for sovereignty alone will allow us to see the truth masked by the morass of glittering deceptions through which we must travel. Christ, Sophia and John were implicitly called forth by this last great conjunction of Jupiter and Saturn in Aries in May 2000, under whose auspices we are still working. It will take Michaelic thinking and knightly courage to realize the new mysteries this conjunction promised. Such is the work of communities who recognize the star-mandate that spreads its influence over two decades of human history. Opponents will fight against the stars, but this will not hinder those who receive their messages and live in accordance with their highborn revelation. Communities gathering in the name of freedom and in obedience to the higher octaves sounding from the stars are the ones laying the foundations leading to the sixth cultural epoch and beyond. We are to follow this path in spite of the cacophony of those laying down a different path that would lead us deeper into the belly of the beast, where culture itself is being torn to pieces in the divisive fires of fragmentation. Freedom on all fronts is to be vigilantly protected, while compassion and love for nature and the Earth are to become the focus of our devotion.

Our freedom is our most precious possession. Each of us is a spark from the one divine flame of love. Each of us is free either to manifest the fullness of who we are, or to squander this through falling into the trap of egoism. Egoism is the signature of communion with the lower spectrums of light. For it is the altruistic light of love that

---

[4] See Rudolf Steiner's "Last Address" (*Karmic Relationships*, vol. 4); also Powell, *Elijah Come Again*.

streams into human beings and their communities when in selflessness we are willing to suffer the pain of others and the pain of the Earth herself. This willingness to suffer calls forth divine inspiration. This is the teaching of the second Beatitude: Blessed are they who mourn, for they shall find comfort.

Are we being prepared for something? It seems this may indeed be the case. We stand at a new turning point in time. It is a time when we may either turn to the stars or miss the illumined path stretching out before us. If the stars have indeed decreed the opening of something new, then we are prudent to wake up to what is actually being proclaimed.

[Since] 2000, we are living in the new period ushered in by the conjunction of Jupiter and Saturn on May 28 of that year—a twenty-year period that promises to be perhaps the most significant in the entire history of the human race. For, as indicated in the *Christian Star Calendar 2002*, all the indications are that it will be during this twenty-year period that the incarnation of the Antichrist,[5] prophesied in the thirteenth chapter of the Book of Revelation, will take place.[6]

The temptation of the will-to-power is evident in the infrared. The ability to take up "Not my will, but thy will be done" is the choice before us, and the stars are our guide.

☙

As we observe what has been established with the sounding in of ultraviolet stellar decrees over the past thirteen years, we witness also the opposite (infrared) to be true. In so many ways freedom is not increasing—it is being stolen. The justification for the stealing of personal and civil liberties is fear—fear of terrorists, disease, different cultures, unpredictable climate changes—and even fear of one another. This state-of-fear vastly accelerated with the event of September 11, 2001. The Jupiter return of that event coincides with this year's opposition between Pluto and Jupiter. Two weeks before the event of 9/11, Jupiter was at the same position (14° Gemini) in which it will be during this year's opposition with Pluto on August 7. At that time the planning of that fateful event would have been in full swing.

The event of 9/11 occurred less than two years after the great conjunction of May 28, 2000. An inversion of what is Christ-like was there evident: instead of one dying for the good of all, many died for the will of one. Whose will this one was is a matter of different opinions. What we know is that it was not the will of The One. Metaphorically speaking, with the twin towers of the World Trade Center of the western financial and commercial empire knocked down, we could have looked compassionately across the great water—and questioned ourselves. Instead, we went to war. We could have stayed with the first effects of the horrible disaster, where people were uniting and hearts were bursting open. Instead of seeing the log in our own eye, however, we brought out the flags and raised our fists against our neighbors, casting off our own shadows and turning our backs on the brotherly/sisterly love that was blossoming out of the tears being spilled around the world. Within a month we (along with NATO) invaded Afghanistan, and in less than three years afterward (in March 2003) we unleashed "shock and awe" as the US struck a preemptive war against Iraq and her people. A precious opportunity was not only wasted, but these actions have unfortunately caused further division within our global family.

There has been much evidence that the infrared has been creating its caricature of evolution over these last few years. In April of 2003 the US government called back all non-essential personnel in their consulate office in Hong Kong and Guangzhou due to the spreading of the SARS (severe acute respiratory syndrome) breakout. Shortly thereafter Saturn marked its return to its position during the birth of the Nathan Jesus child (1° Gemini). Disease is the inversion to the work of the world redeemer. In March 2004, the Madrid commuter rail system was bombed. On December 26, 2004, the Asian earthquake and tsunami

---

5  The use of this term here refers to the incarnation of Ahriman.
6  Powell, *Christian Star Calendar 2003*.

hit, killing hundreds of thousands of people. In 2005 came the July bombings in London; soon after that, hurricane Katrina came, followed a few months later by the Kashmir earthquake.

In 2008, as the Saturn–Uranus influence began, the Nargis cyclone and the Sichuan earthquake occurred in May, followed by more Mumbai attacks in July and the astounding banking crash in September. Soon afterward, the US presidential election culminated. In 2009, we witnessed the inauguration of Barack Obama as well as the longest solar eclipse of the twenty-first century (with Pluto at the exact same place as it was at the baptism of Christ in the River Jordan). This was followed by the fear of H1N1. Then, in 2010, we were approaching the three oppositions to the 2000 great conjunction—along with the Jupiter–Uranus conjunctions, the Pluto transits to the third temptation, and the last two oppositions between Saturn–Uranus. Many aspects were working together and much was afoot!

In January 2010, the Supreme Court ruled to allow corporations personhood status, whereby they were freed to spend without limit in political campaigns (Citizens United). Many felt, and still feel, that this decision was the undoing of democracy. This ruling occurred when the stars were remembering the Adoration of the Magi. For what kind of king does this ruling make way? When the Occupy Wall Street Movement (OWS) swept through the US in 2011, protesting the 1%—the privileged children of the giants (the corporations)—the 99% were dubbed a public nuisance and their camps were bulldozed. It remains to be seen what will be the final chapter of this story. Is protest still allowed in the twenty-first century democracy of the United States? Under the influence of Jupiter opposed Saturn, and Saturn opposed Uranus in 2010, we also saw the Gulf Oil Spill disaster. What is the message? Is gutting the Earth of her life-blood our way forward? Or are there new solutions, as these planetary stories are suggesting? Was the spill the picture of the true cost of refusing to change our ways?

2010 and 2011 were dynamic years among the stars involving Jupiter, Uranus, Saturn, and Pluto.

There are many different ways to interpret any planetary aspect. Could the Pluto transit have been asking if we were truly treating each other, as well as the Earth and her flora and fauna, in ways aligned with the Word of God? Did the Saturn–Uranus opposition ask if our laws, economic systems, and governments were aligned with new imaginations? Were the oppositions of Jupiter and Saturn asking if we had indeed created new communities in alignment with Christ and Sophia? Moreover, was the Jupiter–Uranus conjunction in Pisces asking if we had harmoniously infused these communities with the new revelation coming toward us from the future, welcoming into them new octaves of love?[7]

Also in the years 2010 and 2011, Pluto was opposite its position at the Bolshevik Revolution in Russia.[8] At that time there were floods, cyclones, earthquakes, a nuclear disaster, as well as dreadful tornadoes and other weather anomalies. Osama bin Laden was declared dead, Muammar Gaddafi was killed, and the Iraq war was formally declared over. We witnessed that instead of one country going into revolution, as was the case in the Bolshevik Revolution, parts of the entire globe entered revolution through the Arab Spring and its reverberations throughout the world. With the Saturn–Uranus opposition and the Jupiter-Uranus conjunction (whose signature can be community revolution) also influencing world events, we must ask: What stands behind these revolutions?

At the very onset of 2012 forming forces were beginning. The president signed the highly controversial NDAA bill (National Defense Authorization Act), allowing indefinite detention without charge, thus nullifying the Bill of Rights. Most people seem to have no idea that this has been signed into law. Other civil rights abuses occurred as well, including the possible use of the military against its own citizens. There was also news of an NSA (National Security Agency) Utah Database that is part of a secret NSA surveillance program,

---

7 See Bento, "Contemplations on the Jupiter–Uranus Conjunction," *Journal for Star Wisdom 2010*.

8 See Powell, "The Arising of a Revolutionary Mood in 2010/2011"; http://steinerbooks.org/detail.html?&id=9781584201113.

code-named (interestingly) "Stellar Wind." We came to realize that the NSA has established listening posts throughout the country to collect, store, and examine billions of email messages and phone calls, thereby gathering nearly unlimited data from citizens. In 2012 we also experienced the first election of a US President through corporate funded super-PACs, and received news of the Supreme Court's decision that allowed strip searches for even minor offenses. Moreover, on March 16, 2012, the president signed into effect the National Defense Resources Preparedness Executive Order, the scope of which allows an all-encompassing seizure of US infrastructure, as well as providing for the mobilization of "labor" for the purposes of national defense. On July 6, 2012, another executive order was signed into law authorizing the seizing of communication systems (Assignment of National Security and Emergency Preparedness Communications Functions). On July 20, 2012, a massacre at a Colorado movie complex took place at the opening of the movie The Dark Knight Rises. At this killing spree the Sun was 4° Cancer. When Saturn was at this degree Christ taught the significance of the word Amen:

> This morning Jesus ended his teachings on prayer with a talk on the significance of the word Amen. Jesus received an invitation to go to Bethsaida-Julias. On the way, he went to an inn where the Holy Virgin and some of the holy women were waiting for him. Mary was downcast and begged Jesus not to go to Jerusalem for the Feast of the Dedication of the Temple. Jesus comforted her, saying that he would complete the work of his Father, and that she should be courageous and should strengthen and encourage the others. Jesus and the disciples then continued on to Bethsaida-Julias. There he dined with the Pharisees. That evening, he taught in the synagogue.[9]

As the stars remembered this strong teaching, releasing cosmic memories from the ocean of cosmic forces at rest, a lone gunman appeared before the screen of a perversely violent virtual imagination, The Dark Knight Rises, and killed at least a dozen people, wounding fifty-eight others. Here is evident the contrast between Christ and Antichrist. The Amen is the antidote to possession, and this murderer was certainly possessed. In following the Christ memory of July 20 we can work with Christ in order to assist in completing the work of the Father. We can be courageous and help others. We can dine with those holding views that are intrinsically cold as were the hearts of the Pharisees so long ago, but we are not to commiserate with them, for out of their ranks may rise a Dark Knight.

This massacre also occurred where the Sun was at the longest eclipse of the twenty-first century, when Pluto stood at its Baptism degree. Then Christ entered Jesus. Who entered the wretched being of massacre as the Sun remembered this eclipse? This event offers an example of how the aspecting stars awaken memories, and how the inversion to these memories can be enacted through human beings who are possessed by dark beings. We are living in Grail times, and Grail times prepare us for apocalyptic events.

Two days after the Colorado event marked the anniversary of the Norway massacre of 2011. We can only wonder what part technology and graphic sex and violence play in disintegrating a human "I" to such a breaking point. According to the Wall Street Journal more than half of all young children in the US have access to an iPad, iPhone, or other touchscreen device; and the iPad is predicted to be the children's toy of the year. Apps for children are accelerating at break-neck speed. This heralds an unpredictable cultural phenomenon.

Are we prepared to create change? Where are we working to preserve decency in our culture? Are we witnessing the current events that are affecting our children, our freedom, and our democracy in these waning years of the great conjunction that are now upon us?

I have covered here only some of the notable events of the past thirteen years. I do not mean this article to be exhaustive, but rather that it offer some perspective on several of the puzzle pieces

---

9  *Chron.*, p. 306.

which together depict a pattern reveals what is being put into place.[10]

☙

We can now look at the upcoming opposition between Jupiter and Pluto on August 7th of this year, as well as the Jupiter return of the 9/11 event. As Jupiter at 9/11 was exactly conjunct its position at the Mystery of Golgotha, our response could have been different following the example of Christ, who said from the cross: Father forgive them, for they know not what they do. This is an attitude we are all wise to practice. As it turned out, neither those attacking, nor those reacting to the attack, were aware of what they knew not. The consequence of ignorance casts a long shadow in the ledgers of history.

At the Mystery of Golgotha, the community of Ancient Israel became, in a certain sense, the community of Eternal Israel.[11] The community of Eternal Israel is not a community born of nations or race, but rather here refers to a community born of all individuals of all nations and races, who serve love and peace. The leader of this community was, and is, Jesus Christ—who at the turning point in time, at his death on the cross, became the spirit of the Earth. At his death on the cross, Pluto stood at 17½° Sagittarius, opposite Jupiter 17½° Gemini. This year's opposition between Pluto and Jupiter occurs within 3° of the opposition between these two planets at the Mystery of Golgotha. In the higher spectrums of the ultraviolet, the stellar script over the past thirteen years has summoned those who seek to heal the Earth, who love freedom, and who serve within their communities in the spirit of brotherly/sisterly love. These are communities working with new imaginations of collaboration and stewardship of the Earth, preserving and renewing her resources, who strive to reinstate worldwide moral economics.[12] In the lower spectrums of the infrared, the macro star story has been inverted. Greed and power inspire tyrannical agendas, which compete to take possession of resources—including food, money, and (dare I say it?) souls.

At this upcoming opposition of Jupiter and Pluto, Jupiter will be where it was at the Raising of Lazarus. Pluto will be exactly opposite to where it was when Joseph Stalin took up the position of General Secretary of the Communist Party of the Soviet Union's Central Committee (April 1922)—a position he held from 1922 until his death in 1953. Also opposite this year's Plutonian influence, Mussolini formed a fascist government in Italy, Gandhi was sentenced to six years in prison for civil disobedience, and the Soviet states merged into the USSR. Will we raise ourselves from the dead, or will lower Pluto influences further enslave us? Jupiter is remembering not only the Raising of Lazarus, but also the appointment of Stalin in the USSR. These events depict two different forms the Jupiter forces can express: freedom in community with Christ, or oppressions born of entering the community of the Antichrist (here this term refers to Ahriman).

As Pluto faces off with Jupiter, therefore, communities will also be facing a choice—one given to those who are willing to act. T. S. Eliot wrote his poem *The Wasteland* when Pluto was opposite the degree it will occupy during this year's opposition. It is a poetic description of the fate of those who have lost their hope in the face of oppression from both within and without:

> Unreal City,
> Under the brown fog of a winter dawn,
> A crowd flowed over London Bridge, so many,
> I had not thought death had undone so many,
> Sighs, short and infrequent, were exhaled,
> And each man fixed his eyes before his feet.
> Flowed up the hill and down King William Street,
> To where Saint Mary Woolnoth kept the hours
> With a dead sound on the final stroke of nine.

---

10 As this article was submitted for publication in July of 2012, further contemporary events could not be included. Readers are free to find their independent associations by using the *Journal for Star Wisdom*.

11 The term *Eternal Israel* here denotes the spiritual community of those people choosing to collaborate in the spiritual development of humanity. It in no way reflects any religious or national grouping. This community is devoted to the creation of the "New Jerusalem" mentioned in Revelation 21.

12 See Taft, *Stewardship: Lessons Learned from the Lost Culture of Wall Street*.

There I saw one I knew, and stopped him,
    crying "Stetson!
You who were with me in the ships at Mylae!
That corpse you planted last year in your garden,
Has it begun to sprout? Will it bloom this year?
Or has the sudden frost disturbed its bed?
Oh keep the Dog far hence, that's friend to men,
Or with his nails he'll dig it up again!
You! hypocrite lecteur!—mon semblable—
    mon frere!"

## *The Jupiter–Pluto Opposition*

Jupiter, the planet of wisdom, is an influence that grants the talent to bring order out of chaos, to see the higher Michaelic thoughts behind the little thoughts that tend to entrap us. It is also a planet representing the wisdom of Sophia—whose mantle is the entire starry heavens. The influence of Jupiter inspires us to create communities with benevolent goals and a deep respect for freedom. The tyrannical inversion to Jupiter's benevolence is evident in high places. With Jupiter standing opposite Pluto in August this year, we are being asked to discern whose will we are serving. Pluto has two faces: Phanes and Hades. Phanes is "ultraviolet" Pluto. It is the divine will of our Father. Hades is "infrared" Pluto. It is the personal will—often unwittingly united with sub-earthly power. Humanity is being asked to choose which spectrum of possibilities we will serve. Humanity is also being asked whether tyranny or justice will be the keynote of our societies. Will we allow ourselves to be raised from the dead constriction of materialism, as was Lazarus raised from the dead by Christ when Jupiter was so close to this degree? Or will Plutonian, Stalinistic dictatorships crush the emerging visionary ideals benevolently sounding from the wisdom-filled sphere of Jupiter? The ultraviolet spectrums of Jupiter and Phanes are calling us to unite in love.

Just as Christ founded the community of Eternal Israel and had to face the opposition of Hades at his first coming, so too are these communities of Eternal Israel again facing Pluto and having to decide whom they will follow at this time of the Second Coming. Hades stands in direct opposition to the mission of Christ and new leadership, whereas Phanes stands in union with the mission of Christ and new leadership. We stand between the two in freedom. Will we engage in the aggression of the will-to-power? Will we collaborate by participating in "Not my will but thy will be done?" Or will we surrender to the will of those who want us to do their will, which opens us to possession? What will we see gathering in the world as this opposition draws near? We must remain awake!

## *The Jupiter Return of 9/11*

Twelve years ago, when Jupiter was at 17° Gemini on September 11, 2001, America was faced with an inconceivable attack. No one had a concept for airplanes as weapons. The destruction of the World Trade Center was shocking to the entire free world. And because of this deed of terror, freedom has been lost, and continues to be lost. Therefore, the question confronts us: Are we becoming those we are fighting against?

Jupiter returns to its exact location at 9/11 on August 19, 2013 (at 16°50 Gemini—conjunct Jupiter's position at the Mystery of Golgotha). This is twelve days after the opposition between Jupiter and Pluto (14°26 Gemini) on August 7. Less than 3° will separate the exact Jupiter return of 9/11 from its position at the opposition to Pluto on August 7, 2013. This differential is small enough to create a significant influence connecting the 9/11 event with this opposition. Therefore, Jupiter will be remembering September 11, 2001, as well as Christ's death and resurrection, the dictatorships of Stalin and Mussolini, and the saintly example of Gandhi's life. During this time, Pluto will be remembering the full spectrum of the Mystery of Golgotha as the promise of the victory of good over evil. For communities forming around what the 2000 great conjunction heralded, a renewed determination to work positively, collaboratively, and in freedom will be ignited in souls and spirits of good will. For communities forming around nationalism, fear, and revenge, the result will be greater tyranny and diminishing freedoms. We are indeed witnesses to historical events, and the stellar script can assist us in understanding what is at stake. Jupiter will be asking what we have done with 9/11. Are we applying the wisdom of Michaelic thinking in the world? Or has fear, and the loss of hope, caused us to ignore the suffering of others? Have we bought into propaganda whereby we passively believe the deceptive spin of corporate media? Are we turning toward the outer world in search of one who can save us? We will not find our true leader in the outer world! Rather we are to look to our own heart, for herein lives the One this opposition is remembering as Jupiter returns to its position at the Mystery of Golgotha.

On the surface it appears we are headed in the wrong direction in the US, as is evidenced through the work of political agendas, economic inequality, Supreme Court decisions, and heinous manipulations of nature. In the name of safety, freedom is being replaced with travesties against civil rights, including implementation of surveillance systems. There is work to be done and consciousness must be directed to understanding the larger picture in order for us to participate conscientiously while we still can in the authorship of our future.

Uranus at 17° Pisces will be square (within 3°) to this opposition between Jupiter and Pluto. Uranus at 17° Pisces is exactly square to the Golgotha opposition between Jupiter and Pluto. Uranus at this same degree also saw Russian peasants staging thousands of revolts against Stalin's collectivization that had resulted in the deaths of millions (March 1930). Also during this time, Hitler was mesmerizing the German people with frenzied speeches that would lead to the election of the Nazi Party. Moreover, in America, the crash of 1929 was brewing and poor agricultural practices were setting up conditions that would contribute to the Dust Bowl. The grasses that once covered the prairie lands for centuries were being eliminated by the unwise practices of mechanized farming.

These events give us a sense for the catastrophic results of an intellectualism void of wisdom, where instead inspiration is spawned, wittingly or unwittingly, from subearthly realms, devoid of the water of life. These events also reflect humankind's Uranian proclivity to build Towers of Babel that are based on erroneous foundations—towers that inevitably will fall.

During this Jupiter return of 9/11, and the Jupiter-Pluto opposition squaring Uranus, we must ask: Are we turning to the light-filled revelation of the stars, whereby our response will be to care for our Mother Earth and all her creatures; or, will we continue to push through with the brute force of egoism that seeks to dominate nature, other human beings, and the world, in pursuit of insatiable needs for endless power and profit?

Uranus, in the lower spectrums of the infrared, is the planet of violent revolution and luciferic illusion. In the uppermost spectrums of the ultraviolet, Uranus is the planet bringing the light of radically new imaginations to illumine cultures and expand the boundaries of freedom. We stand in between, to choose freely whether it will be the divine Light, or the inverted light of illusions that will be written into the pages of our history books. We can carefully observe what note on the full spectrum will be sounding from this close square to the Jupiter–Pluto opposition in August.

☙

There is a hostile opposition to wisdom and the work of spiritual communities in our time. In the greater context of major shifts and changes in so many aspects of our lives (climate, economy, government, and culture) we must ask ourselves if we have been loyal to the wisdom of the stars in this twenty-first century. Have we been worthy custodians of the natural world, willing to evolve new ideals, create collaborative cultures, and toll the bells of freedom in these cultures? Are we opening ourselves to receive new paradigms into our social, political, and economic environments? If we are aligned with these high ideals and are Hermetically acting in collaboration with the higher frequencies of star wisdom, we can then trustingly face the Pluto-Jupiter opposition of this year as a source of inner empowerment of spirit.

As we look back, then, on some of the momentous events of the last thirteen years, including the Venus transit of the Sun,[13] we may also look forward to the challenging opportunities ever before us. What part will we play in invoking new, divinely inspired ("ultraviolet") possibilities on behalf of our brothers and sisters in our global family?

The patterns in the language of the stars will continue to teach until the end of time. As we enter the stream of evolution divinely intended, we will learn, again, how to interpret star wisdom. This will help us to understand the spiritual direction in which we are to travel. When we turn back from this stream, we open a chasm through which beasts are allowed to enter our world. It is incumbent upon us to learn how to speak to the stars!

---

[13] See Tresemer, "The Venus Eclipse of the Sun, 2012," *Journal for Star Wisdom 2012*; and his book of the same title.

---

*"Why does a feeling of grandeur, of reverent awe, come over us when we look up into the starry heavens? It is because without our knowing it the feeling of our soul's home awakens in us. The feeling awakens: Before you came down to earth to a new incarnation, you yourself were in those stars, and out of the stars have come the highest forces that are within you. Your moral law was imparted to you when you were dwelling in the world of stars. When you practice self-knowledge, you can behold what the starry heaven bestowed upon you between death and a new birth—the best and finest powers of your soul. What we behold in the starry heavens is the moral law that is given to us from the spiritual worlds, for between death and a new birth we live in these starry heavens. One should contemplate the starry heavens with feelings such as these.... If we then raise our eyes to the starry heavens, we will be filled with a feeling of reverence and will know that this is the memory of the human being's eternal home."*

—RUDOLF STEINER (*Life Between Death and Rebirth*, Nov. 18, 1912)

# COMET ISON

## *Wain Farrants*

Comet ISON was discovered by a Russian observatory on September 21, 2012, and named after the ISON group (International Scientific Optical Network). In November 2013, the Comet ISON is expected to pass within 1.1 million miles (1.8 million km.) of the Sun's surface. Its perihelion (closest distance to the Sun) will be on November 28, 2013. It may not be close enough to the Sun to break up into pieces. It could illuminate the sky just after sunset and just before sunrise in both the Northern and Southern Hemispheres.[1]

As a helpful background to the overall planetary situation during 2013, when Comet ISON will be making its way through our part of the solar system, see Richard Tarnas' contribution to the *Journal for Star Wisdom 2012* and his book.[2]

Georg Blattmann writes in his book on comets:

In the Middle Ages, comets were portents of the worst disasters: wars, pestilence and plagues, foul weather and so on. It was like at school when a teacher lets loose a storm of anger on the class. That is most unpleasant for the pupils at the time—and so it should be, otherwise it would not have the desired effect. The pupils are filled with fear and apprehension, but once the storm is over and everyone has had a bit of a shock, and order has been restored, then the good and salutary effect of such an outburst can be felt. The same can be said about a thunderstorm. There is hardly anyone who looks forward to a thunderstorm with joy or satisfaction.... But once the thunderstorm is over, the benefit is felt. The air all around is clean and fresh, not only from the rain, but also as a result of the tremendous discharge and convulsion of the elements. Afterward, the world seems newly created and we feel the countryside can begin to live afresh and with it all creatures. In the same way, people felt the appearance of a comet.[3]

| DATE IN 2013 | SIDEREAL ZODIAC POSITION |
|---|---|
| Jan. 1 | 29:19 Gemini |
| July 1 | 25:19 Gemini |
| Sept. 1 | 12:18 Cancer |
| Oct. 1 | 25:29 Cancer |
| Nov. 1 | 21:49 Leo |
| Nov. 15 | 19:57 Virgo |
| Nov. 28 | 11:53 Scorpio* |
| Dec. 1 | 10:08 Scorpio |
| Dec. 15 | 2:19 Scorpio |
| Dec. 26 | 14:46 Libra |

\* Perihelion, aligned with the star Theta Lupis in Draco

The date when a new object is first sighted is generally important. On that date, Comet ISON was aligned with the star Alpha Monoceros in the constellation of the Unicorn. Two of the longest

---

1 Google search—Comet Ison.
2 Tarnas, *Cosmos and Psyche*; see also, Tarnas, "World Transits 2000–2020: An Overview," *Journal for Star Wisdom 2012*.
3 Blattmann, *Comets*, pp. 13–14 (trans. revised).

solar eclipses in the last two millennia fell on the longitude/meridian of the star Alpha Monoceros—at the total solar eclipse on June 26 AD 363 just after the death of Julian the Apostate, the last pagan emperor. The rise of the Roman Catholic Church in Rome to become a world power was also underway at the time. More recently, the total solar eclipse on July 21–22, 2009, also occurred on the longitude/meridian of that star. It is noteworthy that the year 2009 was marred by a number of scandals concerning child abuse in the Roman Catholic Church. Moreover, this July 2009 eclipse (the longest total solar eclipse of the twenty-first century) was thought by a number of people to signify the beginning of the fulfilment of Jeane Dixon's prophecy concerning the appearance of the Antichrist on the world stage.

It is also interesting that ISON is a musical term for a drone note, a slow-moving vocal part in Byzantine chant. Because the orbit of this comet is so close to being perfectly parabolic, it could be an entirely new comet. On the other hand, it is following an orbit very similar to the Great Comet of 1600.[4] At that time, in London Denis Papen invented a cast-iron cooking pot with a sealed lid that boiled meat much more quickly. Also a union of Akan states in Ghana formed the Asante Kingdom with the symbol of a golden throne.[5]

When it was discovered, ISON was in the same zodiacal location as was Mars at Christ's Ascension; Mercury was at the same place in the sidereal zodiac as it was at the baptism of Jesus in the River Jordan; the Moon was in the same sidereal location as the Moon at the miracle of the raising of the Youth of Nain; Pluto was at the same zodiacal position as it was at the beheading of John the Baptist; and Venus was at the same place in the zodiac as it was at Christ's Transfiguration.[6]

Thus, it would appear—with all these similarities with important events at the time of Christ—that this comet has a lot of positive potential.

---

4 See the website of James Partridge, http://www.darkstarastrology.com/comet_ison/. NOTE: The ephemeris (opposite) was taken from the same website and converted from the tropical to sidereal zodiac by the author.

5 Burne, *Chronicle of the World*.

6 Powell, *Chron;* this work gives all the planetary positions of those referred to here at the time of Christ.

# WORKING WITH THE STAR CALENDER
## *Robert Powell, Ph.D.*

In taking note of the astronomical events listed in the Star Calendar of the *Journal for Star Wisdom* (*JSW*), it is important to distinguish between long- and short-term astronomical events. Long-term astronomical events—for example, Pluto transiting a particular degree of the zodiac—will have a longer period of meditation than would the five days advocated for short-term astronomical events such as the new and Full Moon. The following describes, in relation to meditating on the Full Moon, a meditative process extending over a five-day period.

### Sanctification of the Full Moon

As a preliminary remark, let us remind ourselves that the great sacrifice of Christ on the Cross—the Mystery of Golgotha—took place at Full Moon. As Christ's sacrifice took place when the Moon was full in the middle of the sidereal sign of Libra, the Libra Full Moon assumes special significance in the sequence of twelve (or thirteen) Full Moons taking place during the cycle of the year. In following this sequence, the Mystery of Golgotha serves as an archetype for *every* Full Moon, since each Full Moon imparts a particular spiritual blessing. Hence the practice described here of *Sanctification of the Full Moon* applies to every Full Moon. Similarly, there is also the practice of *Sanctification of the New Moon*, as described in *Hermetic Astrology, Volume 2: Astrological Biography,* chapter 10.

During the two days prior to the Full Moon, we can consider the focus of one's meditation to extend over these two days as *preparatory days* immediately preceding the day of the Full Moon. These two days can be dedicated to spiritual reflection and detachment from everyday concerns, as one prepares to become a vessel for the in-streaming light and love one will receive at the Full Moon, something that one can then impart further—for example, to help people in need, or to support Mother Earth in times of catastrophe. During these two days, it is helpful to hold an attitude of dedication and service and try to assume an attitude of receptivity that opens to what one's soul will receive and subsequently impart—an attitude conducive to making one a true *servant of the spirit*.

The day of the Full Moon is itself a day of *holding the sacred space*. In doing so, one endeavors to cultivate inner peace and silence, during which one attempts to contact and consciously hold the in-streaming blessing of the Full Moon for the rest of humanity. One can heighten this silent meditation by visualizing the zodiacal constellation/sidereal sign in which the Moon becomes full, since the Moon serves to reflect the starry background against which it appears.

If the Moon is full in Virgo, for example, it reminds us of the night of the birth of the Jesus child visited by the three magi, as described in the Gospel of St. Matthew. That birth occurred at the Full Moon in the middle of the sidereal sign of Virgo, and the three magi, who gazed up that evening to behold the Full Moon against the background of the stars of the Virgin, witnessed the soul of Jesus emerge from the disk of the Full Moon and descend toward Earth. They participated from afar, via the starry heavens, in the Grail Mystery of the holy birth.

In meditating upon the Full Moon and opening oneself to receive the in-streaming blessing from the starry heavens, we can exercise restraint by avoiding the formulation of what will happen or what one might receive from the Full Moon. Moreover, we can also refrain from seeking tangible results or effects connected with our attunement to the Full Moon. Even if we observe only the date but not the exact moment when the Moon is full, it is helpful to find quiet time to reflect alone or to use the opportunity for deep meditation on the day of the full moon.

We can think of the two days following the full moon as a *time of imparting* what we have received from the in-streaming of the full disk of the Moon against the background of the stars. It is now possible to turn our attention toward humanity and the world and endeavor to pass on any spiritual blessing we have received from the starry heavens. Thereby we can assist in the work of the spiritual world by transforming what we have received into goodwill and allowing it to flow wherever the greatest need exists.

It is a matter of *holding a sacred space* throughout the day of the full moon. This is an important time to still the mind and maintain inner peace. It is a time of spiritual retreat and contact with the spiritual world, of holding in one's consciousness the archetype of the Mystery of Golgotha as a great outpouring of Divine Love that bridges Heaven and Earth. Prior to the day of the full moon, the two preceding days prepare the sacred space as a vessel to receive the heavenly blessing. The two days following the day of the full moon are a time to assimilate and distribute the spiritual transmission received into the sacred space we have prepared.

One can apply the process described here as a meditative practice in relation to the full moon to any of the astronomical events listed in the *JSW*, especially as most of these *remember* significant Christ Events. Take note, however, whether an event is long-term or short-term and adjust the period of meditative practice accordingly.

> *"The shadow intellect that is characteristic of all modern culture has fettered human beings to the Earth. They have eyes only for earthly things, particularly when they allow themselves to be influenced by the claims of modern science. In our age it never occurs to someone that their being belongs not to the Earth alone but to the cosmos beyond the Earth. Knowledge of our connection with the cosmos beyond the Earth—that is what we need above all to make our own.... When someone says 'I' to themselves, they experience a force that is working within, and the [ancient] Greek, in feeling the working of this inner force, related it to the Sun;...the Sun and the 'I' are the outer and inner aspects of one being. The Sun out there in space is the cosmic 'I.' What lives within me is the human 'I'.... Human beings are not primarily a creation of Earth. Human beings receive their shape and form from the cosmos. The human being is an offspring of the world of stars, above all of the Sun and Moon.... The Moon forces stream out from a center in the metabolic system.... [The] Moon stimulates reproduction.... Saturn works chiefly in the upper part of the astral body....Jupiter has to do with thinking...Mars [has] to do with speech.... The Mercury forces work in the part of the human organism that lies below the region of the heart...in the breathing and circulatory functions.... Venus works preeminently in the etheric body of the human being."*
>
> —RUDOLF STEINER, *Offspring of the World of Stars*, May 5, 1921

# SYMBOLS USED IN CHARTS

| | Planets | | Zodiacal Signs | | Aspects |
|---|---|---|---|---|---|
| ⊕ | Earth | ♈ | Aries (Ram) | ☌ | Conjunction 0° |
| ☉ | Sun | ♉ | Taurus (Bull) | ✷ | Sextile 60° |
| ☽ | Moon | ♊ | Gemini (Twins) | □ | Square 90° |
| ☿ | Mercury | ♋ | Cancer (Crab) | △ | Trine 120° |
| ♀ | Venus | ♌ | Leo (Lion) | ☍ | Opposition 180° |
| ♂ | Mars | ♍ | Virgo (Virgin) | | |
| ♃ | Jupiter | ♎ | Libra (Scales) | | |
| ♄ | Saturn | ♏ | Scorpio (Scorpion) | | |
| ♅ | Uranus | ♐ | Sagittarius (Archer) | | |
| ♆ | Neptune | ♑ | Capricorn (Goat) | | |
| ♇ | Pluto | ♒ | Aquarius (Water Carrier) | | |
| | | ♓ | Pisces (Fishes) | | |

| | Other | | |
|---|---|---|---|
| ☊ | Ascending (North) Node | ☌' | Sun Eclipse |
| ☋ | Descending (South) Node | ☍' | Moon Eclipse |
| P | Perihelion/Perigee | ⸸ | Inferior Conjunction |
| A | Aphelion/Apogee | ⸸ | Superior Conjunction |
| | Maximum Latitude | ⚷ | Chiron |
| | Minimum Latitude | | |

# TIME

The information relating to daily geocentric and heliocentric planetary positions in the sidereal zodiac is tabulated in the form of an ephemeris for each month, where the planetary positions are given at 0 hours universal time (UT) each day. Beneath the geocentric and heliocentric ephemeris for each month, the information relating to planetary aspects is given in the form of an aspectarian, listing the most important aspects—geocentric and heliocentric/hermetic—between the planets for the month in question. The day and the time of occurrence of the aspect on that day are indicated, all times being given in universal time, which is identical to Greenwich Mean Time (GMT). For example, zero hours universal time is midnight GMT. This time system applies in Britain; however, when summer time is in use, one hour has to be added to all times.

In other countries, the time has to be adjusted according to whether it is ahead of or behind Britain. For example, in Germany, where the time is one hour ahead of British time, one hour has to be added and, when summer time is in use in Germany, two hours have to be added to all times.

Using the calendar in the US, do the following subtraction from all time indications according to time zone: Pacific time subtract 8 hours (7 hours for daylight saving time); mountain time subtract 7 hours (6 hours for daylight saving time); central time subtract 6 hours (5 hours for daylight saving time); eastern time subtract 5 hours (4 hours for daylight saving time).

This subtraction will often change the date of an astronomical occurrence, shifting it back one day. On this account, since most of the readers of this calendar live on the American Continent, astronomical occurrences during the early hours of day x are listed as occurring on days x–1/x. For example, an eclipse occurring at 03:00 UT on the 12th is listed as occurring on the 11/12th since in America it takes place on the 11th.

See *General Introduction to the Christian Star Calendar: A Key to Understanding* for an in-depth clarification of the features of the calendar in the *Journal for Star Wisdom*, including indications as to how to work with it.

> "Immersed in prayer, I saw Christ on the cross. It was as if the cross was hovering in a tremendous amount of light. I was hearing the merging of the divine and human tones of his blood—the earthly and the heavenly commingling in his blood. As his blood fell, the Earth became a chalice, and his blood mingling with the Earth resounded as if the chalice of the Earth became a singing bowl, sending this resonance out into the universe, all the way to the Central Sun at the heart of our Milky Way galaxy. And the Central Sun, which then appeared in resplendent view behind the cross, reflected this resonance back to the Earth with all of its divine tones. I could hear the conversation of divine and earthly harmonies weaving back and forth between the Central Sun and the Earth as Christ's blood merged into the Earth. It was as if the tones were answering each other in seraphic symphony, in consummate supernal order.
>
> "I was given to understand that the tones that were woven between Heaven and Earth are still present. I saw the harmonies stretch out into the cosmos like a highway of light. These harmonies are the way by which we may travel—the narrow way to eternal life. They create the bridge between the worlds. These are the very tones and codes of life itself.
>
> "The cross disappeared. Now Christ hovered above me, gazing into my eyes. He spoke the words "It is fulfilled." These words coursed through the cosmos, harmonizing with the Central Sun and then returned to resound with the Earth. The light of the Central Sun flowed through his eyes and his words, and his light entered completely into my being. His blood in the Earth is eternal. We can know him through the Earth. He gave the gift of his blood to the Earth."
>
> —Estelle Isaacson[*]

[*] See also Estelle Isaacson's vision on page 17. She is a contemporary mystic whose first book was published recently: *Through the Eyes of Mary Magdalene: Early Years & Soul Awakening* (San Rafael, CA: LogoSophia, 2012). In this first book in a trilogy on the life of Mary Magdalene, Estelle Isaacson presents her visions of the life of "the Apostle to the Apostles" as seen through Magdalene's own eyes.

# COMMENTARIES AND EPHEMERIDES
## JANUARY–DECEMBER 2013

*Claudia McLaren Lainson and Sally Nurney*

The commentaries to the ephemerides of the *Journal for Star Wisdom* offer a practical approach for the study of Astrosophy. When various aspects among the planets, as well as the Sun, align with events in the life of Christ, commentaries may serve to illumine these correspondences in light of events in history that have occurred during similar aspects. In this way we are led to understand the tone and tenor of stellar influences. Further, they invite us to participate in the presence of Christ here and now, working in the etheric realms surrounding the Earth.

The etheric sphere of formative forces surrounding the Earth holds the memories of the perfect biography of Jesus Christ. This is called *the Eternal Gospel*—an unwritten Gospel that continues to act as a sculpting force shaping historic rhythms in time. We are wise to become ever more aware of this sphere and the presence of Christ, who dwells therein. This *Journal* is an offering for those seeking to read this Gospel, for the stars are its language. We can imagine that these biographical memories are portals through which the stars above find communion with human beings below, thus fulfilling the Hermetic axiom: *As above, so also below.* Materialistic thinking, on the other hand, creates another sphere around the Earth. This sphere is ruled by a great adversary whose aim is to obscure the presence of Christ, including the memories the stars resound as they align with events of his life.

The commentaries thus serve to focus our thinking toward wisdom-filled realms of light. Wisdom *is* Sophia, for she is the Light that shines into the darkness of our times, leading us to Christ. Thus it is through Sophia that Christ's presence is comprehended. Connecting to the presence of Christ in the etheric is the task of our Age—the Age of the consciousness soul. Another task of our Age is to awaken to the presence of forces opposed to Christ. To move against the will of Heaven will surely deliver us further into trials of escalating intensity that are increasingly manifesting through climate changes, derisive politics, greed-ridden economics, and social upheavals around the world. Like the Grail Knights before us, we are to confront evil and bring forth the good, for knowledge of evil calls forth the good! It is of utmost necessity that we gather the strength needed to endure the truth that stands behind the masks of ordinary reality. The Light of wisdom is streaming toward us, and new Life is rising from the heart of the Mother in the depths of the Earth. The Light and the Life that are now quickening will assist us on our quest to discover the path opening before us.

Though the commentaries refer to specific events in *time*, the information they contain is based on the guidance of Great Teachers, and is therefore *timeless*. Through the effort of remembering Christ's life, his teachings are enlivened for revelatory inspiration. As the stars align with events during his three and one-half years on the Earth, they sound into time as forming forces that affect events on Earth for better or for worse. This all depends on our willingness to move in harmony with these great Star Beings, who rhythmically receive the wandering planets into their twelve-fold constellations—and through them speak to humanity on Earth. A division is gradually occurring. A choice is being made: Will we follow the directives of spiritual beings who sound from the stars and planets, or will we get caught in the web of materialism that cannot imagine a truth beyond the daily news? As we choose this path of remembering the stars, we follow the call of the Grail. As we awaken to star wisdom we learn a new language, and this focus will lead us toward the higher truths that stand behind the veil of sense existence. And it is the Word in these truths—Christ, our Redeemer—who will protect us in the battle for the human soul now taking place on a global level.

Just as Christ was in continual resonance with the beings of the stars, so too can we begin such a quest as we follow the teachings, the warnings, and the promises sounding from the stars in this year of 2013.

## Contributors and Comments

Three people contributed to the commentaries. Sally Nurney wrote the astronomical Skywatch that opens each month. This Skywatch tells us where to see the stars in the sky, and helps us find our way into naked-eye observation. Richard Bloedon served as editor for the commentaries, for which we are deeply grateful. Claudia McLaren Lainson wrote the commentaries with specific attention to major themes of 2013.

It is recommended that the whole sequence of commentaries first be read like a book, in order to gain an overview of the themes highlighted for this year. Having this overview will assist one in deepening into the daily readings of the commentaries as they play out in time through the next twelve months.

The following is a list of abbreviations for books quoted frequently throughout the commentaries:

*CHA*: Refers to Robert Powell's book, *Christian Hermetic Astrology*
*Chron.*: Refers to Robert Powell's book, *Chronicles of the Living Christ*
*ACE*: Refers to Anne Catherine Emmerich
*LBVM*: Refers to the *Life of the Blessed Virgin Mary*, by ACE
*LJC*: Refers to the *Life of Jesus Christ*, by ACE

# JANUARY

We begin the year as usual: with the Sun in the middle of the Archer (Sagittarius) and moving into the Sea Goat (Capricorn) mid-month. Venus begins 2013 as a brilliant morning star in Scorpio, and continues to shine before sunrise until the end of March of this year. Jupiter is retrograde until January 31st and is visible in the night sky now and until the end of April. (We will find Jupiter again mid-July, but by then in the predawn hours.) The Quandrantids meteor shower begins on January 1st and peaks the 3rd to 4th. Look to the northeast, below the Big Dipper into the constellation "Bootes" after dark for a grand show of up to 40 meteors an hour! The New Moon is on the 11th, after the Moon joins with Saturn (on the 6th) and Venus (on the 10th), hidden within the glow of the Sun. A week later, the Sun catches up with Mercury in the first degrees of Capricorn on the 18th. The waxing Moon joins Jupiter on the 22nd, visible together to the south at sunset in the middle of Taurus (The Bull). The red star to their right is Aldebaran, the "Eye of the Bull," one of the Royal Stars of Persia. The Moon appears full on the 27th.

**January 1:** Sun 16° Sagittarius. Today is the 2013th anniversary of the birth of the Nathan Jesus. The year begins with the commemoration of this holy birth. The future of the Earth depends on human beings uniting with the unfathomable love and mercy of Jesus Christ. As we do this our hearts will gradually mature into an open chalice. In this state of humble receptivity we will become more concerned with the needs of others than with our own egoistic selves. In the process of gradually opening, the being of Jesus Christ—he who was the Nathan Jesus—can draw near to us. Blessed are the peacekeepers, for they are the humble servants of this pure and sacrificial divine human being. The peacekeepers are those who strive to regulate human affairs on Earth with the same harmony and love that regulates the community of stars in the heavens. In this way the Hermetic axiom is fulfilled: *As above, so also below.*

May the commemoration of this holy birth, in these times of blatant opposition to what is holy and pure, remind us that there is a choice to be made. Nathan Jesus united with Christ to show the way for all human beings who are choosing to become part of the New Earth—an Earth of Love. He is the gentle shepherd leading us forward in spite of distractions by those who follow a different leader—a shepherd who leads his sheep more deeply into materialism and who grows more desperate as time inches toward the "shift" that is sounding through the world. It may be easier for a camel to pass through the eye of a needle than it will be for some to pass through the changes that have now already begun.

We begin our year with this angelic human, who awakens in us as we awaken to others. May we serve the good, name what is evil, and be blessed to know the difference.

~

**Note:** On this date in 2012, President Obama signed the controversial NDAA bill. The fact that this was just before last year's commemoration of the Union in the Temple (See *Journal for Star Wisdom 2012*) brings to mind the black-magical working of adversary forces that use esoteric events through *inversion*, and bring in their dark agendas riding in the wake of streams laden with divine forces. The question posed in the *Journal for Star Wisdom 2012* article "Possession or Enlightenment" continues to be valid. The NDAA law grants the use of Armed Forces in civilian law enforcement, and the selective suspension of *due process* and *habeas corpus*, as well as other rights guaranteed by the 5th and 6th Amendments to the US Constitution. What will we witness as the ongoing consequences of this new law?

**January 2:** Sun 17° Sagittarius: Conception of the Virgin Mary (Dec/8/22 BC). The Virgin Mary's conception is a star memory that is streaming into the world today. It was at Pentecost that the Virgin Mary became Holy Mary Sophia, for it was Divine Wisdom Sophia who then united with her, bringing the Holy Spirit to ensoul the circle of the disciples of Christ. We receive her in the eternal silence of our own heart. The more we remember these star events, the greater is their ability to send forces of healing grace into us. Today we can open to the blessings of peace that radiate from this being. She serves both human beings and nature beings. Mary-Sophia is the one referred to in the Bible as the Queen from the South:

> The Queen of the South will rise at the judgment with this generation and condemn it, for she came from the ends of the Earth to hear the wisdom of Solomon; and behold, something greater than Solomon is here. (Matt.12:42)

There is much confusion that equates the spiritual world with harsh judgment. This is not the case. The spiritual world only loves. It is the human being who directs harsh judgment against the very *being* of others. *Spiritual judgment is a radiance we encounter each night when we go into sleep, and in greater totality at our death. In both instances we stand before the light of our divine potentiality and we are to develop the courage to witness our true reflection. If we cannot, it is out of our own volition that we flee from the light, not out of condemnation by the spiritual world.* It is out of an inner cowardice that we shrink. We shy away from the light because we cannot face what the light illumines. Mary-Sophia sees our self-condemnation and she holds us in her heart as we—in self-judgment—flee *from* her, for she knows well where this will lead. She does not condemn us, she condemns the false path. As our souls are strengthened we are able to face the light, and the light leads us across the boundary between the world of matter and the world of spirit where both Michael and Sophia stand as guardians to occult secrets. Sophia stands as guardian from the far side of the threshold, and Michael from this side of the threshold. Initiates are able to cross this threshold consciously.

Estelle Isaacson, a modern day visionary, has seen that there are guardians who protect the place where Sophia dwells and who do not allow any to pass who try to approach from a state of fullness. She describes the being who guards the portal into the mysteries of Sophia as:

> A reflective being—like a mirror. As it reflects, one cannot know that the being is there if one is full of self. It shows itself as a portal only when one is empty. If one is full of one's own self, then

## SIDEREAL GEOCENTRIC LONGITUDES : JANUARY 2013 Gregorian at 0 hours UT

| DAY | ☉ | ☽ | ☊ | ☿ | ♀ | ♂ | ♃ | ♄ | ♅ | ♆ | ♇ |
|---|---|---|---|---|---|---|---|---|---|---|---|
| 1 TU | 15 ♐ 49 | 25 ♋ 51 | 0 ♏ 5R | 5 ♐ 43 | 24 ♏ 50 | 9 ♑ 46 | 12 ♉ 51R | 14 ♎ 37 | 9 ♓ 50 | 6 ♒ 9 | 14 ♐ 24 |
| 2 WE | 16 50 | 8 ♌ 29 | 29 ♎ 57 | 7 16 | 26 6 | 10 33 | 12 46 | 14 42 | 9 51 | 6 11 | 14 26 |
| 3 TH | 17 51 | 21 20 | 29 52 | 8 49 | 27 21 | 11 20 | 12 40 | 14 47 | 9 52 | 6 13 | 14 28 |
| 4 FR | 18 52 | 4 ♍ 26 | 29 49 | 10 22 | 28 36 | 12 7 | 12 35 | 14 51 | 9 53 | 6 14 | 14 30 |
| 5 SA | 19 53 | 17 49 | 29 48 | 11 56 | 29 51 | 12 54 | 12 30 | 14 55 | 9 54 | 6 16 | 14 32 |
| 6 SU | 20 54 | 1 ♎ 31 | 29 49D | 13 30 | 1 ♐ 6 | 13 41 | 12 25 | 15 0 | 9 56 | 6 18 | 14 34 |
| 7 MO | 21 55 | 15 34 | 29 50 | 15 5 | 2 21 | 14 29 | 12 20 | 15 4 | 9 57 | 6 19 | 14 37 |
| 8 TU | 22 57 | 29 56 | 29 50R | 16 40 | 3 36 | 15 16 | 12 16 | 15 8 | 9 58 | 6 21 | 14 39 |
| 9 WE | 23 58 | 14 ♏ 37 | 29 49 | 18 15 | 4 52 | 16 3 | 12 11 | 15 12 | 9 59 | 6 23 | 14 41 |
| 10 TH | 24 59 | 29 31 | 29 46 | 19 51 | 6 7 | 16 51 | 12 7 | 15 16 | 10 1 | 6 25 | 14 43 |
| 11 FR | 26 0 | 14 ♐ 32 | 29 40 | 21 27 | 7 22 | 17 38 | 12 3 | 15 20 | 10 2 | 6 27 | 14 45 |
| 12 SA | 27 1 | 29 30 | 29 31 | 23 4 | 8 37 | 18 25 | 11 59 | 15 24 | 10 4 | 6 28 | 14 47 |
| 13 SU | 28 2 | 14 ♑ 17 | 29 22 | 24 41 | 9 52 | 19 13 | 11 55 | 15 27 | 10 5 | 6 30 | 14 49 |
| 14 MO | 29 4 | 28 43 | 29 12 | 26 18 | 11 8 | 20 0 | 11 52 | 15 31 | 10 7 | 6 32 | 14 51 |
| 15 TU | 0 ♑ 5 | 12 ♒ 43 | 29 3 | 27 56 | 12 23 | 20 47 | 11 49 | 15 34 | 10 8 | 6 34 | 14 53 |
| 16 WE | 1 6 | 26 16 | 28 56 | 29 35 | 13 38 | 21 35 | 11 46 | 15 38 | 10 10 | 6 36 | 14 55 |
| 17 TH | 2 7 | 9 ♓ 20 | 28 51 | 1 ♑ 14 | 14 53 | 22 22 | 11 43 | 15 41 | 10 12 | 6 38 | 14 57 |
| 18 FR | 3 8 | 21 59 | 28 48 | 2 54 | 16 8 | 23 10 | 11 40 | 15 44 | 10 13 | 6 40 | 15 0 |
| 19 SA | 4 9 | 4 ♈ 16 | 28 47 | 4 34 | 17 24 | 23 57 | 11 38 | 15 48 | 10 15 | 6 42 | 15 2 |
| 20 SU | 5 10 | 16 18 | 28 48D | 6 14 | 18 39 | 24 44 | 11 36 | 15 51 | 10 17 | 6 44 | 15 4 |
| 21 MO | 6 11 | 28 10 | 28 48R | 7 56 | 19 54 | 25 32 | 11 34 | 15 54 | 10 19 | 6 46 | 15 6 |
| 22 TU | 7 12 | 9 ♉ 57 | 28 48 | 9 37 | 21 9 | 26 19 | 11 32 | 15 56 | 10 21 | 6 48 | 15 8 |
| 23 WE | 8 13 | 21 44 | 28 45 | 11 20 | 22 24 | 27 7 | 11 30 | 15 59 | 10 23 | 6 50 | 15 10 |
| 24 TH | 9 14 | 3 ♊ 36 | 28 40 | 13 2 | 23 39 | 27 54 | 11 29 | 16 2 | 10 25 | 6 52 | 15 12 |
| 25 FR | 10 15 | 15 35 | 28 32 | 14 46 | 24 55 | 28 42 | 11 27 | 16 5 | 10 27 | 6 54 | 15 14 |
| 26 SA | 11 16 | 27 44 | 28 21 | 16 29 | 26 10 | 29 29 | 11 26 | 16 7 | 10 29 | 6 56 | 15 16 |
| 27 SU | 12 17 | 10 ♋ 5 | 28 8 | 18 14 | 27 25 | 0 ♒ 16 | 11 26 | 16 9 | 10 31 | 6 58 | 15 17 |
| 28 MO | 13 18 | 22 38 | 27 54 | 19 58 | 28 40 | 1 4 | 11 25 | 16 12 | 10 33 | 7 0 | 15 19 |
| 29 TU | 14 19 | 5 ♌ 23 | 27 41 | 21 43 | 29 55 | 1 51 | 11 25 | 16 14 | 10 35 | 7 2 | 15 21 |
| 30 WE | 15 20 | 18 19 | 27 29 | 23 29 | 1 ♑ 10 | 2 39 | 11 24 | 16 16 | 10 38 | 7 5 | 15 23 |
| 31 TH | 16 21 | 1 ♍ 27 | 27 20 | 25 14 | 2 26 | 3 26 | 11 24D | 16 18 | 10 40 | 7 7 | 15 25 |

### INGRESSES :

1 ☽ → ♌ 7:55
☊ → ♎ 15: 0
3 ☽ → ♍ 15:55
5 ♀ → ♐ 2:52
☽ → ♎ 21:21
8 ☽ → ♏ 0: 6
10 ☽ → ♐ 0:45
12 ☽ → ♑ 0:48
14 ☽ → ♒ 2:10
☉ → ♑ 22: 9
16 ☿ → ♑ 6: 5
☽ → ♓ 6:46
18 ☽ → ♈ 15:35
21 ☽ → ♉ 3:43
23 ☽ → ♊ 16:44
26 ☽ → ♋ 4:26
♂ → ♒ 15:42
28 ☽ → ♌ 13:55
29 ♀ → ♑ 1:29
30 ☽ → ♍ 21:22

### ASPECTS & ECLIPSES :

1 ☽ S ☊ 7:59
☽ ☍ ♆ 19:38
3 ☿ □ ♅ 16:27
4 ☽ ☍ ♅ 9:51
5 ☉ □ ☽ 3:56
6 ☿ ☌ ♇ 16:39
☽ ☌ ♄ 23: 9
7 ♂ □ ♄ 19:31
☽ ☌ ☊ 23:49
8 ☽ ☍ ♃ 20: 4
10 ☽ ☌ P 10:42
☽ ☌ ♀ 11:30
11 ☽ ☌ ♇ 0:20
☽ ☌ ☿ 12:23
☉ ☌ ☽ 19:42
13 ♀ □ ♅ 4:10
☽ ☌ ♂ 8:36
14 ☽ N ☊ 0:48
☽ ☌ ♆ 13:19
17 ♀ ☌ ♇ 1:24
☽ ☌ ♅ 1:37
18 ☉ S☌ ☿ 8:55
☉ □ ☽ 23:44
19 ☽ ☍ ♄ 23: 3
21 ☽ ☌ ☋ 1:17
22 ☽ ☌ ♃ 3:11
☽ ☌ A 11:10
24 ♂ □ ☊ 19:48
☽ ☍ ♇ 23:17
25 ☿ □ ♄ 18:41
☽ ☍ ♀ 20:34
27 ☉ ☍ ☽ 4:37
☽ ☍ ☿ 18: 8
28 ☽ S ☊ 9:48
☽ ☍ ♂ 16:58
29 ☽ ☍ ♆ 3: 6
30 ☉ □ ♄ 22:48
31 ☽ ☍ ♅ 16:42

## SIDEREAL HELIOCENTRIC LONGITUDES : JANUARY 2013 Gregorian at 0 hours UT

| DAY | Sid. Time | ☿ | ♀ | ⊕ | ♂ | ♃ | ♄ | ♅ | ♆ | ♇ | Vernal Point |
|---|---|---|---|---|---|---|---|---|---|---|---|
| 1 TU | 6:43:14 | 13 ♏ 58 | 25 ♎ 45 | 15 ♊ 49 | 26 ♑ 31 | 18 ♉ 55 | 9 ♎ 34 | 12 ♓ 38 | 7 ♒ 36 | 14 ♐ 21 | 5 ♓ 4'43" |
| 2 WE | 6:47:10 | 16 43 | 27 21 | 16 50 | 27 9 | 19 0 | 9 36 | 12 38 | 7 36 | 14 22 | 5 ♓ 4'43" |
| 3 TH | 6:51: 7 | 19 28 | 28 57 | 17 51 | 27 47 | 19 5 | 9 38 | 12 39 | 7 37 | 14 22 | 5 ♓ 4'43" |
| 4 FR | 6:55: 3 | 22 13 | 0 ♏ 33 | 18 52 | 28 25 | 19 10 | 9 40 | 12 40 | 7 37 | 14 22 | 5 ♓ 4'43" |
| 5 SA | 6:59: 0 | 24 58 | 2 8 | 19 53 | 29 3 | 19 16 | 9 42 | 12 40 | 7 38 | 14 23 | 5 ♓ 4'43" |
| 6 SU | 7: 2:56 | 27 43 | 3 44 | 20 54 | 29 40 | 19 21 | 9 44 | 12 41 | 7 38 | 14 23 | 5 ♓ 4'42" |
| 7 MO | 7: 6:53 | 0 ♐ 28 | 5 20 | 21 56 | 0 ♒ 18 | 19 26 | 9 46 | 12 42 | 7 38 | 14 23 | 5 ♓ 4'42" |
| 8 TU | 7:10:50 | 3 14 | 6 55 | 22 57 | 0 56 | 19 31 | 9 47 | 12 42 | 7 39 | 14 24 | 5 ♓ 4'42" |
| 9 WE | 7:14:46 | 6 1 | 8 31 | 23 58 | 1 34 | 19 37 | 9 49 | 12 43 | 7 39 | 14 24 | 5 ♓ 4'42" |
| 10 TH | 7:18:43 | 8 49 | 10 6 | 24 59 | 2 12 | 19 42 | 9 51 | 12 44 | 7 39 | 14 24 | 5 ♓ 4'42" |
| 11 FR | 7:22:39 | 11 39 | 11 42 | 26 0 | 2 50 | 19 47 | 9 53 | 12 44 | 7 40 | 14 25 | 5 ♓ 4'42" |
| 12 SA | 7:26:36 | 14 30 | 13 17 | 27 1 | 3 28 | 19 52 | 9 55 | 12 45 | 7 40 | 14 25 | 5 ♓ 4'42" |
| 13 SU | 7:30:32 | 17 23 | 14 52 | 28 2 | 4 7 | 19 58 | 9 57 | 12 46 | 7 40 | 14 25 | 5 ♓ 4'41" |
| 14 MO | 7:34:29 | 20 17 | 16 28 | 29 4 | 4 45 | 20 3 | 9 59 | 12 46 | 7 41 | 14 26 | 5 ♓ 4'41" |
| 15 TU | 7:38:25 | 23 14 | 18 3 | 0 ♋ 5 | 5 23 | 20 8 | 10 1 | 12 47 | 7 41 | 14 26 | 5 ♓ 4'41" |
| 16 WE | 7:42:22 | 26 14 | 19 38 | 1 6 | 6 1 | 20 13 | 10 3 | 12 47 | 7 41 | 14 26 | 5 ♓ 4'41" |
| 17 TH | 7:46:19 | 29 16 | 21 14 | 2 7 | 6 39 | 20 19 | 10 5 | 12 48 | 7 42 | 14 27 | 5 ♓ 4'41" |
| 18 FR | 7:50:15 | 2 ♑ 21 | 22 49 | 3 8 | 7 17 | 20 24 | 10 7 | 12 49 | 7 42 | 14 27 | 5 ♓ 4'41" |
| 19 SA | 7:54:12 | 5 30 | 24 24 | 4 9 | 7 55 | 20 29 | 10 8 | 12 49 | 7 43 | 14 27 | 5 ♓ 4'41" |
| 20 SU | 7:58: 8 | 8 42 | 25 59 | 5 10 | 8 33 | 20 34 | 10 10 | 12 50 | 7 43 | 14 28 | 5 ♓ 4'40" |
| 21 MO | 8: 2: 5 | 11 57 | 27 34 | 6 11 | 9 11 | 20 40 | 10 12 | 12 51 | 7 43 | 14 28 | 5 ♓ 4'40" |
| 22 TU | 8: 6: 1 | 15 17 | 29 9 | 7 12 | 9 49 | 20 45 | 10 14 | 12 51 | 7 44 | 14 28 | 5 ♓ 4'40" |
| 23 WE | 8: 9:58 | 18 42 | 0 ♐ 44 | 8 13 | 10 27 | 20 50 | 10 16 | 12 52 | 7 44 | 14 29 | 5 ♓ 4'40" |
| 24 TH | 8:13:54 | 22 11 | 2 20 | 9 14 | 11 5 | 20 55 | 10 18 | 12 53 | 7 44 | 14 29 | 5 ♓ 4'40" |
| 25 FR | 8:17:51 | 25 45 | 3 55 | 10 15 | 11 43 | 21 1 | 10 20 | 12 53 | 7 45 | 14 29 | 5 ♓ 4'40" |
| 26 SA | 8:21:48 | 29 25 | 5 30 | 11 16 | 12 22 | 21 6 | 10 22 | 12 54 | 7 45 | 14 30 | 5 ♓ 4'40" |
| 27 SU | 8:25:44 | 3 ♒ 10 | 7 5 | 12 17 | 13 0 | 21 11 | 10 24 | 12 55 | 7 45 | 14 30 | 5 ♓ 4'40" |
| 28 MO | 8:29:41 | 7 2 | 8 40 | 13 18 | 13 38 | 21 16 | 10 26 | 12 55 | 7 46 | 14 30 | 5 ♓ 4'39" |
| 29 TU | 8:33:37 | 11 1 | 10 15 | 14 19 | 14 16 | 21 21 | 10 27 | 12 56 | 7 46 | 14 31 | 5 ♓ 4'39" |
| 30 WE | 8:37:34 | 15 6 | 11 50 | 15 20 | 14 54 | 21 27 | 10 29 | 12 56 | 7 47 | 14 31 | 5 ♓ 4'39" |
| 31 TH | 8:41:30 | 19 19 | 13 24 | 16 21 | 15 32 | 21 32 | 10 31 | 12 57 | 7 47 | 14 31 | 5 ♓ 4'39" |

### INGRESSES :

3 ♀ → ♏ 15:49
6 ♂ → ♒ 12:21
☿ → ♐ 19:56
14 ⊕ → ♋ 22: 7
17 ☿ → ♑ 5:44
22 ♀ → ♐ 12:46
26 ☿ → ♒ 3:47

### ASPECTS (HELIOCENTRIC +MOON(TYCHONIC)) :

1 ☽ ☍ ♂ 1:19
♀ □ ♂ 18:52
☽ ☍ ♆ 22:20
2 ☽ □ ☿ 19:36
☽ □ ♃ 19:47
☿ ☍ ♃ 20:31
3 ⊕ ☌ P 9:12
4 ☿ ☌ A 4:34
☽ ☍ ♅ 14:49
☽ □ ♇ 17:52
6 ☽ ☌ ♄ 14: 7
8 ☽ □ ♂ 1:43
♀ □ ♆ 10:58
☽ □ ♆ 12:39
☽ ☌ ♀ 12:51
9 ☽ ☍ ♃ 8: 7
10 ☽ ☌ ☿ 18:18
☽ □ ♅ 21: 7
☽ ☌ ♇ 23:48
11 ☿ □ ♅ 9:14
☿ ☌ ♇ 23:19
12 ☽ □ ♄ 16:54
14 ☽ ☌ ♂ 10:42
☽ ☌ ♆ 15:16
15 ☽ □ ♀ 10:34
☽ □ ♃ 13: 7
16 ♀ ☍ ♃ 9:20
17 ☽ ☌ ♅ 6:31
☽ □ ♇ 9:37
♀ ☌ ☋ 9:49
18 ☿ ☍ ⊕ 8:55
♂ ☌ ♆ 16: 7
19 ☽ □ ☿ 3:15
☽ ☍ ♄ 11:40
20 ☿ □ ♄ 11: 3
21 ☽ □ ♆ 19:27
☽ □ ♂ 23:42
22 ☽ ☌ ♃ 22: 8
23 ☽ ☍ ♀ 21: 2
24 ☿ S ☊ 9:22
♂ ☌ P 10:54
☽ □ ♅ 18:37
☽ ☍ ♇ 21:49
25 ⊕ □ ♄ 1:48
27 ☽ □ ♄ 0:36
28 ☿ ☌ ♆ 4:26
29 ☽ ☍ ♆ 4:27
☽ ☍ ☿ 15:17
☽ ☍ ♂ 17:21
☿ ☌ ♂ 22:37
30 ☽ □ ♃ 5:46
♀ □ ♅ 17: 2
31 ☿ □ ♃ 12:37
♀ ☌ ♇ 16:57
☽ ☍ ♅ 20:46
☽ □ ♇ 23:35

one only finds the self reflected by this being, and there is a struggle with what is reflected. If one is empty, then the being appears as a silvery, shimmery portal and grants access. Until one is empty, the reflection of the self will occlude the portal to Sophia. This being is both a mirror and a portal—one does not know it is a portal if one gets caught in the mirror aspect. The being does not call to you. Your soul yearns for it. You cannot at first find this being, because it mirrors. The closer you draw to it, the more you see your own reflection and notice something about yourself. If you become stuck in what you see about yourself, you will only see your reflection and not notice the portal.[1]

As we today remember the descent of the Virgin Mary into incarnation, we are encouraged to find our emptiness (our freedom from attachments to this world) so we may stand before the being who guards the future-born mysteries of Mary-Sophia, and find there an open door. May we remember the constancy of spiritual love and in this light take account of our imperfections so we need not turn from the light. This is a good day to find love for others, and use any darkness we encounter as a mirror that reflects the darkness within our own souls.

**ASPECT:** Heliocentric Mercury 19° Scorpio opposite heliocentric Jupiter 19° Taurus. Heliocentric refers to the spiritual-eye-view; it is as if we were standing on the Sun, and seeing from the "I" of our higher self. From this vantage Jupiter is also remembering the conception of the Blessed Virgin Mary—her purity is streaming from the planet of wisdom. With Jupiter standing opposite Mercury, we are asked to find our way out of any feelings of restlessness and impatience (Mercury), so that we may ease into the solace of wisdom (Jupiter). Agitated thoughts eclipse cosmic thoughts. It is the Virgin Mary who is now guiding us to form new communities. These communities are opening to meet new spiritual capacities that are striving to unite with all human beings of good will. The emblem of her presence in communities is the love of one another within these communities. We can drink in the eternal presence of Mary Sophia and be filled with her love. In the embrace of her peace-bestowing mission, hearts come to stillness. The still heart quiets the mind and a quiet mind is able to reflect heavenly thoughts. Tyranny (negative Jupiter) and mass communication systems (Mercury) are the shadow side of Mercury/Jupiter aspects. We can be mindful of the effects of mass consciousness and direct our minds to images that are true, living, and eternal. These are the cosmic thoughts so urgently needing our attention now. Be mindful of the effects of mass consciousness. This is not the consciousness we are to follow. Tyrants take full advantage of communication systems to seed fear and illusion; and through this they are able to control the thoughts of the masses. Today we are to lift our hearts to the pure, the true and the beautiful. We can be mindful of any disturbing thoughts that are distracting us from the wisdom of cosmic thoughts.

**Venus enters Sagittarius:** In existence growth's power dies (Steiner, *Twelve Moods of the Zodiac*). Venus was in Sagittarius during the forty days in the wilderness and during several of Christ's healing miracles up to the walking on the water. We are to prevail against the restraints of earthly life through will-filled activity directed toward spiritual renewal. This renewal lifts the soul into its eternal becoming.

**January 6:** Epiphany. Today we close the door to the Holy Nights of 2012/13, and venture into the world with all we have gained through these sacred days. A *seedling star* has been born within us. It will grow and ripen throughout the next twelve months. We are to protect this seedling, which represents a spark from our higher self that is striving to unite with our temporal self on Earth. This is the true gift of Christmas, and Epiphany marks the virginal beginnings of new growth in the yearly circle of time. Just as the three kings lost sight of the Star when they entered Herod's fallen realm, so too are we warned that Herodian materialism will predatorily stalk the occult truth of the fact that we have received a gift in these Holy Days and Nights. In this time of Epiphany, we are prudent to protect this new life and hold true to our ideals. As we journey through this new year we are to mature into a fuller expression of who we truly

---

[1] Isaacson, *The Coming Times*, chap. 26.

are. In nine months' time, at Michaelmas, what is now only a possibility, as this Christmas gift, will rise up with strength and power in order to help us battle the dragons that dwell within our soul, and in the world around us. But this can happen only if we protect the light we bring from these depths of winter and successfully avoid the Herods of the world. Like the three kings before us, we are to avoid the enslaving limitations of false kings, false prophets, and false ideals.

**ASPECT**: Mercury conjunct Pluto 14° Sagittarius: The Raising of Lazarus. Heliocentric Pluto was here at the raising of Lazarus from the dead. During the Twelve Holy Nights we breathe in the entire zodiac and conceive new possibilities for the coming year. As these nights come to a close, this year we celebrate the greatest of all of Christ's miracles, the Raising of Lazarus, and ask ourselves if we too can be raised from the death-engendering afflictions of materialism. Herod could not. His realm was one of darkness and deceit. In his attempt to murder the infant Jesus he murdered all the innocent children of Bethlehem, and his stream of wickedness continues to prey on all that is pure. From the view of spirit, this last of the seven healing miracles by Christ is today remembered by Pluto; and Mercury is conjunct Pluto, where this great memory has been inscribed into the living chronicle of the stars. Who is Mercury but the healer, and who is the greatest of all healers if not Christ! *Today the power of healing is intensified if we can turn toward divine love as the source and substance of all healing. In today's communion between Mercury and Pluto we can ask: Will the wing-footed messenger receive teachings of love from Pluto that will bring calming health to us, or will this communion be with the dark side of Pluto, that delivers instead restlessness, fear and hatred?* We are to decide. Will our minds be attuned to the eternal presence of divine love (Phanes/higher Pluto), or will we be distracted (Mercury) by the presence of all that is not love in this world? This is a good day to overcome any animal impulses living in our Centaur nature (Sagittarius), by seizing the archer's bow and aiming it toward the heart of Love (the Galactic Center), which is the true aim of the Sagittarian. Herod did not have this bow, nor would he have known how to aim toward this eternal source of love. Herod sentenced love to death. May our aim be true on this day of Epiphany, and may truth be our constant companion through this coming year.

**January 11:** New Moon 26° Sagittarius. On June 12, AD 32, with the Moon at this same place, Jesus healed 10 lepers. Only one ran after him to thank him. This man became a disciple. Shortly after this healing of the ten lepers, Jesus was summoned to the house of a shepherd in order to raise the man's daughter from the dead. He told the three disciples who accompanied him—Peter, James, and John—that in his name they should do the same. (See *Chron.* p. 313)

On this New Moon we can contemplate the virtue of Sagittarius: Control of Speech, which engenders a feeling for truth. When we speak in union with our conscience, we are speaking in unison with our Angel, and our Angel serves the great Spirits of Time, and these great beings serve Christ. Like Peter, James, and John, we too are urged to heal in Christ's name, and this we do as we learn to control what comes out of our mouth. We live in a world painfully intertwined with lies and deception. Yet disease and afflictions are healed as we raise ourselves from the sleep of forgetfulness and find a willingness to serve the good, the beautiful and the true. May we find our way to freedom in truth. In this way we can raise our consciousness from the grave of denial. In this awakened state we can name the forces weaving insidious webs that further entrap the soul in the *maya* of illusion. As a Full Moon marks a fruition, so does a New Moon mark a beginning. May our words find the feeling for truth in the perfect night of this New Moon.

**January 12: ASPECT:** Venus 10° Sagittarius square Uranus 10° Pisces. Venus was here when Christ told the disciples the parable of the hidden treasure: The kingdom of Heaven is like treasure hidden in a field. When a man found it, he hid it again, and then in his joy went and sold all he had and bought that field. (Matthew 13:44)

The field is the world, and those who find Heaven's treasures in this world will sacrifice all they have to live with these treasures. When Venus is square Uranus she either brings harmony to the living imaginations coming as treasures from Heaven or, in her dark humor, she captivates unsuspecting souls into the alluring false imaginations that masquerade as spiritual treasures. This is a day to discern the difference between the living treasures of cosmic imaginations, and the dead images spinning webs that are increasingly occluding Heaven's treasures.

**January 13:** Sun 27° Sagittarius: Death of Thomas (Dec/18/72).

**January 15:** Sun enters Capricorn: "May the future rest upon the past" (Steiner, *Twelve Moods of the Zodiac*). William Bento illumines Steiner's mantra:

> Although this can be said to be a common sense statement, it holds deeper mysteries into the streams of time. Implicit to this mood is how we all must bear the consequences and deeds of the past as seeds for the future. By being aware of this in the present we can affect the stream of time with conscious intent and not be laid a victim to the past as we step into and through the darkness of the unknown future.

Capricorn, the Goat, is the symbol of sacrificial death and the sign of atonement. Aquila the Eagle extends above the first decan of Capricorn, the main star of Aquila (Altair) being located at 7° Capricorn. The first decan of Capricorn is ruled by Jupiter (Zeus), to whom the Eagle was sacred. Capricorn signifies a special opportunity: Courage becomes the power to redeem, the power to develop conscience, and the insight to know what is right.

Sun 1° Capricorn: Birth of Martin Luther King (Jan/15/29). In a speech directed against the Vietnam war, the words of King illumine us to perceive the beings and motives behind *all* wars:

> Now, let me make it clear in the beginning, that I see this war as an unjust, evil, and futile war. I preach to you today on the war in Vietnam because my conscience leaves me with no other choice. The time has come for America to hear the truth about this tragic war. In international conflicts, the truth is hard to come by because most nations are deceived about themselves. Rationalizations and the incessant search for scapegoats are the psychological cataracts that blind us to our sins. But the day has passed for superficial patriotism. He who lives with untruth lives in spiritual slavery. Freedom is still the bonus we receive for knowing the truth. "Ye shall know the truth," says Jesus, "and the truth shall set you free." Now, I've chosen to preach about the war in Vietnam because I agree with Dante, that the hottest places in Hell are reserved for those who in a period of moral crisis maintain their neutrality. There comes a time when silence becomes betrayal.[2]

The virtue of Capricorn is "Courage becomes the power to redeem." May we find the courage to stand with the truth as redeemers. Today we remember a mighty voice who gave his life for the redemptive power of truth.

**January 16: ASPECT:** Venus conjunct Pluto 15° Sagittarius. On the start of the forty days in the desert Venus was at this degree, also very close to conjunction with Pluto. The planet Venus marks the realm of those we know as the Archai. These beings reached their human stage long ago when the young Earth was a huge body of warmth, expanded to the size marked by the orbit of the present day planet Saturn. The Archai stand above the Archangels and "grail" for the radiance of the Sun. These beings protected Christ—the Sun being—through his trials of temptation, for these are the Time Spirits who guide great evolutionary epochs, and it was he for whom they carry the "grail" who was now being tempted in a wilderness on the Earth.

The Archai that did not complete their evolution at the time of ancient Saturn evolution were held back, and became the beings known as the Asuras. The Asuras hold a disdain for the physical body and the physical world, for they did not achieve this wondrous physicality due to their backwardness. They work through violence and sexual perversion in order to bring harm to the bodies of human beings. When Christ climbed up Mt. Attarus to enter the forty days of continual temptation, he met dark beings who were inspired by the Asuras and

---

[2] Martin Luther King, "Why I Am Opposed to the War in Vietnam," April 30, 1967.

who sought to destroy his mission—for these beings want to shatter the continuity of time. The violence and sexual perversion that has become commonplace in our culture is the signature of the Asuras. With Venus passing the location in the heavens that remembers the forty days, and in conjunction with Pluto, we are wise to take note of the influences of these beings in our midst. To name them is to disempower them. Pluto signifies either the highest realms of divine love or the lowest morbidity of hatred toward anything that is good. Pluto rules the forces of nuclear weapons—and these destructive weapons are fit companions for the Asuras. Together they can spawn great evil. The triumph of these anti-forces is particularly effective when covertly directed toward the masses, as is the case with GMOs. Hermes speaks:

> My son, the powers of evil arose from the abyss in an attempt to disrupt the mission of the Lord, to negate it from the outset. It was only by way of meeting with and overcoming the powers of evil that the mission of Jesus Christ could truly begin. In what did this mission consist? Through the words, miracles, and suffering and death of the Lord, seeds were sown on the Earth for the coming of the Kingdom, Power and Glory of the Heavenly Trinity. And the beasts of the abyss sought—and seek—to prevent this by revealing a false kingdom, a counterfeit power and an illusory glory. Above in the heights is the true Kingdom, the real Power, and the actual Glory of the Divine Trinity, and this is caricatured and falsely reflected in the depths by the false kingdom, counterfeit power, and illusory glory of the beasts of the abyss. Historically the three temptations arose in the mass movements connected with the French Revolution, the Communist Revolution, and the Third Reich of National Socialism.[3]

The Archai are the voice of divine love that speaks to us through our Angel. These beings manifest the highest octaves of love. Today, as Venus and Pluto remember the start of the forty days of temptation, we recall that Christ never once looked at his tempters. Instead he lifted his eyes to Heaven and prayed to his Father. This we are to do as well.

---

3 CHA, The Temptation in the Wilderness.

Place not your eye upon things ugly and degenerate. Turn toward the good and let evil wither in its own degraded trenches. See the good in all you witness today, for only good is eternal. Yet do not deny the temporal *fact* of evil, for this can be a danger. Had Christ not recognized the tempters he would not have called to his Father. We are to name duality's temporal reality while strenuously attending the good. For knowledge of evil calls forth the good!

**January 18: ASPECT:** Superior conjunction of Mercury and Sun 3° Capricorn. This aspect in this degree occurred when Jesus taught in the synagogue. Many friends and relatives were in attendance, including the Holy Virgin Mary:

> You are the light of the world. A city on a hill cannot be hidden. Neither do people light a lamp and put it under a bowl. Instead they put it on its stand, and it gives light to everyone in the house. In the same way, let your light shine before others, that they may see your good deeds and praise your Father in Heaven. (Matthew 5: 13–16)

A superior conjunction between Mercury and the Sun means that Mercury is on the far side of the Sun and open to the intuitive in-streaming of the cosmos. Jesus spoke of our light. Of this we have plenty. If we feel limitation from others we can ask: Where are we willing to be limited? It takes both courage and willingness to shine, and our shining is our praise for our Father in Heaven. In the words of Estelle Isaacson:

> Child of Light! You are the answer, the antidote! Everything is in your divine memory, all the codes are housed within you—you are the hope for future generations. Indeed the future generations have placed you here to prepare for those who will redeem the Earth, and you shall come again in the future. You are planting the seeds for your own futures and shall come again to carry this work forward. You are heralds bearing the message of Christ for this time frame. And the spiritual worlds bear record of you and stand in awe of you; the record that they bear will bless the generations hereafter. The divine memory is imprinted in your very DNA; you can draw from this wellspring. Call upon the sacred magic

that you carry within you to bless the Earth, to sanctify Nature. This wellspring reaches all the way to Shambhala, a never-ending source for you. Exercise wisdom as you reach down into this spring, for you shall be given challenges, lessons, and shall suffer through temptations in order to prepare you, to try you, until you are ready to utilize these sacred powers—even the sacred powers of Shambhala. You will fall in the process. Have no fear. It is a time of learning. You will go through the pain and suffering until you are as pure as glass. This is the journey you are already on. Have faith in yourself. When you fall, repent and move on. Continue forward.

Always hold the Earth in the center of your chalice, your soul, which is being carved to ever greater breadths and depths by your suffering. This suffering gives you greater capacity to hold the Earth in pure Love, and to know what you can do to bless the Earth through these dark times.

Inwardly strive to always be in a state of rest, which means having faith. Be like the infant who easily sleeps in the safety of its mother's arms. She has faith in her mother, for her mother is always concerned for her and always loves her; she knows she will receive nourishment when she needs it and is always protected. And so her mind is at rest. Know this, Child of Light, and have faith that your Divine Mother is holding you now and She will feed you and will never leave you, and Her love has no end. Take strength in knowing this and allow your mind to rest. This will allow the Angels to work through you, for they cannot if your mind is in a state of fear. Rest, O Child of Light, in the bosom of the Mother! Receive Her Light and sustenance into your being.

Peace, Peace, Peace! Hear the AUM resonating from Her heart to yours.

And so it is. Amen.[4]

May we find our will to shine as intuitions stream into us from the wing-footed messenger. Receive the Light! In shining we illumine all that constrains us and we open paths for others to follow.

**January 20:** Inauguration Day. Sun: 5° Capricorn: Private ceremony (due to the 20th falling on a Sunday) to Inaugurate the president of the United States. The Sun today is exactly opposite where the Sun was at the 2009 Solar eclipse. It has been three and half years since the occurrence of this longest solar eclipse of the twenty-first century. We can pray that any darkness this eclipse then birthed is over-lighted now by the good. Also today the Moon is conjunct its south node at 28° Aries. This was the position of Jupiter and Saturn during the great conjunction that began this century in the year 2000, one that heralded a new Christ-like leadership. With the culmination of the three and one-half years that follow the 2009 eclipse, and with Moon and Moon node remembering the great conjunction of 2000, we can pray that today we inaugurate a leader who is willing to serve the good—and not one whose agenda wills to eclipse the Christ.

**ASPECT:** Heliocentric Mercury 10° Capricorn square Saturn 10° Libra. Mercury and Saturn were square to each other, in today's same degree, at the Flight into Egypt of the family of the Solomon Jesus child who was then one year old (Mar. 2, 5 BC). Also, at the conception of this great soul who became the Solomon Jesus—this spiritual king, this master—the waxing Moon stood at 10° Libra. "This was also the subsequent location of the Full Moon at the start of the Mystery of Golgotha, at the carrying of the cross up Mt. Calvary on Good Friday, April 3, AD 33."[5] These three events—the Flight into Egypt, a great soul's conception, and the greatest event in all of Earth evolution (the Passion and death of Jesus Christ) are today remembered through Saturn.

After the flight into Egypt, Herod called for the murder of the innocent children of Bethlehem, which marked the culmination of his evil deeds. This abominable act most certainly falls under the shadow of the 2009 eclipse of the Sun, for this deed proclaimed the fact that Herod's heart was eclipsed by evil forces. Above and beyond this dark memory stands the promise of victory over evil as exemplified by the Passion of Christ. The forces inherent in the Light of the World shall prevail over all evil, and this force dwells within us all. This we can

---

4  Isaacson, *The Coming Times*.

5  CHA, *The Journey of the Three Kings and the Flight of the Holy Family to Egypt*.

remember and pray that this becomes the way of all great leaders.

*Saturn in Libra calls for us to see what is real: to understand relationships, and to find equanimity. The danger with Saturn in Libra is that we fall asleep to relationships forming in our very midst.* Square to Mercury, this aspect offers a dynamic interaction between the two planets. Mercury, the great teacher/healer, is in Capricorn—the constellation of kings. There are kings who crown themselves and there are kings who are crowned by Heaven. The stars beg the question: who today is being crowned?

Today Mercury stimulates our mind and Saturn stirs us to remember the wisdom of the Master Jesus, thus awakening us to the presence of evil forces that are striving to murder all that is innocent and pure in our world. We can take up the Flight into Egypt by opening to the mystery wisdom of the stars, for this is the mystery stream of the great Zarathustra who became the Solomon Jesus. His flight into Egypt is to become our winged-flight into the mysteries of the Holy Grail and the work of becoming modern knights in our fight against the insidious encroachment of materialism. These knights do not follow an outer king, but instead unite with the one true king of kings who inaugurates all his disciples as protectors of life, freedom and goodness. This is a good day to be wakeful and decisive (Mercury), for we know not the moment that shall test the spiritual integrity (Saturn) of humanity.

**January 21:** Sun 6° Capricorn: The Adoration of the Magi (Dec/26/6 BC). Second conversion of Mary Magdalene (Dec/26/30). The magi were those who continued the Chaldean astrological tradition inaugurated in Babylon by Zoroaster in the sixth century BC. They were instructed to wait for the signs in Heaven that foretold the rebirth of their spiritual teacher, and they were to follow this sign (the Star of the Magi) to the birthplace of the new king. At the birth of Jesus they beheld the radiant star of the soul of their spiritual teacher, whose birth they beheld from the sign of the Virgin on the night of the Full Moon in Virgo, and they followed this star to Jerusalem.

The three kings (*magi*) came as representatives of the soul of humankind—of humanity's powers of thought, feeling, and will—faced with the choice between serving the higher Self or collaborating with the lower self in pitting itself against the higher Self. The meeting with Herod represented a temptation for the three kings, a temptation which was of significance for humanity. But with the help of divine intervention the temptation was rendered impotent, and the three magi did not betray their spiritual king.[6]

On the anniversary of this great event, decades later, Mary Magdalene experienced her second and last conversion. Magdalene, as the Apostle to the Apostles, was in mystical union with her teacher—and from this point onward she was therefore not spared from experiencing the trials of the God-Man in her heart. And, like the kings before her, Magdalene most certainly recognized Christ as the true king, one whose kingdom was not of this world.

The events of the Adoration and the Conversion, both occurring at this Sun degree, foretell how necessary is spiritual navigation in these times when lies and deceit are everywhere. Today commemorates the overcoming of the temptation of the lower self, the birth of a true king, and the casting out of demons. May we too overcome the temptation of our lower self and rise to the mission of our higher self. We know not when we will find Herods along the way.

~

**Note:** Today is the public ceremony of the Inauguration of the President of the United States. It is noteworthy to remember the Supreme Court's decision in 2010—at this same Sun degree—that allowed corporations to spend money without limit in political campaigns. This decision most assuredly played a large part in bringing to power the candidate who is today inaugurated. We can be certain that a true king is not being crowned, for the true king is not of this world. We are to become the new kings, crowned with the awakened powers of our consciousness soul, kings who follow the star of spiritual guidance. This is a Grail Path, and a

---

6 Ibid.

Grail Path is one that steadfastly confronts evil and casts out demons. In the words of the Hopi: *We are the ones we have been waiting for.*

**January 25:** Sun 10° Capricorn in conjunction with the mega star 9 Sagittae in the Arrow, above the Goat. Heliocentric Mercury was in conjunction with this mega star at the Resurrection. The Sun enters the second decan of Capricorn. Sagitta the Arrow extends above most of this decan, which is ruled by Mars.

**January 26:** Mars enters Aquarius: "May it raise itself in life's stream" (Steiner, *Twelve Moods of the Zodiac*). Through the power of meditation, the boundless finds its containment in the depths and rises as a sustaining wave of inspiration, which shapes itself to form a chalice for the living word. Growth finds its sacrifice through the forming power of the word. Mars was in Aquarius at the conceptions of both the Solomon Mary and the Nathan Mary, as well as at the summoning of Judas and the raising of the daughter of Jairus. We witness purity, betrayal and miracles. May we form words that become vessels into which the Holy Spirit may find expression through us!

**January 27:** Full Moon 12° Cancer opposite Sun 12° Capricorn. Moon conjunct Praesepe: the Beehive in the middle of the spiraling arms of the constellation of Cancer. Jupiter is exalted at this degree of the zodiac.

> We remember Praesepe, the "Beehive" cradled at the center of the spiraling in and spiraling out of Cancer, and ponder the words of Goethe, "When the inside is in order, the outside takes care of itself." Whereas Gemini's relational aspect is all about the "other," knowing oneself through the reflection of the other, clearly Cancer is about the inside-outside relationship—understanding that what lives within is reflected outwardly. This calls forth the "inner work" of redeeming the outer reality.[7]

Clearly this is a Full Moon filled with the powers of catharsis in order to redeem the fallen aspects of our soul and the fallen aspects of the world's soul.

---

[7] Paul and Powell, *Cosmic Dances of the Zodiac*.

Square to this Full Moon was the *raising of the cross* on the hill of Golgotha. Today a silent cross is raised in the heavens, with today's Full Moon and its invisible companion—the Full Moon of Golgotha. Together the two form a cross. May we encircle this cross with seven roses as our promise to face the purifying fires of catharsis. What 1,980 years ago was one man dying to save the whole of humanity has become, in our time, an array of hostile agendas that seek to sacrifice many in order to preserve their power. What a tragic inversion!

The stars are speaking their patterned language over this past week: We remember the Christ-like leadership heralded at the beginning of the century with the Jupiter/Saturn conjunction; we stand in opposition to the eclipse of the Sun in 2009; the great Zarathustra's rebirth is remembered; Magdalene's demons are cast out; and laws that break the last illusions of democracy are fulfilled. This Full Moon asks us to find Christ in us and see him in all others. It reminds us of agendas that oppose this new leadership and encourages us to remember we have the power to cast out our demons and thereby co-create the shift now occurring. It asks us to find our kingly natures and hold fast to our crowns. It stands as witness to powerful laws that have inveigled their way into society, riding on the devilish motives of the third temptation in the wilderness: turning stones to bread. Will our technologies and our lust for power and money turn us to stone? Or, will we receive the blessings the death on Golgotha bestowed to each of us? Fill your cup with life under the light of this Full Moon!

It is the Capricorn Sun that is illumining today's Moon. Capricorn encourages the soul to hold to its karmic task—which entails transformation. This is the path of the kings, the "Royal Way" that is the path of initiation. May we put the inside in order, so that the outside may take care of itself.

**January 29:** Venus enters Capricorn: May the past feel the future (Steiner, *Twelve Moods of the Zodiac*). When faithfulness to the past can feel the future, the future can then find its rest in the present, in harmony with the World-Being's vigilance. The past imbued with hope becomes the vessel for the possibilities of miracle. This births the blossoming might of change. Venus was in Capricorn at the three temptations in the wilderness and the turning of water into wine at the wedding in Cana.

**Sun 14° Capricorn:** Death of John the Baptist. John the Baptist is the great individuality of whom Rudolf Steiner foretold that he would be with us again at the end of the twentieth century, to lead humanity past the great crisis it would then be facing. As John was there to behold the Light at the First Coming, so is this individuality here again to meet those witnessing the true Light of the Second Coming. When Lazarus was paralyzed in the shadowland of the dead, it was John who united with him, and it was Christ who freed Lazarus from his entombment, by raising him from the dead. This initiation of the Lazarus-John being uniquely prepared him to be our guide as we now endure the meeting with our individual shadow nature; he prepares us as well for the meeting with the collective shadow nature of all humanity. After his beheading, John became the guardian of the circle of Christ's disciples and was therefore aware of the plight of Lazarus—the beloved friend of Jesus. In like manner John is now the guardian of the communities working with Michael and Sophia in the name of Christ. He can lead us out of any darkness that entraps us individually or collectively, but first we must open to his ministration. The Sun is in the middle of the constellation of Capricorn, the constellation that empowers us to transform darkness into light—to steadfastly meet resistance from rigid thought-forms that are holding onto the past. This is our work: to transform the limitations of the brain-bound intellect into forces born of our heart's cognition. The heart will lead us into our intended future, and to find this future we call upon John. The disciples of John are now forming communities that can be recognized in the fact that they love one another. Can we live into the redeeming presence of spiritual guidance? Can we trust what is not seen?

**January 30:** Sun 16° Capricorn square Saturn 16° Libra. News of the death of Lazarus (July/16/32). Saturn was here when "Jesus, accompanied by some apostles, returned to the little village, where the three holy women were waiting for him. Together they received the news of Lazarus's death. It was here that Jesus spoke the words: 'Our friend Lazarus has fallen asleep.'" (John 11:7–13; *Chron.*, p. 315). The Sun was also here when the Sanhedrin appointed a committee to investigate Jesus and concluded that Jesus was in league with the devil. Taking these two events together, today we are faced both with authority figures that live in fear of the truth (Capricorn Sun), and with the *death of soul* necessary to achieve a relationship with higher levels of truth (Saturn in Libra). For it was due to his death and his being raised by Christ, that Lazarus became the bearer of the Rose Cross. The danger is that we remain asleep and do not recognize the forces that are encroaching on our freedom through fear-inducing manipulations.

The holy women represent communities of Sophia, that can withstand the necessity of our soul's death and nurture its transforming rebirth into love-filled courage.

# FEBRUARY

The Sun begins in Capricorn (The SeaGoat) and moves into Aquarius (The WaterHuman) on the 13th. The New Moon is on the 10th and the Full Moon is on the 25th. Jupiter continues to be visible in the south at sunset in front of the Bull (Taurus) until the closing days of April, when it disappears into the Sun's glow. Mercury begins its first of three retrograde cycles in 2013 on February 24th (going direct March 18th.) Saturn also will station retrograde this month; on the 19th Saturn ceases moving forward and will appear to travel backward until early July this year. We'll be able to gaze upon Saturn against the faint stars of Libra, rising in the east about midnight this month. By May, Saturn will rise as the Sun sets, making for earlier gazing opportunities. As you contemplate Saturn in the Scales, open your being to insights regarding fairness, rules, equality and tradition.

**February 4:** Mars conjunct Neptune 7° Aquarius. Healing of the blind youth Manahem (Oct/6/30). "Jesus went this morning from Shiloh to Korea. There he healed the blind youth Manahem, who had the gift of prophecy. That evening, with the beginning of the Sabbath, he spoke in the synagogue about Noah, the ark, and the rainbow as the sign of God's mercy." (*Chron.*, p. 250)

Mars conjunct Neptune represents the Word (Mars) that heals (Neptune). Mars was at the same place of today's conjunction at this healing of Manahem. With this miracle we see that though we have eyes, we may in truth be blind:

> For, generally, either the external world is seen in an illusory way, which is the tendency of the left eye, or in a God-less way, which is the tendency of the right eye, or in the case of blindness the outer world is not seen at all, which gives the possibility of seeing with the third eye, the spiritual organ located in the region of the forehead between the right and left eye. Manahem's blindness meant he saw only with the third eye.[8]

With Mars conjunct Neptune we can ask: Are our words grounded in spiritual Inspiration (higher Neptune/Soul of the World), or are they parroting Ahriman's inspirations—whereby they are attached to magnetized feelings? Such feelings are paralyzed due to their bondage to egoistic sympathies and antipathies that are in consort with power, greed, and self-satisfaction. The former gives true sight, the latter blindness. Pervasive noise, an affliction of our culture, drowns out cosmic Inspirations and increases a growing tendency to see either the godless or illusions, or else causes us to swing madly between the two, ever missing what is right before our very eyes. Manahem was born blind so he would not be distracted by the eyes of Lucifer (illusions) or Ahriman (godlessness) during the incarnation in which he was destined to meet Jesus Christ. We are all Manahem, seeking to see with the eyes of spirit. This means understanding the revelatory stream that has been opened by the great teachers of humanity who have been working in the twentieth century and in our present time.

Mars, as representative of the Word, reminds us of John's message to those at Christ's incarnation in the flesh: "The light shines in the darkness, and the darkness comprehendeth it not" (John 1:5). *Many missed recognizing the light of the world*

---

8  CHA, The Sun Chronicle in the Life of the Messiah.

*at the Turning Point in Time. This blindness has continued to prevent many from participating in the continuous stream of "Christ-imbued teachings" that have been carried by spiritual teachers since the time of Rudolf Steiner. It is a tragedy for both human and spiritual worlds when this continuity goes unseen, for in the living stream of spiritual successorship the mysteries are continually renewed lest they fall into Ahriman's favorite prison—libraries, from whence the past endlessly circles, becoming ever more sclerotic before the light of new revelation.* Those who dare to bring the new light are historically hung on the scaffolds of heresy. This is the blindness Manahem refused to fall into, and therefore he was born blind so he could see the Light and hear the Word that was changing the face of time.

Compassion awakens as we see that what *appears* to be opposition to the light is, in reality, the fate of the darkness in its inability to comprehend the light. Like Manahem we are to be called by the truth emanating from the Tree of Life. This is the tree of the Apocalyptist, who is urging us to find the Morning Star—the light leading us to become builders of the New Heaven and the New Earth.

Sun enters the third decan of Capricorn ruled by the Sun, associated with the constellation of the Dolphin.

**February 6:** Mercury conjunct Neptune 7° Aquarius: The second temptation of Christ (Nov/28/29). Heliocentric Mercury was here at the second temptation in the wilderness. The second temptation was the temptation to have Christ plunge from the pinnacle of the temple with the promise that Angels would catch him. This temptation contributes to the second Fall in our time—the fall into the subearthly realms—and this is the result of misplaced attachments within our etheric bodies:

> Just as in the far-distant past humankind went through the Fall as a result of Lucifer's penetration into the astral body, so in our time humanity is going through a second Fall through Ahriman's intervention into the etheric body. Through materialistic thinking the way was paved for the second Fall. Our thoughts are deposited in the etheric body, and materialistic

| SIDEREAL GEOCENTRIC LONGITUDES : FEBRUARY 2013 Gregorian at 0 hours UT | | | | | | | | | | | |
|---|---|---|---|---|---|---|---|---|---|---|---|
| DAY | ☉ | ☽ | ☊ | ☿ | ♀ | ♂ | ♃ | ♄ | ♅ | ♆ | ♇ |
| 1 FR | 17 ♑ 22 | 14 ♍ 45 | 27 ♎ 13R | 27 ♑ 0 | 3 ♑ 41 | 4 ♒ 14 | 11 ♉ 25 | 16 ♎ 20 | 10 ♓ 42 | 7 ♒ 9 | 15 ♐ 27 |
| 2 SA | 18 23 | 28 15 | 27 10 | 28 46 | 4 56 | 5 1 | 11 25 | 16 22 | 10 45 | 7 11 | 15 29 |
| 3 SU | 19 24 | 11 ♎ 57 | 27 9 | 0 ♒ 31 | 6 11 | 5 48 | 11 26 | 16 23 | 10 47 | 7 13 | 15 31 |
| 4 MO | 20 24 | 25 51 | 27 9 | 2 16 | 7 26 | 6 36 | 11 26 | 16 25 | 10 49 | 7 15 | 15 32 |
| 5 TU | 21 25 | 9 ♏ 58 | 27 9 | 4 0 | 8 41 | 7 23 | 11 27 | 16 26 | 10 52 | 7 18 | 15 34 |
| 6 WE | 22 26 | 24 17 | 27 7 | 5 44 | 9 57 | 8 11 | 11 29 | 16 28 | 10 54 | 7 20 | 15 36 |
| 7 TH | 23 27 | 8 ♐ 46 | 27 2 | 7 26 | 11 12 | 8 58 | 11 30 | 16 29 | 10 57 | 7 22 | 15 38 |
| 8 FR | 24 28 | 23 22 | 26 55 | 9 7 | 12 27 | 9 45 | 11 32 | 16 30 | 11 0 | 7 24 | 15 40 |
| 9 SA | 25 28 | 7 ♑ 57 | 26 44 | 10 46 | 13 42 | 10 33 | 11 33 | 16 31 | 11 2 | 7 27 | 15 41 |
| 10 SU | 26 29 | 22 25 | 26 32 | 12 22 | 14 57 | 11 20 | 11 36 | 16 32 | 11 5 | 7 29 | 15 43 |
| 11 MO | 27 30 | 6 ♒ 39 | 26 20 | 13 55 | 16 12 | 12 7 | 11 38 | 16 33 | 11 7 | 7 31 | 15 45 |
| 12 TU | 28 31 | 20 33 | 26 8 | 15 25 | 17 28 | 12 55 | 11 40 | 16 34 | 11 10 | 7 33 | 15 46 |
| 13 WE | 29 31 | 4 ♓ 4 | 25 58 | 16 51 | 18 43 | 13 42 | 11 43 | 16 35 | 11 13 | 7 36 | 15 48 |
| 14 TH | 0 ♒ 32 | 17 9 | 25 50 | 18 12 | 19 58 | 14 29 | 11 46 | 16 35 | 11 16 | 7 38 | 15 50 |
| 15 FR | 1 33 | 29 50 | 25 46 | 19 28 | 21 13 | 15 17 | 11 49 | 16 35 | 11 18 | 7 40 | 15 51 |
| 16 SA | 2 33 | 12 ♈ 11 | 25 43 | 20 37 | 22 28 | 16 4 | 11 52 | 16 36 | 11 21 | 7 42 | 15 53 |
| 17 SU | 3 34 | 24 16 | 25 43 | 21 40 | 23 43 | 16 51 | 11 55 | 16 36 | 11 24 | 7 45 | 15 55 |
| 18 MO | 4 34 | 6 ♉ 9 | 25 43 | 22 35 | 24 58 | 17 39 | 11 59 | 16 36 | 11 27 | 7 47 | 15 56 |
| 19 TU | 5 35 | 17 58 | 25 42 | 23 22 | 26 13 | 18 26 | 12 3 | 16 36R | 11 30 | 7 49 | 15 58 |
| 20 WE | 6 35 | 29 46 | 25 40 | 24 0 | 27 28 | 19 13 | 12 6 | 16 36 | 11 33 | 7 51 | 15 59 |
| 21 TH | 7 36 | 11 ♊ 40 | 25 35 | 24 28 | 28 43 | 20 0 | 12 11 | 16 36 | 11 36 | 7 54 | 16 1 |
| 22 FR | 8 36 | 23 44 | 25 28 | 24 47 | 29 58 | 20 47 | 12 15 | 16 36 | 11 39 | 7 56 | 16 2 |
| 23 SA | 9 37 | 6 ♋ 1 | 25 18 | 24 56 | 1 ♒ 13 | 21 34 | 12 19 | 16 35 | 11 42 | 7 58 | 16 3 |
| 24 SU | 10 37 | 18 33 | 25 6 | 24 55R | 2 28 | 22 22 | 12 24 | 16 35 | 11 45 | 8 1 | 16 5 |
| 25 MO | 11 37 | 1 ♌ 22 | 24 53 | 24 44 | 3 43 | 23 9 | 12 29 | 16 34 | 11 48 | 8 3 | 16 6 |
| 26 TU | 12 38 | 14 27 | 24 40 | 24 24 | 4 58 | 23 56 | 12 34 | 16 33 | 11 51 | 8 5 | 16 8 |
| 27 WE | 13 38 | 27 46 | 24 29 | 23 54 | 6 13 | 24 43 | 12 39 | 16 33 | 11 54 | 8 7 | 16 9 |
| 28 TH | 14 38 | 11 ♍ 18 | 24 20 | 23 17 | 7 28 | 25 30 | 12 45 | 16 32 | 11 57 | 8 10 | 16 10 |

| INGRESSES : | |
|---|---|
| 2 ☽ → ♎ 3: 5 | 22 ♀ → ♒ 0:33 |
| ☿ → ♒ 16:57 | ☽ → ♋ 12:18 |
| 4 ☽ → ♏ 7: 6 | 24 ☽ → ♌ 21:28 |
| 6 ☽ → ♐ 9:29 | 27 ☽ → ♍ 3:59 |
| 8 ☽ → ♑ 10:54 | |
| 10 ☽ → ♒ 12:42 | |
| 12 ☽ → ♓ 16:42 | |
| 13 ☉ → ♒ 11:20 | |
| 15 ☽ → ♈ 0:18 | |
| 17 ☽ → ♉ 11:32 | |
| 20 ☽ → ♊ 0:27 | |

| ASPECTS & ECLIPSES : | | | |
|---|---|---|---|
| 1 ☿ □ ☊ 2:57 | ☿ □ ♃ 12: 6 | 17 ☽ ☌ ☋ 2:54 | ☉ ☍ ☽ 20:25 |
| 3 ☽ ☌ ♄ 7:43 | 10 ☉ □ ☊ 1: 1 | ☉ □ ☽ 20:29 | ☉ □ ♃ 22:25 |
| ☉ □ ☽ 13:55 | ☽ N ☊ 6:47 | 18 ☽ ☌ ♃ 11:53 | 26 ☿ ☌ ♂ 9: 8 |
| 4 ☽ ☌ ☊ 2:14 | ☉ ☌ ☽ 7:19 | ♀ □ ☊ 14:11 | ☽ ☍ ☿ 17:21 |
| ♂ ☌ ♆ 21: 5 | ♂ □ ♃ 8:11 | 19 ☽ ☌ A 6:46 | ☽ ☍ ♂ 18:11 |
| 5 ☽ ☍ ♃ 2:31 | 11 ☽ ☌ ♆ 1:28 | 21 ☉ ☌ ♆ 7:25 | 28 ☽ ☍ ♅ 1:10 |
| 6 ☿ ☌ ♆ 23: 3 | ♀ □ ♄ 6:41 | ☽ ☍ ♇ 8:41 | ☉ □ Π 9:18 |
| 7 ☽ ☌ ♇ 11:18 | ☽ ☌ ♂ 9:55 | 24 ☽ S ☊ 12: 7 | ♀ ☌ ♆ 13:42 |
| ☽ ☌ P 12:13 | ☽ ☌ ☿ 13:59 | ☉ □ Π 20:17 | |
| 8 ☿ ☌ ♂ 17:55 | 13 ☽ ☌ ♅ 13: 4 | 25 ☽ ☍ ♀ 4:49 | |
| 9 ☽ ☌ ♀ 10:23 | 16 ☽ ☍ ♄ 8:43 | ☽ ☍ ♆ 12:21 | |

| SIDEREAL HELIOCENTRIC LONGITUDES : FEBRUARY 2013 Gregorian at 0 hours UT | | | | | | | | | | | |
|---|---|---|---|---|---|---|---|---|---|---|---|
| DAY | Sid. Time | ☿ | ♀ | ⊕ | ♂ | ♃ | ♄ | ♅ | ♆ | ♇ | Vernal Point |
| 1 FR | 8:45:27 | 23 ♒ 39 | 14 ♐ 59 | 17 ♋ 22 | 16 ♒ 10 | 21 ♉ 37 | 10 ♎ 33 | 12 ♓ 58 | 7 ♒ 47 | 14 ♐ 32 | 5 ♓ 4'39" |
| 2 SA | 8:49:23 | 28 8 | 16 34 | 18 23 | 16 48 | 21 42 | 10 35 | 12 58 | 7 48 | 14 32 | 5 ♓ 4'39" |
| 3 SU | 8:53:20 | 2 ♓ 44 | 18 9 | 19 24 | 17 26 | 21 48 | 10 37 | 12 59 | 7 48 | 14 32 | 5 ♓ 4'39" |
| 4 MO | 8:57:17 | 7 30 | 19 44 | 20 24 | 18 4 | 21 53 | 10 39 | 13 0 | 7 48 | 14 33 | 5 ♓ 4'38" |
| 5 TU | 9: 1:13 | 12 24 | 21 19 | 21 25 | 18 42 | 21 58 | 10 41 | 13 0 | 7 49 | 14 33 | 5 ♓ 4'38" |
| 6 WE | 9: 5:10 | 17 27 | 22 54 | 22 26 | 19 20 | 22 3 | 10 43 | 13 1 | 7 49 | 14 33 | 5 ♓ 4'38" |
| 7 TH | 9: 9: 6 | 22 40 | 24 29 | 23 27 | 19 58 | 22 9 | 10 45 | 13 2 | 7 49 | 14 34 | 5 ♓ 4'38" |
| 8 FR | 9:13: 3 | 28 2 | 26 4 | 24 28 | 20 36 | 22 14 | 10 46 | 13 2 | 7 50 | 14 34 | 5 ♓ 4'38" |
| 9 SA | 9:16:59 | 3 ♈ 32 | 27 38 | 25 29 | 21 14 | 22 19 | 10 48 | 13 3 | 7 50 | 14 34 | 5 ♓ 4'38" |
| 10 SU | 9:20:56 | 9 12 | 29 13 | 26 29 | 21 52 | 22 24 | 10 50 | 13 4 | 7 50 | 14 35 | 5 ♓ 4'38" |
| 11 MO | 9:24:52 | 14 59 | 0 ♑ 48 | 27 30 | 22 30 | 22 29 | 10 52 | 13 4 | 7 51 | 14 35 | 5 ♓ 4'37" |
| 12 TU | 9:28:49 | 20 54 | 2 23 | 28 31 | 23 8 | 22 35 | 10 54 | 13 5 | 7 51 | 14 35 | 5 ♓ 4'37" |
| 13 WE | 9:32:46 | 26 57 | 3 58 | 29 31 | 23 46 | 22 40 | 10 56 | 13 5 | 7 52 | 14 36 | 5 ♓ 4'37" |
| 14 TH | 9:36:42 | 3 ♉ 5 | 5 33 | 0 ♌ 32 | 24 24 | 22 45 | 10 58 | 13 6 | 7 52 | 14 36 | 5 ♓ 4'37" |
| 15 FR | 9:40:39 | 9 18 | 7 8 | 1 33 | 25 2 | 22 50 | 11 0 | 13 7 | 7 52 | 14 36 | 5 ♓ 4'37" |
| 16 SA | 9:44:35 | 15 34 | 8 42 | 2 33 | 25 40 | 22 56 | 11 2 | 13 7 | 7 53 | 14 37 | 5 ♓ 4'37" |
| 17 SU | 9:48:32 | 21 53 | 10 17 | 3 34 | 26 18 | 23 1 | 11 3 | 13 8 | 7 53 | 14 37 | 5 ♓ 4'37" |
| 18 MO | 9:52:28 | 28 12 | 11 52 | 4 34 | 26 56 | 23 6 | 11 5 | 13 9 | 7 53 | 14 37 | 5 ♓ 4'36" |
| 19 TU | 9:56:25 | 4 ♊ 31 | 13 27 | 5 35 | 27 34 | 23 11 | 11 7 | 13 9 | 7 54 | 14 38 | 5 ♓ 4'36" |
| 20 WE | 10: 0:21 | 10 47 | 15 2 | 6 35 | 28 11 | 23 17 | 11 9 | 13 10 | 7 54 | 14 38 | 5 ♓ 4'36" |
| 21 TH | 10: 4:18 | 17 0 | 16 37 | 7 36 | 28 49 | 23 22 | 11 11 | 13 11 | 7 54 | 14 38 | 5 ♓ 4'36" |
| 22 FR | 10: 8:15 | 23 7 | 18 12 | 8 36 | 29 27 | 23 27 | 11 13 | 13 11 | 7 55 | 14 39 | 5 ♓ 4'36" |
| 23 SA | 10:12:11 | 29 8 | 19 47 | 9 37 | 0 ♓ 5 | 23 32 | 11 15 | 13 12 | 7 55 | 14 39 | 5 ♓ 4'36" |
| 24 SU | 10:16: 8 | 5 ♋ 2 | 21 21 | 10 37 | 0 42 | 23 37 | 11 17 | 13 13 | 7 56 | 14 39 | 5 ♓ 4'36" |
| 25 MO | 10:20: 4 | 10 47 | 22 56 | 11 37 | 1 20 | 23 43 | 11 19 | 13 13 | 7 56 | 14 39 | 5 ♓ 4'36" |
| 26 TU | 10:24: 1 | 16 24 | 24 31 | 12 38 | 1 58 | 23 48 | 11 21 | 13 14 | 7 56 | 14 40 | 5 ♓ 4'35" |
| 27 WE | 10:27:57 | 21 51 | 26 6 | 13 38 | 2 35 | 23 53 | 11 22 | 13 14 | 7 57 | 14 40 | 5 ♓ 4'35" |
| 28 TH | 10:31:54 | 27 9 | 27 41 | 14 38 | 3 13 | 23 58 | 11 24 | 13 15 | 7 57 | 14 40 | 5 ♓ 4'35" |

| INGRESSES : |
|---|
| 2 ☿ → ♓ 9:50 |
| 8 ☿ → ♈ 8:40 |
| 10 ♀ → ♑ 11:49 |
| 13 ⊕ → ♌ 11:18 |
| ☿ → ♉ 12: 0 |
| 18 ☿ → ♊ 6:48 |
| 22 ♂ → ♓ 20:59 |
| 23 ☿ → ♋ 3:29 |
| 28 ☿ → ♌ 13:13 |

| ASPECTS (HELIOCENTRIC +MOON(TYCHONIC)) : | | | | |
|---|---|---|---|---|
| 1 ☽ □ ♀ 0:28 | ☽ □ ☿ 12:15 | 14 ☿ □ ♆ 18:31 | ☿ ☍ ♇ 14:50 | 27 ☿ N ☊ 7:40 |
| 2 ☽ ☌ ♄ 21:41 | 9 ☽ □ ♄ 4:43 | 15 ☽ □ ♀ 16:10 | 21 ☽ □ ♅ 3: 1 | ☽ ☍ ♂ 9: 1 |
| 4 ☽ □ ♆ 20:22 | 10 ☿ ☍ ♄ 6:54 | ☽ ☍ ♄ 21:43 | ♀ ☌ A 3:13 | 28 ☽ ☍ ♅ 3:27 |
| 5 ☿ ☌ ♅ 2:54 | ♂ □ ♃ 23:21 | 17 ☿ ☌ P 3:14 | ☽ ☍ ♇ 5:56 | ☿ ☍ ♀ 3:33 |
| ☿ □ ♇ 10:17 | 11 ☽ ☌ ♆ 2: 1 | ☿ ☌ ♃ 4:21 | ⊕ ☍ ♆ 7:25 | ☽ □ ♇ 5:57 |
| ☽ □ ♂ 15:22 | 12 ☽ □ ♃ 3:34 | ♀ □ ♄ 11:56 | ☽ ☌ ☿ 21:33 | |
| ☽ ☍ ♃ 20:16 | ☽ ☌ ♂ 4:45 | ☿ □ ♂ 18:36 | 23 ☽ □ ♄ 10: 6 | |
| 7 ☽ □ ♅ 7: 0 | ☿ ☌ ☊ 10:36 | 18 ☽ □ ♆ 3:31 | 24 ☽ ☍ ♀ 6: 2 | |
| ☽ ☌ ♇ 9:31 | 13 ☿ □ ⊕ 12: 8 | 19 ☽ ☌ ♃ 10:42 | 25 ☿ □ ♄ 2:14 | |
| ☿ □ ♀ 11:37 | ☽ ☌ ♅ 16:29 | ☽ □ ♂ 20:36 | ☽ ☍ ♆ 12: 6 | |
| 8 ☽ ☌ ♀ 4:58 | ☽ □ ♇ 19:15 | 20 ☿ □ ♅ 9:11 | 26 ☽ □ ♃ 17: 0 | |

thinking—by its very nature hardened and empty (devoid of life)—brings about a hardening and hollowing out of the etheric body.[9]

With Mercury remembering this temptation and in conjunction with Neptune (whose fallen nature is Ahriman), we are faced with a choice: To plunge from the pinnacle in order to follow Ahrimanic illusion, or to stand tall on the pinnacle of the temple (our consciousness) in order to receive Inspirations of the World Soul (Neptune). If we plunge it will not be the good Angels who catch us.

Neptune plays an important role this month as Mars, Mercury, Sun, and Venus are all transiting this planet. Neptune was rising at the birth of Johannes Kepler. Kepler is a wonderful example of one who did not plunge from the pinnacle of consciousness, but rather attuned his soul to the harmony of the spheres:

> Kepler pursued a kind of "astral mysticism," and sought the relationships, the comic harmonies, between the human soul and the World Soul. This is an expression of the transcendental impulse of Neptune, which was active in the horizon of [his] consciousness. His world outlook was permeated with the call of the all-pervasive cosmic harmony, associated with Neptune (laid down during the second *manvantara*, that of the goddess Night, according to the cosmology of Orpheus). Kepler's inner life was raised up to become blessed with the Inspiration (corresponding to Neptune) of the World Soul, which led him to discover deep truths about the harmonies of the universe.[10]

Today Neptune is closely trine to the position of Neptune at Kepler's birth:

> Just as the development of thinking depends on overcoming the temptation of the brilliance of "electrified thinking" in order to arrive at Illumination, so does the uplifting of feeling depend on the overcoming of a particular temptation to arrive at Inspiration. This temptation, leading to magnetized feeling, occurs when the human being allows his feelings to dictate his life, in the sense of his becoming a slave of sympathy and antipathy.[11]

Neptune is the planet of Inspiration of one kind or another. Kepler exemplified Inspiration born of the goddess Night/Sophia. We can add to the loss of sight afflicting humanity, the loss of hearing. No longer do most even know there are such things as the harmonies of the spheres.

May we search for the silence of peace and listen to the harmonies of nature. We are surrounded by noise that is in truth "densified sound" from sub-earthly realms (anti-inspiration) where Neptunian harmony becomes a hollow caricature of the loftiness of Sophia's Night. Today we can make use of the power of meditation (Aquarius) in order to find the Inspirations riding on the spiritual airwaves of Aquarius. These Inspirations strengthen our capacity to stand in uprightness on the pinnacle of our individual temple, in order to reach ever higher into the harmonies of the cosmic Temple.

~

**Note:** In Stalinist Russia in the year 1930, Neptune stood opposite to its position this month. During this time great crimes were committed against humanity. Neptune represents divine Inspiration as well as its opposite—demonic inspiration. In the words of the great seer, Daniel Andreev, a prophet for the coming culture of Sophia: "There is a special term—*Hochha*—which means 'Satanic enlightenment.' It is a matter of an ecstatic condition in which a human being communes with lofty demonic powers—not in trance, not in sleep, but in full possession of consciousness."[12]

It is the ahrimanic powers that strive to inspire this kind of communion. And as Ahriman is connected to the planet Neptune, which plays a major role in the stars this month, we are urged to direct our intelligence to the spheres of Michaelic Cosmic Truth. The ahrimanic illusion is to be named and countered. This is our work. Steiner amply warned that our encounter with him would be unavoidable, and other great teachers have sounded similar warnings:

---

9 Powell, *Cultivating Inner Radiance and the Body of Immortality*, p. 118.
10 Powell, *Hermetic Astrology*, vol. 2, p. 313.
11 Ibid., pp. 313-14.
12 Powell, *Prophecy-Phenomena-Hope*, p. 94.

Another important theme is that of the creation of an ahrimanic *maya*, into which a large part of humankind is being drawn. The Sanskrit word *maya* is an age-old concept that describes what is now taking place in our world (*deception* also being a key word here). For the rishis of Ancient India, *maya* signified the illusion we come into by virtue of forgetting our spiritual origin and, in forgetting, that we come to believe in sense perceptible reality as a given, replacing spiritual reality.[13]

And last, to mark the potential influence of Neptune properly this month, Rudolf Steiner speaks in his last lecture to the priests:

> Satan, however, can make use of this great moment in the evolution of humanity to draw the human being across into his own realm through the intellect. Already now we can observe how the satanic power is endeavoring to draw the human being across into its evolution. The method used is to combine human beings into groups the seeds of which are visible everywhere today—groups in which the old group souls cease to exist and in which a new kind of group soul nature can begin. What is happening over in the East of Europe just now [Stalinist Russia] is so terribly satanic because its whole aim is to force human beings together in ways that make it necessary for there to be group souls. Once the most intelligent have been dragged across into the lower realm of Ahriman, then will the groups being formed be allotted to the ahrimanic powers. If this were to happen, the way would be open for the satanic powers to drag humanity away from Earth evolution and take it across to some other planetary evolution. The introduction of this group soul nature will only succeed if the element of intellect can be completely detached from its links in a specific way. Some most cunning beginnings are in progress over in the East today toward the achievement of this.[14]

May we seek wisdom and the profundity of *Michael-Sophia in nomine Christi*, for this is our light in the darkness of *maya*.

**February 9/10:** New Moon 26° Capricorn: The exaltation of Mars. This New Moon is less than 2° from the place in the Heavens known as the exaltation of the planet Mars. Capricorn rules our knees, elbows and vertebrae, suggesting mobility. "Interestingly, the planet Mars is exalted in this watery region at the tail end of Capricorn. Mars is associated with the courage to move toward change. Thus, Mars can help to move humanity and the Earth through this time of great change toward the future of evolution."[15]

Jules Verne (1828—1905), the Father of Science Fiction, was born with the Sun at this degree. Verne, in 1863, wrote a novel called *Paris in the Twentieth Century*, about a young man who lives in a world of glass skyscrapers, gas-powered automobiles, calculators, and a worldwide communications network, yet cannot find happiness and comes to a tragic end. This novel was not published until 1994. As his contemporary Rudolf Steiner knew of that which Vern spoke: "For the concrete implication is that the intellectual, shadow-like thoughts, spun inwardly by human beings today, will one day cover the Earth like a spider's web. Human beings will become entangled in it if they are not willing to rise above these shadowy thoughts."[16]

The orbit of Mars, exalted at this degree in the zodiac, marks the expanded size of the Earth's development when human beings were receiving their astral bodies during the time of old Moon evolution. It is our astral bodies that we are striving to transfigure—and this is connected to the planet Mars. We will be increasingly challenged by the spider's web of intellectual materialism. Jules Verne saw the tragic state that would become our modern culture, and Rudolf Steiner was very overt in his remarks about the dangerous trials we would face due to the work of this spider and the murky web that it would spin around the world.

This New Moon in Capricorn asks us to transform darkness into light. The "L" in eurythmy gestures this work. In accord with Rudolf Steiner we are to open to new revelation carried by those

---

13 Ibid., pp. 57–58.
14 Steiner, *The Book of Revelation and the Work of the Priest*, p. 250.
15 Paul and Powell, *Cosmic Dances of the Zodiac*, p. 85.
16 Steiner, *Materialism and the Task of Anthroposophy*, p. 265.

teachers working out of Platonic streams. To reach into the light of this revelation we must overcome rigid thinking that is imprisoned to the past—the work of Capricorn.

Today we can drink from the living waters pouring into our world from the watery regions of Capricorn. Let us relinquish *personal* certainty and ego attachments chained to the past.

"Knights of the threshold" are gathering in hopes that there can still occur a culmination of Anthroposophy. It will not be culminated until the required collaboration between the Platonists and Aristotelians is accomplished:

> These two groups [Platonists and Aristotelians] must work together, there is no other way for it to be. They will have to work together. They will represent the whole, complete circle—the circle of the new, spiritual knighthood—which can bear the name: "Michae-Sophia in nomine Christi." The men and women of Sophia, of revelation, will walk the path together with the men and women of knowledge; the Platonists will stand guard together with the Aristotelians at the threshold of the spiritual world. They will have to guard the secrets of the spiritual world. In this community, guardianship will involve neither keeping silent nor revealing everything. Instead, it will mean that a living rampart, or wall, will be erected—a wall consisting of steadfast human forms who will stand as a vertical connecting link between the spiritual and the physical worlds. On one side they will open the gates to the authorized, and on the other they will close them to the unauthorized. This community of Knights—this future community of "knights of the threshold"—will be fully realized in the sixth cultural epoch.[17]

This New Moon asks us to pick up the sword of the Word and open to undreamt possibilities born of collaborative efforts. What in the sixth cultural epoch will be fully realized, is now being seeded through the daring courage of those who are armed with the truth and are willing to cut through the spider's web of lies in order to work together. Today we can open to the living stream of the future and test our courage on the blade of the Cosmic Word (Mars).

**February 10:** Sun 26° Capricorn: Presentation in the Temple (January 15, 1 BC). According to Jewish Law, the sanctification of the firstborn should take place traditionally upon the fortieth day after birth. This was also a naming day for the infant. The Holy Family traveled to Jerusalem and stayed in the outskirts of town. The following day they set off for the temple. It was still dark when Mary and Joseph arrived with their infant son. Simeon, the old priest of the temple, had been told in a dream the previous night that the first child presented that morning would be the Messiah. When Simeon saw the infant Jesus he was taken up in rapturous joy. Rudolf Steiner tells us that Simeon was the reincarnation of Asita, who was a sage at the time of Buddha. Asita wept when he saw the little Bodhisattva who was to become Buddha, for he knew he would not live to see the day when the Bodhisattva would walk the Earth as Buddha. But now, in his incarnation as Simeon, he was granted witness to the Buddha. The astral sheath of the Nathan Jesus was filled with the presence of the Buddha. In the words of Rudolf Steiner: "When the Buddha appeared to the shepherds in the image of the "heavenly hosts," he was present not in a physical body, but in an astral body through which he continued to influence the Earth."[18] Thus, Simeon saw the further stages of development of his beloved little Bodhisattva when he blessed the Jesus child in the temple. The next day Simeon died in peace. On this naming day in 1 BC, the name of him who would bear the One was pronounced. Now this name lives in each of us. Christ is in us! Hallowed be Thy Name! May this serve as a reminder to hold respectfully each Name in the community and see the One in each other.

**February 13/14:** Sun enters Aquarius: "May what is bounded yield to the boundless" (Steiner, *Twelve Moods of the Zodiac*). William Bento illumines this mantra:

> All that finds its existence into forms, including all our thoughts, feelings and actions, remains bounded. The bounded are boundaries that too

---

17 Tomberg, *Inner Development*, p. 31.

18 Steiner, *According to Luke*, p. 77.

often confine and define who we are. Yielding to the boundless is not a given. It requires a willingness to let go and trust in the boundless, which is full of new possibilities. And the new possibilities, after all, are what allow us to continue our development and become free from the forms and patterns of our lives that tend to be static and inert.

Discretion becomes silence, becomes meditative force, and becomes power.

The first decan of Aquarius is ruled by Mercury, the planet of movement, and is associated with the Southern Fish, whose main star Fomalhaut is 9° Aquarius.

**February 14:** Sun 1° Aquarius: Healing of the paralyzed man at the Pool of Bethesda. (Jan/19/31). The Sun is conjunct the mega star Sadr (Gamma Cygni) at 0° Aquarius. This is the third of the seven archetypal healings by Christ. At this healing the Sun was in conjunction with the mega star Sadr, marking the breast of the Swan (the center of the Northern Cross).

> Our solar system races at about 140 miles (220 kilometers) per second around the galactic center, taking about 225 million years for a complete circuit of the galaxy. The direction in which the solar system moves lies 90° along the galactic equator from the galactic center, in the direction of the constellation of the Swan. The exact focus of this movement in the direction of the Swan, called the vertex, is near the star Deneb forming the tail of the Swan.[19]

This mega star was a source of power for Christ as he healed the paralyzed man, who had lain at the Pool of Bethesda for 38 years, a pool whose waters could heal the sick. This was not because of its purity (measured by today's standards) for these waters were ripe with bacteria due to the fact that it was also used for livestock, but instead its healing properties were due to the presence of spiritual forces intermittently surging into the waters, and also by the belief the people held of this spiritual truth. Today we would recognize these effects as thermal dynamics, whereas in these times it was understood that what we call a thermal force is in fact the presence of spiritual currents within the Earth. Judith von Halle explains (in *Health and Illness*) that health-threatening microbial pollutants enter water only when it is de-spiritualized, sundered from spirit. Due to our entrenched belief in the increasingly toxic pathogens that have been thoroughly researched and documented, it would be naive to think we could overcome the power we have given these pathogens and safely drink such waters. But, at the Pool of Bethesda, such things were not a part of the belief system. Within this ancient culture, therefore, the healing water was created by the presence of the Angel and the people's belief in these truths.

This miracle is connected to the third chakra—in the region of the solar plexus—the chakra that guards the individual's consciousness and governs movement.

> "I" consciousness of the past, which preserves its activity from the previous incarnation and in which many human beings live and act, is called consciousness of the "dead" in the Gospels, and those who live under the "I" impulse of the past are simply called "the dead." Thus, healing the paralyzed man involved more than merely the present "I"; the "dead," in particular, heard the "voice of the son" and experienced a conversion in his past consciousness.[20]

The paralyzed man had used excessive personal force in his past incarnation, selfishly ignoring both others and the Angels. Now, in the time of Christ's ministry, he was ignored both by others, and by the Angel at the pool of Bethesda. He had lain there for 38 years, asking for help, but to no avail, until Christ visited this pool and asked: "Wilt thou be made whole?"

This healing was intentionally enacted during this conjunction with the star Sadr. This is the mystery of the mega stars, and the work of Christ. Just as Copernicus opened us to the mysteries of the heliocentric system, so are we now being opened to the mysteries of zodiacal consciousness. The heliocentric system was part of the preparation for understanding Christ in his Second Coming, just

---

19 Powell and Dann, *The Astrological Revolution*, p. 105.

20 Tomberg, *Christ and Sophia*, p. 251.

as zodiacal consciousness is part of the preparation for understanding the Sophia mysteries that are now esoterically developing.

> This breakthrough [to understanding of the mega stars] demonstrates the truly cosmic nature of Christ in relation to the stars in the heavens. The initial discoveries of the significance of the sidereal zodiac occurred early in 1970. Then, 33⅓ years later, on May 7, 2003 [21], there came a remarkable expansion in consciousness from the sidereal zodiac to include the entire celestial sphere of the fixed stars (33⅓ years being the rhythm of Christ's life from birth to the resurrection). This signified a quantum leap with respect to the astrological worldview.[22]

This discovery of mega stars will continue to unfold a new level of relationship with the mysteries of the stars—this is a type of galactic consciousness. The extraordinary consequences of this discovery will contribute to our understanding of the cosmic dimension of Christ's work and the work of Sophia that is connected to the sixth cultural epoch—the Slavic cultural period beginning in the astrological Age of Aquarius in 2375. In ancient India we had an unconscious, intuitive relationship with zodiacal consciousness—which later dimmed to solar consciousness, then to lunar consciousness, and finally arrived at the geocentric consciousness prevalent in our time. As we gradually free ourselves from our enchainment to matter we will re-open (consciously) to lunar, solar, and finally zodiacal consciousness as part of our initiation process reaching into the far future (See *Hermetic Astrology Vol. I*, chapter 4). Teachers always come to seed the future in order to make possible the evolution of humanity, and there is always at least a small group of souls who are able to listen.

Today, as the Sun comes into conjunction with this mega star and remembers this healing miracle, we can ask if our deeds are commensurate with the needs of others and with the will of our Angels, or are ghosts from our past shackling us to corpses of egoism? As we become free, our consciousness will expand to as yet undreamt of possibilities.

**February 19:** Saturn stations 16°36 Libra. Solomon Mary enters the temple (Dec/8/18 BC). Neptune was at this exact position in the zodiac when the young Mary (3 years and 3 months of age) was presented in the temple:

> I saw the Blessed Virgin living in the Temple in a perpetual ecstasy of prayer. Her soul did not seem to be on the Earth, and she often received consolation and comfort from heaven. She had an endless longing for the fulfillment of the Promise, and in her humility hardly ventured on the wish to be the lowliest maidservant of the Mother of the Redeemer. Mary's teacher and nurse in the Temple was called Noemi; she was a sister of Lazarus's mother and was fifty years old. She and the other Temple women belonged to the Essenes. Mary learned from her how to knit and helped her when she washed the blood of the sacrifices from the vessels and instruments, or when she cut up and prepared certain parts of the flesh for the Temple women and priests; for this formed part of their food. Later on Mary took a still more active part in these duties.[23]

As Saturn stations at this degree of the zodiac, the memory of young Mary's entry into the temple is highlighted over the next few days. We can hope that more of our young children can find protection, as did the Mary child. Protection prepares them to find their true missions (Saturn). Too many are being sacrificed on the altar of technology, living hurried lives that atrophy the discerning powers of the heart. Today we can remember the Blessed Virgin Mary, and know that a new Temple is waiting for all who have the humility to serve the etheric Christ as humble servants. In this emptiness we are allowed to enter into the new Temple.

**February 21:** Sun conjunct Neptune 7° Aquarius. Earlier this month Mars and Mercury transited Neptune and at the end of the month Venus will do this as well. Today it is the Sun who stands with Neptune. We are being called to lift our perspective to higher realms and from there look down

---

21 It is most interesting to note, that on this date *there was a Mercury transit of the Sun*.
22 Powell and Dann, *The Astrological Revolution*, pp. 143–144.

23 *LBVM*, p. 117 and *Chron*. p. 130.

upon the world of the senses. From this vantage all appears quite differently and our eyes are opened. With the Sun at this degree of the zodiac Christ healed a man with a withered hand; and by driving out a devil from one who was possessed, he caused the man's hearing and speech to be immediately restored. (See *Chron.*, p. 275)

May our Sun-selves breathe in the healing forces of the Sun conjunct Neptune in Aquarius, for Neptune's blessed manna is the antidote for the sucking forces of materialism that hold sway when inspiration falls into the hands of Ahriman. As Mars, Mercury, Sun and Venus all transit the watery realms of Neptune, human beings will have to decide whether the higher tones of Inspiration—or else subearthly magnetism—will fuel their souls' direction. This is a Neptunian month. It will be interesting to notice what becomes activated.

**February 22:** Venus enters Aquarius: "May what is lacking bounds, establish bounds" (Steiner, *Twelve Moods of the Zodiac*) Venus joins Neptune, Sun, Mars and Mercury in Aquarius. Venus was in Aquarius at the death of John the Baptist. In our deepest soul we know what discipline is needed to attain our destiny task. We are encouraged to contemplate what the living currents are asking of us, and to find the reflection of this in our loving relationships with others.

February 23: Sun conjunct Fomalhaut 9° Aquarius: One of the four Royal Stars of Persia. Fomalhaut is the Watcher in the South, who stands with Tat—the loyal student of Hermes (turning to the south):

> Holy Gabriel, thou who carries the spirit-light of the Age of the Moon, whence radiates the fount underlying the life of thought, help illumine our thinking that it be raised to knowledge of the cosmic mystery of the Logos who is the Salvation of humankind and the Earth.[24]

The Age of the Moon (when our astral bodies first manifested) is resurrected in the Age of Jupiter (when the purification of our astral bodies into Spirit Self will be attained), the fifth manifestation of the body of the Earth as depicted in Occult Science: Saturn, Sun, Moon, Earth, future Jupiter, future Venus, future Vulcan. The Aquarian mind thirsts for the wisdom of future Jupiter evolution, which is in its esoteric dawning in our Age of the consciousness soul. This will intensify through the resurrection of the Egyptian mysteries in our time. May we remember the call of star wisdom—the rising gnosis of Egypt.

**February 23:** Sun 10° Aquarius: Feeding of the Five Thousand and the Walking on Water. "Deneb, seen by the Greeks as marking the tail of the Swan, is at the head of the Northern Cross. It is remarkable to consider that the cross is the symbol of Christ, and that—in the sense of "as above, so below"—his central miracles (the feeding of the 5,000 and the walking on the water) were aligned via the sun with Deneb at the head of the cross" (Robert Powell and Kevin Dann, *Astrological Revolution*, p. 151).

These two miracles signify a day side (Feeding of the Five Thousand), and a night side (Walking on Water). Christ feeds five thousand with moral-sensory impressions, and these impressions echo into the night for the twelve disciples.

Rudolf Steiner frequently spoke of spiritualizing sensory impressions; "moral impressions" was the term he gave to sensory impressions of moral and spiritual phenomena.[25] Christ, whose heart was in union with the twelve constellations of the zodiac, filled the twelve senses of the multitude with moral impressions. This satisfied their hunger. They sought to crown him king in this world, whereby they could continue to receive spiritual nourishment passively. His disciples, on the other hand, bore witness to his spiritual kingliness when, later that night, he approached their boat as he walked on water, saying, "It is I; do not be afraid." (John 6:20) These words contain the revelation of Christ's kingly nature.

> [This kingly nature] does not call the Christ to govern (as the five thousand wished), but bestows on the human being the spiritual force of self-determination. The kingly nature of the

---

24 CHA, A Discourse of Hermes to Tat, The Mystery of the Zodiac.

25 On the twelve senses, see Steiner, *Anthroposophy (A fragment)*, chap. 2, "The Human Being as a Sensory Organism."

Christ is his capacity not only to give humankind freedom, but also to give the needed strength to assert that freedom. In the spiritual-moral sense, it would be proper to say that the royal nature of Christ involves giving kingly dignity to human beings.[26]

In the night comes the recognition of the kingly dignity that Christ gives to human beings. His words, "It is I; be not afraid," remind us of who it is that brings us certainty when the winds of change and the waves of uncertainty threaten our equilibrium. We are also reminded of the different natures of sense impressions. Moral impressions echo into the higher hierarchies by night, strengthening the human "I"—whereas immoral impressions, impressions man-made to imitate creation, echo into the sphere of materialism by night, thereby capturing the ego in its *maya*. *What is taken in by day determines which school we enter at night—the school of the Greater Guardian who is Christ, or the school of materialism that is ruled by the tempters. This is a good day to ponder the quality of impressions we place before our senses and, more importantly, the quality of impressions we allow to enter our children's senses. For the nature of these impressions by day will determine who, or what, it is they will meet in the night.*

The Sun at 10° Aquarius enters the second decan of Aquarius, ruled by Venus and associated with the Swan (sacred to Venus). Sun at 10½° Aquarius is conjunct the mega star Deneb, marking the tail of the Swan (the head of the Northern Cross). The Sun was conjunct Deneb at the Feeding of the Five Thousand.

**February 25:** Full Moon: Moon 11° Leo opposite Sun 11° Aquarius. Death of the Nathan Mary (Aug/5/12). This Moon in Leo remembers Mary's death. Mary has made appearances in the nineteenth and twentieth centuries in Lourdes (1858), and Fatima (1917). Another more recent series of visions, still continuing, began on St. John's Day, 1981, in Medjugorje, Yugoslavia.

> At the first appearance on June 24, 1981, Mary appeared to five young people and identified herself with the words: "I am the Queen of Peace. I have come to bring peace to Earth." Since then, the revelation has continued with regular appearances, in the course of which Mary has revealed ten mysteries concerning the future, not yet made public. Several million people have visited Medjugorje. The Virgin's central message is that a renewal of religious life, a new turning toward God, is necessary if the world is to be saved. This renewal is to be attained, above all, through prayer, which, Mary stresses, means "prayer of the heart": "Pray with the heart. Do not let prayer and fasting become a routine or a matter of habit.[27]

The necessity of a renewal of religious life is countered by adversaries:

> Nothing less than the total eradication of Christianity from the world is the aim of Antichrist, in order to establish a world in which egoism alone is the motivating impulse of existence, for the nature of the false self is egoism. A world of banks, universities, factories and clubs, in which egoism holds sway—a world without churches, and where there is no devotion to Christ, no love of neighbor (except for selfish ends), no praise of God, no church bells to sound forth the worship of God, no charitable deed, no prayer, and no religion.[28]

Through prayer and goodness we can toll the bells that are now so desperately needed—the bells of freedom sounding from the constellation of Leo, where the virtue *Compassion becomes Freedom* is practiced. Let this Full Moon remember the purity of Mary. For when we can face our own shadow, we gain compassion for the shadow nature in others. This is freedom. Attachments will increasingly make us vulnerable to the adversaries. Today is a good day to notice any personal agendas that affect our ability to be free. The ten miracles of Mary will be revealed in time. Compassion prepares us to receive *all* miracles.

**February 27:** Sun 14° Aquarius: Birth of Rudolf Steiner and Valentin Tomberg. Jesus taught on the same theme as the Sermon on the Mount: the

---

26 Tomberg, *Christ and Sophia*, p. 254.

27 *Chron.*, p. 114.

28 Powell, *Hermetic Astrology*, vol 2, p. 308.

Beatitudes and the Lord's Prayer (Matt. 5:3–12; 6:9–13).

Both Rudolf Steiner and Valentin Tomberg gave close attention to the Lord's Prayer and the Beatitudes.

> [Valentin Tomberg] can be viewed in the line of the great teachers of humanity. He is one such teacher in our time in the post-Christian era, who is bringing the teaching for the ascending phase of this great movement of Christ on his path of return to the heavenly Father, leading humanity stage by stage on the ascending path leading to the Resurrection. He connected onto the great teacher Rudolf Steiner—this connection shows in their horoscopes, where the Sun's location (14½° Aquarius) at his birth aligned exactly with the position of the Sun (14½° Aquarius) at Rudolf Steiner's birth. Whereas Rudolf Steiner's task was to prepare for the onset of Christ's Second Coming in the etheric aura of the Earth in 1933, the task of the author of *Meditations on the Tarot* was to help humanity align with the etheric Christ in the period after 1933.
>
> As through antiquity Christ descended from the heights of our galaxy down to the Earth, so now he is uniting with the etheric aura of the Earth all the way down to the golden heart of the Earth (Shambhala), from there to begin his ascending movement from the depths in the spiritualization of the Earth, creating the "New Earth."[29]

As true initiates all work together, coming into incarnation in various cultures at various times in order to continue the work of spiritually guiding humanity, it would follow that one of the tasks of an initiate is to assure his successor is recognized. Rudolf Steiner fulfilled this task, without trespassing upon the freedom of his successor, who was still under the age of thirty-three at the time of Steiner's death. (Before this age an individuality may not as yet have accepted the responsibility of a foreordained mission.) Rudolf Steiner said the individuality in the process of becoming the next Buddha was born in 1900 and would begin teaching in the 1930s.

It was more discreetly, and without putting a particular person in the limelight as candidate, that Dr. Rudolf Steiner, founder of the Anthroposophical Society predicted the manifestation—again in the first half of the twentieth century—not of the new Maitreya Buddha or Kalki Avatar, but rather of the Bodhisattva, i.e. the individuality in the process of becoming the next Buddha, whose field of activity he hoped the Anthroposophical Society would serve.[30]

Aquarius is future-oriented and brings something new into the present. Aquarian teachers bear witness to the future. Aquarius is leading us into the next zodiacal age (beginning in 2375), in which the Slavic cultural epoch will open new possibilities for *manas* cognition. We are on the doorstep to this Aquarian Age. Both of these great teachers brought change based on the traditions of the past, but not limited by these traditions. For, to be limited is to become rigidified. *The sanctity of humanity's freedom allows each of us to discern for ourselves whom we recognize as bearers of revelation. Error occurs when those in positions of authority misuse their positions by imposing personal opinions as objective truths, thereby transgressing upon the freedom of others.*

ASPECT: Venus conjunct Neptune 8° Aquarius.

**February 28: ASPECT:** Venus conjunct Neptune 8° Aquarius. The month began with Mars conjunct Neptune followed by Mercury's transit of Neptune, and then the conjunction of the Sun with Neptune. Now the month ends with Venus conjunct Neptune. Three planets and the Sun are transiting Neptune this month, reminding us of three events: The healing of Manahem, the second temptation in the wilderness, the casting out of demons; and now Venus remembers the Adoration of the Magi and the revealing of John's death. As we today celebrate the births of two of the great teachers of the twentieth century, we can rejoice in the love streaming from the goddess of the Night (Neptune)—Sophia. Under the influence of Sophia we will adore the true king, and we will find John's teachings in the apocalyptic stream of revelation moving toward us from the future. Inversely we could find ourselves trapped in

---

29 Powell, *Cultivating Inner Radiance and the Body of Immortality*, p. 192.

30 *Meditations on the Tarot*, p. 614.

the deadening realms of the adversaries who send impostors in place of true kings and who wish to behead any who are speaking from the stream of John. Hear from your heart and know your truth!

# MARCH

The Sun begins March in Aquarius (The Water-Human), moving into Pisces on the 15th. Mercury and Venus come together on the 6th, but cannot be seen by the eyes because they are so close to the bright Sun. Instead, consider other ways to "tap into" their emanations carried by the light of the Sun. The 11th brings the New Moon with Mercury, Neptune and Venus nearby in the WaterHuman. On the 18th a half Moon joins Jupiter in Taurus for a sweet sunset, and Mercury ends its first retrograde cycle stationing direct in the WaterHuman. On the 20th, the whole planet will experience equal day and night: the Vernal Equinox in the Northern Hemisphere and the Autumnal in the Southern. The Archangelic energies tend these "larger" cycles of our planet. How might you feel them near? The Moon grows to Full on the 27th, in Virgo with the Sun in Pisces. Venus is exactly conjunct the Sun on the next day (the 28th), beginning her transition into the evening star. She will emerge for sunset viewing by the 2nd week of May.

**March 4:** Sun 19° Aquarius: Raising an Essene girl from the dead (Feb/7/30) (*Chron.*, p. 219). The Sun is aligned with the mega star 68 Cygnus in the Swan—the second most luminous star visible to us.

> This girl was born into an Essene family, whom Christ Jesus visited at their home in Phasael, six weeks after the wedding at Cana. At that time she was about sixteen years old, and her father's name was Jairus. Jesus warned those present not to speak of what they had witnessed, and this—which took place less than five months into his 3½-year ministry—was therefore not recorded in the Gospels. It is remarkable that this raising from the dead took place when the Sun was aligned with a star which the Hipparcos satellite identified as one of the most luminous stars in our galaxy.[31]

**ASPECT:** Inferior conjunction of Mercury and Sun 19° Aquarius. Mercury was here when Jesus and the apostles made their way to Bethany:

> As he walked, Jesus taught; Mary Salome went on ahead, arriving in Bethany toward evening. She went first to Martha to tell her that Jesus was approaching, Mary Magdalene went with Mary Salome to greet him, but she returned without having spoken to him. Then Martha went to meet him. In the exchange that took place between Martha and Jesus, Jesus spoke the words: "I am the resurrection and the life."[32] (John 11:17–27)

*Inferior conjunction* means that Mercury is between the Sun and the Earth. During such inferior conjunctions, Mercury is active in our consciousness, bestowing cosmic Imaginations from the wellsprings of life.

This day finds Neptune, Venus, Mercury, Sun and Mars in Aquarius. With this Mercury/Sun conjunction and three other planets close by, we can open to the etheric in-streaming from the Water Bearer, who is pouring forth divine nourishment that helps raise us up to the promise of resurrection, which Christ has made possible for all humanity. This divine nourishment is protection against the forces working to enchain us in the "second fall":

> One of the consequences of the second fall that is currently underway through Ahriman's penetration into the etheric body is that humanity and the Earth are coming more and more under the sway of forces of death—the subterranean forces of electricity, electromagnetism, and atomic power, for example. There are also other death forces at work on different levels here, including more subtle, non-physical levels. The expression "death forces" is used here in the wider sense of that which is antithetical to divine life. When Christ came to the Earth, he came to bestow the gift of divine life on humanity and the Earth. The path that he took through the stages of the Passion was for this purpose, to

---

31 Powell and Dann, *The Astrological Revolution*, p. 155.
32 *Chron.*, p. 316.

SIDEREAL GEOCENTRIC LONGITUDES : MARCH 2013 Gregorian at 0 hours UT

| DAY | ☉ | ☽ | ☊ | ☿ | ♀ | ♂ | ♃ | ♄ | ♅ | ♆ | ♇ |
|---|---|---|---|---|---|---|---|---|---|---|---|
| 1 FR | 15 ♒ 38 | 24 ♍ 59 | 24 ♎ 14R | 22 ♒ 31R | 8 ♒ 43 | 26 ♒ 17 | 12 ♉ 50 | 16 ♎ 31R | 12 ♓ 0 | 8 ♒ 12 | 16 ♐ 12 |
| 2 SA | 16 39 | 8 ♎ 48 | 24 11 | 21 40 | 9 58 | 27 4 | 12 56 | 16 30 | 12 3 | 8 14 | 16 13 |
| 3 SU | 17 39 | 22 44 | 24 10 | 20 44 | 11 13 | 27 51 | 13 2 | 16 28 | 12 7 | 8 16 | 16 14 |
| 4 MO | 18 39 | 6 ♏ 44 | 24 10D | 19 44 | 12 28 | 28 38 | 13 8 | 16 27 | 12 10 | 8 19 | 16 15 |
| 5 TU | 19 39 | 20 49 | 24 10R | 18 43 | 13 43 | 29 25 | 13 14 | 16 26 | 12 13 | 8 21 | 16 16 |
| 6 WE | 20 39 | 4 ♐ 57 | 24 10 | 17 41 | 14 58 | 0 ♓ 11 | 13 20 | 16 24 | 12 16 | 8 23 | 16 18 |
| 7 TH | 21 39 | 19 8 | 24 7 | 16 40 | 16 13 | 0 58 | 13 27 | 16 23 | 12 19 | 8 25 | 16 19 |
| 8 FR | 22 39 | 3 ♑ 18 | 24 1 | 15 41 | 17 28 | 1 45 | 13 33 | 16 21 | 12 23 | 8 28 | 16 20 |
| 9 SA | 23 39 | 17 25 | 23 53 | 14 46 | 18 42 | 2 32 | 13 40 | 16 19 | 12 26 | 8 30 | 16 21 |
| 10 SU | 24 39 | 1 ♒ 26 | 23 44 | 13 55 | 19 57 | 3 19 | 13 47 | 16 17 | 12 29 | 8 32 | 16 22 |
| 11 MO | 25 39 | 15 15 | 23 33 | 13 10 | 21 12 | 4 5 | 13 54 | 16 15 | 12 33 | 8 34 | 16 23 |
| 12 TU | 26 39 | 28 49 | 23 24 | 12 30 | 22 27 | 4 52 | 14 2 | 16 13 | 12 36 | 8 36 | 16 24 |
| 13 WE | 27 39 | 12 ♓ 4 | 23 16 | 11 56 | 23 42 | 5 39 | 14 9 | 16 11 | 12 39 | 8 39 | 16 25 |
| 14 TH | 28 39 | 25 0 | 23 10 | 11 28 | 24 57 | 6 25 | 14 17 | 16 9 | 12 43 | 8 41 | 16 26 |
| 15 FR | 29 39 | 7 ♈ 37 | 23 6 | 11 7 | 26 11 | 7 12 | 14 24 | 16 6 | 12 46 | 8 43 | 16 27 |
| 16 SA | 0 ♓ 38 | 19 56 | 23 5 | 10 53 | 27 26 | 7 59 | 14 32 | 16 4 | 12 49 | 8 45 | 16 28 |
| 17 SU | 1 38 | 2 ♉ 1 | 23 5D | 10 45 | 28 41 | 8 45 | 14 40 | 16 1 | 12 53 | 8 47 | 16 28 |
| 18 MO | 2 38 | 13 56 | 23 6 | 10 43D | 29 56 | 9 32 | 14 48 | 15 59 | 12 56 | 8 49 | 16 29 |
| 19 TU | 3 38 | 25 46 | 23 7 | 10 47 | 1 ♓ 10 | 10 18 | 14 57 | 15 56 | 12 59 | 8 52 | 16 30 |
| 20 WE | 4 37 | 7 ♊ 36 | 23 7R | 10 56 | 2 25 | 11 4 | 15 5 | 15 53 | 13 3 | 8 54 | 16 31 |
| 21 TH | 5 37 | 19 31 | 23 6 | 11 11 | 3 40 | 11 51 | 15 13 | 15 50 | 13 6 | 8 56 | 16 31 |
| 22 FR | 6 36 | 1 ♋ 36 | 23 3 | 11 32 | 4 54 | 12 37 | 15 22 | 15 47 | 13 10 | 8 58 | 16 32 |
| 23 SA | 7 36 | 13 56 | 22 58 | 11 57 | 6 9 | 13 23 | 15 31 | 15 44 | 13 13 | 9 0 | 16 33 |
| 24 SU | 8 35 | 26 34 | 22 51 | 12 27 | 7 24 | 14 10 | 15 40 | 15 41 | 13 17 | 9 2 | 16 33 |
| 25 MO | 9 35 | 9 ♌ 33 | 22 44 | 13 1 | 8 38 | 14 56 | 15 49 | 15 38 | 13 20 | 9 4 | 16 34 |
| 26 TU | 10 34 | 22 52 | 22 36 | 13 39 | 9 53 | 15 42 | 15 58 | 15 35 | 13 23 | 9 6 | 16 35 |
| 27 WE | 11 34 | 6 ♍ 30 | 22 30 | 14 21 | 11 8 | 16 28 | 16 7 | 15 32 | 13 27 | 9 8 | 16 35 |
| 28 TH | 12 33 | 20 25 | 22 25 | 15 7 | 12 22 | 17 14 | 16 17 | 15 28 | 13 30 | 9 10 | 16 36 |
| 29 FR | 13 32 | 4 ♎ 33 | 22 21 | 15 56 | 13 37 | 18 0 | 16 26 | 15 25 | 13 34 | 9 12 | 16 36 |
| 30 SA | 14 32 | 18 50 | 22 20 | 16 49 | 14 51 | 18 46 | 16 36 | 15 21 | 13 37 | 9 14 | 16 37 |
| 31 SU | 15 31 | 3 ♏ 10 | 22 20D | 17 44 | 16 6 | 19 32 | 16 46 | 15 18 | 13 40 | 9 16 | 16 37 |

INGRESSES :

1 ☽ → ♎ 8:43
3 ☽ → ♏ 12:28
5 ☽ → ♐ 15:36
♂ → ♓ 18: 8
7 ☽ → ♑ 18:24
9 ☽ → ♒ 21:32
12 ☽ → ♓ 2: 7
14 ☽ → ♈ 9:26
15 ☉ → ♓ 8:35
16 ☽ → ♉ 19:57
18 ♀ → ♓ 1:23
19 ☽ → ♊ 8:36
21 ☽ → ♋ 20:50
24 ☽ → ♌ 6:24
26 ☽ → ♍ 12:37
28 ☽ → ♎ 16:17
30 ☽ → ♏ 18:42

ASPECTS & ECLIPSES :

2 ☽ ☌ ♄ 13:14
3 ☽ ☌ ☊ 2:27
4 ☽ ☍ ♃ 10:59
☉ ♉ ☿ 12:57
♀ □ ♃ 13:51
☉ □ ☽ 21:51
5 ☽ ☌ P 23:31
6 ☽ ☌ ♇ 19:13
7 ☿ ☌ ♀ 4:53
9 ☽ ♉ ☊ 10:55
10 ☿ □ ♃ 3:36
☽ ☌ ♆ 12:19
☽ ☌ ☿ 20:32
11 ☽ ☌ ♀ 11:32
☉ ☌ ☽ 19:50
12 ☽ ☌ ♂ 11:34
13 ☽ ☌ ♅ 1: 4
15 ☽ ☍ ♄ 16:25
16 ☽ ☌ ☋ 6:12
☉ □ Π 15:23
18 ☽ ☌ ♃ 1:47
19 ☽ ☌ A 3:31
☉ □ ☽ 17:25
20 ☽ ☍ ♇ 18: 0
22 ♂ ☌ ♅ 18:13
23 ☽ ♉ ☊ 17: 3
24 ☽ ☍ ♆ 23: 7
25 ☽ ☍ ☿ 6:36
27 ♂ □ ♇ 3:40
☽ ☍ ♀ 8:48
☉ ☍ ☽ 9:26
☽ ☍ ♅ 12: 4
☽ ☍ ♂ 18:13
28 ☉ ♉ ♀ 17: 4
♀ ☌ ♅ 22:58
29 ☉ ☌ ♅ 0:34
☿ □ ♃ 16:55
☽ ☌ ♄ 18:11
30 ☽ ☌ ☊ 5:52
31 ☽ ☌ P 3:27
♀ □ ♇ 10: 7
☽ ☍ ♃ 23: 2

SIDEREAL HELIOCENTRIC LONGITUDES : MARCH 2013 Gregorian at 0 hours UT

| DAY | Sid. Time | ☿ | ♀ | ⊕ | ♂ | ♃ | ♄ | ♅ | ♆ | ♇ | Vernal Point |
|---|---|---|---|---|---|---|---|---|---|---|---|
| 1 FR | 10:35:50 | 2 ♌ 17 | 29 ♑ 16 | 15 ♌ 38 | 3 ♓ 51 | 24 ♉ 3 | 11 ♎ 26 | 13 ♓ 16 | 7 ♒ 57 | 14 ♐ 41 | 5 ♓ 4'35" |
| 2 SA | 10:39:47 | 7 16 | 0 ♒ 51 | 16 39 | 4 28 | 24 9 | 11 28 | 13 16 | 7 58 | 14 41 | 5 ♓ 4'35" |
| 3 SU | 10:43:44 | 12 5 | 2 26 | 17 39 | 5 6 | 24 14 | 11 30 | 13 17 | 7 58 | 14 41 | 5 ♓ 4'35" |
| 4 MO | 10:47:40 | 16 44 | 4 1 | 18 39 | 5 43 | 24 19 | 11 32 | 13 18 | 7 58 | 14 42 | 5 ♓ 4'35" |
| 5 TU | 10:51:37 | 21 15 | 5 36 | 19 39 | 6 21 | 24 24 | 11 34 | 13 18 | 7 59 | 14 42 | 5 ♓ 4'34" |
| 6 WE | 10:55:33 | 25 37 | 7 11 | 20 39 | 6 58 | 24 30 | 11 36 | 13 19 | 7 59 | 14 42 | 5 ♓ 4'34" |
| 7 TH | 10:59:30 | 29 51 | 8 46 | 21 39 | 7 36 | 24 35 | 11 38 | 13 20 | 7 59 | 14 43 | 5 ♓ 4'34" |
| 8 FR | 11: 3:26 | 3 ♍ 57 | 10 21 | 22 39 | 8 13 | 24 40 | 11 40 | 13 20 | 8 0 | 14 43 | 5 ♓ 4'34" |
| 9 SA | 11: 7:23 | 7 55 | 11 57 | 23 39 | 8 51 | 24 45 | 11 41 | 13 21 | 8 0 | 14 43 | 5 ♓ 4'34" |
| 10 SU | 11:11:19 | 11 47 | 13 32 | 24 39 | 9 28 | 24 50 | 11 43 | 13 22 | 8 1 | 14 44 | 5 ♓ 4'34" |
| 11 MO | 11:15:16 | 15 32 | 15 7 | 25 39 | 10 5 | 24 56 | 11 45 | 13 22 | 8 1 | 14 44 | 5 ♓ 4'34" |
| 12 TU | 11:19:13 | 19 10 | 16 42 | 26 39 | 10 42 | 25 1 | 11 47 | 13 23 | 8 1 | 14 44 | 5 ♓ 4'33" |
| 13 WE | 11:23: 9 | 22 44 | 18 17 | 27 39 | 11 20 | 25 6 | 11 49 | 13 24 | 8 2 | 14 45 | 5 ♓ 4'33" |
| 14 TH | 11:27: 6 | 26 11 | 19 52 | 28 39 | 11 57 | 25 11 | 11 51 | 13 24 | 8 2 | 14 45 | 5 ♓ 4'33" |
| 15 FR | 11:31: 2 | 29 34 | 21 28 | 29 39 | 12 34 | 25 16 | 11 53 | 13 25 | 8 2 | 14 45 | 5 ♓ 4'33" |
| 16 SA | 11:34:59 | 2 ♎ 53 | 23 3 | 0 ♍ 39 | 13 11 | 25 22 | 11 55 | 13 25 | 8 3 | 14 46 | 5 ♓ 4'33" |
| 17 SU | 11:38:55 | 6 7 | 24 38 | 1 38 | 13 48 | 25 27 | 11 57 | 13 26 | 8 3 | 14 46 | 5 ♓ 4'33" |
| 18 MO | 11:42:52 | 9 17 | 26 13 | 2 38 | 14 25 | 25 32 | 11 59 | 13 27 | 8 3 | 14 46 | 5 ♓ 4'33" |
| 19 TU | 11:46:48 | 12 24 | 27 49 | 3 38 | 15 2 | 25 37 | 12 0 | 13 27 | 8 4 | 14 47 | 5 ♓ 4'32" |
| 20 WE | 11:50:45 | 15 27 | 29 24 | 4 37 | 15 39 | 25 42 | 12 2 | 13 28 | 8 4 | 14 47 | 5 ♓ 4'32" |
| 21 TH | 11:54:42 | 18 28 | 0 ♓ 59 | 5 37 | 16 16 | 25 48 | 12 4 | 13 29 | 8 5 | 14 47 | 5 ♓ 4'32" |
| 22 FR | 11:58:38 | 21 26 | 2 35 | 6 36 | 16 53 | 25 53 | 12 6 | 13 29 | 8 5 | 14 48 | 5 ♓ 4'32" |
| 23 SA | 12: 2:35 | 24 21 | 4 10 | 7 36 | 17 30 | 25 58 | 12 8 | 13 30 | 8 5 | 14 48 | 5 ♓ 4'32" |
| 24 SU | 12: 6:31 | 27 15 | 5 45 | 8 35 | 18 7 | 26 3 | 12 10 | 13 31 | 8 6 | 14 48 | 5 ♓ 4'32" |
| 25 MO | 12:10:28 | 0 ♏ 6 | 7 21 | 9 35 | 18 44 | 26 8 | 12 12 | 13 31 | 8 6 | 14 49 | 5 ♓ 4'32" |
| 26 TU | 12:14:24 | 2 56 | 8 56 | 10 34 | 19 20 | 26 14 | 12 14 | 13 32 | 8 6 | 14 49 | 5 ♓ 4'32" |
| 27 WE | 12:18:21 | 5 45 | 10 32 | 11 34 | 19 57 | 26 19 | 12 16 | 13 33 | 8 7 | 14 49 | 5 ♓ 4'31" |
| 28 TH | 12:22:17 | 8 32 | 12 7 | 12 33 | 20 34 | 26 24 | 12 17 | 13 33 | 8 7 | 14 50 | 5 ♓ 4'31" |
| 29 FR | 12:26:14 | 11 18 | 13 43 | 13 32 | 21 10 | 26 29 | 12 19 | 13 34 | 8 7 | 14 50 | 5 ♓ 4'31" |
| 30 SA | 12:30:11 | 14 4 | 15 18 | 14 32 | 21 47 | 26 34 | 12 21 | 13 34 | 8 8 | 14 50 | 5 ♓ 4'31" |
| 31 SU | 12:34: 7 | 16 49 | 16 54 | 15 31 | 22 23 | 26 40 | 12 23 | 13 35 | 8 8 | 14 51 | 5 ♓ 4'31" |

INGRESSES :

1 ♀ → ♒ 11: 4
7 ☿ → ♍ 0:54
15 ☿ → ♎ 3: 4
⊕ → ♍ 8:32
20 ♀ → ♓ 9: 4
24 ☿ → ♏ 23: 7

ASPECTS (HELIOCENTRIC +MOON(TYCHONIC)) :

2 ☿ ☍ ♆ 3:27
☽ ☌ ♄ 4:36
3 ☽ □ ♀ 18:45
4 ☽ □ ♆ 2: 6
☿ ☌ ⊕ 12:57
5 ☽ □ ☿ 1: 4
☽ ☍ ♃ 6: 8
☿ □ ♃ 17:37
6 ☽ □ ♂ 3:34
♀ ☌ ♆ 12: 7
☽ □ ♅ 14:10
☽ ☌ ♇ 16:31
8 ☽ □ ♄ 14:13
9 ☿ ☍ ♂ 6:46
10 ⊕ □ ♃ 4:52
☿ ☍ ♅ 10: 4
☽ ☌ ♆ 11:23
☿ □ ♇ 18:52
☽ ☌ ♀ 23:44
11 ☽ □ ♃ 17:11
12 ☽ ☌ ♂ 22:34
13 ☽ ☌ ♅ 2:25
☽ □ ♇ 4:55
14 ☽ ☍ ☿ 3: 3
15 ♀ ♉ ☊ 6:17
☽ ☍ ♄ 8:16
16 ♂ ☌ ♅ 9:24
17 ☽ □ ♆ 12: 7
♀ □ ♃ 13: 0
18 ♂ □ ♇ 13:48
☿ ☌ ♄ 20:56
☽ ☌ ♃ 23:42
19 ☽ □ ♀ 4:48
20 ☽ □ ♅ 11:52
☽ ☍ ♇ 14:31
☽ □ ♂ 17: 8
22 ☿ ☌ ☋ 17:28
☽ □ ♄ 20:30
24 ☽ □ ☿ 1:37
☽ ☍ ♆ 21:21
26 ☽ □ ♃ 6: 0
27 ☽ ☍ ♀ 7:53
☽ ☍ ♅ 12:11
☽ □ ♇ 14:23
☿ □ ♆ 20:24
28 ☽ ☍ ♂ 0:14
♀ ☍ ⊕ 17: 4
♀ ☌ ♅ 21:42
29 ⊕ ☍ ♅ 0:34
☽ ☌ ♄ 13: 6
♀ □ ♇ 16:55
30 ⊕ □ ♇ 7:35
31 ☽ □ ♆ 8:19

open up the gift of divine life—that blossomed forth at the Resurrection. It is to this gift that we open ourselves in taking up the path of putting on the Resurrection body.[33]

Putting on the Resurrection body is a path of spiritual protection developed by Robert Powell and is the focus of his book, *Cultivating Inner Radiance and the Body of Immortality*.

May the blessings of Mercury conjunct Sun in Aquarius be our source for new imaginations that strive to find receptivity in human minds. Today asks us to wisely cultivate stillness—if even for a moment—as our resurrection into new life depends on the inspiration flowing out of the the Waterman's holy urns.

**March 5:** Mars enters Pisces. "And maintain itself in maintaining" (Steiner, *Twelve Moods of the Zodiac*). Mars was in Pisces at the Stilling of the Storm and other miracles, through the death of John the Baptist. With Mars in Pisces we can contemplate the presence of spiritual beings working from behind the threshold of death. This gives us a capacity to penetrate into the unseen. We are urged to maintain our center while experiencing loss, in order to find the treasure of gain therein. This helps us sustain balance between the seen and unseen worlds without succumbing to the lower realms of psychism.

**March 6:** Mercury conjunct Venus 16° Aquarius. Heliocentric Mercury was here after the last three days of the temptations of Christ, and today Mercury and Venus conjoin very close to the place of birth of both Rudolf Steiner and Valentin Tomberg. From the vantage of the Sun (heliocentric), where our higher "I" is ever witness to events on Earth, the wing-footed messenger of the gods poured forth healing on the Son of God after the trial of his last temptation—his encounter with Ahriman.

> On Wednesday, November 30, when Jesus had overcome the last temptation, the twelve Angels of the twelve apostles served him heavenly food. These twelve Angels were accompanied in turn by the seventy-two Angels of the seventy-two disciples. An indescribable blessing and consolation emanated from this heavenly celebration of Jesus' triumphant victory over temptation—a blessing and consolation that was transmitted by the Angels to the apostles and disciples.[34]

With Mercury conjunct Venus at the memory of this momentous event, we are encouraged to feel the loving presence of Christ and Sophia in their current ministrations to all of their children who are facing temptations in our time. The Mercury and Venus chakras are the seat of, respectively, Michael and Sophia, who work in the Name of Christ. May we find the strength of their guiding presence especially highlighted today, and may we radiate their love to all we meet along the way.

In loving memory of Rudolf Steiner and Valentine Tomberg, we can drink deeply from the font of the Holy Spirit, which pours forth its blessed waters in order to enliven today's cosmic memories through the intermediaries of Mercury and Venus.

Sun today enters the third decan of Aquarius, ruled by the Moon. This decan is associated with Pegasus, the Winged Horse.

**March 10:** Sun 24° Aquarius: Healing of the Syrophoenician Woman (Feb/12/31). Here Jesus is approached by a crippled woman who begs him to come and heal her daughter—who is possessed. Concerned about giving offense, Jesus cannot heal the woman's pagan daughter before he heals the Jews. Later that day Jesus exorcises the unclean spirit from the daughter (Matt 15:21-28). Jesus also heals the crippled woman: "Jesus asked her whether she herself wished to be healed, but the Syrophoenician woman replied that she was not worthy, and that she asked only for her daughter's cure. Then Jesus laid one hand upon her head, the other on her side, and said: 'Straighten up! May it be done to you as you also will it to be done!'" (*Chron.*, p. 279)

This is a story about faith and one's willingness to be healed. The shepherding hand of our Angel rests upon our head, and the guiding hand of destiny gently rests upon our side, leading us forward. Feeling into the presence of Christ-imbued spiritual forces makes faith a fact. Our willingness to be

---

[33] Powell, *Cultivating Inner Radiance and the Body of Immortality*, p. 171.

[34] *Chron.*, p. 207.

healed is foreshadowed by our courage to face the forces that have caused our diminishment:

> Should we inquire as to the reason why most people fail to do something, we find that the answer invariably is: love of ease. Whether we consider the most important things of life or mere trifles, we find that love of ease is ubiquitous. To hold on to the old and outdated, not being able to shake it off, is a form of love of ease. Steiner mentions in this connection that people are not always as wicked as they may appear. For instance, those who were responsible for the burning at the stake of Giordano Bruno, or the maltreatment of Galileo, did not necessarily act out of wickedness, but rather out of love of ease. They could not accept the new. It often takes a long time for people to be able to think and feel along new lines and the reason for this tardiness is love of ease! It is those who were prone on Earth to love of ease who have to serve Ahriman in the life after death. For Ahriman, apart from his many other functions, is the "spirit of obstacles." Wherever obstacles arise to true progress, there Ahriman is to be found. He applies the brakes to life and to the spiritual development of human beings. "Those who are subject to love of ease on Earth will become agents to the slowing-down process of everything that comes into the world from the supersensible. So love of ease fetters human souls between death and rebirth to spirits who, under Ahriman, are compelled to serve the powers of opposition and hindrance.[35]

Love of ease is the trial of our times. Where are we harboring an unwillingness to shake off the past in order to receive new paradigms of possibility? These are the places where the ease of disease is a greater yearning in the soul than is the daring it would take to become a vessel through which new inspirations may sound.

Are we worthy to collaborate with Angels? May we dare to become an open book on whose pages the future may inscribe its miracles. The alternative is the crucifixion of those whose courage outshines us.

**March 11:** New Moon 25° Aquarius. Today's New Moon remembers the Moon at the end of the forty days (Nov/30/29), as did the conjunction between Mercury and Venus five days ago. When the Moon is conjunct the Sun as it is at New Moon, we can imagine the Moon (our creative will) receiving spiritual decrees directly from the seed and source of our "I Am"—the Sun. These are forces that we can receive directly into our consciousness today, if we are willing to walk with Angels. As this Moon remembers the celebration of the Angels at the end of the forty days, we may feel strengthened to realize the Angelic presence that around us circles, just as they circled the Christ in his time of great need. The XIV Arcanum (connected to Aquarius) reminds us of our Angel:

> But—and this is the tragic side of Angelic existence—this geniality [of our Angel] shows up only when the human being has need of it, when he makes room for the flashing forth of its illumination. The Angel depends on the human being in his creative activity. If the human being does not ask for it, if he or she turns away from him, the Angel has no motive for creative activity. He can then fall into a stare of consciousness where all his creative geniality remains in potential and does not manifest. It is a state of vegetation or "twilight existence," comparable to sleep from the human point of view. An Angel who has nothing to exist for is a tragedy in the spiritual world.
>
> Therefore, dear Unknown Friend, think of your guardian Angel, think of him when you have problems, questions to resolve, tasks to accomplish, plans to formulate, cares and fears to appease! Think of him as a luminous cloud of maternal love above you, moved by the sole desire to serve you and to be useful to you.[36]

This New Moon is a Moon that invites us to remember the guidance of our Angel, and in the presence of our Angel things can appear quite differently than we may have first assumed. In the words of Estelle Isaacson (who received a vision when the Sun was at the exact place in the heavens as it is today): "Ugliness is the chaos of beauty;

---

35 Nesfield-Cookson, *Rudolf Steiner's Vision of Love*, p. 118.

36 *Meditation on the Tarot*, p. 378.

deception is the chaos of truth; evil is the chaos of good."[37]

This is a day to remember your Angel by carrying her "luminous cloud of maternal love" along with you.

Mercury, Neptune and Venus stand nearby during this New Moon, also in Aquarius.

**March 15:** Sun enters Pisces: "In what is lost, may the loss find itself" (Steiner, *Twelve Moods of the Zodiac*). William Bento illumines this mantra:

> Regardless of the nature of what is let go of there is a sense of accompanying loss. With those losses that have been treasured and valued (such as a loved one), there lives the hope that the object or being that is lost will not be forgotten or forlorn, but will find new life in an entirely new realm. The plea that states, *may the loss find itself* is really a statement of hope in the eternal cycle of life.

Above the first decan is the Square of Pegasus, hence the association of this decan with the body of Pegasus, the Winged Horse, also called the Horse of the Fountain. This decan is ruled by Saturn. Pisces bestows Magnanimity born of Love. The challenge is to stay grounded in reality in the inclination toward the mystical.

**March 18:** Venus enters Pisces. "In what is gained, may gain lose itself" (Steiner, *Twelve Moods of the Zodiac*). Venus was in Pisces throughout the entire Passion of Christ. We must lose ourselves in gain so that we may continue to grow. If we attach to gain, we attach to the temporal and thereby sacrifice our willingness to be one with the flowing stream of eternal growth.

**March 22: ASPECT:** Mars conjunct Uranus 13° Pisces. Mars was here at the commissioning of the twelve (Dec/10/30).

> Today there occurred—for the first time—the sending out of the disciples. At about ten o'clock in the morning, with the twelve and about thirty other disciples, Jesus left Capernaum and went north in the direction of Saphet and Hanathon, accompanied by a large crowd. Around three in the afternoon, they approached Hanathon. Here Jesus and the disciples climbed a mountain used in former times by the prophets. Jesus had taught there less than one year ago. This time, however, the crowd did not go up the mountain. On the mountain, Jesus addressed the disciples, giving them instructions and sending them out into the world with the words found in Matthew 9:36-10:16. Each of the twelve had a small flask of oil, and Jesus taught them how to use it for anointing and also for healing. Afterward, the disciples knelt in a circle around Jesus, and he prayed and laid his hands upon the head of each of the twelve.[38]

As the healing power of the Word, Jesus speaks from high on the mountain, where only disciples were allowed to be present. When the Bible tells us of teachings given on the mountains, we can rightly imagine this means "high" teachings given to those prepared to receive them. Today with Mars conjunct Uranus, such high teachings are potentized, for this aspect promises an in-streaming of the cosmic Word from futuristic realms of cosmic Imagination (Uranus) that are seeking to manifest through the spoken word of human beings on Earth. The mountains of the prophets are calling to those who have been given a small flask of oil. This is the property of all who have made themselves ready to heal through the power of the Word. This requires love, receptivity, and a willingness to kneel in humility before the profundity of cosmic wisdom. Inversely, the lower nature speaks with cloaked hatred, closed-mindedness, and flaring egoism that spills the poison of the anti-Logos—a force of destruction toward what the future is rightly striving to birth. May we choose our words carefully.

**March 25:** Sun enters the second decan of Pisces, ruled by Jupiter. This decan is associated with Cepheus, the Crowned King, located high above, whose head is surrounded and illuminated by the Milky Way.

---

37 Isaacson, *The Coming Times*, chap. 29.

38 *Chron.*, p. 263.

**March 27:** Full Moon 11° Virgo opposite Sun 11° Pisces. Walking on the Water. The Moon was here when Christ walked on the water (Jan/30/31).

The disciples' experience at the miracle of walking on water had five parts: the disciples experienced themselves as a group in the universe, united in one boat, driven over the waves by winds, and meeting with the Christ, who spoke to them. The whole night experience, culminating with the words "It is I," is thus made up of these elements:

> awaking the disciples (self-awareness in sleep)
> perceiving themselves as a group united in destiny (the boat)
> threatened equilibrium (the waves)
> forces pushing in a specific direction (the winds)
> Christ speaking

These five experiences become an *inner* experience of the I AM and the sound emanating from it.[39]

Tomberg goes on to describe the effect that recognition of Christ caused in the innermost being of the disciples in the night after the feeding of the 5,000: how the elemental forces and waves from subconscious depths affected them, and how their consciousness was swept by the blasts of conflicting cosmic forces:

> At this moment, human beings have nothing to oppose that image of stupendous powers and raging cosmic waves in the subconscious, except the incomparable weaker force of their own personality; in this hour, Heaven remains silent and veiled in darkness. Then everything depends on overcoming the fear evoked by that vision through the spring of one's inner forces. There is a force in this spring that will rush out at this moment, not manifesting as "personal" but as cosmic activity. Thus human beings must find within themselves a force of calm courage that can overcome the cosmic waves that assail the subconscious and the cosmic winds that sweep through one's consciousness. This force is contained in the words "I AM" once they have become a real experience of life. These words are the esoteric name of the Christ, who is the spring from which flows the strength of human "I" consciousness that can stand against the fear of cosmic forces.[40]

These images offer strong imaginations for this Full Moon. *The light that is coming will cause upheavals if we cannot find the spring in the heart that flows with the presence of Christ. The adversary that is most effectively working in the world now is Ahriman. It is not the individual that is his aim, but communities—for he works against groups, whereby he separates one from the other.* In this way he is able to capsize the boats of destiny-communities in the stormy seas of change. To know the working of the adversary helps us prevent his success. May we serve our communities and love one another. And may we do what needs to be done in selfless service.

**March 28: ASPECT:** Superior conjunction of Venus with Sun 13° Pisces conjunct Uranus. The Flight into Egypt. Sun and Uranus were conjunct at this same degree when an Angel appeared to Joseph and instructed him to flee with his family into Egypt. That same night, of March 2/3, 5 BC, the Holy Family left Nazareth with their one-year-old son. (See *CHA, The Journey of the Three Kings, and the Flight of the Holy Family to Egypt*).

The Solomon Jesus was filled with great wisdom, for he was the reincarnated Zarathustra. It was imperative for his mission that he absorb the mysteries of Egypt—and he therefore stayed in Egypt for 6½ years. In like manner, the wise of today are re-opening the mysteries of Egypt and Christianizing them. This can be seen in our time as a new Flight into Egypt, for this represents a journey into the future. The Egyptians had a "solar consciousness" and could therefore read the stars and align their culture on Earth with the wisdom of the stars above. This was the foundation for the Hermetic principle: *As above, so also below.* The Christian Hermetic path is a schooling that continues through the work of an anonymous author in his book, *Meditations on the Tarot*—a book that

---

39 Tomberg, *Christ and Sophia*, pp. 254–256.

40 *Ibid.*, pp. 254–256.

serves to unite the attentive reader with the etheric Christ, on the journey toward the Holy Grail.

> From the time of the coming of Christ during the age of Aries (fourth cultural epoch), the onward flow of evolution requires from humanity the fulfillment of the task of Christianizing the religions of old, through bringing the power of Divine Love into the wisdom of antiquity as a force of renewal. Otherwise humanity faces the possibility of a second fall, a fall into the sub-earthly realms. We can see it as a work of divine providence that the book *Meditations on the Tarot* has been written as a guide for us all. This book is an expression of a new form of Christianity. It is a fusion of the Christian and the Egyptian mystery wisdom, and it leads us into a new dimension, a new realm of experience, which has to do with the mystery of Christ's Second Coming.[41]

Today the Sun, Venus, and Uranus stand close together in the heavens, and Mars too is in Pisces. *What our hearts (Sun) love is courage, what our souls (Venus) need is love, what our minds need is for the light to shine upon the path leading us into the new mysteries. With Uranus and Venus united with the Sun in Pisces we must watch for the false path that creates dependency born of neediness. We are being called to find the karmic groups (Venus) that are uniting with this onward movement of evolution.* The new Egyptian mysteries are waiting for the knights of the Grail. Just as the family of the Solomon Jesus was led by an Angel into Egypt, so too are many Angels whispering into the ears of humanity, encouraging them to "look up." The stars are waiting for us to open their book of wisdom, just as did the priests of ancient Egypt. So also did the knights of the Holy Grail become acquainted with star wisdom. This quest begins in the depths of our hearts where love alone is the guiding principle. With this gathering today in Pisces, we are reminded that the entire Earth is evolving into a planet of love. We must be mindful today that we are moving with this direction, lest a greater fall overcome us through dependency or complacency. May we Love with all our heart!

---

41 Powell, *Cultivating Inner Radiance and the Body of Immortality*, p. 192.

**March 29:** Today is Good Friday—Commemoration of Christ's Passion and Death on the Cross. The stars and planets, which bore witness to the events of this day, show us the interconnectedness between Heaven and Earth. It is a profound mystery that the seven classical planets rose in their respective order between Thursday night through Friday afternoon: Moon, Venus, Mercury, Sun, Mars, Jupiter and Saturn (See *CHA:* The Stages of the Passion). This order also reflects the *ascending* order of the chakras. *The Moon rose on the evening of the Last Supper, Venus rose at Peter's first denial, Mercury with Peter's second denial. As the Sun rose that morning, judgement was passed on the Son of Man. As Mars rose he was scourged. Jupiter rose as he was crowned with thorns, and as Saturn rose he was carrying the cross up Mt. Calvary. The rising planets were a perfect prophecy for the different stages of the Passion.* As the Cross was raised upon the hill of Golgotha, Leo was rising—the Lion of Judah, out of unfathomable love and mercy, was hung on a cross between two criminals. Star beings working from the constellation of Leo form the heart as conception begins in a mother's womb. At the crucifixion of Christ, it was the cosmic heart that was being formed—a heart of eternal love and forgiveness. The primal forces of Divine Love rayed forth from the heart of Christ, the Son of God, and the Earth was illumined with grace.

> Hanging there on the holy cross, the crucified Jesus Christ signified the new Tree of Life, raised up for the first time on Earth since the expulsion of man from Paradise. The blood flowed from his wounds for the regeneration of the Earth and Humankind, for the restoration of a new paradise, the Heavenly Jerusalem—in place of the earthly city of Jerusalem—away from which, facing North-West, his gaze was now directed. Thus he could say to the repentant criminal crucified to his right: "Today you will be with me in Paradise." For, on that Good Friday the new Paradise began, a new afterlife for all who unite themselves with Christ. And the repentant criminal was the first human being to die in proximity to Christ, to be taken up by Christ, since the

New Era denoted by the Mystery of Golgotha began.[42]

The death of Jesus on the cross marked the descent of Christ into the underworld. Before he died he was taunted, mocked, and rejected by those he came to redeem. In the subearthly realms, however, he was greeted as the king he truly was. On this Good Friday we remember the Lamb of God who died so that we may find the eternal nourishment of Heaven. It was fulfilled!

**March 30:** Sun 15° Pisces: Birth of the Solomon Jesus (Mar/5/6 BC). The Solomon Jesus was the reincarnation of the great teacher, Zarathustra, who was visited by the Three Kings. The kings brought the wisdom gathered by initiates in the three preceding cultural ages: Myrrh from Ancient India, Frankincense from Ancient Persia, and Gold from Ancient Egypt. *The influence of this great teacher, the Master Jesus, is always present on Earth. It takes discernment to hear his teachings through the cacophony of distractions, but he is always here. There is always an initiate who is working with him, even if he himself is not physically incarnated.* The ideal of Pisces, the Sun sign at this birth, is "Not I, but Christ in me."

Holy Saturday—Commemoration of Christ's Descent into Hell. The descent of Christ to the Mother in the heart of the earthly realm was for the redemption of Nature and the entire Earth. In Paradise the kingdom of the Father and the realm of the Mother were interpenetrated. After the Fall, the two kingdoms fell further and further from each other. Christ descended into the depths of the inner Earth and planted his spirit as a seed in the womb of the Earth. As he began his descent, Virgo was rising in the East. This is the constellation connected to the womb, and to the sowing of seeds that will birth new impulses into the womb of all creation. (See *CHA*, The Mystery of Golgotha.)

The descent into Hell fulfilled the sixth stage of the Passion. In Hell Christ encountered the Antichrist: The power of the Antichrist is, or is almost, equal to that of Christ. The feather that tips the balance is the powerlessness Christ voluntarily takes upon himself in his self-sacrificing deed; and this powerlessness, of which the Antichrist is incapable, ultimately leads to the hair's breadth more power that Christ possesses.[43]

It is incumbent upon each of us to render the Antichrist powerless—through recognizing and resisting his presence in the world. For if left unnamed, this presence causes fear, uncertainty, and denial that such a force even exists. The presence of the Antichrist leads people to seek worldly power and worldly things in a vain attempt to out-run their fear. Avoidance however does not work; instead it divides people and sets each against the other through wars and other inequities. In "powerlessness" we stand together with Christ, and bring the strength of love and courage that pushes fear into the underworld from whence it came.

**March 31:** Sun 16° Pisces: Conception of the Nathan Jesus (Mar/6/2 BC). The Nathan Jesus is the immaculate soul who physically incarnated for the first time as Jesus of Nazareth. It is profound that the birth of the Solomon Jesus and the conception of the Nathan Jesus were so beautifully interwoven in the stars, just as was their interweaving upon the Earth. At the birth of the Solomon Jesus, the Sun was 15° Pisces.

**ASPECT:** Venus 16° Pisces square Pluto 16° Sagittarius. Attarus Arrival/Eclipse 2009: As Christ arrived on the mountain called Attarus to begin his forty days of continual temptation, heliocentric Venus stood witness in the heavens at this same degree, just as she witnessed the longest solar eclipse of the twenty-first century on July 22, 2009 at this same degree. Venus and Pluto were square to each other in these same constellations during the entire Passion and death of Christ.

A somber mood accompanies this aspect and therewith we are called to create the highest possibilities this aspect bestows. Venus as the love that weaves like milk and honey between human hearts, and Pluto as the divine love of the Father, can form a dynamic interaction that allows one to fearlessly stand before danger with an intensity for peace.

---

42 *CHA*, The Mystery of Golgotha.

43 Von Halle, *Descent into the Depths of the Earth*, p. 108.

*And what are temptations if not the testing of one's moral steadfastness? The beings of the constellations of Pisces and Sagittarius ask us to loyally stand in the fire out of which our certainty is born. If tension finds its expression today, our task will be to love the truth no matter how uncomfortable that may be for ourselves or others.*

Easter Sunday—Commemoration of Christ's Resurrection: The spiritual worlds held their breath at the descent of Christ into Hell. A world unknown to the higher hierarchies was being penetrated by Jesus Christ.

> The "gardener" who appeared to the woman made clairvoyant by grief was not a "gardener" from only her perspective. In a deeper sense, he was truly a gardener, because he had acquired the power to cause the Earth's soil to produce the fruits of goodness. From that time forward, the highest human initiates have likewise become "gardeners"; they work for the well-being of humanity—and not just the direct concerns of humanity, but also those that reach indirectly through nature and Earth's soil.[44]

What now occurred was the Resurrection of our Savior and this takes place as a real rhythm of the Earth and as a spiritual power, creating substance every Sunday anew in every single human being. At this moment the Savior of the world revealed the whole immeasurable grandeur of his love to the world with which he had completely united himself, as well as with the human beings living on it. At this moment, as the Christ Spirit arises from the grave in the first Resurrection body, he merges into the innermost heart of every human soul. It is now up to us in humility, in devotion and in joy, to celebrate daily this inner core of holiness by becoming aware that we ourselves bear him—the highest and most precious—in us.[45]

Today we celebrate the Risen One and the work of his "gardeners," as we remember the Sabbath and keep it holy—for the Sabbath Sunday is a day to rest from the toil of daily life, in memory of spiritual worlds and spiritual beings. The fact that materialistic culture has intruded upon this holy day of rest does not mean we need comply.

# APRIL

The Sun begins the month in front of the Fishes (Pisces) moving into Aries on April 14th. Saturn becomes visible in the early night sky by the end of the month, rising around sunset on the 28th. Because it is opposite the Sun, its face will be fully illuminated. This is exactly how a Full Moon is formed: Sun–Earth–Moon. Here we have Sun–Earth–Saturn and it is the best time of year to gaze upon it with the eyes. Saturn will remain easily visible to star gazers until the end of September when it begins to disappear into the Sun's predawn glow. The New Moon is on the 10th (Sun and Moon in Pisces) and the Full upon the 25th with the Moon in Libra. The Full Moon will be a partial lunar eclipse, visible in Europe, Africa, Asia and Australia. Pluto stations retrograde on the 12th, appearing to go backward through the zodiac until September. The Lyrids meteor shower offers meteors from the 16th to 25th and reaches its peak on the 21st to 22nd, promising as many as 20 meteors an hour. With the bright waxing Moon, the best window for viewing is short—between Moon set at about 4 a.m. and sunrise, about 2 hours later. If you are willing to try, look up toward the east into the constellation of Lyra.

**April 4:** The Sun enters the third decan of Pisces, the Mars decan, associated with the constellation Andromeda, the Chained Woman, who—threatened by the sea monster Cetus from below—was rescued by Perseus.

**April 6: ASPECT:** Venus conjunct Mars 24° Pisces: From both the heliocentric (spirit-eye view) and geocentric (Earth's eye view) Venus and Mars are today conjunct at the same place in the zodiac: The Passion of Christ. From this degree Venus watched the judgment, the passion, the crucifixion and the resurrection of Christ. The memory of this event is indelibly inscribed into the Akashic Chronicle for all eternity. Today Mars joins Venus at the place

---

44 Tomberg, *Christ and Sophia*, p. 299.
45 Von Halle, *And If He Had Not Been Raised...*, p. 127.

of this memory from both the vantage of the Sun (heliocentric) as well as from the vantage of the Earth (geocentric).

At the death of John F. Kennedy, heliocentric Jupiter stood at this same degree. This is a man who spoke out against the gathering power of the CIA and the Federal Reserve. Kennedy's wisdom (Jupiter) and his courage to speak the truth (Mars) resulted in his assassination. Five years later Martin Luther King died with the north node at this same degree, suggesting that his angelically guided mission (north node) was in service to the suffering for truth and the freedom won through truth. Two great figures of the 1960s, who spoke out against principles and agencies that were strangling truth, met their death with star alignments remembering Venus during the Passion of Christ.

With Mars joining Venus at this degree we may ask what truth we are willing to speak. When Judas was summoned to be a disciple, Mars was at this same degree. Judas aligned himself with the powers and agendas that both Kennedy and King were striving to thwart. Those who align with the dark side, like Judas, are safe for a time... but what then?

Today we can focus on our "vertical" truth—the truth we would die to defend.

**April 10:** New Moon 25° Pisces: Feeding of the Four Thousand: (Matt. 15:32-39; *Chron.*, 284). At the Feeding of the Four Thousand, seven loaves of bread and seven fish were multiplied. After all had eaten their fill, seven baskets of bread were gathered. Seven indicates communion taking place in the course of *time*, as distinct from the Feeding of the Five Thousand, which depicted communion taking place from cosmic realms of *space* (twelve), where twelve baskets of bread were collected.

In the Feeding of the Four Thousand we see our union with the temporal aspect of evolution connected with the seven days of creation—each day representing one of the seven pillars of Sophia's Temple (from ancient Saturn to future Vulcan). Seven signifies the unfolding of our seven-fold nature: physical, etheric, astral, "I," spirit self, life spirit, and spirit body in time. Physical evolution occurs over the course of time. As we develop we purify our bodies, rendering them fit for continued evolutionary stages of development. As we evolve, our chakras awaken as organs of perception—they become solarized through communion with Christ. As this occurs, we require less nourishment *from* the elemental world and instead become sources of nourishment *for* the elemental world. As we move forward through evolution we will reach ever-higher levels of purity. Of the seven pillars in Sophia's Temple we are currently working with the fourth pillar, Earth. Earth evolution is focused toward the development of the "I." This "I," given to humanity at the *Turning Point in Time*, is to reach ever higher into spiritual realms so as to be nourished by spiritual manna. To do this we must overcome the trial of the third temptation now facing us—"Man does not live by bread alone, but by every word that issues forth from the Word of God."

Today remembers this miracle of honoring the unfolding of Sophia's Temple in time. The beings of nature and all the fruits of Mother Earth are sacred sources of nourishment, and they become sacraments through the human being's communion with Christ. It is what is living that leads humanity to spiritual nourishment. Ahriman said to Christ in the wilderness, at the third temptation: "Look at the dead earthly phenomena, the stones; they can come to life as bread if you only command them to do so. They will become as bread because, from the Earth's interior, I can supply a lifelike force to all dead matter. You must simply will what is dead to live."[46]

Christ rejected the temptation by pointing to the Word of God as the true source of life—the life that gives both nature and humanity the ability to move with evolution toward its fifth manifestation—future Jupiter existence. Today remembers this miracle and the anti-life that today threatens humanity from sub-earthly realms. During this New Moon we can be reminded to say "no" to manipulations that fulfill Ahriman's continual drive to remove *Life* from our daily bread. Instead of participating in the treacherous debasing of our Mother Earth's bountiful gifts, we can spend time in nature taking notice of her every expression with grateful hearts. Which will it be—the bread of life, or the stones

---

46 Tomberg, *Christ and Sophia*, p. 174.

| SIDEREAL GEOCENTRIC LONGITUDES : APRIL 2013 Gregorian at 0 hours UT | | | | | | | | | | | |
|---|---|---|---|---|---|---|---|---|---|---|---|
| DAY | ☉ | ☽ | ☊ | ☿ | ♀ | ♂ | ♃ | ♄ | ⛢ | ♆ | ♇ |
| 1 MO | 16 ♓ 30 | 17 ♏ 30 | 22 ♎ 22 | 18 ♒ 43 | 17 ♓ 20 | 20 ♓ 18 | 16 ♉ 55 | 15 ♎ 14R | 13 ♓ 44 | 9 ♒ 18 | 16 ♐ 37 |
| 2 TU | 17 29 | 1 ♐ 46 | 22 23 | 19 44 | 18 35 | 21 4 | 17 5 | 15 10 | 13 47 | 9 20 | 16 38 |
| 3 WE | 18 28 | 15 58 | 22 24 | 20 48 | 19 49 | 21 50 | 17 15 | 15 6 | 13 51 | 9 21 | 16 38 |
| 4 TH | 19 27 | 0 ♑ 1 | 22 23R | 21 54 | 21 4 | 22 36 | 17 26 | 15 3 | 13 54 | 9 23 | 16 38 |
| 5 FR | 20 27 | 13 57 | 22 22 | 23 3 | 22 18 | 23 21 | 17 36 | 14 59 | 13 58 | 9 25 | 16 39 |
| 6 SA | 21 26 | 27 42 | 22 18 | 24 14 | 23 33 | 24 7 | 17 46 | 14 55 | 14 1 | 9 27 | 16 39 |
| 7 SU | 22 25 | 11 ♒ 17 | 22 14 | 25 27 | 24 47 | 24 53 | 17 57 | 14 51 | 14 4 | 9 29 | 16 39 |
| 8 MO | 23 24 | 24 39 | 22 9 | 26 43 | 26 1 | 25 38 | 18 7 | 14 47 | 14 8 | 9 31 | 16 39 |
| 9 TU | 24 23 | 7 ♓ 47 | 22 5 | 28 0 | 27 16 | 26 24 | 18 18 | 14 43 | 14 11 | 9 32 | 16 39 |
| 10 WE | 25 22 | 20 41 | 22 1 | 29 19 | 28 30 | 27 10 | 18 29 | 14 38 | 14 15 | 9 34 | 16 39 |
| 11 TH | 26 21 | 3 ♈ 20 | 21 59 | 0 ♓ 40 | 29 44 | 27 55 | 18 40 | 14 34 | 14 18 | 9 36 | 16 39 |
| 12 FR | 27 19 | 15 45 | 21 58 | 2 3 | 0 ♈ 59 | 28 41 | 18 51 | 14 30 | 14 21 | 9 37 | 16 39 |
| 13 SA | 28 18 | 27 57 | 21 58D | 3 28 | 2 13 | 29 26 | 19 2 | 14 26 | 14 25 | 9 39 | 16 39R |
| 14 SU | 29 17 | 9 ♉ 58 | 21 59 | 4 55 | 3 27 | 0 ♈ 11 | 19 13 | 14 22 | 14 28 | 9 41 | 16 39 |
| 15 MO | 0 ♈ 16 | 21 52 | 22 0 | 6 23 | 4 42 | 0 57 | 19 24 | 14 17 | 14 31 | 9 42 | 16 39 |
| 16 TU | 1 15 | 3 ♊ 42 | 22 2 | 7 54 | 5 56 | 1 42 | 19 35 | 14 13 | 14 35 | 9 44 | 16 39 |
| 17 WE | 2 13 | 15 32 | 22 3 | 9 25 | 7 10 | 2 27 | 19 47 | 14 8 | 14 38 | 9 46 | 16 39 |
| 18 TH | 3 12 | 27 27 | 22 4 | 10 59 | 8 24 | 3 12 | 19 58 | 14 4 | 14 41 | 9 47 | 16 39 |
| 19 FR | 4 11 | 9 ♋ 31 | 22 4R | 12 34 | 9 38 | 3 57 | 20 10 | 14 0 | 14 45 | 9 49 | 16 39 |
| 20 SA | 5 9 | 21 51 | 22 3 | 14 11 | 10 53 | 4 42 | 20 21 | 13 55 | 14 48 | 9 50 | 16 39 |
| 21 SU | 6 8 | 4 ♌ 28 | 22 2 | 15 50 | 12 7 | 5 27 | 20 33 | 13 51 | 14 51 | 9 52 | 16 38 |
| 22 MO | 7 6 | 17 28 | 22 0 | 17 30 | 13 21 | 6 12 | 20 45 | 13 46 | 14 54 | 9 53 | 16 38 |
| 23 TU | 8 5 | 0 ♍ 52 | 21 58 | 19 12 | 14 35 | 6 57 | 20 57 | 13 42 | 14 57 | 9 54 | 16 38 |
| 24 WE | 9 3 | 14 40 | 21 57 | 20 55 | 15 49 | 7 42 | 21 8 | 13 37 | 15 1 | 9 56 | 16 38 |
| 25 TH | 10 2 | 28 50 | 21 55 | 22 41 | 17 3 | 8 27 | 21 20 | 13 33 | 15 4 | 9 57 | 16 37 |
| 26 FR | 11 0 | 13 ♎ 18 | 21 55 | 24 28 | 18 17 | 9 12 | 21 33 | 13 28 | 15 7 | 9 58 | 16 37 |
| 27 SA | 11 58 | 27 59 | 21 55D | 26 16 | 19 31 | 9 56 | 21 45 | 13 23 | 15 10 | 10 0 | 16 36 |
| 28 SU | 12 57 | 12 ♏ 46 | 21 55 | 28 7 | 20 45 | 10 41 | 21 57 | 13 19 | 15 13 | 10 1 | 16 36 |
| 29 MO | 13 55 | 27 32 | 21 56 | 29 59 | 21 59 | 11 26 | 22 9 | 13 14 | 15 16 | 10 2 | 16 35 |
| 30 TU | 14 53 | 12 ♐ 10 | 21 56 | 1 ♈ 53 | 23 13 | 12 10 | 22 21 | 13 10 | 15 20 | 10 4 | 16 35 |

INGRESSES :

| | |
|---|---|
| 1 ☽ → ♐ 21: 0 | 18 ☽ → ♋ 5: 6 |
| 3 ☽ → ♑ 23:57 | 20 ☽ → ♌ 15:34 |
| 6 ☽ → ♒ 4: 1 | 22 ☽ → ♍ 22:28 |
| 8 ☽ → ♓ 9:44 | 25 ☽ → ♎ 1:57 |
| 10 ☿ → ♓ 12: 8 | 27 ☽ → ♏ 3:16 |
| ☽ → ♈ 17:38 | 29 ☿ → ♈ 0:13 |
| 11 ♀ → ♈ 5: 2 | ☽ → ♐ 4: 2 |
| 13 ☽ → ♉ 4: 4 | |
| ♂ → ♈ 18: 1 | |
| 14 ☉ → ♈ 17:30 | |
| 15 ☽ → ♊ 16:30 | |

ASPECTS & ECLIPSES :

| | | | |
|---|---|---|---|
| 1 ☉ □ ♇ 2:59 | 11 ☽ ☍ ♄ 21:35 | 22 ♀ ☍ ♄ 7:41 | ☽ ☍ ♃ 15: 7 |
| 3 ☽ ☌ ♇ 1: 8 | 12 ☽ ☌ ☋ 12:10 | 24 ☽ ☍ ⛢ 0:36 | ♀ ☍ ☊ 22:53 |
| ☉ □ ☽ 4:35 | 14 ☽ ☌ ♃ 18:56 | ☽ ☍ ☿ 12:10 | 30 ☽ ☌ ♇ 7:18 |
| 5 ☽ N ☊ 14:34 | 15 ☽ ☌ A 22:42 | 25 ☽ ☍ ♂ 16:51 | |
| 6 ☽ ☌ ♆ 20:47 | 17 ☽ ☍ ♇ 2:16 | ☉ ☍ ☽ 19:56 | |
| 7 ♀ ☌ ♂ 4:56 | 18 ☉ ☌ ♂ 0:19 | ☽ ●° P 20: 8 | |
| 8 ☽ ☌ ☿ 4: 8 | ☉ □ ☽ 12:29 | 26 ☽ ☌ ♄ 0:15 | |
| 9 ☽ ☌ ⛢ 11:54 | 20 ☽ S ☊ 0:24 | ☽ ☍ ♀ 8:55 | |
| 10 ☉ ☌ ☽ 9:34 | ☿ ☌ ⛢ 9:18 | ☽ ☌ ☊ 14: 5 | |
| ☽ ☌ ♂ 13: 1 | 21 ☽ ☍ ♆ 10: 3 | 27 ☽ ☌ P 19:51 | |
| ☽ ☌ ♀ 16:23 | ☿ □ ♇ 11:42 | 28 ☉ ☍ ♄ 8:26 | |

| SIDEREAL HELIOCENTRIC LONGITUDES : APRIL 2013 Gregorian at 0 hours UT | | | | | | | | | | | |
|---|---|---|---|---|---|---|---|---|---|---|---|
| DAY | Sid. Time | ☿ | ♀ | ⊕ | ♂ | ♃ | ♄ | ⛢ | ♆ | ♇ | Vernal Point |
| 1 MO | 12:38: 4 | 19 ♏ 34 | 18 ♓ 30 | 16 ♍ 30 | 23 ♓ 0 | 26 ♉ 45 | 12 ♎ 25 | 13 ♓ 36 | 8 ♒ 9 | 14 ♐ 51 | 5 ♓ 4'31" |
| 2 TU | 12:42: 0 | 22 18 | 20 5 | 17 29 | 23 36 | 26 50 | 12 27 | 13 36 | 8 9 | 14 51 | 5 ♓ 4'31" |
| 3 WE | 12:45:57 | 25 3 | 21 41 | 18 28 | 24 13 | 26 55 | 12 29 | 13 37 | 8 9 | 14 52 | 5 ♓ 4'30" |
| 4 TH | 12:49:53 | 27 48 | 23 17 | 19 28 | 24 49 | 27 0 | 12 31 | 13 38 | 8 10 | 14 52 | 5 ♓ 4'30" |
| 5 FR | 12:53:50 | 0 ♐ 34 | 24 52 | 20 27 | 25 25 | 27 6 | 12 33 | 13 38 | 8 10 | 14 52 | 5 ♓ 4'30" |
| 6 SA | 12:57:46 | 3 20 | 26 28 | 21 26 | 26 1 | 27 11 | 12 34 | 13 39 | 8 10 | 14 53 | 5 ♓ 4'30" |
| 7 SU | 13: 1:43 | 6 7 | 28 4 | 22 25 | 26 38 | 27 16 | 12 36 | 13 40 | 8 11 | 14 53 | 5 ♓ 4'30" |
| 8 MO | 13: 5:40 | 8 55 | 29 39 | 23 24 | 27 14 | 27 21 | 12 38 | 13 40 | 8 11 | 14 53 | 5 ♓ 4'30" |
| 9 TU | 13: 9:36 | 11 45 | 1 ♈ 15 | 24 23 | 27 50 | 27 26 | 12 40 | 13 41 | 8 11 | 14 54 | 5 ♓ 4'30" |
| 10 WE | 13:13:33 | 14 36 | 2 51 | 25 22 | 28 26 | 27 32 | 12 42 | 13 42 | 8 12 | 14 54 | 5 ♓ 4'29" |
| 11 TH | 13:17:29 | 17 28 | 4 27 | 26 21 | 29 2 | 27 37 | 12 44 | 13 42 | 8 12 | 14 54 | 5 ♓ 4'29" |
| 12 FR | 13:21:26 | 20 23 | 6 3 | 27 20 | 29 38 | 27 42 | 12 46 | 13 43 | 8 12 | 14 55 | 5 ♓ 4'29" |
| 13 SA | 13:25:22 | 23 20 | 7 39 | 28 18 | 0 ♈ 14 | 27 47 | 12 48 | 13 43 | 8 13 | 14 55 | 5 ♓ 4'29" |
| 14 SU | 13:29:19 | 26 20 | 9 15 | 29 17 | 0 50 | 27 52 | 12 50 | 13 44 | 8 13 | 14 55 | 5 ♓ 4'29" |
| 15 MO | 13:33:15 | 29 22 | 10 51 | 0 ♎ 16 | 1 25 | 27 58 | 12 52 | 13 45 | 8 14 | 14 56 | 5 ♓ 4'29" |
| 16 TU | 13:37:12 | 2 ♑ 27 | 12 27 | 1 15 | 2 1 | 28 3 | 12 53 | 13 45 | 8 14 | 14 56 | 5 ♓ 4'29" |
| 17 WE | 13:41: 9 | 5 36 | 14 3 | 2 13 | 2 37 | 28 8 | 12 55 | 13 46 | 8 14 | 14 56 | 5 ♓ 4'29" |
| 18 TH | 13:45: 5 | 8 48 | 15 39 | 3 12 | 3 12 | 28 13 | 12 57 | 13 47 | 8 15 | 14 57 | 5 ♓ 4'28" |
| 19 FR | 13:49: 2 | 12 4 | 17 15 | 4 11 | 3 48 | 28 18 | 12 59 | 13 47 | 8 15 | 14 57 | 5 ♓ 4'28" |
| 20 SA | 13:52:58 | 15 24 | 18 51 | 5 9 | 4 24 | 28 23 | 13 1 | 13 48 | 8 15 | 14 57 | 5 ♓ 4'28" |
| 21 SU | 13:56:55 | 18 48 | 20 27 | 6 8 | 4 59 | 28 29 | 13 3 | 13 49 | 8 16 | 14 58 | 5 ♓ 4'28" |
| 22 MO | 14: 0:51 | 22 18 | 22 3 | 7 6 | 5 35 | 28 34 | 13 5 | 13 49 | 8 16 | 14 58 | 5 ♓ 4'28" |
| 23 TU | 14: 4:48 | 25 52 | 23 39 | 8 5 | 6 10 | 28 39 | 13 7 | 13 50 | 8 16 | 14 58 | 5 ♓ 4'28" |
| 24 WE | 14: 8:44 | 29 32 | 25 15 | 9 3 | 6 45 | 28 44 | 13 9 | 13 51 | 8 17 | 14 59 | 5 ♓ 4'28" |
| 25 TH | 14:12:41 | 3 ♒ 18 | 26 52 | 10 2 | 7 21 | 28 49 | 13 10 | 13 51 | 8 17 | 14 59 | 5 ♓ 4'27" |
| 26 FR | 14:16:38 | 7 10 | 28 28 | 11 0 | 7 56 | 28 54 | 13 12 | 13 52 | 8 18 | 14 59 | 5 ♓ 4'27" |
| 27 SA | 14:20:34 | 11 8 | 0 ♉ 4 | 11 59 | 8 31 | 29 0 | 13 14 | 13 52 | 8 18 | 15 0 | 5 ♓ 4'27" |
| 28 SU | 14:24:31 | 15 14 | 1 41 | 12 57 | 9 6 | 29 5 | 13 16 | 13 53 | 8 18 | 15 0 | 5 ♓ 4'27" |
| 29 MO | 14:28:27 | 19 27 | 3 17 | 13 55 | 9 41 | 29 10 | 13 18 | 13 54 | 8 19 | 15 0 | 5 ♓ 4'27" |
| 30 TU | 14:32:24 | 23 47 | 4 53 | 14 53 | 10 16 | 29 15 | 13 20 | 13 54 | 8 19 | 15 0 | 5 ♓ 4'27" |

INGRESSES :

| |
|---|
| 4 ☿ → ♐ 19: 8 |
| 8 ♀ → ♈ 5: 8 |
| 12 ♂ → ♈ 14:49 |
| 14 ⊕ → ♎ 17:26 |
| 15 ☿ → ♑ 4:56 |
| 24 ☿ → ♒ 3: 1 |
| 26 ♀ → ♉ 22:57 |

ASPECTS (HELIOCENTRIC +MOON(TYCHONIC)) :

| | | | | |
|---|---|---|---|---|
| 1 ☽ ☌ ☿ 4:17 | 8 ☽ □ ♃ 4:56 | ☽ ☌ ♃ 12:26 | 21 ☽ ☍ ♆ 7: 4 | 28 ☽ □ ☿ 5:33 |
| ☽ ☍ ♃ 15:38 | 9 ☽ □ ☿ 9:23 | ☿ □ ♂ 19:50 | ☿ □ ♀ 20:58 | ⊕ ☌ ♄ 8:10 |
| 2 ☿ ☌ A 3:46 | ☽ ☌ ⛢ 10:56 | 16 ♀ ☍ ♄ 6:50 | 22 ☿ S ☊ 8:36 | 29 ☽ ☍ ♃ 2:41 |
| ☽ □ ⛢ 20: 1 | ☽ □ ♇ 13:11 | ☽ □ ⛢ 20:26 | ☽ □ ♃ 20: 3 | 30 ☽ □ ⛢ 2:52 |
| ☽ ☌ ♇ 22: 8 | ☿ □ ⛢ 16:24 | ☽ ☍ ♇ 22:48 | 23 ☽ ☍ ⛢ 22:35 | ☽ ☌ ♇ 4:42 |
| 3 ☽ □ ♀ 10:58 | 10 ☿ ☌ ♇ 2:33 | 18 ⊕ ☍ ♂ 0:19 | 24 ☽ □ ♇ 0:32 | |
| ☽ □ ♂ 14:40 | ☽ ☌ ♂ 15:23 | ☽ □ ♂ 12: 5 | 25 ☽ ☍ ♂ 14:45 | |
| ☿ ☍ ♃ 16:50 | 11 ☽ ☌ ♀ 2:27 | 19 ☿ □ ♄ 6:45 | ☽ ☌ ♄ 23:50 | |
| 4 ☽ □ ♄ 21:33 | ☽ ☍ ♄ 18:11 | ☽ □ ♄ 6:48 | 26 ☿ ☌ ♆ 6:54 | |
| 5 ♀ ☌ ♂ 13:17 | 13 ☽ □ ♆ 20:29 | ☽ ☍ ☿ 6:50 | 27 ☽ ☍ ♀ 3:47 | |
| 6 ☽ ☌ ♆ 18:29 | 15 ☿ □ ⊕ 10:18 | ☽ □ ♀ 17:21 | ☽ □ ♆ 16:45 | |

of materialism and all the entrapments caused by virtual realities and genetic manipulations? We are surrounded by that which is dead masquerading as the living. May we find the holiness of Life this day, and open our eyes to the activity of the usurper, who causes that which is dead to appear as if living.

**April 11:** Venus enters Aries: "Take hold of growth's being" (Steiner, *Twelve Moods of the Zodiac*). Venus was in Aries at the Ascension, Pentecost, the conception of the Nathan Jesus, and during the Flight into Egypt. We are urged to take hold of the cosmic forces of radiance and through these unite with the highest ideals of love. This growing radiance is to issue forth from our hearts into the whole of nature. In this way we become participants in the evolving presence of Christ and Sophia.

**April 12:** Sun 28: Pisces: Peter receives the keys: (Mar/19/31). Four days after the Feeding of the Four Thousand, Jesus and the disciples had withdrawn to a mountain. At dawn, Jesus went to them and asked, "Who do you say that I am?" Peter saw the majesty of Jesus, and proclaimed his divinity by saying, "You are the Christ, the Son of the living God" (Matthew 16:15-16). Jesus replied:

> Blessed are you, Simon, son of Jonas, because flesh and blood has not revealed this to you, but my Father who is in Heaven! And this I say to you: You are a rock, and upon this rock I will build my church, and the gates of Hell shall not prevail against it. And I will give you the keys of the kingdom of Heaven. And whatsoever you shall bind upon Earth, it shall be bound also in Heaven; and whatsoever you shall loose upon Earth, it shall be loosed also in Heaven!

We can only wonder about what has been loosed on Earth because of humanity's failure to hold the gates of Hell in check. In January of 2010, it was Citizens United; in April of 2010 oil was pouring into the waters of the Gulf of Mexico; in April of 2011 radiation from the Fukushima meltdown was pouring into the ocean off the eastern shores of Japan. In 2012, it was laws that breeched the sovereignty of freedom in the US through the National Defense Appropriations Act. The keys to the kingdom of Heaven signify the power, drawn from the kingdom of the Father, to be able to hold in check the forces of the underworld arising through the gates of Hell. This realm of Hell is guarded by the "gate" of the first chakra, the Moon chakra. "The two keys laid one over the other form a cross, and it is precisely the sign of the cross to which the Father had lent power to banish the evil forces back into the underworld. This can only be achieved in purity and in faith, qualities which Peter had." (*CHA*, The Transfiguration)

It is time to become like Peter and restore our faith in Christ so that we can hold in check the forces of the underworld. First we face our inner underworld, and then we are ennobled to serve the collective underworld whose tentacles weave throughout our culture. Guard the gate!

**Pluto Stations 16°39 Sagittarius:** Pentecost (May/24/33). The descent of the Holy Spirit into the Blessed Virgin Mary. Pluto will remain close to this degree through next month. With Pluto magnifying this cosmic memory, we can imagine a door being held open—a door to realms of cosmic Light. This light illumines truth. Forces of goodness receive the Light and work to release any darkness the Light has revealed. Forces of evil counter the Light by amplifying scenarios born of the serpent's world in order to eclipse the Light. The serpent's sub-earthly realms can be so agitated by the Light that it quakes in rage against the Light. This is a time to be a Light-bearer whose aim (Sagittarius) is the abode of the Father (higher Pluto): the Central Sun.

**April 13:** Sun 29° Pisces: Triumphant entry into Jerusalem: (Mar/19/33). Exactly two years after Peter is given the keys to guard the gates of Hell, the One who would pass through the gates of Hell and descend into the underworld, for the salvation of all humanity, entered Jerusalem as the sacrificial lamb. This was two weeks before his Passion and death.

**Mars enters Aries:** "Ray out awakening life" (Steiner, *Twelve Moods of the Zodiac*). Mars was in Aries at the death of John the Baptist and at the Raising of Lazarus, as well as other healing miracles. With Mars in Aries we are to devote each word we utter to the realization of humanity's triumph over evil. Words become deeds and deeds create history. Our shining light is dependent on the quality of our words. As Mars passes through the sign under which the Sun witnessed the crucifixion, we can remember to serve the living Word.

**April 14:** Sun enters Aries. "Arise, O shining light" (Steiner, *Twelve Moods of the Zodiac*). William Bento illumines this mantra:

> A call is heard as the Sun enters the sign of Aries. It is a call to not merely arise, but to awaken. The Sun effortlessly does this every morning, bestowing light upon us all. Should we not follow the Sun in this way? In the heart of every human being there lives this light that can be made available to others every day. It is our mandate to make it available to all every day and in every way that aids an awakening to the many miracles that take place daily.

Aries—"The Lamb and his Bride"—signifies the process of spiritualization (Christ) and interiorization (Sophia). The teachings of Hermes in ancient Egypt contained a pre-Christian understanding of the relationship between the Lamb and his Bride through the mystery teachings of Isis and Osiris. The first decan is ruled by Mars and is associated with the Girdle of Andromeda, symbolizing the power of unity and purity worn by the Mystic Woman who represents the soul of humanity.

**April 17: ASPECT:** Sun conjunct Mars 2° Pisces: The Blessing of the children and the words of Matthew 19:27-30. Accompanied by Peter, James, and John, Jesus went to Bethabara, where he was joined by Matthew and another apostle. A large crowd had gathered. Jesus healed a great many people. It was here that Jesus spoke of marriage, blessed the children brought to him (Matthew 19:10-15), and advised the rich youth. This last incident was followed by the exchange of words between Peter and Jesus recorded in Matthew 19:28-30, after he had spoken that it would be easier for a camel to pass through the eye of a needle than for a rich man to enter the kingdom of God:

Jesus said to them, "Truly I tell you, at the renewal of all things, when the Son of Man sits on his glorious throne, you who have followed me will also sit on twelve thrones, judging the twelve tribes of Israel. And everyone who has left houses or brothers or sisters or father or mother or children or fields for my sake will receive a hundred times as much and will inherit eternal life. But many who are first will be last, and many who are last will be first."

*As these words came with the blessing of the children, we can see how necessary it is to leave what we have known if we are to align with the coming times. What has become common behavior and activity for ourselves and our children is not what will protect them, but is rather that which is dissolving their spiritual organs of perception. Going the narrow way forward means leaving what is familiar, popular, and comfortable.* The masses follow, as goats, a shepherd leading them into the bowels of materialism—all the while listening to him give the sensible explanation that these are the times and they must go with the flow. There are others who follow a different master, those who are innocent and observant of the forces working against them; they do for the least among them in order to do for the One they follow. This is an arduous path and a lonely one, which forfeits comfort in order to serve truth. Will we protect our families from all that preys on them and damages the spirit? With Mars conjunct Sun at this memory we are wise to summon the courage needed in order to swim against the current.

**April 19:** Sun 4° Aries: Woe Upon the Pharisees: (Mar/24/33). In this address to the crowds and disciples, Jesus Christ threw down the gauntlet before the Pharisees (Matthew 23:2-39). Powerful words echo from this "woe" into our own time. The powerful princes of the material world have nothing but loathing for anything spiritual, and these words from Matthew are words to all that is vainglorious. Jesus, before the Pharisees had gathered around him, had been teaching his disciples of humility, giving these instructions: "They should never boast: 'I have driven out devils in your name!' or 'I have done this and that!' Also, they should not carry out their work publicly" (*Chron.*, p. 345). The moment we forget humility we are vulnerable to inflation, as were the Pharisees. In the seventh Arcanum of *Meditations on the Tarot*, the Chariot, the unknown author speaks of the danger of the fourth temptation—the temptation to come in one's own name—which is the subtlest temptation of all. He calls this "inflation"—a condition fraught with risk:

> Here, then, are the principal dangers of inflation: exaggerated importance attached to oneself, superiority complex tending toward obsession and, lastly, megalomania. The first degree signifies a practical task for work upon oneself; the second degree is a serious trial; whilst the third is a catastrophe.[47]

It is also interesting to note that in this Arcanum reversed inflation is described as negation of the self.

Today we can focus on humility, which from one perspective can be summarized as being *all* that we are and *nothing* that we are not.

**April 20:** Sun 6° Aries: Jesus speaks of his Second Coming (Mar/26/33):

> See that no one leads you onto a wrong path. Many will come and make use of my name. They will say: "I am the Christ." And they will lead many astray. You will become aware of the tumult of war and the cries of battle; see that you do not fail in inner courage. It is necessary that all this should happen, but that is not yet the fulfillment of the aim.
>
> One part of humanity will rise against another, one kingdom against the other. Everywhere there will be famines and earthquakes; and yet these are just the birth pangs of the new world.
>
> Many will appear who will make themselves mouthpieces for deceiving spirits; they will lead many astray. And as the chaos grows ever worse, the capacity for love will grow cold in many. (Matt. 24:4–12)

We are living in a "New Age." This is an expression first used by Rudolf Steiner to describe the time of the Second Coming of Christ. We cannot attribute a time or place for the beginning of this Age, any more than we can appoint a certain leader or sect as its inaugurator. It has been called an inevitable evolutionary leap that cannot be silenced. It seems to be something that cannot stop happening. This shift is a great threat to those who wield power *over* others. The prophet Daniel saw that there would be teachers who would understand the times and preach the Kingdom as a witness unto all nations. "Those who are wise shall shine like the brightness of the sky; and those who lead many to righteousness, like the stars forever and ever" (Daniel 12:3).

We are to know we are in changing times and we are to seek the righteous, whose light ennobles others in order to unify people toward a single ideal: Love. With Sun in Aries, idealism engenders devotion. While the world lowers the bar in order to avoid guilt and maintain comfort, the righteous are to keep the bar high and ever strive to achieve the ideals sounding from the one heart—the heart of eternal love and devotion that beats in harmony with the mission of Earth and humanity.

**ASPECT:** Mercury conjunct Uranus 14° Pisces: The Visitation. Mercury and Uranus were conjunct close to this degree when the Nathan Mary visited her cousin Elizabeth. Both were pregnant: Mary with Jesus and Elizabeth with John. As Mercury is the messenger of the gods and Uranus is the bringer of the light, we can pray that today we hear the messenger bringing the true light and not find, instead, a thief (lower Mercury) approaching in the night:

> The coming tribulations will only come upon us as a "thief in the night" if we have something that can be stolen—if we are in possession of something. In other words, those who are attached to the material world, and love their possessions, have things that may be stolen. This includes whatever the ego may be attached to, including, potentially, everything that we identify ourselves with: positions of power, positions of weakness, the appearance of power or wealth, a victim mentality, relationships of influence, etc.— for all these take the self away from Christ. These are the things that may be taken away by the "thief in the night." Those who are empty vessels, identifying only with Christ, shall be given what they need when they need it; the grace of the Lord shall fill them.[48]

---

47 *Meditation on the Tarot*, p. 153.

48 Estelle Isaacson, *The Changing Times*.

Mercury conjunct Uranus can bring in new imaginations that help free us from the temporal illusions of *maya*, and inversely this aspect can work to further enchain us to the will of tyrants who build false towers to false gods. False towers split peoples into different languages as seen through the story of the Tower of Babel in the Bible. There are languages that speak the poison of money and information-as-power that are reaching new levels of effectiveness through advanced technologies, and there are other languages that are building different kinds of towers that can't be seen with the physical eyes. These towers represent the pinnacle of consciousness upon which the awakened stand in order to find the freedom of truth. We can free ourselves from our attachments to personal power, property, and reputations by standing on this pinnacle. As today remembers the teaching of the Second Coming as well as the Visitation, we can work to serve something noble—and we can tend the inner quickening in our heart that senses *the visitation of the Second Coming*. May we become free and let go! Our "little selves" have never been in charge anyway!

**April 22: ASPECT:** Venus 14° Aries opposite Saturn 14° Libra: Mystery of Golgotha. Today Venus mirrors the Sun at the Crucifixion and Saturn mirrors the Moon at the Crucifixion. *This aspect remembers the bread of eternal life that is Christ's body, and the wine of divine love that is Christ's blood. As Christ entered the depths of the Earth at the death of Jesus on the cross, the entire Earth became the Holy Grail, receiving into itself the divine substance of Heaven.* This is the *Life* we are striving toward, that we too may become the vessels that are able to receive Christ in us.

When Saturn was transiting this position in 1962, thirty-six atmospheric nuclear devices were detonated in the Pacific Proving Ground from April to November of 1962. This was called *Operation Dominic I* and was the largest and most elaborate US testing operation ever conducted. This is the opposite of the life brought to Earth by Christ. Nuclear weapons are the *anti-life* inspired by grave adversaries, and no good will ever come from these devices.

Today we can celebrate the quest for the Holy Grail and be awake to the Grail knights working in the world for peace and protection in times of insane opposition to the divine mission of the Grail. Look into the eyes of the children, for many seem to be bearing a knightly mission. If this be true, what do they need from us? Weapons of destruction, or the bread of life?

**April 24:** Sun 10° Aries: The Visitation (March 30, 2 B.C.). The Nathan Mary, pregnant with Jesus, visited her cousin Elizabeth, who was pregnant with John the Baptist. During that meeting all four of them were filled with holy awe as the Old Adam, John the Baptist in Elizabeth's womb, was quickened by the presence of the New Adam, the Jesus child in Mary's womb. Rudolf Steiner describes how an "I" like that of John's was directly guided by the great mother lodge of humanity, the center of spiritual life on Earth. The John-I and the soul of the Luke Jesus both originated in this mystery center, although the qualities Jesus received were not yet pervaded by the egoistic "I"—that is, the being guided toward incarnation as the New Adam was a young soul.

> The reality of this situation, strange as it may seem, was that the great mother lodge sent out a soul unaccompanied by an actual developed "I," for the same "I" that was reserved for the Jesus of the Luke Gospel was bestowed on the body of John the Baptist, and these two elements—the soul being that lived in the Luke Jesus and the "I" that lived in the Baptist—were intimately related from the very beginning.[49]

The great mystery of the Visitation is the mystery of how the old Adam—who fell from Paradise—is visited by the New Adam, the being holding the forces of purity and love held back at the time of the Fall. The celestial part of John approached him from without, as the child in Mary's womb. Through the immaculate Jesus being, John was enabled to take hold of his incarnation in spite of the conditions on Earth at that time. Through the Jesus child he was quickened to take up his destiny as the forerunner of Christ. This Visitation points us to the fact

---

49 Steiner, *According to Luke*, p. 112.

of heredity becoming subservient to destiny forces in-streaming from Christ. What John experienced at the Visitation is now possible for each human being. Our higher Christ-imbued self shall quicken our lower "I" just as the Jesus child quickened the John child. The Sun today remembers the reunion between the lower and higher self.

This is a good day to serve the quickening in others. May we practice the art of drawing forth the higher in others through questions we can ask today.

Sun enters the second decan of Aries, ruled by the Sun. This decan is associated with Cassiopeia, the Enthroned Woman—a figure of matchless beauty called "the daughter of splendor" or the "glorified woman clothed with the Sun."

**April 25:** Full Moon 10° Libra opposite Sun 10° Aries: Partial Lunar Eclipse visible throughout most of Africa, Europe, Asia, and Australia: The Crowning with Thorns (Apr/3/33). The Moon was at 10° Libra when the crown of thorns was placed upon the head of Christ. This is the third stage of the Passion of Christ, connected to the larynx chakra: the Word. As the Foot Washing comes from above to below and the scourging wrests for the mid-space between left and right, the Crowning with Thorns is the test to hold the center between front and back. Our courage stands in our frontal plane and our devotion in our dorsal (back) plane. Between the two we realize devotional courage. This is what is needed to overcome the two fundamental effects of the Fall: fear and shame. *Since leaving Paradise it is fear that turns us from the light of spirit, and this inability to stand before the light fills us with shame. Shame causes us to turn away from Paradise and fear keeps us from approaching. These same forces are converted to wings when fear turns to reverence and shame to conscience.*

With awakened conscience and reverence we are allowed to meet the Guardian of the Threshold. The Guardian gives us wings that carry us over the abyss that stands at the boundary between our world of the senses and the spiritual world. Facing the Guardian means we are given knowledge of the mysteries—and this we are to safeguard. We are crowned with truth and are to be representatives of truth in the world. Taking this stance between front and back tends to awaken fear and shame in others who then anxiously seek to dethrone the one wearing the crown:

> Once people have taken up the task of "guarding," or representing, spiritual truth, they are exposed to such scrutiny as this. And those who wear the "crown of thorns" must overcome shame and fear under the gaze of such eyes, just as they had to overcome shame and fear at the voice of the spiritual conscience representing the Guardian of the Threshold. They must not allow themselves to be drawn into polemical self-defense, nor must they shrink before the "keen and brazen gaze" of those who wish to expose them and cut to shreds all that they hold most sacred. They must not allow themselves to take a single aggressive step forward nor yield a step backward. The thorny crown of their task requires them to stand firm in the truth. This is the experience of new dignity—that of truth represented by human beings. And this is true human dignity, the dignity of the Son of Man.[50]

With this Full Moon and partial lunar eclipse, we can meditate on the truth we have been called to represent and examine our balance between fear and shame. The crown of truth pierces us due to the knowledge of our unworthiness, and yet we are crowned when the time is ripe. May we find our willingness to serve and not shrink from our destined task.

**April 26:** Sun 12° Aries: The Last Anointing (Apr/1/33). Mary Magdalene's last anointing of Christ set the betrayal by Judas in motion. "Truly, I say to you, wherever this gospel is proclaimed in the whole world, what she has done will also be told in memory of her" (Matt 26:13). Magdalene's devotional understanding stands in opposition to Judas's inability to see what was right before him—Christ. It takes courage to represent the new in the face of those muttering against its possibility, as Judas muttered against Magdalene. Now Christ is present in the etheric realms surrounding the Earth; he is with us. Will we know him? Are we Judas—or

---

50 Tomberg, *Christ and Sophia*, p. 279.

Magdalene? The Crown of Thorns still shines from yesterday's Full Moon.

**April 27/28:** Sun 13° Aries: The Last Supper through the Nailing on the Cross: (Apr/2-3/33). The Sun today remembers the most wretched moments in the life of Christ up to his final victory on the hill of Golgotha. All that Christ then experienced *from* humanity, allows him to *give to* humanity now. The deeds done to him during the Passion created the opening in the laws of karma that allows him—now, in the time of the Second Coming—to spiritually touch us. Christ gives all his love to humanity, as humanity once gave all of its hatred to him. Each step of the way must be contemplated as the greatest mystery of Earth evolution. The Passion of Christ is the path of the initiate. We may pray for the strength to willingly carry the cross of our own burdens, for this lightens the Cross of Christ. In the words of Judith von Halle:

> There can be no fantasy or even wish on the part of the spiritual pupil of entering upon a path of cognition that would be broad and well-trodden, easy and without effort. The path of cognition that one takes is one's own. Hence no one has entered upon it before. At the beginning of the journey, at the time of one's decision to commit, it actually does not exist at all. It is one's task to direct oneself through the morass of one's soul urgings, and to direct one's I through the "soul emptiness of space," through the "destruction of time."[51]

The sacred freedom that Christ brought to all humanity is a force of guidance directing each of us to find our *own way*, upon *our own untrodden path*, to realize *our own initiation*. This demands sobering sanctification for the preservation of free impulses as intended by Rudolf Steiner, in devotion to his founding of the School for Spiritual Science. He could only have founded this school as an affirmation for the necessity of independent research. This is the sacred ground upon which Anthroposophy has been founded.

**April 28:** Sun 14° Aries: Transfiguration and Death on the Cross: (Apr/3/33). This death marks the birth of Christ into the Earth. This birth began with his descent into Hell—a time when the spiritual world held its breath, wondering if the Son of God would ever emerge again from the darkness of the Earth.

> Jesus Christ's "descent into Hell" was the act that overcame Ahriman—not through superiority of power (that was not the issue), but by exposing the extent of Ahriman's true power over an alert and uncompromising consciousness. Since Jesus Christ walked that path, it has been proven that Ahriman's work in the world is hopeless, so long as people are willing to recognize and resist it. This attitude will continue into the future among those who do not succumb to Ahriman, and in this way Ahriman will be "shackled." He will no longer have a point of attack and thus will become ineffective and passive. There will no longer be any motive for kindling activity, even in his consciousness, and (during the future Venus existence) Ahriman will sink into a kind of sleep. Of course, this will not be the end of his destiny, but, for the purpose of this particular meditation, when Ahriman "falls asleep," it may be viewed as the final stage of human conflict with him.[52]

The fact that Ahriman has no power if human beings recognize and resist him, sounds the spiritual decree that most assuredly sets straight the path before us. Where is he? Through whom is he working? What can I *do* to reveal and denounce him? These are the questions that are to be answered now. Just as Christ descended to experience the *kamaloka* of each and every human being, so too are we asked to find the courage to experience just one piece of this—our own piece! The grave danger for humanity in our time is that we "fall asleep" and thereby become an unwitting pawn in Ahriman's game. Where do we bind ourselves to lies, deceptions and cowardice? There comes a time during our individual path of descent when it is as if our hands and feet are nailed down, as the narrow way of redemption opens before us.

**ASPECT:** Sun 13° Aries opposite Saturn 13° Libra: Early this morning, the ringed planet will be at its

---

51 Von Halle, *The Descent into the Depths of the Earth*, p. 20.

52 Tomberg, *Christ and Sophia*, pp. 299–300.

closest approach to Earth and its face will be fully illuminated by the Sun on the western horizon. Today through May 4th three planets (Mercury, Mars and Venus) and the Sun will be in Aries. On ancient Saturn we consisted entirely of the warmth of will. Now, in memory of the descent into Hell and this close approach of the planet Saturn, we are strengthened to warm our will through the power of love. In this way we open our intuitive faculties for recognition and denouncement of Ahriman's presence right here in our midst.

**April 29:** Sun 15° Aries: Descent into Hell. See entry for March 30.

**April 30:** Sun 15½° Aries: Resurrection (Apr/5/33). The depths of this mystery hold the promise that each human being may become a Christ Bearer. The words of the Risen Christ, to Mary Magdalene, sound throughout time: "Touch me not, for I am not yet ascended unto the Father; but go unto my brethren, and say to them, I ascend unto my father and your Father, and my God and your God" (John 20:17). These words contain the powerful fact that Christ, following his descent to the Mother on Holy Saturday, would then, following the Resurrection, ascend to his Father, thereby restoring the unity between the Mother in the depths and the Father in the heights. The coming Ascension (forty days from now) was a deed that would also unite fallen humanity with its divine archetype—an archetype sacrificed at the time of the Fall. From the moment of the Resurrection onward he has been within us. This eternal oneness with Christ interconnects the whole of humanity into brother- and sisterhood. The actual awakening of the disciples to the reality of this oneness came only later at the Holy Whitsun Festival. During the forty days between the Resurrection and the Ascension, the disciples were in a kind of sleep. Images from their daily life with Christ during his three and one-half years on Earth rose into their consciousness (etheric images). These images helped them understand the cosmic teachings Christ was giving during these forty days after the Resurrection. It is just these cosmic teachings that were culled from mainstream Christianity, and these cosmic teachings are resurrecting in this time of the Second Coming through great teachers now working with us.

The forty days between the Resurrection and the Ascension are potent days to work with the budding new life that is moving through us. This is the continuous power of growth that happens in each cycle of the year. We received a spark from our higher self during the Holy Nights of 2012/2013, which is now growing toward its full flowering as it resurrects into new life during the season of Easter. Each of us experiences a micro-resurrection at this time of year. We can liken this to the spark of our higher self that we received at Christmas, now breaking into the light of day. During the forty days between the Resurrection and the Ascension we can experience this new aspect of ourselves in the subtle realms of imagination and inspiration. Just as the disciples of Christ received cosmic teachings during the forty days, so also do we, as disciples of Christ, receive cosmic teachings from this spark of new life we have nurtured since the time of winter now past. Through this higher aspect in us, Christ is teaching—for Christ is the higher self of all of humanity. If we hold silence after a conversation, after an event, or at day's end as we go into sleep, we may experience after-echoes sounding forth from our daily events. These are etheric responses, from Angelic realms, inspiring and informing us of new and hidden dimensions working and weaving through our lives.

**ASPECT:** Mars 13° Aries opposite Saturn 13° Libra: At the Resurrection heliocentric Mars was moving toward conjunction with Saturn. Today it stands in opposition. Our ideals for our future (Aries) are now facing our destiny resolves (Saturn). Do we feel a concordance between the two?

# MAY

As we begin May, the Sun is in the Ram (Aries), entering the Bull (Taurus) on the 15th. We can catch the Eta Aquarids meteor shower, peaking on the 5th and 6th with about 10 shooting stars each hour radiating from the constellation of Aquarius in the east well after midnight. The New Moon is on the 9th and is an annular solar eclipse. Mars and Mercury will be quite close but not visible; what can you sense within the light of this "day gazing" event? The Moon will join Jupiter in Taurus as the evening light wanes on the 12th and Venus emerges as the evening star to their right, near to the western horizon. Venus will be conjunct Jupiter in Taurus on the 28th, reminding us of the beautiful dance we observed between these two and the Moon in February and March 2012. The Full Moon is on the 25th as a penumbral lunar eclipse, visible within the United States and Western Europe (among other places.) The 27th brings Jupiter, Mercury, and Venus extremely close together in the horns of the Bull (Taurus): Mercury—Venus – Jupiter in the west at sunset. Consider observing this stunning group with wonder and senses other than your eyes. Try this also on the 31st, when the Sun will be in front of the star Aldebaran (the "Eye of the Bull" and a Royal Star of Persia). What do you experience as emanating from this star?

**May 2:** Sun 17° Aries: Appearance in Emmaus (Apr/6/33). These days, following the Resurrection, specifically mark the communion of the disciples and holy women with the resurrection body of Christ. There are several different kinds of communion with Christ, of which four are primary:

Communion with Christ's physical body—Bread (resurrection body/forty days)
Communion with Christ's "I"—Wine (descent into Hell)
Communion with Christ's etheric body—the Eternal Gospel (Life Tableau of Christ)
Communion with Christ's astral body—the Eternal Apocalypse (Book of Revelation is a portion of this body)[53]

The day after the Resurrection, Luke and Cleophas were traveling to Emmaus when a third person joined them. That evening the three went to a guesthouse, where they were served food. The third person took the bread, blessed it and broke it into small pieces. Through this act the disciples recognized their traveling companion, who was Christ.

The bread communion is communion with the resurrection body of Christ, given to Luke and Cleophas and accompanied by Christ's words: "I am the bread of life." This bread of life is the substance of the Word of God living in all pure nourishment, as the antidote to destructive manipulation of the Mother's archetypes in seeds. Christ throughout the forty days was ministering the bread of life to his disciples. Through his wounds and from his mouth flowed pure light, giving them the power to forgive sins, to baptize, to heal, and to lay on hands. As communion with the resurrection body was the forty days between the Resurrection and the Ascension, so is communion with the Self of Christ, the wine communion, connected to Christ's descent into Hell. It was the "I," the Self of Christ, that descended after Jesus died on the cross. Christ descended toward the heart of the Mother at the Earth's center. And it was from communion with the Self of Christ that the Grail Knights were schooled to develop the courage to descend into Hell, meet evil, confront and overcome this evil. Parsifal took up this battle with evil for the sake of human beings and the Mother Earth. He is the human being of the future: the future Jupiter human being.

The Self of Christ follows the 12-year rhythm of Jupiter. In 1945 Christ began his penetration of the sub-earthly layers of the Earth on behalf of the Mother in the heart of the Earthly realm. Christ is currently working in the seventh interior sphere, the Earth Mirror (July 23, 2004–June 3, 2016), connected with the *manas* cognition of the spirit self (see Robert Powell's book, *The Christ Mystery*). The Beatitude that is the antidote to the evil of this sphere is *Blessed are the peacemakers for they shall be called the Children of God*. Valentin Tomberg speaks of the peacemakers:

> If the consciousness soul is filled with consciousness of the guilt and need of earthly life, it lifts it like a cup, interceding for the need of Earth. It can then encounter a current descending from above, one that absorbs the darkness of guilt and need into its own clear light, carried upward

---

53 *CHA, The Forty Days After the Mystery of Golgotha.*

SIDEREAL GEOCENTRIC LONGITUDES : MAY 2013 Gregorian at 0 hours UT

| DAY | ☉ | ☽ | ☊ | ☿ | ♀ | ♂ | ♃ | ♄ | ♅ | ♆ | ♇ |
|---|---|---|---|---|---|---|---|---|---|---|---|
| 1 WE | 15 ♈ 52 | 26 ♐ 36 | 21 ♎ 57 | 3 ♈ 48 | 24 ♈ 27 | 12 ♈ 55 | 22 ♉ 34 | 13 ♎ 5R | 15 ♓ 23 | 10 ♒ 5 | 16 ♐ 34R |
| 2 TH | 16 50 | 10 ♑ 46 | 21 57 | 5 46 | 25 41 | 13 39 | 22 46 | 13 1 | 15 26 | 10 6 | 16 34 |
| 3 FR | 17 48 | 24 38 | 21 57R | 7 45 | 26 55 | 14 23 | 22 59 | 12 56 | 15 29 | 10 7 | 16 33 |
| 4 SA | 18 46 | 8 ♒ 13 | 21 57 | 9 45 | 28 9 | 15 8 | 23 11 | 12 52 | 15 32 | 10 8 | 16 33 |
| 5 SU | 19 44 | 21 30 | 21 57 | 11 47 | 29 23 | 15 52 | 23 24 | 12 47 | 15 35 | 10 9 | 16 32 |
| 6 MO | 20 42 | 4 ♓ 31 | 21 56 | 13 51 | 0 ♉ 37 | 16 36 | 23 36 | 12 43 | 15 38 | 10 10 | 16 31 |
| 7 TU | 21 41 | 17 17 | 21 56 | 15 56 | 1 51 | 17 21 | 23 49 | 12 38 | 15 41 | 10 11 | 16 31 |
| 8 WE | 22 39 | 29 50 | 21 56D | 18 3 | 3 4 | 18 5 | 24 2 | 12 34 | 15 43 | 10 12 | 16 30 |
| 9 TH | 23 37 | 12 ♈ 11 | 21 56 | 20 11 | 4 18 | 18 49 | 24 15 | 12 29 | 15 46 | 10 13 | 16 29 |
| 10 FR | 24 35 | 24 22 | 21 56 | 22 19 | 5 32 | 19 33 | 24 28 | 12 25 | 15 49 | 10 14 | 16 29 |
| 11 SA | 25 33 | 6 ♉ 24 | 21 56R | 24 29 | 6 46 | 20 17 | 24 41 | 12 20 | 15 52 | 10 15 | 16 28 |
| 12 SU | 26 31 | 18 20 | 21 56 | 26 39 | 8 0 | 21 1 | 24 53 | 12 16 | 15 55 | 10 16 | 16 27 |
| 13 MO | 27 29 | 0 ♊ 11 | 21 56 | 28 50 | 9 13 | 21 45 | 25 6 | 12 12 | 15 58 | 10 17 | 16 26 |
| 14 TU | 28 27 | 12 0 | 21 55 | 1 ♉ 1 | 10 27 | 22 29 | 25 20 | 12 7 | 16 0 | 10 18 | 16 25 |
| 15 WE | 29 24 | 23 51 | 21 54 | 3 12 | 11 41 | 23 12 | 25 33 | 12 3 | 16 3 | 10 18 | 16 24 |
| 16 TH | 0 ♉ 22 | 5 ♋ 46 | 21 53 | 5 22 | 12 54 | 23 56 | 25 46 | 11 59 | 16 6 | 10 19 | 16 23 |
| 17 FR | 1 20 | 17 50 | 21 52 | 7 32 | 14 8 | 24 40 | 25 59 | 11 55 | 16 8 | 10 20 | 16 22 |
| 18 SA | 2 18 | 0 ♌ 7 | 21 52 | 9 41 | 15 22 | 25 23 | 26 12 | 11 51 | 16 11 | 10 20 | 16 21 |
| 19 SU | 3 16 | 12 41 | 21 52D | 11 49 | 16 35 | 26 7 | 26 25 | 11 46 | 16 14 | 10 21 | 16 20 |
| 20 MO | 4 14 | 25 37 | 21 52 | 13 55 | 17 49 | 26 50 | 26 39 | 11 42 | 16 16 | 10 22 | 16 19 |
| 21 TU | 5 11 | 8 ♍ 57 | 21 53 | 16 0 | 19 3 | 27 34 | 26 52 | 11 38 | 16 19 | 10 22 | 16 18 |
| 22 WE | 6 9 | 22 43 | 21 54 | 18 2 | 20 16 | 28 17 | 27 5 | 11 35 | 16 21 | 10 23 | 16 17 |
| 23 TH | 7 7 | 6 ♎ 56 | 21 55 | 20 3 | 21 30 | 29 1 | 27 19 | 11 31 | 16 24 | 10 23 | 16 16 |
| 24 FR | 8 4 | 21 32 | 21 55R | 22 1 | 22 43 | 29 44 | 27 32 | 11 27 | 16 26 | 10 24 | 16 15 |
| 25 SA | 9 2 | 6 ♏ 27 | 21 55 | 23 57 | 23 57 | 0 ♉ 27 | 27 45 | 11 23 | 16 28 | 10 24 | 16 14 |
| 26 SU | 10 0 | 21 33 | 21 54 | 25 50 | 25 10 | 1 10 | 27 59 | 11 19 | 16 31 | 10 25 | 16 13 |
| 27 MO | 10 57 | 6 ♐ 40 | 21 52 | 27 41 | 26 24 | 1 53 | 28 12 | 11 16 | 16 33 | 10 25 | 16 12 |
| 28 TU | 11 55 | 21 40 | 21 49 | 29 29 | 27 37 | 2 36 | 28 26 | 11 12 | 16 35 | 10 25 | 16 11 |
| 29 WE | 12 52 | 6 ♑ 25 | 21 47 | 1 ♊ 14 | 28 51 | 3 19 | 28 39 | 11 8 | 16 38 | 10 26 | 16 9 |
| 30 TH | 13 50 | 20 49 | 21 45 | 2 56 | 0 ♊ 4 | 4 2 | 28 53 | 11 5 | 16 40 | 10 26 | 16 8 |
| 31 FR | 14 47 | 4 ♒ 48 | 21 44 | 4 36 | 1 18 | 4 45 | 29 7 | 11 2 | 16 42 | 10 26 | 16 7 |

INGRESSES :

| | | |
|---|---|---|
| 1 ☽ → ♑ 5:43 | 20 ☽ → ♍ 7:58 | |
| 3 ☽ → ♒ 9:25 | 22 ☽ → ♎ 12:23 | |
| 5 ♀ → ♉ 12: 5 | 24 ♂ → ♉ 8:58 | |
| ☽ → ♓ 15:37 | ☽ → ♏ 13:40 | |
| 8 ☽ → ♈ 0:19 | 26 ☽ → ♐ 13:24 | |
| 10 ☽ → ♉ 11:11 | 28 ☿ → ♊ 7: 3 | |
| 12 ☽ → ♊ 23:37 | ☽ → ♑ 13:29 | |
| 13 ☿ → ♉ 12:48 | 29 ♀ → ♊ 22:39 | |
| 15 ☽ → ♋ 12:25 | 30 ☽ → ♒ 15:41 | |
| ☉ → ♉ 14:43 | | |
| 17 ☽ → ♌ 23:46 | | |

ASPECTS & ECLIPSES :

| | | | | |
|---|---|---|---|---|
| 1 ♂ ☍ ♄ 5:11 | ☽ ☌ ☋ 19:11 | 17 ☽ [S] ☊ 7:55 | ☉ ☍ ☽ 4:24 | ☉ □ ☽ 18:57 |
| 2 ☉ □ ☽ 11:13 | ☿ ☍ ☊ 19:44 | 18 ☉ □ ☽ 4:33 | 26 ☽ ☌ P 1:55 | |
| ☽ [N] ☊ 19:19 | 10 ☉ ● A 0:25 | ☿ □ ♆ 7:22 | ☽ ☍ ♀ 6:15 | |
| 4 ☽ ☌ ♆ 3:26 | ☉ ☌ ☽ 0:27 | ☽ ☍ ♆ 19:34 | ☽ ☍ ☿ 7:45 | |
| 5 ☿ ☍ ♄ 11:11 | 11 ☽ ☌ ♀ 0:48 | 20 ♅ □ ♇ 22:17 | ☽ ☍ ♃ 10:21 | |
| 6 ☽ ☌ ♅ 20:56 | ☉ [S]☌ ☿ 21: 9 | 21 ☽ ☍ ♅ 12:57 | ☉ □ ♆ 10:33 | |
| 7 ☉ ☍ ☊ 6:27 | 12 ☽ ☌ ♃ 13:31 | 23 ☽ ☌ ♄ 7:33 | 27 ☿ ☌ ♃ 7:55 | |
| 8 ☿ ☌ ♂ 0:32 | 13 ♂ ☍ ☊ 5:50 | 24 ☽ ☌ ☊ 0:37 | ☽ ☌ ♇ 15:10 | |
| 9 ☽ ☍ ♄ 0:35 | ☽ ☌ A 13:55 | ☽ ☍ ♂ 13:54 | 28 ♀ ☌ ♃ 19:28 | |
| ☽ ☌ ♂ 13:51 | ♀ □ ♆ 20:52 | ☿ ☌ ♀ 23:52 | 30 ☽ [N] ☊ 1:35 | |
| ☽ ☌ ☿ 19: 4 | 14 ☽ ☍ ♇ 8:57 | 25 ☽ ☍● PN 4:10 | 31 ☽ ☌ ♆ 9:53 | |

SIDEREAL HELIOCENTRIC LONGITUDES : MAY 2013 Gregorian at 0 hours UT

| DAY | Sid. Time | ☿ | ♀ | ⊕ | ♂ | ♃ | ♄ | ♅ | ♆ | ♇ | Vernal Point |
|---|---|---|---|---|---|---|---|---|---|---|---|
| 1 WE | 14:36:20 | 28 ♒ 16 | 6 ♉ 30 | 15 ♎ 52 | 10 ♈ 51 | 29 ♉ 20 | 13 ♎ 22 | 13 ♓ 55 | 8 ♒ 19 | 15 ♐ 1 | 5 ♓ 4'27" |
| 2 TH | 14:40:17 | 2 ♓ 53 | 8 6 | 16 50 | 11 26 | 29 26 | 13 24 | 13 56 | 8 20 | 15 1 | 5 ♓ 4'26" |
| 3 FR | 14:44:13 | 7 39 | 9 43 | 17 48 | 12 1 | 29 31 | 13 26 | 13 56 | 8 20 | 15 1 | 5 ♓ 4'26" |
| 4 SA | 14:48:10 | 12 33 | 11 19 | 18 46 | 12 36 | 29 36 | 13 27 | 13 57 | 8 20 | 15 2 | 5 ♓ 4'26" |
| 5 SU | 14:52: 7 | 17 37 | 12 56 | 19 44 | 13 10 | 29 41 | 13 29 | 13 58 | 8 21 | 15 2 | 5 ♓ 4'26" |
| 6 MO | 14:56: 3 | 22 50 | 14 32 | 20 43 | 13 45 | 29 46 | 13 31 | 13 58 | 8 21 | 15 2 | 5 ♓ 4'26" |
| 7 TU | 15: 0: 0 | 28 11 | 16 9 | 21 41 | 14 20 | 29 51 | 13 33 | 13 59 | 8 21 | 15 3 | 5 ♓ 4'26" |
| 8 WE | 15: 3:56 | 3 ♈ 42 | 17 45 | 22 39 | 14 54 | 29 57 | 13 35 | 14 0 | 8 22 | 15 3 | 5 ♓ 4'26" |
| 9 TH | 15: 7:53 | 9 22 | 19 22 | 23 37 | 15 29 | 0 ♊ 2 | 13 37 | 14 0 | 8 22 | 15 3 | 5 ♓ 4'25" |
| 10 FR | 15:11:49 | 15 10 | 20 59 | 24 35 | 16 3 | 0 7 | 13 39 | 14 1 | 8 23 | 15 4 | 5 ♓ 4'25" |
| 11 SA | 15:15:46 | 21 5 | 22 35 | 25 33 | 16 38 | 0 12 | 13 41 | 14 2 | 8 23 | 15 4 | 5 ♓ 4'25" |
| 12 SU | 15:19:42 | 27 7 | 24 12 | 26 31 | 17 12 | 0 17 | 13 43 | 14 2 | 8 23 | 15 4 | 5 ♓ 4'25" |
| 13 MO | 15:23:39 | 3 ♉ 16 | 25 49 | 27 29 | 17 46 | 0 22 | 13 44 | 14 3 | 8 24 | 15 5 | 5 ♓ 4'25" |
| 14 TU | 15:27:36 | 9 29 | 27 26 | 28 27 | 18 21 | 0 28 | 13 46 | 14 3 | 8 24 | 15 5 | 5 ♓ 4'25" |
| 15 WE | 15:31:32 | 15 45 | 29 3 | 29 25 | 18 55 | 0 33 | 13 48 | 14 4 | 8 24 | 15 5 | 5 ♓ 4'25" |
| 16 TH | 15:35:29 | 22 4 | 0 ♊ 39 | 0 ♏ 23 | 19 29 | 0 38 | 13 50 | 14 5 | 8 25 | 15 6 | 5 ♓ 4'25" |
| 17 FR | 15:39:25 | 28 23 | 2 16 | 1 20 | 20 3 | 0 43 | 13 52 | 14 5 | 8 25 | 15 6 | 5 ♓ 4'24" |
| 18 SA | 15:43:22 | 4 ♊ 42 | 3 53 | 2 18 | 20 37 | 0 48 | 13 54 | 14 6 | 8 25 | 15 6 | 5 ♓ 4'24" |
| 19 SU | 15:47:18 | 10 58 | 5 30 | 3 16 | 21 11 | 0 53 | 13 56 | 14 7 | 8 26 | 15 7 | 5 ♓ 4'24" |
| 20 MO | 15:51:15 | 17 10 | 7 7 | 4 14 | 21 45 | 0 59 | 13 58 | 14 7 | 8 26 | 15 7 | 5 ♓ 4'24" |
| 21 TU | 15:55:11 | 23 17 | 8 44 | 5 11 | 22 19 | 1 4 | 14 0 | 14 8 | 8 27 | 15 7 | 5 ♓ 4'24" |
| 22 WE | 15:59: 8 | 29 18 | 10 21 | 6 9 | 22 52 | 1 9 | 14 1 | 14 9 | 8 27 | 15 8 | 5 ♓ 4'24" |
| 23 TH | 16: 3: 5 | 5 ♋ 12 | 11 58 | 7 7 | 23 26 | 1 14 | 14 3 | 14 9 | 8 27 | 15 8 | 5 ♓ 4'24" |
| 24 FR | 16: 7: 1 | 10 57 | 13 35 | 8 4 | 24 0 | 1 19 | 14 5 | 14 10 | 8 28 | 15 8 | 5 ♓ 4'23" |
| 25 SA | 16:10:58 | 16 33 | 15 12 | 9 2 | 24 33 | 1 24 | 14 7 | 14 11 | 8 28 | 15 9 | 5 ♓ 4'23" |
| 26 SU | 16:14:54 | 22 0 | 16 50 | 10 0 | 25 7 | 1 29 | 14 9 | 14 11 | 8 28 | 15 9 | 5 ♓ 4'23" |
| 27 MO | 16:18:51 | 27 18 | 18 27 | 10 57 | 25 40 | 1 35 | 14 11 | 14 12 | 8 29 | 15 9 | 5 ♓ 4'23" |
| 28 TU | 16:22:47 | 2 ♌ 26 | 20 4 | 11 55 | 26 14 | 1 40 | 14 13 | 14 12 | 8 29 | 15 10 | 5 ♓ 4'23" |
| 29 WE | 16:26:44 | 7 24 | 21 41 | 12 52 | 26 47 | 1 45 | 14 15 | 14 13 | 8 29 | 15 10 | 5 ♓ 4'23" |
| 30 TH | 16:30:40 | 12 13 | 23 18 | 13 50 | 27 21 | 1 50 | 14 17 | 14 14 | 8 30 | 15 10 | 5 ♓ 4'23" |
| 31 FR | 16:34:37 | 16 52 | 24 56 | 14 47 | 27 54 | 1 55 | 14 18 | 14 14 | 8 30 | 15 11 | 5 ♓ 4'22" |

INGRESSES :

| |
|---|
| 1 ☿ → ♓ 9: 6 |
| 7 ☿ → ♈ 7:56 |
| 8 ♃ → ♊ 15:54 |
| 12 ☿ → ♉ 11:17 |
| 15 ♀ → ♊ 14:14 |
| ⊕ → ♏ 14:39 |
| 17 ☿ → ♊ 6: 7 |
| 22 ☿ → ♋ 2:48 |
| 27 ☿ → ♌ 12:32 |

ASPECTS (HELIOCENTRIC +MOON(TYCHONIC)) :

| | | | | | |
|---|---|---|---|---|---|
| 1 ☿ □ ♃ 5:45 | ☽ □ ♇ 19:45 | 13 ☽ ☌ ♃ 0:23 | 19 ☿ □ ♅ 12: 9 | ☿ □ ♄ 13:26 | ☽ □ ♄ 13: 0 |
| 2 ☽ □ ♂ 1:12 | 8 ☽ ☌ ☿ 13:44 | ☿ □ ♆ 19:51 | ☿ ☍ ♇ 16: 1 | ♀ ☍ ♇ 23: 3 | 30 ☿ □ ⊕ 10:23 |
| ♀ □ ♆ 3:23 | 9 ☽ ☍ ♄ 2:48 | 14 ☽ □ ♅ 4:10 | 20 ☽ □ ♃ 9:48 | 25 ☽ □ ♆ 3:13 | ☽ □ ♂ 11:34 |
| ☽ □ ♄ 4:31 | ☽ ☌ ♂ 6:46 | ☽ ☍ ♇ 6:15 | ☽ □ ♀ 23:34 | ♂ ☌ ☊ 7:39 | 31 ☽ ☌ ♆ 6:29 |
| 4 ☽ ☌ ♆ 0:13 | ☿ ☍ ♄ 17:45 | 15 ♀ ☌ ♃ 23:36 | 21 ☽ ☍ ♅ 9: 7 | 26 ☿ [N] ☊ 6:59 | |
| ☽ □ ♀ 6:19 | 10 ☿ ☌ ♂ 4: 3 | 16 ☿ ☌ P 2:33 | ☽ □ ♇ 10:51 | ☿ □ ♂ 15:40 | |
| ☿ ☌ ♅ 6:42 | ♀ ☌ ☊ 13:20 | ☽ □ ♄ 16: 7 | 22 ☽ □ ☿ 19: 7 | ☽ ☍ ♃ 15:51 | |
| ☿ □ ♇ 11:50 | 11 ☽ □ ♆ 3:58 | 17 ☽ □ ♂ 4:34 | 23 ☽ ☌ ♄ 11:48 | 27 ☽ □ ♅ 12: 0 | |
| 5 ♂ ☍ ♄ 13:53 | ☿ ☌ ☊ 9:54 | ☿ ☌ ♃ 8:58 | 24 ☽ ☍ ♂ 4: 8 | ☽ ☌ ♇ 13:32 | |
| ☽ □ ♃ 15: 8 | ☿ ☍ ⊕ 21: 9 | ☿ ☌ ♀ 19:50 | ♀ □ ♅ 8:35 | ☽ ☍ ♀ 21: 5 | |
| 6 ☽ ☌ ♅ 17:44 | 12 ☽ ☌ ♀ 13:44 | 18 ☽ ☍ ♆ 15:55 | ⊕ □ ♆ 9:42 | 29 ☿ ☍ ♆ 5:22 | |

by the consciousness soul. It may happen then that the ascending darkness and the descending light unite, which leads to a "rainbow" of reconciliation between the two worlds. For example, Goethe, in his soul, carried knowledge of this process of reconciliation and peace between the two worlds. Such knowledge became not only the basis of his theory of color, but also of his fairytale, "The Green Snake and the Beautiful Lily."[54]

The fruition of Earth evolution is the ripening of the consciousness soul to receive into itself the Angelic sphere. We reach this fruition through partaking in communion with Christ, as did the disciples Luke and Cleophas. *If Christ, or an ambassador of Christ, were among us – would we know this? Or, would we persecute such a one in this Second Coming as we did in the first? This is food for thought during these days, remembering the forty days of Christ's cosmic teachings. In remembrance of Christ's appearance in Emmaus, can we open our awareness to sense unseen beings moving among us? We are not alone!*

**May 3:** Sun 18° Aries: Death of Silent Mary (Aug/8/30). "Silent Mary was gifted with clairvoyance and beheld in advance the coming persecution and trials of Jesus, which was more than she could bear. She died in the face of the burden of suffering that she beheld was in store for the Messiah. An arrow of grief pierced through her heart and she was called back to the realm of the Father."[55]

I understood that it was significant that both were named Mary. The Blessed Mother was also a Mary of Silence. These two Marys could both "converse" through Silence. It was because of the Silence of her soul that the Blessed Mother had such towering compassion—for "noisy" souls cannot truly be compassionate. And so it was also with Silent Mary. Her empathy was total. To know and to feel the thoughts and emotions of others—that was her gift.[56]

This day calls us into the eternal silence of the empathetic heart. May we find this place in service to others.

**May 4:** Sun 19° Aries: Conversation with the Pharisee Nicodemus (Apr/9/30). "The wind blows where it wills, and you hear the sound of it, but you do not know whence it comes or whither it goes; so it is with everyone who is born of the Spirit" (John 3:8). In the second Arcanum of *Meditations on the Tarot*, The High Priestess, the unknown author describes the "pure act of intelligence": Like the wind, "the pure act in itself cannot be grasped; it is only its reflection which renders it perceptible, comparable and understandable or, in other words, it is by virtue of the reflection that we become conscious of it."[57]

This seems to fit the nighttime conversations between Jesus and Nicodemus. Three times it is reported in the Bible that Nicodemus comes to Jesus in the night. Rudolf Steiner says this:

> "By night" means nothing else than that this meeting between Jesus and Nicodemus occurred in the astral world: in the spiritual world, not in the world that surrounds us in our ordinary day consciousness. This means that Christ could converse with Nicodemus outside the physical body—by night, when the physical body is not present, when the astral body is outside the physical and etheric bodies.[58]

Jesus approaches Nicodemus in the night. The original forces of the world are living in Jesus—he is bringing not only new teachings, but a kind of teaching that comes from his astral body into the consciousness of others who are prepared to receive these apocalyptic teachings. Jesus makes the preparation for receiving these cosmic teachings clear: "Truly, truly, I say to you, unless one is born of Water and the Spirit, [one] cannot enter the Kingdom of God" (John 3:5).

The "pure act of intelligence" comes like the wind—no one knows whence it comes or whither it goes. It is the spirit of Jesus' teaching in the night. Nicodemus is able to receive these teachings as reflections, and through the reflections he can

---

54 Tomberg, *Christ and Sophia*, p. 220.
55 CHA, Jesus' First Visit to Jerusalem Since the Baptism.
56 Isaacson, *Through the Eyes of Magdalene*, book 1, pp. 243–244.

57 *Meditations on the Tarot*, p. 30.
58 Steiner, *The Gospel of John*, lect. 10.

grasp the wind that blows where it will as *the cosmic teachings of Christ*. Nicodemus was born of Water and of Spirit, as was John—they entered the kingdom of God by letting go of the lower human being and reviving the higher human being. This is the second birth—to be born into spirit consciousness. This is to be "born of Water and the Spirit."

This day calls forth the memory of Nicodemus, who communed with Christ's astral body in the night. The Sun was then in the constellation of Aries, whose virtue is devotion. This constellation is dedicated to the higher ideals that we are all striving toward, knowingly or unknowingly. "This nightly conversation was in fact an initiation of Nicodemus. The task is to be able to read the language spoken by the movements of the heavenly bodies, to grasp their significance intuitively."[59] What material attachments block us from receiving the wind of spirit or believing in the language of the stars?

Sun enters third decan of Aries, ruled by Mercury and associated with Cassiopeia's outstretched legs seated on her throne, so that this decan is sometimes known as Cassiopeia's Throne or Cassiopeia's Chair.

**May 5:** Mercury 12° Aries opposite Saturn 12° Libra: The Last Supper. Mercury remembers the Last Supper and stands opposite Saturn, the planet of cosmic memory, which was at this degree heliocentrically at the birth of the Virgin Mary. At the Last Supper the disciples represented the twelve constellations and therefore the Hermetic correspondence was fulfilled—for the below was a perfect reflection of the above. The order of the disciples depicted by Leonardo da Vinci was incorrect. Among da Vinci's errors was the placement of Jesus between John and James instead of between Peter and John. (This is explained by Robert Powell in his book *CHA, A Discourse of Hermes to Tat: The Last Supper.*)

The significance of Jesus between Peter (representing Taurus) and John (representing Gemini) is a mystery opening in our time. For it was Peter who was to carry the exoteric church and John who was to open the new mysteries of the esoteric church that would guide those working with Christ in his Second Coming. The community of Eternal Israel was sealed at this last communion with the embodied Jesus Christ, and the twelve different world views represented by the disciples were a perfect reflection of the twelve constellations witnessing this event from the realm of the starry heavens. This twelve-fold community continues to work toward the realization of the New Jerusalem, in service to the Virgin Mary-Sophia.

> At the Last Supper, as they received the consecrated bread and wine, the apostles, with the exception of Judas, were filled from above with the radiant Light of the Heavenly Kingdom of the Father [wine], and irradiated from below with the spiritual warmth of the Kingdom of the Mother [bread]. These two spiritual qualities, borne by the bread and wine, met and fused in their hearts. In this way, through the Holy Communion, the Kingdom of the Heart, the New Jerusalem, arises—between the Kingdom of the Father in Heaven and the Kingdom of the Mother within the Earth. This is the new paradise, the Kingdom of the Son.[60]

The union between Peter the Taurus Bull (ruled by Venus), and John the Gemini Twin (ruled by Mercury), who sat on either side of Jesus Christ at the Last Supper, represents the crossing point between the Church of Peter (the way, the truth and the life), and the Church of John (the door, the entrance and the exit). This crossing point is in the heart, where the mysteries of the New Jerusalem seek to dwell. At this crossing point, the exoteric Mass illumines the way, the truth and the life for all pilgrims of Christ; and this Mass is consecrated by the esoteric mysteries of the Holy Grail, which comes through the open door bearing the Sophianic revelations of the future. John is bringing a new dispensation on behalf of the in-streaming mysteries of the Virgin Mary/Sophia. Let us seek this place within our hearts' depths, that we may work out of Peter's strength to become vessels for John's new mysteries.

With Mercury opposed Saturn we can open our minds (Mercury) and seek forgiveness for all trespasses we have visited upon others; for, if we cannot bear our burdens, we risk unwittingly siding

---

59 *CHA,* Jesus' First Visit to Jerusalem since the Baptism.

60 *CHA,* The Last Supper.

with Judas in betrayal of Christ. In this mood of devotion (Aries), we stand before the open door through which the Love of the Father reveals the balancing scales of Libra (Saturn)— where our karmic burdens are weighed.

**May 6:** Venus enters Taurus: "Feel growth's power" (*Twelve Moods of the Zodiac*, Rudolf Steiner). When the horns of the bull become antenna for world thoughts, then Venus can bring to the heart the feeling for the powers inherent in growth. This is not knowledge as power, but rather knowledge as powerlessness. For, to experience the power that lives in growth, one is humbled before the might of spiritual beings and processes. Feeling into this growth allows one to progress in the gentle weaving between above and below.

Venus was in Taurus during the Visitation, the Transfiguration, and the Union in the Temple between the two Jesus children.

**May 9:** New Moon and Annular Solar Eclipse 24° Aries. The path of annularity will begin in western Australia and move east across the central Pacific Ocean. Jesus spoke to a large crowd: "Whoever, He said, wanted to follow Him and be His disciple must love Him more than all his nearest relatives, yes, even more than himself, and must carry his cross after Him."[61]

Under the influence of this New Moon and annular solar eclipse, we may remember our task of carrying our cross, in order to serve the carrying of the cross of Christ. The Moon is the planetary realm where all karma is inscribed. This is the realm of *kamaloka* that we enter after death, or—in the case of initiation—during life. With the Sun fully illumining the dark side of the Moon, we are invited to look into the dark realms of our unconscious in order to see what burdens we can take up on behalf of Christ and the whole of humanity. Too often we project our unwanted baggage onto others, thereby refusing to carry our cross. In such instances we love ourselves more than Christ. Today we can remember our willingness to stand as a connecting link between the heavens and the Earth, that we may serve what Love is asking of us—no matter how foreign this may appear to those with whom we are living. May the invisible light illumine our unwitting compliance with the serpent of egoism, who urges us to exult ourselves over and above others. May we each bear our cross in humble silence, for our trials are a gift from Christ, given in the hope that through them we will find him.

**May 10:** Sun 25° Aries: The appearance of the Risen One to the seven disciples (Apr/15/33). This occurred at the northeast end of the Sea of Galilee (John 21:1-23). Here Peter is bid three times to "Feed my Sheep." He is given the task to be the spiritual leader of the Church, to ensure that the sacraments, Holy Communion above all, continue to be celebrated for all time. Peter asks what will become of John, and the Risen One answers: "If it is my will that he remain until I come, what is that to you?" Implicit here is the task of the Church of John to wait until the Second Coming of Christ in the etheric realm. The Church of Peter has the task to lead human beings *to* the threshold of the spiritual world, and the Church of John has the task of leading them *across* the threshold *into* the spiritual world. John and Peter work together, united in their service to Christ and Sophia.

The Church of John is centered in the heart, and those who choose to join this Church are summoned by the call of the Grail. Corresponding to the Mass in the exoteric church is the Grail Mystery in the esoteric church. Grail communion is communion with the Beings of the stars, which requires a crossing of the threshold—which in turn requires a meeting with the fallen nature of the soul in the depths of the underworld. This is why it is the John being that Rudolf Steiner claims will be with us at the end of the century. For it was John who accompanied Lazarus through the underworld after his death, and before he was raised by Christ.[62]

We live now in the time of the Second Coming, a time when the Church of John is opening, and this is a time when humanity is both collectively and individually crossing the threshold. Moreover, it is a time when star wisdom is being reborn as communion with the beings of the heavens. With the Sun

---

61 Emmerich, *LJC Vol. 3*, p. 315.

62 Isaacson, *Through the Eyes of Magdalene,* book 1, chaps. 27–29.

in Aries, the constellation of self-sacrifice, spiritual strength, and leadership, we may feel inspired to open to the vastness of the mysteries surrounding us in our everyday life. Alternatively we may find we are excessively caught up in the small story of our "little" biography. As our interest in others and in the vastness of other worlds that interact with us increases, new possibilities are revealed. We may ask ourselves: What about John? Where do I stand before the Hermetic mysteries of the stars?

**ASPECT:** Superior conjunction of Mercury with the Sun 25° Aries. On Sunday we remembered the Last Supper, and on Thursday the eclipse asked us to bear our own cross in love of Christ: today, we remember John and the communion with the Grail mysteries—the mystery of star wisdom. This Mercury Sun conjunction approaches the cosmic memory of the Virgin Mary's first communion. May we too find communion with nature, others, and the stars. The Earth is on her way to becoming a star, and to understand this mission we will have to become increasingly fluent in the language of the stars. In order to find the strength we need in order to carry our cross, we must will to be in communion with Christ. And in order to cross the threshold into the mysteries of the Holy Grail, we will need the pierced heart into which new revelation may find its rest. Mercury conjunct Sun is the great awakener. In superior conjunction, Mercury infuses intuitions from cosmic realms into our will (subconscious) nature. May we be alert!

**May 12:** Celebration of Ascension in the Christian Church. The teachings of the forty days come to an end. The little spark of our higher "I" now expands beyond our self-hood's limitation (see entry for April 30). Just as Christ ascended to his Father, so too does an aspect of our being ascend to be infused with spirit. This expansion of new life moving through us, into its full flowering, is utterly necessary. It prepares the new force of will we are developing so it may become the sword of Michael we will bear this autumn. This matured aspect of ourselves is exactly the power that will help us battle our inner dragons when the Earth again in-breathes her soul at summer's end. Something entirely new is striving to become one with us, but first it must make its ascent to the heights. May we let go of all limitation and joyfully dance our way into the communion with spirit that is the gift of summer, and the promise of the Ascension. (See entry for the cosmic remembrance of the Ascension on June 8.)

**May 13: ASPECT:** Venus 10° Taurus square Neptune 10° Aquarius: Uranus tightens its square to Pluto which is exact on the 20th. The seizing of Galileans (Mar/25/31). After teaching in the temple, Jesus and the disciples returned to Bethany. "That afternoon, about fifty Galileans—followers of Judas of Gamala—were seized by Roman soldiers, as Pontius Pilate had been informed that they would try to start an insurrection. However, the people rebelled, attacking the soldiers, and managed to free the captives. Several people died in the melee" (*Chron.*, p. 287).

This was an insurrection against Pilate's use of sacred treasury money to build his aqueduct, which caused many of the people to band together under the Zealot Judas of Gamala. The gathered crowds hurled abuse and insults at Pilate, and he gave a prearranged signal ordering his soldiers to attack. The soldiers laid upon them greater blows than Pilate had commanded and the innocent were punished along with the insurrectionists.

With Venus square Neptune the spectrums of two possibilities are offered: 1. That karmic groups (Venus) follow the peaceful inspirations streaming from the goddess Night (Sophia—high Neptune), or 2. That karmic groups are under the sway of anti-inspirations from the murky realms of Ahriman (lower Neptune), where magnetized feelings cause a destructive frenzy in the behavior of masses.

> When those who are economically powerful are in a position to use their power to wrest privileged rights for themselves, then among the economically weak there will grow up a corresponding opposition to these privileges; and as soon as it has grown strong enough, this opposition must lead to revolutionary disturbances. If the existence of a *special province of rights* makes it impossible for such privileged rights to arise, then disturbances of this sort cannot occur. . . One will never really touch what is

working up through the social movement to the surface of modern life, until one brings about social conditions in which, alongside the claims and interests of the economic life, those of rights can find realization and satisfaction on their own independent basis.[63]

Insurgents are rising around the world under the injustice of an economic life that benefits but the few. Steiner's Three-Fold Social Order preserves the life of rights and cultural life in order to insure that the economic sphere is a reflection of higher ideals rather than an oppressor of the masses. Masses are fraught with the temptation of falling into the control of ahrimanic spirits who are seeking to enslave groups of people through the propaganda of luciferic rights. The way out of the labyrinth of Ahriman is through cultivation of separate but compatible systems that are born of spiritual idealisms. With this square between Venus and Neptune occurring at the time when Pluto and Uranus are approaching an exact square to each other (May 20), a sober warning needs be heard regarding the battle between ahrimanic and luciferic spirits—who use human beings to carry forth their war against creation by instigating revolutions based on illusory rights, using the masses as their puppets.

Let us exercise prudence before the complexities of our times, and endeavor to resurrect an understanding of the three-fold social order rather than engage in insurrection that fails to comprehend the consequences.

**May 15:** Sun enters Taurus: Sun in Taurus: "Shine forth, O glory of being" (Steiner, *Twelve Moods of the Zodiac*): William Bento illumines this mantra:

> The shining light is here defined as a glorious being. It is not a phenomenon dissected as a scientific empirical fact. It is alive with beingness. And surrounding this being is an aura of glory. Can you now gaze at the Sun with new eyes? Can you now look into another's eyes and see a glimmer of this glorious being? When this indeed occurs in our seeing we can experience the awe, wonder, and reverence of the sacredness of the "I/Thou" consciousness out of which each human being shines forth.

[63] Steiner, *Social Threefolding*.

In Taurus, Inner Balance becomes Progress. This is the work of transforming the will, as inner balance is the consequence of the will in obedience to higher will. The first decan is ruled by Venus and is associated with Perseus, who was helped by Athena to overcome the Medusa.

**May 17:** Sun 2° Taurus: The Virgin Mary receives her first communion (Apr/23/33). Shortly after midnight the Blessed Virgin Mary received the holy sacrament from Peter (three weeks after the Last Supper). During this communion, Jesus appeared to her. Later she retired to her room to pray, and toward dawn the Lord appeared to her again and gave her power over the Church, a protective force, such that light flowed from him into her. (See *CHA, The Forty Days After the Mystery of Golgotha*) In this we see a stage in the preparation for the event of Pentecost coming in the weeks that follow. The Virgin Mary could listen to the presence of the Christ. Taurus shapes the larynx and Eustachian tubes, mirrored by the form of the stethoscope. Through the organ of the larynx and its connection to the Eustachian tubes, we can listen to the heart of God. This is the kind of listening of the Virgin Mary. *The assault on hearing from constant noise tends either to draw one into the outer world in covetousness of insatiable desire, or cause the soul to fall into indulgent apathy, obliterating the inspirations sounding from the cosmic periphery. The sacred organs of hearing are being hardened, whereby we cease believing in spiritual thoughts— for we have lost the capacity to attune to these subtle frequencies.*

The sense of hearing is a spiritual sense. The highest expression of hearing is through creating the stillness of inner balance. In this balance, point and periphery commune. This is the stillness of Mary— the stillness that could commune with the Risen One from the very center of her heart. It was into this still-point of centeredness that Mary would receive the Holy Spirit at Pentecost. *Radiant inner stillness is the antidote to our tendency to become victims of the serpent's thoughts—thoughts that are empowered through avarice and work into the apathy of human souls separated from spirit; thus it is this very stillness that "noise" seeks to destroy.*

*The preciousness of the organ of hearing can today be contemplated—as well as the centeredness of holding inner silence.*

**May 20: ASPECT:** Uranus 16° Pisces square Pluto 16° Sagittarius: Pluto at Pentecost. Revolution: A look at history. The keywords of this aspect are revolution, social activism, rebellion vs. authoritarianism, reformation, freedom against oppression, and transformation. Following are some historical events that occurred under the influence of these two planets:

> French Revolution (opposition)
> Harriet Tubman and the Underground Railroad (conjunction)
> Irish Potato Famine: The Great Hunger (conjunction)
> The Indian Wars (square)
> Roosevelt initiates the New Deal (square)
> The Dust Bowl (square)
> The Salt March of Gandhi (square)
> Hitler and the Third Reich (square)
> The Six-Day War (Arab-Israeli conflict) (conjunct)
> The Civil Rights Movement (conjunct)
> Uprisings in the Middle East (square)
> Union Busting in the US (square)
> March 2011 earthquake/tsunami/nuclear disaster (square)
> Occupy Wall Street (square)

These events offer us an understanding of the power generated by Uranus/Pluto aspects. In the life of Christ, Pluto was at this degree at Pentecost (May/24/33), and Uranus was close to today's degree at the conception of John the Baptist. These memories open us to the profundity that is possible when these two planets work together for the good: Pluto/Phanes brings the love of Pentecost, and Uranus signals John's recognition of the Light of the World. The Pentecost event of the year AD 33 will return as a World Pentecost event. *To pass through the trial that the Light of spirit will illumine, we are wise to follow the precedent set by John—who fearlessly brought the light of new thoughts (Uranus)—to free the people from the tyranny of sclerotic Pharisaic laws and oppressions that denied the presence, in their very midsts, of the Light of the World. John was a witness to both the first incarnation of Christ in the flesh, and is also a witness to the Second Coming of Christ in our time—a time when humanity is again vexed by the oppressive Pharisaic laws of the tyrannical elite.*

According to Rudolf Steiner the event of Pentecost, which took place nearly two thousand years ago, is to become a world event. He spoke of this as the coming World Pentecost. What does he mean by this? The World Pentecost is an event comparable to Pentecost two thousand years ago. However, it will be a world event, not just an event that impacts a relatively small group of people in a particular geographical location. At that time in AD 33 it was a matter of many thousands of people, initially the twelve disciples who became apostles, who then went out onto the streets of Jerusalem, to the Pool of Bethesda, and baptized three thousand people that day (and thousands more subsequently). In contrast, the World Pentecost will be an event of the outpouring of Divine Love for the whole of humanity. Will humanity be sufficiently prepared to receive this?

Expressed in a positive way, we have to raise our level of vibration in order to come into and receive the approaching wave of Divine Love. Let us remember that this is an event that is happening on a global scale. Throughout the whole world human beings have to come to terms with the shadow, the lower side of human nature, and at least begin to work upon transforming the negative into something positive.[64]

Clearly there is a force in this world that is anti-Pentecost. We are to be vigilant so as not to fall under its evil sway. The word *agnostic* refers to a state of mind that is anti-gnosis. Unbelievers are unaware that there exists this state of certainty that is the gift of gnosis. *Leadership without gnosis creates cultures that are vulnerable to revolution.*

May we create imaginations of peace that form vessels into which the revelations of John, newly coming into time through teachers voicing these

---

64 Powell, "Sophia and the Rose of the World": http://sophiafoundation.org/articles/mean.

truths, can become reality on Earth. This square between Uranus and Pluto has been active since the middle of 2011 and will continue to influence events on Earth through 2015. We are living in a time when we must choose between revolution and re-evolution (a turning *into* the challenging, yet nurturing, course of humankind's spiritual evolution). May we see the light and wisely align with the powers of Divine Love that sustain the mission of the Earth, which is to become a planet of Love!

**May 24:** Mercury conjunct Venus 22° Taurus: Venus in Taurus remembers the Transfiguration of Christ (Venus 21° Taurus), the 2009 Eclipse (Venus 23° Taurus), and the Venus Transit of 2012 (Venus 20° Taurus). Today Mercury conjoins Venus on the meridian of the mega star Rigel—the western foot of Orion. At the Transfiguration the disciples witnessed the radiant beauty of Christ's pure astral body. At the eclipse of 2009 a shadow passed over the Earth that would be the longest of the 21st century. At the close of the Venus transit last year, communities following the guidance of Sophia became sealed for missions that are most likely becoming clearer as we move into this year of 2013. The third chakra is the Mercury chakra, which is the seat of the astral body that rules the nervous system. The second chakra is the Venus chakra; it is connected with the etheric body of life energies, ruling the glandular system. Ahriman's goal is to destroy the body of life energies, rigidifying the human being and thereby stunting etheric perceptions. We would be wise to now be practicing etheric enlivenment, for the thoughts that are guiding humanity are coming from the etheric realms. This kind of thinking requires a vital etheric body. Eurythmy exercises offered by Robert Powell in his book *Cultivating Inner Radiance* create a protection from ahrimanic influences entering one's etheric body. Further, Powell indicates protection for the thinking (astral/Mercury) from being unduly affected by hindering ahrimanic powers. He quotes Steiner:

> There is a remedy that will hinder ahrimanic beings from penetrating into our consciousness, a symbol that one must enliven within oneself. This is the Staff of Mercury, the luminous staff with a black snake and a bright luminous shining snake. The snake is a symbol of the astral body. Every night the astral body sheds its skin; it throws off the used-up skin. The black snake is a symbol for this. Overnight it gets a new, shimmering skin, and this newly enlivened, beautiful, shining skin of the astral body is symbolized by the shining snake.... [This] symbol, the Staff of Mercury, who is the "messenger of the gods," [is what he] holds in his hand.... [It] bans everything that wants to push into our consciousness and disturb.[65]

With Mercury and Venus together in these very strong positions, we are thus invited to take up practices that protect us. For the shadow cast in 2009 sounded a warning regarding the rising of the collective shadow of humanity. It is a shadow that has been raised from its underworld cavern due to all the spiritual energies humanity has spent by thinking (Mercury) materialistically. Materialistic thinking engenders jealousy (lower Venus) and jealousy rages against the selfless power of purity. There is a battle for the human soul taking place. We can take seriously Christ's advice as he commissioned the twelve apostles (which is commemorated tomorrow): "I am sending you out like sheep among wolves. Therefore be as wise as serpents and as innocent as doves."

Today, on this eve of the Full Moon in Scorpio, we witness Sun, Mars, Mercury, Venus, and Jupiter converging in Taurus. This calls us to listen carefully and to make the effort to digest information we hear in order to make it our own. This is not a day to blindly accept the status quo. We must stand with the strength of the Taurean Bull, with stalwart inner balance, in order to make progress in our search for truth. Covetousness is to be recognized and cast out. Apathy is to be overcome. Thoughts are streaming into the horns of the Bull from spiritual realms. They are urging us to find balance between the astral body (Mercury) of consciousness and the energy body of life force (Venus). *When these two bodies strive against each other we are prey for the wolves. When, however, these two bodies are in harmony we are able to receive the blessings of world thoughts—through which*

---

[65] Powell, *Cultivating Inner Radiance and the Body of Immortality*, p. 123–124.

*we may receive the peace of understanding that streams from the stars.*

**May 25:** Full Moon and Penumbral Lunar Eclipse 9° Scorpio opposite Sun 9° Taurus. The eclipse will be visible throughout most of North America, South America, Western Europe, and West Africa. Commissioning of the Twelve (Dec/30/30). Each Full Moon represents the time of fruit bearing, which realizes the theme inaugurated at the preceding New Moon. These lunar cycles can be seen as vehicles through which our Angel inspires us to accomplish our life tasks. At the last New Moon (Aries) the memory of Christ asking us to take up our cross was heard (May 9). With this Full Moon, we become conscious of what exactly we are being asked to carry. This can be sobering but is nonetheless an organic unfolding for those who are vigilant. This Moon remembers the commissioning of the Twelve. All who recognize Christ as the One through whom all were created can be given a commission this day, and this commission comes from the Scorpion depths. *It is from just these depths that we meet what stands in the way of our own healing—and thereby limits our ability to heal others. These unconscious obstacles, when brought to the light of the Full Moon, become part of the cross we carry; they enlighten us to our own pain, bestowing upon us the gift of compassion toward the pain in others.*

The twelve disciples were given the authority to drive out evil spirits and to heal every disease and sickness with this instruction:

> Do not get any gold or silver or copper to take with you in your belts—no bags for the journey or extra shirt or sandals or a staff, for workers are worth their keep. Whatever town or village you enter, search for some worthy person there and stay at that person's house until you leave. As you enter the home, give it your greeting. If the home is deserving, let your peace rest on it; if it is not, let your peace return to you. If anyone will not welcome you or listen to your words, shake the dust off your feet when you leave that home or town. (Matt. 10: 9–14)

This Full Moon and penumbral lunar eclipse may find us in the home of those who do not carry their cross but instead cast their shadow upon others. If we find this to be true, we are to "let our peace return to us" and we are to "shake the dust off our feet." *Alternatively, we may fall into the trap of allowing our shadow to spar with the shadow of others. Or, even more devastating to our soul, we may carry blame toward the trespasses of others. To "shake off the dust" means we forgive and move on. To dredge up ghosts from the past also brings up demons. Any attachments to these ghosts thwarts us from traveling the path of the healer.* Let the shadow cast by this eclipse restore our peace by showing us the things that are to be placed upon our own cross. We are to carry this cross with the force of silence. At the same time, moreover, we are not to bear the alleged trespasses of others, but rather "shake the past off [our] feet" in order that the future may have a resting place in our heart—as this frees us for revelation.

Sun enters the second decan of Taurus, ruled by the Moon and associated with the constellation of Eridanus the River.

**Mars enters Taurus:** "Into world-imbuing existence" (*Twelve Moods of the Zodiac*, Rudolf Steiner). On May 6th Venus entered Taurus, now follows Mars. What we have taken in as the world-thoughts of the cosmos, Mars asks us to speak into the world. Through bringing world-thoughts to word, our being is brightened into world-imbuing existence, and we make progress upon our path of development.

Mars was in Taurus at the Union in the Temple between the two Jesus children, at the Feeding of the Five Thousand, and at the Transfiguration.

**May 26: ASPECT:** Mercury conjunct Jupiter 28° Taurus: The Blessing of the Children (May/17/32). Mercury and Jupiter were conjunct at this same degree when Jesus blessed the children: "Let the little children come to me, and do not hinder them, for the kingdom of Heaven belongs to such as these" (Matt. 19:14).

Two days ago Mercury conjoined Venus, now it conjoins Jupiter. Jupiter is the great benefactor filled with wisdom. Mercury finds its fulfillment when we are "grailing" for the mighty cosmic thoughts of this planetary giant—home of kings and queens. When we stand before the majesty of cosmic thoughts, we become like children, for our hearts are opened and we are humbled as we bear witness to the might of truth. This day begs us to question our treatment of children in western cultures. They are the innocent ones who know more in their hearts than we care to remember. *Our culture has become like the wicked queen who hated Snow White; for in the presence of Snow White's purity, the queen's own wickedness was a burden she simply could not bear. Solace would not find her until the innocent one was dead. Our culture is eerily similar to this queen, for it is increasingly poisoning innocence. May we question our accommodation of this truth.*

**May 28: ASPECT:** Venus conjunct Jupiter 28° Taurus: The Union in the Temple. Today love and wisdom unite! A great council has been taking place in the heavens with Mars, Sun, Venus, Jupiter and Mercury all gathering together in Taurus. Venus at this degree remembers the Union in the Temple between the two Jesus children (see article in the *Journal for Star Wisdom 2012*). In this union, wisdom (the great Zarathustra individuality) united with love (the pure Nathan Jesus being). This is the ideal for each and every human being—that the wisdom of our higher self unites with the love-imbued heart of mercy beating in the depths of our heart. This can be our personal experience of the Union in the Temple—for the temple is the heart that "grails" for love.

**May 31:** Sun 15° Taurus conjunct Aldebaran, the Bull's eye, known as the Watcher in the East. In a discourse of Hermes to Tat, the opening and closing invocations speak to the four directions and the royal stars of Persia who represent these primal directions: (turning to the East):

> Holy Michael, thou who guards the Evolution of the Earth, during which the Mystery of Golgotha took place, whence comes the inner spirit-birth of the true Self of man, may thy radiant Being guide the Self in freedom and love along the path of human existence which receives its meaning alone through Christ.[66]

---

66 Powell, *CHA*, "A Discourse of Hermes to Tat: The

From the opening invocation: In the holy temple of the Sun, Hermes is standing at the altar in the East, Tat at the altar in the South, Asclepius at the altar in the West, and King Ammon at the altar in the North. Today, with Sun conjunct Aldebaran, we are invited to stand in the East with Hermes, under the watchful eye of Aldebaran.

**Venus enters Gemini:** "Act upon reposing's urge" (*Twelve Moods of the Zodiac*, Rudolf Steiner). This constellation opens to the mysteries of the cosmic heart—the Central Sun—the origin of the Holy Spirit. We are to act in accordance with this urge, which is ignited from above, while here below we are reposed in harmonious stillness of being.

# JUNE

The Sun is in Taurus to begin the month, moving into Gemini (The Twins) on the 15th. Neptune heads retrograde on the 8th, returning to direct motion November 14th. The New Moon (Sun and Moon in Taurus) is on the 8th with Mars, Jupiter, Venus and Mercury close by. Jupiter will be hidden in the bright sunlight; Mars can be seen pre-dawn, Venus and Mercury post-sunset. The evening sky continues to show us Saturn in Libra (The Scales) through the month, with the waxing Moon as partner on the 19th. Also on the 19th, Jupiter and the Sun stand together in Gemini. The Moon continues on its journey, arriving in Sagittarius across from the Sun on the 23rd for the Full Moon. June 21st brings the Solstice; the longest day in the Northern hemisphere, longest night in the Southern. On the 27th, Mercury goes retrograde for the 2nd time this year, turning direct July 21st.

**June 4:** Jupiter enters Gemini. "Toward blissful world-comprehending" (*Twelve Moods of the Zodiac*, Rudolf Steiner). As Jupiter moves into Gemini, the world thoughts of creation are revealed to us if we are willing to turn our mind's eye to the etheric realms of imagination. Gemini holds the mystery of two becoming one. Jupiter in Gemini leads those who persevere in faithfulness into these

---

Mystery of the Zodiac."

light-filled realms of truth where we find strengthening forces for our "I." This work of world-comprehending bestows the bliss of union between our temporal little self and our higher, divine self.

**June 5:** Sun enters the third decan of Taurus, ruled by Saturn, associated with Orion below and Auriga above.

**June 7: ASPECT:** Mercury 16° Gemini opposite Pluto 16° Sagittarius. Pluto was here at both the Ascension and Pentecost. Pluto has been very close to this degree since mid-February and will remain close into July. Mercury and Pluto were in opposition at Pentecost as they are today, in these same constellations. The third chakra is the Mercury chakra, which is related to the astral body. Our work into the far future is the transformation of the astral body into *Spirit Self*.

Mercury is also representative of the *ascending* stream of Earth evolution—a stream leading humanity into future Jupiter evolution, through the guidance of Divine Sophia. Jupiter evolution is the next period that follows after our current period of evolution, where Earth is the planetary sphere upon which humanity is developing. This will not always be so. The *manas* consciousness emanating from this future Jupiter period is bestowing blessings of enlightenment that can lift humanity onto the path of this ascending stream. Our minds (Mercury) must receive this light of spirit consciousness in order to awaken, just as the disciples at Pentecost were awakened.

It is our awakening to spirit that creates a counter force to the increasing power of materialism. The continuation of the materialistic descending stream, which has gripped humanity since the middle of the 19th century, has become a grave danger in our time—for it is long past its time of purpose. Throughout long millennia human beings had to *involve* themselves with matter, and now we are to *evolve* out of matter in order to return to the wellspring of our spiritual heritage—we do this by following the stream of Mercury's ascending path.

With Mercury (representing the human mind seeking light) and Pluto/Phanes (representing the divine Love of the Father) opposing each other at this Pentecost degree, we can imagine the World Thoughts of Sophia (Pentecostal enlightenment) facing the Love of the Father, who gave his only Son that we, too, could find the Light. Inversely, the noise of our ordinary minds may weigh us down—capturing us in the breathless grave of the serpent's world (Pluto/Hades)—whereby the new path that is now to be tread will not be the one taken. Lucifer would like to take control of our astral body and infuse it with egoistical self-seeking. Sophia teaches us the way of transforming our astral body—and this transformation calls us toward this ascending evolutionary stream:

> *Manas*, or spirit self, is the transformed astral body, and it was in the astral body that the intervention of Lucifer took place at the time of the Fall. When we are working on the astral body we are working on the transformation of the luciferic nature within us, which comes to expression as desire, passion, instincts, and so forth. And it is Sophia's purity that helps us to tame our desires and passions and to place ourselves in service of the divine plan.[67]

This is a good day to witness where we direct our thinking, and to take inventory of our sovereign governance over passions, desires, and instincts. Anger is emblematic of Lucifer in our astral body. Through luciferic illusions Pluto/Hades would like to pull us further into the descending stream of materialism, whereby he would be able to possess and use us in his fight against divine creation. Bring the love of Divine Wisdom into your thoughts today, for this leads us into the promise revealed by the Ascension and Pentecost.

**ASPECT:** Mars 10° Taurus square Neptune 10° Aquarius: The Feeding of the Five Thousand and the Walking on Water. The Sun was 10° Aquarius at both of these miracles, and today Mars, the planet of the Word and also aggressions such as military action, is square to these cosmic memories. Just as Lucifer hinders the progress of our Mercury chakra and the work of transforming our astral bodies, so is Ahriman the force of hindrance of those who choose materialism, through which he is able to

---

[67] Powell, *Cultivating Inner Radiance and the Body of Immortality*, p. 117.

SIDEREAL GEOCENTRIC LONGITUDES : JUNE 2013 Gregorian at 0 hours UT

| DAY | ☉ | ☽ | ☊ | ☿ | ♀ | ♂ | ♃ | ♄ | ♅ | ♆ | ♇ |
|---|---|---|---|---|---|---|---|---|---|---|---|
| 1 SA | 15 ♉ 45 | 18 ♒ 22 | 21 ♎ 43 | 6 ♊ 12 | 2 ♊ 31 | 5 ♉ 28 | 29 ♉ 20 | 10 ♎ 58R | 16 ♓ 44 | 10 ♒ 27 | 16 ♐ 6R |
| 2 SU | 16 42 | 1 ♓ 33 | 21 44 | 7 46 | 3 44 | 6 11 | 29 34 | 10 55 | 16 46 | 10 27 | 16 5 |
| 3 MO | 17 40 | 14 22 | 21 45 | 9 16 | 4 58 | 6 54 | 29 47 | 10 52 | 16 48 | 10 27 | 16 3 |
| 4 TU | 18 37 | 26 55 | 21 47 | 10 44 | 6 11 | 7 37 | 0 ♊ 1 | 10 49 | 16 50 | 10 27 | 16 2 |
| 5 WE | 19 35 | 9 ♈ 13 | 21 48 | 12 8 | 7 24 | 8 19 | 0 15 | 10 46 | 16 52 | 10 27 | 16 1 |
| 6 TH | 20 32 | 21 20 | 21 49R | 13 30 | 8 38 | 9 2 | 0 28 | 10 43 | 16 54 | 10 27 | 15 59 |
| 7 FR | 21 30 | 3 ♉ 19 | 21 48 | 14 48 | 9 51 | 9 44 | 0 42 | 10 40 | 16 56 | 10 27 | 15 58 |
| 8 SA | 22 27 | 15 13 | 21 46 | 16 3 | 11 4 | 10 27 | 0 56 | 10 37 | 16 58 | 10 27R | 15 57 |
| 9 SU | 23 24 | 27 4 | 21 43 | 17 15 | 12 17 | 11 9 | 1 9 | 10 34 | 17 0 | 10 27 | 15 55 |
| 10 MO | 24 22 | 8 ♊ 54 | 21 38 | 18 24 | 13 31 | 11 52 | 1 23 | 10 31 | 17 2 | 10 27 | 15 54 |
| 11 TU | 25 19 | 20 44 | 21 32 | 19 29 | 14 44 | 12 34 | 1 37 | 10 29 | 17 3 | 10 27 | 15 53 |
| 12 WE | 26 17 | 2 ♋ 37 | 21 26 | 20 31 | 15 57 | 13 16 | 1 51 | 10 26 | 17 5 | 10 27 | 15 51 |
| 13 TH | 27 14 | 14 35 | 21 20 | 21 29 | 17 10 | 13 59 | 2 4 | 10 24 | 17 7 | 10 27 | 15 50 |
| 14 FR | 28 11 | 26 41 | 21 15 | 22 24 | 18 24 | 14 41 | 2 18 | 10 22 | 17 8 | 10 26 | 15 48 |
| 15 SA | 29 9 | 8 ♌ 59 | 21 11 | 23 16 | 19 37 | 15 23 | 2 32 | 10 19 | 17 10 | 10 26 | 15 47 |
| 16 SU | 0 ♊ 6 | 21 31 | 21 9 | 24 3 | 20 50 | 16 5 | 2 46 | 10 17 | 17 11 | 10 26 | 15 45 |
| 17 MO | 1 3 | 4 ♍ 22 | 21 9D | 24 47 | 22 3 | 16 47 | 3 0 | 10 15 | 17 13 | 10 26 | 15 44 |
| 18 TU | 2 1 | 17 35 | 21 10 | 25 26 | 23 16 | 17 29 | 3 13 | 10 13 | 17 14 | 10 25 | 15 43 |
| 19 WE | 2 58 | 1 ♎ 14 | 21 11 | 26 2 | 24 29 | 18 11 | 3 27 | 10 11 | 17 16 | 10 25 | 15 41 |
| 20 TH | 3 55 | 15 19 | 21 12 | 26 34 | 25 42 | 18 53 | 3 41 | 10 10 | 17 17 | 10 25 | 15 40 |
| 21 FR | 4 52 | 29 50 | 21 11R | 27 1 | 26 55 | 19 35 | 3 55 | 10 8 | 17 18 | 10 24 | 15 38 |
| 22 SA | 5 50 | 14 ♏ 44 | 21 9 | 27 24 | 28 8 | 20 16 | 4 8 | 10 6 | 17 20 | 10 24 | 15 37 |
| 23 SU | 6 47 | 29 54 | 21 6 | 27 42 | 29 21 | 20 58 | 4 22 | 10 5 | 17 21 | 10 23 | 15 35 |
| 24 MO | 7 44 | 15 ♐ 11 | 21 0 | 27 56 | 0 ♋ 34 | 21 40 | 4 36 | 10 3 | 17 22 | 10 23 | 15 34 |
| 25 TU | 8 41 | 0 ♑ 24 | 20 53 | 28 6 | 1 47 | 22 21 | 4 50 | 10 2 | 17 23 | 10 22 | 15 32 |
| 26 WE | 9 38 | 15 23 | 20 46 | 28 10 | 3 0 | 23 3 | 5 3 | 10 1 | 17 24 | 10 22 | 15 31 |
| 27 TH | 10 36 | 0 ♒ 0 | 20 40 | 28 11R | 4 13 | 23 44 | 5 17 | 10 0 | 17 25 | 10 21 | 15 29 |
| 28 FR | 11 33 | 14 9 | 20 35 | 28 6 | 5 25 | 24 26 | 5 31 | 9 59 | 17 26 | 10 20 | 15 28 |
| 29 SA | 12 30 | 27 49 | 20 33 | 27 58 | 6 38 | 25 7 | 5 45 | 9 58 | 17 27 | 10 20 | 15 26 |
| 30 SU | 13 27 | 11 ♓ 1 | 20 31 | 27 44 | 7 51 | 25 49 | 5 58 | 9 57 | 17 28 | 10 19 | 15 25 |

INGRESSES :

| | |
|---|---|
| 1 ☽ → ♓ 21: 9 | 23 ☽ → ♐ 0: 9 |
| 3 ♃ → ♊ 22:14 | ♀ → ♋ 12:50 |
| 4 ☽ → ♈ 5:59 | 24 ☽ → ♑ 23:21 |
| 6 ☽ → ♉ 17:19 | 27 ☽ → ♒ 0: 0 |
| 9 ☽ → ♊ 5:57 | 29 ☽ → ♓ 3:55 |
| 11 ☽ → ♋ 18:44 | |
| 14 ☽ → ♌ 6:30 | |
| 15 ☉ → ♊ 21:30 | |
| 16 ☽ → ♍ 15:54 | |
| 18 ☽ → ♎ 21:52 | |
| 21 ☽ → ♏ 0:16 | |

ASPECTS & ECLIPSES :

| | | | |
|---|---|---|---|
| 3 ☽ ☌ ♅ 4:37 | ☽ ☍ ♇ 14:11 | 21 ☿ ☌ ♀ 2:55 | ☽ ☌ ♅ 12: 1 |
| 5 ☽ ☍ ♄ 3: 1 | ☽ ☌ ☿ 21:13 | 22 ☽ ☍ ♂ 9:13 | |
| 6 ☽ ☌ ☋ 0:57 | 11 ♀ ☍ ♇ 22: 3 | 23 ☽ ☍ ♃ 7: 7 | |
| 7 ☽ ☌ ♂ 13:44 | 12 ♀ □ ♅ 22:46 | ☽ ☌ P 11:16 | |
| ☿ ☍ ♇ 21:58 | 13 ☽ S ☊ 13:18 | ☉ ☍ ☽ 11:31 | |
| 8 ♂ □ ♆ 0: 8 | 15 ☽ ☍ ♆ 2:48 | 24 ☽ ☌ ♇ 0:35 | |
| ☉ ☌ ☽ 15:55 | 16 ☉ □ ☽ 17:22 | ☽ ☍ ☿ 20:18 | |
| ☿ □ ♅ 18:44 | 17 ☽ ☍ ♅ 23:22 | 25 ☽ ☍ ♀ 2:22 | |
| 9 ☽ ☌ ♃ 8:27 | 19 ☽ ☌ ♄ 15:19 | 26 ☽ N ☊ 8:42 | |
| ☽ ☌ A 21:59 | ☉ ☌ ♃ 16:10 | 27 ☽ ☌ ♆ 17:27 | |
| 10 ☽ ☌ ♀ 10:27 | 20 ☽ ☌ ☊ 9:48 | 30 ☉ □ ☽ 4:52 | |

SIDEREAL HELIOCENTRIC LONGITUDES : JUNE 2013 Gregorian at 0 hours UT

| DAY | Sid. Time | ☿ | ♀ | ⊕ | ♂ | ♃ | ♄ | ♅ | ♆ | ♇ | Vernal Point |
|---|---|---|---|---|---|---|---|---|---|---|---|
| 1 SA | 16:38:34 | 21 ♌ 23 | 26 ♊ 33 | 15 ♏ 45 | 28 ♈ 27 | 2 ♊ 0 | 14 ♎ 20 | 14 ♓ 15 | 8 ♒ 30 | 15 ♐ 11 | 5 ♓ 4'22" |
| 2 SU | 16:42:30 | 25 44 | 28 10 | 16 42 | 29 0 | 2 6 | 14 22 | 14 16 | 8 31 | 15 11 | 5 ♓ 4'22" |
| 3 MO | 16:46:27 | 29 58 | 29 48 | 17 40 | 29 33 | 2 11 | 14 24 | 14 16 | 8 31 | 15 12 | 5 ♓ 4'22" |
| 4 TU | 16:50:23 | 4 ♍ 4 | 1 ♋ 25 | 18 37 | 0 ♉ 6 | 2 16 | 14 26 | 14 17 | 8 32 | 15 12 | 5 ♓ 4'22" |
| 5 WE | 16:54:20 | 8 2 | 3 2 | 19 35 | 0 39 | 2 21 | 14 28 | 14 18 | 8 32 | 15 12 | 5 ♓ 4'22" |
| 6 TH | 16:58:16 | 11 53 | 4 40 | 20 32 | 1 12 | 2 26 | 14 30 | 14 18 | 8 32 | 15 13 | 5 ♓ 4'22" |
| 7 FR | 17: 2:13 | 15 38 | 6 17 | 21 30 | 1 45 | 2 31 | 14 32 | 14 19 | 8 33 | 15 13 | 5 ♓ 4'21" |
| 8 SA | 17: 6: 9 | 19 17 | 7 55 | 22 27 | 2 18 | 2 36 | 14 34 | 14 20 | 8 33 | 15 13 | 5 ♓ 4'21" |
| 9 SU | 17:10: 6 | 22 50 | 9 32 | 23 25 | 2 51 | 2 42 | 14 35 | 14 20 | 8 33 | 15 14 | 5 ♓ 4'21" |
| 10 MO | 17:14: 3 | 26 18 | 11 9 | 24 22 | 3 23 | 2 47 | 14 37 | 14 21 | 8 34 | 15 14 | 5 ♓ 4'21" |
| 11 TU | 17:17:59 | 29 40 | 12 47 | 25 19 | 3 56 | 2 52 | 14 39 | 14 21 | 8 34 | 15 14 | 5 ♓ 4'21" |
| 12 WE | 17:21:56 | 2 ♎ 59 | 14 24 | 26 17 | 4 29 | 2 57 | 14 41 | 14 22 | 8 34 | 15 15 | 5 ♓ 4'21" |
| 13 TH | 17:25:52 | 6 13 | 16 2 | 27 14 | 5 1 | 3 2 | 14 43 | 14 23 | 8 35 | 15 15 | 5 ♓ 4'21" |
| 14 FR | 17:29:49 | 9 23 | 17 39 | 28 11 | 5 34 | 3 7 | 14 45 | 14 23 | 8 35 | 15 15 | 5 ♓ 4'21" |
| 15 SA | 17:33:45 | 12 29 | 19 17 | 29 9 | 6 6 | 3 12 | 14 47 | 14 24 | 8 36 | 15 16 | 5 ♓ 4'20" |
| 16 SU | 17:37:42 | 15 33 | 20 54 | 0 ♐ 6 | 6 38 | 3 18 | 14 49 | 14 25 | 8 36 | 15 16 | 5 ♓ 4'20" |
| 17 MO | 17:41:38 | 18 33 | 22 32 | 1 3 | 7 11 | 3 23 | 14 51 | 14 25 | 8 36 | 15 16 | 5 ♓ 4'20" |
| 18 TU | 17:45:35 | 21 31 | 24 10 | 2 1 | 7 43 | 3 28 | 14 52 | 14 26 | 8 37 | 15 17 | 5 ♓ 4'20" |
| 19 WE | 17:49:32 | 24 27 | 25 47 | 2 58 | 8 15 | 3 33 | 14 54 | 14 27 | 8 37 | 15 17 | 5 ♓ 4'20" |
| 20 TH | 17:53:28 | 27 20 | 27 25 | 3 55 | 8 47 | 3 38 | 14 56 | 14 27 | 8 37 | 15 17 | 5 ♓ 4'20" |
| 21 FR | 17:57:25 | 0 ♏ 12 | 29 2 | 4 52 | 9 19 | 3 43 | 14 58 | 14 28 | 8 38 | 15 18 | 5 ♓ 4'20" |
| 22 SA | 18: 1:21 | 3 2 | 0 ♌ 40 | 5 50 | 9 51 | 3 48 | 15 0 | 14 29 | 8 38 | 15 18 | 5 ♓ 4'19" |
| 23 SU | 18: 5:18 | 5 50 | 2 17 | 6 47 | 10 23 | 3 54 | 15 2 | 14 29 | 8 38 | 15 18 | 5 ♓ 4'19" |
| 24 MO | 18: 9:14 | 8 37 | 3 55 | 7 44 | 10 55 | 3 59 | 15 4 | 14 30 | 8 39 | 15 18 | 5 ♓ 4'19" |
| 25 TU | 18:13:11 | 11 24 | 5 32 | 8 41 | 11 27 | 4 4 | 15 6 | 14 31 | 8 39 | 15 19 | 5 ♓ 4'19" |
| 26 WE | 18:17: 7 | 14 9 | 7 10 | 9 38 | 11 59 | 4 9 | 15 8 | 14 31 | 8 40 | 15 19 | 5 ♓ 4'19" |
| 27 TH | 18:21: 4 | 16 54 | 8 47 | 10 36 | 12 31 | 4 14 | 15 9 | 14 32 | 8 40 | 15 19 | 5 ♓ 4'19" |
| 28 FR | 18:25: 1 | 19 39 | 10 25 | 11 33 | 13 2 | 4 19 | 15 11 | 14 32 | 8 40 | 15 20 | 5 ♓ 4'19" |
| 29 SA | 18:28:57 | 22 24 | 12 2 | 12 30 | 13 34 | 4 24 | 15 13 | 14 33 | 8 41 | 15 20 | 5 ♓ 4'18" |
| 30 SU | 18:32:54 | 25 9 | 13 40 | 13 27 | 14 6 | 4 30 | 15 15 | 14 34 | 8 41 | 15 20 | 5 ♓ 4'18" |

INGRESSES :

| |
|---|
| 3 ☿ → ♍ 0:12 |
| ♀ → ♋ 3: 3 |
| ♂ → ♉ 19:24 |
| 11 ☿ → ♎ 2:21 |
| 15 ⊕ → ♐ 21:27 |
| 20 ☿ → ♏ 22:21 |
| 21 ♀ → ♌ 14:14 |

ASPECTS (HELIOCENTRIC +MOON(TYCHONIC)) :

| | | | | |
|---|---|---|---|---|
| 1 ☽ ☍ ☿ 8: 7 | 9 ☽ ☌ ♃ 11:30 | 16 ☽ □ ♃ 22: 9 | ☽ ☍ ♂ 15:54 | 28 ☽ □ ☿ 11:57 |
| 2 ☽ □ ♃ 1: 1 | 10 ☽ □ ♅ 11: 4 | 17 ☽ ☍ ♅ 18:19 | 23 ☽ ☍ ♃ 6:18 | 29 ☿ ☌ A 2:58 |
| ☽ ☌ ♅ 23:48 | ☽ ☍ ♇ 12:52 | ☽ □ ♇ 19:51 | ☽ □ ♅ 22:55 | ☽ □ ♃ 11:57 |
| 3 ☽ □ ♇ 1:33 | 12 ☽ □ ☿ 1: 0 | 18 ☿ ☌ ☋ 16:42 | 24 ☽ ☌ ♇ 0:11 | 30 ☽ ☌ ♅ 6:35 |
| ☿ □ ♃ 13: 9 | ♀ □ ♄ 4:11 | 19 ⊕ ☍ ♃ 16:10 | ☿ □ ♆ 0:12 | ☽ □ ♇ 8: 2 |
| 4 ☽ □ ♀ 10: 3 | 13 ☽ □ ♄ 0:15 | ♂ □ ♆ 16:30 | 25 ☿ ☍ ♂ 0:36 | ♀ □ ♂ 9:25 |
| 5 ☽ ☍ ♄ 10:23 | ☽ ☌ ♀ 3:20 | ☽ ☌ ♄ 23:22 | ☽ □ ♄ 23:34 | |
| 6 ☿ ☍ ♅ 15:26 | ♀ ☌ P 11:42 | 20 ☿ □ ♀ 1:24 | 26 ♀ ☍ ♆ 22:10 | |
| ☽ ☌ ♂ 20:41 | 14 ☽ □ ♂ 18: 9 | ☽ □ ♀ 22:32 | 27 ☽ ☌ ♆ 14:36 | |
| ☿ □ ♇ 21:16 | ☽ ☍ ♆ 23:14 | 21 ☽ ☌ ☿ 0:43 | ☽ ☍ ♀ 16:44 | |
| 7 ☽ □ ♆ 10:30 | 15 ☿ ☌ ♄ 18: 6 | ☽ □ ♆ 14:14 | ☽ □ ♂ 22: 0 | |

inveigle himself into unwitting etheric bodies. Neptune, in its lower expression, is the planet that is representative of this wretched adversarial being:

> It is, in the first place, materialism that gives Ahriman an opportunity to intervene into the human etheric body. By and large, materialistic thinking is of a mechanistic nature—a thinking that applies well to the physical level of existence but is ill suited to come into relationship with the etheric level. This materialistic, mechanistic thought has the effect of hardening the etheric body—ahrimanic influences harden and scleroticize—by way of removing the human being from the living flow of thought activity that belongs naturally to the etheric level of existence.[68]

With Mars square Neptune at the remembrance of these two miracles, we are challenged to rise above the ahrimanic influences in our modern world (lower Neptune), in order to unite with the powerful influences of Christ's fourth and fifth healing miracles. A living flow of thought activity is working into us today and we are to be mindful that our words reflect this harmony. The human being speaking in the sense of *right Word,* as in the *Eightfold noble path,* is in the process of creating peace. At the feeding of the five thousand and the walking on water, Christ was in communion with the mega star Deneb that streamed into him powerful cosmic influences. Neptune today remembers this divine inspiration. We can witness the words we speak and ask if they represent the beauty of Neptune's harmony, or inversely, if they conjure the hardened, aggressive mechanistic world of Ahriman. This can be witnessed in the self, in others, and in the world as well.

With today's aspects (Mercury opposite Pluto and Mars square Neptune), we can face the Father in the heights and bring to word the inspirations of Sophia. Inversely, the world and individuals may find themselves facing the devil (Pluto) in the dark seas of the collective underworld (Neptune). This is a good day to dance in joyful contemplation of miracles.

---

68 Ibid., p. 118.

**June 8:** New Moon 23° Taurus: The Ascension of Christ (May/14/33). Early in the morning of this day, Jesus presented the Blessed Virgin Mary to the apostles and disciples as their advocate and as the center of their community. Here we see another stage in preparation for the coming event of Pentecost—the preceding stage was when Mary received communion (see commentary of May 17). As the Sun climbed higher in the sky, Christ continued to the Mount of Olives and ascended to the top, all the while becoming increasingly radiant with light until he became more radiant than the midday Sun. Then he disappeared into this radiance. Two Angels then appeared saying: "Men of Galilee, why do you stand looking into Heaven? This Jesus, who was taken up from you into Heaven, will come in the same way as you saw him go into Heaven" (Acts 1:11 [ESV]).

The angelic voice sounds again in our time as Christ's appearance in the etheric realm becomes increasingly self-evident. The Resurrection of Christ portrayed by Matthias Grunewald, in his painting of the Isenheim Altarpiece, clearly shows the wounds of Christ. These wounds are the new organs of the will streaming from the ascended Christ. Under the auspices of Taurus, a constellation working with the transformation of the will, this image of Christ with the wounds of Golgotha shows human beings the way toward their own passion and transformation—the way found through obedience of the personal will to the will of God. Through transforming our lower will, we will increasingly find the Christ-Will in the encircling round of Earth and we will find a connection with the life flowing from his sacred wounds. After the Ascension of Christ the disciples were in abject misery:

> That day was the beginning of a sorrowful time for the disciples; they felt forsaken and saddened. The world of imagery [bestowed on them through Christ during the forty days following the resurrection], having so much meaning, was blotted out, and their souls were plunged into silent darkness. Their grief during this time cannot really be compared to any pain we may experience in daily life. It was not the result of affliction or trouble but the absence of all that

enlivened and motivated their souls. In such situations, positive suffering actually brings alleviation. Sharp pain is certainly an experience, but when life is merely an aching emptiness it is not really an experience; rather it is a soul condition that feels like a void. The disciples' experience of soul death preceded the event of Pentecost; it was a necessary preparation for it, since the resurrection of the soul during that event was an experience that could only follow the soul's death. That painful preparation for the Pentecost was alleviated, however, by one thing; the pain was shared by all of the disciples.[69]

Tomberg goes on to describe how their mutual suffering bound them together, whereby the twelve created an organ of Pentecostal revelation.

This New Moon is planting seeds that can mature into deeper understanding of Christ's Ascension. The absence of Christ that caused such pain in the disciples may be comparable to the aching pain, apathy, and emptiness of so many souls today. As depression and soul emptiness is increasingly afflicting both adults *and children*, we can wisely ponder the cause. *The absence of spirit in our culture is creating conditions that mirror the kind of soul death described above by Tomberg. Those who so suffer are diagnosed with an illness. What if they were seen as canaries in the coal mine of the Second Coming, those who have not yet encountered the presence of Christ, and are being taken over by the cynical being that has come into the void created by our cultural agnosticism?* Can young souls (who have come to participate in this event) survive without meeting Christ? Would not the sterile world into which they have come cause illness, not because there is something *wrong* with them, but because there is something *right* with them? Perhaps we can touch someone today who is in need of gentle guidance into these mysteries. Without succumbing to diagnosis and medication, how do we endure the soul's death in preparation for its resurrection? What new forms of healing are we being asked to bring forth? Where is the Christ in our life?

**Neptune stations 10°27 Aquarius** before going retrograde. Neptune stations at the memory of the Feeding of the Five Thousand. The Sun was here at this miracle and conjunct Deneb—a mega star seen as a guiding star for the whole of evolution. Fomalhaut stands close by (9° Aquarius) as one of the four Royal Stars of Persia—the Watcher in the South—as recognized in the opening Hermetic invocations by Hermes: (turning to the South): Holy Gabriel, thou glowing one clothed in silvery moonlight, breathing graciousness, fill us with the ineffable beauty of thy gentle loving piety and reverence.[70]

Let this be our prayer as we turn to the memory of this miracle and the mighty stars that are streaming their energies toward us this day.

**June 11:** Venus 16° Gemini opposite Pluto 16° Sagittarius: The Death of the Solomon Jesus (Jun/5/12). Venus was at this same degree when the great Zarathustra (Solomon Jesus) gave himself up so that he could unite with the pure soul of the Nathan Jesus child (the Union in the Temple) in preparation for the incarnation of Christ. As this memory stands opposite to Pluto, where the Ascension and Pentecost are remembered, we can imagine this beautiful Venusian planet of love and harmony "grailing" for the Love of the Father (Pluto/Phanes). Inversely, jealousy and rivalry (lower Venus) are aroused, calling forth the dark side of Pluto (Hades), the god of the underworld, who loves strife and uses it to dissemble the work of love in communities. "A kingdom divided against itself cannot stand" (Mark 3:24).

On the 7th, Mercury opposed Pluto; and today it is Venus who takes on this task. Venus rules the second chakra and is connected with the etheric body of life energies. These vital forces are the foundation for spiritual thinking, feeling and willing. Ahriman stalks human beings in pursuit of these forces, preying upon etheric life forces and then using these forces he has siphoned—against the same person from whom he has stolen. An etheric body void of life cannot lift itself into the stream of cosmic thinking that is imperative for those choosing the "radiant blue stream" of the etheric Christ. Today we are wise to notice the state of our second chakra. Is it in peace? Are we free of jealousy and rivalry? Are we cultivating inner radiance? If so, we

---

[69] Tomberg, *Christ and Sophia*, pp. 302–303.

[70] Powell, *CHA*, Opening Invocation.

can feel the in-streaming of the etheric Christ, who, having ascended to his Father, is with us again—in the etheric realms of vital life energies. We can touch into these realms of vibrant flowing cognition through finding inner peace. The great Zarathustra individuality became the Master Jesus and into his sheaths was the Christ incarnated. This mighty individuality will meet us in our efforts to find Christ. Just as he served at the first coming, so too is he serving at this time of the Second Coming of Christ.

**June 12:** Venus 17° Gemini square Uranus 17° Pisces. Yesterday's theme may be carried into today as Venus still stands so very close to the death of the Solomon Jesus. Today, however, she is square to Uranus (as well as still in close opposition to Pluto). Uranus at this degree recalls the peasant uprisings in Russia and the establishment of the "GULAG"; also the days of the American Dust Bowl in the early thirties; and the rising popularity of the young Hitler in Germany. Could any of this have occurred if humanity were following the teachings of the Master Jesus? No! The teachings born of this individuality, bring fluidity to human souls from light-filled realms raying toward us from the future. This kind of thinking-with-spirit creates harmony amongst human beings and also in the elemental kingdoms of Natura. Tyrants and dust bowls were not possible in the Garden of Eden, for there harmony reigned within all kingdoms. It is human beings themselves who create phenomena on Earth, through the collective content of their soul life:

> Much is taking place, and anyone who is truly paying attention can see this. In nature, much happens every year that increasingly contradicts the whole traditional process of nature in the past. Springtime is different from what it used to be. Summer, autumn, and winter are changing as well. In March, we experience the sultry days of summer. People talk of mysterious manifestations; the whole divine revelation of spring, summer, autumn, and winter is mixed up. Chaos is setting in, and this comes not from Heaven, but from the interior of the Earth. People think that these are merely climate changes, but this is not the case. When orderly changes take place again in nature, these will be the outer signs of Christ's etheric return.[71]

Chaos is rising from the sub-earthly interior of the Earth. Much of humanity is involved in pacts with the devil of materialism. This pact occludes the teachings of the Master Jesus (who works with Michael and Sophia, as well as Christ). This severance from divine thinking is the cause of tyrants and dust bowls, for the dry intellect renders barren the soil of the Earth's body, just as it renders barren the soil of our etheric life bodies (Venus). Uranus square Venus asks us to open and receive the true light—bringing new revelation—by wresting ourselves free from the egoistical electric light (Uranus) of intellects in consort with hellish adversaries.

**June 15:** Sun enters Gemini the Twins. "Reveal thyself, Sun life" (Steiner, *Twelve Moods of the Zodiac*) William Bento characterized this mantra:

> Within this phrase there is a hidden mystery. How does the Sun hide from our view? It is certainly not the physical Sun we see daily that is being referred to here—but the living, etherically permeated Sun, felt and experienced, though rarely perceived. Within this Sun exist the threefold sources of health, life and goodness. How easily we forget to place our trust in this ever-present stream of divinity when we are faced with illness, death and evil! For this reason alone, it is well worth reminding ourselves to see beyond appearances and behold the true revelation of the Sun, which reveals itself to our hearts, where its life resides.

The first decan of Gemini is ruled by Jupiter and associated with Orion, whose bright star Betelgeuse is located at 4° Gemini.

**June 18/19:** Sun 3° Gemini: Cosmic Pentecost (May/24/33). The Sun was 2½° Gemini at Pentecost, when the Holy Spirit descended into the Blessed Virgin Mary. At this degree, the Sun is directly opposite the Galactic Center (2° Sagittarius). The Galactic center, also known as the Central Sun, is the Divine Heart of the galaxy, which is the source of the Holy Spirit. The Blessed Virgin Mary, who was presented by Jesus Christ (before the Ascension) as

---

71 Tomberg, *Christ and Sophia*, pp. 399–400.

the center of the community, served here—at Pentecost—as this heart-center and as the bearer of Divine Sophia.

> Because of extremely complicated influences and experiences coming from the spiritual world, Mary had an astral body that was so purified it could receive the revelations of Sophia and pour them out again as inspirations of the soul. This faculty was the very reason why, at the time of Pentecostal revelation, the Virgin Mary occupied the central position in the circle of the twelve. Without her, the revelation would have been only spiritual; there would have been twelve prophets, united in the Holy Spirit as was ancient prophecy. Through the cooperation of Mary, however, something more could happen; the disciples' hearts beat in harmony with hers while they experienced the Pentecostal revelation as *personal* human conviction. Through this experience, they became not prophets but specifically apostles.[72]

The difference between prophets and apostles is that prophets proclaim revelations impersonally, whereas apostles reveal the Holy Spirit *within* their own souls. This was possible only because the Virgin Mary transmitted *ensouled* revelation to the disciples—through her, revelation became personal and yet maintained its objective spiritual truth.

From the moment of Pentecost onward, the silence imposed on Sophia through Lucifer's intervention in human destiny was released. Sophia became free to reach down into groups of earthly human beings. This was a great event for both the earthly and spiritual worlds.

The sparks of fire that issued from her blessed soul were the ensouled manifestation of Christ's cosmic I Am. This eternal "I" of the world was born into the disciples through the immaculate heart of the divine Mary-Sophia, who was standing at the heart of their community. Since that first Pentecost, the Christ spirit has lived within human souls on Earth. Pentecost was the awakening of Christ's disciples from a dreamlike state, whereby they united with the principle of Christ's love as an experience within their own being. We also are to awaken from our dream-like sleep to meet the challenge of our time with hearts filled with love.

Emanations from the heart of the galaxy are increasing in our time, leading up to a Pentecost on a world scale (See Robert Powell's article "World Pentecost," *Journal for Star Wisdom 2010*; or at articles, www.sophiafoundation.org). In remembrance of this profound moment, which today quickens, we are encouraged to live into this Sophianic awakening to Christ. It is our "I" that receives the new revelation, and it is the sense of ego (the "I") that is represented by the constellation of Gemini.

Can we find the strength of self to radiate from our center while all the while remaining open to the periphery?

**ASPECT:** Sun 3° Gemini conjunct Jupiter. On this day of remembering Pentecost, Jupiter joins the Sun. Jupiter is a planet that emanates influences of holy wisdom, enlivening our minds to perceive truths newly being born into time. To receive the World Pentecost we need this Jupiterian type of thinking, for this is what illumines the inner human being, awakening conscience. In this way our hearts (Sun) are prepared to receive new revelation born of a World Pentecost:

> The order of events now is the reverse of their occurrence nineteen centuries ago. The series begins now with the Pentecost; the actual meeting with Christ, as an experience, comes later. At the time of the Mystery of Golgotha, Christ first descended into the realm of death [descent into Hell], and then the Pentecost followed as the last in the series of events. Pentecost was a resurrection in the human soul; this time it happens in reverse. First, the Christ must be understood in his return in the etheric. Then the meeting in space with Christ, moving in the etheric, can happen consciously. The significance of his etheric return must now come first to human beings inwardly; only then will people be able to perceive Christ in the etheric realm. Consequently, it is extremely important that these questions remain at the center of our inner efforts and search; in this way, the return of Christ will not go unnoticed. To realize this, a general knowledge of spiritual science (knowledge of the ether body, karma, and so on) is not

---

72 Ibid., p. 306.

enough; people must concern themselves with the matters and connections we have been discussing, and intensive work is needed in relation to this event. Christology today is not an area of knowledge that may or may not be cultivated according to one's preference; it is a need of human destiny, so that we can avoid the misfortune of allowing these events to go unnoticed by human consciousness.[73]

Our souls are resurrected through the higher thinking Jupiter represents—Jupiter mediates the revelation. Once we turn to this wisdom stream, we gain the knowledge that leads us further into the mystery of the Second Coming—the meeting with Christ. Let today find us celebrating the gift of the Christ imbued "I," through which we understand the Second Coming. It rests heavily upon our shoulders (ruled by Gemini) that this truth not go unnoticed.

**June 21: ASPECT:** Mercury conjunct Venus 27° Gemini: Death of the Nathan Mary (Aug/5/12). Venus was here when the young Mary departed into the spiritual world shortly after the Union in the Temple between the two Jesus children. Venus imparts to Mercury the preciousness of purity. May we find our minds (Mercury) filled with love (Venus). As this conjunction occurs in Gemini, we can put special attention on seeing the star of the higher self that shines above each of us.

**June 23: Full Moon:** Sun 7° Gemini opposite Moon 7° Sagittarius: Second Temptation of Christ (Nov/28/29). This Full Moon remembers the position of the Sun at the second temptation of Christ in the wilderness. At this temptation both Lucifer and Ahriman approached, and asked Christ to plunge from the pinnacle of the temple, assuring him that Angels would catch him. Here the deceitfulness of all that springs from ahrimanic influences is revealed. *The pinnacle of the temple is the pristine clarity of consciousness. To plunge is to be caught by Angels of a fallen sort. The Bolsheviks called their people to plunge into the splendor of communism; instead they fell into the arms of a dragon. The western world is asking their people to plunge into a brilliant world of electrically-magnetized virtuality; instead we are falling into a spiders web:*

> To conceal from humankind that in modern intellectual, rationalistic science with its supplement of a superstitious empiricism, one is dealing with a great illusion, a deception—that men should not recognize this is of the greatest possible interest to Ahriman. It would be a triumphant experience for him if the scientific superstition that grips all circles today and by which men even want to organize their social science, should prevail into the third millennium. He would have the greatest success if he could then come as a human being into Western civilization and find the scientific superstition. But I ask you not to draw false conclusions from what I have just said. It would be a false conclusion to avoid the science of the day; that is the very falsest conclusion that could be drawn. We must get to know science; we should get an exact knowledge of all that comes from this direction—but with the full consciousness that we are receiving an illusory aspect, an illusion necessary for our education as human beings. We do not safeguard ourselves against Ahriman by avoiding modern science, but by learning to know its character. For modern science gives us an external illusion of the universe, and we need this illusion. Do not imagine that we do not need it. We must only fill it in from quite another side with actual reality gained through spiritual research; we must rise from the illusory character to the true reality. You will find reference in many of my lecture-courses to what I am telling you today, and you will see how everywhere it has been sought to enter fully into the science of our time, but also to lift it all to the sphere where one can see its real value. You cannot wish to get rid of the rainbow because you know it to be an illusion of light and color! You will not understand it if you do not realize its illusory character. But it is just the same with all that modern science gives you for your imagination of the universe; it gives only illusions, and that must be recognized. It is by educating oneself through these illusions that one arrives at the reality.[74]

---

73 Ibid., p. 401.

74 Steiner, *The Ahrimanic Deception*.

This Full Moon illumines our task to include the science of the spirit with the science of the illusory sense world. If we do not add the spirit to the sciences, we will find our lower ego strengthened at the cost of losing our connection with our higher self. Gemini carries the promise that the lower "I" and the higher "I" may unite. If we plunge wantonly into the illusory enticements that are capturing the masses, this promise will pass us by. We can remember to live in faithful perseverance toward the higher laws indwelling all *maya*.

**Venus enters Cancer:** "Engender warmth of life" (*Twelve Moods of the Zodiac*, Rudolf Steiner).

Venus in Cancer asks that we feel into the full flowering of each day, each summer, and each lifetime. Every flowering is an expression of life's warmth, and this warmth is to be lovingly shared with others. Venus was here at the death of the Virgin Mary, at the conception of the Solomon Jesus and at the birth of John the Baptist.

**June 24:** Celebration of St. John's Day.

**June 28:** Sun 12½° Gemini: Birth of John the Baptist (Jun/4/2 BC). John the Baptist was revealed by Christ to be the reincarnated Elijah, and later came to Earth as the Renaissance painter Raphael, and still later as Novalis. John fulfilled his mission when he baptized Christ in the Jordan River in the year AD 29, bearing witness to the incarnation of Christ—the true Light of the World and the Lamb of God. After the fulfillment of this mission, his new mission began, which was in service to Sophia. Just as John was the guide and preparer for those who would recognize the incarnated Christ, so too is he the preparer and guide for those working on behalf of Sophia, in recognition of the etheric return of Christ. This is a day to open our eyes and ears to the truth ringing through the world—a truth enlightened by wisdom and born of love. John works in the apocalyptic realms where the *Book of Revelation* lives eternally. He needs us to wake up to the presence of adversaries and to face this truth as would the Grail Knights. To know evil, is to bring forth the good. This is true for those following a Christ-centric Grail path. For those who do not know Christ, such knowledge regarding evil is imprudent. John is the bearer of strength and works through the power of the Word. May we find our fullness of voice and proclaim the Light, lest we become swallowed in the shadows of illusion!

# JULY

The Sun begins July in Gemini (the Twins), moving into Cancer (The Crab) on the 18th. Uranus turns retrograde on the 18th until mid-December. The New Moon in Gemini is on the 8th and Saturn stations direct on the 9th. The waxing Moon can be seen in the evening sky meeting up with Saturn again in Libra on the 16th. Mercury goes direct on the 21st, ending its 2nd retro-cycle. Early morning risers on the 22nd will observe Jupiter and Mars on top of one another in the east with Mercury nearby. All are in Gemini in the early morning pre-dawn glow and will be all month, becoming easier to view as the Sun moves through Gemini into Cancer. The Full Moon is on the 22nd (Sun in Cancer and Moon in Capricorn.) The Southern Delta Aquarid meteor showers begin July 18th and offer shooting stars through August 18th; July 28th and 29th bring the peak of twenty meteors each hour. Look to the constellation of Aquarius, which will rise about 9 p.m.. The waning Moon's light may obscure the meteors, so consider sky watching before its rise about 11 p.m. on the 28th and midnight on the 29th.

**July 1:** Sun 14° Gemini: Death of the Solomon Jesus (June/5/12). Robert Powell refers to the death of the Solomon Jesus shortly after the Union in the Temple between the two Jesus children:

> In the case of a highly developed individuality such as Zarathustra, who reincarnated as the Solomon Jesus, death signifies merely a translation of activity from one realm to another. This individuality worked on, after the death of the body on June 5, AD 12, in union with the Nathan Jesus. Thus, the Solomon Jesus was active in preparing the way for the unfolding of the earthly mission of Jesus Christ—the mission which began with the Baptism in the Jordan and culminated in the death on the cross on Golgotha.[75]

---
75 *Chron.*, p. 91.

Today we are reminded of the presence of initiates working from behind the veil of sense existence. Faithfulness and perseverance (Gemini) are virtues that guide us to develop our "I." As our "I" develops we become more aware of the continuous interaction between ourselves and with beings in the spiritual worlds. Today we can bring our attention to the weaving between worlds and how this vertical communion increases the harmony between all beings—inclusive of the beings of nature.

**ASPECT:** Venus 9°56 Cancer square Saturn 9°56 Libra. Conversation at Jacob's Well with Dina (July/26/30). Venus was here when Jesus met a Samaritan woman, Dina, at Jacob's well. He asked her to draw water for him. She was most surprised and responded: "You are a Jew and I am a Samaritan woman. How can you ask me for a drink?" (For Jews did not associate with Samaritans.) Jesus responded: "Everyone who drinks this water will be thirsty again, but those who drink the water I give them will never thirst. Indeed, the water I give them will become in them a spring of water welling up to eternal life." (John 4: 7-14) This eternal spring is the source of inspiration welling forth from the waters of our etheric bodies.

In his conversation with the Samaritan woman Jesus crossed the boundary of convention (Saturn), exemplifying the fact that karmic groups (Venus) were henceforth to be determined by spiritual measure and by no other standard. With Venus square Saturn we have an opportunity to experience any tension between our inner soul nature (Venus) and our conscience (Saturn). Venus is related to our second chakra and the etheric body, which finds healing in the words from the second beatitude: *"Blessed are those who bear suffering, for they shall be comforted."*:

> The level of inspiration (Pentecost) comes about in that the human being overcomes the sleep of Gethsemane and feels himself as a participant and receives soul education through the life body [etheric body]. This is the prerequisite for the human being's faculty of Inspiration. Every inspiration is initially painful and then gives knowledge. This knowledge is always a comfort, an awakening of the soul. Inspiration is thus a consequence of becoming conscious in the "school of suffering." Through the pain, Inspiration is a hearing of the kingdom of Heaven. The kingdom of Heaven becomes the Word.[76]

*The sleep of Gethsemane is the condition of those unwilling to bear the world's suffering. Without this we cannot find the water of life as did Dina. This water is the elixir bestowed by the comfort we receive when we are willing to suffer. It is this water that enlivens the etheric body and quenches the thirst of the soul. This is the capacity to feel empathy, to experience the pain and suffering of the external world—it is this that awakens us from the sleep of Gethsemane.* With Venus square Saturn, the thirst in the collective soul nature of humanity is heightened. This unquenchable thirst is caused by the soul being enclosed within itself, unable to feel compassion for the suffering of nature, others and the world. Ghoulish headlines, increases in addiction, and a growing apathy toward violence suggest we are still sleeping while Christ suffers the fate of our ignorance. May we awaken!

**ASPECT:** Sun 15° Gemini opposite Pluto 15° Sagittarius. The healing of two possessed youths from Gergesa (Dec/5/30). The Sun was at this Pluto degree when Jesus met two youths who were possessed by ahrimanic demons, inhabiting tombs beside a path. Because of the two, none could pass—owing to the demons' exceeding force. When they saw Jesus they cried out: "What have you to do with us. O Son of God?" (Matthew 8:29). Jesus cast out the demons into a nearby herd of swine, whereon the whole herd rushed down a steep bank into the sea.

In this healing, the relationship of Ahriman to the element of water becomes clear. The perceptive demons recognized the Son of God and experienced him as a direct threat to their activity. Ahriman called out from the possessed, asking to be thrown into the swine, so that through the people eating of the swine meat, he would find more than just two bodies to possess. It was known in ancient wisdom that Ahriman could enter the human lymph system (the fluid system) through the pinworms in pork. This was the knowledge behind the Jewish prohibition against eating pork. Those laws were

---

[76] Tomberg, "The Human Being as a Trinity of Body, Soul, and Spirit," *Starlight*, Spring 2011.

SIDEREAL GEOCENTRIC LONGITUDES : JULY 2013 Gregorian at 0 hours UT

| DAY | ☉ | ☽ | ☊ | ☿ | ♀ | ♂ | ♃ | ♄ | ♅ | ♆ | ♇ |
|---|---|---|---|---|---|---|---|---|---|---|---|
| 1 MO | 14 ♊ 24 | 23 ♓ 48 | 20 ♎ 32 | 27 ♊ 27R | 9 ♋ 4 | 26 ♉ 30 | 6 ♊ 12 | 9 ♎ 56R | 17 ♓ 29 | 10 ♒ 18R | 15 ♐ 23R |
| 2 TU | 15 22 | 6 ♈ 15 | 20 33 | 27 5 | 10 17 | 27 11 | 6 26 | 9 55 | 17 30 | 10 17 | 15 22 |
| 3 WE | 16 19 | 18 26 | 20 33 | 26 40 | 11 29 | 27 52 | 6 39 | 9 55 | 17 30 | 10 17 | 15 20 |
| 4 TH | 17 16 | 0 ♉ 26 | 20 33R | 26 12 | 12 42 | 28 34 | 6 53 | 9 54 | 17 31 | 10 16 | 15 19 |
| 5 FR | 18 13 | 12 19 | 20 31 | 25 41 | 13 55 | 29 15 | 7 7 | 9 54 | 17 32 | 10 15 | 15 17 |
| 6 SA | 19 10 | 24 8 | 20 26 | 25 7 | 15 7 | 29 56 | 7 20 | 9 54 | 17 32 | 10 14 | 15 16 |
| 7 SU | 20 8 | 5 ♊ 57 | 20 18 | 24 31 | 16 20 | 0 ♊ 37 | 7 34 | 9 53 | 17 33 | 10 13 | 15 14 |
| 8 MO | 21 5 | 17 48 | 20 9 | 23 54 | 17 33 | 1 18 | 7 47 | 9 53 | 17 33 | 10 12 | 15 13 |
| 9 TU | 22 2 | 29 42 | 19 58 | 23 16 | 18 45 | 1 59 | 8 1 | 9 53D | 17 34 | 10 11 | 15 11 |
| 10 WE | 22 59 | 11 ♋ 41 | 19 46 | 22 38 | 19 58 | 2 39 | 8 14 | 9 54 | 17 34 | 10 11 | 15 10 |
| 11 TH | 23 57 | 23 47 | 19 35 | 22 1 | 21 10 | 3 20 | 8 28 | 9 54 | 17 34 | 10 10 | 15 8 |
| 12 FR | 24 54 | 6 ♌ 0 | 19 25 | 21 25 | 22 23 | 4 1 | 8 41 | 9 54 | 17 35 | 10 8 | 15 7 |
| 13 SA | 25 51 | 18 24 | 19 17 | 20 50 | 23 35 | 4 42 | 8 55 | 9 55 | 17 35 | 10 7 | 15 5 |
| 14 SU | 26 48 | 1 ♍ 0 | 19 12 | 20 18 | 24 48 | 5 22 | 9 8 | 9 55 | 17 35 | 10 6 | 15 4 |
| 15 MO | 27 46 | 13 51 | 19 10 | 19 50 | 26 0 | 6 3 | 9 21 | 9 56 | 17 35 | 10 5 | 15 2 |
| 16 TU | 28 43 | 27 1 | 19 9 | 19 24 | 27 13 | 6 43 | 9 35 | 9 56 | 17 35 | 10 4 | 15 1 |
| 17 WE | 29 40 | 10 ♎ 32 | 19 9D | 19 3 | 28 25 | 7 24 | 9 48 | 9 57 | 17 35 | 10 3 | 14 59 |
| 18 TH | 0 ♋ 37 | 24 26 | 19 9R | 18 46 | 29 37 | 8 4 | 10 1 | 9 58 | 17 35R | 10 2 | 14 58 |
| 19 FR | 1 35 | 8 ♏ 45 | 19 8 | 18 34 | 0 ♌ 50 | 8 45 | 10 15 | 9 59 | 17 35 | 10 1 | 14 56 |
| 20 SA | 2 32 | 23 27 | 19 4 | 18 28 | 2 2 | 9 25 | 10 28 | 10 0 | 17 35 | 9 59 | 14 55 |
| 21 SU | 3 29 | 8 ♐ 27 | 18 58 | 18 26D | 3 14 | 10 5 | 10 41 | 10 1 | 17 35 | 9 58 | 14 53 |
| 22 MO | 4 26 | 23 37 | 18 50 | 18 30 | 4 26 | 10 46 | 10 54 | 10 3 | 17 35 | 9 57 | 14 52 |
| 23 TU | 5 24 | 8 ♑ 48 | 18 40 | 18 40 | 5 38 | 11 26 | 11 7 | 10 4 | 17 35 | 9 56 | 14 51 |
| 24 WE | 6 21 | 23 48 | 18 29 | 18 56 | 6 50 | 12 6 | 11 20 | 10 6 | 17 35 | 9 54 | 14 49 |
| 25 TH | 7 18 | 8 ♒ 29 | 18 20 | 19 17 | 8 2 | 12 46 | 11 33 | 10 7 | 17 34 | 9 53 | 14 48 |
| 26 FR | 8 15 | 22 44 | 18 12 | 19 45 | 9 14 | 13 26 | 11 46 | 10 9 | 17 34 | 9 52 | 14 47 |
| 27 SA | 9 13 | 6 ♓ 30 | 18 6 | 20 18 | 10 26 | 14 6 | 11 59 | 10 11 | 17 33 | 9 51 | 14 45 |
| 28 SU | 10 10 | 19 46 | 18 3 | 20 57 | 11 38 | 14 46 | 12 12 | 10 13 | 17 33 | 9 49 | 14 44 |
| 29 MO | 11 7 | 2 ♈ 36 | 18 1 | 21 43 | 12 50 | 15 26 | 12 25 | 10 14 | 17 32 | 9 48 | 14 43 |
| 30 TU | 12 5 | 15 4 | 18 1 | 22 33 | 14 2 | 16 6 | 12 38 | 10 17 | 17 32 | 9 46 | 14 41 |
| 31 WE | 13 2 | 27 14 | 18 1 | 23 30 | 15 14 | 16 46 | 12 50 | 10 19 | 17 31 | 9 45 | 14 40 |

INGRESSES :

| | | | |
|---|---|---|---|
| 1 | ☽ → ♈ | 11:52 | |
| 3 | ☽ → ♉ | 23: 7 | |
| 6 | ♂ → ♊ | 2:31 | |
| | ☽ → ♊ | 11:54 | |
| 9 | ☽ → ♋ | 0:36 | |
| 11 | ☽ → ♌ | 12:15 | |
| 13 | ☽ → ♍ | 22: 6 | |
| 16 | ☽ → ♎ | 5:21 | |
| 17 | ☉ → ♋ | 8:22 | |
| 18 | ♀ → ♌ | 7:32 | |
| | ☽ → ♏ | 9:24 | |
| 20 | ☽ → ♐ | 10:31 | |
| 22 | ☽ → ♑ | 10: 4 | |
| 24 | ☽ → ♒ | 10: 2 | |
| 26 | ☽ → ♓ | 12:33 | |
| 28 | ☽ → ♈ | 19: 3 | |
| 31 | ☽ → ♉ | 5:31 | |

ASPECTS & ECLIPSES :

| | | |
|---|---|---|
| 1 | ♀ □ ♄ | 17: 2 |
| 2 | ☉ ☍ ♇ | 0: 0 |
| | ☽ ☍ ♄ | 7:10 |
| 3 | ☽ ☌ ☋ | 4:13 |
| 4 | ☉ □ ♅ | 6:19 |
| 6 | ☽ ☌ ♂ | 12:29 |
| 7 | ☽ ☌ A | 0:49 |
| | ☽ ☌ ♃ | 3:19 |
| | ☽ ☍ ♇ | 18:46 |
| 8 | ☉ ☌ ☽ | 7:13 |
| | ☽ ☌ ☿ | 11:42 |
| 9 | ☉ ☌ ☿ | 18:40 |
| | ♀ □ ☊ | 20:42 |
| 10 | ☽ S ☊ | 15:49 |
| | ☽ ☌ ♀ | 18:17 |
| 12 | ☽ ☍ ♆ | 8: 2 |
| 15 | ☽ ☍ ♅ | 6:52 |
| 16 | ☉ □ ☽ | 3:17 |
| | ☽ ☌ ♄ | 22:59 |
| 17 | ☽ ☌ ☊ | 14:57 |
| 21 | ☽ ☍ ♂ | 2:43 |
| | ☽ ☍ ♃ | 3:36 |
| | ☽ ☌ ♇ | 10:11 |
| | ☽ ☍ ☿ | 15:52 |
| | ☽ ☌ P | 20:22 |
| 22 | ♂ ☌ ♃ | 7:34 |
| | ☉ ☍ ☽ | 18:14 |
| 23 | ☽ N ☊ | 15:32 |
| 24 | ☽ ☍ ♀ | 23:11 |
| 25 | ☽ ☌ ♆ | 2:18 |
| 26 | ♀ ☍ ♆ | 12:13 |
| 27 | ☽ ☌ ♅ | 19:55 |
| | ♂ ☍ ♇ | 22:43 |
| 28 | ☉ □ ♄ | 1: 4 |
| 29 | ☽ ☍ ♄ | 14:40 |
| | ☉ □ ☽ | 17:42 |
| 30 | ☽ ☌ ☋ | 5:47 |

SIDEREAL HELIOCENTRIC LONGITUDES : JULY 2013 Gregorian at 0 hours UT

| DAY | Sid. Time | ☿ | ♀ | ⊕ | ♂ | ♃ | ♄ | ♅ | ♆ | ♇ | Vernal Point |
|---|---|---|---|---|---|---|---|---|---|---|---|
| 1 MO | 18:36:50 | 27 ♏ 54 | 15 ♌ 17 | 14 ♐ 25 | 14 ♉ 37 | 4 ♊ 35 | 15 ♎ 17 | 14 ♓ 34 | 8 ♒ 41 | 15 ♐ 21 | 5 ♓ 4'18" |
| 2 TU | 18:40:47 | 0 ♐ 39 | 16 55 | 15 22 | 15 9 | 4 40 | 15 19 | 14 35 | 8 42 | 15 21 | 5 ♓ 4'18" |
| 3 WE | 18:44:43 | 3 25 | 18 32 | 16 19 | 15 40 | 4 45 | 15 21 | 14 36 | 8 42 | 15 21 | 5 ♓ 4'18" |
| 4 TH | 18:48:40 | 6 12 | 20 9 | 17 16 | 16 11 | 4 50 | 15 23 | 14 36 | 8 42 | 15 22 | 5 ♓ 4'18" |
| 5 FR | 18:52:36 | 9 1 | 21 47 | 18 13 | 16 43 | 4 55 | 15 25 | 14 37 | 8 43 | 15 22 | 5 ♓ 4'18" |
| 6 SA | 18:56:33 | 11 50 | 23 24 | 19 11 | 17 14 | 5 0 | 15 26 | 14 38 | 8 43 | 15 22 | 5 ♓ 4'17" |
| 7 SU | 19: 0:30 | 14 41 | 25 2 | 20 8 | 17 45 | 5 5 | 15 28 | 14 38 | 8 43 | 15 23 | 5 ♓ 4'17" |
| 8 MO | 19: 4:26 | 17 34 | 26 39 | 21 5 | 18 16 | 5 11 | 15 30 | 14 39 | 8 44 | 15 23 | 5 ♓ 4'17" |
| 9 TU | 19: 8:23 | 20 29 | 28 16 | 22 2 | 18 47 | 5 16 | 15 32 | 14 40 | 8 44 | 15 23 | 5 ♓ 4'17" |
| 10 WE | 19:12:19 | 23 26 | 29 53 | 23 0 | 19 19 | 5 21 | 15 34 | 14 40 | 8 45 | 15 24 | 5 ♓ 4'17" |
| 11 TH | 19:16:16 | 26 26 | 1 ♍ 31 | 23 57 | 19 50 | 5 26 | 15 36 | 14 41 | 8 45 | 15 24 | 5 ♓ 4'17" |
| 12 FR | 19:20:12 | 29 28 | 3 8 | 24 54 | 20 20 | 5 31 | 15 38 | 14 41 | 8 45 | 15 24 | 5 ♓ 4'17" |
| 13 SA | 19:24: 9 | 2 ♑ 34 | 4 45 | 25 51 | 20 51 | 5 36 | 15 40 | 14 42 | 8 46 | 15 25 | 5 ♓ 4'17" |
| 14 SU | 19:28: 5 | 5 42 | 6 22 | 26 48 | 21 22 | 5 41 | 15 41 | 14 43 | 8 46 | 15 25 | 5 ♓ 4'16" |
| 15 MO | 19:32: 2 | 8 54 | 7 59 | 27 46 | 21 53 | 5 46 | 15 43 | 14 43 | 8 46 | 15 25 | 5 ♓ 4'16" |
| 16 TU | 19:35:59 | 12 11 | 9 36 | 28 43 | 22 24 | 5 52 | 15 45 | 14 44 | 8 47 | 15 26 | 5 ♓ 4'16" |
| 17 WE | 19:39:55 | 15 31 | 11 14 | 29 40 | 22 54 | 5 57 | 15 47 | 14 45 | 8 47 | 15 26 | 5 ♓ 4'16" |
| 18 TH | 19:43:52 | 18 55 | 12 51 | 0 ♑ 37 | 23 25 | 6 2 | 15 49 | 14 45 | 8 47 | 15 26 | 5 ♓ 4'16" |
| 19 FR | 19:47:48 | 22 25 | 14 28 | 1 35 | 23 56 | 6 7 | 15 51 | 14 46 | 8 48 | 15 27 | 5 ♓ 4'16" |
| 20 SA | 19:51:45 | 25 59 | 16 4 | 2 32 | 24 26 | 6 12 | 15 53 | 14 47 | 8 48 | 15 27 | 5 ♓ 4'16" |
| 21 SU | 19:55:41 | 29 40 | 17 41 | 3 29 | 24 57 | 6 17 | 15 55 | 14 47 | 8 49 | 15 27 | 5 ♓ 4'15" |
| 22 MO | 19:59:38 | 3 ♒ 25 | 19 18 | 4 26 | 25 27 | 6 22 | 15 57 | 14 48 | 8 49 | 15 28 | 5 ♓ 4'15" |
| 23 TU | 20: 3:34 | 7 18 | 20 55 | 5 24 | 25 58 | 6 27 | 15 58 | 14 49 | 8 49 | 15 28 | 5 ♓ 4'15" |
| 24 WE | 20: 7:31 | 11 16 | 22 32 | 6 21 | 26 28 | 6 32 | 16 0 | 14 49 | 8 50 | 15 28 | 5 ♓ 4'15" |
| 25 TH | 20:11:28 | 15 22 | 24 9 | 7 18 | 26 58 | 6 38 | 16 2 | 14 50 | 8 50 | 15 29 | 5 ♓ 4'15" |
| 26 FR | 20:15:24 | 19 35 | 25 45 | 8 16 | 27 28 | 6 43 | 16 4 | 14 50 | 8 50 | 15 29 | 5 ♓ 4'15" |
| 27 SA | 20:19:21 | 23 56 | 27 22 | 9 13 | 27 59 | 6 48 | 16 6 | 14 51 | 8 51 | 15 29 | 5 ♓ 4'15" |
| 28 SU | 20:23:17 | 28 25 | 28 59 | 10 10 | 28 29 | 6 53 | 16 8 | 14 52 | 8 51 | 15 30 | 5 ♓ 4'14" |
| 29 MO | 20:27:14 | 3 ♓ 2 | 0 ♎ 35 | 11 7 | 28 59 | 6 58 | 16 10 | 14 52 | 8 51 | 15 30 | 5 ♓ 4'14" |
| 30 TU | 20:31:10 | 7 48 | 2 12 | 12 5 | 29 29 | 7 3 | 16 12 | 14 53 | 8 52 | 15 30 | 5 ♓ 4'14" |
| 31 WE | 20:35: 7 | 12 43 | 3 48 | 13 2 | 29 59 | 7 8 | 16 13 | 14 54 | 8 52 | 15 31 | 5 ♓ 4'14" |

INGRESSES :

| | | |
|---|---|---|
| 1 | ☿ → ♐ | 18:20 |
| 10 | ♀ → ♍ | 1:36 |
| 12 | ☿ → ♑ | 4: 7 |
| 17 | ⊕ → ♑ | 8:19 |
| 21 | ☿ → ♒ | 2:12 |
| 28 | ☿ → ♓ | 8:17 |
| | ♀ → ♎ | 15:16 |
| 31 | ♂ → ♊ | 0:49 |

ASPECTS (HELIOCENTRIC +MOON(TYCHONIC)) :

| | | |
|---|---|---|
| 1 | ⊕ □ ♅ | 4:10 |
| | ⊕ ☌ ♇ | 23:43 |
| 2 | ☽ ☍ ♄ | 17:51 |
| 3 | ☿ ☍ ♃ | 11:48 |
| 4 | ☽ □ ♆ | 16:41 |
| 5 | ⊕ ☌ A | 0:27 |
| | ♀ N ☊ | 1:21 |
| | ☽ ☌ ♂ | 9:19 |
| | ☽ □ ♀ | 22:16 |
| 6 | ☽ ☌ ♃ | 22:14 |
| | ☿ □ ♅ | 23:33 |
| 7 | ☿ ☌ ♇ | 5:46 |
| | ☽ □ ♅ | 17:37 |
| | ☽ ☍ ♇ | 19: 7 |
| | ☽ ☍ ☿ | 23:24 |
| 9 | ☿ ☌ ⊕ | 18:40 |
| 10 | ☽ □ ♄ | 7:45 |
| 12 | ☽ ☍ ♆ | 5:21 |
| 13 | ☽ □ ♂ | 4:55 |
| | ♀ □ ♃ | 13:18 |
| 14 | ☽ □ ♃ | 8:52 |
| | ☽ ☌ ♀ | 11:33 |
| 15 | ☽ ☍ ♅ | 1:36 |
| | ☽ □ ♇ | 2:53 |
| 17 | ☿ □ ♄ | 1:58 |
| | ☽ ☌ ♄ | 9:10 |
| | ☽ □ ☿ | 11:28 |
| 19 | ☽ □ ♆ | 0: 4 |
| | ♀ ☍ ♅ | 4:35 |
| | ☿ S ☊ | 7:46 |
| | ♀ □ ♇ | 14:41 |
| 20 | ☽ ☍ ♂ | 1:39 |
| | ☽ ☍ ♃ | 20:32 |
| 21 | ☽ □ ♅ | 10: 3 |
| | ☽ ☌ ♇ | 11: 6 |
| | ☽ □ ♀ | 16:22 |
| 23 | ☿ ☌ ♆ | 9:17 |
| | ☽ □ ♄ | 11:27 |
| 25 | ☽ ☌ ♆ | 0:34 |
| | ☽ ☌ ☿ | 16:18 |
| 26 | ☽ □ ♂ | 8:28 |
| 27 | ☽ □ ♃ | 0:31 |
| | ☽ ☌ ♅ | 15: 0 |
| | ☽ □ ♇ | 16: 9 |
| 28 | ☿ □ ♂ | 0:21 |
| | ☽ ☍ ♀ | 19:36 |
| 29 | ☿ □ ♃ | 20:10 |
| 30 | ☽ ☍ ♄ | 2:12 |
| 31 | ☿ ☌ ♅ | 10:24 |
| | ☿ □ ♇ | 13:18 |
| | ☽ □ ♆ | 23:20 |

disregarded in this region. When the people of Gergesa heard of the death of their swine, and the lost profit this caused, they asked Jesus to leave. In the words of Judith von Halle:

> The fact that the Gergesenes finally urged the Lord to leave their district, expresses the tragic aspect which the Christ impulse already bore at the dawn of the new era, and must always bear whenever it encounters evil. People had then degenerated to such an extent that they could not properly value the benefits of his deed, but, happy to violate the laws, were more interested in the profit and loss attached to their herd of swine than in their own healing and wellbeing.[77]

With Sun opposing Pluto at this memory, we must ask ourselves: Where does love of profit overshadow moral law? Motives solely for profit will continue to lead humanity into the arms of demons. Mercury, which rules Gemini (today's Sun), is often found on plaques at the entrance to banks. (Mercury, god of merchants and thieves—you be the judge). As long as we are driven by profit, we will be driven into a different stream than the one that is guiding us toward a golden future. We will become like a herd of swine rushing into the seas of the underworld. This is a good day to reflect upon our relationship to money.

**July 2:** Sun 16° Gemini: Conception of Solomon Jesus (June/7/7 BC). Last year commemorated the Union in the Temple between the two Jesus children. This continues to sound through time. The Jesus being, after the union, traveled and taught, learning the deepest truths. His soul suffered from all that he saw. He saw people were afflicted with all kinds of terrible diseases that affected their souls and also their bodies. After an encounter at the altar of the pagans he heard words sounding within his soul from the spheres of Sun existence:

> Amen.
> The evils hold sway,
> Witness of egoity freeing itself.
> Selfhood guilt through others incurred,
> Experienced in the daily bread,
> Wherein the will of the heavens does not rule,
> Because man separated himself from your realm,
> And forgot your names,
> You Fathers in the heavens.[78]

This prayer came as he witnessed the decadence that had come into the different streams of worship, and this prayer was an inversion of what would later come (after the Baptism in the Jordan) as the Lord's Prayer. Through this prayer human beings would find protection from evil forces that would continue to prey upon them—until the end of Time. We have been told: "Heaven and Earth shall pass away but my words shall not pass away." Turning to this prayer creates a connection to Christ.

**July 3:** Sun 17° Gemini square Uranus 17° Pisces. Uranus was at this degree when Joseph Stalin, then dictator of the Union of Soviet Socialist Republics (USSR), had collectivized 90% of Russia's rural farms (March 1930). Along with their farms, their livestock and other assets came under government control. In the years following this seizure of lands and property, peasants, including hungry children who hand-collected grain in the collective fields after the harvest, were arrested for damaging the state grain production. In 1945 it is said that Stalin confided to Churchill at Yalta that ten million people had died in the course of collectivization. None of this mattered to the evil heart of this sub-human dictator whose inspirations possessed him from dark depths of Hell.

*With Sun square Uranus, under the sorrowful akashic chronicle of these years, we can remember to protect our freedom, and to watch carefully for the rise of evil ones who rhythmically reappear in the annals of history. No country or continent is beyond the scope of their tyrannical machinations. No time is exempt from yet another attempt at the unthinkable realization of their callous pursuits of power.*

We can turn our hearts to the light of unexpected revelation. For this is the gift of Uranus when aspecting the Sun.

---

[77] Von Halle, *Illness and Healing*, pp. 132–138.

[78] Steiner, *The Fifth Gospel*, p. 51.

**July 6:** Sun 19° Gemini: This position is aligned exactly with the most radiant star in our heavens, Sirius, known as the star of the Master Jesus and revered by the Egyptians as the star of Isis (a pre-Christian manifestation of Sophia). Today we celebrate Sun conjunct Sirius, which closely follows the commemoration of both the conception of the Master Jesus (he who would unite with the Nathan Jesus at the Union in the Temple, and later bear the Christ) and the work of the dictator who was under the spell of the Antichrist.

There is a mysterious connection among the star Sirius, our Sun, and Shambhala—the golden realm at the heart of the Earth, the Earth's heart chakra. When Sun aligns with Sirius we can imagine a conversation amplifying between the Daughter in the heights and the Mother in the depths, through our Sun-heart. Sun in Gemini proclaims: "Reveal thyself, Sun life" (Steiner, *Twelve Moods of the Zodiac*). The inversion to the radiance of the cosmic Sun/Son, is well known, and the puppets of this anti-Son demon fill too many pages in the darker remembrances of history. Today, however, the power of great spiritual beings and great masters can illumine our hearts.

Sun enters third decan of Gemini, ruled by the Sun and associated with the constellation of the Lesser Dog, Canis Minor. The second star in this constellation, Gomeisa, signifying redemption, marks the neck of the dog at 27½° Gemini. The Lesser Dog was seen by the Egyptians in connection with Horus, just as the Greater Dog was seen to be the dwelling place of Isis, and Orion was seen as the cosmic abode of Osiris.

**Mars enters Gemini:** "Toward mighty life-movement" (Steiner, *Twelve Moods of the Zodiac*). Mars was in Gemini throughout the Passion of Christ. Mars gives us the capacities that allow us to manifest our highest intentions. We are to direct these capacities in harmony with divine will, so as to co-create the mighty life-movement guiding us toward the future. This will bring us face to face with our personal passion as a way of preparation.

~

Note: Last year with the Sun conjunct Sirius, on this very day, President Obama signed an executive order (Assignment of National Security and Emergency Preparedness Communications Functions) that guaranteed him the authority to seize communication systems. On this same day in 2012 Uranus (connected to communication systems) was remembering a reported 1,778,000 people who were convicted of crimes during the year 1929 under Stalin. What is actually happening with our right to privacy? Communication systems work with sub-earthly forces of trapped light. When the Sun is conjunct Sirius we remember a higher form of radiant light that works with revelation. As Sirius is the star of the Master Jesus and Isis-Sophia, we have to question whether this order serves an anti Christ-like leadership, or is it simply a harmless measure targeting disaster preparedness?

**July 8:** New Moon 21° Gemini: The raising of the pagan child (June/12/32). As a prelude to the raising of Lazarus from the dead, this raising from the dead took place six weeks previously:

> This took place in a shepherd village northwest of Jericho. Jesus was approached by a man from this village, whose daughter had died. She was about seven years old. The same disciples—Peter, James and John—who had been with him at the transfiguration were with him on this occasion. Jesus and the three disciples accompanied the man to his house, where the corpse of his daughter lay. Jesus placed one hand on the child's head and the other on its breast, and directed his prayers toward Heaven. The child raised itself up, alive. It was the day of the Full Moon, just as it had been Full Moon at the raising of the daughter of the Essene Jairus in the town of Phasael.[79]

At New Moon and Full Moon there is a special facilitation between the cosmic world and the earthly world. This alignment facilitates the incarnation of the soul, coming from the Moon sphere down to the Earth. The Moon is the portal of souls between these two worlds. The Raising of Lazarus also occurred at a New Moon.

---

[79] CHA, The Raising of Lazarus.

At this event Jesus told the apostles that in his name they should do as he did. These were the same three (Peter, James and John) that had witnessed his Transfiguration—they were told that they should do this, too. It seems that we are being told that as we transfigure our astral bodies, we will receive the heavenly manna that comes to us from spiritual worlds, preparing us, as healers, even to raise the dead—all in the name of Christ. Before we reach this level, we must first seek to heal the darkness in ourselves. This is our first task: to raise ourselves from the dead. Let this be a reminder, today, of our imperfection and our willingness to work toward the divine enlightenment that casts the light of perfect love into the darkness of our estranged souls.

**July 9:** Inferior conjunction of Sun and Mercury 22° Gemini: The First Temptation (Nov/27/29). Mercury was directly opposite today's conjunction at the first temptation in the wilderness. An inferior conjunction means that Mercury passes between the Earth and the Sun. In the Hermetic chart this appears as an *opposition between Sun and Mercury*. Therefore, Hermetically, Mercury today stands at the exact place of the first temptation. During inferior conjunctions, imaginations come into conscious clarity:

> When [Mercury] is in opposition to the Sun in the Hermetic chart [inferior conjunction], the planet is closest to the Earth and it is the consciousness aspect of the planet which then comes to expression in the microcosm. Using an analogy drawn from the realm of psychology, drawing near the Earth signifies penetration into consciousness, while disappearance beyond the Sun [superior conjunction] signifies withdrawal from the sphere of consciousness into the subconscious realm of the will.[80]

Mercury represents the third chakra, which is the 10-petalled lotus flower. This lotus flower has two pentagrams, one upon the other, configuring two poles: the pole of will (superior conjunction) and the opposite pole, the pole of consciousness (inferior conjunction). As today is an inferior conjunction between Sun and Mercury, it is consciousness that lights up, intensifying the work of coordination of thought.

**May 10/11** was the last superior conjunction between Sun and Mercury. During that superior conjunction we remembered the mysteries of the Holy Grail and the Church of John. This is the church that leads us to understanding of star wisdom—the call into the new Egypt—the place of revelation. Whatever was then seeded into our will, today emerges into the clarity of thought. Be vigilant regarding any temptation to bow before the golden calf of power that is lingering from outdated traditions. Since the Venus transit last year, Hermetic messengers are speaking into communities of the Grail, where all sit in circle together, no one raised above the other. This is our safeguard against the temptation to have others bow before us—as the Prince of Darkness tempted Christ to do.

Saturn stations 9°53 Libra: Saturn's location at the Birth of the Solomon Mary (Sept/7/21 BC). This degree activates a cosmic cross: With Saturn *square* to this degree in Capricorn, we are reminded of hard times: The Russian winter of 1932/33 found Stalin imposing terror and famine in the Ukraine, which mournfully led to the starvation of millions of people. In Germany, Hitler was about to become chancellor (January 30, 1933). In the US, the Dust Bowl was building up to the full disaster it would become (late December 1932). With Saturn *opposite* to this degree in Aries: The Flight into Egypt of the Solomon Jesus family took place (Mar/2/5 BC). In *square* to today's constellation of Libra, in Cancer, Parzival was seeking the Castle of the Grail: "What was this time? The saga itself tells us—it was a Saturn time. Saturn and the Sun stood together in Cancer, approaching culmination. So we see how in the most intimate effects a connection between the Earth and the Stars is established. It was a Saturn Time!"[81]

> The individuality who once in the mystery places of Egypt raised the eyes of his soul up to the stars, and sought to unravel their secrets in celestial space after the manner of those days under the guidance of the Egyptian sages, lived again in

---

80 Powell, *Hermetic Astrology*, vol.1, p. 149.

81 Steiner, *Christ and the Spiritual World: The Search for the Holy Grail*, p. 128.

our own epoch as Kepler. What had existed in another form in his Egyptian soul appeared in a newer guise as the great laws of Kepler, which today are such an integral part of astro-physics. It came to pass also that within the soul of this man there arose something which forced these words to be uttered—words which may be read in the writings of Kepler—"Out of the holy places of Egypt I have brought the sacred vessel; I have transported it to the present time, so that men may understand something in these days of those influences that are able to affect even the most distant future."[82]

As Saturn stations in Libra, it activates these three other points in the zodiac that hold the above mentioned events: Stalin, Hitler, and the dust bowl; the flight into Egypt; and Parsifal seeking the Grail Castle. Saturn remembers the pinnacle in today's starry heavens: the birth of wisdom—the birth of the Solomon Mary. There will always be distractors to the manifestation of goodness. Yet, goodness will prevail! Today we can remember the Grail and its roots in Egypt, and take stock of any signs indicating anti-Grail activity. Dictators are the antithesis of the Grail leadership we are striving to emulate. Ignorant custodianship of our soils (both the soil of our souls and the soils of our Earth) brings us to starvation—both physically and spiritually. *The Grail, however, leads us into divine nourishment rising on the tides of a Christianized Egypt; and the wisdom of the Solomon Mary leads us to our distant future—Heavenly Jerusalem. Like Kepler we can bring the sacred vessels into the present time! This is the work of uniting above and below, and through this union we become a source of redemption for nature.*

**July 18:** Sun enters Cancer: "Thou resting, luminous glow" (Steiner, *Twelve Moods of the Zodiac*). William Bento illumines this mantra:

> As the Sun reaches its zenith in the summer sky it appears to rest and emit a luminous glow of warmth and light. This high point of the yearly cycle offers us the opportunity to express our gratitude for all the life we see around us, knowing that its existence is due to the Sun's luminosity. This phrase opens the breast and allows our heart to enter into dialogue with the mighty orb of warmth and light that bestows life to all.

In Cancer "Selflessness becomes Catharsis" is the virtue to be practiced in order to purify oneself. The Cathars were the "pure ones." The first decan is ruled by Mercury and is associated with the constellation of Argo the Ship—in which, according to Greek mythology, Jason and the Argonauts recovered the Golden Fleece.

**Uranus stations 17°35 Pisces:** Uranus remembers the Sun at the Conception of the Nathan Jesus (Mar/6/2 BC). Uranus at this position is exactly square to the Jupiter-Pluto opposition during the Mystery of Golgotha. The planet of revolution stations, square to the powerful opposition of Jupiter and Pluto during Christ's death on the cross, and also this station occurs at the Sun memory of the conception of the Nathan Jesus, who was a pure and chaste being. These two events intensify teachings pouring from these degrees in the akashic memory. It was the body of the Nathan Jesus that would hang on the cross that sorrowful day in AD 33. As Uranus calls forth these events, it stimulates a creative dynamic in the stars—a dynamic that can manifest the light of purity, thus overshadowing all that works against this. Inversely, it can bring revolutions.

Gandhi's "Salt March" (Mar/12/30) ended while Uranus was at this degree (April 5th, 1930). Gandhi and his *satyagrahis* (activists of truth and resolution) reached the coast of the Arabian Ocean after a 240-mile journey. The Salt Tax imposed by the British made it illegal for workers to freely collect their own salt from their own coasts, making it necessary for them to buy salt they could not afford. The Salt March started a series of protests that resulted in horrible violence. The non-violent *satyagrahis* did not defend themselves against the clubs of policemen, and many were killed instantly.

As Saturn is still remembering the beginning of the Dust Bowl, Stalin's collectivization of agriculture, and the rise of Hitler as the German Chancellor (see commentary for July 9), intensity is activated today. It offers us the tasks of actively serving

---

82 Steiner, *The East in the Light of the West,* chap. 8.

purity, bearing love toward nature, cultivation of peace, and preservation of freedom. Uranus standing square to the Jupiter-Pluto opposition of Golgotha asks: What new light can you offer in contribution to the change we all must create as the fulfillment of the Second Coming?

~

**Note:** Today the Sun is aligned with Procyon (redeemed or redeeming) in the Lesser Dog. This is where the Sun was when Jesus taught the need to be awake to the signs of the times.

**Venus enters Leo:** "Existing grounds of worlds" (Steiner, *Twelve Moods of the Zodiac*). Venus here asks that we bring the ground of the world into the senses' might. Venus was in Leo at the birth of the Nathan Mary. She is our exemplar for compassion so great she spared herself nothing. To live fully into the streaming of worlds, is to brave the wisdom achieved through pain.

**July 21:** Sun 4° Cancer: Jesus teaches the significance of the word *Amen* (*Chron.*, p. 306). This is also where the Sun was at the July 2009 eclipse, when Pluto stood exactly where it was at the Baptism of Christ. Tomorrow marks the Sun directly opposite its position at the inauguration of the US President earlier this year. This day rests between the memory of dictators who oppose the work of the Archangel Jesus, and tomorrow's remembrance of the night in Gethsemane. And, with the Sun at today's degree, we remember Jesus teaching the significance of the word Amen! This word represents Christ and he is the antidote to dictators and the one who calls us to take up the cross, just as on the night of Gethsemane he took up the sins of the world. Valentin Tomberg addresses the *Amen*: "A: The risen head; M: The risen hands; E: The inner life of the resurrection body; N: The force of [the resurrection body's] denial of evil."[83]

We can look around and ask if we are headed in the right direction both personally and collectively. Is freedom and peace expanding? Are we working toward the redemption of nature in her time of great travail? With Venus now in Leo we can strengthen our heart that it may receive Christ just as did Jesus receive him at the Baptism. We are to be vigilant in recognizing anti-forces.

The *Amen* is Christ in his cosmic robes. This is a day to experience the presence of the *Amen* and the power of the eurythmy gesture "N" as "No" to forces rising from the abyss. This is the gesture for the constellation of Pisces—making this the gesture of our time, as we are living in the Piscean Age of the Consciousness Soul.

**July 22:** Full Moon: Sun 5° Cancer opposite Moon 5° Capricorn: The Night in Gethsemane (Apr/2/33). This Full Moon stands square to the approaching Full Moon on the night in Gethsemane, when Christ sweated blood. Who then approached him? Ahriman! A silent cross is raised in the heavens today, remembering four events: Gethsemane (Moon 5° Libra), the 2009 eclipse (Sun 4° Cancer—the longest eclipse of the 21st century), the inauguration of the US president in January (Sun 5° Capricorn), and the enmity of the Pharisees (5° Aries—Mar/26/31). During the night in Gethsemane:

> As he knelt and prayed, he was faced with wave upon wave of the most loathsome scenes portraying the depths of guilt and sin in the world since the Fall of Adam. At the same time this was accompanied by the mocking voice of the Evil One, who taunted Jesus, depicting his deeds of love as completely worthless. Jesus, shocked on the one hand by the abominableness and sheer volume of sin and on the other hand by the unspeakable ingratitude shown by human beings toward God, cast himself down in fear and trembling, and prayed: "Abba, Father! If it be possible, let this cup pass from me. My Father, all things are possible with thee, remove this cup from me; nevertheless not my will, but thine, be done." His will and the will of the Father were one, as he offered himself up in love for the sake of humankind, but he was shaken to the core in the face of death and the onslaught of temptation from the depths of Hell.[84]

As his tormentor continued to assault him, he was shown the incredible suffering that was before

---

83 Tomberg, *Christ and Sophia*, p. 300.

84 Powell, *CHA*, Gethsemane Night.

him and all the future deeds and abominations that would be done in the future—in his name!

This Full Moon asks us to find courage when confronting falsehoods by turning to Our Father and Our Mother, so that we will not be swayed by the madness of the masses who are too easily fooled by wolves wearing sheep's clothing. In this way we will find the path of catharsis that is illuming this Capricorn Moon. The disciples fell asleep, in spite of Christ's need for them. We are to remain awake with Christ as we find our way through the shift we are here to serve. Enmity will cast its dispersion, the Sun will darken as we face our shadow, and we will be tempted to follow earthly rulers rather than the voice of our conscience; yet the night in Gethsemane can be the lantern at the prow of our ship, leading us ever forward. This is a Moon through which stillness of thought can enlighten us to our work of transformation.

ASPECT: Mars conjunct Jupiter 11° Gemini: Mars was coming into conjunction with Jupiter very close to this degree on this night in Gethsemane. Let this encourage us to manifest (Mars) wisdom (Jupiter).

**July 26: ASPECT:** Venus 9°52 Leo opposite Neptune 9°52 Aquarius: Venus stood where Neptune is today when Jesus visited the cave of Machpelah near Hain Mambre—where Abraham, Sarah, Isaac, and Jacob were buried. All entered the cave barefoot and stood in reverential silence. Only Jesus spoke (*Chron.*, p. 272).

Today Neptune is close to conjunction with the mega star Deneb (10½° Aquarius). This is a very powerful guiding star under whose influence the Feeding of the Five Thousand and the Walking on Water were accomplished, and Venus at this degree remembers Jesus entering the cave of the three patriarchs. These were the three patriarchs who worked together to form the twelve-fold community of ancient Israel, in preparation for the coming of Christ at the turning point in time. They can be likened to the three teachers of the 20th century who also work together (incarnated or not) to help form the community of Eternal Israel at this time of the Second Coming. Abraham could be seen as Rudolf Steiner, Isaac as the second teacher, and Jacob as the now incarnated John being. This is *not* to say that these individualities are the reincarnations of the patriarchs, but by way of analogy we could say that the father of spiritual science in the twentieth century is like Abraham; Isaac, who was offered for sacrifice, could be seen as the reincarnated Bodhisattva Jesu ben Pandira; and Jacob, who battled lies and falsehoods, reflects the battle of the John being against deception in our time. These three modern teachers of the twentieth century are the teachers of the karmic community (Venus) of the Second Coming. Naturally, with the onset of the Second Coming, there would be a reflection of the Patriarchs and the Trinity:

> Against this background we can understand on a deeper level the tasks of the three teachers and the challenges confronting them. For the present time it is especially the task of the third teacher that concerns us. Here we may see, by way of analogy with the life of the patriarch Jacob, who had to battle continually against the falsehood of the luciferic sphere, that the third teacher is confronted especially with the challenge presented by this sphere, which works to distort and corrupt truth. At the same time the third teacher seeks to inspire the Sophianic impulse of community, just as through Jacob the twelve founding fathers of the community of Israel came into being. The third teacher has the task, following on from the moral impulse of the word (sixteen-petalled lotus) brought by the second teacher (the Bodhisattva individuality Jeshu ben Pandira), to mediate the pure love impulse of the heart center, the twelve-petalled lotus. This means becoming a bearer of the Nathan Jesus, who is the source of the pure love impulse of the twelve-petalled lotus. According to Valentin Tomberg, this signifies an incarnation in female form:
>
> In the earthly sphere one human being (female organization) has to take up the Nathan Jesus, after the Bodhisattva has worked and impulsated twelve human beings through his words. Then the Nathan Jesus will radiate out twelve rays of his light to twelve human beings.[85]

Today we recall the profundity of these thoughts with Venus streaming from the Lion—the

---

[85] Powell, *The Most Holy Trinosophia*, pp. 68-69.

heart—where the Nathan Jesus is the source of the pure love impulse. Let us find love this day on behalf of Venus. On behalf of Neptune, we ask for inspiration from Sophia, who is working through the third teacher. On behalf of all of humanity we listen for the twelve voices impulsated by the Bodhisattvas, who are carrying on this work through the rays of light emanating from the Nathan Jesus being. May we find reverential silence in the depths of these mysteries, as did those who entered the cave of Machpelah with Jesus.

**July 27:** Mars 14° Gemini opposite Pluto 14° Sagittarius: Appearance to the eleven (Apr/11/33). Mars was here (four days before an opposition with Pluto) when Christ, in his resurrection body, appeared to his disciples while they were celebrating a love-feast (agape) for the second time:

> During a brief pause the Risen One entered, resplendent with light. He greeted them with the words: "Peace be with you!" Thomas drew back, frightened at the sight of the Lord. Yet Jesus took hold of Thomas's hands and laid them in his wounds, at which Thomas exclaimed: "My Lord and God!" Then the Lord requested something to eat, as he had done at the previous appearance in the hall of the Last Supper.[86]

Christ went on to impart strength and power to Peter and gave him a mantle that would continue to represent to him the power he had then been given.

With Mars opposing Pluto we too can be strengthened to overcome our doubt. Our lower astral desires and yearnings (Mars) can be lifted, through faith (the virtue of Gemini) into new heights of communion with our Father in Heaven (Pluto/Phanes). We are to connect ourselves to the blue mantle of the etheric Christ as the mantle of protection offered to each of us.

Sun enters second decan of Cancer, ruled by Venus. This decan contains the star cluster Praesepe, the Beehive (12½° Cancer). According to Rudolf Steiner in his lectures on bee-keeping: "Bees surrender themselves entirely to Venus, unfolding a life of love through the whole beehive." This decan is associated with the neck of the Lesser Bear, Ursa Minor.

Praesepe, the beehive, is at the center of the spiraling arms of Cancer, the heart of the crab. It was through this gateway that the Greeks believed human souls entered earthly incarnation in order to gather the golden nectar of earthly experience to take back to Sophia, the Queen of the cosmic realm. Cancer marks a point of decision in our yearly journey through the zodiac: development or envelopment? The spiraling arms of Cancer invite us to breathe in the Light and to move forward with the evolution of life and consciousness. The opposite is envelopment, whereby we are arrested in our progress and are thus relegated to the dark corridors of rigidified convention—if we stay here too long, our atrophied forces may eventually turn toward the unrighteous.

**July 31: ASPECT:** Mars 17° Gemini square Uranus 17° Pisces: Mars now comes into square with Uranus as did the Sun on July 3rd, and on the 18th Uranus stationed at this same degree. What does Mars bring to the memories we covered on the 3rd and 18th? Mars brings the memory of Christ's teachings regarding the Church of Peter and the Church of John (Apr/15/33). This was four days after his appearance to the disciples at their agape feast mentioned above. At that time Mars and Jupiter were close together in the Twins, as they are today; and Mars was opposite Pluto, just as they were four days ago.

At this appearance Christ told Peter to: "Feed my Sheep," which indicated his task to continue the celebration of the sacraments for all time. Then Peter asked the Lord, indicating John: "And what will become of him?" The Risen One replied: "If it is my will that he remain until I come, what is that to you?" Here John was prophesied as the head of the Church of the Second Coming, and Peter was instructed not to worry about who is appointed to what and when. This applies to us all. It is senseless to worry about our various positions, as there is a season for each of us in the course of time. The event of the Second Coming is now upon us, and with Mars square Uranus we are encouraged to open to the Words (Mars) of Christ now bringing

---

86 CHA, The Forty Days After the Mystery of Golgotha.

new revelation (Uranus) specific to the work of John at this time.

# AUGUST

The month begins with the Sun in the Crab (Cancer) and moves into the Lion (Leo) on the 17th. The New Moon is the 6th this month, (Sun and Moon in Cancer) and the Full Moon is on the 20th. In a word, August is packed with stargazing opportunities! The month starts with a lovely predawn show of the tiny waning crescent Moon in Gemini conjunct Jupiter, with Mars and Mercury very close by on the 4th. They will rise in the east together about 3:30 am and disappear into the Sun's light about two hours later. This grouping can be observed by the early birds all month; by the end of the month, the Moon will have gone all the way around the zodiac to join again with Jupiter in the morning light. Mars will still be observable to the left in Cancer while Mercury will have moved on into Leo, conjunct the Sun on the 24th. And of course, August always brings the Perseid Meteor Showers which peak on August 13/14th. With as many as sixty meteors/hour and sweet summer evenings, this is THE time to lie upon the ground, gazing to the north east into the constellation of Perseus to receive the blessings within these shooting stars. We've got great conditions this year, with a waxing Moon setting just before midnight on the 13th. (And catch this crescent Moon conjunct Saturn in the west as the light wanes at twilight on the 12th!) For the diehards among us, realize that the Perseid Shower offers shooting stars from July 23rd until August 22nd, overlapping with the Southern Delta Aquarids! What a dream!

**August 6:** New Moon: 18° Cancer: Parsifal's first visit to the Grail Castle (Jul/15/828). This date is considered to be correct by some researchers, and it does reflect Saturn and Sun in conjunction. Steiner proclaimed: "It was a Saturn time; Saturn and Sun were conjunct in Cancer." Not only were Saturn and Sun conjunct but also Jupiter, Venus, Moon and North Node stood together in Cancer. The virtue of Cancer—*Selflessness becomes catharsis*—certainly applies to the path of initiation upon which Parsifal was led into the Grail Castle.

When the Christ Impulse entered into the evolution of humanity in the way known to us, one result was that the chaotic forces of the Sibyls were thrust back for a time, as when a stream disappears below ground and reappears later on. These forces were indeed to reappear in another form, a form purified by the Christ Impulse.... "Yes, a time is coming when the old Astrology will live again in a new form, a Christ-filled form, and then, if one can practice it properly, so that it will be permeated with the Christ Impulse, one may venture to look up to the stars and question them about their spiritual script."

At this point Rudolf Steiner introduces two personalities whose soul forces were transformed under the influence of the Christ Impulse: the Maid of Orleans as a Christianized Sibyl, and Johannes Kepler as the one who was able to read the new stellar script. We may regard it as our future task to practice for ourselves the mode of thinking infused with the Christ Impulse as modeled for us by Kepler, and to learn to read the new stellar script.[87]

What is the contemplation for this Moon? It is the Grail legend, for this is the story of our time. We are to become *Knights of the Threshold*. Valentin Tomberg addressed this knighthood and characterized its nature as being the union between Platonistic and Aristotelian world views. When these two different streams work together, one is master of both Space and Time—one is on the cross and in the *crossing point*. This is the crossing point known to the Apocalyptist who wrote the revelation. The mysteries of Time bestow a phenomenological clairvoyance of nature, and the mysteries of Space bestow clairvoyance of karma. Tomberg speaks of how the Platonists will stand guard together with the Aristotelians at the threshold of the spiritual world:

On one side they will open the gates to the authorized, and on the other they will close them to the unauthorized. This community of knights—this future community of "knights of

---

[87] Ellen Schalk, "Kyot and the Stellar Script of Parsifal"; http://sophiafoundation.org/articles/mean.

the Threshold"—will be fully realized in the sixth cultural epoch.

But let us keep one province free from compromise; let us remain true to the spirit, independent of all teachings and teachers, of all organizations in the world. Let us remain faithful to the inner voice of truth and conscience! Then we are in the school that is preparing for the future Michael Community—the community that will bear the motto: "Michael-Sophia in nomine Christi."[88]

This is our calling: to assure it is Christ and Christ alone who stands at the center of all teachings by all teachers. True teachers honor his centrality. This will rightfully lead us through our trials of initiation in selflessness (Cancer). Let this New Moon plant the seed of catharsis.

**August 7:** Jupiter 14° Gemini opposite Pluto 14° Sagittarius: The Mystery of Golgotha. See the article in this *Journal*: "Patterns in the Language of the Stars: The 2013 Jupiter Pluto Opposition and the Jupiter Return of 9/11." For the next few days we stand as communities (Jupiter) before Our Father (Phanes). He is asking us what we have done for His Son as this Golgotha memory sounds again into time. Have we helped carry his burden? Or have we added to it? Wisdom is the grace born of suffering truth. Tyranny is the curse of those who refuse their suffering. There is a threshold between worlds, which is becoming thinner due to the weight of great ideas pressing into time. The illusory world of *maya* is falling. Situated between wisdom and tyranny are the agnostics who do not concern themselves with whether there is a Heaven or Hell. This growing disinterest in spiritual truth may be our proof that Hades/Pluto is preparing many souls for his world:

> Intensive engagement with and study of the most incisive occult problems of our time is still largely suppressed and avoided in today's anthroposophic movement. Likewise the equally significant and striking utterances by Steiner about the mystery of the reappearance of the etheric Christ and the impulse of his adversary, the Antichrist, in the twentieth and twenty-first centuries, are only seldom examined, illumined or cited, although the drastic nature of these comments, along with the radical form in which they were expressed, ought to place every student of Anthroposophy on the highest alert. In perception of and engagement with this highly topical phenomenon of our times, a scarcely explicable kind of paralysis seems to have taken hold of human spirits. There seems no other way to explain this paralysis than as the latent effect of the power of the Antichrist himself.[89]

If the work of adversarial beings is not countered they achieve a victory that has grave consequences for the Earth and her people. Humanity is now collectively facing Ahriman, who tempted Christ to turn stones into bread:

> This can be seen as substituting what is dead for what is living. If we consider the forces of evil involved in this process we realize that they are particularly directed against the world of nature, and are creating a fifth realm alongside the four kingdoms (mineral, plant, animal, human) which could be called the "Kingdom of Technology." The world of nature nurtures us with food and water and air. The Kingdom of Technology cuts us off from the world of nature and offers us a "virtual reality" in its place.[90]

Robert Powell wrote this astonishing passage seventeen years ago!

Rudolf Steiner spoke of how the activity of the etheric Christ would lead to a new connection with the lost Kingdom of Shambhala. Christ is coming to commune with the Divine Mother. We are to strengthen our connection to the kingdoms of nature and forbid Ahriman his success in spinning humanity into the dark caverns of a fifth kingdom. As Jupiter opposes Pluto near the Mystery of Golgotha, we can live into the promise that nature is awakening and new life forces are rising from the heart of the Earth (Shambhala). Those who know these truths are participating in something that makes the virtual worlds a mere cartoon. We can ask ourselves: What are we doing to connect to Christ, Natura, and wisdom?

---

88 Tomberg, *Inner Development*, p. 32.

89 Von Halle, *Descent into the Depths of the Earth*, p. 49.

90 Powell, *Christian Star Calendar 1996*.

| SIDEREAL GEOCENTRIC LONGITUDES : AUGUST 2013 Gregorian at 0 hours UT | | | | | | | | | | | |
|---|---|---|---|---|---|---|---|---|---|---|---|
| DAY | ☉ | ☽ | ☊ | ☿ | ♀ | ♂ | ♃ | ♄ | ⛢ | ♆ | ♇ |
| 1 TH | 14 ♋ 0 | 9 ♉ 12 | 18 ♎ 0R | 24 ♊ 32 | 16 ♌ 26 | 17 ♊ 25 | 13 ♊ 3 | 10 ♎ 21 | 17 ♓ 31R | 9 ♒ 44R | 14 ♐ 39R |
| 2 FR | 14 57 | 21 3 | 17 56 | 25 40 | 17 38 | 18 5 | 13 16 | 10 23 | 17 30 | 9 42 | 14 37 |
| 3 SA | 15 54 | 2 ♊ 52 | 17 50 | 26 53 | 18 49 | 18 45 | 13 28 | 10 26 | 17 29 | 9 41 | 14 36 |
| 4 SU | 16 52 | 14 42 | 17 42 | 28 12 | 20 1 | 19 24 | 13 41 | 10 28 | 17 28 | 9 39 | 14 35 |
| 5 MO | 17 49 | 26 36 | 17 31 | 29 35 | 21 13 | 20 4 | 13 53 | 10 31 | 17 27 | 9 38 | 14 34 |
| 6 TU | 18 47 | 8 ♋ 37 | 17 18 | 1 ♋ 3 | 22 24 | 20 44 | 14 6 | 10 34 | 17 27 | 9 36 | 14 33 |
| 7 WE | 19 44 | 20 45 | 17 4 | 2 36 | 23 36 | 21 23 | 14 18 | 10 36 | 17 26 | 9 35 | 14 31 |
| 8 TH | 20 42 | 3 ♌ 3 | 16 51 | 4 13 | 24 47 | 22 2 | 14 31 | 10 39 | 17 25 | 9 33 | 14 30 |
| 9 FR | 21 39 | 15 29 | 16 39 | 5 54 | 25 59 | 22 42 | 14 43 | 10 42 | 17 24 | 9 32 | 14 29 |
| 10 SA | 22 37 | 28 6 | 16 29 | 7 39 | 27 10 | 23 21 | 14 55 | 10 45 | 17 23 | 9 30 | 14 28 |
| 11 SU | 23 34 | 10 ♍ 54 | 16 23 | 9 27 | 28 22 | 24 0 | 15 7 | 10 48 | 17 21 | 9 28 | 14 27 |
| 12 MO | 24 32 | 23 54 | 16 19 | 11 19 | 29 33 | 24 40 | 15 19 | 10 52 | 17 20 | 9 27 | 14 26 |
| 13 TU | 25 30 | 7 ♎ 8 | 16 18 | 13 12 | 0 ♍ 44 | 25 19 | 15 31 | 10 55 | 17 19 | 9 25 | 14 25 |
| 14 WE | 26 27 | 20 39 | 16 18 | 15 8 | 1 56 | 25 58 | 15 43 | 10 58 | 17 18 | 9 24 | 14 24 |
| 15 TH | 27 25 | 4 ♏ 27 | 16 18 | 17 6 | 3 7 | 26 37 | 15 55 | 11 2 | 17 17 | 9 22 | 14 23 |
| 16 FR | 28 23 | 18 35 | 16 17 | 19 5 | 4 18 | 27 16 | 16 7 | 11 5 | 17 15 | 9 21 | 14 22 |
| 17 SA | 29 20 | 3 ♐ 0 | 16 13 | 21 5 | 5 29 | 27 55 | 16 18 | 11 9 | 17 14 | 9 19 | 14 21 |
| 18 SU | 0 ♌ 18 | 17 41 | 16 7 | 23 6 | 6 40 | 28 34 | 16 30 | 11 13 | 17 13 | 9 17 | 14 20 |
| 19 MO | 1 16 | 2 ♑ 32 | 15 59 | 25 8 | 7 51 | 29 13 | 16 41 | 11 17 | 17 11 | 9 16 | 14 19 |
| 20 TU | 2 13 | 17 25 | 15 49 | 27 9 | 9 2 | 29 52 | 16 53 | 11 20 | 17 10 | 9 14 | 14 18 |
| 21 WE | 3 11 | 2 ♒ 12 | 15 39 | 29 10 | 10 13 | 0 ♋ 31 | 17 4 | 11 24 | 17 8 | 9 12 | 14 17 |
| 22 TH | 4 9 | 16 44 | 15 29 | 1 ♌ 11 | 11 24 | 1 9 | 17 16 | 11 28 | 17 7 | 9 11 | 14 16 |
| 23 FR | 5 7 | 0 ♓ 54 | 15 20 | 3 12 | 12 34 | 1 48 | 17 27 | 11 33 | 17 5 | 9 9 | 14 15 |
| 24 SA | 6 4 | 14 39 | 15 14 | 5 11 | 13 45 | 2 27 | 17 38 | 11 37 | 17 3 | 9 7 | 14 15 |
| 25 SU | 7 2 | 27 56 | 15 11 | 7 10 | 14 56 | 3 5 | 17 49 | 11 41 | 17 2 | 9 6 | 14 14 |
| 26 MO | 8 0 | 10 ♈ 49 | 15 10 | 9 8 | 16 6 | 3 44 | 18 0 | 11 45 | 17 0 | 9 4 | 14 13 |
| 27 TU | 8 58 | 23 19 | 15 10D | 11 5 | 17 17 | 4 22 | 18 11 | 11 50 | 16 58 | 9 3 | 14 12 |
| 28 WE | 9 56 | 5 ♉ 31 | 15 10 | 13 0 | 18 27 | 5 1 | 18 22 | 11 54 | 16 57 | 9 1 | 14 12 |
| 29 TH | 10 54 | 17 31 | 15 10R | 14 55 | 19 37 | 5 39 | 18 33 | 11 59 | 16 55 | 8 59 | 14 11 |
| 30 FR | 11 52 | 29 23 | 15 8 | 16 48 | 20 48 | 6 18 | 18 43 | 12 4 | 16 53 | 8 58 | 14 10 |
| 31 SA | 12 50 | 11 ♊ 13 | 15 4 | 18 40 | 21 58 | 6 56 | 18 54 | 12 8 | 16 51 | 8 56 | 14 10 |

INGRESSES :

| | |
|---|---|
| 2 ☽ → ♊ 18:10 | 20 ♂ → ♋ 5: 4 |
| 5 ☽ → ♋ 6:48 | ☽ → ♒ 20:24 |
| ☿ → ♋ 6:53 | 21 ☿ → ♌ 9:52 |
| 7 ☽ → ♌ 18: 5 | 22 ☽ → ♓ 22:27 |
| 10 ☽ → ♍ 3:35 | 25 ☽ → ♈ 3:47 |
| 12 ♀ → ♍ 9: 2 | 27 ☽ → ♉ 13: 5 |
| ☽ → ♎ 11: 6 | 30 ☽ → ♊ 1:14 |
| 14 ☽ → ♏ 16:18 | |
| 16 ☽ → ♐ 19: 2 | |
| 17 ☉ → ♌ 16:34 | |
| 18 ☽ → ♑ 19:55 | |

ASPECTS & ECLIPSES :

| | | | |
|---|---|---|---|
| 1 ♂ □ ⛢ 3: 4 | 9 ☽ ☌ ♀ 22: 3 | ☽ N□ ☊ 21:26 | ☽ ☌ ☋ 8:16 |
| 3 ☽ ☌ A 8:58 | 11 ☽ ☍ ⛢ 11:57 | 20 ☽ ☍ ☿ 18:16 | ♀ ☍ ⛢ 17:53 |
| ☽ ☌ ♃ 21:54 | ☿ □ ♄ 18: 3 | 21 ☉ ☍ ☽ 1:43 | 27 ☉ ☍ ♆ 1:50 |
| ☽ ☍ ♇ 23:45 | 13 ☽ ☌ ♄ 6:47 | ♃ □ ⛢ 7: 4 | ♀ □ ♃ 21:52 |
| 4 ☽ ☌ ♂ 10: 4 | ☽ ☌ ☊ 16:19 | ☽ ☌ ♆ 11:29 | 28 ☉ □ ☽ 9:34 |
| ☉ □ ☊ 17:32 | 14 ☉ □ ☽ 10:55 | 23 ☽ ☍ ♀ 22:15 | 30 ☽ ☌ A 23:48 |
| 5 ☽ ☌ ☿ 6:48 | ☿ □ ☊ 14:14 | 24 ☽ ☌ ⛢ 4:17 | 31 ☽ ☍ ♇ 5:57 |
| 6 ☽ □S ☊ 16:52 | 17 ☽ ☌ ♇ 18:33 | ♀ □ ♇ 9:56 | ☽ ☌ ♃ 15:45 |
| ☉ ☌ ☽ 21:49 | ☽ ☍ ♃ 22: 3 | ☉ S☌ ☿ 20:55 | |
| 7 ♃ ☍ ♇ 23:24 | 18 ☽ ☍ ♂ 18:24 | 25 ☿ ☍ ♆ 23:15 | |
| 8 ☽ ☍ ♆ 12:33 | 19 ☽ ☌ P 1:37 | 26 ☽ ☍ ♄ 1:48 | |

| SIDEREAL HELIOCENTRIC LONGITUDES : AUGUST 2013 Gregorian at 0 hours UT | | | | | | | | | | | |
|---|---|---|---|---|---|---|---|---|---|---|---|
| DAY | Sid. Time | ☿ | ♀ | ⊕ | ♂ | ♃ | ♄ | ⛢ | ♆ | ♇ | Vernal Point |
| 1 TH | 20:39: 3 | 17 ♓ 47 | 5 ♎ 25 | 14 ♑ 0 | 0 ♊ 29 | 7 ♊ 13 | 16 ♎ 15 | 14 ♓ 54 | 8 ♒ 52 | 15 ♐ 31 | 5 ♓ 4'14" |
| 2 FR | 20:43: 0 | 23 0 | 7 1 | 14 57 | 0 59 | 7 18 | 16 17 | 14 55 | 8 53 | 15 31 | 5 ♓ 4'14" |
| 3 SA | 20:46:57 | 28 22 | 8 37 | 15 54 | 1 29 | 7 24 | 16 19 | 14 56 | 8 53 | 15 32 | 5 ♓ 4'14" |
| 4 SU | 20:50:53 | 3 ♈ 53 | 10 14 | 16 52 | 1 59 | 7 29 | 16 21 | 14 56 | 8 54 | 15 32 | 5 ♓ 4'14" |
| 5 MO | 20:54:50 | 9 33 | 11 50 | 17 49 | 2 28 | 7 34 | 16 23 | 14 57 | 8 54 | 15 32 | 5 ♓ 4'13" |
| 6 TU | 20:58:46 | 15 21 | 13 26 | 18 47 | 2 58 | 7 39 | 16 25 | 14 58 | 8 54 | 15 33 | 5 ♓ 4'13" |
| 7 WE | 21: 2:43 | 21 17 | 15 2 | 19 44 | 3 28 | 7 44 | 16 27 | 14 58 | 8 55 | 15 33 | 5 ♓ 4'13" |
| 8 TH | 21: 6:39 | 27 19 | 16 38 | 20 42 | 3 57 | 7 49 | 16 29 | 14 59 | 8 55 | 15 33 | 5 ♓ 4'13" |
| 9 FR | 21:10:36 | 3 ♉ 28 | 18 14 | 21 39 | 4 27 | 7 54 | 16 30 | 15 0 | 8 55 | 15 34 | 5 ♓ 4'13" |
| 10 SA | 21:14:32 | 9 41 | 19 50 | 22 37 | 4 56 | 7 59 | 16 32 | 15 0 | 8 56 | 15 34 | 5 ♓ 4'13" |
| 11 SU | 21:18:29 | 15 57 | 21 26 | 23 35 | 5 26 | 8 4 | 16 34 | 15 1 | 8 56 | 15 34 | 5 ♓ 4'13" |
| 12 MO | 21:22:26 | 22 16 | 23 2 | 24 32 | 5 55 | 8 10 | 16 36 | 15 1 | 8 56 | 15 34 | 5 ♓ 4'12" |
| 13 TU | 21:26:22 | 28 35 | 24 38 | 25 30 | 6 25 | 8 15 | 16 38 | 15 2 | 8 57 | 15 35 | 5 ♓ 4'12" |
| 14 WE | 21:30:19 | 4 ♊ 54 | 26 14 | 26 27 | 6 54 | 8 20 | 16 40 | 15 3 | 8 57 | 15 35 | 5 ♓ 4'12" |
| 15 TH | 21:34:15 | 11 10 | 27 50 | 27 25 | 7 24 | 8 25 | 16 42 | 15 3 | 8 58 | 15 35 | 5 ♓ 4'12" |
| 16 FR | 21:38:12 | 17 22 | 29 26 | 28 23 | 7 53 | 8 30 | 16 44 | 15 4 | 8 58 | 15 36 | 5 ♓ 4'12" |
| 17 SA | 21:42: 8 | 23 29 | 1 ♏ 1 | 29 20 | 8 22 | 8 35 | 16 45 | 15 5 | 8 58 | 15 36 | 5 ♓ 4'12" |
| 18 SU | 21:46: 5 | 29 29 | 2 37 | 0 ♒ 18 | 8 51 | 8 40 | 16 47 | 15 5 | 8 59 | 15 36 | 5 ♓ 4'12" |
| 19 MO | 21:50: 1 | 5 ♋ 22 | 4 13 | 1 16 | 9 20 | 8 45 | 16 49 | 15 6 | 8 59 | 15 37 | 5 ♓ 4'11" |
| 20 TU | 21:53:58 | 11 7 | 5 48 | 2 13 | 9 49 | 8 50 | 16 51 | 15 7 | 8 59 | 15 37 | 5 ♓ 4'11" |
| 21 WE | 21:57:55 | 16 43 | 7 24 | 3 11 | 10 19 | 8 55 | 16 53 | 15 7 | 9 0 | 15 37 | 5 ♓ 4'11" |
| 22 TH | 22: 1:51 | 22 10 | 8 59 | 4 9 | 10 48 | 9 0 | 16 55 | 15 8 | 9 0 | 15 38 | 5 ♓ 4'11" |
| 23 FR | 22: 5:48 | 27 27 | 10 35 | 5 7 | 11 17 | 9 6 | 16 57 | 15 9 | 9 0 | 15 38 | 5 ♓ 4'11" |
| 24 SA | 22: 9:44 | 2 ♌ 35 | 12 10 | 6 4 | 11 45 | 9 11 | 16 59 | 15 9 | 9 1 | 15 38 | 5 ♓ 4'11" |
| 25 SU | 22:13:41 | 7 33 | 13 46 | 7 2 | 12 14 | 9 16 | 17 1 | 15 10 | 9 1 | 15 39 | 5 ♓ 4'11" |
| 26 MO | 22:17:37 | 12 21 | 15 21 | 8 0 | 12 43 | 9 21 | 17 2 | 15 10 | 9 1 | 15 39 | 5 ♓ 4'10" |
| 27 TU | 22:21:34 | 17 0 | 16 56 | 8 58 | 13 12 | 9 26 | 17 4 | 15 11 | 9 2 | 15 39 | 5 ♓ 4'10" |
| 28 WE | 22:25:30 | 21 30 | 18 32 | 9 56 | 13 41 | 9 31 | 17 6 | 15 12 | 9 2 | 15 40 | 5 ♓ 4'10" |
| 29 TH | 22:29:27 | 25 52 | 20 7 | 10 54 | 14 10 | 9 36 | 17 8 | 15 12 | 9 3 | 15 40 | 5 ♓ 4'10" |
| 30 FR | 22:33:24 | 0 ♍ 5 | 21 42 | 11 52 | 14 38 | 9 41 | 17 10 | 15 13 | 9 3 | 15 40 | 5 ♓ 4'10" |
| 31 SA | 22:37:20 | 4 11 | 23 18 | 12 50 | 15 7 | 9 46 | 17 12 | 15 14 | 9 3 | 15 41 | 5 ♓ 4'10" |

INGRESSES :

| |
|---|
| 3 ☿ → ♈ 7: 9 |
| 8 ☿ → ♉ 10:31 |
| 13 ☿ → ♊ 5:22 |
| 16 ♀ → ♏ 8:36 |
| 17 ⊕ → ♒ 16:31 |
| 18 ☿ → ♋ 2: 4 |
| 23 ☿ → ♌ 11:49 |
| 29 ☿ → ♍ 23:30 |

ASPECTS (HELIOCENTRIC +MOON(TYCHONIC)) :

| | | | | | |
|---|---|---|---|---|---|
| 2 ☽ ☌ ♂ 21: 3 | ☿ ☌ ☊ 9: 7 | ♀ □ ⊕ 8:20 | 19 ☽ ☍ ☿ 7:29 | ☿ ☍ ⊕ 20:55 | ☽ □ ⛢ 8: 7 |
| 3 ☽ ☌ ♃ 9:15 | ♀ ☌ ♄ 21:30 | ☽ ☌ ♀ 11: 3 | ☽ □ ♄ 23: 5 | 25 ☿ ☍ ♆ 7:17 | ☽ ☌ ♂ 8:13 |
| ⊕ □ ♄ 10:39 | 8 ☽ ☍ ♆ 11:22 | ☿ ☌ ♃ 13:18 | 21 ☿ □ ♄ 0:42 | 26 ☽ ☍ ♄ 11:54 | ☽ ☍ ♇ 9: 1 |
| 4 ☽ □ ⛢ 0:28 | 9 ☿ □ ♆ 21: 7 | 15 ☽ □ ♆ 7:42 | ☽ □ ♀ 9:34 | ☿ □ ♀ 23:30 | |
| ☽ ☍ ♇ 1:41 | 10 ☽ □ ♂ 13:23 | ☿ □ ⛢ 15: 4 | ☽ ☌ ♆ 11:10 | 27 ⊕ ☌ ♆ 1:33 | |
| 5 ☿ ☍ ♀ 13: 7 | ☽ □ ♃ 18:42 | ☿ ☍ ♇ 17: 8 | 22 ♀ □ ♆ 0:10 | 28 ☽ □ ♆ 7: 0 | |
| 6 ☿ ☍ ♄ 4:21 | 11 ☽ ☍ ⛢ 7:38 | 17 ☽ ☍ ♂ 9: 7 | ☿ N□ ☊ 6:16 | 29 ☽ ☍ ♀ 6: 3 | |
| ☽ □ ♀ 11: 1 | ☽ □ ♇ 8:40 | ☽ ☍ ♃ 9:13 | 23 ☽ □ ♃ 14:18 | 30 ☽ □ ☿ 2:11 | |
| ☽ □ ♄ 15:29 | 12 ☿ ☌ P 1:47 | ♂ ☌ ♃ 12:56 | ☽ □ ♂ 18:42 | ♀ ☌ ☋ 2:32 | |
| ☿ □ ⊕ 16:37 | 13 ☽ ☌ ♄ 16:57 | ☽ □ ⛢ 19:46 | 24 ☽ ☌ ⛢ 0:54 | ☽ ☌ ♃ 21: 2 | |
| 7 ☽ □ ☿ 2: 1 | 14 ☿ ☌ ♂ 8:19 | ☽ ☌ ♇ 20:37 | ☽ □ ♇ 1:46 | 31 ♂ □ ⛢ 5:47 | |

Sun enters third decan of Cancer, ruled by the Moon and associated with the flank of the Great Bear (Ursa Major).

**August 10:** Sun 22° Cancer: Death of Lazarus (July/15/32). Lazarus lay in the sleep of initiation that led to his death and later to his resurrection through Christ. What happened in these eleven days between his sleep and his being raised from the dead? A contemporary seer speaks words that pierce many hearts with their truth. She speaks of the three days of an initiation trial that were to culminate in Lazarus returning to his body. But this was not to be. After having descended to the heart of the Mother in the depths of the Earth, Lazarus was dangerously distracted:

> But as he passed upward through the dark spheres of the sub-earthly world, he forgot to honor John's [the Baptist] admonitions to turn away his ears from the cries of the fallen souls.
>
> Having felt always a deep concern for humanity, he wanted only to save these lost souls. Poised for a time on the precipice of indecision, wondering how he might aid at least some few of these souls, he was swept away suddenly in a tornado of darkness.
>
> At first, just one soul reached out for him. But as he gave heed to this one soul's cry, others joined in, until Lazarus was overwhelmed and overtaken by their entreaties.
>
> Their cries were strange, as if sounding through mire. It was as if the depths of the Earth swallowed their cries. And yet, Lazarus could not turn his ears away. The souls could perceive his light, and they wanted that light for themselves.
>
> As Lazarus was swept away, I saw John reach out for him. But he reached in vain, for the dark forces had waxed too powerful—Lazarus was enshrouded in the darkness, and John could not retrieve him.
>
> And so was Lazarus lost in Hell. He witnessed many horrors, the horrors of all humanity's works of darkness. Holocausts and wars passed before my spiritual eyes, just as they were being projected by the wretched souls at Lazarus. I saw the most degenerate of desires acted out, desires that would moreover remain always unfulfilled.
>
> Lazarus lost touch with the love of the Mother that he had come to know. His memory of Her love was being rapidly snuffed out in the darkness. I saw him grow rigid, lying in a spiritual grave surrounded by the spiritually dead. His light became as the guttering flame of a candle, about to expire for want of air.[91]

On this day, and for the next eleven days, we can imagine the magnetic spell of forces from beings working into our time from the darkness of the underworld. We are to follow the admonitions of John, and turn our ears from this. We are to "grail" for the light in spite of the presence of dark adversarial forces. We are not to be distracted. The Light is the only eternal truth!

Midway through the time Lazarus spent entrapped in darkness, the Sun opposed Neptune (See the article in this *Journal* by David Tresemer). William Bento also has an article in this *Journal*: "Finding Ahriman's Influence in the Dark Shadows of Neptune." Both of these articles address the realm of Hades and the influence of ahrimanic beings in our time. Just as Lazarus faced the devil in the depths of Hades, so, too, are we to face his presence in the world and find the courage to name what is evil.

**August 11:** Mercury 10°48 Cancer square Saturn 10°48 Libra: Jesus faces the Pharisees (June/9/32). When Mercury was at this same location, Jesus was in Jericho for the last time. He was healing many people and pouring his love out to all he met.

> The disciples, on the contrary [in contrast to the peace of Jesus], were anxious and dissatisfied on account of Jesus' so unconcernedly exposing himself to the snares that the enraged Pharisees, of whom almost a hundred were gathered here from different parts of the country, sought to prepare for him. They sent messengers to Jerusalem to consult as to how they could take him into custody. The Apostles too were in a certain dread, as if they thought that Jesus laid himself open to danger and treated with the people rather rashly.[92]

---

91 Isaacson, *Through the Eyes of Mary Magdalene*, book 1, pp. 189–190.
92 Emmerich, *TLJC*, vol. 3, p. 475.

With Mercury at this degree, the greatest of all healers was working in spite of the presence of his enemies. His courage and selflessness (Cancer) made his disciples nervous. The Pharisees (Saturn) could not bear to see him exercising free and certain authority, utilizing the laws that they were to guard and protect. Therefore, a stormy tension was brewing.

We can become attuned to any restraint that may bind us from expressing freely what lives in our heart. We are to selflessly proclaim these truths in spite of enemies in our midsts. There will always be authority figures who feel that guarding past truths is more important than hearing the new truths. As creation is continuous, we can trust that there will always be new truths and new heretics. Where do our minds (Mercury) allow us to be limited in our service to our mission (Saturn)? We must use caution, courtesy, diplomacy, and intelligence, but we are not to hold back due to fear.

**August 12:** Sun 25° Cancer: Birth of the Nathan Mary (July/17/17 BC). The Nathan Mary bore the vessel for the Logos. Purity and gentleness are remembered today. At this birth, Venus, Mars and Moon were all conjunct Regulus, the heart of the Lion, providing a beautiful contemplation for the purity of heart we are all striving to attain—the purity of the Nathan Mary.

Venus enters Virgo: "May the soul fathom worlds" (Steiner, *Twelve Moods of the Zodiac*). Venus was in Virgo at the conception of the Virgin Mary. This is an imagination of the purity we achieve when our souls unite with the World Soul. Venus in the Virgin seeks to comprehend the phenomenon of the world in order to bring peace to the phenomena of the inner soul life. When inner and outer are in communion, the soul moves in harmony with Sophia—the World Soul—the Virgin.

**August 17:** Sun enters Leo: "Invigorate with senses' might" (Steiner, *Twelve Moods of the Zodiac*). William Bento illumines this mantra:

> One of our most primal gifts we received from the Cosmos was the possibility to be endowed with senses, to have the capacity to witness the creation of all things upon the Earth. It is a gift we can so easily take for granted. Yet, when we ponder how the Sun being has gathered the forces of the entire zodiac and poured them down upon our uprightness in such a way as to create portals into the external world, we can sensitize ourselves to feel how this streaming of forces has never ceased. It is there in the infusion and invigoration of our senses' activity in grasping the world with all its beauty.

The first decan, ruled by Saturn, is associated with the faint constellation of Leo Minor, the Lesser Lion, above Leo and below the Great Bear. The virtue: *Compassion becomes Freedom*. This freedom is the foundation of the spiritualized "I."

**August 19: ASPECT:** Jupiter 16°50 Gemini: The Jupiter return of 9/11. Since 9/11, Jupiter has traveled through all twelve constellations and today returns to where it was on September 11, 2001. In these twelve years Sophia has woven a new revelation through the gathering path of wise old Jupiter. This benevolent giant of cosmic wisdom has collected teachings from each of the twelve colonies of beings who rule the mighty forces of the stars. At the time of the attacks, in Gemini, she bore witness to the effects of ungoverned duality that had torn asunder the fabric of world consciousness, and had thus allowed entrance to dark adversarial forces. As Jupiter traveled onward to the great beings in the constellation of Cancer, Sophia beheld the grace of selflessness through which a willing humanity would find the catharsis necessary for us to overcome our inner adversaries. In Leo she beheld how freedom is the reward of compassion; for, freedom signifies we have overcome our inner antipathies. In Virgo she beheld the new language of nature, so that she could teach humanity how to hear the travails of Mother Earth. In Libra she rested at the great fulcrum point of equilibrium, from whence streams the power of Michaelic thoughts into earthly reality. In Scorpio she was shown all that stands as the working of occult dynamics behind seemingly ordinary events and circumstances, and how perception of these secrets is gained through the power of patience. In Sagittarius she was shown how the animal nature must be tamed lest it come to speech and cause greater divisiveness. In Capricorn she beheld the courage that is necessary in order to push back the old thinking and awaken to a new thinking. In Aquarius the Holy Spirit breathed upon Jupiter and thus opened a portal revealing the apocalyptic future. In Pisces Sophia heard the resounding tones of love as they expanded through the watery firmament of Earth; she saw, too, the torment that could grasp souls who dove too deeply into matter. In Aries she beheld the Word of Christ as a healing force that could awaken human devotion, through which people would found new ideals. And in Taurus the world thoughts of the spirit echoed to her the understanding that could create progress into hitherto unexplored dimensions of harmony in union with divine will.

With all these gifts, Jupiter has today returned to us. She is shining from the octave of Gemini—where two, the higher and the lower "I," can become one, pouring forth the wisdom gained from the twelve constellations over these past twelve years. We are to take stock of what has become in the world since 9/11. What do we see? Have the towers of greed and power continued to fall, or have they instead been fortified?

*Jupiter knows what stood behind the events of 9/11 and is bearing witness for Sophia, who is urging us to wake up so we can receive her holy wisdom and become open to new possibilities. She is gathering her armies of peace. She wonders if we will be among them, or if the sleep of Gethsemane will fall upon us, thus leading us further into the deepening ruts of materialism.* Let us honor Jupiter, this planet of wisdom, by laying aside what we think we know, in order to seek a higher knowing—a knowing whose time must come! Throughout Jupiter's twelve-year journey, Christ has been present, for as he hung on the cross, Jupiter was quite near to where it began and ended its twelve-year journey. Sophia is offering us a choice, for she can no longer bear our suffering. Some will hear her call, others will falter. This is a day to joyfully celebrate an expansive opening, born of faithfulness, to the star of our higher self. Do we have the perseverance to allow the two to become, ever more, one? (See the opening article to the commentaries: "The Patterns in the Language of the Stars.")

**August 20:** Full Moon: Sun 3° Leo opposite Moon 3° Aquarius: The Raising of Lazarus (Jul/26/32).

The Raising of Lazarus was an archetypal event for humanity, demonstrating the possibility in the future, following Golgotha, for the human being to receive the breath of life from the creative source of the living Word, received as an initiatory breath from the etheric life body of Christ Jesus. This was the octave of the baptism in the Jordan, wherein a new consciousness was to be born of water, understanding water as the physical agent of cleansing and the faithful bearer of vibratory imprint.

The importance of the desert experience for the Israelites was a movement forward away from the Egyptian mystery tradition where the spiritual aspirant left the physical body during the three-day temple sleep to unite with the spiritual world, which could be born as an imprint thereafter as a source of inspiration throughout life. In contrast, the Israelite's mission under the guidance of Yahweh was to make a step forward, undertaking the work of calling down the spiritual world into the physical body—with the goal of bringing an imprint of the spiritual world into the "I" of the individual.[93]

Dr. Powell goes on to explain how the miracle of the Raising of Lazarus was a baptism by air, which denotes a rebirth, after which the transformed consciousness of the one initiated develops the ability to work with conscience (a bestowal from the beings of Saturn), which means working with the spiritual world. How does this apply to us?

The miracle of The Raising of Lazarus works irrespective of time and place, where that which is forgotten is remembered, where that which sleeps is awakened, and where that which is dead is brought to life. Lazarus, according to Rudolf Steiner, was the individuality who became Christian Rosenkreutz, he who brought the Rose Cross and founded Rosicrucianism. The mysteries of the depths open as the heights are revealed; and as the heights are opened, so also are the depths. This is the work before us: facing the darkness in pursuit of the Light, as "Knights of the Threshold."

---

93 Powell, *Elijah Come Again*, p. 133.

This is a day to listen for the world call to awaken from our sleep in the increasingly ominous illusions of materialism. Are we willing to be called from the grave of our entombment?

**ASPECT**: Jupiter 17° Gemini square Uranus 17° Pisces: The Last Anointing through Pentecost.

Jupiter was at this degree during the entire Passion of Christ, his death and resurrection, all the way to Pentecost. These solemn and profound memories today square Uranus at the degree that remembers the work of two historical figures who worked with heinously anti-Christian forces—Joseph Stalin and Adolf Hitler. Uranus at this degree found Hitler, the master speech-maker, letting loose his talents on the German people in a whirlwind campaign that resulted in a later victory of the Nazi party, propelling Hitler into the national spotlight. Meanwhile in Russia, at this same time, man-made famine devastated the Ukraine through Stalin's collectivization project.

With Jupiter square to Uranus under the influence of these strong memories, and on the day when the Sun remembers the monumental imprint of the Raising of Lazarus, we are encouraged to free our minds from our temporary concerns and turn to spiritual thoughts and practices. Uranus's revolutionary propensities will work for the Light to the degree there are human beings on Earth who are willing to receive its revelation from *above*. If "ten righteous people" cannot be found, tyranny (lower Jupiter) can seed destructive revolution (lower Uranus) in order to open the door to an even greater evil, thus working against the divine principles of unity that Christ offered at the Mystery of Golgotha.

**Mars enters Cancer**: "Toward powerful self-probation" (Steiner, *Twelve Moods of the Zodiac*). Mars was in Cancer at the Ascension, at Pentecost, and at the death of the Nathan Mary. Mars is asking us to penetrate deeper levels of our soul with the light-filled warmth of spirit, just as it completely enveloped those who were present at these above-mentioned events. This leads us to powerful self-probation, which is the act of testing our conduct and character—allowing us to redeem our failures.

**August 22**: Sun 5° Regulus; the Lion's Heart. In the closing invocation by Hermes to Tat on the mysteries of the zodiac, Hermes opens to the great beings who indwell the constellation of Leo: (turning to the North):

> Holy Uriel, thou who bears the memory of the Golden Age of Saturn, whence streams the foundation of human will, pray strengthen the will of all who humbly seek to unite themselves with Christ and His Mission.[94]

Regulus is one of the four Royal Stars of Persia.

> Already then in ancient Persia, Zarathustra spoke of the four royal stars as the four "foundation stones" of the zodiac—Aldebaran, the Bull's eye, the central star of the Bull; Regulus, the Lion's heart, shining from the breast of the Lion; Antares, the red-glowing Scorpion's heart, the central star of the Scorpion; and bright Fomalhaut in the mouth of the Southern Fish, beneath the stream of water flowing from the urn of the Waterman.[95]

In the Foundation Stone Meditation, given by Rudolf Steiner, the spirits of the elements in the East, West, North and South are to hear the prayer, and the beings in the cosmos above are "trigger points" for the directions mirrored upon the Earth below:

Aldebaran: The Bull's eye is the watcher in the East—15° Taurus.
Antares: The Scorpion's heart is the watcher in the West—15° Scorpio.
Regulus: The Lion's heart is the watcher in the North—5° Leo.
Fomalhaut: The Southern Fish is the watcher in the South—9° Aquarius.

**August 24: ASPECT**: Venus 14° Virgo square Pluto 14° Sagittarius: Conception of the Nathan Mary (Oct/24/18 BC). Venus rules the waters of life in the soul: "The serpent poured water like a river out of his mouth after the woman, to sweep her away with the flood. But the Earth came to the help of the woman, and the Earth opened its mouth and swallowed the river which the dragon had poured from his mouth" (Revelation 12:15–16).

---

94 *CHA*, Closing Invocation; The Mystery of the Zodiac.
95 *CHA*, The Mystery of the Zodiac.

Water carries sound, and the waters of Venus thus organize souls into karmic groups through the compatible resonance between their respective soul-toning. There are two primary types of water: The sea of glass that surrounds the throne of God, and the fanatical, agitated waters of aggression that seek to sweep others away in the flood of their selfish desires and zealotry:

> The difference between the waters of the "sea of glass" before the throne and the waters poured forth by the serpent is that the former are the calm, peace and stability of contemplation, or pure perception—they are "as glass, like crystal"—whilst the latter are in movement, "poured forth," "like a river," in the pursuit of an aim, namely that of sweeping away the woman.[96]

With Venus square Pluto, there is a tension between the peaceful toning of divine Love (Pluto/Phanes), which begets contemplation and stability, and the aggressive agitation that seeks to sweep away the souls (Venus) of the masses in the frenzy of amped-up distractions and dramas; behind which specific agendas are operating (Pluto/Hades). With Venus very close to where it was at the conception of the Nathan Mary, contemplation of her being calms our souls, thus edging us nearer to the "sea of glass."

ACPECT: Superior conjunction Mercury and Sun 6° Leo: Regulus. This potent position in the zodiac quakes with the power of the heart. This superior conjunction is within 3° of the Sun's position at the Raising of Lazarus, and one degree from the regal star of Regulus. Superior conjunction means Mercury is on the far side of the Sun—furthest from Earth. During superior conjunctions it is the will pole in the human being that is quickened. We can imagine ourselves receiving spiritual intuitions into the unconscious depths of our will. Such content may be found in the night through dreams and lucid experiences, or may rise to consciousness in flashes of understanding. We are encouraged to open our hearts to receive divine in-streaming from the cosmos. On November 1st an inferior conjunction will occur. Ideally, we nurture the intuitions now gained in order to follow them into conscious flowering in approximately 2½-months' time. We can give our minds (Mercury) over to our Angels in hopes of being raised from the sleep of forgetfulness that has come like a pall over the world. Even the dead heard when Jesus called out: "Lazarus come forth!" May the deadened parts of our soul awaken to the call of the Sun/Son.

**August 25: ASPECT:** Mercury 9° Leo opposite Neptune 9° Aquarius: Conception of John the Baptist (Sept/9/3 BC). Heliocentric Mercury was at this degree when the individuality of Elijah was conceived into this world as he who would become known as John the Baptist. The loss of John's spiritual vision contributed to his death, for without this perception John did not will to live longer:

> As far as he was concerned, he had already fulfilled his mission, having recognized and baptized the Messiah. He had said, with respect to the Messiah, "He must increase, and I must decrease." Here, already, he had renounced the deeper will to live. The Angels and higher spiritual beings, who had helped him up until the Baptism, were obliged gradually to withdraw. Thus John the Baptist was already "spiritually beheaded" before he became actually beheaded.[97]

As the loss of John's angelic support withdrew, he lost his certainty that Jesus was the Messiah. The loss of John's vision for his future contributed to his death. Yet all this was as it was to be, for John was to become the guardian soul of the disciples of Christ after his death. With heliocentric Mercury remembering John's conception, we are strengthened in our efforts to pass through the density of material thinking. This enables us to find the spiritual guidance that empowers us to imagine a benevolent future and apply our minds (Mercury) to forming imaginations that serve not only our personally intended future, but also the future intended for the whole of humanity.

Heliocentric Neptune was at this same degree during the second temptation of Christ in the wilderness (Nov/28/29). This was the temptation to plunge from the pinnacle of the temple. Mercury aspecting Neptune can bring forth astounding

---

96 Anon, *Meditations on the Tarot*, p. 271.

97 CHA, The Ministry up to the Beheading of John the Baptist.

inspirations (Neptune/Night), or the lowest cults of inspiration from the sub-earthly realms. The dragon that Ahriman has unleashed upon the world would like us to think only materialistically, therefore beheading us and plunging us from the pinnacle of the consciousness soul. Sophia, on the other hand, inspires us with the formative and toning in-streaming from the future, forming vessels within our souls into which her divine inspiration may resound.

With Neptune conjunct Fomalhaut (one of the Royal Stars of Persia), our minds can find their way into the divine aspects of Neptune. This means that draconian ahrimanic noise is silenced through the grace of Mary-Sophia (higher Neptune). This is our task this day; to bear the harmonies of peace, and sound them into each moment of our day. Aquarius is the bearer of the holy waters of the Spirit who approaches on spiritual airwaves. May we find quietude!

**August 26: ASPECT:** Venus 17° Virgo opposite Uranus 17° Pisces: Uranus remembers Stalin and Hitler. From an historical perspective it would seem that these two evil beings were competing for the attention of the Antichrist. Stalin's collectivization caused untold misery, using starvation as an unrivaled form of genocide. The famine affected forty million people, including those who died from it and those who suffered its consequences. It extended throughout all of Ukraine, much of Kazakhstan, and the plains of the Don, the Kuban, and the northern Caucasus. In 1933 alone, six million people died of famine-related causes. It is notable that the areas which had resisted collectivization most vigorously in 1929-1930 were, for the most part, those that suffered the worst effects of the famine. For example, some 14,000 riots and peasant revolts protesting collectivization had taken place in 1930; more than eighty-five percent of these occurred in regions that were hardest hit by the famine that would come later, in 1932-33. Quite simply put, this was *not* a natural disaster but rather a calamity carefully engineered by Stalin himself. Also at this degree, Uranus remembers the Russian NKVD (The People's Commissariat for Internal Affairs) repressing an uprising in Chechnya. The NKVD conducted mass extrajudicial executions, ran the Gulag, suppressed resistance, conducted mass deportation, and engaged in espionage and political assassinations at home and abroad.

Meanwhile, in Germany, Hitler was busy preparing his rise to infamy in a whirlwind campaign that brought the Nazis to power as the second largest political party in Germany. No good would come of this.

With Venus opposing the planet of both revelation and revolution, we can take care to protect our rights and form karmic affiliations (Venus) that are immune from the propaganda perpetuated by mass media (Uranus).

**Sun 9° Leo opposite Neptune 9° Aquarius:** The Sun faces either Sophia, or the dragon that sought to sweep her away. In the articles in this Journal by William Bento and David Tresemer, it becomes evident that the lower influences of Neptune cast dark shadows, possessing souls and writing infamous history. Neptune represents the realm of the Goddess Night/Sophia, and inversely the murky waters of the ahrimanic hoards. Neptune was opposite to this degree in the 1930s when both adversaries to Christ—Hitler and Stalin—were weaving their fateful webs around the people of the USSR and Germany. America was recovering from the crash of '29 and the agricultural practices that would contribute to the dust bowl were accelerating. The demonic side of Neptune is here obvious. With the Sun standing where Neptune was during these dreadful times, we can open ourselves to receive the light of Christ-filled heart forces, bestowing the courage needed to bring the dragon under our feet.

With Neptune and Uranus in close relationships to the rising of evil forces in the 1930s, this entire year is one in which caution and wakefulness are required in the spirit of *Michael-Sophia in nomine Christi.*

**August 27: ASPECT:** Venus 18° Virgo square Jupiter 18° Gemini: The Passion of Christ. Jupiter at 18° Gemini is still within 1° of its position at the Passion of Christ, and at this degree Christ was appearing to his disciples in his resurrection body. With Venus facing the memory of the founding of the community of Eternal Israel (Jupiter), we can reflect upon the nature of our acquaintances and ask if the inspirations streaming from these affiliations are in line with our values. We are encouraged to find the Christ in his etheric presence, and to form communities seeking the same goals.

Sun enters the second decan of Leo, ruled by Jupiter and associated with the tail of the Great Bear, Ursa Major.

**August 28: Sun 10° Leo:** The Healing of the Nobleman's Son (Aug/3/30) (John 4:46-54). In this second miracle of Christ, he healed the stream of heredity—the present worked back onto the past. Selathiel (the nobleman) had given himself to his king. He came to Christ to beg that his son Joel be healed. Joel had been adopted by his King, Zorobabel; even this he had given away. Selathiel was a *kings-man*. This meant he had to suppress his own "I" to serve his master's "I." This suppression weakens the "I." The weakness of the father's "I" created a physical weakness in the son's *body*. The boy's blood was too weak to carry an "I" and therefore his blood became inflamed. In his illness the boy constantly repeated: "Jesus, the prophet of Nazareth, alone can help me!" In desperation Selathiel rode to find Jesus. Jesus spoke: "Go, thy son liveth!" When Selathiel asked if this was really true, Jesus responded: "Believe me, in this very hour he has been cured." The nobleman's faith in Christ restored his "I" to uprightness, and simultaneously healed his son. Jesus Christ gave the nobleman a new name. Instead of *basilikos* (Kings Man) he was called *pater* (father); he became "father of his own house." This fatherhood involves not only responsibility in the physical world, but also the appointment of being a spiritual authority in the home. This story teaches the absolute necessity of fathering children with spiritual authority. This healing reveals the fact of the power of the vertically aligned, Christ-centered "I" over any horizontal influence in the hereditary stream. We may contemplate today where we may be compromising our true self with excuses born of some hereditary story, or to gain favor with any powers of this world. Have we become a satellite of any person or bloodline, or collective body of thought? There is a great deal of reality being created by satellite-humans. Are we moons, or suns? Do we create, or are we puppets of another's creation? Are we taking up the responsibility of spiritually fathering our children?

**August 30: Sun 12° Leo:** Death of the Nathan Mary (Aug/5/12). "Not long after the event in the Temple at the Passover of AD 12, the Nathan Mary died. Rudolf Steiner describes how, seventeen years later, at the baptism in the Jordan, the Nathan Mary was spiritually united with the Solomon Mary." (*Chron.*, p.116)

> At the moment of this baptism in the Jordan, the mother (the Solomon Mary) was aware of something like the climax of the change that had come about in her. She was then between her forty-fifth and forty-sixth years. She felt as though pervaded by the soul of that mother (the Nathan Mary) who had died, the mother of the Jesus child who in his twelfth year had received the Zarathustra individuality. Thus the spirit of the other mother had come upon the mother with whom Jesus had held that conversation. And she felt herself as the young mother who had once given birth to the Jesus child of Saint Luke's Gospel.[98]

The Nathan Mary comes as Grace for those who seek her.

## SEPTEMBER

The Sun begins in Leo and enters Virgo on the 17th. The outer planets of Uranus, Neptune and Pluto begin the month still retrograde; Pluto stations direct on the 21st. The waning crescent Moon will conjunct Mars in Cancer before sunrise to begin the month, and the Moon is New on the 5th in Leo. The new crescent will conjunct Venus on the 8th in Virgo and should make a fantastic sunset view. Saturn is about 15° farther to the south, within the stars of Libra; the growing Moon catches up to Saturn the next day (the 9th). Then, Venus moves to join Saturn on the 18th, a sparkling diamond best seen as the day fades into night in the west. The next day (the 19th) brings the Full Moon (Sun in

---

[98] Steiner, *The Fifth Gospel*, p. 93.

Leo, Moon in Aquarius.) September 22nd brings the Equinox: equal day and night throughout the globe, marking an important place on our journey around the Sun—an opportunity to sink into the larger energies of the Archangelic powers. By the end of the month, the waning Moon again joins Jupiter in Gemini in the pre-dawn glow.

**September 5:** New Moon 18° Leo: The Pharisees turn against Jesus (Aug/11/30). This morning, Pharisees from Upper and Lower Sepphoris drew Jesus into a great dispute concerning the strict teaching on marriage and divorce that he had recently expounded in Lower Sepphoris:

> Some Pharisees came to him and asked, "Is it lawful for a man to divorce his wife for any cause:" He answered, "Have you not read that the one who made them at the beginning made them 'male and female', and said, 'For this reason a man shall leave his father and mother and be joined to his wife, and the two shall become one flesh'? So they are no longer two, but one flesh. Therefore what God has joined together, let no one separate." They said to him, "Why then did Moses command us to give a certificate of dismissal and to divorce her?" He said to them, "It was because you were so hardhearted that Moses allowed you to divorce your wives, but from the beginning it was not so. And I say to you, whoever divorces his wife, except for unchastity, and marries another commits adultery."[99]

How do we understand these words in our times?

The male has a feminine etheric body, and the female a masculine etheric body. How did it come about? This differentiation, this separation into male and female, came about relatively late, after the "days" of creation. There was no such differentiation in the human being who arose on the sixth "day" as the common purpose of the Elohim. At that time all human beings had a bodily nature in common. We can best describe it (so far as representation is possible at all) by saying that the physical body was more etheric and the etheric body somewhat denser than is the case today. A differentiation between physical and etheric, a densification on the side of the physical, only occurred later under the influence of Jahve-Elohim. You will appreciate that we cannot speak of the human creation of the Elohim as separately male and female in the sense of today; the Elohim-man was at the same time both male and female, undifferentiated. Thus man, in the sense expressed by the Elohim in the words "Let us make man," was still undifferentiated, still male and female at the same time. Through this deed of the Elohim the bisexual man was created. That is the meaning of the words translated *male and female created he them*. The words do not refer to man and woman in the sense of today, but to the undifferentiated human being, the male-female human being.[100]

Thus this passage illumines the statement: "But from the beginning it was not so." It was the common purpose of the Elohim to create a being both male and female—in the image of the Elohim. We are to tend both of these natures within us. We had to leave our Father and Mother and descend into Earth evolution in order to gain our freedom. In order for us to free ourselves from enchainment to matter, it will take this union of the two principles working harmoniously within us. This can be seen as a reflection of Christ (our masculine spirit) and Sophia (our feminine soul) working together as the Lamb and his Bride. One cannot separate one from the other. What God has joined together must not be separated.

Perhaps what Moses recognized in his people was that some had become so rigid and hardhearted that they had caused suffering to their soul—their wives. And this divorce from their inner Sophia is a form of adultery in the world of spirit where Christ and his Bride are One; therefore they were given a certificate that formally declared the unchaste nature of their own souls, allowing them to divorce. The day after this encounter, the Pharisees sought to murder Jesus, so estranged had become their souls due to their hardheartedness.

*It is the heart that unites the two poles of male and female within us. With this New Moon occurring in Leo, our hearts can be quickened for the work of reconciliation. We can contemplate the state of*

---

99 Matthew 19: 3-9.

100 Steiner, *Genesis: Secrets of the Bible Story of Creation*, lect. 10.

SIDEREAL GEOCENTRIC LONGITUDES : SEPTEMBER 2013 Gregorian at 0 hours UT

| DAY | ☉ | ☽ | ☊ | ☿ | ♀ | ♂ | ♃ | ♄ | ♅ | ♆ | ♇ |
|---|---|---|---|---|---|---|---|---|---|---|---|
| 1 SU | 13 ♌ 48 | 23 ♊ 6 | 14 ♎ 58R | 20 ♌ 31 | 23 ♍ 8 | 7 ♋ 34 | 19 ♊ 4 | 12 ♎ 13 | 16 ♓ 49R | 8 ♒ 54R | 14 ♐ 9R |
| 2 MO | 14 46 | 5 ♋ 4 | 14 50 | 22 21 | 24 18 | 8 13 | 19 14 | 12 18 | 16 47 | 8 53 | 14 9 |
| 3 TU | 15 44 | 17 12 | 14 40 | 24 9 | 25 28 | 8 51 | 19 25 | 12 23 | 16 45 | 8 51 | 14 8 |
| 4 WE | 16 42 | 29 31 | 14 29 | 25 57 | 26 38 | 9 29 | 19 35 | 12 28 | 16 43 | 8 49 | 14 8 |
| 5 TH | 17 40 | 12 ♌ 2 | 14 19 | 27 43 | 27 48 | 10 7 | 19 45 | 12 33 | 16 41 | 8 48 | 14 7 |
| 6 FR | 18 39 | 24 45 | 14 10 | 29 27 | 28 58 | 10 45 | 19 55 | 12 38 | 16 39 | 8 46 | 14 7 |
| 7 SA | 19 37 | 7 ♍ 40 | 14 2 | 1 ♍ 11 | 0 ♎ 8 | 11 23 | 20 5 | 12 43 | 16 37 | 8 45 | 14 6 |
| 8 SU | 20 35 | 20 48 | 13 57 | 2 53 | 1 18 | 12 1 | 20 14 | 12 48 | 16 35 | 8 43 | 14 6 |
| 9 MO | 21 33 | 4 ♎ 7 | 13 55 | 4 34 | 2 27 | 12 39 | 20 24 | 12 54 | 16 33 | 8 41 | 14 5 |
| 10 TU | 22 32 | 17 36 | 13 55D | 6 14 | 3 37 | 13 17 | 20 33 | 12 59 | 16 31 | 8 40 | 14 5 |
| 11 WE | 23 30 | 1 ♏ 17 | 13 55 | 7 53 | 4 46 | 13 54 | 20 43 | 13 5 | 16 29 | 8 38 | 14 5 |
| 12 TH | 24 28 | 15 9 | 13 56 | 9 31 | 5 55 | 14 32 | 20 52 | 13 10 | 16 26 | 8 37 | 14 4 |
| 13 FR | 25 27 | 29 13 | 13 57R | 11 8 | 7 5 | 15 10 | 21 1 | 13 16 | 16 24 | 8 35 | 14 4 |
| 14 SA | 26 25 | 13 ♐ 26 | 13 55 | 12 43 | 8 14 | 15 47 | 21 10 | 13 21 | 16 22 | 8 33 | 14 4 |
| 15 SU | 27 24 | 27 48 | 13 52 | 14 18 | 9 23 | 16 25 | 21 19 | 13 27 | 16 20 | 8 32 | 14 4 |
| 16 MO | 28 22 | 12 ♑ 15 | 13 47 | 15 51 | 10 32 | 17 3 | 21 28 | 13 33 | 16 18 | 8 30 | 14 4 |
| 17 TU | 29 21 | 26 42 | 13 41 | 17 24 | 11 41 | 17 40 | 21 37 | 13 38 | 16 15 | 8 29 | 14 4 |
| 18 WE | 0 ♍ 19 | 11 ♒ 4 | 13 34 | 18 55 | 12 50 | 18 17 | 21 45 | 13 44 | 16 13 | 8 27 | 14 3 |
| 19 TH | 1 18 | 25 14 | 13 27 | 20 25 | 13 58 | 18 55 | 21 54 | 13 50 | 16 11 | 8 26 | 14 3 |
| 20 FR | 2 16 | 9 ♓ 7 | 13 22 | 21 54 | 15 7 | 19 32 | 22 2 | 13 56 | 16 8 | 8 24 | 14 3 |
| 21 SA | 3 15 | 22 40 | 13 18 | 23 22 | 16 15 | 20 9 | 22 10 | 14 2 | 16 6 | 8 23 | 14 3D |
| 22 SU | 4 13 | 5 ♈ 52 | 13 17 | 24 49 | 17 24 | 20 47 | 22 18 | 14 8 | 16 4 | 8 21 | 14 3 |
| 23 MO | 5 12 | 18 42 | 13 16D | 26 15 | 18 32 | 21 24 | 22 26 | 14 14 | 16 1 | 8 20 | 14 3 |
| 24 TU | 6 11 | 1 ♉ 12 | 13 17 | 27 40 | 19 40 | 22 1 | 22 34 | 14 20 | 15 59 | 8 19 | 14 3 |
| 25 WE | 7 10 | 13 25 | 13 19 | 29 4 | 20 48 | 22 38 | 22 41 | 14 27 | 15 57 | 8 17 | 14 4 |
| 26 TH | 8 8 | 25 27 | 13 20 | 0 ♎ 26 | 21 56 | 23 15 | 22 49 | 14 33 | 15 54 | 8 16 | 14 4 |
| 27 FR | 9 7 | 7 ♊ 21 | 13 21 | 1 47 | 23 4 | 23 52 | 22 56 | 14 39 | 15 52 | 8 14 | 14 4 |
| 28 SA | 10 6 | 19 13 | 13 21R | 3 8 | 24 12 | 24 29 | 23 4 | 14 45 | 15 49 | 8 13 | 14 4 |
| 29 SU | 11 5 | 1 ♋ 7 | 13 19 | 4 26 | 25 19 | 25 6 | 23 11 | 14 52 | 15 47 | 8 12 | 14 4 |
| 30 MO | 12 4 | 13 8 | 13 16 | 5 44 | 26 27 | 25 42 | 23 18 | 14 58 | 15 45 | 8 11 | 14 5 |

INGRESSES :

| | | | | | | | |
|---|---|---|---|---|---|---|---|
| 1 | ☽ → ♋ | 13:52 | 19 | ☽ → ♓ | 8:11 | | |
| 4 | ☽ → ♌ | 0:56 | 21 | ☽ → ♈ | 13:14 | | |
| 6 | ☿ → ♍ | 7:32 | 23 | ☽ → ♉ | 21:41 | | |
| | ☽ → ♍ | 9:47 | 25 | ☿ → ♎ | 16:21 | | |
| | ♀ → ♎ | 21:18 | 26 | ☽ → ♊ | 9: 9 | | |
| 8 | ☽ → ♎ | 16:37 | 28 | ☽ → ♋ | 21:46 | | |
| 10 | ☽ → ♏ | 21:45 | | | | | |
| 13 | ☽ → ♐ | 1:20 | | | | | |
| 15 | ☽ → ♑ | 3:39 | | | | | |
| 17 | ☽ → ♒ | 5:29 | | | | | |
| | ☉ → ♍ | 16:10 | | | | | |

ASPECTS & ECLIPSES :

| | | | | | | | | | | | |
|---|---|---|---|---|---|---|---|---|---|---|---|
| 2 | ☽ ☌ ♂ | 6:35 | 12 | ☉ □ ☽ | 17: 7 | | ♀ ☌ ♄ | 20:52 | 28 | ☽ ☌ ♃ | 7:51 |
| | ☽ S ☊ | 19: 5 | 14 | ☽ ☌ ♇ | 1: 3 | 19 | ☉ ☍ ☽ | 11:11 | | ♀ □ ♂ | 13:30 |
| 4 | ☽ ☍ ♆ | 17:51 | | ☽ ☍ ♃ | 13: 4 | 20 | ☿ □ ♃ | 2:19 | 30 | ☽ S ☊ | 0:15 |
| 5 | ☉ ☌ ☽ | 11:35 | | ☿ □ ♇ | 20:25 | | ☽ ☌ ♅ | 12:19 | | ☉ □ Π | 8:56 |
| 6 | ☽ ☌ ☿ | 10: 8 | 15 | ☽ ☌ P | 16:55 | 21 | ☽ ☍ ☿ | 1:24 | | | |
| 7 | ☽ ☍ ♅ | 16:21 | 16 | ☽ N ☊ | 2:31 | 22 | ☽ ☌ ☋ | 13:46 | | | |
| 8 | ☽ ☌ ♀ | 20:44 | | ☿ ☍ ♅ | 6:39 | | ☽ ☍ ♄ | 15:31 | | | |
| 9 | ♂ □ ♄ | 11: 5 | | ☽ ☍ ♂ | 8:18 | | ☽ ☍ ♀ | 23:40 | | | |
| | ☽ ☌ ♄ | 15:46 | 17 | ♄ ☌ ☊ | 4:11 | 27 | ☉ □ ☽ | 3:54 | | | |
| | ☽ ☌ ☊ | 17:27 | | ☽ ☌ ♆ | 19:37 | | ☽ ☍ ♇ | 13:35 | | | |
| 11 | ♂ □ ☊ | 0:40 | 18 | ♀ ☌ ☊ | 14: 2 | | ☽ ☌ A | 18:23 | | | |

SIDEREAL HELIOCENTRIC LONGITUDES : SEPTEMBER 2013 Gregorian at 0 hours UT

| DAY | Sid. Time | ☿ | ♀ | ⊕ | ♂ | ♃ | ♄ | ♅ | ♆ | ♇ | Vernal Point |
|---|---|---|---|---|---|---|---|---|---|---|---|
| 1 SU | 22:41:17 | 8 ♍ 9 | 24 ♏ 53 | 13 ♒ 48 | 15 ♊ 36 | 9 ♊ 51 | 17 ♎ 14 | 15 ♓ 14 | 9 ♒ 4 | 15 ♐ 41 | 5 ♓ 4'10" |
| 2 MO | 22:45:13 | 12 0 | 26 28 | 14 46 | 16 4 | 9 56 | 17 16 | 15 15 | 9 4 | 15 41 | 5 ♓ 4'10" |
| 3 TU | 22:49:10 | 15 44 | 28 3 | 15 44 | 16 33 | 10 2 | 17 17 | 15 16 | 9 4 | 15 42 | 5 ♓ 4' 9" |
| 4 WE | 22:53: 6 | 19 23 | 29 38 | 16 42 | 17 1 | 10 7 | 17 19 | 15 16 | 9 5 | 15 42 | 5 ♓ 4' 9" |
| 5 TH | 22:57: 3 | 22 56 | 1 ♐ 13 | 17 41 | 17 30 | 10 12 | 17 21 | 15 17 | 9 5 | 15 42 | 5 ♓ 4' 9" |
| 6 FR | 23: 0:59 | 26 23 | 2 48 | 18 39 | 17 58 | 10 17 | 17 23 | 15 18 | 9 5 | 15 43 | 5 ♓ 4' 9" |
| 7 SA | 23: 4:56 | 29 46 | 4 23 | 19 37 | 18 26 | 10 22 | 17 25 | 15 18 | 9 6 | 15 43 | 5 ♓ 4' 9" |
| 8 SU | 23: 8:53 | 3 ♎ 4 | 5 58 | 20 35 | 18 55 | 10 27 | 17 27 | 15 19 | 9 6 | 15 43 | 5 ♓ 4' 9" |
| 9 MO | 23:12:49 | 6 18 | 7 33 | 21 34 | 19 23 | 10 32 | 17 29 | 15 19 | 9 7 | 15 44 | 5 ♓ 4' 9" |
| 10 TU | 23:16:46 | 9 28 | 9 8 | 22 32 | 19 51 | 10 37 | 17 31 | 15 20 | 9 7 | 15 44 | 5 ♓ 4' 8" |
| 11 WE | 23:20:42 | 12 35 | 10 43 | 23 30 | 20 20 | 10 42 | 17 32 | 15 21 | 9 7 | 15 44 | 5 ♓ 4' 8" |
| 12 TH | 23:24:39 | 15 38 | 12 18 | 24 29 | 20 48 | 10 47 | 17 34 | 15 21 | 9 8 | 15 45 | 5 ♓ 4' 8" |
| 13 FR | 23:28:35 | 18 38 | 13 53 | 25 27 | 21 16 | 10 52 | 17 36 | 15 22 | 9 8 | 15 45 | 5 ♓ 4' 8" |
| 14 SA | 23:32:32 | 21 36 | 15 28 | 26 25 | 21 44 | 10 57 | 17 38 | 15 23 | 9 8 | 15 45 | 5 ♓ 4' 8" |
| 15 SU | 23:36:28 | 24 32 | 17 3 | 27 24 | 22 12 | 11 3 | 17 40 | 15 23 | 9 9 | 15 46 | 5 ♓ 4' 8" |
| 16 MO | 23:40:25 | 27 25 | 18 38 | 28 22 | 22 40 | 11 8 | 17 42 | 15 24 | 9 9 | 15 46 | 5 ♓ 4' 8" |
| 17 TU | 23:44:22 | 0 ♏ 16 | 20 13 | 29 21 | 23 8 | 11 13 | 17 44 | 15 25 | 9 9 | 15 46 | 5 ♓ 4' 7" |
| 18 WE | 23:48:18 | 3 6 | 21 48 | 0 ♓ 19 | 23 36 | 11 18 | 17 46 | 15 25 | 9 10 | 15 47 | 5 ♓ 4' 7" |
| 19 TH | 23:52:15 | 5 55 | 23 23 | 1 18 | 24 4 | 11 23 | 17 48 | 15 26 | 9 10 | 15 47 | 5 ♓ 4' 7" |
| 20 FR | 23:56:11 | 8 42 | 24 57 | 2 16 | 24 32 | 11 28 | 17 49 | 15 27 | 9 11 | 15 47 | 5 ♓ 4' 7" |
| 21 SA | 0: 0: 8 | 11 28 | 26 32 | 3 15 | 25 0 | 11 33 | 17 51 | 15 27 | 9 11 | 15 48 | 5 ♓ 4' 7" |
| 22 SU | 0: 4: 4 | 14 14 | 28 7 | 4 14 | 25 28 | 11 38 | 17 53 | 15 28 | 9 11 | 15 48 | 5 ♓ 4' 7" |
| 23 MO | 0: 8: 1 | 16 59 | 29 42 | 5 12 | 25 56 | 11 43 | 17 55 | 15 29 | 9 12 | 15 48 | 5 ♓ 4' 7" |
| 24 TU | 0:11:57 | 19 44 | 1 ♑ 17 | 6 11 | 26 24 | 11 48 | 17 57 | 15 29 | 9 12 | 15 49 | 5 ♓ 4' 6" |
| 25 WE | 0:15:54 | 22 28 | 2 52 | 7 10 | 26 52 | 11 53 | 17 59 | 15 30 | 9 12 | 15 49 | 5 ♓ 4' 6" |
| 26 TH | 0:19:51 | 25 13 | 4 27 | 8 9 | 27 19 | 11 58 | 18 1 | 15 30 | 9 13 | 15 49 | 5 ♓ 4' 6" |
| 27 FR | 0:23:47 | 27 58 | 6 1 | 9 7 | 27 47 | 12 3 | 18 3 | 15 31 | 9 13 | 15 49 | 5 ♓ 4' 6" |
| 28 SA | 0:27:44 | 0 ♐ 44 | 7 36 | 10 6 | 28 15 | 12 8 | 18 4 | 15 32 | 9 13 | 15 50 | 5 ♓ 4' 6" |
| 29 SU | 0:31:40 | 3 30 | 9 11 | 11 5 | 28 42 | 12 14 | 18 6 | 15 32 | 9 14 | 15 50 | 5 ♓ 4' 6" |
| 30 MO | 0:35:37 | 6 17 | 10 46 | 12 4 | 29 10 | 12 19 | 18 8 | 15 33 | 9 14 | 15 50 | 5 ♓ 4' 6" |

INGRESSES :

| | | |
|---|---|---|
| 4 | ♀ → ♐ | 5:31 |
| 7 | ☿ → ♎ | 1:41 |
| 16 | ☿ → ♏ | 21:41 |
| 17 | ⊕ → ♓ | 16: 7 |
| 23 | ♀ → ♑ | 4:32 |
| 27 | ☿ → ♐ | 17:40 |

ASPECTS (HELIOCENTRIC +MOON(TYCHONIC)) :

| | | | | | | | | | | | | | | |
|---|---|---|---|---|---|---|---|---|---|---|---|---|---|---|
| 1 | ♂ ☍ ♇ | 4:38 | | ☽ □ ♂ | 20:26 | | ♀ ☌ ♇ | 4:20 | 21 | ☽ □ ♂ | 4:20 | 30 | ⊕ □ ♃ | 6:27 |
| | ☿ □ ♃ | 10:49 | 9 | ☽ ☌ ☿ | 5: 8 | | ☽ ☍ ♂ | 14:21 | | ☽ □ ♀ | 7:54 | | ☽ □ ♄ | 9:55 |
| 2 | ☿ ☍ ♅ | 20:52 | | ☽ ☌ ♄ | 23:49 | | ☿ ☌ ☋ | 16: 2 | 22 | ☽ ☍ ♄ | 22:31 | | | |
| | ☿ □ ♇ | 23:42 | 10 | ♀ ☍ ♃ | 23:42 | 16 | ☽ □ ♄ | 9: 3 | 24 | ☽ □ ♆ | 15:40 | | | |
| 3 | ☽ □ ♄ | 0:10 | 11 | ☽ □ ♆ | 13:36 | 17 | ☽ □ ☿ | 7:24 | 25 | ☿ ☌ A | 2:19 | | | |
| | ☿ □ ♂ | 6: 1 | 12 | ☿ ☌ ♄ | 15:36 | | ☽ ☌ ♆ | 20:48 | | ☽ ☍ ☿ | 23:24 | | | |
| 4 | ☽ ☍ ♆ | 18:23 | 13 | ☽ ☍ ♃ | 19:48 | 19 | ♀ ☍ ♂ | 15: 0 | 27 | ☽ ☌ ♃ | 9:35 | | | |
| 6 | ☽ □ ♀ | 17: 5 | | ♀ □ ♅ | 22:37 | 20 | ☿ □ ♆ | 4: 7 | | ☽ □ ♅ | 16:32 | | | |
| 7 | ☽ □ ♃ | 4:58 | 14 | ☽ □ ♅ | 3:15 | | ☽ □ ♃ | 4: 8 | | ☽ ☍ ♇ | 17: 9 | | | |
| | ☽ ☍ ♅ | 14: 0 | | ☽ ☌ ♀ | 3:49 | | ☽ ☌ ♅ | 11: 7 | 28 | ☽ ☌ ♂ | 18:58 | | | |
| | ☽ □ ♇ | 14:45 | | ☽ ☌ ♇ | 3:52 | | ☽ □ ♇ | 11:43 | 29 | ☽ ☍ ♀ | 18:36 | | | |

*harmony between our spirit and soul natures. This will be reflected to us from those around us—especially our spouses.* Are we chaste (loyal and decent to both our soul and the souls of others)? Are we tolerant and loving in the world? This is a day to honor both the sword and the chalice, for we need both to travel the path as Grail Knights seeking Christ and Sophia.

**September 6: ASPECT:** Venus conjunct Spica 29° Virgo: Jesus visited the two remaining Magi (Sept/21/32). The ancient clairvoyants saw Virgo as a young woman holding an ear of corn or shaft of wheat. The tip of the shaft of wheat marks the star Spica. This heavenly Virgin holds the mysteries of feminine wisdom, and the star Spica blesses us with the grace and love of this wisdom. Beneath the feet of this woman we find the body of Hydra—"the Serpent"—stretching its undulating life force throughout the entire region beneath Virgo. To find the blessing of the wheat, the daily bread, we must overcome the temptation of the serpent. This is a day that calls our attention to the awakening of the Divine Feminine within and without, in nature, in the depths of the Earth, and in the heights of Heaven.

The Sun was conjunct Spica at the conversation between Master Jesus and the Virgin Mary just before the Baptism in the Jordan, as well as when Jesus visited the two remaining kings in their tent city in September of AD 32. Mysteries of esotericism surround both of these events. The meeting of Christ Jesus with the Magus who had borne the gift of gold to the "Radiant Star" babe he had sought those many years before, was especially momentous:

> He knew what lay ahead for Christ Jesus; it had been written in the stars—what would happen and when.
>
> Up to this time, Jesus had been gradually receiving the Christ Being into his spiritual bodies, which began to happen at the Baptism in the Jordan. The Being of Christ was descending more and more into Jesus' body—this could be likened to the gestation period before birth—it was as if the Being of Christ was gestating within the spiritual bodies of Jesus. This aspect of his Incarnation is a very challenging and sensitive thing to explain. I gained the understanding that as the Christ entered more and more into the physical body, he encountered limitations he had never before experienced.
>
> At this very important juncture in Jesus' ministry, the Magus was there to bring to his consciousness what was written in the stars about his ultimate sacrifice, and when it would take place. Jesus knew of this sacrifice of course, but it was brought to the forefront of his consciousness during his visit with the grandfatherly sage, who revered Jesus, recognizing him as the bearer of the Christ. The Magus knew that Jesus would come to visit him.[101]

Not only did the Magus bestow knowledge to Christ, but Christ also bestowed knowledge to the Magus, for in this meeting, the heathen religions of old were brought into the light of Christ for their development into the far future.

Sophia, Divine Wisdom, works and weaves in mysterious ways and it is this divine being that is potentized when any of the planets or the Sun transit the memories she has inscribed into the akashic chronicle at this degree where lies Spica. As it is Venus, the planet of love, who today transits these profound memories, we can know that divine Light is striving to illumine us. This is a day to attend to the presence of Wisdom and Love in all the subtleties of natural phenomena (Virgo).

**September 7:** Sun enters third decan of Leo, ruled by Mars and associated with the constellation of the Hunting Dogs (Canes Venatici).

Venus enters Libra: "Being beholds itself within Being" (*Twelve Moods of the Zodiac*, Rudolf Steiner). With Venus in Libra we seek the middle ground—the absolute fulcrum—where our soul finds it inner balance. Here is the place where Michaelic thoughts find entrance to the soul. Only in balance can we perceive the subtle, and in this quiet place we behold ourselves within the Beings of the spiritual worlds.

Venus was in Libra at the raising of Nazor and at the healing of the blind.

---

[101] Isaacson, *Through the Eyes of Mary Magdalene*, book 2.

**Sept. 8:** Sun 20° Leo. Uranus was at 20° Leo at the conversion of Lucifer. Christ on the cross signified the Tree of Life, raised up for the first time on Earth since the expulsion of human beings from Paradise. God had set up his cross in the wilderness of the world, as the seed of redemption—a sign for all posterity. And it was this situation to which the planet Uranus (20° Leo) bore witness as it rose about two o'clock that afternoon. Lucifer, beholding the innocent Son of Man on the cross, was overcome by his guilt and underwent a profound conversion. This conversion can be conceived of as the beginning of the redemption of the Cosmic Lucifer (see *CHA, The Mystery of Golgotha*). Uranus brings lightning bolts to either illumine or destroy the works of human beings, depending upon their moral character.

> In order to arrive at Illumination, a subtle temptation must be met. Instead of thinking becoming a vehicle for divine truth, it can become "brilliant" and then "electrified." And there is a world of difference between an illumined person and a brilliant thinker. The brilliant thinker is able to combine thoughts to his own pleasing, to make everything conform to the way in which he wants to see things, whilst an illumined person is interested solely in divine truth, for which he sacrifices his personal viewpoints.[102]

Lucifer has a profound connection to the planet Uranus, and it is the unredeemed aspects of Lucifer that are able to twist truth into knots that cannot easily be untangled. The world is intricately woven with these distortions of truth. Media provide a vehicle through which "brilliant thinkers" can fashion mass opinion. When the truth is altered even just one degree, the arc of projection will cause it to miss its mark. This is a very good day to meditate on the uncompromising power of truth. How do we live it, and how do we protect our children from becoming pawns of the virtual world's brilliance? The heart is the great thinker and Uranus in Leo points us to this future potential. Negative Uranus works against this potential, luring human souls into enticing webs spun by a spider who is the master of illusions. Can we sacrifice our attachment to our personal viewpoints so that our minds can open to the mighty revelations of Cosmic Thoughts? Can we spend this day detached from technology (Uranus)?

**September 9: ASPECT:** Mars 12°54 Cancer square Saturn 12°54 Libra: The Raising of Lazarus (July/26/32). Chernobyl nuclear disaster (April/26/1986). Pluto was at this degree (12° Libra) three weeks before the Chernobyl disaster, as subearthly forces were swelling. The catastrophic accident occurred as the Sun, shortly thereafter, came into opposition with retrograde Pluto (11°). Pluto governs both the spiritually radiant constructive powers of a transformed physical body (resurrection body), and its opposite, the destructive inversion that is nuclear power born of Hades. The Chernobyl accident rivals Fukushima; they are the two worst non-military nuclear disasters in history.

In contrast to nuclear forces stands the raising of Lazarus from the dead. This occurred with Mars square Saturn (Aries/Libra) in close square to today's Mars position (11° Aries). Through the contrast between these two events, we witness the incredible work of divine forces of goodness in juxtaposition to the heinous work of evil forces.

With nuclear reactors operating across the globe, and with nuclear-tipped weapons loosed in ordinary warfare, we can ask: From where do we find protection against these subearthly forces? The subearthly realm was addressed by Rudolf Steiner in a conversation with Countess Johanna von Keyserlingk at the end of the *Agricultural Course* (Pentecost 1924):

> Keyserlingk: "Is the Earth's interior of gold, originating from the empty space within the Sun, actually belonging back there again?" He replied, "Yes, the interior of the Earth is of gold." For the sake of certainty, I asked him further, "Herr Doctor, if I stand here upon the ground, then beneath me, deep in the interior of the Earth, is the golden land. If I were to attain to freedom from sin and were to remain standing in the depths, the demons would not [get] me and I would be able to pass through them to the golden land. Is this so?" He replied, "If one passes through them together with Christ,

---

102 Powell, *Hermetic Astrology* vol.2, p. 312.

then the demons are unable to harm one, but otherwise they would be able to destroy one!" He added the significant words, "However, they are able to become our helpers. Yes, this is so. The path is right, but it is very difficult."[103]

These subearthly forces are able to tear us apart if we are not enveloped in protective forces—protection emanating from the Christ. It is just this protection that is the essence of Dr. Powell's book, *Cultivating Inner Radiance and the Body of Immortality*. We can begin to create a connection, through the etheric Christ, to the golden heart of the Mother in the depths of the Earth. Here the substance of the Sun has been breathed in by the Earth, as one of the many gifts we received through the Mystery of Golgotha. This golden substance will eventually form the planet known in *Occult Science* as future Vulcan existence—when the Earth will have achieved its mission of becoming a planet of Love—a Sun.

In this conversation with the Countess Keyserlingk, Steiner indicates the necessity of calling upon Christ as these subearthly powers become ever more present in daily life, and he speaks also of the future Manichaean mission of transforming evil.... "The path is right, but it is very difficult." We can contemplate the power of the resurrection body and begin our work in developing a strong field of protection through our connection to Christ. The healthy soul must partake in moral nourishment in food, in images, in thoughts, in feelings and in deeds. The planet Mars marks the expanded size of our Earth at the time of ancient Moon evolution when humanity was receiving their astral bodies. The content of soul nourishment determines whether these bodies are healthy or ill:

> If the world brings impressions that are not satisfying into the soul, then the inner fire of wishes [desires] in the soul is felt more strongly on account of the lack of satisfaction, and one can speak of the "thirst" of the soul. On the other hand, if the world does not bring any new impressions arousing wishes into the soul so that the life of wants finds less and less to desire in the world and thus the inner life of the soul focuses upon itself, then a "hunger" arises in the soul. However, if it is a matter of deeper moral demands, expectations, and longings of the soul, then such a soul feels the balance between inner demands upon the world and the stream of impressions from without as *righteousness*. If the soul's primary focus is morality, then it will be the life question of morality which will govern the relationship between inner drives and outer reality. Then the constantly changing "hunger" and "thirst" of the soul becomes a "hunger and thirst for righteousness." For righteousness is the condition of the moral harmonization of the sentient soul, just as the satisfaction of hunger and thirst is the condition of the natural harmonization of the body. The sentient soul – that part of the soul which lives in perceptions from without and impressions and perceptions from within – is morally oriented toward righteousness, just as the body is oriented toward food and drink.[104]

In these profound thoughts, Tomberg gives answers to pressing challenges in psychology. *The soul that naturally hungers and thirsts for righteousness must find this reflected in the outer world, or else the soul will turn against itself in hopeless reaction to the abandonment it has experienced as a consequence of the hollow world that surrounds it. If the soul's thirst is not quenched it will be overcome by the desire nature. If the soul's hunger is not appeased it will lose interest in life.* Does the former inform us about the causes of addiction? Does the latter inform us about the causes of depression? What impressions are we feeding the soul? Why are pathologies increasing? The astral body must find its sustenance through inner desire for, and contemplations of, truth! To the extent a culture fails in nourishing souls with moral impressions, the culture will be ill. An ill culture reflects soul sickness.

Today Lazarus, impressions representative of divine truth, and the golden center of the Earth, come together as the antidote to forces working into our cultures from subearthly realms. May we remember that our work is to establish catharsis

---

103 Powell, *The Christ Mystery*, p. 33.

104 *Starlight*, Advent 2011, excerpts from previously unpublished material by Valentin Tomberg.

born of purification (Mars) so that we may find the path of the Rose Cross—a cross seeded by Lazarus in his descent to the Mother in the golden center of the Earth. In this way we will be true to our destiny (Saturn).

**Sept. 10:** Sun 22° Leo: Death of the Virgin Mary (Aug/15/44). After the Ascension of Christ, John (the son of Zebedee) took the Blessed Virgin Mary to Ephesus where she lived until her death. This great being, the Virgin Mary, goes before us into future Jupiter evolution. She ascended at her death to take up this mission on behalf of all who are uniting into the stream of Eternal Israel. She who was Eve, the mother of all, prepares the way. It is the Blessed Virgin who helps all her children find their way home:

> A short time before the Blessed Virgin's death, as she felt the approach of her reunion with her God, her Son, and her Redeemer, she prayed that there might be fulfilled what Jesus had promised to her in the house of Lazarus at Bethany on the day before his Ascension. It was shown to me in the spirit how at that time, when she begged him that she might not live for long in this vale of tears after he had ascended, Jesus told her in general what spiritual works she was to accomplish before her end on Earth. He told her, too, that in answer to her prayers the apostles and several disciples would be present at her death, and what she was to say to them and how she was to bless them.... After the Blessed Virgin had prayed that the apostles should come to her, I saw the call going forth to them in many different parts of the world.... I saw all, the farthest as well as the nearest, being summoned by visions to come to the Blessed Virgin.[105]

We are encouraged to keep our focus on the mission we have come to serve, and not be unduly burdened by the "vale of tears" that is the world in which we must continue our striving. May we keep the light of goodness shining for all, and especially for the children. Today we remember to behold our common Mother, the Earth, and all her elemental beings—for her redemption rests upon each of us.

In the still heart compassion pours from an eternal spring.

**September 15: ASPECT:** Mercury 16° Virgo opposite Uranus 16° Pisces: The blessing of the Virgin Mary. Heliocentric Mercury was at this degree the day following Pentecost. Always before the apostles departed to perform baptisms, as well as when they returned at day's end, they were blessed by the Blessed Virgin Mary:

> Before departing for the Pool of Bethsaida to consecrate the water and administer Baptism, they received on their knees the benediction of the Blessed Virgin. Before Jesus' Ascension, this ceremony was performed standing. On the following days I saw this blessing given whenever the apostles left the house, and also on their return.[106]

The apostles of Christ, on bended knee, received this blessing before and after their daily work. There is a story that emerges from this picture telling of the spiritual power that was working in Mary after Whitsun. It was then that she united with Holy Sophia. In order to receive a blessing from one so united, one would have to be on one's knees.

Also today, Uranus is square to where Jupiter was on September 11, 2001 (16° Gemini); and Uranus has been at this degree for the past few weeks. The Jupiter return of this event occurred this past August 19th. With the wing-footed messenger reminding us of the blessings of Sophia (Virgo), and Uranus stimulating the memory of 9/11, we can fall on our knees before the mysteries of world events in hopes that we receive the blessings of Inspiration, which reveal to our humbled minds (Mercury) just what stands behind what appears to be explainable. *Many events are showing the work of adversaries who seek to destroy all that is holy and pure. Since 2001 our world has changed drastically, our freedoms have diminished, and headlines speak of the work of the Asuras—the dreaded beings whose trademark is acts of destructions against the physical body of humanity and the Earth. May we find the solace of kneeling before Sophia, that we may find the strength and courage to perceive new*

---

105 Emmerich, *LBVM*, pp. 363–364.

106 Emmerich, *LJC*, vol. 4, p. 431.

*revelations (Uranus) unveiling who it is that stands behind the mask of illusion in the gathering storm of a world that has forgotten how to love (Pisces).*

**Sept. 17:** Sun enters Virgo: "Behold worlds, O soul!" (Steiner, *Twelve Moods of the Zodiac*)

William Bento illumines this mantra:

> The more engaged we are with the phenomena of Natura, the accompanying rhythms of social life, and the planetary and starry celestial dances above us, the more awe and wonder arise in our soul. This beholding is more than a seeing; it is an immersion into a conscious participation-mystique. The mystery of worlds is precisely what the longing of the soul seeks to know; and so this beholding is indeed not a static event, but the movement of the soul into worlds known and unknown.

The first decan is ruled by the Sun, and associated with the constellation of the Cup (Crater): here we can think of the Grail chalice held by the Queen of Peace, represented by the Virgin. The virtue of Virgo: *Courtesy becomes tactfulness of heart*. The inner work of descent (Persephone) brings the awareness of self-knowledge. Hydra "the Serpent" stretches its undulating life force throughout the entire region beneath Virgo. To become self-aware, we must confront the serpent.

**Sun 0° 19' Virgo:** The Moon (portal to both Angels and demons) stood here at the beginning of the forty days in the wilderness. In describing these forty days of continual temptation of Christ, Anne Catherine Emmerich depicts how Christ never once looked at his tempters. Instead he addressed himself directly to his Father in Heaven. This is a powerful example for humanity, who is now facing the united activity of the tempters on a global scale. May we remember to keep our attention on the in-streaming of spiritual Light and Love! This is what guides us through the changes so very necessary in our time. What we attend to will grow, and as the Sun enters Virgo, the sign of the Divine Sophia, we are to tend our garden gate. This means having proper boundaries. Our boundaries protect us and allow us to choose what shall enter and what shall not. The "B" in eurythmy is the gesture for the constellation of Virgo. This gesture characterizes the forming of our essential cloak of protection. May we thus practice wrapping ourselves in the protecting mantle of Sophia. And may we stand with the serpent underfoot!

**September 18: ASPECT:** Venus conjunct Saturn 13° Libra: Healing of the blind youth Manahem (Oct/6/30). The Sun was at 14° Libra at this healing, directly opposite its position two-and-a-half years later at the Crucifixion. Dr. Powell explains this as a prophetic shining in of the Son/Sun of righteousness, the Light of the World:

> Human souls living in paradise prior to the Fall saw spiritually, beholding the world as a revelation of God. But with the Fall a transformation of man's seeing took place, whereby the eyes of human beings were opened, and henceforth they saw the "bare facts" of the world without the illumination of God. They no longer saw the world as an expression of God, which is spiritual seeing, but for its own sake, estranged from God, which is ordinary seeing. Manahem did not want to see this God-estranged world, and be being born blind he retained spiritual seeing. For, generally, either the external world is seen in an illusory way, which is the tendency of the left eye, or in a God-less way, which is the tendency of the right eye, or in the case of blindness the outer world is not seen at all, which gives the possibility of seeing with the third eye, the spiritual organ located in the region of the forehead between the right and left eye. Manahem's blindness meant he saw only with the third eye.[107]

Due to Manahem's faith in Jesus Christ his sight was restored without dampening his ability to see also with his spiritual eye. With Venus and Saturn mediating this memory we too can be quickened by the shining in of the Sun of righteousness that stands opposite to today's conjunction from the place of the Crucifixion. Venus governs our desire nature. Saturn places the weight of the iron necessity of our destiny onto the scale of justice (Libra). Are we willing to cast off the light of illusory seeing that is born of ego attachments? Are we willing to

---

107 *CHA*, The Sun Chronicle in the Life of the Messiah.

cast off the dark light of godlessness that is born of believing in matter over spirit?

**September 19: Full Moon:** Sun 1° Virgo opposite Moon 1° Pisces: Behold the Lamb of God (Oct/7/29). Nine days after his baptism by John, Jesus and his followers drew near to that baptismal place, where John was teaching. As John saw Christ in the distance he cried out "Behold the Lamb of God," and spoke the following words:

> This is the one I meant when I said, "A man who comes after me has surpassed me because he was before me." I myself did not know him, but the reason I came baptizing with water was that he might be revealed to Israel.
>
> Then John gave this testimony: "I saw the Spirit come down from Heaven as a dove and remain on him. And I myself did not know him, but the one who sent me to baptize with water told me, "The man on whom you see the Spirit come down and remain is the one who will baptize with the Holy Spirit." (John 1:30–34)

On this day of the Full Moon in Pisces, remembering John's testimony, we can remember to keep awake to the presence of spiritual teachers who come in succession—one after the other. *Just as the Great Teachers of humanity collaborate to bring forth the mission of the Earth, so too may we participate by recognizing these teachers; for each has his/her own language, and each language prepares us to recognize the one that will follow. Cynicism and doubt can be triggered against new teachers. The Moon holds our karmic indebtedness, and from these unconscious depths we can be steered away from the path our Angel had hoped we would follow. The Lamb of God is here in his etheric body. Can we see him on the far side of the river that divides the world of matter from lunar spheres of etheric cognition? He speaks with the Great Teachers.* This is a Moon that serves to let oneself open to the higher sense of hearing called Inspiration. And this is potentized in a Piscean Moon. Listen into the secrets that live in silence!

**September 21:** Pluto stations before going direct at 14°3 Sagittarius: The death and Raising of Lazarus. Heliocentric Pluto was here when Lazarus died on July 15, 32; it remained here through July 26th when he was raised by Christ. As this memory is heightened by Pluto, we can carefully discern whose will we are following. It requires sacrifice to follow divine will. Others are often sacrificed when instead we follow our own will. The Lord's Prayer states "Thy will be done"; yet we see everywhere its inversion: "My will be done." It is worth the effort to take inventory as to where we may be under the spell of the tempter.

**Sept. 26:** Sun 9° Virgo: The Raising of Nazor (1/Sept/32). Jesus went to the field in which Nazor had died, and he prayed there. Returning to the house, Jesus and his followers found Nazor sitting upright in his coffin. Nazor was raised from a distance. Christ went to where his soul and spirit lingered over the field of his death. This is similar to how thoughts and words linger over locations in which they were expressed. We live in times when it is prudent to surround oneself with a protective sheath born of one's conscious attention to the etheric Christ:

> May the outer sheath of my aura grow stronger.
> May it surround me with an impenetrable vessel
>     against all impure, self-seeking thoughts and
>     feelings.
> May it be open only to divine wisdom

This meditation is particularly significant in relation to the "radiant blue steam" of the etheric Christ. Imagining a protective sheath of radiant blue aura thus links us directly to the in-streaming of the etheric Christ.[108]

Wrapping oneself in this manner also invokes the mantle of Sophia's (Virgo) protection—the "B" gesture in eurythmy for the constellation of Virgo. As we become more skilled in creating this connection with Christ and Sophia, we are protected from corrupt thoughts, feelings and deeds in our environment. Within such a conscientiously tended aura, the voice of spiritual guidance is more easily heard. This voice warns us to know when certain spaces and beings need to be cleared of ill will. By cleansing our environments, we help raise from the

---

[108] Powell, *Cultivating Inner Radiance and the Body of Immortality*, p. 124.

dead that which is fallen. This can be done while in the location or even from a distance, as was the case in this healing of Nazor. New healing capacities are awakening as gifts from Sophia. Nazor was instructed, after his raising, to be kinder to his servants. We can remember to be more courteous in our words, thoughts and deeds, so as to preserve the environments of this kingdom of Our Mother (Virgo). Elemental beings are longing to serve the good, and they look to us for their redemption. Today we can be particularly attentive to them as we surround ourselves in the radiant blue mantle whose source is Christ.

**Sept. 28: ASPECT:** Venus 24° Libra square Mars 24° Cancer: Summons of Judas (Oct/24/30). Neptune was 24° Capricorn (square to today's Venus and Mars) when Judas was brought before Christ. It is interesting to note that five disciples were called when Venus was square Mars: the summons of Peter, Andrew, Matthew, Phillip and Thomas, and also the call of Zacchaeus. This was not the case for Judas. Bartholomew and Simon approached Jesus to introduce him to Judas:

> "Master, this is Judas of whom we have spoken." Jesus was most friendly toward Judas, but was filled with an indescribable sorrow. Judas bowed and said: "Master, I pray that you may allow me to take part in your teaching." Jesus replied most gently the prophetic words: "You may take a place, unless you would prefer to leave it to another." Here Jesus was alluding prophetically to Judas's betrayal, forsaking his place among the Twelve, leaving it to Matthias.[109]

Venus in square to Mars deepens language, allowing it to become more inward and full of soul. When the five disciples were called during this aspect, they were profoundly moved by the depth of soul manifesting through Christ; and they must have experienced his words, inwardly, as a destiny call. For Judas it was different, however, as he was filled with desire for personal glory. This was not the case with the others. Venus calls karmic groups together. The Sun had just entered Scorpio when Judas became a disciple and it was the sting of the Scorpion that got to him in the end. Mars (the Word) spoke gently through Jesus to Judas, however, for Jesus knew of his mission and knew that it was a role someone had to fulfill. It was due to Judas's desire for money that he was led to betray Jesus to the Pharisees.

With Mars and Venus square to each other and to the memory of Judas becoming one of the Twelve, we can ask ourselves if we hear the summons that is calling through the world in our time—the call to unite under the banner of truth in the name of Christ.

Today Venus works through Libra. Libra holds the scales, and at the fulcrum of balance—at this exact point—cosmic truths sound through Michael, shining light on the path we are to follow, while all the while illuminating the reality of diversions that around us swirl. Judas swung between left and right—the center point eluded him. He was distracted to death by his own hand; earthly rewards were the obsession that drove him to the gallows. Let us strive for equanimity of soul and let Mars illumine what stands in the way of this balance, as it lives in our words; for the Judas in us betrays first our own heart, and then goes after the hearts of others.

~

Note: Venus and Mars were square to today's positions, very close to this degree, when Joseph Stalin became the Premier of the Soviet Union (May/6/1941). He had previously been the General Secretary of the Communist Party of the Soviet Union's Central Committee.

Sun enters the second decan of Virgo, ruled by Mercury and associated with the constellation of Corvus the Raven, the messenger of Apollo and the bird that fed the prophet Elijah (I Kings 17:3).

**Sept. 29:** Sun 12° Virgo: Healing of Mara the Suphanite (Sept/4/30). Michaelmas.

> She was converted through her encounter with Jesus Christ in the town of Ainon. She was wealthy and came from the region of Supha in the land of the Moabites, who were descendants of Lot. Because she was from the region of Supha, she was called the Suphanite. Her Jewish husband, who lived in Damascus, had rejected

---

[109] CHA, The Sun Chronicle in the Life of the Messiah.

her because she had had four lovers, one after the other. Through these liaisons she had given birth to three children—a son and two daughters, all born out of wedlock. Filled with remorse and anguish, she had lived in Ainon for some time. She tried to live an exemplary life. Hearing the preaching of John the Baptist against adultery had intensified her sense of wanting to do penance. Nevertheless, she became possessed from time to time, as was the case when Jesus arrived in Ainon. He freed her of the demonic influence and blessed her three illegitimate children. Following Mara's conversion, Dina and Seraphia (Veronica) welcomed her warmly into the circle of holy women.[110]

May we, on this day of Michaelmas, lift the sword of truth against our inner dragons in order to banish them. Then we are to seek the circle in which we find support for our new ways of being.

# OCTOBER

The Sun begins in Virgo, moving into Libra (The Scales) on the 18th. October rivals August this year for star and planetary delights to gaze upon in awe. The New Moon (Sun and Moon in Virgo) is on the 4th. The Full Moon on the 18th is a penumbral lunar eclipse, visible from most everywhere on the planet (except Australia). The month offers a couple of "double headers" as October starts and ends with Moon conjunct Mars; beginning on the 1st in Cancer and again on the 29th in Leo. These can be viewed about 3 hours before sunrise. Also twice this month, Saturn is in conjunction with Mercury: on the 8th and the 29th. The Moon joins in from the 7th to the 8th, streaming past Mercury, Saturn and Venus in these 2 evenings. This beautiful show is visible after sunset in the dusky light. (Mercury will be farthest to the right, then Saturn in the middle, and shiny Venus farthest left.) Mercury also begins its 3rd and final retrograde cycle on the 22nd in Libra, going direct on November 11th. Finally, October brings the Orionids Meteor shower, with shooting stars visible from the 20th to 24th. However, this year the waning Moon (conjunct with Jupiter on the 25th) will be too bright for any but the brightest shooting stars. Hopefully you will still choose to gaze, looking to the southeast toward the constellation Orion, after midnight, far away from city lights.

**October 3:** Sun 15° Virgo square Pluto 14° Sagittarius, opposite Uranus 15° Pisces: The Cosmic Cross of Holy Births: Birth of the Solomon Jesus, Sun 15° Pisces; birth of the Virgin Mary, Sun 16° Virgo; birth of the Nathan Jesus, Sun 15° Sagittarius; conception of the Solomon Jesus, 16° Gemini. Heliocentric Jupiter stands close to this cosmic cross at 12° Gemini—the place of John the Baptist's birth Sun. Two of the planets of hindrance (Pluto and Uranus) stand on this cross today. They bring possibilities for Divine Love and Divine Revelation. Inversely, they could manifest as hatred and revolution. The former serves the births of the holy ones today remembers, and the latter serves the great adversaries of these holy beings. We can bring this cross into our meditation today in remembrance of the love (Nathan Jesus), wisdom (Solomon Jesus), wild revelatory capacities (John), and purity (Virgin Mary) that are today in-streaming.

**Venus enters Scorpio:** "In Being, existence yet endures" (Steiner, *Twelve Moods of the Zodiac*). Venus in Scorpio represents the life forces that are consumed through Earth existence, and yet endure within the human soul who is in communion with the source of all life—Christ. Here Venus asks us to seek the occult truths lying beneath the surface of all things, and to open our souls to find the maintaining growth that endures existence.

Venus was in Scorpio at the summons of both Judas and Thomas, the birth of the Nathan Jesus, the Baptism, and Magdalene's first conversion.

**October 4:** Sun 16° Virgo: Birth of Solomon Mary (Sept/7/21 BC). The Solomon Mary is the one referred to as the Blessed Virgin Mary, who is the mother of the Master Jesus (the reincarnated Zarathustra individuality who was called Zaratas in Babylon). It is the Virgin Mary who goes before us to future Jupiter existence in order to create a new star-temple for humanity, which will develop in the

---

110 *Starlight*, The Holy Women at Christ's Death and Resurrection, Spring 2011.

orbit currently inscribed by the planet called Venus. Her son, the great teacher of star wisdom, revealed the way:

> Zaratas's clairvoyance allowed him a panoramic vision of Time as well as Space, and he saw the imminent arrival of a period when humanity would no longer see these Holy Beings of the cosmos, nor even accept that such Beings existed. He understood that in this approaching period of spiritual darkness, humanity would need a science of the cosmos that would in veiled form express the cosmic mysteries, since the spiritual reality standing behind them would be lost. The mathematical exactitude that emerges from the astronomical texts of this period of ancient Babylon shows that Zaratas succeeded in this, the heart of his task as a teacher of the Babylonian astronomer-priests.[111]

Our awakening to the stars is thus necessary in order for us to be able to climb their stairway to the realms of future Jupiter existence being prepared for us by the Virgin Mary. The Virgin Mary's son revealed the way; and she prepares us through in-streaming moral forces that we are to take up on behalf of our brothers and sisters, the elemental beings, and in service to the entire evolution of the Earth. May we hear this as a serious call to follow the Morning Star (Venus).

**New Moon 17° Virgo:** Conception of John the Baptist (9/Sept/3 BC). Under the darkness of this New Moon, we celebrate the presence of the John being in our time, for he will not be seen in the light of day, but in the spiritual light of darkness. John is the guide and protector of those seeking to awaken to the apocalyptic challenges we are facing. Just as John came before Herod and was beheaded, so too are we facing a type of Herod in the collective activity of a world-wide, power-based, domination system—a system that fragments the spiritual capacities of the human nerve/sense system—resulting in a kind of beheading of our individuality. This means that the personality loses its hold on itself and sinks down rather than lifting itself into spiritual worlds. Rudolf Steiner saw how the third temptation (related to money) would play out in the future through the economic sphere:

> This may be illustrated by the most mundane things. I could prove it to you, for example, in the details of the development of the banking system in the second half of the nineteenth century. Perhaps it is only for future historians to show clearly that a fundamental change then came about, which we may describe by saying that in banking affairs the personality was gradually shattered. I should have to draw your attention to the time when the four Rothschilds went out into the world from Frankfurt, one to Vienna, another to Naples, the third to London, the fourth to Paris. The whole banking system was then brought into a personal sphere by the personal talent directed to it. The personality immersed itself in finance. Today you see banking affairs becoming impersonal. Capital is passing into the hands of joint stock companies; it is no longer managed by the individual personality. Capital is beginning to control itself.
>
> Now the personality may yet save itself and ascend again. It can save itself, for example, by really learning to strengthen its inner soul-forces and depend upon itself and make itself independent of the objective forces of capital. But the personality may also throw itself into these forces; it may in a certain way sail into and plunge into the abyss by allowing itself to be ensnared by the forces active in capital.[112]

Astonishing insight was delivered by Steiner in 1908. Consider how one hundred years later, in 2008, the banking system crashed. As mortgages, which represent personal property, are scattered into investment sub-classes, they become the abstract property of various institutions. There is no longer a personal relationship between ourselves and our banker. Our very personhood is in this way shattered as we are powerless against the might of corporate finances.

Money is connected to the third temptation in the wilderness, where Ahriman approached Christ and asked him to turn stones into bread. The success of this temptation is evident in the economic sector, GMOs, fracking, and weather modification

---

111 "Origins of Star Wisdom," Robert Powell www.astrogeographia.org.

112 Steiner, *The Apocalypse of St. John*, p. 123.

SIDEREAL GEOCENTRIC LONGITUDES : OCTOBER 2013 Gregorian at 0 hours UT

| DAY | ☉ | ☽ | ☊ | ☿ | ♀ | ♂ | ♃ | ♄ | ♅ | ♆ | ♇ |
|---|---|---|---|---|---|---|---|---|---|---|---|
| 1 TU | 13 ♍ 3 | 25 ♋ 20 | 13 ♎ 11R | 7 ♎ 0 | 27 ♎ 34 | 26 ♋ 19 | 23 ♊ 24 | 15 ♎ 5 | 15 ♓ 42R | 8 ♒ 9R | 14 ♐ 5 |
| 2 WE | 14 2 | 7 ♌ 46 | 13 7 | 8 15 | 28 41 | 26 56 | 23 31 | 15 11 | 15 40 | 8 8 | 14 5 |
| 3 TH | 15 1 | 20 27 | 13 2 | 9 28 | 29 48 | 27 33 | 23 37 | 15 18 | 15 37 | 8 7 | 14 6 |
| 4 FR | 16 0 | 3 ♍ 26 | 12 58 | 10 39 | 0 ♏ 55 | 28 9 | 23 44 | 15 24 | 15 35 | 8 5 | 14 6 |
| 5 SA | 16 59 | 16 42 | 12 55 | 11 49 | 2 2 | 28 46 | 23 50 | 15 31 | 15 32 | 8 4 | 14 6 |
| 6 SU | 17 58 | 0 ♎ 13 | 12 53 | 12 57 | 3 8 | 29 22 | 23 56 | 15 37 | 15 30 | 8 3 | 14 7 |
| 7 MO | 18 58 | 13 57 | 12 52 | 14 2 | 4 15 | 29 59 | 24 2 | 15 44 | 15 28 | 8 2 | 14 7 |
| 8 TU | 19 57 | 27 51 | 12 53D | 15 6 | 5 21 | 0 ♌ 35 | 24 7 | 15 51 | 15 25 | 8 1 | 14 8 |
| 9 WE | 20 56 | 11 ♏ 54 | 12 54 | 16 7 | 6 27 | 1 11 | 24 13 | 15 57 | 15 23 | 8 0 | 14 9 |
| 10 TH | 21 55 | 26 3 | 12 55 | 17 6 | 7 33 | 1 47 | 24 18 | 16 4 | 15 20 | 7 59 | 14 9 |
| 11 FR | 22 55 | 10 ♐ 14 | 12 56 | 18 1 | 8 39 | 2 24 | 24 23 | 16 11 | 15 18 | 7 58 | 14 10 |
| 12 SA | 23 54 | 24 26 | 12 56R | 18 54 | 9 44 | 3 0 | 24 28 | 16 18 | 15 16 | 7 57 | 14 10 |
| 13 SU | 24 53 | 8 ♑ 37 | 12 56 | 19 43 | 10 50 | 3 36 | 24 33 | 16 25 | 15 13 | 7 56 | 14 11 |
| 14 MO | 25 53 | 22 45 | 12 54 | 20 29 | 11 55 | 4 12 | 24 38 | 16 32 | 15 11 | 7 55 | 14 12 |
| 15 TU | 26 52 | 6 ♒ 46 | 12 53 | 21 10 | 13 0 | 4 48 | 24 42 | 16 38 | 15 8 | 7 54 | 14 12 |
| 16 WE | 27 52 | 20 39 | 12 51 | 21 47 | 14 5 | 5 23 | 24 47 | 16 45 | 15 6 | 7 53 | 14 13 |
| 17 TH | 28 51 | 4 ♓ 21 | 12 49 | 22 19 | 15 9 | 5 59 | 24 51 | 16 52 | 15 4 | 7 52 | 14 14 |
| 18 FR | 29 51 | 17 49 | 12 47 | 22 45 | 16 14 | 6 35 | 24 55 | 16 59 | 15 1 | 7 51 | 14 15 |
| 19 SA | 0 ♎ 50 | 1 ♈ 2 | 12 46 | 23 6 | 17 18 | 7 10 | 24 59 | 17 6 | 14 59 | 7 50 | 14 16 |
| 20 SU | 1 50 | 13 59 | 12 46D | 23 20 | 18 21 | 7 46 | 25 2 | 17 13 | 14 57 | 7 49 | 14 17 |
| 21 MO | 2 49 | 26 39 | 12 46 | 23 27 | 19 25 | 8 22 | 25 6 | 17 20 | 14 54 | 7 48 | 14 17 |
| 22 TU | 3 49 | 9 ♉ 4 | 12 47 | 23 26R | 20 28 | 8 57 | 25 9 | 17 27 | 14 52 | 7 48 | 14 18 |
| 23 WE | 4 49 | 21 16 | 12 48 | 23 18 | 21 31 | 9 32 | 25 12 | 17 34 | 14 50 | 7 47 | 14 19 |
| 24 TH | 5 48 | 3 ♊ 17 | 12 49 | 23 1 | 22 34 | 10 8 | 25 15 | 17 42 | 14 48 | 7 46 | 14 20 |
| 25 FR | 6 48 | 15 12 | 12 49 | 22 35 | 23 37 | 10 43 | 25 17 | 17 49 | 14 46 | 7 46 | 14 21 |
| 26 SA | 7 48 | 27 3 | 12 50 | 21 59 | 24 39 | 11 18 | 25 20 | 17 56 | 14 43 | 7 45 | 14 22 |
| 27 SU | 8 48 | 8 ♋ 57 | 12 50 | 21 15 | 25 41 | 11 53 | 25 22 | 18 3 | 14 41 | 7 44 | 14 23 |
| 28 MO | 9 48 | 20 58 | 12 50R | 20 23 | 26 42 | 12 28 | 25 24 | 18 10 | 14 39 | 7 44 | 14 25 |
| 29 TU | 10 48 | 3 ♌ 9 | 12 50 | 19 22 | 27 44 | 13 3 | 25 26 | 18 17 | 14 37 | 7 43 | 14 26 |
| 30 WE | 11 48 | 15 36 | 12 50 | 18 14 | 28 45 | 13 38 | 25 28 | 18 24 | 14 35 | 7 43 | 14 27 |
| 31 TH | 12 48 | 28 22 | 12 50D | 17 1 | 29 45 | 14 13 | 25 30 | 18 32 | 14 33 | 7 42 | 14 28 |

INGRESSES :

| | | | | | |
|---|---|---|---|---|---|
| 1 | ☽ → ♌ | 9: 4 | | ☽ → ♈ | 22: 6 |
| 3 | ♀ → ♏ | 4:17 | 21 | ☽ → ♉ | 6:25 |
| | ☽ → ♍ | 17:41 | 23 | ☽ → ♊ | 17:24 |
| 5 | ☽ → ♎ | 23:37 | 26 | ☽ → ♋ | 5:56 |
| 7 | ♂ → ♌ | 0:58 | 28 | ☽ → ♌ | 17:50 |
| 8 | ☽ → ♏ | 3:40 | 31 | ☽ → ♍ | 3: 1 |
| 10 | ☽ → ♐ | 6:41 | | ♀ → ♐ | 5:49 |
| 12 | ☽ → ♑ | 9:24 | | | |
| 14 | ☽ → ♒ | 12:23 | | | |
| 16 | ☽ → ♓ | 16:20 | | | |
| 18 | ☉ → ♎ | 3:46 | | | |

ASPECTS & ECLIPSES :

| | | | | | | | | | | | |
|---|---|---|---|---|---|---|---|---|---|---|---|
| 1 | ☽ ☌ ♂ | 2: 2 | | ☿ ☌ ♄ | 19:38 | 17 | ☽ ☌ ♅ | 19: 0 | | ☽ ☌ ♃ | 20:29 |
| 2 | ☽ ☍ ♆ | 0:42 | 10 | ♀ □ ♆ | 9:11 | 18 | ☉ ☍ ☽ | 23:36 | 26 | ☉ □ ☽ | 23:39 |
| | ☉ □ ♇ | 1:22 | | ☽ ☌ P | 23: 2 | | ☽ ● PN | 23:48 | 27 | ☽ S ☊ | 7:47 |
| 3 | ☉ ☍ ♅ | 14: 9 | 11 | ☽ ☌ ♇ | 6:38 | 19 | ☽ ☌ ☋ | 21:44 | 29 | ☽ ☍ ♆ | 8:52 |
| 4 | ☽ ☍ ♅ | 21:55 | | ☉ □ ☽ | 23: 1 | 20 | ♂ ☍ ♆ | 2: 5 | | ☽ ☌ ♂ | 20: 4 |
| 5 | ☉ ☌ ☽ | 0:33 | 12 | ☽ ☍ ♃ | 0: 3 | | ☉ □ Π | 2:31 | | ☿ ☌ ♄ | 20:46 |
| | ☿ ☌ ☊ | 22:35 | | ☉ □ ♃ | 15: 8 | | ☽ ☍ ♄ | 6: 9 | 31 | ☉ ☌ ☊ | 0:47 |
| 6 | ☽ ☌ ☊ | 22: 7 | 13 | ☽ N ☊ | 7:17 | | ☽ ☍ ☿ | 17:51 | | | |
| 7 | ☽ ☌ ☿ | 0:10 | 14 | ☽ ☍ ♂ | 20:27 | 23 | ☽ ☍ ♀ | 0:33 | | | |
| | ☽ ☌ ♄ | 3: 7 | 15 | ☽ ☌ ♆ | 1:55 | 24 | ☽ ☍ ♇ | 22:18 | | | |
| 8 | ☽ ☌ ♀ | 13:54 | 16 | ☉ □ Π | 8:58 | 25 | ☽ ☌ A | 14:28 | | | |

SIDEREAL HELIOCENTRIC LONGITUDES : OCTOBER 2013 Gregorian at 0 hours UT

| DAY | Sid. Time | ☿ | ♀ | ⊕ | ♂ | ♃ | ♄ | ♅ | ♆ | ♇ | Vernal Point |
|---|---|---|---|---|---|---|---|---|---|---|---|
| 1 TU | 0:39:33 | 9 ♐ 5 | 12 ♑ 21 | 13 ♓ 3 | 29 ♊ 38 | 12 ♊ 24 | 18 ♎ 10 | 15 ♓ 34 | 9 ♒ 14 | 15 ♐ 51 | 5 ♓ 4' 6" |
| 2 WE | 0:43:30 | 11 55 | 13 56 | 14 2 | 0 ♋ 5 | 12 29 | 18 12 | 15 34 | 9 15 | 15 51 | 5 ♓ 4' 5" |
| 3 TH | 0:47:26 | 14 46 | 15 31 | 15 1 | 0 33 | 12 34 | 18 14 | 15 35 | 9 15 | 15 51 | 5 ♓ 4' 5" |
| 4 FR | 0:51:23 | 17 39 | 17 6 | 16 0 | 1 0 | 12 39 | 18 16 | 15 36 | 9 16 | 15 52 | 5 ♓ 4' 5" |
| 5 SA | 0:55:20 | 20 34 | 18 41 | 16 59 | 1 28 | 12 44 | 18 18 | 15 36 | 9 16 | 15 52 | 5 ♓ 4' 5" |
| 6 SU | 0:59:16 | 23 31 | 20 15 | 17 59 | 1 55 | 12 49 | 18 19 | 15 37 | 9 16 | 15 52 | 5 ♓ 4' 5" |
| 7 MO | 1: 3:13 | 26 31 | 21 50 | 18 58 | 2 23 | 12 54 | 18 21 | 15 38 | 9 17 | 15 53 | 5 ♓ 4' 5" |
| 8 TU | 1: 7: 9 | 29 34 | 23 25 | 19 57 | 2 50 | 12 59 | 18 23 | 15 38 | 9 17 | 15 53 | 5 ♓ 4' 5" |
| 9 WE | 1:11: 6 | 2 ♑ 39 | 25 0 | 20 56 | 3 17 | 13 4 | 18 25 | 15 39 | 9 17 | 15 53 | 5 ♓ 4' 4" |
| 10 TH | 1:15: 2 | 5 48 | 26 35 | 21 55 | 3 45 | 13 9 | 18 27 | 15 39 | 9 18 | 15 54 | 5 ♓ 4' 4" |
| 11 FR | 1:18:59 | 9 0 | 28 10 | 22 55 | 4 12 | 13 14 | 18 29 | 15 40 | 9 18 | 15 54 | 5 ♓ 4' 4" |
| 12 SA | 1:22:55 | 12 16 | 29 45 | 23 54 | 4 39 | 13 19 | 18 31 | 15 41 | 9 18 | 15 54 | 5 ♓ 4' 4" |
| 13 SU | 1:26:52 | 15 37 | 1 ♒ 20 | 24 54 | 5 7 | 13 24 | 18 33 | 15 41 | 9 19 | 15 55 | 5 ♓ 4' 4" |
| 14 MO | 1:30:49 | 19 1 | 2 55 | 25 53 | 5 34 | 13 29 | 18 34 | 15 42 | 9 19 | 15 55 | 5 ♓ 4' 4" |
| 15 TU | 1:34:45 | 22 31 | 4 30 | 26 52 | 6 1 | 13 35 | 18 36 | 15 43 | 9 20 | 15 55 | 5 ♓ 4' 4" |
| 16 WE | 1:38:42 | 26 6 | 6 5 | 27 52 | 6 28 | 13 40 | 18 38 | 15 43 | 9 20 | 15 56 | 5 ♓ 4' 3" |
| 17 TH | 1:42:38 | 29 46 | 7 40 | 28 51 | 6 55 | 13 45 | 18 40 | 15 44 | 9 20 | 15 56 | 5 ♓ 4' 3" |
| 18 FR | 1:46:35 | 3 ♒ 32 | 9 15 | 29 51 | 7 23 | 13 50 | 18 42 | 15 45 | 9 21 | 15 56 | 5 ♓ 4' 3" |
| 19 SA | 1:50:31 | 7 25 | 10 51 | 0 ♈ 50 | 7 50 | 13 55 | 18 44 | 15 45 | 9 21 | 15 57 | 5 ♓ 4' 3" |
| 20 SU | 1:54:28 | 11 24 | 12 26 | 1 50 | 8 17 | 14 0 | 18 46 | 15 46 | 9 21 | 15 57 | 5 ♓ 4' 3" |
| 21 MO | 1:58:24 | 15 30 | 14 1 | 2 50 | 8 44 | 14 5 | 18 48 | 15 47 | 9 22 | 15 57 | 5 ♓ 4' 3" |
| 22 TU | 2: 2:21 | 19 43 | 15 36 | 3 49 | 9 11 | 14 10 | 18 49 | 15 47 | 9 22 | 15 58 | 5 ♓ 4' 3" |
| 23 WE | 2: 6:18 | 24 5 | 17 11 | 4 49 | 9 38 | 14 15 | 18 51 | 15 48 | 9 22 | 15 58 | 5 ♓ 4' 3" |
| 24 TH | 2:10:14 | 28 34 | 18 46 | 5 49 | 10 5 | 14 20 | 18 53 | 15 49 | 9 23 | 15 58 | 5 ♓ 4' 2" |
| 25 FR | 2:14:11 | 3 ♓ 11 | 20 21 | 6 48 | 10 32 | 14 25 | 18 55 | 15 49 | 9 23 | 15 59 | 5 ♓ 4' 2" |
| 26 SA | 2:18: 7 | 7 58 | 21 57 | 7 48 | 10 59 | 14 30 | 18 57 | 15 50 | 9 23 | 15 59 | 5 ♓ 4' 2" |
| 27 SU | 2:22: 4 | 12 53 | 23 32 | 8 48 | 11 26 | 14 35 | 18 59 | 15 50 | 9 24 | 15 59 | 5 ♓ 4' 2" |
| 28 MO | 2:26: 0 | 17 57 | 25 7 | 9 48 | 11 53 | 14 40 | 19 1 | 15 51 | 9 24 | 16 0 | 5 ♓ 4' 2" |
| 29 TU | 2:29:57 | 23 11 | 26 43 | 10 48 | 12 20 | 14 45 | 19 3 | 15 52 | 9 25 | 16 0 | 5 ♓ 4' 2" |
| 30 WE | 2:33:53 | 28 33 | 28 18 | 11 48 | 12 46 | 14 50 | 19 4 | 15 52 | 9 25 | 16 0 | 5 ♓ 4' 2" |
| 31 TH | 2:37:50 | 4 ♈ 4 | 29 53 | 12 48 | 13 13 | 14 55 | 19 6 | 15 53 | 9 25 | 16 1 | 5 ♓ 4' 1" |

INGRESSES :

| | | |
|---|---|---|
| 1 | ♂ → ♋ | 19:27 |
| 8 | ☿ → ♑ | 3:26 |
| 12 | ♀ → ♒ | 3:44 |
| 17 | ☿ → ♒ | 1:28 |
| 18 | ⊕ → ♈ | 3:42 |
| 24 | ☿ → ♓ | 7:31 |
| 30 | ☿ → ♈ | 6:21 |
| 31 | ♀ → ♓ | 1:43 |

ASPECTS (HELIOCENTRIC +MOON(TYCHONIC)) :

| | | | | | | | | | | | | | | |
|---|---|---|---|---|---|---|---|---|---|---|---|---|---|---|
| 2 | ☽ ☍ ♆ | 2:50 | | ☽ □ ♇ | 22:30 | 13 | ☽ ☌ ☿ | 15:37 | | ☽ □ ♂ | 12:59 | | ☿ □ ♃ | 8:16 |
| | ☿ ☍ ♃ | 4:53 | 5 | ☽ □ ☿ | 8:51 | | ☽ □ ♄ | 16:53 | 20 | ☽ ☍ ♄ | 9: 1 | | ☿ ☌ ♅ | 14: 7 |
| 3 | ☿ □ ⊕ | 3: 9 | 6 | ☽ □ ♂ | 3: 6 | | ☿ □ ♄ | 20:50 | | ☿ ☌ ♀ | 9:56 | | ☿ □ ♇ | 14:48 |
| | ☿ □ ♅ | 6:48 | 7 | ☽ ☌ ♄ | 7:39 | 14 | ☽ ☌ ♀ | 19:36 | 22 | ☽ □ ♆ | 0:35 | | ☽ □ ♄ | 20: 7 |
| | ☿ ☌ ♇ | 9: 5 | | ☽ □ ♀ | 15:23 | 15 | ☽ ☌ ♆ | 4:24 | | ☽ □ ♀ | 14:43 | 29 | ☽ ☍ ♆ | 12: 8 |
| | ⊕ ☌ ♅ | 13:53 | 8 | ☽ □ ♆ | 19:32 | | ☿ S ☊ | 7: 3 | 23 | ☽ □ ☿ | 8:51 | 31 | ☽ ☍ ♀ | 3:12 |
| | ♀ ☌ A | 19:54 | 9 | ☿ ☍ ♂ | 5:44 | 17 | ☽ □ ♃ | 16:48 | 24 | ☽ ☌ ♃ | 22:25 | | ⊕ □ ♂ | 18:26 |
| | ⊕ □ ♇ | 20:32 | 11 | ☽ ☍ ♃ | 5: 6 | | ☽ ☌ ♅ | 20:16 | 25 | ☽ □ ♅ | 1:15 | | | |
| 4 | ☽ □ ♃ | 16:49 | | ☽ □ ♅ | 9:11 | | ☽ □ ♇ | 20:37 | | ☽ ☍ ♇ | 1:35 | | | |
| | ♀ □ ♄ | 18: 4 | | ☽ ☌ ♇ | 9:34 | 18 | ♀ ☌ ♆ | 1:18 | | ♀ S ☊ | 22:53 | | | |
| | ☽ ☍ ♅ | 22: 2 | 12 | ☽ ☍ ♂ | 17:51 | 19 | ☿ ☌ ♆ | 11:45 | 27 | ☽ ☌ ♂ | 5:10 | | | |

(to name a few). Those possessed by their intellects think man can rival God's creation. This is proving to be a grave mistake and such practices will continue to reveal just who it is that stands behind such inspirations. *With giant corporations and financial institutions using our money to increase their profits, we have become pawns in Ahriman's game—and the signs of the cost of this type of shattering are everywhere. Where do we turn when the stones of finances are successfully splitting the personality?* We may turn to the unifying forces streaming from the John being. John works on behalf of Sophia, whose presence is represented by Virgo. We are not in danger of becoming physically beheaded, as was John, but rather we are in danger of our thinking becoming ensnared in the brittle, dry, abstract intellect that encumbers our ability to rise into spiritual thinking. The abstraction that has become financing, makes room for great demons to occupy monied realms. Where can we serve new paradigms that restore personhood again to our financial affairs? An example of this is the *Slow Money* movement.

**October 7:** Sun enters third decan of Virgo, ruled by Venus and associated with Hydra the Serpent. Here it is the tail of the Serpent, and the Biblical image is of the Woman standing upon the serpent (Gen. 3:15). Likewise, the Chinese goddess of mercy, Kwan-Yin, is depicted riding upon a dragon. For the Chinese, Sophia is Kwan-Yin.

Mars enters Leo: "Toward will's resolution of being" (Steiner, *Twelve Moods of the Zodiac*). In this mantra Steiner awakens us to the power of the will in our sense nature. This is the work of transforming desires of egoism into compassion. This allows us to bear the World Word in self-affirming resolutions free of selfishness. In this manner we are able to fully engage in the power of the senses in obedience to our higher "I"—the "I" that lives in our heart.

**October 8:** Mercury conjunct Saturn 16° Libra: The Transfiguration (Apr/3/31). Heliocentric Mercury was at this same degree at the Transfiguration on Mt. Tabor. It was just past an inferior conjunction between the Sun and Mercury, a time when Mercury was reaching down toward the Earth. This configuration activates the ten-petalled lotus flower of the astral body. At the Transfiguration, Mercury was indeed reaching downward into the Christ, bringing from the Sun the forces that were at this moment transfiguring his astral body into its higher, purified state of the Spirit Self: "A shining pathway of light reached down from Heaven upon Jesus Christ, comprising the different choirs of Angelic beings in descending order from Heaven down to the Earth. Among the shining figures that approached Jesus in the light were Moses and Elijah."[113]

The disciples cast themselves upon the ground in fear and trembling before the power of this moment, and before the whispering voice that spoke: "This is my beloved Son in whom I am well pleased. Listen to him!" Such is the power of the light on humble beings of Earth. It is actually the increasing intensity of light in-streaming from the Central Sun that is creating the inverse activity of rising evil. *Humanity will increasingly be choosing between the revealing brilliance of spiritual light, and the sucking forces from sub-earthly realms that relentlessly seek to pull us down. We must choose! Will we face the trials of the Light, or the splintering of the dark? Peter, James and John cast themselves upon the ground in fear and trembling. This is choosing the light. This takes courage. This only the humble can achieve.*

Today Saturn stands with Mercury, quickening the destiny resolves (Saturn) we have pledged to uphold in our sojourn upon the Earth. There will always be teachers (Mercury) to help guide us in the accomplishment of our sacred tasks. At the Transfiguration the twelve leaders of humanity gathered around the Cosmic Christ: "These twelve leaders encircling Christ are the great teachers of humankind, who periodically incarnate upon the Earth in order to bring new spiritual impulses for the sake of humanity's evolution. Together they comprise the 'white lodge.'"[114]

It is interesting to note that the Transfiguration was 15 days after Peter was given the keys as head of the Church. Hermes reveals to Tat that the

---
113 *CHA*, The Transfiguration.
114 Ibid.

Church of Peter works under the Father principle of unity (the highest principle of unity) where *one* is appointed as the head who speaks for the others in unity with the Father principle. The Son principle, however, is an ideal for the future. This can only be realized when a Judas-type betrayal is no longer possible. Eventually the Son principle of unity will be able to replace the Father principle. An example of this Son ideal actualized in the present is the Church of John, where in contrast to the Father principle of unity working through *one*, prevailing in the Church of Peter, *three individuals, united in Christ, work together*. None of these individuals acts as a personality, that is, in his/her own name; each acts instead in the spirit of Christ. (See *CHA*, The Transfiguration.)

We can meditate on the profound meaning of this. The Son principle is awaiting those who are united in the name of the Holy Grail, where betrayal is no longer possible—for all are united together in Christ. On this path, we are learning how to move over to make room for others who join us, ever widening a circle. We can strive for these ideals in light of today's memory of the Transfiguration where the Great Teachers exemplify the work of togetherness in Christ. *Saturn and Mercury today are holding the unity of the White Lodge present at the Transfiguration. In preparation for this reality, three individualities are working together in the name of Christ. They are communicating through the holy citadel of the Church of John—speaking into the Church of Peter—calling the awakened to the great council that is forming where these two churches meet. May we find the humility to cast ourselves to the ground in reverence for the unity that lies beyond the graveyard of egoism.*

**October 10:** Sun 23° Virgo: The Little Transfiguration (Sept/16/29). Here we find Jesus walking with Eliud, who was one of the best-instructed of the Essenians.

> Around midnight, Jesus said to Eliud that he would reveal himself, and—turning toward Heaven—he prayed. A cloud of light enveloped them both and Jesus became radiantly transfigured. Eliud stood still, utterly entranced. After a while, the light melted away, and Jesus resumed his steps, followed by Eliud, who was speechless at what he had beheld.[115]

In this "Little Transfiguration" Jesus reveals himself to his friend and confidant, Eliud, who did not live to see the Crucifixion. The light encompasses Eliud as well as Christ. Perhaps there is a story here for us. Perhaps we are encouraged to be Eliuds ourselves, and walk with Christ. In small steps this will lead us toward the light.

**ASPECT:** Venus 8° Scorpio square Neptune 8° Aquarius: It takes Neptune approximately 164 years to orbit the Sun. Therefore it takes approximately 82 years for Neptune to travel halfway around the Sun. This was the case in the early 1930s. Neptune was in Leo opposite to where it is today. These years remember the rising of the beasts; Joseph Stalin and Adolf Hitler. Evil was afoot.

Venus, however, at this degree remembers Jesus visiting the Gold King, Mensor, in his tent city while he was journeying in pagan lands. Here a beautiful juxtaposition opens before us. On the one hand we have loving Venus remembering the king who brought the secrets of Egypt to the newborn Solomon Jesus child. On the other hand, we have the rising of wickedness through the possessed dictators of the 1930s. Venus is in Scorpio, the constellation of occult secrets and hidden dynamics. *There is much we can do in these trying times to protect ourselves against negativity. We can stand with Venus (karmic groups), the Gold King (Egypt), and the Master Jesus (Solomon Jesus) and know we can gain insight into the work of evil that is brewing. With this knowledge we are able to become knights in the battle for the human soul now being waged. The "Little Transfiguration" that Eliud witnessed is the radiance promised when we invert negative Neptune (representative of Ahriman), into its righteousness, whereby it becomes the sphere of divine inspiration.* May we attune to loving inspirations and turn from the deadening effects of pretend realities!

**October 12:** Sun 24° Virgo square Jupiter 24° Gemini: The Ascension of Christ (May/14/33). Jupiter was at this degree at the Ascension and the Sun was

---
[115] *Chron.*, pp. 197–198.

very close to this degree at the "Little Transfiguration" mentioned above, which was one week before the Baptism in the Jordan River. The period of time between the Baptism and the Resurrection is 1290 days:

> He said, "Go your way, Daniel, for the words are to remain secret and sealed until the time of the end. Many shall be purified, cleansed, and refined, but the wicked shall continue to act wickedly. None of the wicked shall understand, but those who are wise shall understand. From the time that the regular burnt offering is taken away and the abomination that desolates is set up, there shall be one thousand two hundred ninety days. (Daniel, 12:9–11)

This number, 1290 days, represents three and one-half years. This is the time in which Christ was building up his resurrection body. It was forty days after his crucifixion, after having descended into Hell where he laid a seed in the kingdom of his Mother, that the Ascension took place. In these 1290 days of his life on Earth the Hermetic axiom—*as above, so below*—applied to his every step:

> The period of 1290 days extending from the Baptism to the Resurrection—looked at in terms of the ministry, and in relation to the corresponding movements of the heavenly bodies—holds the key to the historical events that have taken place on the Earth since the Mystery of Golgotha. In fact, closer study of the correspondence between the ministry and the subsequent unfolding of the Christ Impulse reveals that Christianity is still at an early stage of development; and applying this correspondence in historical terms, we are now living in the period of temptation, which began 28⅓ days after the Baptism and lasted forty days. The three temptations which presented themselves to Jesus Christ during the forty days in the wilderness have also arisen historically, mirrored in the French Revolution, the Communist Revolution and the rise of National-Socialism. But as well as taking on social forms, the three temptations also present themselves in an individual way to each person. The culmination of the period of temptation is signified by the simultaneous emergence of all three temptations combined, which historically betokens the meeting with Antichrist, a choice which each individual and humankind as a whole has to face—the choice between Christ and Antichrist.[116]

The practices Dr. Powell has given us in his book, *Cultivating Inner Radiance and the Body of Immortality*, are exactly what humanity now needs in order to find protection against the incredible onslaught of forces from Ahriman. As Jupiter and Sun remember the Ascension and the Little Transfiguration, we can join the community (Jupiter) of Eternal Israel, who are serving Christ (Sun) and are practicing protective measures put forth in the above-mentioned book. These are not times when active attention to the light is a choice. Inactivity is a form of "not choosing," and not choosing brings near the possibility that we will *be chosen*. May we practice!

**October 15:** Sun 27° Virgo: The death of John the Baptist (Jan/4/31).

> That night, during the festivities to celebrate Herod's birthday at Machaerus, John the Baptist was beheaded at the request of Herodias's daughter, Salome. After witnessing the spectacle of Salome dancing before him, Herod had said to her: "Ask what you will, and I will give it to you. Yes, I swear, even if you ask for half my kingdom, I shall give it to you." Salome hurriedly conferred with her mother, who told her to ask for the head of John the Baptist on a dish.[117]

Even after the death of John, Herod was uneasy, for he could still feel the mighty spirit of John, and this caused him great distress.

The Sun remembers Herod and the power of the desire nature, which has the ability to completely overwhelm us. If this were to happen, we would be given "half of Herod's kingdom" as was given to Salome. This is *not* the kingdom we are seeking. With the Sun in Virgo we can cast the knowing glance to the cunning of the serpent, Hydra, that stretches his undulating forces beneath this constellation. Crater—"the Cup" and a Grail symbol—is balanced on the serpent's back along with

---

116 *CHA*, The Start of Christ's Ministry.
117 *Chron.*, p. 270.

Corvus—"the Raven" and a symbol for intuitive feminine wisdom. The memory of John's death calls forth the Cup and the Raven: the Grail quest seeks the cup, and the Raven leads the Grail seeker to the mysterious and holy Castle of the Grail. It is in the realms where John is working that the Grail is preserved. John leads us to the Grail. Perhaps he speaks through the Raven. Inversely, Hydra can lead us into the dark castle of Klingsor, and once one is in this realm it is very difficult to get out—as exemplified with Herod and Herodias. *We can pay particular attention to the phenomena (Virgo) of nature in our surroundings and read the story the Mother is always telling. The headlines in our newsfeeds are ample evidence of the presence of Hydra amongst us. Seek the Grail wisdom in the living story of the stars; this is the greatest of the Virgin's phenomenological storytelling, for here she opens the book of Holy Wisdom Sophia—and the starry mantle worn by Sophia shows the path to the Holy Grail.*

**October 16:** Sun 29° Virgo conjunct the star Spica. This is a good day to tend to all mysteries. In two days' time the penumbral lunar eclipse will occur very close to this great star in the tip of the shaft of wheat held by the Virgin.

**October 18:** Sun enters Libra. "Worlds are sustaining worlds" (Steiner, *Twelve Moods of the Zodiac*). William Bento illumines this mantra:

> Everything is connected to everything, and so it is with any attempt to grasp how the Cosmos has given birth to worlds that sustain worlds. Nothing can be truly understood when it is taken out of the context of relatedness. Modern scientific thinking has unfortunately lost this understanding and continues to attempt to explain the complexity of nature, man and the heavens by abstracting it from its natural habitat. The result is a kind of lifelessness. The antidote to this edifice of abstractions is to apply the principles of a spiritual scientific thinking, which is based on the premise that "worlds sustain worlds."

The first decan is ruled by the Moon and associated with the constellation of Bootes the Ploughman. The deeper meaning of Bootes has to do with the Hebrew *Bo*, which means *coming*; hence Bootes is the Coming One. How appropriate that the Baptism of the *Coming One*, the Messiah, took place when the Sun entered this decan! Libra calls for balanced thought, which becomes balanced action, as well as a certain standard of uprightness that requires an alignment with higher consciousness. In Libra *contentment becomes equanimity*, whereby we enter the connectivity of all creation.

**October 18:** Full Moon and Lunar eclipse: Sun 0°50 Libra opposite Moon 0°50 Aries: This penumbral lunar eclipse will be visible from the Americas, Europe, Africa, and most of Asia. This is the last of three lunar eclipses in 2013, and *it occurs exactly where the Sun was at the Baptism in the Jordan* (Sept/23/29). Jesus, having become an empty vessel, makes his way to the Jordan accompanied by Lazarus. At the moment of the Baptism a voice of thunder sounds from the heavens: "This is my beloved Son; today I have begotten thee!" Christ, the Great Spirit of the Sun, entered into the vessel vacated by the Master Jesus through his conversation with the Virgin Mary directly preceding the Nathan Jesus' walk to the Jordan River. At the Baptism, the Son of God was conceived within a human being. Anne Catherine Emmerich speaks of how perfectly transparent, entirely penetrated by light, the Jesus being became. She also sees:

> But off at some distance on the waters of the Jordan, I saw Satan, a dark, black figure, as if in a cloud, and myriads of horrible black reptiles and vermin swarming around him. It was as if all the wickedness, all the sins, all the poison of the whole region took a visible form at the outpouring of the Holy Ghost, and fled into that dark figure as into their original source.[118]

This is a profound day to meditate on the Divine Light that came into the world at this Baptism. We may ponder as well how the equal opposite to the light witnessed the event from the opposite shore of the Jordan. As the dark being Anne Catherine saw spreads his poisons so blatantly in our time, right before our very eyes, it is clear who the antidote is. It has always been clear. This is a day to focus on the presence of Christ. At the threshold into Libra

---

118 *LJC*, Anne Catherine Emmerich, pp. 441–442.

stands the Michaelic star of Arcturus, whose name means "the Watcher" (or Guardian). Christ, the Greater Guardian of the threshold, was born this day. Emblazoned in the stars is the story of *Michael* (Arcturus), *Sophia* (Spica), *in nomine Christi* (in the name of Christ).

**October 19:** Mars 7°49 Leo opposite Neptune 7°49 Aquarius: On the 10th, Venus squared Neptune at this degree and today Mars stands in opposition to Neptune. On the 12th, the 1290 days were remembered, as was the collective temptation of humanity in our time. The three temptations were said to have been reflected into history by the French Revolution, the Communist Revolution, and the rise of National-Socialism. Neptune at this degree is opposite its position at the time of Stalin and Hitler. These two dictators not only personally succumbed to the tempter, but they took whole nations along with them. These are the dictators that brought the world the Communist Revolution and National-Socialism. Mars stands close to Regulus, the great royal star in the constellation of Leo. In order to pass through the trials brewing on a global level, we will need to reclaim the royalty we were bestowed by Christ. The extent to which we are unaware of the undulating movements of the serpent's currents in the rhythms of history, may be the degree to which we have already been swallowed by his propaganda. The Word (Mars) in our heart (Leo) is Christ, and he lived his entire three and one-half years on Earth in communion with the inspirations of Sophia and the wisdom of the stars. Christ and Sophia are the antidote to the lower forces of Neptune that inspire evil. May we hear and speak truth!

**October 23:** Sun 6° Libra: The healing of Theokeno (Sept/28/32). Theokeno was one of the three kings who visited the birth of the Solomon Jesus child. He was the king known as Caspar, whose name means "born of God." It was Theokeno who brought frankincense to the newborn child. The three kings had been pupils of Zoroaster in their previous incarnations in Babylon, and Theokeno was famed in that incarnation for his reverence and piety as a mighty Persian king. His gift of frankincense was an offering from the Persian wisdom stream. The three kings reincarnated again in the eighth/ninth centuries AD as collaborators in the spiritual stream of the Holy Grail.

At this healing we find the Sun exactly square to where it was when the kings came to adore Jesus thirty-seven years earlier (6° Capricorn). Thirty-seven years marks the second nodal return (18.6-year cycles); this nodal point heralds the soul's need to fine-tune itself in order to meet its destiny task. This meeting between Jesus and Mensor was transfiguring to the souls of them both.

Jesus and Mensor then visited Theokeno in his tent, where he was confined to his bed. Jesus took Theokeno by the hand and raised him up. Thereafter, the three went to the local temple, where Jesus taught.

He explained that when the good Angels withdraw, Satan takes possession of a temple service. He said that they should remove the various animal idols and teach love and compassion and give thanks to the Father in Heaven. Jesus now took bread and wine, which had been prepared beforehand. Having consecrated the bread and wine, he placed them upon a small altar. He prayed and blessed everyone. Mensor, Theokeno, and the four priests knelt before him with their hands folded across their chests.[119]

Satan not only takes possession of a temple service, but also of human beings if they allow animal instincts to rule in the temple of the human body. From the time of Christ forward, the "I" is to govern the animal forces in the astral body. Those who have animals on their altars will not attract good Angels. It is no longer animals we offer for sacrifice, but our lower human passions instead. Christ now works in the "I." The "I" that governs the animal nature, in turn, shows compassion toward the animal kingdoms. The "I" enmeshed in the human animalistic nature will be deaf to the suffering of animals. Our hearts are the altars in our human temple, and upon this altar we give thanks, and partake in communion with the spiritual world. Human beings are now to rise from their beds of contentment and work for the salvation of the Earth and humanity. This will attract the good Angels.

---

119 *Chron.*, p. 328–329.

The square of the Sun's position between the Adoration of the Magi and Christ's visit to the kings, thirty-seven years later, exemplifies the awakening to a new relationship (Libra) in the mystery traditions. It is a relationship founded on a new covenant with the Sun mysteries. May we rise from our love of ease in order to forge Michaelic resonances into a world gone deaf.

~

**Note:** The Sun is square to its degree at the inauguration of the US President.

**October 27:** Sun enters the second decan of Libra, ruled by Saturn and associated with the constellations of Corona the Crown (above) and Crux the Southern Cross (below), representing the "crown of life" (Rev. 2:10) that is bestowed on those who "take up the cross" (Matt. 10:38) and follow the Anointed One, remaining "faithful unto death" (Rev. 2:10).

**October 29:** Mercury conjunct Saturn 18° Libra: In 1933 with Saturn square to today's degree (18° Capricorn) the beast was rising in Germany—as prophesied by Rudolf Steiner. The rising of the beast (Hitler) distracted humanity to such a magnitude as to render the etheric return of Christ imperceptible. With Saturn today in square to the incredible events of 1933, we can lean into the truth of the etheric Christ. *We must live into the tension of this square and ask ourselves where we are participating with the egoistic illusions in the name of power, wealth, comfort, and/or apathetic contentedness. If knighthood was our pre-birth intention, then this is the year to suit up and brandish the sword of truth against the unholy alliances that riddle our realities with lies, deceptions and all manner of falsehoods.* Possession is increasing. Wouldst thou sleep while the dragon devours all that is holy and pure?

# NOVEMBER

The Sun begins conjunct Mercury on the 1st in Libra, and moves into Scorpio on the 16th and on the 17th opposes the Moon for our Full Moon this month. Saturn is also hidden here, and is exactly conjunct the Moon during the Leonid Meteor shower peak; this annual shower reaches its peak on the 17th to 18th. Look to the constellation of Leo in the east after midnight. The Full Moon's light will obscure some of the meteors, but at up to forty shooting stars an hour, still worth it! The New Moon is on the 3rd in Libra and is a "hybrid" solar eclipse (a mix of annular and total) visible in some parts of the eastern US, Africa and South America. The Sun catches up to Saturn on the 6th, presenting daytime stargazing opportunities for developing capacities of the heart, in complement to the physical eyes. What of Saturn's qualities can be sensed in the light of the Sun? Also on the 6th, the new crescent Moon joins Venus, visible in the west as the Sun sets. Neptune stations direct on the 14th in Aquarius (the WaterHuman) retrograde since June. Mercury returns to direct motion in Libra on the 18th, ending its last retrograde cycle of 2013. The Moon joins Jupiter (which has turned retrograde on the 8th) on the 22nd, Mercury and Saturn come together on the 25th, and the Moon conjuncts Mars on the 27th.

**November 1: ASPECT:** Uranus 14° Pisces square Pluto 14° Sagittarius: The rise of Hitler in Germany and mass starvation in Russia due to Stalin's forced collectivization. In 1932/33 a square between these two planets occurred with Pluto opposite today's constellation (Pluto in Gemini, Uranus in Pisces). This aspect is a signature of revolution. Hitler promised his suppressed people freedom from their economic predicament, and the suppressed peasants of the USSR rose up against Stalin's collectivization—both of these scenarios occurred at an incomprehensibly great cost. These two planets have been dancing in and out of this aspect of tension since last year, and will continue to do so through March of 2015. Let this remind us to exercise prudent caution toward revolutionary-sounding ideas and the dynamic personalities who talk a good talk that they do not walk. We must penetrate to the origins and forces that stand behind the speech of the powerful. It is certainly time for revolutions in many areas of life. Nonetheless, there are constructive revolutions and destructive ones; and many are seeded by the adversaries in order to lead the people into the hands of even greater oppressors.

Uranus is connected to technology. In relationship to Pluto it can spawn evil technologies. We are wise to remember that what we use against our enemies will eventually be used against us. This follows the unavoidable karmic law that what we sow we will reap. Often this reciprocity comes as an inversion. For example, the precision of a single drone surgically killing one person can return as imprecise weaponry killing many.

We can pray that the intensity of the good powers of Phanes (higher Pluto) can penetrate the darkness, and that the enlightening powers of Uranus can find human beings ready to receive this planet's en-Christed revelation. In this way Steiner's threefold social order may yet find us, and implementing this wisdom will show us how to forge the new path forward. We are either going to prepare the way for the Light, or we will suffer in the darkness. This choice is upon us, and the Light stands ready to serve.

**Sun 13° Libra**: Healing of the Blind (Oct/6/30 and 31). At this Sun degree Christ twice healed the blind. We can pray to be liberated from blindness. The Earth is suffering as are far too many of her people. We are not to feign sleep before this reality! This is a good day to pray for peace. (See entry for September 18 for the healing of the blind.)

**Venus enters Sagittarius**: "In existence becoming's power dies" (Steiner, *Twelve Moods of the Zodiac*). One can imagine the centaur, poised on his horse, with bow in hand and arrow pointed to the Galactic Center—the heart of the galaxy. The spiritual force this exemplifies, and with which we are born, dies into the material world; and it is not until we remember our aim, and work from the discipline this bestows, that we will find the power which lives eternal, weaving through all existence.

**ASPECT**: Inferior conjunction Mercury and Sun 14° Libra: Mercury and Sun were also conjunct, very close to today's degree, at the healing of the blind mentioned above.

**November 3**: New Moon and solar eclipse 16° Libra: Totality of this eclipse will be visible from the northern Atlantic Ocean east of Florida to Gabon and Africa. The Mystery of Golgotha (Apr/3/33). The Moon was 14° Libra when Christ hung on the cross. At that time, however, it was a Full Moon:

> To the left of Jesus, the Sun, which stood high in the heavens, had begun to be covered by a reddish cloud formation from about noon onward. Now it began visibly to darken. This was not an eclipse of the Sun, however, for the Full Moon was on the opposite side of the Earth, and a solar eclipse can only take place around New Moon, when the Moon passes between the Sun and the Earth. The darkening of the Sun was accompanied not only by clouds and mists, but also by other mysterious signs in the whole world of nature. Around half-past one the heavens became quite dark. Terrified cattle began bellowing, and swarms of birds flew around unusually close to the ground. The darkness had grown to such an extent that it seemed to be night. The jeering, mocking taunts of the Pharisees faded away, and the whole atmosphere around the cross became quite still. This was the situation: God had set up his sign for all posterity.
>
> As Christ's death neared:
>
> The Sun was still shrouded with red mist, but the Sun's rays began to break through here and there. And now Jesus Christ spoke his last words from the cross. He bowed down his head and gave up his spirit. At this moment it was just after three o'clock; an earthquake rent a gaping hole in the ground between Jesus' cross and that of the criminal crucified to his left. It was fulfilled! This was God's sign of the fulfillment of Christ's ministry for man and the sign of the start of his deed of love for the Earth.[120]

Whenever there is an eclipse of the Sun, its effect is world-wide, regardless of whether or not it is visible in a particular geographic location. Today a Golgotha Moon eclipses the Sun everywhere in the world. Already there is a spiritual earthquake rumbling: It is the growing divide between those who follow Christ and those, like the criminal on his left, who do not recognize who it is that is in their presence.

This is a day to consciously carry the cross. The place between the vertical and the horizontal beams expresses the place where the essence of the

---
120 *CHA*, The Mystery of Golgotha.

SIDEREAL GEOCENTRIC LONGITUDES : NOVEMBER 2013 Gregorian at 0 hours UT

| DAY | ☉ | ☽ | ☊ | ☿ | ♀ | ♂ | ♃ | ♄ | ⛢ | ♆ | ♇ |
|---|---|---|---|---|---|---|---|---|---|---|---|
| 1 FR | 13 ♎ 48 | 11 ♍ 29 | 12 ♎ 50 | 15 ♎ 44R | 0 ♐ 46 | 14 ♌ 48 | 25 ♊ 31 | 18 ♎ 39 | 14 ♓ 31R | 7 ♒ 42R | 14 ♐ 29 |
| 2 SA | 14 48 | 24 58 | 12 50 | 14 26 | 1 45 | 15 23 | 25 32 | 18 46 | 14 29 | 7 41 | 14 31 |
| 3 SU | 15 48 | 8 ♎ 49 | 12 50 | 13 10 | 2 45 | 15 57 | 25 33 | 18 53 | 14 27 | 7 41 | 14 32 |
| 4 MO | 16 48 | 22 57 | 12 50R | 11 57 | 3 44 | 16 32 | 25 34 | 19 0 | 14 25 | 7 41 | 14 33 |
| 5 TU | 17 48 | 7 ♏ 21 | 12 50 | 10 49 | 4 43 | 17 6 | 25 34 | 19 7 | 14 23 | 7 40 | 14 34 |
| 6 WE | 18 48 | 21 53 | 12 49 | 9 50 | 5 41 | 17 40 | 25 35 | 19 15 | 14 21 | 7 40 | 14 36 |
| 7 TH | 19 48 | 6 ♐ 27 | 12 49 | 9 0 | 6 39 | 18 15 | 25 35 | 19 22 | 14 19 | 7 40 | 14 37 |
| 8 FR | 20 49 | 20 59 | 12 48 | 8 21 | 7 36 | 18 49 | 25 35R | 19 29 | 14 17 | 7 40 | 14 38 |
| 9 SA | 21 49 | 5 ♑ 23 | 12 47 | 7 54 | 8 33 | 19 23 | 25 34 | 19 36 | 14 16 | 7 39 | 14 40 |
| 10 SU | 22 49 | 19 35 | 12 46 | 7 38 | 9 30 | 19 57 | 25 34 | 19 44 | 14 14 | 7 39 | 14 41 |
| 11 MO | 23 49 | 3 ♒ 34 | 12 47D | 7 34D | 10 25 | 20 31 | 25 33 | 19 51 | 14 12 | 7 39 | 14 43 |
| 12 TU | 24 50 | 17 19 | 12 47 | 7 40 | 11 21 | 21 5 | 25 32 | 19 58 | 14 10 | 7 39 | 14 44 |
| 13 WE | 25 50 | 0 ♓ 49 | 12 48 | 7 58 | 12 15 | 21 38 | 25 31 | 20 5 | 14 9 | 7 39 | 14 46 |
| 14 TH | 26 51 | 14 5 | 12 49 | 8 25 | 13 10 | 22 12 | 25 30 | 20 12 | 14 7 | 7 39D | 14 47 |
| 15 FR | 27 51 | 27 8 | 12 51 | 9 0 | 14 3 | 22 46 | 25 29 | 20 19 | 14 6 | 7 39 | 14 49 |
| 16 SA | 28 51 | 9 ♈ 57 | 12 51 | 9 44 | 14 56 | 23 19 | 25 27 | 20 27 | 14 4 | 7 39 | 14 50 |
| 17 SU | 29 52 | 22 35 | 12 51R | 10 35 | 15 48 | 23 52 | 25 25 | 20 34 | 14 3 | 7 39 | 14 52 |
| 18 MO | 0 ♏ 52 | 5 ♉ 1 | 12 50 | 11 32 | 16 39 | 24 26 | 25 23 | 20 41 | 14 1 | 7 39 | 14 54 |
| 19 TU | 1 53 | 17 17 | 12 47 | 12 34 | 17 30 | 24 59 | 25 21 | 20 48 | 14 0 | 7 40 | 14 55 |
| 20 WE | 2 53 | 29 23 | 12 44 | 13 41 | 18 20 | 25 32 | 25 18 | 20 55 | 13 58 | 7 40 | 14 57 |
| 21 TH | 3 54 | 11 ♊ 21 | 12 41 | 14 52 | 19 9 | 26 5 | 25 16 | 21 2 | 13 57 | 7 40 | 14 59 |
| 22 FR | 4 54 | 23 15 | 12 37 | 16 7 | 19 58 | 26 38 | 25 13 | 21 9 | 13 56 | 7 40 | 15 0 |
| 23 SA | 5 55 | 5 ♋ 6 | 12 33 | 17 25 | 20 45 | 27 11 | 25 10 | 21 16 | 13 55 | 7 41 | 15 2 |
| 24 SU | 6 56 | 16 59 | 12 31 | 18 45 | 21 32 | 27 43 | 25 7 | 21 23 | 13 53 | 7 41 | 15 4 |
| 25 MO | 7 56 | 28 57 | 12 29 | 20 7 | 22 18 | 28 16 | 25 3 | 21 30 | 13 52 | 7 41 | 15 6 |
| 26 TU | 8 57 | 11 ♌ 5 | 12 29D | 21 31 | 23 2 | 28 48 | 25 0 | 21 37 | 13 51 | 7 42 | 15 7 |
| 27 WE | 9 58 | 23 27 | 12 29 | 22 57 | 23 46 | 29 21 | 24 56 | 21 44 | 13 50 | 7 42 | 15 9 |
| 28 TH | 10 58 | 6 ♍ 9 | 12 31 | 24 24 | 24 29 | 29 53 | 24 52 | 21 51 | 13 49 | 7 43 | 15 11 |
| 29 FR | 11 59 | 19 14 | 12 33 | 25 52 | 25 10 | 0 ♍ 25 | 24 48 | 21 58 | 13 48 | 7 43 | 15 13 |
| 30 SA | 13 0 | 2 ♎ 45 | 12 34 | 27 20 | 25 51 | 0 57 | 24 43 | 22 5 | 13 47 | 7 44 | 15 15 |

INGRESSES :

| | | | |
|---|---|---|---|
| 2 ☽ → ♎ 8:47 | 25 ☽ → ♌ 2: 6 | | |
| 4 ☽ → ♏ 11:47 | 27 ☽ → ♍ 12:27 | | |
| 6 ☽ → ♐ 13:22 | 28 ♂ → ♍ 5:22 | | |
| 8 ☽ → ♑ 15: 0 | 29 ☽ → ♎ 19:10 | | |
| 10 ☽ → ♒ 17:49 | | | |
| 12 ☽ → ♓ 22:31 | | | |
| 15 ☽ → ♈ 5:20 | | | |
| 17 ☉ → ♏ 3:15 | | | |
| ☽ → ♉ 14:16 | | | |
| 20 ☽ → ♊ 1:14 | | | |
| 22 ☽ → ♋ 13:39 | | | |

ASPECTS & ECLIPSES :

| | | | | |
|---|---|---|---|---|
| 1 ☽ ☍ ⛢ 5:26 | 7 ☽ ☌ ♀ 0:20 | 16 ☽ ☌ ☋ 5:28 | ☉ ☐ ☽ 19:26 | |
| ⛢ ☐ ♇ 11:10 | ☽ ☌ ♇ 13:29 | ☽ ☍ ♄ 20: 5 | 26 ☿ ☌ ♄ 1:53 | |
| ☉ ⚻ ☿ 20:18 | 8 ☽ ☍ ♃ 7:37 | 17 ☉ ☍ ☽ 15:14 | 27 ☽ ☌ ♂ 11:42 | |
| 3 ☿ ☌ ☊ 6:18 | 9 ☽ ᴺ☐ ☊ 12:27 | 19 ☿ ☌ ☊ 4:35 | 28 ♀ ☍ ♃ 12: 0 | |
| ☽ ☌ ☿ 6:49 | 10 ☉ ☐ ☽ 5:56 | 21 ☽ ☍ ♇ 7:18 | ☽ ☍ ⛢ 14: 8 | |
| ☽ ☌ ☊ 6:52 | 11 ☽ ☌ ♆ 7: 4 | ☽ ☍ ♀ 16:52 | 30 ☽ ☌ ☊ 16:57 | |
| ☉ ● AT12:45 | 12 ☽ ☍ ♂ 6:55 | 22 ☽ ☌ ♃ 3:57 | | |
| ☉ ☌ ☽ 12:49 | 14 ☽ ☌ ⛢ 0: 3 | ☽ ☌ A 9:47 | | |
| ☽ ☌ ♄ 17:17 | 15 ♀ ☐ ⛢ 1: 9 | 23 ☽ ☐ₛ ☊ 15: 1 | | |
| 6 ☽ ☌ P 9:42 | ♀ ☌ ♇ 21:27 | 24 ☉ ☐ ♆ 17:59 | | |
| ☉ ☌ ♄ 12: 0 | ☽ ☍ ☿ 23:33 | 25 ☽ ☍ ♆ 17:20 | | |

SIDEREAL HELIOCENTRIC LONGITUDES : NOVEMBER 2013 Gregorian at 0 hours UT

| DAY | Sid. Time | ☿ | ♀ | ⊕ | ♂ | ♃ | ♄ | ⛢ | ♆ | ♇ | Vernal Point |
|---|---|---|---|---|---|---|---|---|---|---|---|
| 1 FR | 2:41:47 | 9 ♈ 44 | 1 ♓ 29 | 13 ♈ 48 | 13 ♋ 40 | 15 ♊ 0 | 19 ♎ 8 | 15 ♓ 54 | 9 ♒ 26 | 16 ♐ 1 | 5♓ 4' 1" |
| 2 SA | 2:45:43 | 15 33 | 3 4 | 14 48 | 14 7 | 15 5 | 19 10 | 15 54 | 9 26 | 16 1 | 5♓ 4' 1" |
| 3 SU | 2:49:40 | 21 29 | 4 39 | 15 48 | 14 34 | 15 10 | 19 12 | 15 55 | 9 26 | 16 2 | 5♓ 4' 1" |
| 4 MO | 2:53:36 | 27 31 | 6 15 | 16 48 | 15 0 | 15 15 | 19 14 | 15 56 | 9 27 | 16 2 | 5♓ 4' 1" |
| 5 TU | 2:57:33 | 3 ♉ 40 | 7 50 | 17 48 | 15 27 | 15 20 | 19 16 | 15 56 | 9 27 | 16 2 | 5♓ 4' 1" |
| 6 WE | 3: 1:29 | 9 53 | 9 26 | 18 48 | 15 54 | 15 26 | 19 18 | 15 57 | 9 27 | 16 2 | 5♓ 4' 1" |
| 7 TH | 3: 5:26 | 16 10 | 11 1 | 19 49 | 16 21 | 15 31 | 19 19 | 15 58 | 9 28 | 16 3 | 5♓ 4' 0" |
| 8 FR | 3: 9:22 | 22 29 | 12 37 | 20 49 | 16 47 | 15 36 | 19 21 | 15 58 | 9 28 | 16 3 | 5♓ 4' 0" |
| 9 SA | 3:13:19 | 28 48 | 14 12 | 21 49 | 17 14 | 15 41 | 19 23 | 15 59 | 9 29 | 16 3 | 5♓ 4' 0" |
| 10 SU | 3:17:16 | 5 ♊ 6 | 15 48 | 22 49 | 17 41 | 15 46 | 19 25 | 15 59 | 9 29 | 16 4 | 5♓ 4' 0" |
| 11 MO | 3:21:12 | 11 22 | 17 23 | 23 50 | 18 7 | 15 51 | 19 27 | 16 0 | 9 29 | 16 4 | 5♓ 4' 0" |
| 12 TU | 3:25: 9 | 17 34 | 18 59 | 24 50 | 18 34 | 15 56 | 19 29 | 16 1 | 9 30 | 16 4 | 5♓ 4' 0" |
| 13 WE | 3:29: 5 | 23 41 | 20 35 | 25 50 | 19 1 | 16 1 | 19 31 | 16 1 | 9 30 | 16 5 | 5♓ 4' 0" |
| 14 TH | 3:33: 2 | 29 41 | 22 10 | 26 51 | 19 27 | 16 6 | 19 33 | 16 2 | 9 30 | 16 5 | 5♓ 3'59" |
| 15 FR | 3:36:58 | 5 ♋ 34 | 23 46 | 27 51 | 19 54 | 16 11 | 19 34 | 16 3 | 9 31 | 16 5 | 5♓ 3'59" |
| 16 SA | 3:40:55 | 11 18 | 25 22 | 28 52 | 20 20 | 16 16 | 19 36 | 16 3 | 9 31 | 16 6 | 5♓ 3'59" |
| 17 SU | 3:44:51 | 16 54 | 26 57 | 29 52 | 20 47 | 16 21 | 19 38 | 16 4 | 9 31 | 16 6 | 5♓ 3'59" |
| 18 MO | 3:48:48 | 22 20 | 28 33 | 0 ♉ 52 | 21 13 | 16 26 | 19 40 | 16 5 | 9 32 | 16 6 | 5♓ 3'59" |
| 19 TU | 3:52:45 | 27 37 | 0 ♈ 9 | 1 53 | 21 40 | 16 31 | 19 42 | 16 5 | 9 32 | 16 7 | 5♓ 3'59" |
| 20 WE | 3:56:41 | 2 ♌ 45 | 1 45 | 2 53 | 22 7 | 16 36 | 19 44 | 16 6 | 9 32 | 16 7 | 5♓ 3'59" |
| 21 TH | 4: 0:38 | 7 42 | 3 21 | 3 54 | 22 33 | 16 41 | 19 46 | 16 7 | 9 33 | 16 7 | 5♓ 3'59" |
| 22 FR | 4: 4:34 | 12 30 | 4 56 | 4 55 | 22 59 | 16 46 | 19 48 | 16 7 | 9 33 | 16 8 | 5♓ 3'58" |
| 23 SA | 4: 8:31 | 17 9 | 6 32 | 5 55 | 23 26 | 16 51 | 19 49 | 16 8 | 9 34 | 16 8 | 5♓ 3'58" |
| 24 SU | 4:12:27 | 21 39 | 8 8 | 6 56 | 23 52 | 16 56 | 19 51 | 16 8 | 9 34 | 16 8 | 5♓ 3'58" |
| 25 MO | 4:16:24 | 26 0 | 9 44 | 7 57 | 24 19 | 17 1 | 19 53 | 16 9 | 9 34 | 16 9 | 5♓ 3'58" |
| 26 TU | 4:20:20 | 0 ♍ 13 | 11 20 | 8 57 | 24 45 | 17 6 | 19 55 | 16 10 | 9 35 | 16 9 | 5♓ 3'58" |
| 27 WE | 4:24:17 | 4 18 | 12 56 | 9 58 | 25 12 | 17 11 | 19 57 | 16 10 | 9 35 | 16 9 | 5♓ 3'58" |
| 28 TH | 4:28:14 | 8 16 | 14 32 | 10 59 | 25 38 | 17 16 | 19 59 | 16 11 | 9 35 | 16 10 | 5♓ 3'58" |
| 29 FR | 4:32:10 | 12 7 | 16 8 | 11 59 | 26 5 | 17 21 | 20 1 | 16 12 | 9 36 | 16 10 | 5♓ 3'57" |
| 30 SA | 4:36: 7 | 15 51 | 17 44 | 13 0 | 26 31 | 17 26 | 20 3 | 16 12 | 9 36 | 16 10 | 5♓ 3'57" |

INGRESSES :

| | |
|---|---|
| 4 ☿ → ♉ 9:43 | |
| 9 ☿ → ♊ 4:34 | |
| 14 ☿ → ♋ 1:17 | |
| 17 ⊕ → ♉ 3:11 | |
| 18 ♀ → ♈ 21:45 | |
| 19 ☿ → ♌ 11: 3 | |
| 25 ☿ → ♍ 22:45 | |

ASPECTS (HELIOCENTRIC +MOON(TYCHONIC)) :

| | | | | | |
|---|---|---|---|---|---|
| 1 ☽ ☐ ♃ 6:22 | ☿ ☐ ♆ 22:21 | 10 ♀ ☌ ⛢ 2:57 | ☽ ☐ ♃ 3:41 | 21 ☿ ☍ ♆ 9: 9 | 28 ☽ ☌ ☿ 5:37 |
| ☽ ☍ ⛢ 7:55 | 6 ⊕ ☍ ♄ 12: 0 | ♀ ☐ ♇ 4: 2 | ♂ ☐ ♄ 5: 9 | ☽ ☐ ⛢ 9:34 | ☽ ☐ ♇ 18:26 |
| ☽ ☐ ♇ 8: 8 | 7 ☽ ☐ ♀ 8:27 | 11 ☽ ☌ ♆ 10:16 | ☽ ☌ ♀ 16:54 | ☽ ☍ ♇ 9:36 | ☽ ☍ ⛢ 18:29 |
| ☿ ☐ ♂ 17:39 | ☽ ☍ ♃ 15: 1 | ☿ ☌ ♃ 17:32 | 16 ☽ ☐ ☿ 4:35 | ☽ ☌ ♃ 10:48 | ☽ ☐ ♃ 20:34 |
| ☿ ☌ ⊕ 20:18 | ☽ ☐ ⛢ 15:41 | ☿ ☐ ⛢ 17:56 | ☽ ☍ ♄ 18:21 | 23 ☽ ☐ ♀ 3:21 | 30 ☿ ☐ ♇ 2: 4 |
| 2 ☿ ☍ ♄ 14:47 | ☽ ☌ ♇ 15:50 | ☿ ☍ ♇ 18:11 | ☽ ☐ ♂ 20:25 | ⛢ ☐ ♇ 13:45 | ☿ ☍ ⛢ 2:17 |
| 3 ☿ ☌ ☊ 8:19 | 8 ☿ ☌ P 0:59 | 12 ☿ ☐ ♀ 7:28 | 17 ☿ ☐ ♄ 12: 2 | 24 ☽ ☐ ♄ 5:48 | ☿ ☐ ♃ 10:36 |
| ☽ ☐ ♂ 10: 8 | ♃ ☌ ☊ 22:36 | 13 ♃ ☐ ⛢ 3:17 | ☿ ☌ ♂ 18:34 | ☽ ☌ ♂ 14:23 | |
| ☽ ☌ ♄ 17:42 | 9 ☽ ☍ ♂ 20:39 | ♃ ☍ ♇ 20:17 | 18 ☿ ᴺ☐ ☊ 5:29 | 25 ☽ ☍ ♆ 21: 3 | |
| 4 ☽ ☍ ☿ 13:19 | ♀ ☐ ♃ 23:26 | 14 ☽ ☌ ⛢ 3:33 | ☽ ☐ ♆ 8:48 | ♂ ᴺ☐ ☊ 22:43 | |
| 5 ☽ ☐ ♆ 3:29 | ☽ ☐ ♄ 23:42 | ☽ ☐ ♇ 3:39 | 20 ☿ ☐ ⊕ 0:53 | 26 ⊕ ☐ ♆ 14:53 | |

Grail blood poured from Christ's heart into the entire world—resulting from the lance that struck him through his right side. Christ's blood carries the essential Light from the kingdom of the Father. This is nectar for those of goodwill, and is experienced as poison for those who bear ill will. Let us be mindful that a red mist is rising due to all the disharmony humanity has sown and continues to sow upon the living Earth and all elements of her creation; yet, through Christ, we are untouched by its vapors. Let this Moon remind us of the infinite possibilities that are within our reach. May we find gratitude for every spark of love we find, for this is Christ!

**November 6:** Sun conjunct Saturn 19° Libra: The Sanhedrin investigates Jesus (Oct/9/29). Two days after John's proclamation, "Behold the Lamb of God," when he recognized Christ on the far side of the river, Jesus went on to Gilgal and began baptizing, causing much jubilation from the people. This was sixteen days after his baptism. The jubilation caused agents of the Sanhedrin to feel threatened:

> Agents reported back to the Sanhedrin in Jerusalem about the jubilation Jesus evoked at Gilgal and his baptizing activity there. The Sanhedrin, composed of seventy-one priests and scribes, appointed a committee of twenty to investigate Jesus. They concluded that Jesus was in league with the devil. On this day, Jesus and about twenty followers left Gilgal. Traveling eastward, they crossed the Jordan on a large raft. Coming to a place where many tax collectors lived—they had already been baptized by John—Jesus taught them the parable of the sower (Matthew 13).[121]

After this parable Jesus spoke: "Those who have will be given more, and they will have an abundance. As for those who do not have, even what they have will be taken from them."

With Sun conjunct Saturn at this degree, we learn of the abundance that is given to those who are striving to know truth, as well as of the increasing barrenness that is the scorching reality of those who turn away from truth. *A stern warning sounds: the devil one sees in the other is often the devil one will not meet in one's own heart. This causes great misery in our world. We must bear our own truth so we can open to the world truth. With today's aspect in Libra, we are invited to feel into the interconnectedness of all things. This brings jubilation. There will always be those who cast their devils onto others.*

Sun enters third decan of Libra, ruled by Jupiter and associated with the constellation of Centaurus the Centaur. The most famous centaur was Chiron, to whom was ascribed great wisdom.

**November 14: ASPECT:** Venus conjunct Pluto 14° Sagittarius square Uranus 14° Pisces: Uranus was here during the peasant wars that caused more than one thousand riots in two years. These uprisings were in protest to Stalin's collectivization of farms throughout the USSR. This was 84 years ago (which is the time it takes Uranus to orbit the Sun). *Now Uranus is back in Pisces and this planet of revolution, sudden change, and technological advances is remembering the grim and evil winds that then brought torment to millions.* Pluto was opposite to this degree when in 1922 the Soviet government ordered the confiscation of valuables from churches, which was later followed by Soviet troops shooting into crowds of church supporters. At this same degree (April 1922), Stalin was appointed general secretary of the Central Committee of the Communist Party.

Venus was at this degree when Christ asked Simon Peter to cast out his net, whereby he pulled up the miraculous draught of fishes. This is a guiding imagination that can help us maintain our equilibrium no matter how challenging the shift before us may become. We have taken the draught of forgetfulness; and having done this, we have been led further and further into materialism, all the while becoming increasingly blind, deaf and dumb to higher worlds. It is the Miraculous Draught that Christ gives, and this is the draught of remembrance. We can cast our nets into etheric realms and he will show us the abundance of protection and grace that is the spiritual armor adorning the knights of Christ. We are to put on this armor in order to meet the challenges of the dark forces in our time.

---
121 *Chron.*, p. 204.

The Miraculous Draught is an imagination for the antidote to what the outer planets are remembering. If we can *dare* to ask, have the *will* to seek, and become *silent* in order to hear inspirations, we will then *know* when the door has opened to the new mysteries. This is the formula of the synthesis of effort and grace. This is Sacred Magic. We are to cast our nets into the living stream of Christ and there find the way out of the dragon's lair. As we read in Matthew 7; 7–8:

> Ask and it will be given you; seek, and you will find; knock, and it will be opened to you. For everyone who asks receives, and he who seeks finds, and to him who knocks it will be opened.

NEPTUNE STATIONS 7°39 Aquarius: It takes Neptune approximately 165 years to orbit the Sun. Opposite to this degree we find that Neptune (84 years ago) was in Leo at this same degree when Stalin was calling for mass collectivization and had ordered the persecution of "kulaks" (rich farmers), a campaign that would cause the deportation of 15 million peasants to the Arctic regions and the death of 6.5 million peasants (fall 1929). At this same time the government began an anti-religious campaign. Much more was happening as the Stalin net was tightening throughout the USSR.

With Pluto and Uranus aspecting, and with Neptune accentuating 1929, we can remember that this planet, in its lower expression, is connected to Ahriman. The higher forces of Neptune work out of the pure stream of inspiration that is entering the world through the influence of Divine Sophia—the Bride of Christ. Dr. Powell's book, *Cultivating Inner Radiance and the Body of Immortality,* is offered as an antidote to the hardening forces of Ahriman that are ramping up as his desperate attempt to distract us from the Light now descending from cosmic realms. Rudolf Steiner made it clear that we cannot avoid the incarnation of Ahriman but rather must go through it as part of our awakening out of our sleep in the world of mammon. All is as it should be, yet we are called to be active. We are to practice etheric health in order to find our protection in the community of Eternal Israel that Christ has been opening since his appearance in the early 30s of the 20th century. Stalin and Hitler were specifically working in opposition to the reality of this momentous event in the history of humanity.

May today find us willing to awaken to what lies hidden in the waters of our sub-conscious, for here we will find the truth, and the truth will show us the forces and principalities that are raging behind the realities we are facing. For in truth it is not "flesh and blood" that is causing world strife, but mighty principalities are in a great conflict against the powers of good. This is written in Ephesians 6:12: "*For we wrestle not against flesh and blood, but against principalities, against powers, against the rulers of the darkness of this world, against spiritual wickedness in heavenly places*" And we have all that we need to rise above the deadening afflictions of our times. First, we must turn to Christ. Our task is to send light into the world, for this alone causes the darkness to fade.

With today's memory of the Miraculous Draught and the outer planets remembering hard times, we are wise to seek the quiet power of silence:

> It is the profound silence of desires, of preoccupations, of the imagination, of the memory, and of discursive thought. One may say that [one's] entire being becomes like the surface of calm water, reflecting the immense presence of the starry sky and its indescribable harmony. And the waters are deep, they are so deep! And the silence grows, ever-increasing...what silence![122]

**November 16:** Sun enters Scorpio: "Existence consumes being" (Steiner, *Twelve Moods of the Zodiac*). William Bento illumines this mantra:

> What a riddle this phrase proposes to us! Existence as a term expressing the state of life and the experience of living has a primary activity that cannot be denied. It does not preserve as much as it consumes. It is a force of changing all things. As the force empowering life it is always aiming at the inevitable end, death. And so it is, life begets death and in death springs forth new existence. This is a riddle that is equally valid in understanding the passage of human life on Earth as it is in understanding the forces playing out through the course of nature.

---

[122] Anon., *Meditations on the Tarot*, p. 10.

The first decan is ruled by Mars and is associated with the constellation of Lupus the Wolf. Sun entering Scorpio began the forty days in the wilderness. With Sun in Scorpio, we are asked to be patient in order to gain insight.

**November 17:** Full Moon: Sun 0°31 Scorpio opposite Moon 0° 31 Taurus: Attarus arrival (Oct/23/29). Mount Attarus is the place of the temptations in the wilderness suffered and overcome by Christ:

> These temptations in the wilderness result from the trials of loneliness. Their essence is an ardent longing for fullness that arises from inner emptiness. One "hungers" for the fullness of life, and this hunger may expose a person to the illusion of discerning the fullness of life in the development of power. Those who are thus isolated and emptied stand at a crossroad, between the possibility of either recognizing that, as human beings, we are in fact beggars and must surrender humbly to the love revelation of the suprahuman spiritual world, or turning to the forces of the instinctual life to fill the void. The essence of the human instinctual life, however, is power—the will to power. Such will is rooted deep in the instinctual nature of the human life. Just as the interior of the Earth is filled with the forces of nine subterranean spheres, similarly the human subconscious is filled with the will to power. This is more than just a parallel, since in this guise the forces of the Earth's interior are projected into the human being. Those forces are a source of a kind of fullness (different from that of the spiritual world) that confronts individuals as a temptation in the wilderness. Those same forces confronted Nietzsche, who assented to them and became the herald of the will to power, the fullness of "this life," and the "superman" who denies everything that counters the instinct and eternal earthly existence.[123]

Tomberg goes on to describe how the present is haunted by the past, for it is always specters that rise from the interior of the Earth when anything from the past is seen to live anew. In this light, we can ask ourselves, under the influence of this Full Moon, whether we are carrying ghosts from the past. These ghosts manifest as resentments directed toward others, and in and of themselves prove our attachments to specters. For, here we cling to perceptions whose time is long gone, and it is not the other to whom we are a victim; rather, we are victims of the ghosts who live within us through our "will to power." To dredge up these beings who live in our instinctual life is *not* the way of the knight; it is the way of attachment and self-denial. Forgive and let go! There is nothing good that comes from dancing with ghosts. To forgive means to cut the rope that binds one to the instinctual forces. May we cast our gaze to the Father and the Mother and pray for their intercession on our behalf. In this way we will find the hidden dynamics (Scorpio) that reveal what we need to know about our own self.

**November 18:** Sun 2° Scorpio: Immaculate Conception of the Nathan Mary (Oct/24/18 BC). This is the Mary, born to Joachim and Anna, who bore a high degree of love and the ability for self-sacrifice. At an early age she married Joseph of Nazareth, and bore one child, the Nathan Jesus. This pure, loving soul received the wisdom bearing body of the Solomon Jesus youth at the Union in the Temple.

**November 19:** Sun 3° Scorpio: Death of Johannes Kepler (Nov/5/1630). As the death horoscope is an expression of the fulfillment of an individuality's life, it is interesting to note Kepler's death horoscope with Sun, Mars, South Node, and Mercury in Scorpio. Kepler is one who penetrated into hidden realms to understand mysterious dynamics working in the movements of the planets and in the depths of the Earth. In his lecture cycle *Christ and the Spiritual World, the Search for the Holy Grail,* Rudolf Steiner spoke about Kyot, then wove in Kepler, and then he again wove back through the Grail, and then he wove into the hidden realms of Presbyter John, into whose realms the Grail has been taken—a realm beyond sense existence. Steiner called Kepler "a man in whom lived and pulsed the Christ-filled Astrology which draws after it, merely as its shadow, astrological superstition." The Kyot being led Steiner to "a thing called the Grail" and Kepler worked with forces that spring from the elemental world that maintain communication between the stars and the Earth. And as we follow

---
123 Tomberg, *Christ and Sophia*, p. 165.

the stars we find Presbyter John as the keeper of the Grail Mysteries. Such rich content to inbreathe! Mars was conjunct Kepler's death Sun in Scorpio. At the birth of the Nathan Jesus, who later became Jesus Christ at the Baptism in the Jordan, Mars and Venus were conjunct, in the tail of the Scorpion, at the location of Kepler's death Sun. Jesus Christ is the highest manifestation of the work of reaching into realms of hidden dynamics, for it was he who descended into Hell. Steiner notes that the indications given by Kepler are spiritual revelations permeated by Christ.

Kepler did not view science and spirituality as mutually exclusive. His laws renewed the ancient Pythagorean concept of universal harmony. Today we can imagine the elemental beings rejoicing in the symphony of stars, and the stars rejoicing in the chorus of the elementals—and somewhere between the two we may find the mysteries of the Holy Grail. Kepler's music of the spheres is the music that sounds through Heaven and Earth: "The heavenly motions are nothing but a continuous song for several voices, perceived not by the ear but by the intellect, a figured music which sets landmarks in the immeasurable flow of time."[124]

The Grail Knight, Kyot, was trained to confront evil, as were all Grail Knights. These knights must be returning, for it is time to confront evil and unmask lies in order to restore harmony between Heaven and Earth. We can look into the eyes of the children we meet, and we may see that there are knights among them. This is a day to remember the harmony inherent in all archetypal life and to find the penetrating insight to notice forces working against divinity, the Grail, and harmony. The human being, as mediator between the stars above and the elemental beings below, have a sovereign part to play in the drama of discord resounding throughout our world. What part can we play?

**November 22:** Sun 5° Scorpio: 50th Anniversary of the Kennedy assassination. See Kevin Dann's article in this *Journal*: "Contemplating America's Camelot at Fifty: The JFK Years and the Christ Rhythm."

**November 24:** Sun 7° Scorpio square Neptune 7° Aquarius: The summons of Thomas (Oct/29/30). With Sun at this degree we remember Thomas, who asked Jesus if he could be a disciple. John was in prison at Machaerus, and had sent two of his disciples to also become followers of Christ at this same time. Together Jesus and his disciples then went to Mount Gilboa: "Here he was met by a group of about fifteen elderly people, family relatives. Jesus spoke much with these pious, simple-hearted people, who expressed their concern on account of the Pharisees' hostility toward Jesus."[125]

With the planet Neptune (representing Ahriman) square to this memory, we are warned to overcome our doubts, as did Thomas, and open to the new miracles awaiting our attention. What are miracles?

> They are the love of two wills, distinct and free— divine and human will. Thus miracles require two united wills! They are not manifestations of an all-powerful will *ordaining*, but are due to a new power which is *born* whenever there is unity between divine will and human will.[126]

John told his disciples whom to follow and in like manner Rudolf Steiner pointed us to John. He mentioned John as the one who would lead humanity through the great trial they would face at the end of the twentieth century. John will help us overcome our doubt. There are pharisaic forces rising as ghosts from the past that are today remembered by the planet Neptune, which continues to hover opposite its position of the early 1930's. Neptune is the planet representing both the greatest inspiration from the Goddess Night (Sophia), as well as the greatest anti-inspiration from sub-regions of the Earth. At this degree, Neptune remembers how, following Stalin's call for full collectivization, the purge of engineers began and the government launched a campaign against entrepreneurs. Shortly after this was the establishment of the GULAG (Chief Administration of Corrective Labor Camps and Colonies), where millions of prisoners were inhumanely interned.

Labor camps can exist on a soul/spiritual level as well as on a physical level. Souls who have

---

124 Kepler, *The Harmony of the World*.

125 *Chron.*, p. 254.
126 *Meditations on the Tarot*, p. 56.

given themselves over to the serpent's world have enfolded themselves into closed circles and are in conditions of repetitive and endless labor. It was through divine intervention, at the time of the Fall, that the serpent's enfolding circle retained the possibility of opening into a spiral:

> For the reality and entirety of *evolution* consists on the one hand of the enfolding activity of the serpent, which has formed the brain and produced cerebral intellectuality; and on the other hand of the activity of the light from above, which *opens* the enfolded and illumines cerebral intellectuality. The serpent and the dove: these are, in the last analysis, the factors underlying the *whole* process of evolution.[127]

We are now in the second half of Earth evolution, which means we are evolving out of matter, and this will require the presence of "miracles," the union of human and divine will. *In the world of the circle, the serpent rules, and the serpent works to obstruct the miracle, thereby maintaining his world-wide Gulag.*

Today we can be wise as serpents and innocent as doves, opening to the reality of cerebral illumination, for a will higher than our own is striving to work miracles with us.

**November 25:** Mercury conjunct Saturn 21° Libra: Jesus speaks of the will of the Father (Dec/12/30). The Sun was at this degree, conjunct Mercury and Venus (trine to Saturn) when Jesus healed many sick people in Hucuca.

> In the synagogue, he spoke of the Messiah and of the significance of prayer. He said that the Messiah was already here; indeed, that they were living at the time of the Messiah, and that he, Jesus, was proclaiming the Messiah's teachings. He taught them devotion to God in spirit and in truth. The doctors of the synagogue asked Jesus, in a friendly way, whether he himself were the Messiah, the Son of God. Jesus did not answer directly. He said that they should not inquire into his origin but consider his teachings and actions. He spoke of the will of the Father (Matt. 12:50; John 5:30).[128]

Here it the essence of our time—the time of the consciousness soul. We are to become free of dependency strictly based upon earthly measures. We are to hear in each other the voice of Christ and bring Christ to all our relationships. In Hermeticism we strive to resuscitate the union of sympathy and love that never accuses others, but rather seeks to intuit the worthiness that indwells each human spirit.

Hermeticism also is called to live—not only as a reminiscence, but also as a resuscitation. This will take place when those who are faithful to it—i.e. in whom reminiscences of its past are living—comprehend the truth that man is the key to the world, and that Jesus Christ is the key to man, and that Jesus Christ is the key to the world, and that the world—such as it was before the Fall and such as it will be after its Reintegration—is the Word, and that the Word is Jesus Christ, and that, lastly, Jesus Christ reveals God the Father who transcends both the world and man.[129]

Mercury, the great teacher, and Saturn, the portal to the Father, both shine from Libra today. Libra offers us insights into the realities of life, and helps us balance our relationships to these realities. It was a reality that the Messiah was before the doctors of the synagogue, just as it is a reality that the Messiah is with all peoples of the Earth in our time. The scales represent the balance between two opposing actions, and the fulcrum represents a third action—Christ. We are not to be swayed by listening to what is condoned or condemned by self-appointed authorities enforcing their personal biases in order to influence the thoughts of others, and we are also to be prudent so as not to be swept away by the torrents of mass thought. The Messiah lives in each heart and it is our task to draw him forth. We can judge actions but never a being. Beings are always with Christ even if their actions betray this truth. Let this be our contemplation—to reclaim the mercy of the heart. It is from this center of our being that we can find the third way between two opposing forces.

---

127 Ibid., p. 251.
128 *Chron.*, p. 264.

129 *Meditations on the Tarot*, p. 195.

**November 26:** Sun enters the second decan of Scorpio, ruled by the Sun and associated with the constellation of Hercules, the Mighty Sun Hero.

**November 28:** Venus 24°52 Sagittarius opposite Jupiter 24°52 Gemini: Power on the twelve (Dec/4/30). Venus at this degree was square to Jupiter when Christ bestowed his power on the twelve.

> Jesus continued the Sermon on the Mount near Bethsaida-Julias. He spoke on the fourth beatitude. Afterward, he went with the twelve to a place on the east shore of the lake. There he gave the twelve authority to cast out unclean spirits (Matthew 10:1-4). Jesus then sailed with the twelve and about five other disciples to Magdala, where he exorcised some people who were possessed. Peter, Andrew, James, and John also cast out unclean spirits. Jesus and the disciples then spent the night on board the boat.[130]

After casting out unclean spirits they spent the night aboard the boat…on the water. Why is this mentioned?

The duality of "unclean spirits" (possession) creates convulsions that toss one from one extreme to another. This can tear the soul apart. This can happen within individuals, in groups, in communities, in nations and in the world itself. Stark contrasts are becoming increasingly prevalent in politics, in economic inequality, and in the cultural life. The center is being lost, and the center is the place where equilibrium is maintained. Opposition can reach a tearing point—a point in which the middle tears open from the intensity of two forces striving against each other. Through the tear, "unclean spirits" can enter into the individual and/or into various aspects within the three-fold social order. We witness this in the rise of derisive ridicule in politics, in increasing economic fears and anxieties, and in atrocities born of hatred in the social spheres. When the middle has been lost, all is in peril. As extremism is growing it is imperative from a spiritual perspective that we bring down forces from spiritual realms in order to hold the balance of center between any two extremes. This acts to *cast out* what would otherwise rise from below and shatter the person, or group, community or nation. This is what a good mediator does: establish a center born of the ideal that is the equal opposite to the opposition being acted out from below. We can see how Christ empowered the Twelve to hold this absolute middle space of the heart in order to restore equilibrium to those being torn apart by unclean spirits.

In like manner we, too, are empowered to cast out the demons of the abyss by restoring centeredness. This empowerment comes now from Christ just as it did over two thousand years ago. Human beings gather into karmic groups (Venus) and serve in communities (Jupiter) of like mind. The communities of the etheric Christ are serving the community of Eternal Israel. In this stream we are learning how to speak *with* Christ, and through his power we will learn how to *cast out demons*. It is delicate work, for the personality must *only be the vehicle* through which the Word sounds. If it gets in the way it will instead draw its power from below; and rather than creating a center that reflects above, it will form a new tyranny born from below. Herein the comment "they spent the night aboard the boat" may have its purpose.

After casting out demons they spent the night aboard the boat. An image rises of a karmic group holding the center of balance on the vacillating waters of reality. Their calm is like waters that reflect the starry heaven above, and at the same time the calm waters allow them to see what lies beneath the surface. They rest into center in order to restore balance to the agitated waters of souls suffering the tearing forces of duality. This is the way of the disciples of Christ—they rest in equilibrium before the trails of life.

> The duality [convulsiveness] of the demon is also very vividly expressed in the description of the Evangelist Mark, where he writes: "And when the unclean spirit had torn him…" Between two extremes we are torn back and forth, paralyzed and rendered passive, so that we become incapable of maintaining self-control. This formulation shows the human soul condition in which, without the balancing, Trinitarian and mediating power of Christ, we find ourselves caught between the polarities of Lucifer and Ahriman.

---

[130] *Chron.*, p. 262.

The influx of the Christ impetus into the human being always mediates between these two dark forces, placing itself between them as a wholesome and healing soul element and, by bringing the polarities back into equilibrium, not only halts their destructive power but also leads them toward redemption.[131]

*The antidote to ridicule, fear, and hatred, is praise, courage and love, which is the way of the twelve-fold community Venus and Jupiter today remember.* Christ is asking us to restore equilibrium in all quarters of the world. The model for this work is Rudolf Steiner's carving of the statue, the Representative of Man. For the middle *is* Christ!

**November 28:** Mars enters Virgo: "Work out of life's powers" (Steiner, *Twelve Moods of the Zodiac*). Here we are given a mandate. After attending conscious perception of the natural world, we are to take hold of its essence and work out of its life powers, in order to become co-creators with its blossoming existence. This asks that we first unite with the World Soul (Sophia/Virgo) in order that we align with the good powers of creation.

Mars was in Virgo all through Christ's forty days of temptation in the wilderness.

# DECEMBER

**December 1:** Today is the beginning of Advent.

The Sun begins the month in the Scorpion, standing in front of the star Antares in the 2nd (the "Heart of the Scorpion" and a Royal Star of Persia). The Sun moves into Sagittarius (The Archer) on the 16th. Uranus stations direct on the 18th (retrograde since July), Venus in Capricorn stations retrograde on the 22nd and Jupiter remains retrograde in Gemini. The waning crescent Moon joins with Saturn and Mercury on the 1st before joining the Sun on the 2nd for the New Moon in Scorpio. The emerging new crescent then swings by evening star Venus in Sagittarius on the 5th. The Full Moon is on the 17th and the large face of the Moon journeys on to join Jupiter in Gemini on the 19th. The Moon ends the month as she began, conjunct Mars on the 25th, and Saturn on the 29th. On that same day, Mercury dives into the Sun, conjunct in Sagittarius. December brings us the Geminids Meteor Shower that stretches from the 6th to the 19th and is considered by some to be the best of the year on account of its sixty multicolored-trailed shooting stars each hour during the peak on the 13th/14th! This year, we need to contend with a Full Moon that will obscure the dimmer meteors streaking through the sky, but is nonetheless worth looking up for! Look to the constellation of Gemini in the east after midnight to close this year in wonder, sensing the love and celebration showering down upon us on Earth from our friends in the starry worlds!

**December 2:** New Moon 16° Scorpio: Antares, one of the four Royal Stars of Persia 15° Scorpio. The Sun has just passed 15° Scorpio before coming into conjunction with the Moon. They stand less than one degree from this Royal Star at today's New Moon. Antares is known as the Watcher in the West. Here stands Asclepius, a disciple of Hermes, as guardian. Today we are invited to stand with him, under the watchful eye of Antares. In the closing invocation of Hermes to Tat, spoken from "the holy temple of the Sun," we turn to the West: "Holy Raphael, thou who embodies the power of the Age of the Sun, whence flows the spiritual stream underlying feeling, may thou imbue human feeling with never-ending devotion to the Christ Being and His Healing Work of Redemption."[132]

What a beautiful contemplation for this first week of Advent, as new seeds are being planted under the auspices of the Scorpio Sun raying into the dark side of the Moon, which now stands directly before the Sun! On this far side of the Moon we can imagine a grand citadel where great beings dwell. They keep the books wherein our karma is inscribed, and bestow this upon us as we come into their realms after death and right before birth. Their book can also be opened during transformational opportunities in life. Through the work of transforming ourselves, we become open to fully receive the

---

131 Von Halle, *Illness and Healing and the Mystery Language of the Gospels*, pp. 83-84.

132 CHA, The Mystery of the Zodiac.

teachings given in the School of the Greater Guardian of the Threshold—and find thereby the path of redemption. May we settle into devotion to the being of Christ, that he may walk with us as we call forth from the depths all that eclipses our light. The great Watcher in the West is with us today.

~

**Note:** Opposite today's Sun, and one day before the Sun came into conjunction with Aldebaran (15° Taurus) on May 29, 2012, the New York Times released an article exposing President Obama's "kill list." This means that at this time the Earth was opposite the Sun in Aldebaran; therefore it was conjunct Antares. Venus, Mercury, Sun, South Node, and Jupiter were all in Taurus on that day. The *kill list* exemplified "my will be done," as opposed to "thy will be done." Today's New Moon is opposite where the Sun was when the fact of this list was revealed, and this fact has caused great consternation in the moral conscience of many.

**December 3:** Sun 17° Scorpio: First conversion of Mary Magdalene (Nov/8/30). Jesus arrived at the mountain beyond Gabara, and delivered a powerful discourse with the words: "Come! Come to me, all who are weary and laden with guilt! Come to me, O sinners! Do penance, believe, and share the kingdom with me!" (*Chron.*, p. 256).

Magdalene was deeply moved by these words and experienced her first conversion. Later that evening, when Jesus was at a banquet at the home of a Pharisee named Simon Zabulon, Magdalene entered the room to anoint Jesus' head. This is a sign that she recognized him as a true King, and as the Messiah. It is astonishing, given the times, that Magdalene walked uninvited into a room where men were gathered. Women of those times were not allowed such privilege. The certainty of Magdalene is an example for us all. No matter where the old rules stultify, we are to walk in truth and without fear. This is a good day to contemplate where it is that we may allow ourselves to be limited due to soul contractions incurred long ago.

*We contract in order to defend. As we mature we often carry these defensive soul postures long after their time of necessity has passed. Thus, we will find others falling into these contracted spaces; and rather than seeing the offender as the teacher pointing out our self-limitations, we often project our fear outwardly as antipathy toward the alleged offender. How foolish we can be when we fail to notice that the outer is a divine reflection of the inner!* Magdalene, after being freed from a demon by Christ, redeemed her contracted soul that had allowed demons entrance, and she vowed to abstain from the behaviors of her past so that the presence of Christ could increase within her. For a time she experienced a greater expression of her full self and therefore could enter into places uninvited, in order to serve the One for whom she was making way in her heart. Where do we fear to enter, due to the limits we self-impose? Judgements often have their origin in selfhood's guilt. We must not be distracted by the limitations in others who cast aspersions toward us. May we walk with Christ in full expression of his presence within us!

On this first Monday of Advent we may reflect upon our inner world and our openness for conversion. Magdalene fell after this first conversion and it was not until her second conversion, 2½ weeks later, that she would find her ever-lasting peace and become the apostle to the apostles—the *spiritual sister* of Jesus.

**December 5:** Sun 19° Scorpio: Healing of the centurion's servant (Nov/10/30). Remarkable insights come to light with this healing. At the beginning of the new era in which Christ lived, there was a connection between the illness of a child and his parents, just as there was a connection between a master and his servant. A sick daughter meant a soul sickness in the parents, and a sick servant referred to an illness in the will of the master. This was understood in these days of old. At this time, humanity was in a transitional process in which it was still separating itself from the last effects of previous lives in ancient Lemuria and Atlantis. In these ancient cultures the will life was focused wholly outside the human being. Objects could be moved without being touched. Among the people at the time of Christ this was still found primarily amongst heathen peoples, who could dispatch their will into a servant.

## SIDEREAL GEOCENTRIC LONGITUDES : DECEMBER 2013 Gregorian at 0 hours UT

| DAY | ☉ | ☽ | ☊ | ☿ | ♀ | ♂ | ♃ | ♄ | ♅ | ♆ | ♇ |
|---|---|---|---|---|---|---|---|---|---|---|---|
| 1 SU | 14 ♏ 1 | 16 ♎ 43 | 12 ♎ 34R | 28 ♎ 50 | 26 ♐ 30 | 1 ♍ 29 | 24 ♊ 39R | 22 ♎ 12 | 13 ♓ 46R | 7 ♒ 44 | 15 ♐ 16 |
| 2 MO | 15 2 | 1 ♏ 6 | 12 33 | 0 ♏ 20 | 27 8 | 2 1 | 24 34 | 22 19 | 13 46 | 7 45 | 15 18 |
| 3 TU | 16 3 | 15 50 | 12 30 | 1 51 | 27 45 | 2 32 | 24 29 | 22 26 | 13 45 | 7 45 | 15 20 |
| 4 WE | 17 3 | 0 ♐ 48 | 12 26 | 3 22 | 28 21 | 3 4 | 24 24 | 22 32 | 13 44 | 7 46 | 15 22 |
| 5 TH | 18 4 | 15 51 | 12 21 | 4 54 | 28 55 | 3 35 | 24 19 | 22 39 | 13 43 | 7 47 | 15 24 |
| 6 FR | 19 5 | 0 ♑ 49 | 12 15 | 6 25 | 29 28 | 4 6 | 24 14 | 22 46 | 13 43 | 7 48 | 15 26 |
| 7 SA | 20 6 | 15 34 | 12 10 | 7 57 | 29 59 | 4 37 | 24 8 | 22 53 | 13 42 | 7 48 | 15 28 |
| 8 SU | 21 7 | 0 ♒ 0 | 12 6 | 9 30 | 0 ♑ 29 | 5 8 | 24 3 | 22 59 | 13 42 | 7 49 | 15 30 |
| 9 MO | 22 8 | 14 5 | 12 4 | 11 2 | 0 57 | 5 39 | 23 57 | 23 6 | 13 41 | 7 50 | 15 32 |
| 10 TU | 23 9 | 27 46 | 12 4D | 12 35 | 1 23 | 6 10 | 23 51 | 23 12 | 13 41 | 7 51 | 15 34 |
| 11 WE | 24 10 | 11 ♓ 5 | 12 5 | 14 7 | 1 48 | 6 40 | 23 45 | 23 19 | 13 40 | 7 52 | 15 36 |
| 12 TH | 25 11 | 24 6 | 12 7 | 15 40 | 2 10 | 7 11 | 23 38 | 23 25 | 13 40 | 7 53 | 15 38 |
| 13 FR | 26 12 | 6 ♈ 50 | 12 8 | 17 13 | 2 31 | 7 41 | 23 32 | 23 32 | 13 40 | 7 54 | 15 40 |
| 14 SA | 27 13 | 19 20 | 12 8R | 18 46 | 2 50 | 8 11 | 23 25 | 23 38 | 13 40 | 7 55 | 15 42 |
| 15 SU | 28 14 | 1 ♉ 40 | 12 6 | 20 19 | 3 7 | 8 41 | 23 19 | 23 45 | 13 39 | 7 56 | 15 44 |
| 16 MO | 29 15 | 13 52 | 12 1 | 21 53 | 3 22 | 9 11 | 23 12 | 23 51 | 13 39 | 7 57 | 15 46 |
| 17 TU | 0 ♐ 16 | 25 56 | 11 54 | 23 26 | 3 34 | 9 40 | 23 5 | 23 57 | 13 39 | 7 58 | 15 48 |
| 18 WE | 1 17 | 7 ♊ 55 | 11 45 | 24 59 | 3 45 | 10 10 | 22 58 | 24 4 | 13 39D | 7 59 | 15 50 |
| 19 TH | 2 18 | 19 50 | 11 35 | 26 33 | 3 53 | 10 39 | 22 51 | 24 10 | 13 39 | 8 0 | 15 52 |
| 20 FR | 3 19 | 1 ♋ 43 | 11 24 | 28 7 | 3 58 | 11 8 | 22 44 | 24 16 | 13 39 | 8 1 | 15 54 |
| 21 SA | 4 20 | 13 34 | 11 14 | 29 41 | 4 2 | 11 37 | 22 36 | 24 22 | 13 39 | 8 3 | 15 56 |
| 22 SU | 5 21 | 25 27 | 11 6 | 1 ♐ 15 | 4 3R | 12 6 | 22 29 | 24 28 | 13 40 | 8 4 | 15 58 |
| 23 MO | 6 22 | 7 ♌ 25 | 10 59 | 2 49 | 4 1 | 12 34 | 22 21 | 24 34 | 13 40 | 8 5 | 16 0 |
| 24 TU | 7 23 | 19 31 | 10 55 | 4 24 | 3 57 | 13 3 | 22 14 | 24 40 | 13 40 | 8 6 | 16 2 |
| 25 WE | 8 25 | 1 ♍ 49 | 10 53 | 5 58 | 3 51 | 13 31 | 22 6 | 24 46 | 13 41 | 8 8 | 16 4 |
| 26 TH | 9 26 | 14 24 | 10 53D | 7 33 | 3 42 | 13 59 | 21 59 | 24 52 | 13 41 | 8 9 | 16 6 |
| 27 FR | 10 27 | 27 21 | 10 54 | 9 9 | 3 31 | 14 27 | 21 51 | 24 57 | 13 41 | 8 10 | 16 9 |
| 28 SA | 11 28 | 10 ♎ 43 | 10 54R | 10 44 | 3 17 | 14 54 | 21 43 | 25 3 | 13 42 | 8 12 | 16 11 |
| 29 SU | 12 29 | 24 35 | 10 54 | 12 20 | 3 1 | 15 22 | 21 35 | 25 9 | 13 42 | 8 13 | 16 13 |
| 30 MO | 13 30 | 8 ♏ 56 | 10 50 | 13 56 | 2 42 | 15 49 | 21 27 | 25 14 | 13 43 | 8 15 | 16 15 |
| 31 TU | 14 32 | 23 44 | 10 45 | 15 32 | 2 21 | 16 16 | 21 19 | 25 20 | 13 44 | 8 16 | 16 17 |

### INGRESSES :

1 ☿ → ♏ 18:37
☽ → ♏ 22:11
3 ☽ → ♐ 22:43
5 ☽ → ♑ 22:41
7 ♀ → ♑ 0:48
☽ → ♒ 23:59
10 ☽ → ♓ 3:59
12 ☽ → ♈ 11: 4
14 ☽ → ♉ 20:43
16 ☉ → ♐ 17:42
17 ☽ → ♊ 8: 7
19 ☽ → ♋ 20:31
21 ☿ → ♐ 4:54
22 ☽ → ♌ 9: 8
24 ☽ → ♍ 20:30
27 ☽ → ♎ 4:49
29 ☽ → ♏ 9: 8
31 ☽ → ♐ 9:59

### ASPECTS & ECLIPSES :

1 ☽ ☌ ♄ 9:18
☽ ☌ ☿ 22:35
3 ☉ ☌ ☽ 0:21
4 ☽ ☌ P 10:13
☽ ☌ ♇ 23:17
5 ☽ ☍ ♃ 13:28
☽ ☌ ♀ 21:44
6 ☽ N ☊ 18:27
☿ □ ♆ 21:34
8 ☽ ☌ ♆ 13:15
9 ☉ □ ☽ 15:10
10 ☽ ☍ ♂ 15:39
11 ☽ ☌ ♅ 4:43
13 ☽ ☌ ☋ 10: 8
14 ☽ ☍ ♄ 8:24
16 ☽ ☍ ☿ 18:15
17 ☉ ☍ ☽ 9:27
18 ☽ ☍ ♇ 15:57
19 ☽ ☌ ♃ 6: 0
20 ☽ ☌ A 0:10
☽ ☍ ♀ 4:35
☽ S ☊ 19:20
23 ☽ ☍ ♆ 1:20
25 ♂ ☍ ♅ 8:28
☉ □ ☽ 13:46
☽ ☍ ♅ 22:39
☽ ☌ ♂ 23:11
28 ☽ ☌ ☊ 0:19
29 ☽ ☌ ♄ 0:57
☉ ☌S ☿ 6:26
☿ □ ♅ 20:46
30 ☉ □ ♅ 5: 2
31 ♂ □ ♇ 1:10
☿ ☌ ♇ 11:22
☿ □ ♂ 14:58

## SIDEREAL HELIOCENTRIC LONGITUDES : DECEMBER 2013 Gregorian at 0 hours UT

| DAY | Sid. Time | ☿ | ♀ | ⊕ | ♂ | ♃ | ♄ | ♅ | ♆ | ♇ | Vernal Point |
|---|---|---|---|---|---|---|---|---|---|---|---|
| 1 SU | 4:40: 3 | 19 ♍ 30 | 19 ♈ 20 | 14 ♉ 1 | 26 ♋ 57 | 17 ♊ 31 | 20 ♎ 4 | 16 ♓ 13 | 9 ♒ 36 | 16 ♐ 11 | 5 ♓ 3'57" |
| 2 MO | 4:44: 0 | 23 2 | 20 57 | 15 2 | 27 24 | 17 36 | 20 6 | 16 14 | 9 37 | 16 11 | 5 ♓ 3'57" |
| 3 TU | 4:47:56 | 26 30 | 22 33 | 16 3 | 27 50 | 17 41 | 20 8 | 16 14 | 9 37 | 16 11 | 5 ♓ 3'57" |
| 4 WE | 4:51:53 | 29 52 | 24 9 | 17 4 | 28 16 | 17 46 | 20 10 | 16 15 | 9 38 | 16 12 | 5 ♓ 3'57" |
| 5 TH | 4:55:49 | 3 ♎ 10 | 25 45 | 18 5 | 28 43 | 17 51 | 20 12 | 16 16 | 9 38 | 16 12 | 5 ♓ 3'57" |
| 6 FR | 4:59:46 | 6 24 | 27 21 | 19 5 | 29 9 | 17 56 | 20 14 | 16 16 | 9 38 | 16 12 | 5 ♓ 3'56" |
| 7 SA | 5: 3:43 | 9 34 | 28 58 | 20 6 | 29 35 | 18 1 | 20 16 | 16 17 | 9 39 | 16 13 | 5 ♓ 3'56" |
| 8 SU | 5: 7:39 | 12 40 | 0 ♉ 34 | 21 7 | 0 ♌ 2 | 18 6 | 20 17 | 16 18 | 9 39 | 16 13 | 5 ♓ 3'56" |
| 9 MO | 5:11:36 | 15 43 | 2 10 | 22 8 | 0 28 | 18 11 | 20 19 | 16 18 | 9 39 | 16 13 | 5 ♓ 3'56" |
| 10 TU | 5:15:32 | 18 44 | 3 47 | 23 9 | 0 54 | 18 16 | 20 21 | 16 19 | 9 40 | 16 14 | 5 ♓ 3'56" |
| 11 WE | 5:19:29 | 21 42 | 5 23 | 24 10 | 1 20 | 18 21 | 20 23 | 16 19 | 9 40 | 16 14 | 5 ♓ 3'56" |
| 12 TH | 5:23:25 | 24 37 | 6 59 | 25 11 | 1 47 | 18 26 | 20 25 | 16 20 | 9 40 | 16 14 | 5 ♓ 3'56" |
| 13 FR | 5:27:22 | 27 30 | 8 36 | 26 12 | 2 13 | 18 31 | 20 27 | 16 21 | 9 41 | 16 15 | 5 ♓ 3'55" |
| 14 SA | 5:31:18 | 0 ♏ 21 | 10 12 | 27 13 | 2 39 | 18 36 | 20 29 | 16 21 | 9 41 | 16 15 | 5 ♓ 3'55" |
| 15 SU | 5:35:15 | 3 11 | 11 49 | 28 14 | 3 6 | 18 42 | 20 31 | 16 22 | 9 41 | 16 15 | 5 ♓ 3'55" |
| 16 MO | 5:39:12 | 6 0 | 13 25 | 29 15 | 3 32 | 18 47 | 20 32 | 16 23 | 9 42 | 16 15 | 5 ♓ 3'55" |
| 17 TU | 5:43: 8 | 8 47 | 15 2 | 0 ♊ 16 | 3 58 | 18 52 | 20 34 | 16 23 | 9 42 | 16 16 | 5 ♓ 3'55" |
| 18 WE | 5:47: 5 | 11 33 | 16 39 | 1 17 | 4 24 | 18 57 | 20 36 | 16 24 | 9 43 | 16 16 | 5 ♓ 3'55" |
| 19 TH | 5:51: 1 | 14 19 | 18 15 | 2 18 | 4 51 | 19 2 | 20 38 | 16 25 | 9 43 | 16 16 | 5 ♓ 3'55" |
| 20 FR | 5:54:58 | 17 4 | 19 52 | 3 19 | 5 17 | 19 7 | 20 40 | 16 25 | 9 43 | 16 17 | 5 ♓ 3'55" |
| 21 SA | 5:58:54 | 19 49 | 21 29 | 4 20 | 5 43 | 19 12 | 20 42 | 16 26 | 9 44 | 16 17 | 5 ♓ 3'54" |
| 22 SU | 6: 2:51 | 22 33 | 23 5 | 5 21 | 6 9 | 19 17 | 20 44 | 16 27 | 9 44 | 16 17 | 5 ♓ 3'54" |
| 23 MO | 6: 6:47 | 25 18 | 24 42 | 6 23 | 6 35 | 19 22 | 20 46 | 16 27 | 9 44 | 16 18 | 5 ♓ 3'54" |
| 24 TU | 6:10:44 | 28 3 | 26 19 | 7 24 | 7 2 | 19 27 | 20 47 | 16 28 | 9 45 | 16 18 | 5 ♓ 3'54" |
| 25 WE | 6:14:41 | 0 ♐ 49 | 27 56 | 8 25 | 7 28 | 19 32 | 20 49 | 16 28 | 9 45 | 16 18 | 5 ♓ 3'54" |
| 26 TH | 6:18:37 | 3 35 | 29 33 | 9 26 | 7 54 | 19 37 | 20 51 | 16 29 | 9 45 | 16 19 | 5 ♓ 3'54" |
| 27 FR | 6:22:34 | 6 22 | 1 ♊ 9 | 10 27 | 8 20 | 19 42 | 20 53 | 16 30 | 9 46 | 16 19 | 5 ♓ 3'54" |
| 28 SA | 6:26:30 | 9 10 | 2 46 | 11 28 | 8 46 | 19 47 | 20 55 | 16 30 | 9 46 | 16 19 | 5 ♓ 3'53" |
| 29 SU | 6:30:27 | 12 0 | 4 23 | 12 29 | 9 13 | 19 52 | 20 57 | 16 31 | 9 47 | 16 20 | 5 ♓ 3'53" |
| 30 MO | 6:34:23 | 14 51 | 6 0 | 13 31 | 9 39 | 19 57 | 20 59 | 16 32 | 9 47 | 16 20 | 5 ♓ 3'53" |
| 31 TU | 6:38:20 | 17 44 | 7 37 | 14 32 | 10 5 | 20 2 | 21 1 | 16 32 | 9 47 | 16 20 | 5 ♓ 3'53" |

### INGRESSES :

4 ☿ → ♎ 0:57
7 ♀ → ♉ 15:32
♂ → ♌ 22:31
13 ☿ → ♏ 20:58
16 ⊕ → ♊ 17:38
24 ☿ → ♐ 16:58
26 ♀ → ♊ 6:48

### ASPECTS (HELIOCENTRIC +MOON(TYCHONIC)) :

1 ☽ ☍ ♀ 4:59
☽ ☌ ♄ 5:40
♀ ☍ ♄ 11:11
☽ □ ♂ 17:41
2 ☽ □ ♆ 13:55
5 ☽ ☌ ♇ 0:33
☽ □ ♅ 0:39
☽ ☍ ♃ 3:13
6 ☽ □ ☿ 11:30
7 ☽ □ ♄ 7:45
♀ □ ♂ 12:54
8 ☽ ☍ ♂ 0: 2
☽ □ ♀ 1: 3
☽ ☌ ♆ 16:23
10 ☿ ☌ ♄ 13:15
11 ☽ □ ♇ 9:25
☽ ☌ ♅ 9:36
☽ □ ♃ 13:26
☿ ☌ ☋ 15:19
13 ♀ □ ♆ 16:11
14 ☽ ☍ ♄ 2:12
☿ □ ♂ 23: 2
15 ☽ □ ♂ 2:53
☽ ☍ ☿ 3:51
☽ □ ♆ 15:46
☽ ☌ ♀ 23: 0
17 ☿ □ ♆ 7:59
18 ☽ ☍ ♇ 16:48
☽ □ ♅ 17: 4
☽ ☌ ♃ 22:20
21 ♀ ☌ ☊ 5:51
☽ □ ♄ 14:26
22 ☿ ☌ A 1:37
☿ ☍ ♀ 11:21
☽ ☌ ♂ 22:17
23 ☽ ☍ ♆ 4:38
24 ☽ □ ♀ 15:20
☽ □ ☿ 21:30
26 ☽ □ ♇ 3:36
☽ ☍ ♅ 3:55
☽ ☌ ♃ 9:49
28 ☽ ☌ ♄ 17:45
29 ☿ ☍ ⊕ 6:26
30 ☽ □ ♂ 1:12
☽ □ ♆ 1:23
♂ ☍ ♆ 7:28
☿ ☌ ♇ 12:22
☿ □ ♅ 14: 1
31 ☿ ☍ ♃ 19:24

The centurion's will inhabits the servant, so that when the former says: "Do this!" he does it. But now the servant has fallen ill, and cannot do what the master says; for, as we are told, he has "the palsy" (paralysis). He is incapable of acting, for the will is paralyzed. Then the centurion says: "Lord, I am not worthy that thou shouldest come under my roof; but speak the word only, and my servant shall be healed." This means that his roof covers and protects his house. But he is himself his house in which the will is sick. The centurion acknowledges this and asks the Christ to help him: to speak just *one* word so that his servant, his will, can recover. Through this one word the Lord will not enter physically into the centurion's house, but certainly will do so spiritually. This same process, already vouchsafed to the centurion before the Mystery of Golgotha, will come to every person on Earth through the Resurrection on Easter morning. The Word that is spoken and enters the "house" of the centurion is the same Word celebrated in the prologue to the St. John Gospel, the I AM. This I enters the habitation of the human being, enters the new house of the centurion, enlivening his sick servant—in other words, healing his sick will.[133]

With the Sun in Scorpio, the constellation that plummets the depths in order to reveal the heights, we can invite Christ into our house—our bodies—in order to experience a healing of our wills and our souls. This can happen only if we have faith: "And I say unto you, that many shall come from the east and west and shall sit down with Abraham, and Isaac, and Jacob, in the kingdom of Heaven. But the children of the kingdom shall be cast out into outer darkness" (Matt. 8: 5–13).

The "outer darkness" refers to the fate of those in the community of ancient Israel who were children of the kingdom and yet placed not their faith in the Messiah who was sent into their kingdom at the Turning Point in Time. Again we face this situation—the etheric Christ is here. Are we going to enter the community of Eternal Israel, or are we going to be "cast out into outer darkness." This is a day to make commitments to our spiritual practice.

**December 6:** Sun 19° Scorpio: Meeting with Maroni, the widow of Nain (Nov/10/30).

Today marks the place of the Sun when Jesus met Maroni (the mother of the Youth of Nain) in the Valley of the Doves, south of Capernaum. She begged him to come and heal her twelve-year-old son. As Jesus taught in the synagogue when the Sabbath began, a possessed man ran in, causing great commotion (*Chron.*, p. 256). Images we can work with are: the Valley of the Doves, the widow, and the possessed man. The Holy Spirit (dove) can find us as we renew our relationship with the Father, thus becoming widows no more. This process sets us upon the path of deliverance from possessive forces in our lower nature (the Scorpion becomes the Eagle). As we begin to find Christ, as did Maroni, we will be widows no longer. First we remember, then we awaken, then we are reborn. Where does our soul feel widowed from the divine love of our Father? We are to seek the Holy Spirit, heal ourselves of possessing forces born of falsehoods, and reunite with our Father in Heaven.

**ASPECT:** Mercury 7° Scorpio square Neptune 7° Aquarius: Conversation with Nicodemus (Apr/9/30). Mercury and Neptune were square when Christ and Nicodemus conversed in the night. This was just after the death of Silent Mary. "The wind blows where it wills, and you hear the sound of it, but you do not know whence it comes or whither it goes; so it is with everyone who is born of the Spirit" (John 3:8).

In the second Arcanum of *Meditations on the Tarot*, The High Priestess, the unknown author describes the "pure act of intelligence": "[Like the wind,] the pure act in itself cannot be grasped; it is only its reflection which renders it perceptible, comparable and understandable—or, in other words, it is by virtue of the reflection that we become conscious of it."[134]

This seems to fit the nighttime conversations between Jesus and Nicodemus. Three times it is reported in the Bible that Nicodemus came to Jesus *in the night*. Rudolf Steiner says this:

> "By night" means nothing else than that this meeting between Jesus and Nicodemus occurred in the astral world: in the spiritual world, not

---

133 Von Halle, *Illness and Healing and the Mystery Language of the Gospels*, pp. 119–120.

134 *Meditations on the Tarot*, p. 30.

in the world that surrounds us in our ordinary day consciousness. This means that Christ could converse with Nicodemus outside the physical body—by night, when the physical body is not present, when the astral body is outside the physical and etheric bodies.[135]

Jesus approaches Nicodemus in the night. The original forces of the world are living in Jesus—he is bringing not only new teachings, but a kind of teaching that comes from his astral body into the consciousness of others who are prepared to receive these teachings. Jesus makes the preparation for receiving these cosmic teachings clear: "Truly, truly, I say to you, unless one is born of Water and the Spirit, [one] cannot enter the Kingdom of God" (John 3:5).

The "pure act of intelligence" comes like the wind—no one knows whence it comes or whither it goes. It is the spirit of Jesus' teaching in the night. Nicodemus is able to receive these teachings as reflections, and through the reflections he can grasp the wind that blows where it will as the cosmic teachings of Christ. Nicodemus was born of Water and of Spirit, as was John—they entered the kingdom of God by letting go of the lower human being and reviving the higher human being. This is the second birth; to be born into spirit consciousness. This is to be "born of Water and the Spirit."

*At night we are reliving our previous day. If our day is filled with agitation and attention to primarily material concerns, we will find what comes out of us in sleep creates filmy clouds that obscure our ability to perceive the spiritual beings who are then striving toward us. The waters of our soul are to become still, for through stillness these waters become a surface that is able to reflect the above. Our spirits are to be actively attending what the waters of our soul are reflecting. This is the way of the Hermeticist.* When one's consciousness bears witness to the perfect reflection of above and below, one is fulfilling the Hermetic axiom: *as above so also below*. This is being born of water and spirit.

This day calls forth the memory of Nicodemus, who communed with Christ's astral body in the night. This was his initiation. His eagerness to learn (Mercury), and his ability to bring stillness to his soul, brought before his consciousness the Inspired (Neptune) teachings of Christ. This day reminds us of right preparation for sleep—for entering sleep is entering the great School of the Night.

**December 7:** Sun enters the third decan of Scorpio, ruled by Mercury and associated with the constellation of Ophiucus the Serpent Holder. Ophiucus, sometimes also called Aesclepius, has a healing mission.

**Venus enters Capricorn:** "May the past feel the future" (Steiner, *Twelve Moods of the Zodiac*). Here we are being asked to know that in our thoughts the future is present. *Each thought is a kind of death, and just as the soul and spirit leave the human body at death, so too does the soul-spiritual element within a thought rise like a spirit from our thinking—for thinking is a death process. It is this subtle body of thought that feels the future, such thought having been freed from the brain. In order to sense this subtle realm we must engage "stillness of thought"—the mantra for the third verse of the Foundation Stone Meditation, and for Capricorn.* In this stillness we can feel the future as it indwells the soul-spiritual element of thinking, creating an inner resilience that helps us endure what the future is revealing.

Venus was in Capricorn during the temptations of Christ, thus making clear the way that is opened before us as the spiritual heights are revealed.

**December 9:** Sun 22° Scorpio: Raising of the Youth of Nain (Nov/13/30). The Youth of Nain was the Son of the Widow, who is a significant figure for the entire history of humanity. We can follow the incarnations: Youth of Nain, Mani, Parsifal. Rudolf Steiner called Mani one of the greatest beings ever to incarnate upon the planet. Further, he indicates that this individuality will most likely incarnate again in the twenty-first century if conditions are right. (Has he perhaps incarnated already?) Parsifal was also a son of a widow. What does the "son of the widow" indicate? In this regard, Rudolf Steiner noted:

---

135 Steiner, *The Gospel of St. John*, lect. 10.

During the fifth Root Race,[136] the father withdraws. The soul is widowed. Humanity is thrown back onto itself. It must find the light of truth within its own soul in order to act as its own guide. Everything of a soul nature has always been expressed in terms of the feminine. Therefore this self-directing feminine element (which exists only in a germinal state today and will later be fully developed) is no longer confronted by the divine fructifier, and is called by Mani the "Widow." Therefore he calls himself "Son of the Widow."

Steiner then quotes the words of Mani: "You must lay aside everything that you have acquired as outer revelation by means of the senses. You must lay aside all things that come to you via outer authority; then you must become ripe to gaze into your own soul."[137]

Clearly the teachings of Mani direct widowed souls to unite with the return of the etheric Christ and the in-streaming wisdom of Divine Sophia. *We are now to become spiritual investigators in our own right through the inner ripening of our souls. Mani teaches the redemption of evil. The first step toward this great aspiration begins when one is able to confront evil in one's own nature.*

The Venus transit of the Sun that occurred last year, at 20° Taurus, was very close to opposition with where the Sun was at the Raising of the Youth of Nain. This is a clear signal that the "feminine element" that has been widowed from spiritual worlds must now create its own relationship with the teachings of Divine Sophia that are streaming toward us from the future. Past teachings are the foundation upon which the new revelations will find their ground, but these teachings are not to push into the future. They are to become the vessels into which the future finds its rest in the present. When Venus transits of the Sun occur, we could say that Venus and the Sun give birth to a pentagram of love—a star—and this star pulses with vital forces urging the soul to create new paradigms of cultural harmony. Since June of last year this star had been born and we are to follow it. This is the new star of Sophianic inspiration, and it will crest to its waxing and then descend to its waning over the next hundred years. Clearly it is the feminine wisdom of Sophia that pulses from this new cultural beacon. We are urged to found communities into which these impulses can flourish.

The Sun today remembers this raising of the Youth of Nain. We may ask: *What ails thee and me? Where am I widowed from my spiritual aims? Where does my faithfulness to my spiritual resolves need resurrection?*

In following the continuous sequence of spiritual teachings, we develop greater abilities in understanding the new language that is constantly forming. A deepening is occurring due to the effects of the etheric Christ, wherein Platonic resonances are ensouling new dispensations. This is creating a renaissance of wisdom, and the language of wisdom is quite different from the abstractions of past theologies. *Just as we need to develop an organ for comprehending the wisdom of fairy tales, so too do we need to develop an organ for comprehending the wisdom streams now flowing from cosmic heights. Great teachers are preparing us. Each teacher brings a thread contributing to the masterpiece that is leading us toward the future. To renounce even one of these teachers hampers our ability to understand the next—renunciation can actually affect our ability to stay on course with the "spiritual trajectory" of Earth evolution.* The Youth of Nain is coming. Teachers are now preparing those who are to become his disciples. The new teachings may seem foolish at first; then they become obvious, but by that time there is already a new foolishness to follow in the continuous unfolding of time. We are to follow the Morning Star—Venus—and her pentagram of love!

**December 14:** Sun 27° Scorpio: First raising of the daughter of Jairus (Nov/18/30). In Biblical times a child might become ill as a result of a transgression (a moral failure) on the part of one of its parents—instead of the parent becoming ill. Children had

---

136 The Fifth Great Epoch ("fifth Root Race") refers to the post-Atlantean Great Epoch, comprising seven smaller cultural ages beginning with the ancient Indian cultural epoch and ending with the future American cultural epoch. We are currently in the fifth cultural epoch— the European cultural epoch— within this post-Atlantean Great Epoch.

137 Steiner, *The Temple Legend*, p. 62.

great importance at this time, as they were links in the generational chain leading to the incarnation of the Messiah; and it was just this chain that caused such transference of illness from parent to child. After Christ performed his miracles he would offer a mantric prayer that was to help in sustaining the healing he had given, until the time when the Mystery of Golgotha would change everything:

> If we think back to the general condition of humanity shortly before the Mystery of Golgotha, we can gain a tangible sense of the reason for giving special mantra and prayers and urging people to remember these. The empty sheaths of the gods' dwelling places [chakras], which human beings had brought with them in their astral bodies through the succession of cultural epochs, had progressively been occupied by demons, and these could exert particularly destructive effects if those who led an immoral life supplied these demons improvident astral nourishment. At the moment a healing was performed and Christ had driven these demons out of the bodies of sick people, these sheaths of the dwelling places of the gods remained behind in an empty state, cleansed of the adversarial beings. Thus they were empty, and each person needed to fill them with something new to prevent them being re-occupied by the luciferic and ahrimanic spirits. They were therefore to fill them with the prayers and esoteric exercises which Christ Jesus had given them, until the day when they would *behold the whole glory of the Son of the Father*; in other words, until the Mystery of Golgotha, when the divine spirit would itself enter and inhabit these sheaths of one's body.[138]

The family of Jairus fell into their old attitude of disrespect and disbelief toward Jesus—and so their daughter again fell ill and died two weeks later.

The special mantras and prayers that were to sustain soul health in those ancient times is applicable as well to our times. Due to humanity's disrespect and disregard of their spiritual well-being, demons again occupy the chakras. Materialism, false teachings, and immoral developments in all aspects of life have provided nourishment for demons. The vast amount of spiritual attention transferred to the world of mammon is engendering possessions in our chakras. We have forgotten our lofty origins and have given ourselves over to unholy alliances. *As a matter of spiritual hygiene, in this time of the second coming of Christ, it is essential that we call the good powers again into our being through the practice of reciting prayers and mantras. This is no longer a mere option, for the adversary has grown too strong to be ignored. Our chakras need spiritual nourishment in order to maintain a connection, in freedom, to the divine-spiritual beings who would manifest within and through us.* In his book *Inner Radiance and the Body of Immortality*, Dr. Powell offers practices that bring the manna from Heaven that sustains us in maintaining our connection to Christ. We can counter the battle for the human soul now taking place on a global level by asking Christ to indwell us on a daily basis. Either we turn toward the spiritual world, or we will be taken up by the anti-spiritual beings that are rampantly swallowing many individuals and whole groups. Apathy toward this reality is a choice in and of itself.

**December 16:** Sun enters Sagittarius: "Becoming achieves the power to be" (Steiner, *Twelve Moods of the Zodiac*). William Bento illumines this mantra:

> When existence is regarded not merely as a noun, but as a verb, we enter the realm of becoming.
>
> It is being, in dynamic movement. Such movement is purposeful, for being seeks a state in which it can be a power of "presence," a reality of the here and now. This achievement "to be" is the drama of human potential. Each human being seeks "to be" what he or she has resolved to become. The arrival of that becoming is both a joyful and empowering experience where there is nothing to do but be.

*Control of Speech becomes Feeling for Truth.* Blessed are the self-disciplined, for they shall know the truth.

**December 17:** Full Moon: Sun 0°39 Sagittarius Moon 0°39 Gemini: Stilling of the storm (Nov/21/30). The Sun was at this degree in Sagittarius when Christ

---

138 Von Halle, *Illness and Healing and the Mystery Language of the Gospels*, pp. 113–114.

stilled the storm. In this miracle reported in the Gospel of Luke (8:22-25), Jesus and his disciples crossed a lake. While they were sailing he fell asleep and a great storm mounted, casting great waves that endangered the little boat. The disciples awakened Jesus saying: "Master, Master, we are perishing!" Jesus rose up, raised his hand—and a great calm ensued. The disciples were amazed at his command over the elements. Powerful images are contained in this story.

In changing times much will be asked of human beings striving to keep their destiny communities (the boat) intact. Astral forces of wind and etheric forces of water will surge from the depths of both individual and collective human nature. Change requires that we decide between fear and conviction. The nature of one's conviction will determine the course of one's destiny. Unshakeable belief in Christ and Sophia calms the storms in both human and earthly kingdoms.

> The eurythmy gesture "G" (Sagittarius) uses the force of the upper arms to push away the forces of darkness, to open the veiled secrets and the curtains of deception, with an aim to reveal the light of clarity and to understand the truth.[139]

Solutions to complex world dilemmas become possible as we part the curtains of deception. This is a day to remember and rekindle our willingness to aim our arrows (Sagittarius) with conviction toward solutions living beyond worldly possibilities. Storms of one sort or another always accompany change. It is rare that the nature of the change is perceived correctly as it is occurring. An example is this:

> People talk of mysterious manifestations; the whole divine revelation of spring, summer, autumn, and winter is mixed up. Chaos is setting in, and this comes not from Heaven but from the interior of the Earth. People think that these are merely climate changes, but this is not the case.[140]

Here is a great contemplation for the connection between the Earth's behavior and human thinking. If we cannot part the curtains of deception in order to bring forth the light, our thinking will remain shallow and the causes of Earth-change will be misinterpreted. When the winds of change threaten equilibrium, to whom would you turn?

**December 18:** Uranus stations 13°39 Pisces: With Uranus at this degree the USSR was in upheaval under the rule of rabid dictators. Stalin was persecuting the peasants; new camps for alleged dissidents were being built; a Five-Year-Plan for rapid industrialization was launched; mass collectivization was announced; the government began an anti-religion campaign; deportation and deaths listed in the millions; and revolts were measured in the hundreds. *Uranus has been transiting back and forth through these degrees since last year and throughout this year.*

The planet Uranus offers us a choice between "building" something in order to exalt one's self and through which we are given temporary advantages; or to "grow" something in order to exalt Heaven and through which we are moved by a hunger and thirst for truth, beauty, and goodness. The former is temporary, the latter eternal.

> Now, we occultists, magicians, esotericists and Hermeticists—all those who want to "do" instead of merely waiting, who want "to take their evolution in their own hands" and "to direct it toward an aim"—are confronted with this choice in a much more dramatic way, I should say, than is so for people who are not concerned with esotericism. Our principal danger (if not the *only* true danger) is that of preferring the role of "builders of the tower of Babel" (no matter whether personally or in a community) to watching over, "as gardeners or vine-growers, the garden or the vine of the Lord." Truth to tell, the only truly morally founded reason for keeping esotericism "esoteric," i.e. for not bringing it to the broad light of day and popularizing it, is the danger of the great misunderstanding of confusing the *tower* with the *tree*, as a consequence of which "masons" will be recruited instead of "gardeners."[141]

---

139 Paul and Powell, *Cosmic Dances of the Zodiac*, p. 74.
140 Tomberg, *Christ and Sophia*, p. 399–400.
141 *Meditations on the Tarot*, pp. 449-450.

*It is astonishing to witness those whose will "to do" is so driven that they convince themselves the mysteries can be popularized without causing harm—the result is the summons of a guild of masons. It is far better to patiently allow for the growth that leads toward an inner awakening, than it is to force this time before the soil has been properly prepared. If something is forced, esotericism is placed in harm's way. As esotericists we are to protect these mysteries.* Humanity is to learn how to rise up to meet the mysteries, for if mysteries are prematurely brought into the concrete world they will be killed. There is a fertile ground between above and below that is the living garden of esotericism. If the mysteries descend lower than this sphere, they will be trivialized and this is a tragedy. It may exalt the one doing the killing, for he/she is then seen as someone important. But evolution is not to be taken into our own hands. It has a season and must be gently grown into its fruition. Herod exalted the material world by sparing the Pharisees the threat posed by Christ. And hurried occultists exalt themselves at the expense of esotericism.

The power hungry, both large and small, who have striven to build towers of Babel, have therein made pacts with the devil—all who build from this ground will fail. Much in our world has been built to amass power and to exalt egoists; but these are *temporary* fortifications no matter how powerful those inhabiting these towers may feel. We are to find that which is quietly growing as the natural maturing of esotericism and tend this new life as gardeners—for in *growth* eternity finds its reflection.

Today we can seek the *light* within the budding *life* that is promising new growth in our souls; and this growth is to be tended as gardeners would tend a newly sprouted plant. Ignore the saber rattling and posturing of snakes and thieves—their world is temporal. We remember: "He who exalts himself will be abased, and he who humbles himself will be exalted" (Luke XIV, 11).

**December 19:** Sun 2° Sagittarius conjunct the Galactic Center. The Archer's arrow aims at the Galactic Center: the heart of the Milky Way. This is opposite to where the Sun was at Pentecost.

**December 23:** Sun 6°51 Sagittarius: First Temptation in the Wilderness (Nov/27/29): There are forces that originated in cosmic aeons prior to that of the human being. Remnants of these forces live in densified forms within the interior of the Earth, and from here they work negatively against the human being. The remnants from previous aeons that work negatively with the will-nature of human beings are those of "trapped life." Through the transformation of the will, whereby it becomes obedient to Divine Will, "trapped life" becomes united with cosmic love (Pluto/Phanes). The first temptation in the wilderness was the temptation to bow to the Prince of this World. This is the temptation to use the personal will in service of self-gain—a temptation that continues in our time through all forms of tyranny.

> Humanity has the task to bring to realization that which Nature does not bring to realization. Nature becomes conscious in us and we have to create further. The kingdoms of Nature are beneath the human being. The ideal to strive for is the kingdom of God (*regnum Dei*)—as in the Lord's Prayer: "Thy kingdom come!" To bring this to realization—this is the task which the human being has to fulfill on Earth, following his/her highest ideal. This world that is not yet there is what the human being has to learn to build.[142]

May we become the "handmaids of the Lord" so that our deeds reflect what is best for all of humanity and all of Earth's creatures. In this way we become builders of the "world that is not yet there." The brick and mortar of this building are not those sculpted on Earth, but rather the forces that are freed when moral will holds sway in our deeds.

**December 24:** Christmas Eve and the opening to the Holy Nights. May we consciously enter into the wonder of this portal that leads us into the mysteries of the Holy Days and Nights that stretch before us.

**Sun 7°53 Sagittarius:** The Second Temptation in the Wilderness (Nov/28/29). Forces from past aeons that work negatively against the feeling nature of

---
142 *Starlight*, vol. 10, translations of unpublished works by Valentin Tomberg.

human beings are the forces in the inner Earth that work from "trapped sound" (Neptune/Night). *Through the transformation of our heart, our feeling life becomes permeated with cosmic sound, whereby we hear spiritual beings working with us.* The second temptation in the wilderness was the temptation to plunge from the pinnacle of the temple, with the assurance that Angels would catch us. This is the temptation to fall from consciousness, forsaking the Angels, and instead become pawns in magnetic attractions to fallen, and, densified forces. This can result in terrible polarization in the feeling life, as happened with those who were behind the communist revolution of 1917 in Russia.

> Circumstances are always influenced by the subconscious if the human being is not active. If he does not strive continually with respect to his subconscious, he succumbs to some kind of inertia, which leads to a darkening of the subconscious. Thus, the human being can find himself in complete darkness. "The pinnacle of the temple" (Luke 4:11) is the superconscious. The temptation [of casting oneself from the pinnacle of the temple] of Christ Jesus in the wilderness is that of believing in the wisdom of the subconscious.[143]

May our heart beat as one with the hearts of others, in spirit awareness. And may we reach for the true pinnacle of our temple!

**December 25:** Christian Celebration of the Birth of Christ. This day a seed is planted in the inner sanctuary of our heart. May we believe in this gift and tend it through the coming weeks. It will quicken at Candlemas, and then sprout, revealing its new life at Easter. We can follow the flowering as we move through the coming summer, and this will come to fruition at Michaelmas (nine months from this time of our conceiving). This is the seed of our future spiritual potential for the coming year. What in childhood came from without as gifts becomes, in our adulthood, our recognition of a new aspect of our eternal being that is born from the depths of winter's night, and seeks to become one with us as the year unfolds.

---

143 Ibid.

**ASPECT:** Mars and Moon 13° Virgo opposite Uranus 13° Pisces: The Flight into Egypt. Uranus was at this degree when the family of the Solomon Jesus family fled to Egypt after having been visited by the three kings. Mars was close to today's degree at the temptations in the wilderness. *As we come to the close of the year 2013 we can see today's inscription in the stars as guidance for our moving into 2014. We are to overcome the tempters who are so blatantly working everywhere around us, and turn our hearts to the reincarnation of the wisdom teachings of ancient Egypt. These new teachings, now Christianized, are guiding us to the new city—Heavenly Jerusalem—the holy city that we enter by opening to Christ in his second coming in union with his Bride—Sophia. Christ and Sophia are leading us to this golden future. We are living in the time when our forgetting of the stars is coming to an end. Sophia is opening her great book—the book of the stars. As this book is opening, so too is our ability to remember how to read its star-born language.*

The Solomon Jesus child was taken into Egypt in order to be spared the murder of the innocents that took place shortly thereafter throughout Bethlehem. We are to avoid the murderous activity of the adversaries by also finding sanctuary in the unfolding mysteries of Christ and Sophia, whose teachings are revealed through the stars—and this great wisdom has its origins in Egypt.

Look up tonight and find your wonder as the stars of Heaven delight in your attention. May we find the peace of heart that hears the silence of love weaving its glistening threads of wisdom throughout the world as the Grail nourishment that ennobles the soul:

> The legend of the Holy Grail tells us of that miraculous food, prepared from the finest effects of the sense impressions and the finest effects of the mineral extracts, whose purpose it is to nourish the noblest part of human beings throughout life on Earth. All other nourishment would kill them. This celestial food is contained in the vessel of the Holy Grail. [Lecture 6: The Paradise Legend and the Holy Grail Legend]
>
> The content of the Holy Grail has been mentioned. It is the substance that nourishes

the physical instrument of the earthly human being—it is the pure mineral extract derived from the food that, in the purest part of the human brain, unites with the finest sense impressions. To whom should this food be served? If we turn to the esoteric presentation in the Mysteries instead of the external description, we discover that the Grail should be offered to the person who has come to understand the maturity necessary to lift oneself gradually and with increasing awareness to knowledge of what the Grail is.[144]

**Sun 8°54 Sagittarius:** The Third Temptation in the Wilderness (Nov/29/29). Forces from past aeons that work negatively against the thinking life of human beings are the forces in the inner Earth that work out of "trapped light" (Uranus/Ouranos). These forces can cause a poverty of thought, whereby thinking is torn from cosmic thoughts. Through the transformation of our thinking we can become a vehicle for cosmic light. The third temptation in the wilderness was the temptation to turn stones to bread:

> The temptation of "turning stones to bread" is that of "producing" the living and organic from the dead and material. For example, one does precisely this if one conceives of thinking as a mechanical process in the brain. That is, if one supposes that the brain produces thoughts just as the glands produce secretion. Thus, the third temptation has to do with materialism, just as the second temptation has to do with the force of moral irresponsibility, and the first temptation with the will to power.[145]

May our thinking be illumined by truth, and our contemplation ennobled through spirit beholding.

**December 26:** Sun enters the second decan of Sagittarius, ruled by the Moon and associated with the constellation Corona Australis, the Southern Crown, forming a moonlike chalice beneath the central part of the Archer.

**Sun 9°58 Sagittarius:** End of the forty days in the wilderness. In 2010 Pluto's transit of 8° 54 Sagittarius was of special significance, as it recalled Pluto's actual position at the climax of the temptation period in the wilderness, when the Sun and Pluto were in conjunction. On this fortieth day in the wilderness, however, we celebrate the end of the period of temptation when Angels came to minister to Christ:

> Just as Jesus Christ triumphed in the confrontation with evil and emerged victorious on the fortieth day—to be consoled by the heavenly nourishment of the Angels—so there is every hope that humankind as a whole will successfully navigate a course through the historical period of temptation [ending historically in 2018]. It is only after passing through this that the real unfolding of the Christ Impulse will come to manifestation. Then, for example, a historical mirroring of the miracle at the wedding at Cana will take place during the Aquarian age.[146]

May we all find the wings of the dove—the presence of the Holy Spirit—during these blessed days and nights we have now entered. Let this peace enfold and envelop us.

**December 27:** Sun 11° Sagittarius: Second raising of the daughter of Jairus (Dec/1/30) Thirteen days after her first raising from the dead, Salome was again close to death. At this second raising from the dead, Salome was deeply moved and shed tears:

> Jesus exhorted the parents to receive God's mercy thankfully, to completely renounce vanity and worldly pleasure, to do penance, and to beware of again compromising their daughter's life, now restored for the second time. Jesus told Salome that in the future she should no longer live according to the dictates of her flesh and blood, but that she should eat the Bread of Life—the Word of God—and she should repent, believe, pray, and do good deeds. Salome's parents became inwardly transformed and expressed their determination to change their ways.[147]

---

144 Steiner, *The Effects of Esoteric Development*, lect. 7: Astrality's Struggle with Egoism.

145 *Starlight vol. 10*, translations of unpublished work by Valentin Tomberg.

146 *CHA*, The Temptation in the Wilderness.

147 *CHA*, The Raising of the Youth of Nain and of the Daughter of Jairus.

There is a universal teaching in this miracle:

> In this example of Jairus's daughter is contained a teaching concerning the Second Coming of the Lord. Many are those who received the grace of Jesus Christ through his First Coming, but in later incarnations have forgotten it. Like Jairus and his wife, they have lived frivolous lives based on worldly concerns, even mocking the memory of the Holy One of Israel, the Saviour of mankind. But misfortune is bound to strike whosoever turns away from the Source of all Goodness. And this is the situation in which many find themselves in their incarnations in the Age of the Second Coming. Salvation can be found only by turning to Jesus Christ, and as in the case of Jairus, a second opportunity will be given to all who sincerely seek him. And in the case of those who have missed the grace of Jesus Christ in their incarnations up until now, there is now another opportunity—as in the case of the pagan woman Enue[148]—to seek out Jesus Christ and make contact with him. However great the throng, he notices each one, and his healing power of love and compassion goes forth to each who seeks it and needs it.[149]

Pagans, Jews, Christians, Buddhist, Hindus—and all the other religious groups who are devoted to the various petals of the *Rose of the World*—can touch him now. Christ, the being of Love, is the center of all groups of people until the end of time. Where Christ has been usurped, the soul of the person, the circle, organization, or society is dying, just as Salome died when her father dismissed the presence of Christ. We are given a second chance.

As the year comes toward its end, we can contemplate how we may strive to change our ways to become more of who we truly are. May we receive the blessed nourishment of these holy days and nights.

**December 29:** Superior conjunction Mercury and Sun 13° Sagittarius square Uranus 13° Pisces: Jesus in Megiddo (Nov/15/30). Mercury and Sun are conjunct where Mercury remembers Jesus in Megiddo—a city now known as the valley of Jezreel—and also known as Armageddon (derived from the Hebrew for Har Megiddo) and mentioned in Revelation 16:14-16. Historians believe that more battles were fought at this location than anywhere else on the Earth. This day in AD 30 was two days after the raising of the Youth of Nain:

> During the afternoon Jesus wandered in the fields east of Megiddo, teaching the workers who were busy sowing seeds. He taught them in parables. As he was thus engaged, some disciples of John the Baptist arrived and accompanied Jesus into Megiddo. Many sick people were gathered there: lame, blind, dumb, deaf, and others. Jesus cured them all.[150]

With Mercury and Sun together remembering this dark valley, and Uranus still remembering the dark times of Stalin and Hitler, we can celebrate the power of Christ that works through all darkness to bring the light of love and faith into all human beings of good will.

**December 30: ASPECT:** Mars 16° Virgo square Pluto 16° Sagittarius, and opposite heliocentric Uranus 16° Pisces: Pentecost and Whitsun. Pluto was here at both Ascension and Pentecost. Orpheus described Phanes (higher Pluto) as an androgynous creator god, the source of the primal will, the fire of love that underlies the whole of existence:

> Phanes is the creator of all, from whom the world has its first origin.... He is imagined as marvelously beautiful, a figure of shining light.... He is of both sexes, since he is to create their race of gods unaided, "bearing within himself the honored seed of the gods" (Orphic Fragment 85).... He made an eternal home for the gods and was their first king.... Phanes bore a daughter, Night, whom he took as his partner and to whom he gave great power. She assisted him in the work of creation, and he finally handed over his sceptre to her, so that she became the next in order to the rulers of the universe.... Night bore to Phanes Gaia and Ouranos (Earth and

---

148 Enue was the woman healed of the issue of blood whose destiny was intricately intertwined with that of Salome.
149 Ibid.

150 *Chron.* p. 257.

Heaven).... To Ouranos Night handed over the supreme power.[151]

With Mars, the planet of the Word, square Pluto and opposite Uranus, we can live into the beauty of creation in its Inspiration (Night/Sophia) and in its Imagination (Ouranos/Uranus) and in its Intuitive origins (Phanes/Pluto). With these three higher aspects of thinking, feeling and willing, we will be initiated into *the Harmony of the Spheres*—the region in which the divine origins of creation sound together with the unfallen archetype of the human soul.

At the Ascension, Christ rose into these realms, and at Pentecost he brought down to Earth and humanity the possibility that all may achieve this blessedness.

**December 31: ASPECT:** Mercury conjunct Pluto 16° Sagittarius: Commissioning of the Twelve (Nov/10/30). Pluto and Mercury were conjunct when Jesus had comforted Martha, who was very sad due to Magdalene's relapse. On this day he commissioned the twelve:

> Today there occurred—for the first time—the sending out of the disciples. At about ten o'clock in the morning, with the twelve and about thirty other disciples, Jesus left Capernaum and went north in the direction of Saphet and Hanathon, accompanied by a large crowd. Around three in the afternoon, they approached Hanathon. Here Jesus and the disciples climbed a mountain used in former times by the prophets. Jesus had taught there less than one year ago, on Tebeth 12. This time, however, the crowd did not go up the mountain. On the mountain, Jesus addressed the disciples, giving them instructions and sending them out into the world with the words found in Matthew 9:36-10:16. Each of the twelve had a small flask of oil, and Jesus taught them how to use it for anointing and also for healing. Afterward, the disciples knelt in a circle around Jesus, and he prayed and laid his hands upon the head of each of the twelve. Then he blessed the remaining disciples. After embracing one another, the disciples set off, having received indications from Jesus as to where they should go and when they should return to him. Peter, James the Lesser, John, Philip, Thomas, Judas, and twelve other disciples remained with him. They all came down the mountain together. At the bottom, they met up with a crowd of people returning home from Capernaum. That night Jesus stayed in Bethanat (Matthew 11:11).[152]

On this last day of 2013 we can all become disciples, commissioned to go into the world, and in this coming new year we can bless, heal, and make peace with every word we utter and with every step we take. The flask of oil we carry is the flame of love in our heart. May we spend this endlessly in pursuit of service to our Mother and the mission of the Earth and humanity.

---

151 *Hermetic Astrology*, vol. 2, pp. 290–291.

152 *Chron.* p. 263.

# GLOSSARY

This glossary of entries relating to Esoteric Christianity lists only some of the specialized terms used in the articles and commentaries of the *Journal for Star Wisdom*. For reasons of space, the entries are very brief, and the reader is encouraged to read the works of Rudolf Steiner for a more complete understanding of these terms.

**Ahriman:** An adversarial being identified by the great prophet Zarathustra during the ancient Persian cultural epoch (5067–2907 BC) as an opponent to the Sun God, *Ahura Mazda,* or *Ahura Mazdao* (obs.), ("Aura of the Sun"). Also called Satan, Ahriman represents one aspect of the Dragon. Ahriman's influence leads to materialistic thinking devoid of feeling, empathy, and moral conscience. Ahriman helps inspire science and technology, and works through forces of sub-nature such as gravity, electricity, magnetism, radioactivity—forces that are antithetical to life. The influence of Ahriman's activity upon the human being limits human cognition to that which is derived from sense perception, hardens thinking (materialistic thoughts), attacks the etheric body by way of modern technology (electromagnetic radiation, etc.), and hardens hearts (cold and calculating).

**ahrimanic beings:** Spiritual beings who have become agents of Ahriman's influences.

**Angel Jesus:** A pure immaculate Angelic being who sacrifices himself so that the Christ may work through him. This Angelic being is actually of the status of an Archangel, who has descended to work on the Angelic level in order to be closer to human beings and to assist them on the path of confrontation with evil.

**Ascension:** An unfathomable process at the start of which, on May 14, AD 33, Christ united with the etheric realm which surrounds and permeates the earth with Cosmic Life. Thus began his cosmic ascent to the realm of the heavenly Father, with the goal of elevating the Earth spiritually and opening pathways between the Earth and the spiritual world for the future.

**astral body:** Part of the human being that is the bearer of consciousness, passion, and desires, as well as idealism and the longing for perfection.

**Asuras:** Fallen Archai (Time Spirits) from the time of Old Saturn, whose opposition to human evolution comes to expression through promoting debauched sexuality and senseless violence among human beings. So low is the regard that the Asuras have for the sacredness of human life, that as well as promoting extreme violence and debauchery (for example, through the film industry), they do not hold back from the destruction of the physical body of human beings. In particular, the activity of the Asuras retards the development of the consciousness soul.

**bodhisattva:** On the human level a bodhisattva is a human being far advanced on the spiritual path, a human being belonging to the circle of twelve great teachers surrounding the Cosmic Christ. One who incarnates periodically to further the evolution of the Earth and humanity, working on the level of an angelic, archangelic, or higher being in relation to the rest of humanity. Every 5,000 years one of these great teachers from the circle of bodhisattvas takes on a special mission, incarnating repeatedly to awaken a new human faculty and capacity. Once that capacity has been imparted through its human bearer, this Bodhisattva then incarnates upon the earth for the last time, ascending to the level of a Buddha in order to serve humankind from spirit realms. See also Maitreya Bodhisattva.

**Central Sun:** Heart of the Milky Way, also called the Galactic Center. Our Sun orbits this Central Sun over a period of approximately 225 million years.

**chakra:** One of seven astral organs of perception through which human beings develop higher levels of cognition such as clairvoyance, telepathy, and so on.

# Glossary

**Christ:** The eternal being who is the second member of the Trinity. Also called the *Divine I AM*, the Son of God, the Cosmic Christ, and the Logos/Word. Christ began to fully unite with the human vessel (Jesus) at the Baptism in the Jordan, and for 3½ years penetrated as the *Divine I AM* successively into the astral body, etheric body, and physical body of Jesus, spiritualizing each member. Through the Mystery of Golgotha Christ united with the Earth, kindling the spark of Christ consciousness (*Not I, but Christ in me*) in all human beings.

**Christ Jesus:** The Divine-Human being; the God-Man; the union of the Divine with the Human. The presence of the Cosmic Christ in the physical body of the human being called the Nathan Jesus during the 3½ years of the ministry.

**consciousness soul:** The portion of the human soul in which "I" consciousness is awakening not only to its own sense of individuality and to the individualities of others, but also to its higher self—spirit self (Sanskrit: *manas*). Within the consciousness soul, the "I" perceives truth, beauty, and goodness; within the spirit self, the "I" becomes truth, beauty, and goodness.

**crossing the threshold:** a term applicable to our time, as human beings are increasingly encountering the spiritual world—in so doing, crossing the threshold between the sense-perceptible realm and non-physical realms of existence. To the extent that spiritual capacities have not been cultivated, this encounter with non-physical realms beyond the sense world signifies a descent into the subconscious (for example, through drugs) rather than an ascent to knowledge of higher worlds through the awakening of higher levels of consciousness.

**Decan:** The zodiac of 360° is divided into twelve signs, each of 30°. A decan is 10°, thus one third of one sign or 1/36 of the zodiac.

**Devil:** Another name for Lucifer.

**Dragon:** As used in the Apocalypse of John, there are different appearances of the dragon, each one representing an adversarial being opposed to Michael, Christ, and Sophia. For example, the great red dragon of chapter 12 opposes Sophia, the woman clothed with the Sun (Sophia is the pure Divine-Cosmic Feminine Soul of the World). The imagery from chapter 12 of Revelations depicts the woman clothed with the Sun as pregnant and that the great red dragon attempts to devour her child as soon as it is born. The child coming to birth from the woman clothed with the Sun represents the Divine-Cosmic "I AM" born through the assistance of the pure Divine Feminine Soul of the World. The dragon is cast down from the heavenly realm by the mighty Archangel Michael. Cast down to the Earth, the dragon continues with attempts to devour the cosmic child (the Divine-Cosmic "I AM") coming to birth among humankind.

**ego:** The soul sheath through which the "I" begins to incarnate and to experience life on Earth (to be distinguished from the term *ego* used in Freudian and Jungian psychology—hence written capitalized "Ego" in order to make this distinction). The terms *ego*, "*I*," and *soul* are often used interchangeably in spiritual science. The ego maintains threads of integrity and continuity through memory, while experiencing new sensations and perceptions through observation and thinking, feeling, and willing. The ego is capable of moral discernment and also experiences temptation. For this reason it is often stated that the "I" comprises a higher nature ("Ego") and a lower nature ("ego").

**Emmerich, Anne Catherine** (also "Sister Emmerich"): A Catholic stigmatist (1774–1824) whose visions depicted the daily life of Jesus, beginning some weeks before the event of the descent of Christ into the body of Jesus at the Baptism in the River Jordan and extending for a period of several weeks after the Crucifixion.

**Ephesus:** The area in Asia Minor (now Turkey) to which the Apostle John (also called John Zebedee, the brother of James the Greater) accompanied the Virgin Mary approximately three years after the death of Christ Jesus. Ephesus was a very significant ancient mystery center where cosmic mysteries of the East found their way into the West. Initiates at Ephesus were devoted to the goddess Artemis, known as "Artemis of Ephesus," whose qualities are more those of a Mother goddess than is the case with the Greek goddess Artemis, although there is a certain degree of overlap between Artemis and Artemis of Ephesus with regard to many of their respective characteristics. A magnificent Ionic mystery temple was built in honor of Artemis of Ephesus at a location close to the Aegean Sea. Mary's house, built by John, was located high up above, on the nearby hill known as Mount Nightingale, about six miles from the temple of Artemis at Ephesus.

etheric body: The body of life forces permeating and animating the physical body. The etheric body was formed during Ancient Sun evolution. The etheric body's activity is expressed in the seven life processes permeating the seven vital organs. The etheric body is related to the movements of the seven visible planets.

Fall, The: A fall from oneness with spiritual worlds. The Fall, which took place during the Lemurian period of Earth evolution, was a time of dramatic transition in human evolution when the soul descended from "Paradise" into earthly existence. Through the Fall the human soul began to incarnate into a physical body upon the earth and experience the world from "within" the body, perceiving through the senses.

Fifth Gospel: The writings and lectures of Rudolf Steiner based on new spiritual perceptions and insights into the mysteries of Christ's life on earth, including the second coming of Christ—his appearance in the etheric realm in our time, beginning in the twentieth century.

Golgotha, Mystery of: Rudolf Steiner's designation for the entire mystery of the coming of Christ to the Earth. Sometimes this term is used more specifically to refer to the events surrounding the Crucifixion and Resurrection. In particular, the Crucifixion—the sacrifice on the cross—marked the birth of Christ's union with the Earth. Also referred to as the "Turning Point of Time," whereby at the Crucifixion Christ descended from the sphere of the Sun and became the "Spirit of the Earth."

Grail: An etheric chalice into which Christ can work to transform earthly substance into spiritual substance. The term *Grail* has many deep levels of meaning and refers on the one hand to a spiritual stream in service of Christ, and on the other hand to the means by which the human "I" penetrates and transforms evil into good. The power of transubstantiation expresses something of this process of transformation of evil into good.

Grail Knights: Those trained to confront evil and transform it into something good, in service of Christ. Members of a spiritual stream that existed in the past and continues to exist—albeit in metamorphosed form—in the present. Every human being striving for the good can potentially become a Grail Knight.

I AM: One's true individuality, that—with few exceptions—never fully incarnates but works into the developing Ego and its lower bodies (astral, etheric, physical). The **Cosmic I AM** is the "I AM" of Christ, through which—on account of the Mystery of Golgotha—we are all graced with the possibility of receiving a divine spark therefrom.

Jesus (see Nathan Jesus and Solomon Jesus): The pure human being who received the Christ at the Baptism in the River Jordan.

Jesus Christ: See Christ Jesus.

Jesus of Nazareth: The name of the human being whose birth is celebrated in the Gospel of Luke, also referred to as the Nathan Jesus. When Jesus of Nazareth reached the age of twelve, the spirit of the Solomon Jesus (Gospel of Matthew) united with the body and sheaths of the pure Nathan Jesus. This union lasted for about 18 years, until the Baptism in the River Jordan. During these 18 years, Jesus of Nazareth was a composite being comprising the Nathan Jesus and the spirit ("I") of the Solomon Jesus. Just before the Baptism, the spirit of the Solomon Jesus withdrew, and at the Baptism Jesus became known as "Christ Jesus" through the union of Christ with the sheaths of Jesus.

Jezebel: Wife of King Ahab, approximately 900 BC, who worked through the powers of black magic against the prophet Elijah.

Kali Yuga: Yugas are ages of influence referred to in Hindu cosmography, each yuga lasting a certain numbers of years in length (always a multiple of 2500). The Kali Yuga is also known as the Dark Age, which began with the death of Krishna in 3102 BC (-3101). Kali Yuga lasted 5,000 years and ended in AD 1899.

## Glossary

**Kingly Stream:** Biblically, the line of heredity from King David into which the Solomon Jesus (Gospel of Matthew) was born. The kings (the three magi) were initiates who sought to bring the cosmic will of the heavenly Father to expression on the Earth through spiritual forces working from spiritual beings dwelling in the stars. The minds of the wise kings were enlightened by the coming of Christ Jesus.

**Krishna:** A cosmic-human being, the sister soul of Adam that overlighted Arjuna as described in the Bhagavad Gita. The overlighting by Krishna of Arjuna could be described as an incorporation of Krishna into Arjuna. An incorporation is a partial incarnation. The cosmic-human being known as Krishna later fully incarnated as Jesus of Nazareth (Nathan Jesus—Gospel of Luke).

**Lazarus:** The elder brother of Mary Magdalene, Martha, and Silent Mary. At his raising from the dead, Lazarus became the first human being to be fully initiated by Christ (see Lazarus–John).

**Lazarus–John:** At the raising of Lazarus from the dead by Christ, the spiritual being of John the Baptist united with Lazarus. The higher spiritual members of John (Spirit Body, Life Spirit, Spirit Self) entered into the members of Lazarus, which were developed to the level of the consciousness soul.

**Lucifer:** The name of a fallen spiritual being, also called the Light-Bearer, who acts as a retarding force within the human astral body and also in the sentient soul. Lucifer inflames egoism and pride within the human being, often inspiring genius and supreme artistry. Arrogance and self-importance are stimulated, without humility or sacrificial love. Lucifer stirs up forces of rebellion, but cannot deliver true freedom—just its illusion.

**luciferic beings:** Spiritual beings who have become agents of Lucifer's influences.

**magi:** Initiates in the mystery school of Zarathustra, the Bodhisattva who incarnated as Zoroaster (Zaratas, Nazaratos) in the sixth century BC and who, after he came to Babylon, became a teacher of the Chaldean priesthood. At the time of Jesus, the magi were still continuing the stargazing tradition of the school of Zoroaster. The task of the magi was to recognize when their master would reincarnate. With their visit to the new-born Jesus child in Bethlehem (Gospel of Matthew), to this child who was the reincarnated Zarathustra/Zoroaster, they fulfilled their mission. The three magi are the "priest kings from the East" referred to in the Gospel of Matthew.

**Maitreya Bodhisattva:** The bodhisattva individuality that is preparing to become the successor of Gautama Buddha and will be known as the Bringer of the Good. This bodhisattva was incarnated in the second century BC as Jeshu ben Pandira, the teacher of the Essenes, who died about 100 BC. Rudolf Steiner indicated that Jeshu ben Pandira reincarnated at the beginning of the twentieth century as a great bodhisattva individuality in order to fulfill the lofty mission of proclaiming Christ's coming in the etheric realm, beginning around 1933: "He will be the actual herald of Christ in his etheric form" (lecture about Jeshu ben Pandira held in Leipzig on November 4, 1911). There are differing points of view as to who this individuality actually was in his twentieth century incarnation.

**manas:** Also called the Spirit Self; the purified astral body, lifted into full communion with truth and goodness by becoming the true and the good within the essence of the higher self of the human being. Manas is the spiritual source of the Ego ("I"), and as it is the eternal part of the human being that goes from life to life, Manas bears the human being's true "eternal name" through its union with the Holy Spirit. The "eternal name" expresses the human being's true mission from life to life.

**Mani:** The name of a lofty initiate who lived in Babylon in the third century AD. The founder of the Manichean stream, whose mission is the transformation of evil into goodness through compassion and love. Mani reincarnated as Parzival in the ninth century AD. Mani/Parzival is one of the leading initiates of our present age—the age of the consciousness soul (AD 1414–3574). One of the highest beings ever to incarnate upon the earth, he will become the future Manu beginning in the astrological age of Sagittarius. This future Manu will oversee the spiritual evolution of a sequence of seven ages, comprising the seven cultural epochs of the Sixth Great Age of Earth evolution from the Age of Sagittarius to the Age of Gemini—lasting a total of 7 x 2,160 years (15,120 years), since each zodiacal age lasts 2,160 years.

**Manu:** Like the word Buddha, the word Manu is a title. A Manu has the task of spiritually overseeing one Great Age of Earth evolution, comprising seven astrological ages (seven cultural epochs)—lasting a total of 7 x 2,160 years (15,120 years), since each zodiacal age lasts 2,160 years. The present Age of Pisces AD 215–2,375—with its corresponding cultural epoch (AD 1414–3574)—is the fifth epoch during the Fifth Great Age of Earth evolution. (Lemuria was the Third Great Age, Atlantis the Fourth Great Age, and since the great flood that destroyed Atlantis, we are now in the Fifth Great Age). The present Manu is the exalted Sun-initiate who guided humanity out of Atlantis during the ancient flooding that destroyed the continent of Atlantis formerly in the region of the Atlantic Ocean—the Flood referred to in the Bible in connection with Noah. He is the overseer of the seven cultural epochs corresponding to the seven astrological ages from the Age of Cancer to the Age of Capricorn, following the sequence: Cancer, Gemini, Taurus, Aries, Pisces, Aquarius, Capricorn. The present Manu was the teacher of the Seven Holy Rishis who were the founders of the ancient Indian cultural epoch (7227–5067 BC) during the Age of Cancer. He is known in the Bible as Noah, and in the Flood story belonging to the Gilgamesh epic he is called Utnapishtim. Subsequently this Manu appeared to Abraham as Melchizedek and offered Abraham an agape ("love feast") of bread and wine. Jesus is designated as "high priest after the order of Melchizedek" (Hebrews 5:10).

**Mary:** Rudolf Steiner distinguishes between the Nathan Mary and the Solomon Mary (see corresponding entries). The expression "Virgin Mary" refers to the Solomon Mary, the mother of the child Jesus whose birth is described in the Gospel of Matthew.

**Mary Magdalene:** Sister of Lazarus, whose soul was transformed and purified as Christ cast out seven demons who had taken possession of her. Christ thus initiated Mary Magdalene. Later, she anointed Christ Jesus. And she was the first to behold the Risen Christ in the Garden of the Holy Sepulcher on the morning of his resurrection.

**megastar:** Stars with a luminosity greater than 10,000 times that of our Sun.

**Nain, Youth of:** Referred to in the Gospel of Luke as the son of the widow of Nain. The Youth of Nain—at the time he was 12 years old—was raised from the dead by Jesus. The Youth of Nain later reincarnated as the Prophet Mani (third century AD) and subsequently as the Grail King Parzival (ninth century AD).

**Nathan Jesus:** From the priestly line of David, as described in the Gospel of Luke. An immaculate and pure soul whose one and only physical incarnation was as Jesus of Nazareth (Nathan Jesus).

**Nathan Mary:** A pure being who was the mother of the Nathan Jesus. The Nathan Mary died in AD 12, but her spirit united with the Solomon Mary at the time of the Baptism of Jesus in the River Jordan. From this time on, the Solomon Mary—spiritually united with the Nathan Mary—was known as the Virgin Mary.

**New Jerusalem:** A spiritual condition denoting humanity's future existence that will come into being as human beings free themselves from the *maya* of the material world and work together to bring about a spiritualized Earth.

**Osiris:** Osiris and Isis are names given by the Egyptians to the preincarnatory forms of the spiritual beings who are now known as Christ and Sophia.

**Parzival:** Son of Gahmuret and Herzeloyde in the epic *Parzival* by Wolfram von Eschenbach. Although written in the thirteenth century, this work refers to actual people and events in the ninth century AD, one of whom (the central figure) bore the name Parzival. After living a life of dullness and doubt, Parzival's mission was to seek the Castle of the Grail and to ask the question "What ails thee?" of the Grail King, Anfortas—moreover, to ask the question without being bidden to do so. Parzival eventually became the new Grail King, the successor of

## Glossary

Anfortas. Parzival was the reincarnated prophet Mani. In the incarnation preceding that of Mani, he was incarnated as the Youth of Nain (Luke 7:11-15). Parzival is a great initiate responsible for guiding humanity during the Age of Pisces, which has given birth to the cultural epoch of the development of the consciousness soul (AD 1414-3574).

Pentecost: Descent of the Holy Spirit fifty days after Easter, whereby the cosmic "I AM" was birthed among the disciples and those individuals close to Christ. They received the capacity to develop Manas or Spirit Self within the community of striving human individuals, whereby the birth of the Spirit Self is facilitated through the soul of the Virgin Mary. See also World Pentecost.

phantom body: The pure spiritual form of the human physical body, unhindered by matter. The far-distant future state of the human physical body when it has become purified and spiritualized into a body of transformed divine will.

Presbyter John: Refers to Lazarus-John who moved to Ephesus about twenty years after the Virgin Mary had died there. In Ephesus he became a bishop. He is the author of the Book of Revelations, the Gospel of St. John, and the Letters of John.

Risen One: The initial appearance of Christ in his phantom body (resurrection body), beginning with his appearance to Mary Magdalene on Easter Sunday morning. Christ frequently appeared to the disciples in his phantom body during the 40 days leading from Easter to Ascension.

Satan: The traditional Christian name for Ahriman.

Serpent: Another name for Lucifer, but sometimes naming a combination of Lucifer and Ahriman, as in Revelations 12:9: "And the great dragon was cast out, that old serpent, called the Devil, and Satan, which deceiveth the whole world...."

Shepherd Stream: Biblically, the genealogical line from David the shepherd through his son Nathan. It was into this line that the Nathan Jesus was born, whose birth is described in the Gospel of Luke. Rudolf Steiner describes the shepherds, who—according to Luke—came to pay homage to the new-born child, as those servants of pure heart who perceive the good will streaming up from Mother Earth. The hearts of the shepherd were kindled with the fire of Divine Love by the coming of the Christ. The shepherds can be regarded as precursors of the heart stream of humanity that now intuits the being of Christ as the spirit of the earth.

Solomon Jesus: Descended from the genealogical line from David through his son Solomon. This line of descent is described in the Gospel of Matthew. The Solomon Jesus was a reincarnation of Zoroaster (sixth century BC). In turn, Zoroaster was a reincarnation of Zarathustra (6000 BC), the great prophet and founder of the ancient Persian religion of Zoroastrianism. He was a Bodhisattva, who as the founder of this new religion that was focused upon the Sun Spirit Ahura Mazdao, helped prepare humanity for the subsequent descent into incarnation of Ahura Mazdao, the cosmic Sun Spirit, as Christ.

Solomon Mary: The wise mother of the Solomon Jesus, who adopted the Nathan Jesus after the death of the Nathan Mary. At the time of the Baptism of Jesus in the River Jordan, the spirit of the Nathan Mary united with the Solomon Mary. Usually referred to as the Virgin Mary or Mother Mary, the Solomon Mary bore witness at the foot of the cross to the Mystery of Golgotha. She died in Ephesus eleven years after Christ's Ascension.

Sophia: Part of the Divine Feminine Trinity comprising the Mother (counterpart of the Father), the Daughter (counterpart of the Son), and the Holy Soul (counterpart of the Holy Spirit). Sophia, also known as the Bride of the Lamb, is the Daughter aspect of the threefold Divine Feminine Trinity. To the Egyptians Sophia was known as Isis, who was seen to belong to the starry realm surrounding the earth. In the Book of Proverbs, attributed to King Solomon, Sophia's temple has seven pillars (Proverbs 9:1). The seven pillars in Sophia's temple represent the seven great stages of Earth evolution (from Ancient Saturn to Future Vulcan).

Sorath: The great enemy of Christ who works against the "I" in the human being. Sorath is identified with the two-horned beast that rises up from the depths of earth, as described in the Apocalypse of St. John. Sorath is the Sun

Demon, and is identified by Rudolf Steiner as the Antichrist. According to the Book of Revelations his number is 666.

**Sun Demon:** Another name for Sorath.

**Transfiguration:** The event on Mt. Tabor where Christ Jesus was illumined with Divine Light raying forth from the purified etheric body of Jesus, which the Divine "I AM" of Christ had penetrated. The Gospels of Matthew and Luke describe the Transfiguration. The sunlike radiance that shone forth from Christ Jesus on Mt. Tabor was an expression of the purified etheric body that had its origin during the Old Sun period of Earth evolution.

**Transubstantiation:** Sacramental transformation of physical substance—for example, the transubstantiation of bread and wine during the Mass to become the body and blood of Christ. During the Holy Eucharist the bread and wine are transformed in such a way that the substances of bread and wine are infused with the life force (body) and light (blood) of Christ. Thereby the bread and wine are re-united with their divine archetypes and are no longer "merely" physical substances, but are bearers on the physical level of a spiritual reality.

**Turning Point of Time:** Transition between involution and evolution, as marked by the Mystery of Golgotha. The descending stream of involution culminated with the Mystery of Golgotha. With the descent of the Cosmic Christ into earthly evolution, through his sacrifice on Golgotha an ascending stream of evolution began. This sacrifice of Christ was followed by the events of his Resurrection and Ascension, which were followed in turn by Whitsun (Pentecost)—all expressing the ascending stream of evolution. This path of ascent was also opened up to all human beings by way of the power of the divine "I AM" bestowed—at least, potentially—on all humanity by Christ through his sacrifice on the cross.

**Union in the Temple:** The event of the union of the spirit of the Solomon Jesus with the 12-year-old Nathan Jesus. This union of the two Jesus children signified the uniting of the priestly (Nathan) line and the kingly (Solomon) line—both lines descended from King David.

**Whitsun:** "White Sunday"; Pentecost.

**World Pentecost** is the gradual event of cosmic revelation becoming human revelation as a signature of the end of the Dark Age (Kali Yuga). Anthroposophy (spiritual science) is a language of spiritual truth that could awaken a community of striving human beings to the presence of the Holy Spirit and the founding of the New Jerusalem.

**Zarathustra:** The great teacher of the ancient Persians in the sixth millennium BC (around 6000 BC). In the sixth century BC, Zarathustra reincarnated as Zoroaster. He then reincarnated as the Solomon Jesus (6 BC–AD 12), whose birth is described in the Gospel of Matthew.

**Zoroaster:** An incarnation of Zarathustra. Zarathustra/Zoroaster was a Bodhisattva. Zoroaster lived in 6th century BC. He was a master of wisdom. Among his communications as a teacher of wisdom was his specification as to how the zodiac of living beings in the heavens comes to expression in relation to the stars comprising the twelve zodiacal constellations. Zoroaster subsequently incarnated as the Solomon Jesus, whose birth is described in the Gospel of Matthew, to whom the three magi came from the East bearing gifts of gold, frankincense, and myrrh.

# REFERENCES

*See "Literature" on page 10 for an annotated list of books on Astrosophy.*

Andreev, Daniel. *Rosa Mira: Die Weltrose.* Frankeneck. Germany: Vega, 2009.

——. *The Rose of the World.* Great Barrington, MA: Lindisfarne Books, 1997.

Anonymous. *Meditations on the Tarot.* New York: Tarcher/Putman, 2002.

——. *The Mysterious Story of X7.* Berkeley, CA: North Atlantic Books, 2009.

Baudrillard, Jean. *The Illusion of the End.* Stanford, CA: Stanford University, 1994.

——. *Simulacra and Simulation.* Ann Arbor: University of Michigan, 1994.

Bento, William, Robert Schiappacase, and David Tresemer. *Signs in the Heavens: A Message for Our Time.* www.StarWisdom.org, 2001.

Blattmann, Georg. *Comets: Their Appearance and Significance.* Edinburgh: Floris Books, 1985.

Boardman, Terry. *Kaspar Hauser: Where Did He Come From?* Stourbridge. UK: Wynstones Press, 2007.

Bock, Emil. *The Three Years: The Life of Christ between Baptism and Ascension.* Edinburgh: Floris Books, 2006.

Bryant, William A. *A Journey Through Time: Biographical Rhythms.* Fair Oaks, CA: Rudolf Steiner College, 2006.

Burne, Jerome. *Chronicle of the World.* Mount Kisco, NY: ECAM Publications, 1990.

Carey, John (ed.). *Eyewitness to History.* New York: Avon, 1987.

Coon, Robert. *Earth Chakras.* self published, dist. by Lulu.com, 1967–2009.

*Der Europäer.* Basel: Perseus Publishing, periodical.

Dorsan, Jacques. *The Clockwise House System: A True Foundation for Sidereal and Tropical Astrology.* Great Barrington, MA: Lindisfarne Books, 2011.

Douglass, James. *JFK and the Unspeakable: Why He Died and Why It Matters.* Maryknoll, NY: Orbis Books, 2008.

Edwards, Ormond. *The Time of Christ: A Chronology of the Incarnation.* Edinburgh: Floris Books, 1986.

Ginzberg, Louis. *The Legends of the Jews: From Joshua to Esther* (vol. 4). Baltimore: John Hopkins University, 1998.

Goldhill, Simon. *The Temple of Jerusalem.* London: Profile, 2004.

Greene, Liz. *The Astrological Neptune and the Quest for Redemption.* Boston: Weiser, 1996.

Hauser, Kaspar. *Kaspar Hauser Speaks For Himself; Kaspar's Own Writings.* North Yorkshire, UK: Camphill Books, 1993.

Jung, Carl. *The Archetypes and the Collective Unconscious.* Princeton: Bollingen, 1981.

Kirchner-Bockholt, Margarete, and Erich Kirchner-Bockholt. *Rudolf Steiner's Mission and Ita Wegman.* London: Rudolf Steiner Press, 1977.

LeGrice, Keiron. *The Archetypal Cosmos.* Edinburgh: Floris, 2010.

Marx, Karl and Friedrich Engels. *Communist Manifesto.* New York: Penguin, 2012.

Meyer, Rudolf. *Die Wiedergewinnung des Johannesevangeliums.* Stuttgart: Verlag Urachhaus, 1962.

Mill, John Stuart. *Principles of Political Economy.* London: Oxford Classics, 1982.

O'Leary, P. V. (ed.) *The Inner Life of the Earth: Exploring the Mysteries of Nature, Subnature, and Supranature.* Great Barrington, MA: SteinerBooks, 2008.

Postman, Neil. *Amusing Ourselves to Death: Public Discourse in the Age of Show Business.* New York: Penguin, 1985.

Powell, Robert. *The Christ Mystery.* Fair Oaks, CA: Rudolf Steiner College, 1999.

——. *Christian Hermetic Astrology: The Star of the Magi and the Life of Christ.* Great Barrington, MA: Lindisfarne Books, 2009.

——. *Chronicle of the Living Christ: The Life and Ministry of Jesus Christ: Foundations of Cosmic Christianity.* Hudson, NY: Anthroposophic Press, 1996.

——. *Cultivating Inner Radiance and the Body of Immortality: Awakening the Soul through Modern*

*Etheric Movement*. Great Barrington, MA: Lindisfarne Books, 2012.

——. *Elijah Come Again: A Prophet for Our Time: A Scientific Approach to Reincarnation*. Great Barrington, MA: Lindisfarne Books, 2009.

——. *Hermetic Astrology*, vols. 1 and 2. San Rafael, CA: Sophia Foundation Press, 2006.

——. *History of the Zodiac*. San Rafael, CA: Sophia Academic Press, 2007.

——. *The Most Holy Trinosophia: The New Revelation of the Divine Feminine*. Great Barrington, MA: SteinerBooks, 2000.

——. *The Mystery, Biography, and Destiny of Mary Magdalene: Sister of Lazarus John & Spiritual Sister of Jesus*. Great Barrington, MA: Lindisfarne Books, 2008.

——. *The Sophia Teachings: The Emergence of the Divine Feminine in Our Time*. Great Barrington, MA: Lindisfarne Books, 2007.

Powell, Robert, and David Bowden. *Astrogeographia: Correspondences between the Stars and Earthly Locations: Earth Chakras and the Bible of Astrology*. Great Barrington, MA: SteinerBooks, 2012.

Powell, Robert, and Kevin Dann. *The Astrological Revolution: Unveiling the Science of the Stars as a Science of Reincarnation and Karma*. Great Barrington, MA: SteinerBooks, 2010.

——. *Christ and the Maya Calendar: 2012 & the Coming of the Antichrist*. Great Barrington, MA: SteinerBooks, 2009.

Powell, Robert, and Lacquanna Paul. *Cosmic Dances of the Planets*. Sophia Foundation Press: San Rafael, CA, 2006.

Schulz, Joachim, and Emil Funk. *Zeitgeheimnisse im Christus-leben: Chronologie und 33-jähriger Rhythmus* [Secrets of Time in the Life of Christ: Chronology and the 33-Year Rhythm]. Dornach: Verlag am Goetheanum, 1970.

Schwaller de Lubicz, R. A. *The Temple of Man*. Rochester, VT: Inner Traditions, 1998.

Sheen, A. Renwick. *Geometry and the Imagination* (revised ed.). Fair Oaks, CA: AWSNA, 2002.

Steiner, Rudolf. *According to Luke: The Gospel of Compassion and Love Revealed*. Great Barrington, MA: SteinerBooks, 2006.

——. *The Ahrimanic Desception*. Spring Valley, NY: Anthroposophic Press, 1985.

——. *Anthroposophical Leading Thoughts*. London: Rudolf Steiner Press. 1985.

——. *Anthroposophy (A Fragment): A New Foundation for the Study of Human Nature*. Hudson, NY: Anthroposophic Press, 1996.

——. *The Apocalypse of St. John: Lectures on the Book of Revelation*. Hudson, NY: Anthroposophic Press, 1993.

——. *The Book of Revelation: And the Work of the Priest*. London: Rudolf Steiner Press, 2008.

——. *Christ and the Spiritual World: And the Search for the Holy Grail*. London: Rudolf Steiner Press, 2008.

——. *Christianity as Mystical Fact: And the Mysteries of Antiquity*. Great Barrington, MA: SteinerBooks, 2006.

——. *Cosmic Memory: The Story of Atlantis, Lemuria, and the Division of the Sexes*. Great Barrington, MA: SteinerBooks, 2006.

——. *Esoteric Christianity and the Mission of Christian Rosenkreutz*. London: Rudolf Steiner Press, 2000.

——. *Esoteric Lessons 1904–1909*. Great Barrington, MA: SteinerBooks, 2007.

——. *Esoteric Develpment: Selected Lectures and Writings*. Great Barrington, MA: SteinerBooks, 2003.

——. *Et Incarnatus Est: The Time Cycle in Historic Events*. Spring Valley, NY: Mercury Press, 1983.

——. *The Fall of the Spirits of Darkness*. London: Rudolf Steiner Press, 2008.

——. *The Fifth Gospel: From the Akashic Record*. London: Rudolf Steiner Press, 1998.

——. *"Freemasonry" and Ritual Work: The Misraim Service*. Great Barrington, MA: SteinerBooks, 2007.

——. *From Crystals to Crocodiles…: Answers to Questions*. London: Rudolf Steiner Press, 2002.

——. *From the History & Contents of the First Section of the Esoteric School 1904–1914*. Great Barrington, MA: SteinerBooks, 2010.

——. *The Gospel of St. John*. New York: Anthroposophic Press, 1962.

——. *How to Know Higher Worlds: A Modern Path of Initiation*. Hudson, NY: Anthroposophic Press, 1995.

——. *The Incarnation of Ahriman: The Embodiment of Evil on Earth*. London: Rudolf Steiner Press, 2006.

———. *Intuitive Thinking as a Spiritual Path: A Philosophy of Freedom.* Hudson, NY: Anthroposophic Press, 1995.

———. *The Karma of Untruthfulness: Secret Societies, the Media, and Preparations for the Great War,* vol. 1. London: Rudolf Steiner Press, 2005.

———. *Karmic Relationships: Esoteric Studies,* vol. 3. London: Rudolf Steiner Press, 2009.

———. *Karmic Relationships: Esoteric Studies,* vol. 4. London: Rudolf Steiner Press, 1997.

———. *Materialism and the Task of Anthroposophy.* Hudson, NY: Anthroposophic Press. 1987.

———. *Menschheitsentwickelung und Christus-Erkenntnis* ("Human Evolution and Knowledge of Christ"). Dornach, Switzerland: Rudolf Steiner Verlag, 2005.

———. *The Mission of the Folk-Souls in Relation to Teutonic Mythology.* London: Rudolf Steiner Press, 2005.

———. *An Outline of Esoteric Science.* Hudson, NY: Anthroposophic Press, 1997.

———. *Rethinking Economics: Lectures and Seminars on World Economics.* Great Barrington, MA: SteinerBooks, 2012.

———. *The Social Future: Culture, Equality, and the Economy.* Great Barrington, MA: SteinerBooks, 2013.

———. *The Spiritual Guidance of the Individual and Humanity: Some Results of Spiritual-Scientific Research into Human History and Development.* Hudson, NY: Anthroposophic Press, 1991.

———. *The Spiritual Hierarchies and the Physical World: Zodiac, Planets & Cosmos.* Great Barrington, MA: SteinerBooks, 2008.

———. *Theosophy: An Introduction to the Spiritual Processes in Human Life and in the Cosmos.* Hudson, NY: Anthroposophic Press, 1994.

———. *Twelve Moods of the Zodiac.* Eschborn, Germany: Verlag Gerhold, 1987.

———. *Das Verhältnis der verschiedenen naturwissenschatlichen Gebiete zur Astronomie* ["The Astronomy Course"], Dornach, Switzerland: Rudolf Steiner Verlag, 1997.

Steiner, Rudolf, and Edouard Schuré. *The East in the Light of the West/Children of Lucifer: A Drama.* Blauvelt, NY: Garber, 1986.

Sucher, Willi. *Isis Sophia I: Introducing Astrosophy.* Meadow Vista, CA: Astrosophy Research Center, 1999.

———. *Isis Sophia II: An Outline of a New Star Wisdom.* Meadow Vista, CA: Astrosophy Research Center, 1985.

Taft, John G. *Stewardship: Lessons Learned from the Lost Culture of Wall Street.* Hoboken, NJ: Wiley, 2012.

Tarnas, Richard. *Cosmos and Psyche.* New York: Viking, 2006.

Tomberg, Valentin, *Christ and Sophia: Anthroposophic Meditations on the Old Testament, New Testament, and Apocalypse.* Great Barrington, MA: SteinerBooks, 2006.

Toynbee, Arnold. *A Study in History.* London: Oxford, 1972.

Tradowsky, Peter. *Christ and Antichrist: Understanding the Events of Our Time and Recognizing Our Tasks.* London: Temple Lodge, 1999.

———. *Kaspar Hauser: The Struggle for the Spirit.* London: Temple Lodge, 1997. Reprint expected by 2012.

von Halle, Judith. *Descent into the Depths of the Earth on the Anthroposophic Path of Schooling.* London: Temple Lodge, 2011.

———. *Illness and Healing: And the Mystery Language of the Gospels.* London: Temple Lodge, 2008.

Tresemer, David. *The Venus Eclipse of the Sun 2012.* Great Barrington, MA: Lindisfarne Books, 2011.

Tresemer, David, and Robert Schiappacasse. *Star Wisdom & Rudolf Steiner: A Life Seen through the Oracle of the Solar Cross.* Great Barrington, MA: SteinerBooks, 2007.

Tucker, Linda. *Mystery of the White Lions.* Mapumulanga, South Africa: Npenvu Press, 2003.

von Manen, Hans Peter. *Transparent Realities: The Anthroposophical Impulse in the Environmental Movement: The 33-Year Rhythm in the History of the Anthroposophical Society.* London: Temple Lodge, 1994.

Waitz, Theodor. *Foundations of Psychology.* London: Oxford Classics, 1967.

# ABOUT THE CONTRIBUTORS

DANIEL ANDREEV (1906-1959) was born in Berlin. His father was the well-known Russian writer Leonid Andreev. His mother Alexandra Veligorsky died during childbirth. Daniel's father, overcome with grief, gave up Andreev to Alexandra's sister Elizabeth Dobrov, who lived in Moscow. It was a critical event in Daniel Andreev's life, for in contrast to many of the Russian intelligentsia at the time, the family maintained its Russian Orthodox faith. Daniel's childhood included contact with persons such as his godfather Maxim Gorky. Daniel was conscripted as a noncombatant in the Soviet Army in 1942, and after the war he returned to writing fiction and poetry. He was arrested in 1947, along with his wife and many of his relatives and friends, and sentenced to twenty-five years in prison, while his wife received twenty-five years of labor camp. All of his previous writings were destroyed. With the rise of Khrushchev, Andreev's case was reviewed and his sentence reduced to ten years. He was released to his waiting wife in 1957, his health ruined following a heart attack in prison. While in prison, he had written the first drafts of *The Rose of the World* and *Russian Gods* (a collection of poetry), as well as *The Iron Mystery,* a play in verse. Andreev spent the last two years of his life finishing these works. Andreev's wife Alla, realizing the negative reception the books would get from the Soviet authorities, hid them until the mid-1970s and did not publish them until Gorbachev and glasnost. The first edition of *The Rose of the World* (100,000 copies) quickly sold out, and since then several editions have been equally popular in Russia.

WILLIAM BENTO, Ph.D., has worked in the field of human development for more than thirty years. He is a recognized pioneer and a published author in psychosophy (soul wisdom) and astrosophy (star wisdom) and travels extensively as a speaker, teacher, and consultant. He currently resides in Citrus Heights, California. Dr. Bento is the Associate Dean of Academic Affairs at Rudolf Steiner College, Fair Oaks, California and works as a transpersonal clinical psychologist at the Center for Living Health in Gold River, California. His involvement in guiding social therapy seminars for Camphill Communities has been well received over the last two decades. He is coauthor of *Signs in the Heavens: A Message for Our Time* and author of *Lifting the Veil of Mental Illness: An Approach to Anthroposophical Psychology.* His forthcoming book is *Psychosophy: A Primer for an Extended Anthroposophical Psychology,* to be published by SteinerBooks.

DAVID BOWDEN is a teacher of phenomenological physics and projective geometry and has taught at Orana School for Rudolf Steiner Education in Canberra, the Mount Barker Waldorf School in Adelaide, Australia, and at Lorien Novalis School in Sydney. He originally trained in electronics and telecommunications and is currently a researcher and a teacher of projective geometry and the new Goethean physics.

 **KEVIN DANN**, Ph.D., has taught history at SUNY Plattsburgh, the University of Vermont, and Rutgers University. His books include *Bright Colors Falsely Seen* (1998); *Across the Great Border Fault* (2000); *Lewis Creek Lost and Found* (2001); *A Short Story of American Destiny, 1909–2009* (2008); and (with Robert Powell) *Christ & the Maya Calendar: 2012 & the Coming of the Antichrist* (2009) and *The Astrological Revolution: Unveiling the Science of the Stars as a Science of Reincarnation and Karma* (2010).

 **WAIN FARRANTS** discovered astrology (both tropical and sidereal) and Anthroposophy during his first years at the University of Toronto. After completing a B.Sc. in psychology and mathematics, he spent the next few years teaching math at a secondary school in Mochudi, Botswana. Later, he traveled to England and became a biodynamic gardener in a Camphill Community for disabled adults in the North York Moors National Park. After a few years there, he assumed responsibility for the Botton Village Bookshop. He has edited and coedited numerous books written by Karl König, Peter Roth, Baruch Urieli, Peter Tradowsky, and Andrea Damico Gibson. Wain has also contributed a number of articles to the *Christian Star Calendar*. He has considerable experience in a wide variety of orthodox, complementary medical, and alternative therapies, without which he would not have made his contribution to the *Journal*.

 **BRIAN GRAY** trained an architect and environmental planner who also has deep interests in astrology, art, music and anthroposophy. Since 1981, he has taught at Rudolf Steiner College in Fair Oaks, California. His research topics include cosmology, sacred architecture, the constitution of the human being, biography, life cycles, karma and reincarnation, esoteric Christianity and astro-geographia. A student of astrology since 1967, Brian has interpreted astrological charts for thousands of people and offers classes in star wisdom and observation of the stars. He has discovered hidden astrological keys in Wolfram von Eschenbach's *Parzival* and in the Bible, particularly Genesis, the Gospel of St. John, and the Book of Revelation. Brian currently directs the Foundation Program in Anthroposophy Program at Rudolf Steiner College. Brian's lecture on compassion and forgiveness can be viewed on YouTube at "Compassion and Forgiveness by Brian Gray.mov."

 **CLAUDIA MCLAREN LAINSON** is a teacher and Therapeutic Educator. She has been working in the field of Anthroposophy since 1982, when she founded her first Waldorf program in Boulder, Colorado. She lectures nationally on various topics related to spiritual science, human development, the evolution of consciousness and the emerging Christ and Sophia mysteries of the twenty-first century. Claudia is the founder of Windrose Farm and Academy near Boulder. Windrose is a biodynamic farm and academy for collaborative work in anthroposophic courses, therapeutic education, cosmic and sacred dance and nature-based educational programs. Claudia most recently founded the School for the Sophia Mysteries at Windrose.

 SALLY NURNEY has been interested in astrology all her life, beginning her research with her "Sun sign" in elementary school. After several years of travel and exploration, she arrived at The StarHouse in Boulder, Colorado, in 1997 and quickly transitioned to the Sidereal perspective of reading the stars. Along with her studies in the Path of the Ceremonial Arts, she has deepened her direct understanding of the stars through research with David Tresemer at The Star-House and study with Brian Gray at the Rudolf Steiner College in Fair Oaks, California. She currently lives in the Rocky Mountain foothills near the StarHouse of Boulder.

 LAQUANNA PAUL is a teacher of various forms of healing movement. As a graduate of the Choreocosmos School of Cosmic and Sacred Dance, Lacquanna has discovered astonishing correspondences between the ancient healing art of Qigong and the modern healing movements of Eurythmy, both working with the flow of etheric life force (prana, or chi). Her most recent work has centered on introducing the art of coming into connection with the vital realm of the etheric (life) body of the Earth, the mantle of Mother Earth, which bears the formative patterns of life on Earth. It is through our connection with the etheric realm of life forces that we can express our gratitude and take up a "response-able" life of service to one another and to Mother Nature. Together with Robert Powell, she has coauthored *Cosmic Dances of the Planets; Cosmic Dances of the Zodiac; The Foundation Stone Meditation in the Sacred Dance of Eurythmy;* and *The Prayer Sequence in Sacred Dance* (all available at Fields Bookstore/Sophia Foundation).

 ROBERT POWELL, Ph.D., is an internationally known lecturer, author, eurythmist, and movement therapist. He is founder of the Choreocosmos School of Cosmic and Sacred Dance, and cofounder of the Sophia Foundation of North America. He received his doctorate for his thesis *The History of the Zodiac,* available as a book from Sophia Academic Press. His published works include *The Sophia Teachings,* a six-tape series (Sounds True Recordings), as well as *Elijah Come Again: A Prophet for Our Time; The Mystery, Biography, and Destiny of Mary Madgalene; Divine Sophia—Holy Wisdom; The Most Holy Trinosophia and the New Revelation of the Divine Feminine; Chronicle of the Living Christ; Christian Hermetic Astrology; The Christ Mystery; The Sign of the Son of Man in the Heavens; The Morning Meditation in Eurythmy;* and the yearly *Journal for Star Wisdom* (previously *Christian Star Calendar*). He translated the spiritual classic *Meditations on the Tarot* and co-translated Valentin Tomberg's *Lazarus, Come Forth!* Robert is also coauthor with Kevin Dann of *The Astrological Revolution: Unveiling the Science of the Stars as a Science of Reincarnation and Karma* and *Christ & the Maya Calendar: 2012 & the Coming of the Antichrist;* and coauthor with Lacquanna Paul of *Cosmic Dances of the Zodiac* and *Cosmic Dances of the Planets.* He teaches a gentle form of healing movement: the sacred dance of eurythmy, as well as the *Cosmic Dances of the Planets* and signs of the zodiac. Through the Sophia Grail Circle, Robert

facilitates sacred celebrations dedicated to the Divine Feminine. He offers workshops in Europe, Australia, and North America, and with Karen Rivers, cofounder of the Sophia Foundation, leads pilgrimages to the world's sacred sites: Turkey, 1996; the Holy Land, 1997; France, 1998; Britain, 2000; Italy, 2002; Greece, 2004; Egypt, 2006; India, 2008; Turkey, 2009; the Grand Canyon, 2010; and South Africa, 2012. Visit www.sophia-foundation.org and www.astrogeographia.org.

DAVID TRESEMER, Ph.D., has a doctorate in psychology. In 1990, he cofounded the StarHouse in Boulder, Colorado, for community gatherings and workshops (www.TheStarHouse.org) and cofounded, with his wife Lila, the Healing Dreams Retreat Centre in Australia (www.healingdreams.com.au). He has also founded the Star Wisdom website (www.StarWisdom.org), which offers readings from the Oracle of the Solar Crosses, an oracle relating to the heavenly imprint received on one's day of birth. Dr. Tresemer has written in many areas, including *The Scythe Book: Mowing Hay, Cutting Weeds, and Harvesting Small Grains with Hand Tools* and a book on mythic theater, *War in Heaven: Accessing Myth Through Drama*. With his wife, he also coauthored several plays produced in the U.S., including *My Magdalene* (winner of Moondance 2004, Best Script). With William Bento and Robert Schiappacasse, he wrote *Signs in the Heavens: A Message for Our Time*. He is also the author, with Robert Schiappacasse, of *Star Wisdom & Rudolf Steiner: A Life Seen through the Oracle of the Solar Cross*, and with his wife, the recent book, *One-Two-ONE: A Guidebook for Conscious Partnerships, Weddings, and Rededication Ceremonies*.

> *A star is above my head.*
> *Christ speaks from the star:*
> *"Let your soul be borne*
> *Through my strong force.*
> *I am with you.*
> *I am in you.*
> *I am for you.*
> *I am your I."*
> —RUDOLF STEINER

## ASTROGEOGRAPHIA
### Correspondences between the Stars and Earthly Locations
### A Bible of Astrology and Earth Chakras

*Robert Powell and David Bowden*

"As above, so below" is the foundation of all star wisdom. It was known in ancient times that there are correspondences between the macrocosm (heavenly realm) and the microcosm (human being) and the Earth. Astrogeographia is a modern form of that ancient star wisdom.

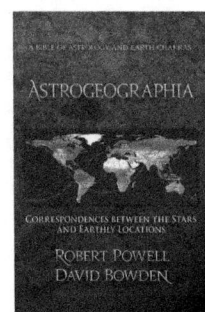

According to the astronomer Johannes Kepler:

"There radiates into the Earth soul an image of the sense-perceptible zodiac and the whole firmament as a bond of sympathy between Heaven and Earth.... This imprint into the Earth soul through the sense-perceptible zodiac and the entire sphere of fixed stars is also confirmed through observation."

Moreover, Rudolf Steiner said in his course on astronomy, "We can conceive of the active heavenly sphere mirrored in the Earth." The authors of *Astrogeographia* set out to determine the correspondences between the starry heavens and the earthly globe: *As above, so below.*

There are numerous books on the sacredness and the spirituality of our Earth. However, few books deal with the relationship between the Earth and the cosmos, which is the central theme for the research presented in *Astrogeographia*. Its point of departure is the one-to-one correspondence between the encircling starry heavens—the celestial sphere—and the sphere of the earthly globe. David Bowden has not only worked out the mathematics of this one-to-one correspondence, but has also written a computer program that applies it in practice. Thus, a new science has been born—Astrogeographia—concerning the one-to-one correspondence between the earthly sphere and the celestial sphere.

ISBN: 9781584201335 | 360 pages | pbk | $25.00

## CULTIVATING INNER RADIANCE AND THE BODY OF IMMORTALITY
### Awakening the Soul through Modern Etheric Movement

*Robert Powell*

The human being is an expression of the ever-unfolding wisdom of the creative Logos, the Word. The whole of creation bears the imprint of the cosmic sounding. This book describes a way, through movement and gesture, to work with the creative, sounding principle

that manifests in the Earth's enveloping life sphere. Today, the increasingly binding and hardening conditions of modern life now threatens the divine seed of life here on Earth, which has been fructified and developed over the millennia. Creation—coming to expression through the flowering of the cosmic breath—is losing its natural connection with humanity and with Mother Earth, which are increasingly given over to anti-life forces, comprising destruction, inversions, and lifeless replicas of creation's gifts.

The sacred movements described in this book arise from the modern art of movement known as eurythmy (Greek: "good movement"), which came into the world in 1912. These sacred gestures, when practiced with the words gifted to humanity by the incarnated Logos two thousand years ago, lead us back to our connection with the fullness of creation and toward the goal of developing the body of immortality, the resurrection body. In 2012, we celebrate the one-hundredth anniversary of the birth of eurythmy. This book invites us to partake of the richness of the sacred through life-enhancing movement and gesture as a path to reconnect with the cosmic formative forces that sound the call of resurrection.

The wealth of material included in this book educates the soul toward awaking to a conscious understanding of humanity's divine heritage and true calling. The exercises in this work provide a training that ennobles and refines the qualities of the human soul.

ISBN: 9781584201175 | 240 pages | pbk | $25.00

## PROPHECY · PHENOMENA · HOPE
### The Real Meaning of 2012
### *Christ & the Maya Calendar*—An Update

#### Robert Powell

Robert Powell, explores what 2012 really means, updating the research presented in the groundbreaking book, *Christ & the Maya Calendar: 2012 and the Coming of the Antichrist* (coauthored with Kevin Dann). Here, Powell focuses on two significant prophecies by Rudolf Steiner. The first (from 1909) concerns the Second Coming of Christ, his appearance to humanity as the Etheric Christ. The second (from 1919) represents the shadow side of Christ's Second Coming—the incarnation in human form of Ahriman.

Powell points to the steady, multifaceted encroachment of ahrimanic forces today, especially as the harmful effects of modern technology on the etheric body. After looking into Steiner's prophetic remarks on the Book of Revelation, Powell looks into the prophecies of the Russian poet/mystic Daniel Andreev and examines the prophecy of the American clairvoyant Jeane Dixon concerning the human birth of the Antichrist. He also includes spiritual research by Judith von Halle regarding an earlier incarnation of Jospeh Stalin, as well as Andreev's indications relating to Stalin's earlier incarnations, which may be seen as preparation of this individuality for his role as "Mr. X," the human vessel for the incarnation of Ahriman.

Applying the astrological rules of reincarnation, Powell's research supports Jeane Dixon's prophecy, that Mr. X was born in 1962, a finding whose accuracy was also confirmed by Willi Sucher, Powell's mentor in Astrosophy. This finding, seen in relation to various contemporary phenomena, confirms Rudolf Steiner's prophetic statement that the incarnation of Ahriman into his human vessel would take place shortly after the year 2000.

Nonetheless, great hope for humankind is offered by the return of Christ in the etheric realm, an event to which human beings can connect, as humanity and the Earth pass through the great trials associated with 2012.

ISBN: 9781584201113 | 138 pages | pbk | $16.00

## THE ASTROLOGICAL REVOLUTION
### Unveiling the Science of the Stars as a Science of Reincarnation and Karma

#### Robert Powell & Kevin Dann

The reader is invited to question the basis of modern astrology—the tropical zodiac, which emerged through Greek astronomers from what was originally a calendar dividing the year into twelve solar months. Ninety-eight percent of Western astrologers use the tropical zodiac, meaning that it is based on a calendar system that no longer embodies the reality of the stars.

Astrology needs to be brought back into alignment with the stars in the heavens. The first step in this astrological revolution is to recognize the sidereal zodiac. In antiquity, the Babylonians, Egyptians, Greeks, Romans, and Hindus used the sidereal zodiac, and today Hindu (Vedic) astrologers still use the sidereal zodiac. Based on recognition—through the newly discovered rules of astrological reincarnation, that the sidereal zodiac presents an authentic astrological zodiac—a new practice of astrology is possible that offers tools to reestablish a wisdom-filled astrology in the modern world. This new astrology, based on the sidereal zodiac, is similar to the classic sidereal form but in a modern form, as that practiced by the three magi, who—prompted by the stars—journeyed to Bethlehem two thousand years ago.

Drawing on specific biographical examples, *The Astrological Revolution* reveals new understandings of how the starry heavens work into human destiny. The book points to the astrological significance of the entire celestial sphere, including all the stars and constellations beyond the twelve zodiacal signs. This discovery is revealed by studying the megastars, the most luminous stars of our galaxy, illustrating how megastars show up in an extraordinary way in Christ's healing miracles by aligning with the Sun at the time of those miraculous events.

KEVIN DANN, Ph.D., has taught history at SUNY Plattsburgh, the University of Vermont, and Rutgers University. He is also the coauthor of *Christ & the Maya Calendar* with Robert Powell.

ISBN: 9781584200833 | 254 pages | pbk | $25.00

# THE CLOCKWISE HOUSE SYSTEM
## A TRUE FOUNDATION FOR SIDEREAL AND TROPICAL ASTROLOGY

*Jacques Dorsan*
*Wain Farrants and Robert Powell, editors*

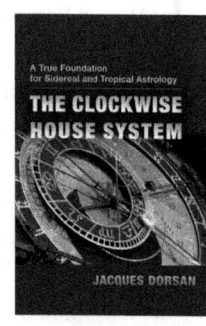

Jacques Dorsan, a leading pioneer of sidereal astrology in France, uses more than eighty sidereal horoscopes to illustrate his clockwise house system. With charts from the original French edition and many added, this book embodies one of the most important astrological discoveries of twentieth and twenty-first centuries. Astrology normally views the twelve houses in astrology in a counterclockwise direction, the direction of the zodiac signs. According to Dorsan, however, we should view them in a clockwise direction.

By using this clockwise house system along with the sidereal zodiac, everything falls into place in a horoscope, unlocking the mystery of the horoscope. We are given access to a true form of astrology, enabling a giant leap forward in the practice of astrology. It allows us to recover the original astrology. Moreover, Rudolf Steiner's indications, as well as the research of the French statistician Michel Gauquelin, confirm that the astrological houses run in a clockwise direction.

This English translation includes more than eighty charts, both those in Dorsan's original work in French and more added by the editor of this edition.

JACQUES DORSAN was born December 22, 1912, in Orléans, France. In 1936, he moved to the Ivory Coast, where he drew his first horoscope. It was more than seven years before he began to do consultations. Fourteen years later, after intense practice in Brazil and before returning to France, he had become convinced that the houses actually move in the direction opposite the zodiacal signs. He put his idea to the test for more than twenty years before publishing the original version of this book *Le véritable sens des maisons astrologiques* (1984). Jacques Dorsan lived in Morocco, New York City, Monaco, Luxembourg, Belgium, Zaire, and New Caledonia. He died September 8, 2005, in Nice.

ISBN: 9781584200956 | 330 pages | pbk | $30.00

# ELIJAH COME AGAIN
## A PROPHET FOR OUR TIME
## A SCIENTIFIC APPROACH TO REINCARNATION

*Robert Powell*

The research presented by Robert Powell in this book shows that a new science of the stars is possible, based on a study of reincarnation and karma. Willi Sucher did much to pioneer the development of a new star wisdom, or astrosophy, as a scientific tool for the investigation of karma. Powell has discovered that applying the science of astrosophy to the findings of karma research reveals—through the discovery of astrological reincarnation rules—the foundations underlying star wisdom. Once these foundational findings relating to astrological reincarnation research have been assimilated, a reformation of traditional astrology will inevitably take place. Once the new astrology is established, there will be a similar feeling in looking back upon traditional Western astrology that modern astronomers have when looking back upon the old geocentric astronomy.

The purpose of this book is to contemplate the incarnations of the prophet Elijah, with the goal of laying the foundation for a new "science of the stars" as the "science of karma." At the close of his last lecture, after discussing the sequence of incarnations of Elijah–John the Baptist–Raphael–Novalis, Rudolf Steiner spoke of this individuality as "a radiant and splendid forerunner...with whom you are to prepare the work that shall be accomplished at the end of the [twentieth] century, and will lead humankind past the great crisis in which it is involved." These words indicate that, from the end of the twentieth century and into the twenty-first century (that is, now), the Elijah-John individuality is to be a "radiant forerunner" for humanity in the next step underlying our spiritual evolution.

*Elijah Come Again* presents a scientific approach toward unveiling the mystery of human destiny. This theme is timeless in nature—yet timely, nevertheless, in the recounting of the unfolding destiny and mission of the Old Testament prophet Elijah.

ISBN: 9781584200703 | 260 pages | pbk | $35.00

# Holy Nights Journal 2012-2013
## By William Bento, PhD

This year's *Holy Nights Journal* theme is focused on finding the light in the dark. There has been a collective angst and fear pervading many dialogues concerning the future throughout the year 2012. There is no doubt that we have entered an era that is unprecedented and unpredictable. Yet in all that may be experienced as darkness there is an inner light to be ignited, an inner light that resides and radiates in and from the conscious heart, a light that has the potential to set the world aright. This light is not a given, but a choice we must make in the darkest moments of our life. As we share in this dark hour of 2012 it becomes imperative that we join in the endeavor to light the dark with a consciousness of loving so fierce that a path into a bright and better future is assured. A series of meditative thoughts for igniting the inner light is presented in a sequential manner throughout the Holy Nights.

A guide is given for consciously working through meditations, questions and journaling topics for each of the Holy Nights. There are correspondences given of the Holy Nights to signs of the zodiac, human virtues, and dedications to the Saints accompanying each journaling page. It is a wonderful way to celebrate the Holy Nights and can be an equally wonderful gift for those who wish to enter more deeply into the significance of this sacred time. **$22.95 + shipping & handling**

**Available from the Bookstore at Rudolf Steiner College**
**Phone: 916-961-8729 | Fax: 877-782-1890 | E-mail: orders@steinercollege.edu**

www.ingramcontent.com/pod-product-compliance
Lightning Source LLC
Chambersburg PA
CBHW081208170426
43198CB00018B/2886